ECONOMICS
with Islamic Orientation

Zubair Hasan

OXFORD
UNIVERSITY PRESS

Oxford New York
Auckland   Cape Town Dar es Salaam   HongKong
Karachi   Kuala Lumpur Madrid Melbourne   Mexico City
Nairobi   New Delhi   Shanghai Taipei Toronto

© Oxford University Press 2015
First published 2015

ISBN 978 983 47 1405 5

Perpustakaan Negara Malaysia   Cataloguing-in-Publication Data

Zubair Hasan
    ECONOMICS With Islamic Orientation / Zubair Hasan.
    ISBN 978-983-47-1405-5
    1. Economics--Religious aspects--Islam.
    2.Finance--Religious aspects--Islam. I. Title.
    332.088297

Impression: 9 8 7 6 5 4 3 2 1

Text set in 11 point Bembo Std by
Chitra Computers, India
Printed by Vivar Printing Sdn. Bhd., Selangor Darul Ehsan
Published by Oxford Fajar Sdn. Bhd. (008974-T),
under licence from Oxford University Press,
4 Jalan Pemaju U1/15, Seksyen U1
40150 Shah Alam
Selangor Darul Ehsan, Malaysia

To my students, past and present

Preface

For me, the publication of the text *Economics with Islamic Orientation* is a mission accomplished. During my six decades in teaching and research at several institutions of higher education at home and abroad, my first professional concern has always been my students—their learning progress and welfare. To experience the glow born of understanding on their faces is the greatest reward for a teacher. Teaching is a difficult task, especially in a nascent subject like Islamic economics. The subject became my cup of tea ever since I joined the International Islamic University, Malaysia in its formative years in 1990. It was pleasant and inspiring to work under Prof. Datuk Dr. Abdul Hamid Abu Sulaiyman, the Rector (1989–1998) whose earnest and untiring efforts contributed mostly to the stature and status the IIUM enjoys today.

In September 1997, the Rector assigned me the task of writing a paper on 'Islamization of knowledge in Economics'. It was this assignment which made me think hard on the line of argument and direction I should take. My experience of teaching Islamic economics over the years has convinced me of a few things. The religion has not divided knowledge as Islamic and non-Islamic. Rather, existing stock of knowledge has to be evaluated from an Islamic point of view—accept what is evidently allowed and reject what is patently not. Then, accept what can be after modification. Finally, in the areas where the religion passes no judgement, let rationality operate commensurate with the spirit and intent of the Shari'ah. It was also clear that however we separate Islamic economics from the mainstream, we cannot keep our students ignorant of the latter, so long as mainstream economics thoughts and practices, despite all their ills—actual or perceived—dominate the global economic scene.

With this in mind, I could not forget the predicament of hapless students who were being fed ill-conceived and erroneous concepts and theories. So, I raised the issues of curricula development and integrative writings, especially textbooks for the undergraduate students, in my write up. After its publication, titled *Islamization of Knowledge in Economics: Issues and Agenda,* 1998, I increasingly used the integrative approach in my class lectures and articulated it in my writings and conference presentations. In my classes, I found students to be more interested and receptive to comparisons of the mainstream and Islamic positions on an issue. And I saw the glow I expected on their faces.

I completed the first textbook, *Introduction to Microeconomics – An Islamic Perspective*, integrating Islamic and mainstream knowledge. However, it was hard to convince peers on its efficacy and difficult to find an international publisher, until one offered to publish it. But they declined a second edition. I sent the book to the Islamic Economics Research Centre of KAU in Jeddah, but their reviewers found it more mainstream in content and approach; they advised an increase in its Islamic content. I felt as though my mission was failing. More so, because efforts at Islamic universities to produce an Islamic economics textbook had by now picked up momentum: teams of scholars had already been working on such projects.

But in the face of setbacks, came a ray of hope when I had just shifted to INCEIF. Oxford University Press, Malaysia approached me to write a textbook for them on macroeconomics. It was a project which I decided to take up. I expressed the desire to include Islamic perspectives where appropriate in the chapters. To this, the publishers agreed, but politely declined to insert Islamic in the title of the book. The book was released in November 2009.

Macroeconomics did well and Oxford commissioned *Fundamentals of Microeconomics*, also as a textbook. 'Islamic' could not again appear in the title. The book was released in 2011, and received elating reception. Oxford commissioned yet another book, but in a new area for me, under the title *Islamic Banking and Finance – An Integrative Approach*. It hit the international markets in February 2014.

The story narrated above is not the success story of an individual and his mission. More than that, it is the success story of mutual trust and cooperation, between a teacher author and a renowned University (Press), wherein a key role was played by Mr. Tanweer Ahmad of Oxford Fajar, South East Asia, Kuala Lumpur. He and his team deserve credit and praise for the work done. He was instrumental in the continuation of my mission. Oxford commissioned one more book. They requested to combine both the *Macroeconomics* and *Fundamental of Microeconomics* texts in one volume, *Economics with Islamic Orientation*. The subtitle announces: 'mission accomplished'.

Spread over twenty four chapters, the present book is the first presentation of economics with Islamic orientation cast in a modern textbook frame, to serve undergraduate students taking courses in business and economics in universities. The material of the earlier texts has been revised and updated. Analysis has been improved and more diagrams and illustrations have been added. The improvements are so many, at places innovative, that *Economics with Islamic Orientation* can claim to be a textbook in its own right.

Key Features

- Written in simple language, with explanatory illustrations and descriptive diagrams.
- Learning outcomes are stated at the beginning of each chapter and checks on them are provided in the form of exercises throughout the chapters.
- Boxes in each chapter provide Islamic input on topics discussed, while keeping the flow of the text smooth and unhindered for the reader.
- The running texts contain occasional posers throughout to make readers pause and think for a moment. The posers may also sustain their interest in continuing with the chapter.
- Each chapter provides test questions to help students assess their learning levels and see if the same reasonably match the expected outcomes.
- Relevant and recent case studies and a Web-based task are provided at the end of each chapter.

As Islamic economics has emerged and is gaining ground in teaching and research, especially in the Muslim world, the integrative approach of this book will be found, it is hoped, acceptable and rewarding by its readers. The table of contents provides the details of coverage in each chapter in adequate measure. The book provides, where appropriate, a historical linkage of the concepts and theories discussed, providing at the same time the latest position. This feature may not only make the narration interesting for the students, but may attract other readers as well.

Zubair Hasan
17 October 2014

Acknowledgements

Acknowledgement of the contribution of others to the publication of a book is as difficult as it is an unfailing duty. It is difficult because the debts are too numerous to remember. My learned teachers made immense contribution to the development of my knowledge and work culture; it helped me achieve what little I could in my professional career and beyond. It is my lament that I do not reflect more than a shade of their erudition in my writings. Likewise, the borrowings from other writers are indeed numerous, which I took care to record in the bibliography. But, I hasten to say that the list is by no means exhaustive and I earnestly seek pardon if I fail on any of these accounts.

The environment of an educational institution is crucial to the achievement levels of its faculty. This depends very much on top management. I have been privileged to find brother Daud Vicary Abdullah, CEO and President of INCEIF; an epitome of appreciation and encouragement for faculty performance. No less is the contribution of Prof. Datuk Dr. Syed Othman Alhabshi, CAO of INCEIF who generously provided the time, space and assistance required to complete the work. Assoc. Prof. Dr. Ahcene Lahsasna, popularly known as Hasan, is a worthy colleague and friend. He has always been at hand to assist me with his insight on *fiqh* matters; he has saved me from many pitfalls along the way. Errors, if any, are of course mine.

Thanks are due to Ms. Nurhafiza Abdul Kader Malim, my research assistant who has intermittently been working for me in that capacity since 2006. This is my fifth book where I am obliged to appreciate her assistance in my work. She went through the manuscript minutely and helped weed out many errors, despite the fact that she is currently very much occupied with the completion of her PhD dissertation. This time, she was greatly helped by two other students currently in my PhD course—Messrs. Mohammed Anouar Gadhoum and Mazen et Khatib. They took care of marginal notes and diagrams, and deserve praise for the work done.

I have already expressed my gratitude in the preface to Mr. Tanweer Ahmad, Director of Higher Education, OUP Malaysia for his personal interest in the project and seeing to it that the book is one of the best publications from his company. His editor Ms. Levinia Ann deserves a special mention for her cooperation, efficiency and hard work.

About the Author

Prof. Dr. Zubair Hasan, *MA (Economics), M.Com., PhD* is an Indian economist with an outstanding academic and professional record. Having worked worldwide in a number of institutions—mainly the University of Delhi, and the International Islamic University of Malaysia—he joined INCEIF, the Global University of Islamic Finance as a Professor of Islamic Economics and Finance on 1 July 2008.

Prof. Dr. Hasan has published several books and a monograph including *Theory of Profit* (Vikas, 1975), *Introduction to Microeconomics: An Islamic Perspective* (Pearson, 2006), *Macroeconomics* (Oxford, 2009), *Fundamentals of Microeconomics* (Oxford, 2011) and *Islamic Banking and Finance: An Integrative Approach* (Oxford, 2014). *Economics with Islamic Orientation* (Oxford, 2015) is his latest work.

Moreover, he has published over 60 articles in peer reviewed academic journals on topics in economics and finance—Islamic and mainstream—in addition to numerous working papers, commentaries and book reviews. He is a resource person with a number of Islamic financial institutions. He sits on the advisory board of several international journals of repute and works as a referee for some others. He has presented papers at more than 50 local and international conferences including the prestigious 21st World Islamic Banking Conference (WIBC) 2014. His articles have appeared in 18 edited works as chapters in reputed publications. Many of his works are downloadable free from the site 'ZubairHasan at IDEAS'.

Prof. Dr. Hasan won the Best Researcher faculty level award (2003) at the IIUM. He was awarded the prestigious Islamic Development Bank (IDB) Prize in Islamic Economics (2009) in recognition of his outstanding contributions to the subject. Recently, he has been selected as a recipient of The Standing Committee for Economic and Commercial Cooperation of the Organization of Islamic Conference (COMCEC) Academic Award 2014.

He has a passion for Urdu poetry and published his own compositions under the title *Aaeena* (The Mirror) in 2007 (Modern Publishing House, New Delhi).

Contents

| **CHAPTER 12** | **Markets, Environment and Sustainability** | **316** |

| **CHAPTER 13** | **Money Banking and Prices** | **347** |

CHAPTER 14   **Macroeconomics: Nature and Significance**   **373**

CHAPTER 15   **National Income: Variants and Measurement**   **395**

CHAPTER 16   **Aggregate Demand and Aggregate Supply**   **428**

CHAPTER 21   Fiscal Policy: Public Revenue and Expenditure   570

CHAPTER 24

Open Economies: International Trade, Balance of Payments and Exchange Rates

List of Tables

List of Figures

What is Economics About?

LEARNING OUTCOMES

This chapter should enable the student to understand:

- The bases of economic activity: Human wants and scarcity
- Choice-making and economics
- Controversy on values in economics
- What economics deals with?
- Problems economists seek to resolve
- Methods used to establish economic laws
- The distinction between microeconomics and macroeconomics
- The nature of the language economists use
- Capitalism, socialism and Islamic system: A comparison

1.1 WANTS AND SCARCITY

Economists see the source of all economic activities in the scarcity of resources and multiplicity of human wants. Scarcity is the result of our desire to consume more goods and services than we can produce. We work to earn our living but our incomes are not sufficient to satisfy our never-ending wants. Likewise, a country has limited resources in men, money and materials; it cannot produce each and every thing people may desire to have. Also, in many cases, the situation is aggravated by the rapid increase in population. Thus, we find that resources are insufficient or scarce for both individuals and nations because wants grow beyond satisfaction. Note that scarcity does not mean being limited in quantity. Some species of plants for which man has not yet discovered any use may be there in much smaller quantities than wheat in the world; yet such plants are not scarce, wheat is because we need it. *Relativity* is *an inherent attribute of scarcity.*

Islam is not a dry religion; rather it encourages believers to create wealth and enjoy all good things in life. Production of wealth and its protection is considered one of the five most important objectives of the Shari'ah. Ibn Khaldun (1406) followed by Adam Smith (1776) counted wealth among the factors directly responsible for the rise and fall of nations. Thus, wants–scarcity inequality is clearly relevant to Islamic economics as well. But some writers do not agree with this view, believing that admitting the scarcity of resources would be a denial of the benevolence of God who has stored the earth (and heavens) with inexhaustible resources for all times to come, not only for mankind but also for other creatures. He also created various things in a mould that they would readily submit to the human will. He has been infinitely merciful in the provision of resources.

Still, resources are scarce from an Islamic viewpoint as well because what matters is not their divine *provision* but their *availability* to mankind from the inexhaustible stocks of God. Availability depends on human knowledge about the location of resources, methods of obtaining them and their uses. But all knowledge of resources (and other matters) is with God and he releases it to those who seek—if he wants—bit by bit, so that men may not get illusions of self-pride. And, *reward depends on effort* (Qur'an 55:38). Thus, scarcity is part of the divine scheme: the history of mankind is largely the history of conquering nature and pushing outwards the frontiers of scarcity through continual explorations, inventions and innovations. Islam instructs us to avoid wastage (*israf*) and stop from hoarding in recognition of resources being scarce in terms of their *availability*. It is scarcity that has made toil both the means and the want for life.

1.1.1 Choice-making

Scarcity imposes economization of resources on mankind and creates the unending problem of *choice-making* for individuals as well as society. As individuals, we have to decide which of our wants we shall satisfy, in what order and to what extent because resources are not only scarce, they also have alternative uses. Likewise, a nation has to decide how best it can use its available resources. It has to make a choice: what goods will be produced, in what quantities and for whom will it be produced. In other words, a decision has to be made regarding the relative importance of the competing needs of different social groups—the rich, the not so rich and the poor. For example, an obligatory first demand on national resources from the Islamic viewpoint is to produce enough goods and services to meet the *basic needs* of people including food, clothing, shelter, education and health care. The vision and mission of an economic system is what differentiates one system from another.

As there often are several ways of producing a commodity, a technological choice is also involved, i.e. how to produce the selected mix of goods. The choice becomes all the more important as we can use the same resource for several purposes. It is also influenced by the nature and availability of various resources. Since a number of resource owners must come together to contribute to productive effort, they have to share the output according to some prior arrangement. Distribution of wealth and income therefore, also becomes an important question for a society. The answer to questions of what or how to produce and distribute the product depends on the economic system a country chooses for development. We shall briefly discuss these systems later. Suffice to note here that fulfilment of needs and justice in distribution are to be the hallmark of an Islamic economic system.

1.1.2   Values and Economics

As explained above, economics is the science of how society produces and distributes scarce means for the satisfaction of human wants. It follows that economics necessarily requires the making of value based judgements—what is fair and what is unfair—when prescribing economic policies. However, most present day writers on the subject hold that economics is ethics-neutral. The view separates economics from ethics. But this view seems to be dissolving into the new currents of thought. Multiplicity of wants and scarcity of resources may give rise as we now see to greed and dishonesty in the society. For this reason, principles of economics cannot remain free of value judgements, explicit or implicit. The problem is: what values (moral judgements) are considered socially relevant and what decision-making processes would determine them? Private ownership of property, freedom of enterprise, competition in markets and distributive justice are some of the leading values underlying most economic systems that operate today in various economies of the world. Even spiritual considerations may be part of economic decisions. Today, there hardly seems to exist anything that could be called 'pure' economics. To talk of neutrality towards the end is self-deception. Values are implicit in the assumptions of economic theories. An economist is expected to explain the actual situation and state the effects of alternative policies if action were taken. His social and political views may influence his analysis and conclusions. The important question is not whether economics has values or not, but how a discipline selects its values or rejects them. Mainstream economics is claimed to be value-free. However, *not to have values is itself a value*, as Kenneth Joseph Arrow puts it. For Islamic economics, faith provides the rules of the game; it is conditioned by morality and specified norms. In mainstream economics, it is the reason and majority endorsement that decide them.

> Economics has never been value-free. The difference between Islamic and mainstream disciplines lies only in the process of value selection.

1.2   DEFINITION AND SCOPE

Given the above facts, we may now proceed to define economics. In general, the subject is concerned with the promotion of human well-being. The difference between the two economic disciplines—mainstream and Islamic—essentially centres on their notion of human well-being and this difference emanates from their worldview differences that shape their respective objectives institutions and operational frameworks. Here, we do not go into the details of those differences. Suffice it to say that the Islamic view of well-being encompasses both the mundane and spiritual aspects of living while mainstream view ignores the latter. Presumably, the gap can be bridged. Note that the multiplicity of wants and scarcity of resources are undeniable both are a part of the divine scheme of living on earth. The primary difficulty with the mainstream approach to economics is that it claims as being neutral towards the ends and ignores spiritual aspirations of humans. Both can easily be covered if we define Islamic economics as follows.

Islamic economics is the subject that studies human behaviour in relation to multiplicity of wants and scarcity of resources with alternative uses so as to maximize falah that is the well-being both in the present world and the hereafter.

The notion of *falah* is the essence of Islamic teachings; it covers all aspects of human life, here and in the hereafter. The definition mirrors the content and spirit of the following prayer from the Qur'an that believers so frequently address to God: *Our Lord! Give us in this world that which is good and in the hereafter that which is good and save us from the torment of fire* (2: 201).

Decision-making in the face of multiplicity of human wants and scarcity of available resources constitutes the subject matter of economics. The decision-making process involves a comparison of the advantages and disadvantages that would follow the decision; we have to strike a *balance* between the two. Advantages imply benefits, while disadvantages impose costs. Cost here means *opportunity cost* which is a key concept in economics and is also welcome to Islamic thought. The concept refers to the gains of the second best alternative that we have to give up in favour of what we choose to do. Thus, the gain that we forego or give up for implementing a choice is called the *opportunity cost* of that choice. For example, if we use a piece of land to grow wheat that could also grow rice, the income that we forego for not growing rice is the opportunity cost of growing wheat.

Choice or decision-making cannot be independent of the objectives an economic organization aims at achieving. Formally, all economies, irrespective of the way they are organized—religious or secular—work for four basic objectives: *growth, full employment, stability and distributive justice.* Self-reliance and national esteem are recent additions to the list. We provide here an illustration of the general problem of choice that confronts all economies in achieving such objectives due to the scarcity of resources. Let us assume that at any point in time, t, an economy has a fixed stock of natural resources, labour hours and machines that it can use to produce combinations of two goods, tanks and houses; tanks representing war materials and houses the goods for civilian consumption. Table 1.1 provides six imaginary combinations of these goods—A, B, C, D, E and F—each of which, if chosen for production, will exhaust the given resources completely.

Economics studies the behaviour of human beings in relation to the use of scarce resources for satisfying their wants. The ultimate objective of all economic activity—mainstream or Islamic—is to promote human welfare. While mainstream economics focuses only on the mundane part of welfare, Islamic economics includes in it the spiritual aspect as well; it sees material prosperity as a means for spiritual attainments.

Scarcity makes the allocation of resources among various uses a basic issue in economics. The concept of opportunity cost assumes importance.

Table 1.1 *Production possibilities for tanks and houses (imaginary data)*

Combinations of tanks and houses	Number of tanks	Number of houses (per thousand unit)	Marginal opportunity cost of T in H unit
A	1	35	–
B	2	32	3
C	3	27	5
D	4	20	7
E	5	11	9
F	6	0	11

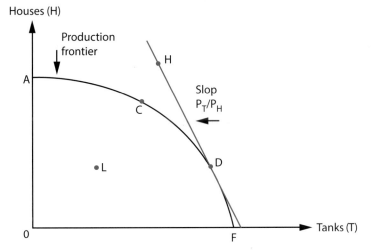

Figure 1.1 *Production possibilities curve for houses and tanks*

Figure 1.1 rests on the following assumptions:

1. Resources of the economy are fully employed at each point on the curve.

2. The technology of producing the two goods, tanks and houses, remains unchanged in time (t).

3. All resources are not equally efficient in producing each of the good, tanks (T) and houses (H). Therefore, as we move from A towards F we have to transfer from the production of houses to the production of tank resources that are progressively more efficient in producing houses than tanks. Thus, we sacrifice each time, more houses than before to produce one more tank as the last column of Table 1.1 shows. This column provides what we call the marginal rate of transformation of houses into tanks or MRT_{HT}. The behaviour of this rate gives us the law of increasing opportunity cost. In general, the opportunity cost for any commodity such as tanks (T),may be defined as the quantity of any other commodity such as houses (H) that we have to give up for acquiring one more unit of T.

Marginal rate of substitution of X for Y is the quantity of Y given up to have one more unit of X.

4. All resources are efficiently used, i.e. the opportunity cost is minimized.

Which combination of tanks (T) and houses (H) will actually be produced on the frontier will depend on the prices of tanks (P_T) and houses (P_H) respectively. The price line has to be tangent to the production frontier at any point such as D. Here, the slope of the transformation curve equals the price ratio: $MRT_{HT} = P_T/P_H$. We find that at D, four tanks and sixteen houses are produced. The MRT_{HT} is 5:1, so that should also be the price ratio of the two goods.

Efficiency in the allocation of resources is achieved on the production frontier, where the marginal rate of substitution of two goods equals the ratio of their prices.

Exercise 1.1

Add a column to the right of Table 1.1 showing the marginal opportunity cost of H in terms of T moving upwards from F to A. What relationship do you find between the two marginal costs? Are they reciprocals of one another?

Exercise 1.2

Suppose in the example of Table 1.1, the market price of a tank is RM3.5 million and a house is RM0.5 million. Which combination of tanks and houses—A, B, C, D, E or F—will the economy produce if the price line were tangent to the production frontier?

Mainstream economics essentially rests on the assumption of harmony between the interests of the individual and the society.

If the economy produces at point L, resources will not be efficiently used because some of them will remain unemployed. Again, the economy will not be able to operate at point H due to the insufficiency of resources. Changes in technology or in the availability of resources will change the shape and position of the production frontier in the plane (why?), but the curve will remain concave to the origin. This is so because the marginal opportunity cost or rate of product transformation rises as we move down the frontier, as explained above. (See Table 1.1.)

BOX 1.1

Religion and Economics

Alfred Marshall made, on page 2 of his *Principles*, a passing observation that the course of world history was mainly determined by two forces—economic and religious, of the two economic forces were perhaps more significant. The debate went into hibernation for decades. However, the failure of more and more conventional models to account for economic performance through time and the devastating collapse of developed economies in recent years has induced many economists to look to more non-traditional explanations of economic performance, including religion.

Several recent surveys of published literature find both theoretical arguments on the economic role of religion and empirical studies equally inconclusive on the point. But the inquisitions of the learned continue unabated.

It will not perhaps surprise people that economists have something to say about the economics of religion, since economists believe they have something to say about everything; what is surprising is that religion has something to say about economics (Deirdre N. McCloskey, University of Illinois, Chicago).

Muslim economists are insistent that Islam provides a model of economic development constrained by a moral code of conduct that can ensure growth on a smooth path with peace and equity for all. The claim is pious and laudable but demonstration alone can win conviction.

1.2.1   Behavioural Norms

Until recently, economists had used human behaviour guided by reason (rationality) alone as the foundation for their theoretical work. Also, one was regarded as being rational only if he pursued his self-interest and attempted to maximize the same. It was thought that the *invisible hand* of self-interest guided people to promote interest of others as well. Adam Smith wrote in his *Wealth of Nations* (1776): *An individual generally neither intends to promote the public interest, nor knows how much he is promoting it... he intends only his own gain and he is in this, as in many other cases, led by an invisible hand to promote an end which was no part of his intention... by pursuing his own interest he frequently promotes that of the society more effectually than when he really intends to promote it.*

Islamic economists, in evaluating the above passage, invariably lose sight of the fact that Smith did not believe in self-interest alone being relevant as a regulator of human conduct. He spoke movingly about the compassion one feels for others and thought that even the most hardened violators of the law of society were not altogether without sympathy for others. Presumably, there is a need to get rid of the unwanted bifurcation of human motives into self-interest and concern for others: the first being wicked and the second virtuous. For, there are some surprising affinities between self-interest and morality. The principal force that puts a check on self-interest is often found to be self-interest itself. Indeed, a famous Islamic dictum says *cause no harm, get no harm*. Self-interest reinforces the commands of morality. It promotes civility and consideration for others.

> Islam endorses the pursuit of self-interest within the confines of its code of conduct. Also, it gives priority to the promotion of social interest if individual interest conflicts with it.

Indeed, no moral objection can in principle be raised to the pursuit of self-interest. Even religious prayers one performs are meant for pleasing God and for self-salvation in the hereafter. Self-interest does not mean selfishness; it does not bar one from being altruistic or benevolent. People make personal sacrifices to help the needy and the poor; they generously contribute to charities. For example, the world has seen the largest voluntary mobilization of resources in history to help the victims of the colossal natural calamity, the Asian Tsunami (2004). Also, the maximization principle is in itself, value neutral. The judgement would depend on what is maximized, by whom and to what end.

Negligent self-interest is not only bad economics; it may lead to bad morals as well. However, it is also true that relentless pursuit of maximizing self-interest on the part of economic entities—consumers or entrepreneurs—has led to greed, acquisitive passions and discontentment. For example, how counterproductive the over-seeking of material prosperity could become is displayed through the current massive demonstrations (BBC, 19 December 2013) in China against government insistence that people must strive hard for attaining material status: they are instead demanding time for spiritual pursuits beyond the fulfilment of their basic needs; their slogans echoing religion.

To operate as controls, Islam insists on moderation, contentment, cooperation and mutual support, promising prosperity with solace in life. Today, rationality based on self-interest alone as the regulator of human behaviour is being widely questioned even in mainstream economics. A classic example is the essay of Amartya Kumar Sen, *Rational Fools,* where he has *inter alia* projected *commitment* to a cause as no less important a force, motivating people into action. And commitment to any *noble* cause may more than cover the Islamic notion of justice and morality. We shall have occasion to highlight such Islamic norms to regulate human conduct in the following chapters.

1.2.2   Nature and Scope

Economics is a science, for it is a body of knowledge that systematically deals with cause and effect relationships in the ordinary business of life and searches for uniformities in human behaviour to establish hypotheses, theories and laws. Islamic economics studies laws according to which a Muslim society could develop economically. It seeks to investigate whether economic laws in conformity with the scripture and its moral norms would be different from those studied in the mainstream economics to describe the functioning of an economy. If there are differences, what modification or rejections are needed to erect an Islamic economic order? One cannot think of an economy working in such an Islamic order entirely independent of the conventional stock of knowledge.

With science and economics come two important aspects: positive and normative. As a *positive* science, it deals with the 'what is' of an economy and with the forces that govern *factual* situations. It asks questions such as: How does the economy work? What are the forces that determine things such as the level of national output, distribution of income, or flow of materials, commodities and capital across national borders? The sole purpose of such queries is to obtain information and understanding about the economy as one finds it. Positive economics observes and states but does not prescribe. There are many statements in the Qur'an, inviting men to observe, think and learn.

However, as economics is ultimately concerned with human beings and their welfare, it has to have a *normative* aspect as well. Normative economics discusses questions such as what *should* be produced and how *should* it be distributed. With the increasing interest of psychologists, political scientists, sociologists and environmentalist on the subject and the urge for promoting interdisciplinary research, normative questions are assuming importance in economic discussions. Men of ethics and religion raise moral issues concerning consumption, finance and business conduct. It is the philosophical branch of economics that integrates the subject with other branches of knowledge and paves the way for interdisciplinary studies, the hallmark of Islamic approach to learning and research.

If 'what is' is not what it should be, the normative aspect of economics instantly raises the questions of policy: What policy could correct the situation, for instance, in the case of the 2008 worldwide financial meltdown? Policy is action designed to achieve a given objective such as promoting growth, reducing distributive inequalities or ensuring full employment. As no policy is worth more than what it is in practice, the role of the state becomes important in running an economy.

> Economics is an art as well because it also deals with policy designs and their implemental aspects.

Policy questions lead us to the *art* component of economics. The component links the positive elements of economics to its normative content. The linkage is important. Consider this example. We observe that inflation is speeding up in the economy and feel that it may be injurious to economic development of the country. As a remedy, we might suggest reduction in money supply or imposition of price controls. The discussion of such measures becomes an integral part of economic discourse. Thus, you see how the three facets of economics—positive, normative and art (policy)—integrate in this simple case. Their complete separation in economics could never be possible because the subject was primarily developed as a discipline to throw light upon questions of policy. As different policies suit different nations, economics by its very nature operates in national frames. For example, the developing countries aspire for more independence of action and national respect than for mere bread and butter. Their interests need not always be the same as of developed countries. Conflict of interests has often caused much confusion and controversy in economic theory and practice.

1.3 METHODOLOGICAL PITFALLS

The terms *methodology* and *methods* are often used in place of one another in textbook economics. This is somewhat misleading. Methods refer to the ways economists use to formulate economic hypotheses, theories and laws. They are part of the subject, i.e. *internal* to it. Methodology, on the other hand, is part of the theory of knowledge. Methodology of a subject oversees it from *outside* the subject and is philosophical in nature. It consists of rules, criteria and procedures to assess how well a subject—economics for example—is performing with reference to its objectives.

> Methodology is not a part of economics. Rather, it examines the performance of economics from the outside.

It is to be noted that methodology of mainstream economics developed mostly after the middle of the twentieth century, when the science of economics had already matured and its structure had hardened. Methodologists largely struggled to uphold and justify what the economists and economies had all along been doing. It was too week to reverse or modify the tide of actuality. Here, the glide was from reality to doctrine. In contrast, Islam being a way of life, reality was supposed to conform to its doctrine.

As Islamic economics is based on Qur'anic injunctions, prophetic sayings and their juristic interpretations, its methodology cannot go beyond screening the existing stock of knowledge to decide what could be acceptable out of it, what needs outright rejection and what could possibly be absorbed after due modification. However, what precautions economists must take to avoid pitfalls of the sort exemplified below seems relevant to both disciplines of economics—mainstream and Islamic.

> Economics being a science deals with cause and effects relationships. As such, logical reasoning plays a crucial role in arriving at valid conclusions. It is imperative to know and avoid pitfalls in economic reasoning.

1.3.1   Fallacy of Composition

A common pitfall in economic reasoning is the assumption that what is true for one individual or part of a whole is necessarily true for the group of individuals or the whole. This is called fallacy of composition. For example, in a group of students, Fareed may prefer carrot juice to pineapple juice but it does not mean that all in the group or even the majority have the same preference. Again, money is wealth for an individual, but a nation cannot become rich merely by printing more of its own currency notes. Likewise, a favourable balance of trade usually benefits a country but all nations cannot have a favourable balance of trade simultaneously. (Why?)

1.3.2   Causation Fallacies

Post hoc fallacy

You might observe that event A follows event B. But you must think carefully before you conclude that B *causes* A. Before spring every year, migratory birds from Siberia flock to some lakes in north India. However, you cannot safely conclude that migratory birds bring spring to that country. The sort of reasoning 'after this therefore because of this' may be false and is called a *post hoc fallacy*.

Covariation versus causation

> The movement together of two variables does not necessarily mean that one causes the other.

Do not treat covariation or 'movement together' of two variables, as a cause and effect relationship. Statistical correlation only informs us that the variables, e.g. A and B, tend to change together. This, however, need not always mean that one *causes* the other. Suppose, a sample result shows that the proportion of boys was more among total births when the moon was rising than when it was waning. Would you say, on that evidence alone, that the rising or waning of the moon affects the sex of the child?

Take another example. A time series containing data for the last thirty years relating to the number of woman drivers and road accidents in Kuala Lumpur shows a continual increase in both the series and correlation between the two is found as high as +0.93. Should we conclude that women make bad drivers? Surely, such a conclusion may be grossly unfair to the fairer sex. Certainly, it is not the number of women drivers alone but also the number of men drivers that must have been rising over the years and the total number of drivers—men and women—may have even had a higher degree of correlation with road accidents. The reason may or may not be the fall in the efficiency of the drivers; it may well be the fast growth in the traffic volume relative to the carrying capacity of roads.

1.3.3 Tautological Reasoning

We should avoid tautological reasoning or statements. A tautology means saying of the same thing twice over in different words as fault of style. Here are some illustrations of tautological arguments. Black is black because we see it black. Most demand curves slope downwards because people buy more at lower prices. Here, the real issue is to provide reasons as to why people buy more when prices fall. Likewise, it carries us nowhere to say that people prefer to buy what they are seen as buying. This sort of reasoning is not uncommon in economic discussions, more so in popular debates. You must study economics carefully and should be able to recognize *tautologies*.

> Tautology means repeating the same thing in different words or ways.

1.3.4 Exclusionist Argumentation

Exclusivity in argumentation means shutting out from consideration other possible reasons that may cause an event. The use of exclusionist reasoning in economics has increased over time in the name of promoting scientific accuracy. While putting across our arguments, we often tend to forget that economic activity is an arbitrarily separated part of a much larger social dynamics. Economic phenomena influence and are influenced by a host of non-economic factors—moral, religious, political and social. For example, fixation of minimum wages, control of rents or profits, grant of subsidies to crops, fulfilment of basic needs and so on may not meet economic logic of free markets but may have justification on other grounds, say, social or political.

> Exclusion means leaving out other factors except one that may cause an event.

The Islamic emphasis on adopting a holistic approach in studying social sciences helps in avoiding the pitfalls of the exclusionist approach in economic analysis. It is helpful to keep in mind the relationship of economic issues we deal with which have ethical, political, psychological, religious and other social factors attached to it.

1.4   METHODS OF ECONOMICS

Deduction and induction are both needed for scientific analysis. In fact, both are now combined in a single investigation depending on the stage of inquiry. Classical Islamic researches have used both; the modern empirical method was indeed perfected in the Muslim Spain.

There has been much debate in economics on what method—pure logic (deduction) or empirical analysis (induction)—is suitable for economic inquiries. It is now agreed that economics must use what is called the *scientific method* that stems from the old debate, deduction versus induction. The approach harmonizes the two methods in a logical sequence. Deduction and induction can each be used at different stages in the same inquiry. The *scientific method* involves the following steps:

1. Start with some obvious truth about the economic phenomenon. For example, people are motivated into action by self-interest, so they are likely to buy less when the price of a commodity rises and vice versa. This can be the hypothesis to start with.

2. Observation of facts, i.e. collection of real world data on prices and sales.

3. Based on the data, formulate a possible cause and effect explanation to uphold or reject the hypothesis. For example, test if price and quantity demanded were positively associated. Your empirical analysis may reject the hypothesis in favour of the alternative hypothesis that price and quantity demanded do not have a positive relationship, rather they have a negative relationship.

4. If repeated experiments confirm the alternative hypothesis, it may be treated as an economic theory.

5. Finally, if over time and space the experiments fail to refute the theory, it may be accorded the status of an economic law: the law of demand.

This entire procedure is also available for Islamic economics. The empirical method which is the darling of mainstream economics today was evolved and perfected essentially in Muslim Spain. Of course, elements of faith cannot be put to any sort of testing.

1.5   MONEY AND EXCHANGE

Money helps separate the buying and selling of commodities.

Economics is distinct from other social sciences in an important way. It has a scale that is money to measure values of goods and services. Measurement makes economics relatively a more accurate science than other social disciplines like psychology, political science, ethics, philosophy or sociology.

Goods that satisfy our wants have value for us. But value can be thought of in two ways. First, how much satisfaction do we get from consuming or having a thing. This is the concept of *value-in-use*. There is no direct measure of value-in-use: who can measure, for example, the satisfaction a glass of water would give to a person dying of thirst? Second is the notion of *value-in-exchange*: how much of one commodity a person is willing to give for having a given quantity of another commodity, e.g. how many pencils for a notebook or how many chocolate bars for a cricket bat? But settling and expressing exchange value of a good in terms of all other goods are a tedious work and hinder progress. Money provides a common expression for values of goods in the form of their prices. It *separates* buying from selling in the act of exchange. You can sell your goods in the market for money and spend that money as and when you choose to buy goods you need. The ultimate exchange is still of goods for goods, money just serves as a medium or go-between in the process of exchange.

> Money helped to overcome the difficulties of barter; it separates the sale and purchase aspects of transactions by measuring the exchange value of goods called prices. Remember that the exchange value of goods is not the same thing as their value in use.

Money evolved over time as a matter of social convention—from hides and skins through gold and silver to paper money and finally to bank deposits of today which are just a 'promise to pay'. The most important thing about money is *stability* in its value or purchasing power, i.e. of prices in the economy. Given that, it is of little significance of what *material* money is made. To insist, as some still do, that money should be made of something valuable, e.g. gold or silver, is like insisting that air tickets should be printed on chocolates so that if we do not travel we may eat them..

> Money evolved over time as a social convention. The universality of its definition does not lie in what commodity was used as money; it lies in the functions that it performed. General acceptability and stability in the value of money are two main characteristics of money.

1.6 MICROECONOMICS AND MACROECONOMICS

To study the problems of scarcity and choice, economics is divided into its micro and macro branches. Microeconomics is concerned with the behaviour of individual economic entities like consumers, firms, industries, individual prices for commodities and factors of production in the markets. It considers questions of allocation of resources within firms and industries with reference to *what* to produce and *how*. It also sees how income is distributed among individuals, groups and regions of a country. On the other hand, macroeconomics focuses in a blanket sense on issues of growth, employment and stability. It deals with aggregates of demand and supply, savings, investment, price levels, money volume, balance of payments and the like for the economy *as a whole* to analyze and assess its performance.

> Scarcity of resources gives rise to the problem of choice.

There is a close relationship between the two branches of the subject. After all, aggregates of incomes, expenditures, or demand and supply of products are all sums of individual values. Most economic decisions are made by individual entities such as consumers, producers and institutions in a society and macro variables reflect the sum effect of these decisions. Figure 1.2 shows the connection between micro and macroeconomics via the circular flow in a closed economy that assumes away the existence of savings, investments or public finances. Numerous decisions made daily *within* the boxes of firms and households are dealt with in microeconomics. What flows as the result out of the two boxes becomes the subject matter of macroeconomics. Firms make decisions about the hiring (employing) of various factors of production—land, labour hours and machines—from the households for producing goods and services. The sum of these payments including profits to factors constitutes income of the nation. Firms use the services of the hired factors to produce the goods and services that the individual recipients of income purchase with their money in the product market. The aggregate of these purchases becomes national expenditure as well as the aggregate value of goods and services that the system produced. Markets convert individual decisions into national aggregates. Firms buy their services in the factor market for wages, rent, interest and profit.

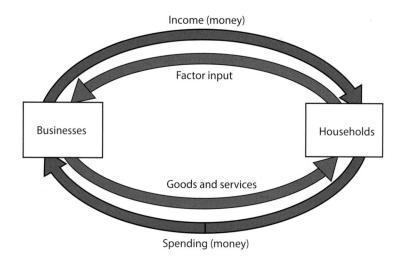

Figure 1.2 *Real flow and money flow in a two-sector closed economy*

In a simple closed model of an economy that Figure 1.2 represents, you can see that: *National income = National expenditure = Value of national output.* (How?) Also notice, that each real flow in the economy is matched with a corresponding money flow; the two always running in opposite directions as the arrow heads show.

Indeed, the relationship between the two branches of the subject is so close that the study of micro foundations of macroeconomics is gaining prominence in modern researches as a separate subject. There are issues that are studied in both micro and macroeconomics or lie at the border line between them. For example, the general equilibrium analysis, i.e. the study of interactions between individual markets *simultaneously,* is becoming the common property of the two branches. So is the case with environmental issues or welfare economics.

This book provides an introductory presentation of the principles of microeconomics from Islamic perspectives. It uses economic environment in developing economies as the backdrop for analysis and illustrations.

1.7   PROBLEMS ECONOMISTS SEEK TO RESOLVE

Among the questions that continue to confront economists, the following have been of significance and are largely philosophical in nature.

1. What is the source of wealth? It is apparent that work creates wealth while nature provides in her benevolence the resources from the universe. But profits are also there. Where do profits come from? Does capital create wealth, like labour, or are profits merely an appropriation from the wealth that labour creates? Wealth is a stock in economics while income is a flow. Does Islam recognize this distinction?

2. We face the problem of prices too. The prices of individual commodities are the phenomenon of economic life we all experience. Microeconomics explains them. But prices as a whole are seen varying over time randomly? What then is the underlying principle of value that accounts for such fluctuations? Can we always maintain full employment; how do we manage aggregate demand for the purpose? Why the world experiences economic turmoil like the one it has faced since 2008?

3. Again, what is the role of money in an economy? What is the relation of individual money incomes to the societal wealth as a whole? Should money be related to something valuable? Was gold standard better than the current fiat money systems? Should or can we go back to the era of gold-linked money? A United Nations (UN) Commission is considering such issues for recommending reforms in the monetary arrangements at the global level. The focal points of attention in the matter are of course the International Monetary Fund (IMF) and the World Bank. How relevant is the talk of reviving gold dinar in Muslim countries? Can the Islamic Development Bank (IDB) contribute to a solution; if yes, how?

4. Also, we have the problem of economic justice: how do we define it? Can it be right that some families live in extravagant luxury while others can scarcely find food for their children? Are such situations ethically valid? Not only there are gross inequalities in the distribution of wealth and incomes within developing economies, the absolute gap between them on the one hand and the developed economies on the other continue to widen: it has almost doubled since 1990 as Table 1.2 demonstrates. World Bank reports (2010) that twelve countries now produce more than two-thirds of the world's output. Do you think this is a fair win–win situation for all?

> Despite tremendous growth of economics over the centuries, we have not been able to explain let alone solve a number of problems the world faces. These especially include among others, the real source of wealth and profits, price level variations over time, distributional inequalities, poverty and the ever increasing pollution.

> Achieving justice is the most difficult of economic objectives.

Table 1.2 *Per capita income data for selected years in US dollars*

Country type	Year					
	1990	1995	2000	2005	2010	2015★
Developing countries (a)	840	1,090	1,230	2,363	2,781	3,371
Developed countries (b)	19,590	24,930	27,510	34,962	38,360	40,617
Gap: (b) − (a)	18,750	23,840	26,280	32,599	35,579	37,246
(b)/(a)		23.32	22.87	22.37	14.80	13.79	12.0

Source: Construction is based on the data in World Development Reports. Developed countries include the 'high income' classification and developing countries include the 'low and middle income' classifications (★estimated).

5. What about the ever increasing pollution humanity faces with ever increasing production? Can there be a system of nations sharing the pollution consequences equitably, if some of the largest polluters stay out of the international protocols that most countries abide by?

6. Finally, can universal privatization and globalization benefit all nations—developed and developing—in equal measure? If not, what can be a fair basis for allowing differences? Can promotion of global interest bypass the interests of individual nations? For example, can some countries alone have the option of having atomic energy and insist on denying the same to others?

The sort of questions we raised above requires deep thought. We do not have any agreed answers to them yet. Let us hope for the future.

1.8   THE LANGUAGE OF ECONOMICS

An important source of confusion and controversy in economics is that unlike natural sciences, economists draw their terminology from the language in everyday use.

Unlike physical sciences, economics picks up its notions such as scarcity, production, consumption, utility, satisfaction, firm, cost, profit, income, savings, investment, growth, employment, demand, supply, maximization, etc. from the common man's language. You must know that when we use these words in economics they often assume *different* meanings. Not many of us understand that economists may be talking about altogether different things when they use the same words as the common man. Even among economists, differences in opinion can at times be traced back to the divergence in the meaning each attaches to the same term. This may happen because terms assume different meanings depending on a number of things, such as the goals of an economic study or the type of market structure one is dealing with. For example, the notion of a firm, you will see, does not remain the same when you think of it under competition among many producers rather than competition among a few of them or just between the two.

To avoid confusion, concepts, notions and terms economists use have to be clearly explained and understood. They are *coined* to facilitate analysis: they are *heuristic* in nature. A coined or heuristic concept need not always state or contain reality. Similarly, we have a kind of reasoning common in social sciences including economics that may be called *metaphysical*. The word has been used in various senses. In economics, it refers to the use of language that carries no *factual* content and describes no logical relations. Metaphysics gives no precise instructions but it is widely used to influence the opinion and behaviour of people. The early French economists, called the Physiocrats (1750–1773), preached natural order that implied almost no role for the state in running an economy. Likewise, Adam Smith believed in the natural harmony between individuals and social interests. Both ideas—natural order and harmony of interest—were metaphysical in formulation. So are many of the present concepts such as the 'greatest good of the greatest number'. How do we say what is good or measure it? Or how can we balance more good of a few against less good of many?

> Many economic concepts lack real content.

Expressions such as harmony, common good, altruism and commitment have no scientific content but do create perceptions that cannot be ignored. For perceptions, conditioned reality have at times, caused social turmoil, even revolutions. An upcoming variant of economics—Islamic economics—often uses this sort of perceptive language and is fast winning adherents, especially in the areas of banking and finance.

There hardly is anything novel about this development. Economics has been mixed up with politics from its very inception: it is mixed up with patriotism. Economics is increasingly assuming political overtones. Talks about the general good, win-win situations, universality for economic laws or the world reducing to a global village often conceal the advocacy of national or stratified interests. This fact was kept under wraps for centuries. But now the wrap seems to be coming off.

1.9   ECONOMIC SYSTEMS

Economic activity operates within the confines of an organizational framework. This framework is often referred to as an economic system. Such a system consists of economic entities, components and institutions such as households, manufacturers, farms, banks, transportation units, markets and so on placed in relation to one another. They rest on and operate in line with some axioms and observe a set of rules. The axioms refer to the fundamental principle that the proponents of the system regard as self-evident truths. They have ideological underpinnings and provide legitimacy to the rules designed to regulate the mutual relations of the entities and institutions of the system with a view to achieving the objectives of running an economy.

> An organizational framework is needed to conduct the economic activity. The framework is based on some axioms and fundamental principles having an ideological base. The framework is called an economic system. It is inspired by the world view a community has.

Axioms that make a system what it is intended to be, come from the world view a society holds. World view broadly refers to how a community visualizes the mission of its existence on the globe and what path it considers suitable to achieve the goals of that mission. World view conditions the doctrine or theoretical base of the economic system the community chooses to follow and promote. The doctrine clarifies its position on such matters as property rights and their ownership, basic freedoms or restrictions on them, motivational scheme, the role of the state and the vision of a social order that it aims to establish. The prevalent economic systems—capitalism and socialism—both have positional and methodological differences from Islam. For example, in capitalism any method of promoting growth and acquiring wealth that conflicts with its principle of individuals' economic freedom is resisted: it treats market as the prime arbiter in economic matters. In Islam, individual freedom and markets are respected but face constraints if broader social interests so demand. Socialism is not opposed to the capitalist insistence on growth but advocates forms of organizing economic activity with public ownership of material means of production and labour dominance. Islam, on the other hand, denounces regimentation of life and procedures that would humble its norms of distributive justice and fair play.

> A specific worldview lies behind each economic system.

The words, capitalism, socialism and Islamic system, are essentially generic in nature; they have no precise meaning. One can theoretically define these words with some accuracy but then any one society, e.g. Indian or Pakistani, does not exactly fit into any particular description: theory and practice differ in each case. Interestingly, the advocates of each system provide arguments for the system of their choice in *theoretical* terms but present arguments against the rival systems on the basis of what they are in *practice*. Such a pitfall must be avoided.

Despite the above details, the question remains: what precisely is the nature of an Islamic system and where does it exactly fall? How far it is valid to claim as some do, that Islam provides the framework for a unique economic order that is neither capitalist nor socialist? We may debate the point but it is difficult to dispute that definition of such an order still remains unclear. The most significant controversy in the way on the juridical front concerns the limits of private property rights. In essence, the Islamic economic system seems to be capitalistic. Reforms proposed by Islamic economists are, at most, a blueprint for a capitalist economy with an interventionist state defence. Islamic jurisprudence is explicit in its defence of private property rights and endorses many regulatory functions common in modern capitalist economies. Below, we shall present a comparison of the three systems largely in terms of their basic *principles*.

The basic differences in the three systems may be broadly discussed under four heads: ownership of property rights, operational framework, motivation scheme and social priorities. We begin the discussion with an explanation regarding the axioms of the various systems. As indicated earlier, axioms are norms that a system regards as self-evident, requiring no proof.

1.9.1   Axiomatic Differences

In principle, capitalism believes in freedom of enterprise, public non-intervention in economic affairs, market arbitration and competition as a regulatory force. Also, it sees in general no clash between individual and social interests.

In contrast, socialism sees private enterprise as an unwelcome institution leading to exploitation of the masses. It sees labour in inevitable conflict with capital owners in which labour is believed to emerge victorious. Workers eventually capture political power, the state owns natural resources and instruments of production. It directs the economy to meet social objectives and priorities.

Islam strikes the middle course; it allows axioms of capitalism to operate in a reformed and modified shape in the light of the Shari'ah requirements: unity, freedom of action, moderation and balance, *amanah* and justice, and social responsibility are its foundational norms.

> The Islamic system in terms of axioms strikes a middle course between capitalism and socialism.

1.9.2   Property Rights

Property refers to natural resources and all man-made instruments used for producing wealth. Rights in property consist of the ability to acquire, use or sell it, or receive or give it in gift or inheritance, or deal with it in any other way the law permits. Capitalism allows private ownership of property while socialism puts property rights mostly in the hands of the state agencies.

The Islamic system is closer to capitalism in this matter but with a difference. It allows private ownership in property but enjoins on owners to hold it in *trust* for the society as a whole. The Qur'an says: *He (Allah) is who has created for you, all that is in the earth'* (2:29). Unlike capitalism, Islam assigns rights (*haq*) to others in one's wealth and insists that these rights are to be honoured. Thus, Islam puts in principle more restrictions on individual property rights than other free systems. Furthermore, Islam encourages the creation of trusts (*awqaf*) to serve specific or general social purposes. Even though establishing trusts is not prohibited or absent in capitalist societies, historical evidence confirms its prominence in Muslim communities as a third sector in addition to the private and public sectors.

> Islam allows private ownership of property but it is held in *amanah* or trust, as others' rights are invoked in one's property.

1.9.3   Operational Mechanism

The institution of private ownership of property in capitalism implies freedom of enterprise for personal gain. It operates through the mechanism of prices determined in the market by the competitive forces of demand and supply. Business firms work as a go-between the two sets of prices: (i) the one at which they sell what they produce and (ii) the other at which they buy factor inputs they use for production. The owners of the firm take the difference, i.e. (i − ii) as profit if positive or suffer a loss if negative. Thus, capitalism is a profit and loss system: profits are the carrots for the right decision makers while losses are the sticks for those who go wrong. The market is the main arbiter of the system in matters of allocating resources and distributing the fruits of production.

As Islam also allows private ownership of property, even if with a trusteeship constraint, it too relies on price mechanism and competitive markets for resource allocation and output distribution. However, its output mix gives prominence to goods for the fulfilment of basic needs, curtailment of luxuries and exclusion of what it regards as *haram* (prohibited) goods. To achieve its objectives, it does not put any limits on the expansion of the public sector; freedom of enterprise though encouraged is not a social imperative.

> Markets, price mechanism and profit motive are allowed to operate in an Islamic system but subject to the observation of its moral code of conduct.

In socialism, resources being virtually owned by the organs of the state, it is the Central Planning Authority of the country that mostly allocates resources including labour to various uses according to a plan that sets priorities and targets for production. They decide what to produce, how much, for whom and using what techniques. Prices are there but play a passive accounting role in socialist decision-making processes. The mechanism is more costly and less efficient in performance compared to market arbitration that both capitalism and the Islamic system make use of. The main advantage of the Islamic system is that it brings about a relatively more equitable distribution of wealth and income in the society. Compared to capitalism, socialism has much varied structures melting into mixed economies of all sorts, the distinguishing feature being a wider public sector in the economy and greater control of the state over private enterprise in the economy. Its potential for better distribution of income and pro-poor stance has led some Muslim countries to view the Islamic system closer to socialism, and on that perception one finds some among the Muslim countries also wearing the socialist garb.

1.9.4   Motivation Scheme

We talked about the pursuit of self-interest as the regulator of human behaviour above. In capitalism, based on freedom of enterprise, self-interest translates into profit motive. Property owners employ their possessions for enhancing them through profit earned on investment in productive activities. However, the future being uncertain, it is not necessary that investment should result in profit. There is also the risk of loss. So, profit is often regarded as the reward for risk-bearing in business. We shall return to this point in Chapter 11.

To be a just reward, there ought to be a one-on-one correspondence between profit and risk. In capitalism, such correspondence mostly does not exist nor can it be ensured. The position is no different in an Islamic system. We shall discuss this behavioural aspect in detail in the following chapters.

Therefore, Islam seeks to moderate the profit motive and promote the perception of a fair return on investment. In capitalist societies, sharing of profit with labour is gaining ground to promote fairness and win industrial peace. The Islamic system would only encourage the trend.

> Social good and the promotion of Shari'ah objectives work as the main motivational force in the Islamic system.

Socialist societies are in a state of transition to a market system after the collapse of socialism in the USSR (1989) and its subsequent disintegration. The pace of privatisation and liberalisation in these economies is on the increase. Profit motive is fast replacing the socialist norm: the largest good of the largest numbers.

1.9.5 Societal Priorities

Capitalism, as its name indicates, is a system that works primarily for safeguarding and promoting the interests of private capital or property owners. Profit maximization, allocation of resources and distribution of output according to the distribution of purchasing power in the society are its basic norms. Socialism on the other hand aims at working for advancing the well-being of the society as a whole, individual interest is of secondary importance.

The Islamic system falls in between: it uses capitalist structures to achieve overall social welfare. It invokes the trusteeship notion, grants rights to the deprived in the wealth of the rich and puts the *ultimate* responsibility for the fulfilment of basic needs of *all* its citizens on the state. Constitutions of Iran and Pakistan incorporate this duty among the responsibilities of the state towards achieving the objectives of the Islamic law (Shari'ah). Islam is a *din*, i.e. a way of life. It is wrong to presume, as some do, that if we take out interest and add *zakat* to capitalism, it will become an Islamic system. Cultural and social priorities of nations may differ much on the basis of faith and custom.

The following chapters explain basic principles of microeconomics in a capitalistic framework interfaced with moral norms and requirements of Islam.

BOX 1.2

Economic Problem and Its Solution: Secular versus Islamic

The secularist market system, with its undue emphasis on individual self-interest and disregard for the healthy role that moral values can play in reforming individual tastes and preferences as well as social norms and attitudes, has failed to bring about an equitable balance between unlimited wants and limited resources. It has inadvertently put the entire burden on the price mechanism. This has tipped the balance in favour of the rich. Critiques of the system have, therefore, rightly indicated that the system has on the whole been highly unjust and has aggravated the inequalities of income and wealth. Its utilitarian philosophy, combined with the enormous power of its advertising machine and the high social status enjoyed by conspicuous consumption, has led to a large-scale multiplication of wants, most of them superficial and unnecessary for human well-being. Credit to both the public and private sectors has risen excessively to satisfy this expansion in wants. This has been the result of a built-in flaw in the interest-based financial system, where banks do not share in the risk and have, therefore, an incentive to lend as much as they can to maximize their profit. The acceleration of demand at a rate far beyond the ability of the economy to supply goods and services tends to generate inflationary pressures. Efforts are then made to reduce aggregate demand in a value-free, across-the-board manner. This leads to recession and unemployment, adding further to the woes of the poor.

A role for the government has now become generally recognized under the influence of socialism, the Great Depression, economic downtowns and financial crises. This is undoubtedly a welcome change in capitalist thinking. However, it has also led to a substantial rise in government spending. Without a corresponding decrease in inessential spending elsewhere, it has led to unduly large budgetary deficits in many countries around the world. The total world debt has consequently risen substantially—a phenomenon which has been generally recognized as one of the major causes of financial crises. Only social health at a deeper level can help bring about a just economic system that is capable of satisfying the needs of all without creating economic imbalances.

In the Islamic economic system, the primary emphasis has to be on the difficult but indispensable moral transformation of individuals and society and the establishment of appropriate social and economic institutions to curb inessential spending and improve the condition of the poor. The government should also play an active and constructive role but depend more on the moral reform of society and the development of appropriate social and economic institutions rather than its coercive power which should be used only to the extent to which it is necessary. The government machinery should not be allowed to degenerate into despotism and to perpetuate injustice in the same manner as blind market forces do.

Source: Chapra, M. U. (2011), The economic problem: Can Islam play an effective role in solving it efficiently and equitably? *IRTI Working Paper*, p. 1432-01.

Summary

- Human wants are unlimited while resources to satisfy them are scarce and have alternative uses. This forces choice-making on human beings. Wherever there is a problem of choice there is an economic problem.

- Economics is the subject that deals with decision-making in three important areas: (i) What to produce and how much? (ii) What technology is to be used to produce goods? (iii) How is the output to be divided among individuals, functional groups and regions? These decisions involve questions of efficiency and equity.

- The nature of these problems can be broadly studied through the production possibilities curve including its shape, slope and shifts.

- All economies operate to achieve growth, full employment, stability, equity and self-reliance in a national aspirations framework that may include spiritual considerations as well.

- Pursuit of self-interest at the individual and national level regulates economic behaviour. However, there need not always be an automatic harmony between individual and social interests. This gives importance to the role of state in the economic life of the community.

Pursuit of self-interest does not bar or deny altruism or commitment being part of the motivation in an economic scheme.

- Economics has both positive and normative aspects and has also had a policy orientation from its very inception.

- Methodology of economics provides a set of rules, criteria and procedures to evaluate from outside if the discipline of economics is performing satisfactorily at the theoretical level to promote in practice the objectives it is meant to achieve. Methods of economics are, on the other hand, *internal* to the subject to help erect its hypotheses, theories and laws.

- The controversy as to which of the methods, induction or deduction is to be used or is better is no more relevant. Different methods can be and are used at different stages in the same economic inquiry. Such a procedure is called the scientific method. However, certain obvious pitfalls in economic reasoning are to be avoided.

- Economics has two main divisions: microeconomics and macroeconomics. The two are closely related. Microeconomics provides foundations for macroeconomics. Microeconomics deals with the behaviour and performance of individual economic agents like firms and the households while macroeconomics concentrates on their collective behaviour. This can be illustrated with a circular flows diagram for a simple closed economy.

- Some of the crucial problems economists have all along been struggling with include who produces wealth, for what profit is the reward, how can we explain erratic fluctuations in price levels, what constitutes economic justice and why a state of full employment cannot always be maintained. Other issues include how we can deal effectively with externalities like pollution and its consequences, or how is privatisation plus globalisation equally beneficial for all nations, developed and developing.

- One difficulty in why people often fail to understand economists is that the latter mostly use the words of common language but give them technical meanings to explain their theories and policies. Economic concepts are often made heuristic to facilitate analysis and have little real content.

- Economic activity operates within the confines of an organizational framework or economic system. Three economic systems—capitalist, socialist and Islamic—differ considerably from one another with reference to property rights, operation mechanism, motivation scheme and social priorities. Islamic system follows the middle course. These differences arise because they rest on different axiomatic positions.

Glossary

Scarcity of resources Some writers deny that Islam upholds the concept of scarcity, presumably in reaction to Lionel Robbins who in his *Nature and Significance of Economic Science* (1932) lamented that nature has been niggardly; it has not provided us all that we need to satisfy our wants. This patently is not correct. True, God has created inexhaustible stocks for all times to come (Qur'an 15:20) but resources do become *available* to mankind from the provision on search (Qur'an 29:17; 62:10; 73:20) and remain limited in relation to human wants. The Qur'an seems to endorse the distinction between provision of resources and their availability to mankind, otherwise why should it, for example, denounce wasteful expenditure (*israf*), condemn hoarding, exhort men to search for God's bounties and distinguish between the rich and the poor? Alternatively, if resources were not scarce, why could not poverty be removed from the face of the earth despite all efforts? And finally, why should we study economics at all?

World view This refers to how an individual or a community looks at the purpose of life, especially the relationship between man, universe and the creator of both. Mainstream world view divides human conduct into economic and non–economic; Islam sees life as a whole where moral values determine action in all affairs including economic. In mainstream, world view doctrine follows practice; in the Islamic the glide is from doctrine to reality. Finally, reason in Islam is subject to revelation; in mainstream economics reason conditioned by self-interest alone is the guide to action.

Well-being The concept of human well-being is not clear and precise even in mainstream economics. It arbitrarily separates economic from the non–economic using monetary valuations. Also, it focuses only on the material or mundane component of well-being; Islamic economics sees well-being from a spiritual prism. The Qur'an is explicit on the point: *But seek with the wealth which God has provided thee the home of the hereafter, and forget not thy portion of the present world* (28:77). The Islamic term for well-being is *falah that* integrates the mundane and the spiritual aspects of human personality.

Amanah (trusteeship) The concept of trusteeship or *amanah* is fundamental to Islam; it is the soul of religion. God created the universe and stocked it with his treasures for all living beings on the earth. When man volunteered to take charge of affairs on the earth as God's vicegerent, he got the job as a trustee. The resources of the universe were meant for the use of all humans. For, the Qur'an said: *He is who has created for you all that is in the earth* (2:29). Thus seen, we own wealth in which the *rights* of others are explicitly invoked. To give others their indicated *due* is an obligation, not an act of mercifulness or charity. The logic of most Islamic injunctions follows from the all-pervading notion of *amanah*. It is this concept that helps glorify Islamic system as a via media that utilizes the means of the capitalistic order to achieve the egalitarian objectives of socialistic patters.

Tautology The word tautology is used to show that a proposition is claimed to be true merely by saying the same thing twice. No logical deduction is involved; same idea is repeated in different words, e.g. people buy what they are seen as buying or annual poetry symposium is held each year.

Invisible hand Adam Smith argued that in a free market economy an individual by pursuing self-interest tends to also promote the good of his community as a whole through coining a metaphor that he called 'the invisible hand'. He thought that each individual by maximizing revenue for self maximizes the total revenue of society as well because the latter is identical with the sum total of individual revenues. Smith used the term 'invisible hand' only three times in his *Wealth of Nations*, but the metaphor later gained widespread use. Islamic economists tried to create a contrast by talking of the 'hand of God'. In fact the invisible hand (of self-interest) in Smith's is in itself the creation of God.

Opportunity cost The opportunity cost of a resource refers to the value of the next-highest-valued alternative use of that resource. If, for example, you spend time and money going to a movie, you cannot spend that time on reading a book or money on buying chocolates. If your next-best alternative to seeing the movie is reading the book and enjoying chocolates, then the opportunity cost of seeing the movie is the money not spent on chocolates plus foregone pleasure of reading the book. The word 'opportunity' in 'opportunity cost' is actually redundant. The cost of using something is already the value of the highest-valued alternative use. But redundancy can at times be a virtue. Here, its virtue is to remind us that the cost of using a resource arises from the value of what it could be used for instead.

Concepts for Review

- Axioms
- Capitalism
- Economic system
- Fallacy of composition
- Induction and deduction
- Macroeconomics heuristic concepts
- Marginal rate of transformation
- Methodology
- Opportunity cost
- Ownership of property
- Post hoc fallacy

- Production frontier
- Production possibilities
- Rational behaviour
- Scarcity
- Self-interest
- Social priorities
- Socialism
- Tautology microeconomics
- Transformation curve

Case Study   1.1

The Worsening Unemployment

GENEVA As of last year, some 12.4 per cent of people aged 15 to 24 worldwide were unemployed, up from 12.3 per cent in 2011 and is estimated to reach 12.6 per cent by 2013. Global youth unemployment is likely to touch 12.8 per cent by 2018, wiping out gains made in the recent economic recovery.

In six of 10 developing countries surveyed, more than 60 per cent of the young people were either unemployed or trapped in low-paying jobs; for many of them 'a job does not necessarily equal a livelihood'. The highest regional rates in 2012 were 28.3 per cent in the Middle East and 23.7 per cent in North Africa. The lowest rates were South Asia, with 9.3 per cent, and East Asia at 9.5 per cent.

Source: UN Business News: <http://www.huffingtonpost.com/2013/05/08/global-youth-unemployment_n_3236229.html> accessed 12 December, 2013 (edited from the web).

Case Questions
1. For many of them,'a job does not necessarily equal livelihood'. Elaborate.
2. In your opinion, to what extent has the recent rising unemployment of the young aggravated the recent unrest in the affected countries? Give reasons to support your answer.

Case Study   1.2

What Caused the Iraq War— Presence of Weapons or Oil?

LONDON Hans Blix, who led the UN weapons inspection team in the run-up to the 2003 invasion (of Iraq) told the *Daily Mail* that the then two leaders—Bush and Blair—had 'misled themselves and then they misled the public' about the reasons for the conflict.

The presence of weapons of mass destruction was the main justification for the US-led war in the absence of explicit UN approval, but the Blix team found nothing in the run-up to the invasion nor was such weapons found afterwards.

Blix said he warned Blair not to invade because 'it would prove paradoxical and absurd if 230,000 troops were to invade Iraq and find very little'. However, the leaders eventually had so much military in the Gulf that they felt they had to invade.

Source: Adapted from the *New Straits Times*, 6 December, 2009, p. 39.

Case Questions
1. It is widely believed that the prime cause of the US-led invasion of Iraq was the oil wealth of that country rather than the weapons. Do you agree? Give reasons for your answer.
2. What in your opinion have been the consequences of invasion (economic and non-economic)?
3. Can such invasions of weaker countries be avoided in future? Argue your case.

Test Questions

1.1 Why is choice-making the central feature of economics? Explain. What would happen if resources were not scarce or did not have alternative uses?

1.2 With the passage of time the shifts shown by outer curves (unbroken) in Figure 1.3 took place in the production possibilities curves of three economies. How would you explain each change?

1.3 Assume that Figure 1.3 shows the production possibilities curves of Iraq before and after the American invasion of that country. Which curve in your opinion shows the shift after the invasion and why?

1.4 Figures in Table 1.1 represent the production frontier $Y = 36 - X^2$ with $X \leqslant 6$. Find and plot the frontier values if the function changes over time as (a) $Y = 33 - X^2$, (b) $Y = 27 - 0.8 X^2$ and (c) $Y = 27 - 1.2 X^2$, where $0 \leq X \leq 6$ in each case. Plot the new frontier in each case on the same graph as shows the initial frontier and interpret the change. (Approximate the obtained values to whole numbers.)

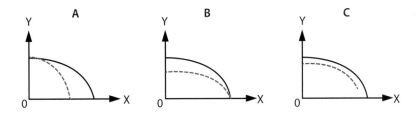

Figure 1.3 *Shift in the production possibilities curves of three imaginary economies*

1.5 If $Y = 26 - X^2$ is a production frontier linking goods Y and X, find the combinations of Y and X falling on the frontier, keeping $X < 6$, and plot the curve. Find the marginal rate of transformation of Y into X for each combination. If the slope of the price line $P_y - P_x$ is 6, what combination of Y and X quantities will the economy produce?

1.6 Is the pursuit of self-interest or its maximization always unethical? Argue your case from an Islamic viewpoint.

1.7 In what sense is economics a science? Can economics be neutral towards the ends? Give reasons for your answer.

1.8 Comment on the following statements:

(a) Among the MPs who voted against the Agriculture Reforms Bill in the parliament, 75% were the farmers. So the bill was opposed to the interests of the farmers.

(b) In a community, most of the people who drink wine die before reaching eighty years of age. So, drinking is injurious to health and the sale of wine must be banned in the country.

(c) Most cost curves are U-shaped because they first fall over a range of output, remain constant for a while and then rise as output increases.

(d) The death rate among the American soldiers in occupied Iraq is much lower than in New York City. Therefore, it is safer to be fighting in Iraq than living in New York.

1.9   Distinguish between methodology and methods of economics. Explain how scientific method can combine deduction and induction in the same piece of economic inquiry.

1.10   What do you understand by the circular flow in an economy? Distinguish between real flows and money flows; which of the two is more important and why? Suppose people invest less than what they save from their incomes, how will this affect the level of money flow in a simple closed economy?

1.11   Is it valid that economic theory has nothing to do with economic reality? Illustrate your answer. It is said that economists have not been able to solve important problems of modern economies. Do you agree? If yes, name some of the problems. In defence of economists, especially when you have chosen to be one of the tribe, do you see any non-economic reasons contributing to the failures? Explain.

1.12   One reason of public mistrust of economists is that they use the same language as the man in the street. Explain and illustrate this statement.

1.13   What do you understand by an economic system? Explain how an economic system is conditioned by the axioms it rests on. Compare the Islamic economic system with capitalism with reference to property rights and motivation schemes. Is it valid to say that the Islamic system is nothing but Capitalism + *Zakat* – Interest? Give reasons for your answer.

Web Exercise

Search the Internet for literature on self-interest and explain the concept in the light of Islamic norms.

Forward Link

Economics is called the queen of social sciences as it seeks to measure human motives in terms of money and lends analyses of the phenomena it tackles with more objectivity and precision. It has a tool kit for constructing theories and testing them. In this kit, the most important instruments are of demand and supply. Make a parrot learn two words—demand and supply—and you will convert him into an economist (Samuelson). The following chapter explains what these tools are, how they are used and what factors influence them. Islamic economics is not opposed to the use of these tools or the factors that lie behind them.

2

Demand and Supply

LEARNING OUTCOMES

This chapter should enable the student to understand:

- Markets: Their role and limitations
- Demand for and supply of a commodity
- Relationship between price, demand and supply
- Demand and supply interaction to determine price
- Factors that determine and change demand and supply
- Role of time element in price determination
- Need for markets regulation
- Administered prices: Its meaning, merits and limitations

2.1   MARKETS, GOODS AND PRICES

The sort of decisions scarcity of resources imposes on people in their economic life broadly have three facets.

1. First, goods and services cannot be produced without making payments to the resource owners for their contribution to the productive effort. These payments constitute the costs which producers attempt to recover through the sale of what they produce.

2. Second follows from the first, one must be able and willing to pay for what one wants to have; there is no free lunch, so to say. Also, one has to rank his wants and decide the extent of satisfying each of them because income/wealth of the buyers is limited. Thus, in the market, we have prices at which people may want to buy (*demand*) goods, and prices at which producers could be willing to sell (*supply*) them.

One must pay for what one uses because resources are scarce. There is a price for everything one uses. Demand and supply of goods determine their prices in the market.

3. Finally, markets provide space to buyers and sellers for contacting each other, and forge linkages between demand and supply of goods, business firms operate as a go-between. The forces of *demand* and *supply* determine prices at which commodities are bought and sold. Markets keep price, demand and supply in balance like three balls placed in a bowl. Change in the position of any of the balls forces the others to change theirs.

> Market for a commodity in economics refers to an entire area where its buyers and sellers are in constant communication with one another that the price of the commodity readily tends to be equal throughout the area.

The notion of a market in economics is not essentially that of a *specific place* like a shopping complex where you go to make your daily purchases. Rather, market is seen in economics as an entire area where the buyers and sellers of a commodity are in such communication with each other that its price instantly tends to equality throughout the area without any special inquiries. Improvements in the means of communication and transportation, cold storage facilities, wide recognition of trademarks, patents, and copy rights, spread of multinational corporations, international payment arrangements, and of late the internet facilities have in general expanded much the market size for all goods and services. Still, the peculiarities of commodities matter. Things such as gold, silver, diamonds and pearls that combine high value with small bulk have vast international markets. So is the case with national currencies, and equity shares of many multinational corporations. Fresh milk and vegetables, fruits and poultry have narrower markets. The market for bricks is local. (Why?)

Demand and supply are the basic tools for analyzing market behaviour of economic agents. The notions are not of recent origin; we find much insightful discussion on them in earlier writings. For example, Ibn Taymiyyah wrote:

If people are selling their goods according to commonly accepted manner without any injustice on their part and the price rises due to the decrease of the commodity (fall in supply) or due to increase in population (rise in demand), this is due to Allah (natural causes; explanation added).

Later economists only sharpened the demand and supply concepts and gave them formal definitions. We must have a closer look at the nature and significance of these notions. Remember that they are as value-neutral as knives or guns; there can hardly be any objection to their use in Islamic economics.

Markets exist for real goods and services as also for monetary transactions. However, different considerations shape demand and supply forces in each case. Presently we restrict our discussion to the markets for goods only.

2.2   EARLY MARKETS: EXAMPLE

Market preceded Islam and the religion recognized them as social institutions of value and significance but with the insistence on subjecting the conduct of participants—consumers and producers—involved in the process of exchange to the moral code of Islam. The Prophet (pbuh) established a market in Medina for Muslims run on Islamic principles of fair play and social commitment because a Jewish market already operating in the locality was found to be involved in malpractices. Under Islamic norms, purely speculative transactions are to be avoided. Undue praise of one's merchandise must be eschewed. Defects in goods if known to the seller have to be revealed to the customer; 'buyers beware' is not an exclusive principle in Islam.

Economics treats what one is willing to pay for a commodity in the market as the measure of the intensity of his want. For example, if Anees is willing to pay more for a kilogram of apples in the market than Yunus, his need for apples is taken as more urgent than of the latter. So, market allocation of resources to various uses and distribution of goods to people is considered not only efficient but also equitable. This could be accepted as valid if income distribution too was fair but the market fails to ensure this. Islam distinguishes the *needs* of people from wants in general. The former are to be independent of the purchasing power to meet them. Islamic system insists that *basic needs* of all those living in a country must be fulfilled. If society cannot somehow ensure this, it becomes a state obligation.

Furthermore, market determined prices are acceptable as fair if they were not affected by what Islam regards as unfair trade practices. Natural abundance or scarcity affecting prices from the demand or supply side is legitimate; state intervention in the market is uncalled for but is needed if public interest otherwise demands.

2.3　DEMAND FOR COMMODITIES

The existence of a want is a necessary but not sufficient condition that gives rise to market demand for a commodity. Demand for anything cannot exist independent of price. If wishes were horses then beggars would ride, so goes the saying. It follows that in addition to want, the consumer must have the purchasing power to pay for the commodity and should be willing to do so. Also note that demand is not a 'one-price-one-quantity' notion. It is a *schedule* concept. We may define demand as under:

Demand for a commodity is a schedule of quantities consumers (users) are willing to buy at all possible prices at a given point of time. The *point of time* can be anything, e.g. an hour, a day, a week, a month or a year.

Table 2.1 presents a market demand schedule giving alternative combinations of price P and quantity Q. It also shows that market demand for a commodity is a horizontal summation of individual demand schedules such as A, B and C. Figure 2.1 shows the market demand curve for the table. Notice that the curve slopes downwards to the right in accordance with a fundamental law of economics: the law of demand that we explain below.

Table 2.1 *Demand for commodity X (imaginary data)*

Price RM per unit P	Individual demand (units)			Market demand units A + B + C + Q
	A	B	C	
10	–	–	20	20
9	–	10	30	40
8	–	20	40	60
7	–	30	50	80
6	10	30	60	100
5	15	35	70	120
4	20	40	80	140
3	25	45	90	160
2	30	50	100	180
1	35	55	110	200

2.4   THE LAW OF DEMAND

The relationship between price and quantity demanded in the list is normally negative. The quantity demanded increases if the alternative price offered is lower and vice versa. The relationship is so universal that it is called the law of demand. The inverse relationship shows a downward sloping demand curve in economic diagrams.

The law of demand says, *other things remaining the same, people purchase more of a commodity if its price falls and less if it rises.*

Thus, there is an inverse relationship between price and quantity demanded of a commodity. A demand curve, therefore, has a *negative* slope. The relationship between P and Q in Table 2.1 is given by the equation $Q = 220 - 20P$; $(0 < P < 11)$. Therefore, the slope of the demand curve shown in Figure 2.1 is -20 with reference to X-axis.

Exercise   2.1

Can we write the demand function for Table 2.1 as $Q = 11 - P$? Why or why not? Rewrite the equation with P as a function of Q and state its slope.

In the above statement of the law of demand, two things need explanation: (i) what do we mean by the phrase 'other things remaining the same' and (ii) why should there be an inverse relationship between price and quantity demanded or in other words why should most demand curves slope downwards?

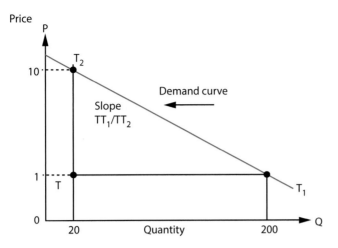

Figure 2.1 *Market demand for X*

2.4.1   Assumptions

The law of demand focuses only on the relationship between price and quantity demanded. So, it rests on assumptions that isolate influences other than price that may cause a change in quantity demanded of a commodity even when there is no change in its price. In the case of any good X under consideration, the phrase *other things remaining the same* covers the assumptions of the law. These are:

1. That the tastes or preferences of consumers for any good X in the market remain unchanged.
2. That the income of consumers does not change.
3. That the prices of all goods other than X remain constant.
4. That the number of consumers in the group buying X does not change.

> The law of demand rests on a number of simplifying assumptions. The fulfilment of these assumptions keeps the consumer movement restricted to the demand curve; he cannot leave it despite a change in price.

The implication of these assumptions is that with a rise in the price of X people will buy less quantity of it in the market and with a fall more.

The assumptions of the law of demand as stated above are quite hard to come true in practice. We shall see later what happens if they do not remain intact.

2.4.2   Why Do Most Demand Curves Have a Negative Slope?

To understand the law of demand we must know why people should normally purchase more when the price of X falls and less when it rises. To put the same thing differently, we should be able to explain why most demand curves have a negative slope or slope downwards. There are four reasons for an inverse price and quantity relationship that the law of demand states.

1. **Common sense explanation**: Price is a barrier to purchases. If the T-shirts become cheaper, i.e. the barrier is lowered, people in

> Why most demand curves slope downwards implies the question: why quantity demanded increases for a lower price in the demand schedule? There are several reasons, but the more important ones normally are income effect and the substitution effect.

general may like to have more of them. Businesses open clearance 'sales' for limited periods in that expectation and experience proves them correct: people do buy more at reduced prices.

2. **Utility and demand**: People buy things because they expect to derive satisfaction or utility from their consumption or possession. Utility prompts us to buy goods on the market. As we consume or possess more and more units of a good, our want for it decreases. *Utility is relative to the intensity of our want.* So, the utility from each additional unit of a good that we buy progressively declines. The tendency is called the law of *diminishing marginal utility.* The law reflects the declining intensity of our want as we have more and more of the commodity that satisfies it. Remember that the price we pay for each additional unit remains unchanged. The utility from the constant amount of money spent on each additional unit progressively decreases. When the declining marginal utility of the commodity and of money spent on it becomes equal, there is no point in buying more of it unless the price falls to compensate for the reduction in its (marginal) utility. *Diminishing marginal utility* thus provides an explanation for the inverse relationship between price and quantity demanded of a commodity.

> If a vendor offers to sell at a lower price, he may expect a rise in sales. The buyers at a lower price would spend less on the same quantity of the commodity than at a higher price. Of the money saved, they are likely to spend a part if not full, on the same commodity increasing its quantity demanded.

3. **Income effect**: Suppose Ahmad buys seven pencils when their price is 10 cents per pencil, thus spending 70 cents in all on them. Now, if the price of pencils falls to 7 cents a unit, Ahmad can have the seven pencils he was buying before for just 49 cents and save 21 cents on his purchases. Out of this saving he can buy up to three more pencils without affecting his purchase of other commodities. Assume he purchases two more pencils, i.e. 9 in all, making additional expenditure of 14 cents on them out of the income the fall in the price released. Such increase in quantity demanded is because of what we call *income effect.*

4. **Substitution effect**: In the market goods compete for the income of the consumer as more than one commodity can satisfy the same want. For example, tea and coffee (meat and fish) can be used one for the other. Now, if the price of coffee (fish) falls some of the buyers of tea (meat) may switch their choice to coffee (fish) and raise its demand. Such increase in quantity demanded of a commodity with a fall in the price of another commodity is called *substitution effect.*

> Goods in the market compete for the consumers' income and many are good substitutes for others. If the price of a good remains unchanged but its substitute rises, people are likely to buy more of it as replacement for the substitute.

Exercise 2.2

When the price of bananas falls from Taka 10 to Taka 5 a dozen in Bangladesh, Tasneem increases her purchase of bananas from four to seven dozen. How much income is released for her by the fall in price of bananas? If the increase of a dozen the bananas in her purchase is due to substitution of bananas for oranges, how much more does she spend on the bananas under the income effect?

2.4.3 Exceptions

The law of demand is a fundamental law of economics independent of time and place. Still, it does not apply in certain cases. For example, the law may not apply if people—rightly or wrongly—take a rise in the price of a commodity as an indication of further rise in its price, i.e. *the market becomes speculative.* People buy more of the commodity even at a higher price to avoid the loss of buying it later at an even higher price. Likewise, if an initial fall in the price of a commodity is somehow taken as a signal for a further fall in its price, people may like to postpone if possible their purchase of the commodity for the future to take advantage of still lower price. The law of demand may not again apply. This sort of speculative behaviour of the buyers is quite common in stock markets and provides an exception to the law of demand. Prices of goods such as rare paintings or coins, large cut diamonds, costly jewellery and designer dresses that carry prestige value in society for those who possess them tend to defy the law of demand. They sell because of their high prices that keep them out of the commoners' reach.

The law of demand does not apply to certain cases including speculative markets, rare coins or paintings or very costly jewellery.

2.5 CHANGES IN DEMAND

Figure 2.1 specifies the combinations of P and Q of the sort Table 2.1 provides. You move up and down on the *same* demand curve opting to buy different quantities of the commodity in response to a change in its *price*. Demand does not change. *A change in demand means increase or decrease in all Qs in the table, while Ps remain unchanged.* The demand curve *shifts* upwards or downwards. You move not *on* the *initial* demand curve but you move *off* that curve. Table 2.2 illustrates the concept of a change in demand. An *increase* in demand takes place when:

Increase in demand takes place if people buy more of the commodity than before at the current price or continue buying the same quantity as before even after a rise in price.

1. People purchase more quantity of the commodity X than before at the *same* price. For example, in Table 2.2 they buy 324 units of it instead of the initial 180 units even when the price remains unchanged at INR 2 per unit. This is shown in Figure 2.2 as the movement from T to T_1.

Table 2.2 *Change in demand (imaginary data)*

Price per unit (INR) P	Change in demand (Q)		
	Decrease in demand Q_1	Initial demand Q_0	Increase in demand Q_2
10	11	20	36
8	33	60	108
6	44	100	180
4	55	140	252
2	66	180	324

As demand for a commodity is a schedule represented by a downward sloping curve, a change in demand implies a shift of the entire curve in the plane. If the shift is upwards demand has increased and if downwards it has decreased.

2. People continue to purchase the *same quantity* of X as before even when its price has gone up. For example, in Table 2.2 they continue to buy the same 180 units of it as before though the price rises from INR 2 to 6 per unit. In Figure 2.2, this is shown as the movement from T to T_2.

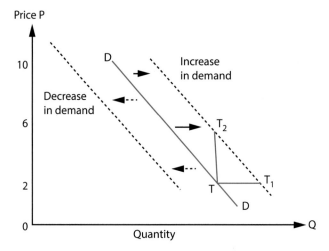

Figure 2.2 *Increase or decrease in demand causes shift of the entire curve upwards or downwards*

Exercise 2.3

Construct a definition of decrease in demand along the same lines as we have defined an increase in it. Construct a figure to illustrate the definition.

2.5.1   Causes

What brings about a change—increase or decrease—in demand? The answer lies in the phrase 'other things remain the same' that conditions the law of demand. The assumptions the phrase implies are, in fact, the *determinants* of demand. Let us see what happens as we drop these assumptions one by one.

1. **Change in tastes**: If you prefer a commodity to satisfy a particular want, you have a *taste* for it not *distaste*. Tastes often become a matter of habit and take time to change. For a hot drink you may, for example, have a taste or *preference* for tea, not coffee. Uniformity in the tastes of consumers finds expression in the formation of market demand for goods including their brand names and associated facilities such as the after-sale services. Tastes may change, sometimes even abruptly, for a variety of factors, known or unknown. Logic need not always be the basis of change. Experience, observation and persuasion are all important. However, technological improvements dominate the scene. Better ways of doing things, ease of handling, more attractive designs

and resale value may for instance shift demand from one product to another. Hand phones replacing fixed phones, compact discs replacing bulky cassettes, ball points replacing fountain pens, and so on, all exemplify changes in consumer tastes. They shift the demand for a product independent of its price.

2. **Change in income**: The assumption that income of *all* consumers remains constant is quite stiff; societies are characterized with dynamic change in economic variables, including personal incomes. An increase or decrease in the income of consumers may cause a corresponding increase or decrease in the market demand for X even if its price remains unchanged. A commodity whose demand varies directly with income of the consumers is termed as a *positive, normal* or *superior* commodity. But sometimes the demand–income relationship could be negative as well. The commodity is then called an *inferior* commodity. For example, with a rise in their income people may buy less of used clothes, coarse rice, second-hand automobiles and so on even when the prices of these goods fall. They may prefer to purchase more of new dresses, quality rice or automobiles straight from the producers. The law of demand may not hold good for *inferior* goods.

3. **Change in the prices of related goods**: The demand for a commodity is invariably related to the demand for other commodities. Goods are related to other goods in two ways: they are (a) substitute for one another or (b) supplement each other. Beef and mutton are substitutes for one another. So are tea and coffee. Automobiles and petrol or cups and saucers, on the other hand, supplement each other: they are *complementary goods*.

The demand for a commodity is directly related to the changes in the price for its substitutes. If the price of coffee—a substitute for tea—goes up, the market demand for tea will rise as its price has *relatively* fallen. Here you must be clear about a relative rise or fall in the price of a commodity, its own price remaining constant. Study Figure 2.3 carefully. Notice that even as the height of P_X remains the same in the three blocks A, B and C, it becomes smaller in B and larger in C *relative* to P_Y as P_Y increases or decreases as shown by its broken portions. In contrast to substitutes, if the price of petrol a complement for auto-bikes rises the market demand for the bikes may fall.

> Many factors may bring about change in demand, the important ones are: change in the taste of consumers, in their income or in their number. Change in the price of related goods also matter.

> Related goods could either be substitutes for the commodity in question or complementary to it. Relative price may change if the price of related goods alone changes, the price of the commodity remaining unchanged.

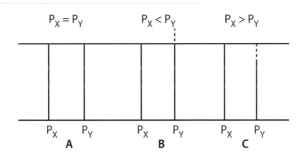

Figure 2.3 *Relative change in the price of X*

Exercise 2.4

Reconstruct Figure 2.3 to show the relative change in the price of commodity Y, keeping P_Y unchanged.

4. **Number of buyers**: An increase in the number of buyers of a commodity in a market is most likely to increase the demand for a commodity and vice versa. For example, improvements in the means of communication have given range and depth to financial markets. The demand for many equity shares and bonds has become international. Storage facilities have enlarged the demand for perishable goods. Likewise, increase in lifespan has increased the demand for spectacles and dentures. Examples can be multiplied.

Exercise 2.5

What will change the demand in the following cases?
(i)   Abdullah gives up smoking because it is injurious to health.
(ii) More people have started giving milk to their children due to a public health campaign.
(iii) People are buying more bicycles as petrol prices rise in Karachi.
(iv) Some families are using more honey than sugar with the rise in their income.

2.6   SUPPLY OF COMMODITIES

> The concept of supply like the concept of demand is also a schedule concept with the difference that the relationship between price and supply is positive in the supply schedule, i.e. quantity supplied increases with a rise in price and decreases with a fall in price.

Like demand for commodities, supply is also not a one-price-one quantity notion.

Supply of any commodity X may be defined as a schedule of its quantities that the sellers are able and willing to sell at each of the possible prices at any point in time.

We may conceive the supply schedule of an individual seller or of the market. Market supply of a commodity is the horizontal summation of the individual supply schedules. Table 2.3 presents imaginary supply schedules of three individual sellers R, W and Z and their summation as the market supply in the last column as Q.

Notice that the sellers are willing to supply more and more of X as its price rises upwards from RM1 per unit, one possible reason being that higher price promises more profit.

2.6.1   Law of Supply

The law of supply says that *other things remaining the same, sellers will be willing to supply more of a commodity as its price goes up and less if its price goes down.*

Table 2.3 *Supply of commodity X (imaginary data)*

Price (RM) per unit P	Individual supply (units)			Market supply (units) R + W + Z Q
	R	W	Z	
10	40	50	70	160
9	35	45	65	145
8	30	40	60	130
7	25	35	55	115
6	20	30	50	100
5	15	25	45	85
4	10	20	40	70
3	5	15	35	55
2	–	10	30	40
1	–	5	20	25

Thus, there is a direct or positive relationship between price, P, and quantity supplied, Q of Table 2.3. The supply function for the table can be written as: $Q = 10 + 15P$, where $P \geq 0$. Figure 2.4 shows the supply curve for commodity X.

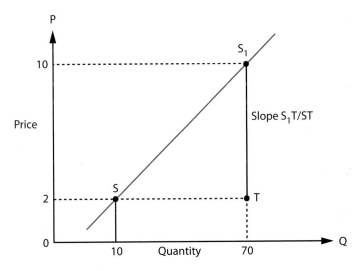

Figure 2.4 *Supply curve for X*

2.6.2   Assumptions

The phrase *other things remain the same* in the law of supply means that:
1. Input prices remain unchanged,
2. Technology for producing various commodities remains the same,
3. Prices of other commodities do not change,
4. Taxes and subsidies remain fixed,

The law of supply based on diminishing returns says that more can be supplied only at a higher price, other things remaining unchanged. The things remaining unchanged include technology, prices of other commodities, taxes and subsidies, number of sellers and absence of speculation. These are called the assumptions of the law of supply.

5. The number of sellers in the market does not change, and
6. Expectations of sellers do not become speculative.

There are virtually no exceptions to the law of supply. It is more universal than the law of demand. However, here too you must make a distinction between a change in quantity supplied and a change in supply, i.e. movement *on* and movement *off* a supply curve. In Figure 2.4, SS_1 shows the supply schedule, PQ of Table 2.3. It is upward sloping; it has a positive slope, S_1T/ST. The movement from S to S_1 keeps you on the *same* curve and shows a change in *quantity* supplied in response to a rise in the price of X. It does not depict a change in supply.

2.7 CHANGES IN SUPPLY

As in the case of demand, a change in supply also implies a shift in the supply curve. It shifts downward to the right if supply increases and upward to the left if it decreases.

In contrast, Table 2.4 illustrates the change in supply and Figure 2.5 presents it in the form of curves. The illustration enables us to define a change in supply along the same lines as we defined earlier for a change in demand. For example, a decrease in supply of commodity X takes place if:

Table 2.4 *Change in supply (imaginary data)*

Price per unit (INR) P	Change in supply (Q) (units)		
	Decrease in supply Q_1	Initial supply Q_0	Increase in supply Q_2
10	68	84	90
8	52	68	84
6	36	52	68
4	20	36	52
2	4	20	36

1. Sellers are willing to sell less than before, price of X remaining the same. This is shown in the figure by the movement from T_2 on the original supply curve S_0 to T on the S_D curve. Check in Table 2.4 that the quantity sellers are now willing to supply decreases from 52 to 36 units of X, while the price stays at RM6 per unit. Or,
2. Sellers are not willing to sell more than the initial quantity of X even when its price goes up. This situation is shown in the figure by the movement from T_1 to T, showing again a movement *off* the supply curve S_0 to S_D. In the table, sellers sell the same quantity of X as before, i.e. 36 units, even though the price of X rose from RM4 to 6 a unit.

Thus, we find that supply curve shows a decrease in supply when it bodily shifts upwards to the left of its original position in the plane. The opposite will happen when there is an increase in supply; the curve will shift downwards to the right.

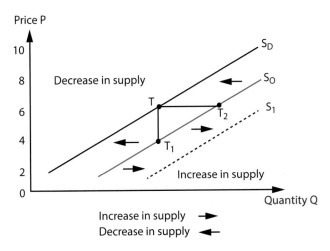

Figure 2.5 *Increase or decrease in supply implies the shift of the entire curve*

Exercise   2.6

Define an increase in supply and construct a figure to explain it. You may use the data given in Table 2.4 for the purpose. State which way the curve shifts from its original position.

2.7.1   Causes of Change in Supply

There are numerous factors—from weather to the whims of sellers—that may bring about a change in supply of a commodity in the market. The main factors, however, are contained in the assumptions of the law stated above. These are briefly as under.

 1. **Change in the prices of inputs**: Firms use resources or inputs for producing a commodity. These inputs have to be paid for their services. The sum of such payments including normal profit constitutes the cost of production of what the firm produces. Therefore, a change in input prices may change, under profit motive, the assortment of commodities the economy might choose to produce. It may choose to produce more of a commodity whose *relative* cost of production has gone down and vice versa.

Factors causing changes in supply (or in demand) mostly arise from assumptions on which the law is based.

Exercise 2.7

$Y = 49 - X^2$ (X < 8) is a production frontier showing alternative output combinations of Y and X produced using two inputs, labour, L and capital, K. Prepare the table for alternative output combinations including the marginal rate of transformation of Y into X, (MRT_{YX}). Construct the frontier to scale. What quantities of Y and X will be produced if the price ratio of X to Y i.e. (P_x/P_y) were 5? How will supply of the two goods change if this ratio changed to 9?

(*Hint*: Equate the marginal rate of transformation MRT_{YX} and the capital–labour price ratio.)

These include change in input prices, change in technology, change in the prices of other goods, change in taxes and subsidies, change in the number of suppliers and future expectations.

2. **Improvement in technology**: Improvements in techniques of production enable firms to produce a good with lesser resources than before or they can produce more of a good with the same resources. In either case, there is a reduction in the cost of production per unit and the firms are able to sell more without increase in price. Recently technological breakthrough in producing flat-screen computer monitors has enabled manufacturers to offer more such monitors for sale than before at lower prices. However, technological improvements are not uniform for all products.

3. **Change in prices of other goods**: Sometimes a firm is producing a variety of goods using the same facilities. For example, a firm in sports industry in Pakistan may be producing balls for both hockey and cricket. Now if the price of cricket balls rises, promising higher profits, the firm may reduce the supply of hockey balls to increase those for cricket.

4. **Impact of taxes and subsidies**: Sellers are usually able to pass in part or full to their customers the taxes public authorities impose on the production or sale of goods to raise revenue for meeting public expenditure. To the extent sellers succeed in transferring taxes forward to their customers, prices of goods rise even without a change in their supply (refer to Figure 2.5). If the government imposes a tax TT_1 on commodity X, the sellers will offer the same quantity of the commodity at each old price plus TT_1. In other words, the same quantity of X will be offered for sale as before at the enhanced price. The supply curve will shift upwards to S_D in line with point (2), supporting the definition of decrease in supply of X as explained earlier.

Sometimes the government meets, in part, the cost of producing certain goods through grant of subsidies. Examples are, provision of mid-day meals to school children living in city slums, construction of low-cost houses for the poor, growing of crops vital for the national economy and so on. Subsidies are intended to reduce prices for the targeted sections of population to meet some social objective. For example, in an Islamic economy, goods that are needed to meet the basic needs of people may attract subsidies. Here, supply remains the same as before even though the purchasers pay lower prices. This is equivalent to an increase in supply: the supply curve shifts downwards. Whether the full benefit of subsidy will reach the target groups depends on many factors including the integrity of the business managers.

5. **Change in the number of sellers**: If new firms enter an industry, there shall be an increase in supply. Supply curve will shift downwards to the right. On the other hand, if some firms leave the industry supply of the product may decrease, shifting the supply curve upwards to the left.

6. **Change in price expectations**: If the sellers take the initial rise in the price of a commodity as an indicator of a further rise in the price, they may hold back stocks for more profit in that expectation. Interestingly, Islam does not allow hoarding of goods, especially food articles, to effect a rise in prices. If prices rise for natural causes reducing supply as bad weather may do in the case of agricultural products, prices could be raised by sellers to equate demand with supply. In fact, Islam does not approve of speculative market behaviour.

2.8   MARKET EQUILIBRIUM

The notion of *equilibrium* is basic to economics. Equilibrium means 'resting-in-balance'. The market for a commodity is in a state of equilibrium when price equates its demand with supply. In fact, all the three—price, demand and supply—are in a state of mutual balance. The beauty of market equilibrium is that, if it is disturbed, it tends to get restored automatically. Let us see how market equilibrium is established. We have shown above, *separately,* the relationship between (a) price and quantity demanded of a commodity, and (b) price and the quantity supplied. The key point is that price is a common element in the two relationships and helps them *rest in balance.* Let us put together the price, demand and supply data for X given earlier in Table 2.1 and Table 2.3. It is clear that the price of RM6 per unit of X alone is such at which the buyers are willing to purchase the *same* quantity of X as sellers are willing to sell (100 units). RM6 is then the equilibrium price; it clears the market in the sense that it equates demand with supply. At prices higher than RM6 buyers are not willing to purchase what sellers want to sell; *surpluses* of good X are piling on their shelves. On the other hand, at prices lower than RM6 buyers are eager to purchase more than what sellers are willing to sell; there are shortages in the market from the viewpoint of the buyers. Figure 2 .6 gives us the picture of market equilibrium with price at RM6 and quantity bought and sold of X at 100 units. It explains

> Equilibrium is a state of rest i.e. when the two or more forces operating on something, like price balance each other to stop the movement.

Literally, equilibrium means 'resting in balance'. The market for a commodity is in a state of equilibrium when its price is such that the demand for the commodity equals its supply. In other words, the market is cleared.

that if supply were more than demand, there will be downward pressure on price due to the competition among sellers, until the price falls back to the equilibrium level at RM6 a unit. Likewise, if the price falls for any reason, there will be scarcity of X in the market and buyers who are willing to pay a higher price rather than go without it, will compete to push up price until it again attains the old level. Thus, free competition keeps the balance between price and quantity of a commodity bought and sold in the market.

Table 2.5 *Market demand and supply of X (units)*

Price per unit P	Quantity demanded Q_D	Quantity supplied Q_S	Surplus + Deficit − $(Q_S - Q_D)$
10	20	160	+ 140
9	40	145	+ 105
8	60	130	+ 70
7	80	115	+ 35
6	**100**	**100**	**0**
5	120	85	− 35
4	140	70	− 70
3	160	55	− 105
2	180	40	− 140
1	200	25	− 180

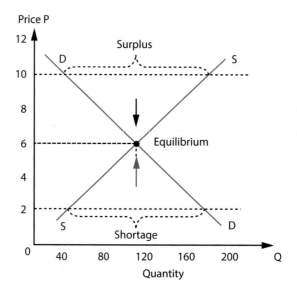

Figure 2.6 *Market equilibrium*

Demand and supply functions express the relationship between the price of the commodity and its demand and supply separately. Here is a numerical illustration of how their interaction determines equilibrium price.

We may also use demand and supply functions of a commodity to find its equilibrium price and quantity bought and sold in the market. The process is simple; we only have to equate the two functions and solve the equation to find the needed values.

For our illustration (Table 2.5), the solution is as follows:

The demand function for commodity X is $Q_D = 220 - 20P$ and the supply function is $Q_S = 10 + 15P$. Now in equilibrium, $Q_D = Q_S$. So, we may set up:

$$220 - 20P = 10 + 15P$$

This we can put as, $220 - 10 = 15P + 20P$

That is, $35P = 210$

Therefore, $P = 210/35$

$$= RM6 \text{ per unit}$$

If we put the value of P in the equation for demand or supply and solve for Q; the answer will be the same in either case. Let us substitute the value of P in the supply equation: $Q_S = 10 + 15 \times 6$

Thus, in equilibrium $Q_S = 100 \text{ units of } X = Q_D$

Exercise 2.8

The following is the imaginary demand and supply schedules for tea bags in India.

Table 2.6 *Demand and supply of tea bags in India*

Price P (INR hundred)	5	10	15	20	25	30	35	40	45	50
Demand Q_D (thousand bags)	650	600	550	500	450	400	350	300	250	200
Supply Q_S (thousand bags)	150	225	300	375	450	525	600	675	750	825

Using the information,

(i) Construct a diagram showing the equilibrium market price, P and quantity of tea bags bought and sold at that price.

(ii) Is it correct to say that $Q_D = 700 - 10P$ and $Q_S = 75 + 15P$ are respectively, the demand and supply functions specifying the data in the above table? Find the equilibrium price and quantity of tea bags bought and sold at that price. Does the table confirm your results?

2.9   DEMAND AND SUPPLY: RELATIVE IMPORTANCE

If demand and supply have a role in the determination of market price, you may reasonably ask if the two forces are of equal importance; if not which one has greater importance and why? There was a time when economists were sharply divided even on whether it was demand *or* supply that was the primary factor in price determination. Alfred Marshall (1842–1924) in his book *Principle of Economics,* provided an answer to the question. Paraphrasing him, we may as reasonably dispute whether it is the upper blade or the under blade of a pair of scissors that cuts a piece of paper as to whether it is demand or supply that determines value; both were needed for price formation. For that reason, the depiction of demand and supply curves showing market equilibrium as in Figure 2.6 is called the *Marshall cross*.

Regarding the *relative* importance of demand and supply in price determination, Marshall thought that demand can change rapidly, even abruptly, but supply of necessity takes more time to respond. Therefore, it is better to investigate why the response of supply to changes in demand is slow. It takes time to make arrangements for increasing or decreasing supply. To explain, he divided the time span into four periods with reference to the sort of restrictions applied in the supply side of the market. He used the fishing industry to illustrate his argument.

1. **Very short period**: This period is by definition so short that the supply of the commodity is limited just to its *stock* available in the market. For example, the supply of the fish on a day is limited to the overnight catch the fishermen put on the market for sale. Supply being fixed for the day, the price of fish will be completely dominated by change in demand. Figure 2.7 explains the case of an increase in demand. We find from Figure 2.7 that in the very short period supply by definition being fixed, an increase in demand will push up its price from P_0 to P_1, but the quantity bought and sold will remain unchanged at Q_0.

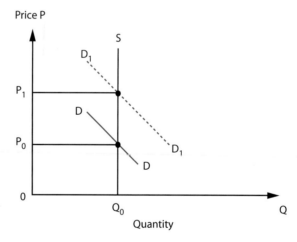

Figure 2.7 *Price–quantity relationship in a very short period*

Exercise   2.9

The supply function for X in the very short period is $Q_S = C$, where C is a positive constant equal to 20. The demand function for X is $Q_D = 25 - P$. Now the demand function falls by 3 units; its slope remaining unchanged. Write the function after the fall in price. Find the price before and after the fall for X. Explain your results with the help of a figure such as Figure 2.7.

2. **Short period**: The short period is defined as the one which would allow increase or decrease in supply within the *existing* production capacity of the industry without any change in the technique of production. For example, if the rise in the demand for fish and its high price P_1 persists for a few days, the fishermen may stay at sea and as a result quantity bought and sold *increases* from 1 to 2 for longer hours than before, may press into service idle boats, may repair old nets and boats, more family members may go out to sea or new workers may be employed on a temporary basis. All these would increase the daily quantity of fish the industry can now put on the market. There will be relative flexibility for supply to adjust to the change in demand. Figure 2.8 shows the tilt of the supply curve to the right, labelled as S_{SHP}. Notice that when the price decreases from 1 to 2, the quantity bought and sold increases from 1 to 2.

3. **Long period**: If the increase in the demand for fish still persists for several months, and the fishermen take it as an indicator of a durable shift in consumer tastes for fish relative to say meat, more people will enter the industry, and more modern ways, such as powered boats, improved nets, etc., can be introduced into the picture. Thus, the long period is long enough to allow fresh entrants into the industry and absorb improvements in technology. Now, the influence of supply will dominate the determination of price and corresponding volume of output of fish in the market. In the long run, price could even be $\leq P_0$, the initial market price. Marshall also talked of very long periods which we have not included in discussion here. Marshall concluded that the longer the period we allow for supply to adjust with change in demand, the greater will be the share of our attention devoted to supply in the determination of price; on the other hand, the shorter the time granted for adjustment, the greater the share of our attention devoted to demand.

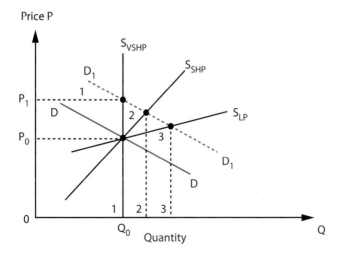

Figure 2.8 *As we allow more and more periods to supply for response, its impact on price, and quantity bought and sold increases*

2.9.1   Role of Price

We have seen how price equates demand with supply. In addition, prices are believed to measure the intensity of our wants for various goods and services sold in markets. Following this view, price mechanism is presumed to allocate the scarce resources of the economy to various uses and distribute goods among the consumers in an *efficient* manner. This way, market-determined prices present a cost-free rationing system that ensures social justice. Do you support this view? Is it distribution of incomes or intensity of wants that has the upper hand in operating the price mechanism in the market? Discuss these questions among yourselves.

2.10   EQUILIBRIUM: STATIC VERSUS DYNAMIC

If the conditions of demand and supply remain unchanged—the curves do not leave their respective places in the plane—market equilibrium is *static*: it has, as we saw, self-correcting properties, if disequilibrium takes place. However, an economy and its various sectors are invariably in a process of dynamic change. Over time, markets move from one position of equilibrium to another. Dynamism is the reality of equilibriums. This is so because *conditions* of demand and supply both change continually. Let us take a few examples to explain dynamics of equilibrium.

> Cases of a dynamic equilibrium could be numerous: we can study them by keeping supply fixed with change in demand or vice versa. But mostly, both demand and supply change together over time in the same or opposite direction.

1. **Change in demand alone**: Demand is more susceptible to shifts because consumer tastes do not need much time or preparation to change, supply does. So, this case is more relevant for the short run. Figure 2.9 explains the impact of such changes on price and quantity of commodity X bought and sold in the market. The demand curve may shift upwards, i.e. increase in demand D_1, or downwards, decrease in demand D_D, supply SS remaining the same. If demand increases, both price P and quantity Q increases, and if demand decreases both fall. P and Q are *positively* related.

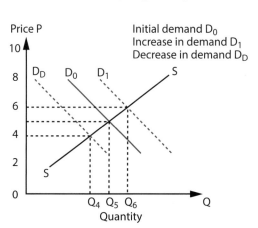

Figure 2.9 *Impact of increase or decrease in demand on equilibrium*

2. **Change in supply alone**: Next, let us assume that demand for X remains unchanged while there is a change in supply. Here, if supply increases, price falls and quantity bought and sold increases. It is the opposite effect if supply decreases: price rises while quantity decreases. Notice that there is an *inverse* relationship between equilibrium price and quantity, as in the law of demand. (See Figure 2.10.)

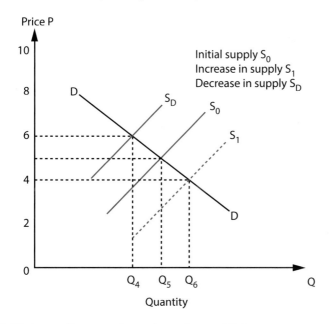

Figure 2.10 *Impact of increase or decrease in supply on equilibrium*

3. **Mixed cases**: Changes in demand and supply can and do take place simultaneously. However, the contrast in the equilibrium price–quantity relationship provides the clue to the fact that mixed cases can be quite complex for making predictions. The net effect of simultaneous changes in demand and supply on equilibrium price and quantity will depend on their *relative* strength and *direction*. Numerous cases can emerge. Figure 2.11 provides a few illustrations. Here, unbroken straight lines show the initial demand and supply curves and broken ones indicate their simultaneous shifts. Following is the explanation of the impact of such shifts on equilibrium price and quantity in each case:

    (a) Decrease in both demand and supply reduces quantity, but the impact on price is uncertain.
    (b) Increase in both demand and supply increases quantity, but the impact on price is uncertain.
    (c) Decrease in demand and increase in supply reduces price, but the impact on quantity is uncertain.
    (d) Increase in demand and decrease in supply increases price, but the impact on quantity is uncertain.

Imaginably, mixed cases could be innumerable and the net effect on price and output could in most cases be indeterminate.

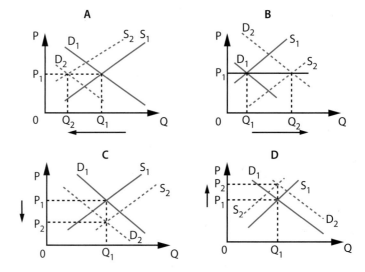

Figure 2.11 *Illustrative combinations of simultaneous changes in demand and supply, and their impact on the price of the product*

Exercise **2.10**

$Q_0 = 35 - P$ and $Q_S = 5 + 2P$ are respectively, the initial demand and supply functions for a digital clock.
(i) Find the equilibrium price–quantity combination and construct an illustrative diagram.
(ii) Subsequently, if the following changes in the demand and supply functions take place, show how equilibrium price and quantity would change in each case. Also, make explanatory diagrams.
   (a) The demand curve intercept increases by 5 and supply curve decreases by 5.
   (b) The demand curve intercept decreases by 5 and supply curve increases by 5.
(iii) If the initial equilibrium quantity does not change, but price rises to 12, how will the demand and supply functions change, their slopes remaining intact?

BOX
2.1

Limitations of Markets

Fair practices and the state of competition in the markets determine the extent of their contribution to social welfare. Perfect competition is the benchmark in the matter. In the absence of perfect competition, markets fail on a number of fronts. Unrestrained pursuit of self-interest often creates a gap between the individual and social interest; it causes market failure on many fronts. Indeed, there is no dearth of literature in mainstream economics expressing dismay on the performance of free markets and on enumerating their weaknesses. Of these, we refer here to failures which are especially relevant for the present work. Most writings on Islamic economics dealing with the subject frequently refer to them.

- Market produces and distributes goods and services not in accordance with the hierarchy of human needs, but proportionate to the purchasing power of individuals, unequal within and among nations, there is insufficient production of goods to meet all the basic necessities of life—food, clothing and shelter—for the poor masses while luxury for the much smaller clusters of the rich are made in abundance. In other words, allocation of resources is distorted. The economic notion of the efficiency requires a relook.
- The celebrated marginal productivity theory does not distribute income according to the contribution each factor makes to the total output even if competition in the factor market were perfect. The demonstration that a factor is paid equal to the value of its marginal product revenue does not by itself prove that the marginal product *determines* that payment, because it is not the contribution of a factor to output but its scarcity relative to other values, which are themselves determined together with the general forces of demand and supply. Characteristics: (i) if a unit is purchased by A, the *same* unit cannot be purchased by B. We call this the principle of *exclusion*; and (ii) if C is using a commodity, D cannot use it simultaneously, for example, if I am eating an apple, you cannot eat it too. We call this the principle of *rivalry*. However, many goods do not have the characteristics of exclusion or rivalry but society may need them. Non-excludability and non-rivalry may cause problems for the production of such goods. It is argued that they may lead to instances of market failures, as self-interest, the driving force of the system, may not allow their production in desired quantities. Such goods are provided by the government and are called public goods, provision of civil administration or defence are leading examples.
- Market includes in production costs only the payments made for goods and services in which the law recognizes as the property or rights of individuals or institutions. Many natural resources such as fresh air, water, forests and the atmosphere that remain free gifts of nature are also used in the production process for releasing or depositing wastes that are injurious to all forms of life. Their ever increasing volume has long crossed the absorption and self-cleansing capacity of natural agents and environmental damage has brought in the properties of non-exclusion and non-rivalry but they cannot be treated as public goods. The balance and proportions God had created in the natural phenomena (the Qur'an refers to such balance and proportions time and again), man has tampered with impunity only to face disaster. It is now widely recognized that environmental goods must pass through the market so that the payment for their use becomes part of production costs. This implies an extension of the concept of scarcity. But how to do so remains a question.

Source: Hasan, Z. (2008), *Contribution to the Islamic Encyclopedia of Islamic Economics*, Islamic Foundation, Leicester, UK.

2.11   APPLICATIONS

Demand and supply together constitute the basic analytical apparatus for economics of any sort. The tools have often been used to demonstrate the inefficacy of public policies if they go against the market for achieving objectives with non-economic content. Such demonstrations are of special interest to the people living in developing countries where market results concerning allocation of resources or distribution of income at times, run against wider public interest. While the results of demand and supply applications may apparently look correct, their limitations

Free play of the forces of demand and supply in the market at times leads to results not conducive to social interest. The role of the state to modify the results thus becomes very important, more so in an Islamic economy.

cannot be ignored in arriving at balanced conclusions. Two important limitations of demand and supply analyses you must always keep in mind.

First, the explanatory diagrams that support a conclusion generally have no time dimension. They are snapshots of a running train showing *still* backgrounds; they are not a movie of the train's entire journey. Even when time is brought into the picture, changes during the period are assumed away, or restricted, to keep the analysis simple. Obviously, the implications of a simple, virtually static, depiction need not be the same as of a complex dynamic situation.

Second, the departures from a market solution may be less efficient on the cost–profit criteria economists often use for the purpose. However, there are gains too, that could more than make up for the loss of efficiency defined in cost–profit terms. The problem is that social consequences of public policies are difficult to evaluate because these gains cannot always be quantified for comparison with efficiency losses to arrive at a firm conclusion. But the principle is clear: pecuniary loss due to departures from the market solutions is not a complete story; the gain part of the story must also be considered. It is comparison of one piece of the story with the other that alone can help arrive at right conclusions on public policies.

2.11.1   Administered Prices

The prices that government action brings into existence as a departure from the free market results a fall in the administered prices category.

Textbook economics maintains that it is mostly in the interest of the society that market prices are allowed to fall or rise to their equilibrium levels, no matter how low or high those levels might be. Islamic economists tend to subscribe to this view on the strength of a tradition where the Prophet (pbuh) refused to fix prices lower than the market, for food grains in Medina when they tended to rise too high creating hardship for the common man. His decision is seen in the context of scarcity caused by drought in countries from where merchants brought in the grains. Natural factor was the cause of high prices, not the greed of the merchants. However, the Prophet (pbuh) appealed to the merchants to keep prices as low as possible in social interest, and the appeal had a moderating impact.

The spirit of the tradition remains valid even today. However, the rise or fall in prices of most individual commodities is no longer attributable to *natural causes,* the core of the tradition. Modern textbook economics is opposed to government intervention in the market, as that could hurt the very cause it seeks to promote. Intervention may result, it is argued, in two sorts of market distortions.

Administered prices may lead to the emergence of corruption and black markets in the economy. In principle, Islam is opposed to the government intervention in the market unless it becomes imperative in social interest.

1. **Price ceilings create shortages**: Figure 2.12 helps explain how fixing of ceilings on the market price of a commodity, say sugar, will lead to its shortage. Here, P_0 and Q_0 are the initial price and quantity in equilibrium for sugar. The government feels that this price is too high to make sugar available to the poorer sections that constitute the majority of population in the country, say Bangladesh. Also, the country imports most

of its sugar from abroad and cannot afford a further drain on its meagre foreign exchange reserves. Under the circumstances, the government puts a ceiling on the price of sugar at P_1. A shortage of supply, which is the same thing as an excess of demand, T_1T_2, must appear on the market. This would result in a two-tier price system. One is the open price, the ceiling P_1. But a black market in sugar is most likely to develop as there are people willing to buy it at a higher price. This price will tend to rise and may even cross P_0. The lower the ceiling, the more will be the diversion for selling sugar at an illegal price. Thus, the objective of the ceiling would be defeated.

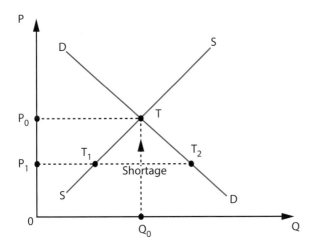

Figure 2.12 *Price ceiling creates deficit*

Now, the fixing of price ceiling is invariably accompanied by introduction of formal rationing of the commodity, here sugar, to be sold at a fixed price (P_1). Of course, the rich can always buy extra sugar from the willing poor at the higher price. But the poor benefit in any case: they get extra money to spend. Also, the black market argument is based on the assumption that people *en mass* indulge in immoral activities for pecuniary gains. This may not always be true; there at least is scope to soften immorality through appropriate moral education. Finally, we must weigh the social gains of price ceiling against market distortions to arrive at a valid conclusion.

Fixation of maximum price for a commodity or ceiling may cause shortages of the commodity in the market and part of demand remaining unmet.

An alternative to ceiling fixation for selected commodities in agriculture is to grant subsidies—financial assistance—to farmers for meeting part of the production cost so that market prices could be kept lower for the buyers. Subsidies have some advantages over price ceilings. For example, it may do away with the need of introducing cumbersome rationing or procurement system and their accompanying difficulties. Farm subsidies are very common even in developed economies such as the US, France and Japan. In fact, the issue of abolition of farm subsidies which France opposed vehemently in 2005 is posing a serious threat to the unity of Europe.

Social concern is clearer in the case of rent controls commonly imposed in metropolitan towns of developed and developing countries. In towns such as Karachi, Delhi or Dhaka, maximum legal rent is fixed to make housing affordable to the weaker sections of society. Democratic governments continue with them for that reason, despite the ills associated with them. Reforms are introduced from time to time to curb the ills and strike a balance between the interests of the landlords and the tenants.

Fixing a minimum or floor price for a commodity may cause unsold surpluses in the market.

2. **Price floors cause surpluses**: A price floor refers to the minimum price the government fixes for a commodity. A price paid below it is illegal. Minimum price is fixed for a commodity when the government feels that the free market price does not provide sufficient income or incentive to the producers. Minimum price is obviously higher than the equilibrium price in the market and leaves unsold surpluses of the commodity with the producers as shown in Figure 2.13. Here, P_0 is the equilibrium price; it clears the market, equating the quantity bought and sold to Q_0 at price P_0. If the government fixes the minimum price for the commodity at P_1, less will be demanded than the producers would be willing to sell at that price. An unsold surplus measured as $T_1 - T_2$ will emerge. Competition among the sellers may compel them to sell the commodity at a price even lower than the initial P_0, thus defeating the very purpose of state intervention in the market.

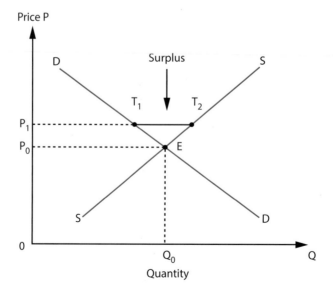

Figure 2.13 *Floor fixing creates surpluses*

This argument is valid but incomplete. A price floor is often accompanied by a procurement policy ensuring the producers that state agencies would buy from them at the minimum price any quantity of the commodity they may want to sell to public authorities. The state enters the market as a competitor. In India, for example, the procurement mechanism has successfully been operating for over half a century in the case of many agricultural products including wheat, oilseeds and cotton among others. The commodities in state-owned warehouses have helped keep stable the long-run price and supply position of the commodities covered. The system has contributed to the welfare of millions of villagers in the country and kept adequate land allocated to national priority uses. As a long-run impact of the policy, Indian agriculture, the backbone of the economy, is booming today.

> Government intervention in the market is needed to maintain floor prices.

BOX 2.2

Demand and Supply

A number of Muslim scholars seem to have clearly understood the role of both demand and supply in the determination of prices. For example, Ibn Taymiyyah (d. 1328) wrote: 'The rise or fall of prices may not necessarily be due to injustice by some people. They may also be due to the shortage of output or the import of commodities in demand. If the demand for a commodity increases, and the supply of what is demanded declines, the price rises. If, however, the demand falls and the supply increases, the price falls'. Even before Ibn Taymiyyah, al-Jahiz (d. 869) wrote nearly five centuries earlier that: 'Anything available in the market is cheap because of its availability (supply), and dear by its lack of availability, if there is need (demand) for it' (1983, p. 13), and that 'anything the supply of which increases, becomes cheap except intelligence, which becomes dearer when it increases'.

Ibn Khaldun went on further to emphasize that both an increase in demand or a fall in supply leads to a rise in prices, while a decline in demand or a rise in supply contributes to a fall in prices. He believed that while continuation of 'excessively low' prices hurts the craftsmen and traders and drives them out of the market, the continuation of 'excessively high' prices hurts the consumers. 'Moderate' prices between the two extremes were, therefore, desirable, because they would not only allow the traders a socially-acceptable level of return but also lead to the clearance of the market by promoting sales and thereby generating a given turnover and prosperity. Nevertheless, low prices were desirable for necessities because they provide relief to the poor who constitute the majority of the population. If one were to use modern terminology, one could say that Ibn Khaldun found a stable price level with a relatively low cost of living to be preferable, from the point of view of both growth and equity in comparison with bouts of inflation and deflation. The former hurts equity, while the latter reduces incentive and efficiency. Low prices for necessities should not, however, be attained through the fixing of prices by the state; this destroys the incentive for production. (References omitted)

Source: Chapra, M.U. (2011), *Islamic economics: What it is and how it has developed over the centuries*; <http://eh.net/encyclopedia/eh.net/encyclopedia/whaples@wfu.edu>, accessed April 2014.

Summary

- Scarcity of resources gives rise to cost of production which the buyers of a commodity must pay as price of a commodity. Also, consumers have to rank their wants for their satisfaction because of limited income.

- Prices are determined in the market by the forces of demand and supply. Market refers to a space where buyers and sellers of a commodity are in such communication that the price rapidly tends to equality without any special inquiry. A number of factors determine the extent of a market.

- Demand for a commodity is a schedule of its quantities that buyers are willing to buy at different prices at any point in time.

- Other things being equal, the quantity demanded of a commodity normally decreases as its price rises and increases as its price falls. This statement of an inverse relationship between the price and the quantity demanded of a commodity is called the law of demand.

- The reasons for an inverse relationship between price and quantity demanded of a commodity are (i) common sense explanation is that price is a barrier and the lower the barrier the more crossings are expected and vice versa. (ii) Lower price allows the falling marginal utility of the commodity to be equal to the money paid. So, more of it can now be purchased. (iii) Lower price may make a commodity cheaper relative to another commodity for which it can now be substituted. So, more of it may be purchased. This is called the operation of substitution effect. (iv) The fall of price allows having the initial quantity of the commodity for lesser money than before. It releases income, and a part or whole of this income can be used to buy additional quantity of the same commodity. The operation is called the income effect.

- The law of demand does not apply in the case of *inferior goods*; things having high prestige value, rare antiques and in speculative situations.

- Change in quantity demanded refers to movement *on* the *same* demand curve in response to a change in the price of a commodity alone, i.e. in harmony with the law of demand. On the other hand, change in demand takes place when we move from the *initial* demand curve to a higher or lower demand curve, i.e. there is a movement *off* the *initial* demand curve.

- Increase in demand takes place when consumers buy more of a commodity without any change in its price or continue to buy the same quantity as before even with a rise in its price. Likewise, a decrease in demand takes place when consumers reduce the purchases without any change in its price or continue to buy the same quantity of the commodity as before, even when its price has fallen.

- The factors that cause changes in the demand for a commodity are change in consumer taste and preference, their number in the market, change in consumer income and change in the price of related goods.

- Supply of a commodity is defined as the schedule of its quantities sellers are willing to sell at various prices at any point in time. The supply of a commodity varies directly with a rise or fall in its price. The relationship is expressed as the law of supply. The law assumes that there is no change in the input prices, state of technology, prices of other commodities, taxes or subsidies and the number of sellers in the market. Also that the market does not become speculative.

- Change in supply means the shift of the supply schedule without any change in the prices of the commodity. When there is an increase in supply, the curve shifts downwards to the right and when there is a decrease, it shifts upwards to the left.

- Changes in input prices, technology, prices of other goods, taxes or subsidies, number of sellers in the market and price expectations cause changes in the supply of a commodity.

- If the price of a commodity in the market is such that demand equals supply at that price, the market is in a state of equilibrium. Dynamic economic conditions keep destroying equilibrium while demand and supply mechanism continually tends to restore it.

- Demand and supply both are needed for price formation but their relative importance depends on the time we allow supply to harmonize with changes in demand. The shorter the period, the greater the impact of changes in demand on price. On the other hand, the longer the period, the greater the influence of supply on price.

- There is positive relationship between price of a commodity and change in its demand, supply remaining unchanged. On the other hand, the relationship between price and change in supply is negative. So, if both demand and supply change simultaneously their net impact on equilibrium quantity and price is quite uncertain. It will depend on the relative strength of the two opposing forces.

- State intervention in the market may not in principle be desirable, but it becomes often essential to promote social good. The criterion for decision is a comparison between private costs and social gain.

- Fixation of price ceilings and floors creates market disequilibria and misallocation of resources. But such losses ial gains before passing judgment on the issues modern societies currently face.

- Farm subsidies are now increasingly used as alternative to price ceilings as they have relative superiority over the latter.

Glossary

Market The concept of market has been in existence since the dawn of human civilization. In common parlance, it was and remains associated with a place or location where goods and services were freely exchanged. The location usually referred to an open space earmarked for traders to set up stalls and buyers flocked there to browse the merchandise for purchase. The marketplace had no permanent structures of any sort; any site there could be occupied on a first come first occupy basis. Countless markets of this sort still operate in many countries of Asia and Africa, more so in rural areas. Many of them spring to life on specified week days. They often trade in a single type of commodity: grains such as wheat, vegetables, fruits, food or cattle, to name a few.

With the rise of economics as a discipline, the term market no longer remained restricted to a location or place. Instead, market is seen as a social institution that allows exchange of goods, services and information between buyers and sellers who are in such communication with one another that the price instantly tends to equality throughout an area, local, regional or international. Human interaction in markets formalizes the transference of *ownership rights* in goods and services. Broadly, we have markets, national and international for commodities including services, for factors (inputs) of production and finally for purely financial deals.

Market equilibrium Equilibrium is a state of balance; a position of no change unless the object in question is disturbed. Even so it has a tendency to return to equilibrium like the pendulum of a clock. Market equilibrium is a situation where price is such that demand for a commodity equals its supply.

Market regulation Supervision of markets emerged quite early in history. Committees composed of influential people in the locality were organized to frame rules and regulations for doing business in a market and supervised their observance in practice. The regulations in the first instance related mainly to the standardization of weights and measures and their correct use. Market charges and fees for stalls and display, resting places, drinking water and provision of other facilities came next. With the growth of population, spread of education, progress in science and technology, advancement of inventions and innovations, rapid expansion of means of transportation and communication and the rise of corporate form of business enterprise, market concepts, volume and variety of goods traded in them as also the modes of regulation underwent a sea change. Legal frameworks developed and acts proliferated for various markets.

Movement on or off a demand curve Movement on a demand curve takes place when quantity demanded increases with a fall in price and vice versa. We remain on the same demand curve only moving up or down on it in response to a change in price and quantity demanded. On the other hand, if buyers demand more than before at the *same* price there is an increase in demand; we move to a higher curve and vice versa. In either case, we do not remain on the original demand curve but move off the original curve.

Price This is the amount of money for which a commodity is bought and sold in the market, i.e. it is the *value-in-exchange* of a commodity for money. The satisfaction one derives from the possession or consumption of a commodity is called its *value-in-use*. Economists treat price of a commodity as a measure of its use value albeit the two are not mostly identical. The economic function of price is to equate demand with supply. Sometimes the government fixes a *ceiling* above which the sellers legally cannot charge a price. At times it fixes a *floor* below which the sellers will not accept a price for the commodity. Fixation of ceilings and floors distorts the free market allocation of resources by creating artificially the surplus or shortage of supply depending on the sort of intervention.

In principle, Islam stands for free markets and does not allow state intervention in the market to influence price if it changes due to purely natural causes affecting its demand or supply. However, there is no bar or limit of state action to promote or safeguard public interest as Islamic system does not promote individualism at social cost.

Concepts for Review

- Changes in market equilibrium
- Decrease in supply
- Demand
- Functions and curves
- Increase in demand
- Laws of demand and supply

- Market
- Market equilibrium
- Price
- Price ceilings
- Price floors
- Supply

Case Study   2.1

The 1973 Oil Crisis

The 1973 oil crisis started in October when the members of the Organization of Arab Petroleum Exporting Countries or OPEC (consisting of the Arab members of OPEC, plus Egypt and Syria) proclaimed an oil embargo in response to the US decision to resupply the Israeli military during the Yom Kippur war; it lasted until March 1974. The OPEC declared it would limit or stop oil shipments to the US and other countries if they supported Israel in the conflict. The OPEC members decided independently to use their leverage over the world price-setting mechanism for oil in order to stabilize their real income by raising the prices.

With the US actions seen as initiating the oil embargo, the long-term possibility of high oil prices, disrupted supply and recession created a strong rift within the North Atlantic Treaty Organization; both European nations and Japan sought to disassociate themselves from the US Middle East policy.

Source: Adapted from Wikipedia, <en.wikipedia.org/wiki/1973_oil_crisis>, accessed April 2014.

Case Questions
1. Was it the OPEC's decision to put an embargo on oil supply alone that caused the price of oil shoot up in 1973? If not, what other factors contributed to the rise? Explain.
2. What in your opinion is likely to be the trend in oil prices in the years ahead and why? Explain your answer in light of the current politico–economic situation in the Arab world.

Case Study   2.2

Price Mechanism and Free Markets

The demand and supply mechanism is the most basic investigative tool in economics. Economists use them to analyze issues in such diverse areas as inflation and employment, the effect of taxation on prices, government regulation of business, issues concerning the environment, education, marriage, and healthcare, even crime.

Adam Smith was all praise for free markets, which guided by the invisible hand of self-interest ensured, he believed, efficient allocation of scarce resources to various uses and distributed the fruits of production equitably. Samuelson thought: if you make a parrot learn two words—demand and supply—you will convert him into a perfect economist.

However, governments of all shades across the world have over time and space tempered with the price mechanism—prices, wages, rentals, interest rates, incomes etc.; hardly any economic variable remained untouched giving rise to what we call 'control economics'. The battles have mostly resulted in undesirable side effects.

Case questions

1 'Markets operate in the best social interest; demand and supply allocate resources where they are most needed'. Comment on this statement.

2 Markets do not allocate resources according to the societal preferences: demand is determined by the purse, not by the needs of the people. When income is unevenly distributed in society, markets cannot ensure the maximization of social good. Do you agree? Elaborate the reasons for your answer, especially from an Islamic perspective.

Test Questions

2.1 What is a market? Explain the factors that determine the size of a market. Indicate in each of the following cases, which of the goods will have comparatively smaller markets. Give reasons for your choice.
(a) Book editions published with paperbacks or hard covers
(b) Sugarcane or powdered milk
(c) Cotton or cloth
(d) Gold or cars

2.2 Why do most demand curves slope downwards? Explain your reasons adequately. Discuss cases when a demand curve may not have a negative slope?

2.3 (a) Distinguish between movement along a demand curve and movement off a demand curve. What in your view is the importance of this distinction? Explain.
(b) Reconcile the following statements:
(i) Demand decreases with a rise in price.
(ii) Price rises with an increase in demand.

2.4 Explain why the impact of changes in demand and supply on equilibrium price and quantity is indeterminate. Trace the impact of the following shifts in demand and supply on the equilibrium price and quantity of the commodity Y. (Use the Marshallian cross of Figure 2.5 as your starting point.)
(a) Both demand and supply increase,
(b) Demand increases but supply decreases,
(c) Supply increases but demand decreases, and
(d) Both demand and supply decrease.

2.5 In a dynamic situation, why do economists consider the adjustment of supply to demand as more important than of demand to supply? Explain how time element is important for the adjustment process to complete. Define supply for each time segment precisely and clearly. Illustrate your answer with a suitable example and diagrams.

2.6 A cinema hall has 100 seats of one class only. It is half filled if the price of ticket is fixed at RM30 but 20 seats remain unfilled if the price is reduced to RM20 a seat. At what price for the ticket would (a) the hall will be fully occupied, and (b) only 10 seats remain vacant? (Use the equation P − 1/3 (140 − Q). Try to obtain this equation from the given information.)

2.7 The publisher of a book estimates the demand function for the book as Q = 1,150 − 0.5P. If he plans to print 1,100 copies of the book, what price should fix to sell the whole stock? If his supply function is Q = 1,123 + P, find the equilibrium price and quantity for him. Draw a diagram to illustrate your results.

2.8 Discuss why the government sometimes fixes a maximum price for a commodity? Would state intervention in the market be always undesirable?

2.9 Many developing countries do not allow the prices of some agricultural good to fall below a minimum, why? How do they achieve their objective? Do you think that providing farm subsidies is a better instrument to promote economic interests of the country than fixing price floors? Give reasons for your answer.

2.10 Revisit Q2.7. Suppose the government finds that the book serves some social cause and must be read by more people. So, it asks the publisher to sell it for not more than RM15 a piece, with a commitment to give RM2.5 to him maintain that price. How will it affect the price of the book and its sale? Will the profit of the publisher go up or down? Explain your answer.

Web Exercise

Search the Internet for concepts of demand and supply and explain the same in the light of Islamic norms.

Forward Link

Chapter 3 explains an economic concept—elasticity—related to demand and supply of a commodity. Elasticity is free of any ethical content. It helps us answer such questions of why one continues to purchase for the kitchen the same quantity of salt even when the price of salt in the market, say doubles, but postpones the purchase of a car if its price rises by 10% and believes that it may fall soon. We shall consider several types of elasticity and their implications. The notion of elasticity is a helpful guide in drawing up various public policy measures and studying their implications.

3

Elasticity of Demand and Supply

LEARNING OUTCOMES

This chapter should enable the student to understand:

- The notion of elasticity in economics
- The price elasticity of demand for a commodity and its kinds
- Methods of measuring price elasticity of demand
- Determinants of price elasticity of demand and its significance
- Non-price concepts of elasticity of demand
- Price elasticity of supply, types and measurement
- Factors influencing price elasticity of supply
- Cost of production and elasticity of supply
- Elasticity and Islamic economics

3.1 THE CONCEPT OF ELASTICITY

> Elasticity refers to the extent of flexibility of a thing in response to the measure of force operating on it.

In common language, elasticity refers to the characteristic of a substance to expand or contract in response to a change in the force operating on it. Expansion or contraction may be proportionate to the change in the force or it could be more than proportionate in some cases and less in others. Thus seen, things may not be equally elastic. Here are a few examples of elastics in common use.

Ladies use rubber bands to keep their hair in place; banks use them to make stacks of currency notes. Elastic is used in garments too. A balloon or a rubber tube swells proportionate to the air pumped in and contracts to the extent it is released. Our skin is also elastic to some measure: people gain weight and lose it, the skin remaining in place. Cases can be multiplied infinitely. Which would you think is more elastic: a bicycle tube or that of a truck if pressed by the hand increasingly?

In economics, demand and supply have a similar property: both are elastic. Price is a force, along with others, where a change may cause an expansion or contraction in the quantity of goods bought and sold in the market. The extent of responsiveness of quantity demanded or supplied of any good showed in relation to a change in price is called its price elasticity. Elasticity can be measured, we shall see, in a number of ways. Remember that the concept of elasticity is purely *technical*; it has no moral content, Islamic or non-Islamic.

This force could, for example, be price in the case of demand or supply of a commodity.

3.2   PRICE ELASTICITY OF DEMAND

The law of demand that you learnt in the preceding chapter tells us only the *direction* of change in quantity demanded of a commodity in response to a change in its price. It does not tell us anything about the *extent* of that change, i.e. if the increase or decrease in quantity demanded for a given change in price shall be *large* or *small*. This information we get from the price elasticity concept of demand. The information has significance for the formulation of economic policies because the response of quantity demanded to price change is not the same in all cases. For example, if the price of common salt doubles, we do not expect any significant fall in its use in our kitchens. On the other hand, if the price of cloth rises by only 20% we may find expenditure visibly reduced on new dresses. Thus, the demand for common salt is, so to say, much less elastic compared to that for dresses. There are several methods to know how elastic the demand for a commodity is. Figure 3.1 shows how the response of quantity demanded of a commodity could relatively be more or less to a change in price.

The law of demand tells us the direction of change—not its magnitude—in quantity demanded in response to a given change in price.

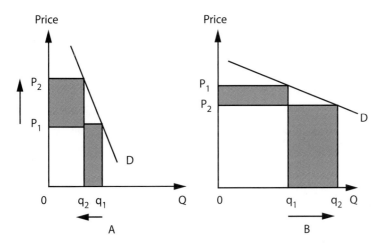

Figure 3.1 *Response of demand to a change in price*

However, as price and quantity demanded normally have an inverse relationship, price elasticity of demand, E_{DP}, invariably has a negative

The law of demand informs us only about the direction of change in the quantity demanded of a commodity in response to a change in its price. It does not tell us if the quantity will change by the same proportion as price or more (less) than that. Elasticity of demand provides us this additional information because it can be measured.

sign. But we use the absolute value of E_{DP}, ignoring its negative sign. We know that the negative sign is the consequence of an inverse relationship between the price and quantity demanded for *normal* goods and services. To interpret a negative coefficient may be confusing; for example, which is greater –5 or –2? Once we know the reason for the sign being negative, it is the magnitude of the coefficient that would matter, not its sign. Compare the degree of responsiveness of quantity demanded to change in price in sections A and B of Figure 3.1. Do you need to know the sign for the comparison? However, later we shall see that there is a situation where the sign of the coefficient does matter.

3.3 THE MEASUREMENT

We use the following methods to measure the price elasticity of demand.

3.3.1 Proportionate Change Method

The following formula is commonly used for estimating the price elasticity of demand or E_{DP}:

$$E_{DP} = \frac{\text{Proportionate change in quantity demanded}}{\text{Proportionate change in price}} \qquad (3.1)$$

(percentage change can be used in place proportionate change in the equation)

Putting values for initial quantity and price of the commodity as Q_0 and P_0 respectively, and their values after the change as Q_1 and P_1, the above equation can be written as:

If the percentage change in quantity demanded equals the percentage change in price, elasticity of demand is 1. If it is more, demand is more elastic (> 1), if it is less demand is less elastic (< 1).

$$E_{DP} = \frac{\dfrac{Q_0 - Q_1}{Q_0}}{\dfrac{P_0 - P_1}{P_0}} = \frac{\dfrac{\Delta Q}{Q_0}}{\dfrac{\Delta P}{P_0}} = \frac{\Delta Q}{\Delta P} \cdot \frac{P_0}{Q_0} \qquad (3.2)$$

Conventionally, we omit the suffix 0 in P_0/Q_0 of the formula and just write P/Q. Here, Δ indicates the difference of the two values of variable Q or P. At any given P, the ratio $\Delta Q/\Delta P$ gives us the slope of the demand curve over the relevant *price range* P_0 to P_1. If we know the demand function, its first derivative gives us the slope of the curve at any *point* P. If demand function is linear, the first derivative will be a constant. For instance, if

$$Q_D = a - bP$$
$$dQ/dP = -b \ \ (\text{a constant})$$

We may reverse the function and have $P = (1/b)(a - Q_D)$. Derive dP/dQ. Is it 1/b?

If we use the derivatives instead of differences in the formula, we obtain *point elasticity* of demand.

Example 3.1 The demand function $Q_D = 700 - 10P$ is linear and its first derivative is 10, a constant; we can easily find the quantity demanded for any value of P. But P should not exceed 70. (Why?) Now, consider the function $Q_D = 34 - 0.5P^2$. The first derivative dQ/dP for this function will be P. Table 3.1 provides the numerical values of the function and the derivative or the slope of the function for selected values of P:

Table 3.1 *Values for the demand function* $Q_D = 34 - 0.5P^2$

Price (P)	1	2	3	4	5	6	7	8
P^2	1	4	9	16	25	36	49	64
Quantity demanded (Q_D)	33.5	32.0	29.5	26.0	21.5	16.0	9.5	2.0
$dQ/dP = P$	1	2	3	4	5	6	7	8
P/Q	–	–	–	–	–	–	–	–
$E_{DP} = (dQ/dP)(P/Q)$	–	–	–	–	–	–	–	–

Using the table values, we may find E_{DP} at say P = 6 as:

$$E_{PD} = \frac{dQ}{dP} \cdot \frac{P}{Q}$$

$$= 6 \times (6/16)$$

$$= 2.25 \text{ (The numerical value is called the coefficient of elasticity.)}$$

> The use of differential calculus helps us to measure elasticity more precisely at any point on a demand curve.

Exercise 3.1

(i) Using information in Table 3.1, plot the demand curve and the values of the first derivative as separate graphs. What difference do you notice between the two figures? Explain.
(ii) Fill in the missing values in the last two rows of Table 3.1.
(iii) Find elasticity of demand when P = 4.

Example 3.2 The demand function for cinema tickets at a hall is $Q_D = 85 - 0.05P^2$. Find the elasticity of demand when the price of the ticket is reduced from RM30 to RM25.

At price RM30, the number of tickets demanded is 40. When the price is reduced to RM25, the demand rises to 54. We have $\Delta Q = Q_0 - Q_1 = 40 - 54 = -14$. Likewise, $\Delta P = P_0 - P_1 = 30 - 25 = 5$. Given the initial values of Q and P as 40 and 30, respectively, we get elasticity of demand:

(i) When price pair or *range* = 25 to 30

$$E_{DP} = \frac{\Delta Q}{\Delta P} \cdot \frac{P}{Q}$$

$$= \frac{-14}{5} \times \frac{30}{40}$$

$$= -2.1$$

However, if we use the first derivative $\frac{dQ}{dP} = 0.1P$ in place of $\frac{\Delta Q}{\Delta P}$ we have:

(ii)   When P = 30

$$E_{DP} = \frac{dQ}{dP} \cdot \frac{P}{Q}$$

$$= -3 \times \frac{30}{40}$$

$$= -2.25$$

(iii)   When P = 25

$$E_{DP} = \frac{dQ}{dP} \cdot \frac{P}{Q}$$

$$= -2.5 \times \frac{25}{54}$$

$$= -1.15$$

Notice that the value of E_{DP} is not the same at P = 30 in (ii) and at P = 25 in (iii). Also, the two differ over their range in (i). We can well conclude that the elasticity at any two points on a demand curve would be different. (Why does it fall in case (i) between E_{DP} at cases (ii) and (iii)?)

Exercise   3.2

Using the demand function of Example 3.2, find the elasticity of demand when the price falls from RM25 to RM20 a ticket. Also notice that the value of E_{DP} is now smaller. Can you say why?

Exercise   3.3

Following is the imaginary demand schedule for tea bags in India taken from Exercise 2.8. Is it a linear demand curve? State the reason for your answer. Find elasticity of demand when (a) price rises from 10 to 25, and (b) quantity demanded falls from 400 to 250.

Price P (INR hundred)	5	10	15	20	25	30	35	40	45	50
Demand Q_D (thousand bags)	650	600	550	500	450	400	350	300	250	200

(Use the proportionate change method in both cases.)

The advantage of using dQ/dP in place of DQ/DP is that the value of elasticity would not vary with the choice of a price range (P_0-P_1) for estimation. Assume that in Example 3.2, the price falls from 30 to 20 (instead of to 25), the value of E_{DP} would change from 2.25 to 1.87 (verify from your answer in Exercise 3.2). If we use the derivative as slope of the demand curve, the measurement at each price remains precise. For a straight line demand curve, the slope DQ/DP and dQ/dP are identical constants in the calculation of E_{DP}, but the multiplier P/Q does change with a change in price of the commodity. Thus, price elasticity of demand is different at each points of a straight line demand curve also (as hinted earlier). It follows that a comparison of any two demand curves for price elasticity may not be appropriate except over the *same* range of price. Figure 3.2 illustrates the point. Here, the two demand curves D_1 and D_2 cross each other at point T_1 so that at price P_1 the quantity demanded Q_1 is the same for each of the curves and would keep P/Q equal for calculating the two elasticities. But when price falls from P_1 to P_2, quantity demanded expands more on D_2 than on D_1 as $Q_3 > Q_2$. In other words, the slope T_2T_4/T_1T_2 of D_2 with reference to the price axis is greater than the slope of D_1 which is T_2T_3/T_1T_2.

> Since elasticity is not the same at various points of a demand curve, we can compare the two demand curves for elasticity only over a common price range.

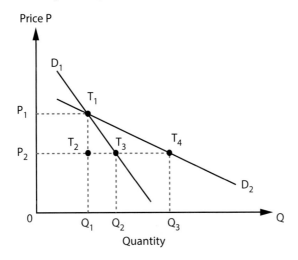

Figure 3.2 E_{DP} *over the same price range on different demand curves*

Thus, in (DQ/DP)(P/Q), even as the ratio Q/P (initial values) is identical in both cases, the other term DQ/DP or the slope is greater for D_2. Demand over the *same* price range P_1 to P_2 is therefore, more elastic on the curve with the greater slope. Thus, E_{DP} over the same price range on the two demand curves differs because their slopes are unequal. An interesting question is, what will be the consequence if the slopes of the two demand curves were the same? Clearly, the equality of slopes will make straight line demand curves parallel to one another, having no common point as T_1 in Figure 3.2.

We show in Figure 3.3 that on two demand curves, the E_{DP} at *any* price will be *smaller* for the one that is farther away from the origin. Here, we have two demand curves D_1 and D_2 with identical slopes. However, the ratio P_1/Q_1 for D_1 is greater than the ratio P_1/Q_2 for D_2. Therefore, E_{DP} for any price like P_1 will be *smaller* for D_2 than for D_1. The message of this result is that attempt at expanding the market may prove an increasingly difficult task because as the effort intensifies, expenditure on marketing tends to become progressively less rewarding.

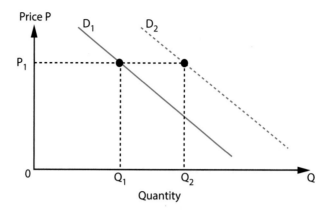

Figure 3.3 *Elasticity of demand on parallel demand curves*

Exercise   3.4

Consider the following demand functions:

$$Q = 10 - 2P$$
$$P = 7.5 - 0.5Q$$

(i)   Show that these functions have equal slopes.
(ii) Find elasticity of demand in each case when price is RM3 per unit.
(iii) Construct a figure similar to Figure 3.2 to explain your results.

Average elasticity of demand

We have argued above that the elasticity of demand on different points of a curve would be different and any two demand curves can therefore, be compared over the same price range. However, the concept of *average* elasticity helps us to compare the two demand curves in their totality. The formulae for average elasticity of demand is:

$$\text{Average E}_{DP} = \frac{\Delta Q}{\Delta P} \cdot \frac{\bar{P}}{\bar{Q}}$$

Where $\frac{\Delta Q}{\Delta P}$ is the slope of the demand curve, $\bar{P}$ is the price average $[(P_1 + P_2)/2]$ and $\bar{Q}$ the quantity average $[(Q_1 + Q_2)/2]$. This method is known as the Marshall–Edgeworth solution to the problem of choosing from the pair of Ps and Qs to set up the ratio P/Q in the elasticity formula. The formula they provided can be written as:

$$E_{DP} = \frac{\Delta Q}{\Delta P} \cdot \frac{\dfrac{P_1 + P_2}{2}}{\dfrac{Q_1 + Q_2}{2}} = \frac{\Delta Q}{\Delta P} \cdot \frac{P_1 + P_2}{2} \cdot \frac{2}{Q_1 + Q_2} = \frac{\Delta Q}{\Delta P} \cdot \frac{P_1 + P_2}{Q_1 + Q_2} \quad (3.3)$$

For example, in the linear demand schedule of Exercise 3.3 (a) the slope of the curve is 50, a constant, the mean of two prices 10 and 25 is 17.5 and of the corresponding quantities 600 and 450 is 525. Thus,

$$\text{Average E}_{DP} = 50 \times (17.5/525)$$
$$= 1.67$$

We find that the given demand curve is on the whole fairly elastic. The concept can be used in the case of non-linear demand curves as well. (Calculate the average elasticity for the demand function of Table 3.1.) The concept is useful for measuring the relative elasticity of such variables as the imports and exports of a country. You will learn in your econometric course that in log-linear analyses the coefficient of independent variable gives the average elasticity measure of the function.

> Average price elasticity of demand measures the overall elasticity of the demand function.

Types of EDP

The value of E_{DP} ranges from zero to infinity. Demand is considered inelastic if $E_{DP}<1$. Abdul Hamid Abu Ghazali indeed presented an early version of price inelasticity of demand for certain goods. Demand is unit elastic when $E_{DP} = 1$ and it is elastic if $E_{DP}> 1$. The extreme cases arise when $E_{DP} = 0$ or ∞. In the first case demand is perfectly inelastic and in the second it is perfectly elastic. Figure 3.4 is a *schematic* depiction of various types of elasticity. Here, the depiction of unit elasticity—entry C—requires explanation as the curve drawn is to be a rectangular hyperbola, i.e. it is the locus of a point that moves in the plane in such a way that the product of its distance from two straight lines perpendicular to each other remains equal. In our case, axes P and Q are such lines. It is a characteristic of such curves that the area the coordinates of any point on it enclose is always a constant.

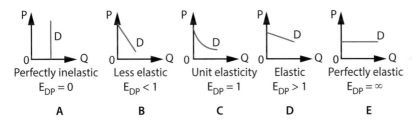

Figure 3.4 *Types of price elasticity of demand*

It is easy to demonstrate that elasticity of demand on any point of such curve will be unity. The proof is as follows. We have by definition:

$PQ = \beta$, where β is a constant.

$Q = \beta/P$

$$\frac{dQ}{dP} = -\frac{\beta}{P^2}$$

Multiplying both sides by $\frac{P}{Q}$ we have:

$$\frac{dQ}{DP} \cdot \frac{P}{Q} = -\frac{\beta}{P^2} \cdot \frac{P}{Q}$$

$$= -\frac{\beta}{PQ}$$

But $dQ/dP \cdot P/Q = EDP$ and $PQ = \beta$ by definition.

$\therefore EDP = -\beta/\beta$

> Normally, elasticity is different on each point of a demand curve. The exception is if the demand curve is a rectangular hyperbole. On such a curve, the quantity-price product remains constant. In other words, the expenditure on the commodity does not change.

Thus, we have:

$E_{DP} = -1$ (On any point of the curve.)

The above demonstration is intimately related to, rather it is based on, another method employed to measure price elasticity of demand that we now discuss.

Exercise **3.5**

$PQ = 36$ is a demand function. Fill in the blank cells in the following table.

P	1	2	3	4	6	9	12	18	36
Q_D									
P/Q									
dQ/dP									
E_{DP}									

3.3.2 Total Outlay Method

Table 3.2 *Total outlay and elasticity of demand*

Price (RM per unit P)	10	9	8	7	6	5	4	3	2	1
Quantity demanded (Q)	1	2	3	4	5	6	7	8	9	10
Total outlay (PQ)	10	18	24	28	30	30	28	24	18	10
Type of elasticity (E_{DP})	Elastic (>1) A				Unit elastic (51) B		Inelastic (<1) C			

In Table 3.2, as price decreases steadily from 10 to 1, quantity demanded increases from 1 to 10. The impact of the operation on total revenue is interesting. To begin with, in segment A, it increases as price falls, implying that the demand expands faster than the fall in price but clearly at a slowing rate, the outlay reaching a maximum of 30 in segment B. Then it no longer rises with a fall in price and stays at the same level, i.e. 30 indicating that demand increases at the same rate as price falls: elasticity is unity. As we move to the last segment C, outlay falls despite continuation of decrease in price: quantity is slower to respond, i.e. demand is inelastic. Figure 3.5 sketches the relationship between total outlay and elasticity of demand as price falls. Segment B in the table presents a unique case because it does not arise in A or C. Let us apply the proportion method to find elasticity when P decreases from 6 to 5 raising the Q from 5 to 6. Slope of the curve being 1, E_{DP} becomes P/Q or 5/6 = 0.83, i.e. less than unity. But the outlay method estimates it as 1. The contradiction does not arise if for calculating the proportions we use the Marshall–Edgeworth method. Here, we use *average* of the relevant prices and quantities as under:

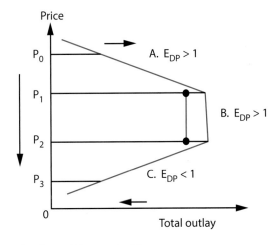

Figure 3.5 *Total outlay and E_{DP} as price falls*

$$E_{DP} = \frac{\dfrac{Q_0 - Q_1}{(Q_0 + Q_1)/2}}{\dfrac{P_0 - P_1}{(P_0 + P_1)/2}} = \frac{Q_0 - Q_1}{(Q_1 + Q_0)/2} \cdot \frac{(P_1 + P_0)/2}{P_0 - P_1}$$

$$= \frac{Q_0 - Q_1}{P_0 - P_1} \cdot \frac{P_0 + P_1}{Q_0 + Q_1} = \frac{\Delta Q}{\Delta P} \cdot \frac{P_1 + P_0}{Q_1 + Q_0} \qquad (3.4)$$

Notice that the 2s used as denominator for averaging cancel out each other in the simplification process. The end result, therefore, need not convey that the relevant ratio is of the sum of values, not their averages.

Exercise **3.6**

Estimate E_{DP} using the Marshall–Edgeworth formula for the information in segment B of Table 3.2. Compare with the result of the total outlay method.

Exercise **3.7**

For a demand law, $P = a - bQ^2$ of the normal form show that E_{DP} decreases as Q increases. (**Hint**: Find dP/dQ and use the inverse function rule to estimate dQ/dP.)

3.3.3   The Line Segment Ratio or the Point Method

If we are using calculus, the slope will be given by the first derivative of the demand function at a *point* on the curve. The point will divide the curve into two parts: the upper left segment and the lower right segment. We state without proof the following simple formula for estimating E_{DP}.

$$E_{DP} = \frac{\text{Lower segment}}{\text{Upper segment}}$$

If the two segments are of equal length, E_{DP} will be equal to 1. In Figure 3.6, based on data in Table 3.2, this point is D, lying halfway between A and B; elasticity will be more than 1 at points above D on the line and less than 1 at points below D. (Why?) Segment ratio or point method is a useful tool for measuring the price elasticity of demand. We can assess E_{DP} by merely looking at the figure. We may use the segment ratio even when the curve is not a straight line. Figure 3.7 helps us to understand the procedure; here the demand curve DD is non-linear.

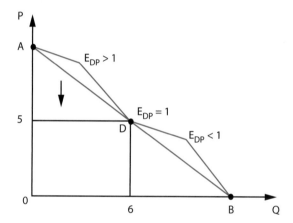

Figure 3.6 *E_{DP} at segments of a straight line demand curve*

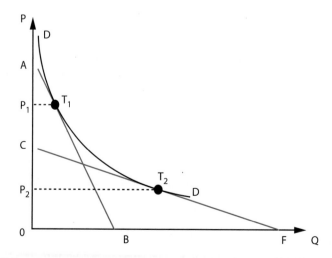

Figure 3.7 *Measuring E_{DP} on a smooth curve: graphic method*

We draw a tangent to the curve DD at the point where we want to measure the elasticity E_{DP} and extend it both ways to meet the axes. The point divides the tangent in two parts: the upper and the lower. These can be used to find the E_{DP}. To illustrate, let AB be a tangent to the demand curve DD at T_1 price, while CF is tangent to the same curve at T_2. Notice that the lower segment T_1B is larger than T_1A, the upper segment. Demand is elastic (>1) at P_1 price, but it is less elastic (<1) at P_2 price because the lower segment T_2F is smaller than the upper segment T_2C. Again, note that demand is elastic at higher prices and less elastic at the lower ones. This method was first employed by Alfred Marshall in his *principles* (1898).

If the demand curve is non-linear, we draw a tangent to it at the given point such that it meets the axes. The point method can then be used, taking the tangent as the demand curve.

3.3.4 Average Revenue and Marginal Revenue Rule

An advantage of the total revenue method is that it helps link the concept of price elasticity of demand to the supply side of the commodity through comparisons of various revenue concepts: total, average and marginal with their cost counterparts. We reproduce here Table 3.2 in the vertical form (see Table 3.3) adding revenue columns to it. It can be shown that at any point on a demand curve:

$$E_{DP} = \frac{AR}{AR - MR} \tag{3.5}$$

Example 3.3 The result is important as it enables us to interpret the nature of demand at a price if we know the corresponding elasticity. Note the following points from Table 3.3.

Since there is a mathematical relationship between average revenue (price) and marginal revenue, their values help construct a formula for measuring demand elasticity.

Table 3.3 *Price, quantity, revenues and price elasticity of demand (imaginary data)*

Price per unit RM P	Quantity demanded (Thousand units)	Total revenue P × Q TR	Average revenue TR/Q AR	Marginal revenue MR	Elasticity of demand E_{DP}
10	1	10	10	10	
9	2	18	9	8	
8	3	24	8	6	>1
7	4	28	7	4	
6	5	30	6	2	
5	6	30	5	0	1
4	7	28	4	−2	
3	8	24	3	−4	<1
2	9	18	2	−6	
1	10	10	1	−8	

1. If $E_{DP} > 1$, a small decrease in price results in a more than proportionate increase in demand, marginal revenue dTR/dQ

is positive and total revenue increases as output (= demand) expands.

2. If $E_{DP} = 1$ for a given price–demand combination, a small decrease in price and corresponding increase in quantity are proportional, marginal revenue is zero and total revenue maximum. Output expansion is not indicated.

3. If $E_{DP} < 1$ for a given price and quantity demanded, a small decrease in price is accompanied by a less than proportionate increase in quantity, marginal revenue is negative and total revenue decreases if output (= demand) were increased. Figure 3.8 helps us understand these points.

> Elasticity of demand is more than 1 if MR >1, is unity if MR 5 0 and is more than 1 if MR < 0.

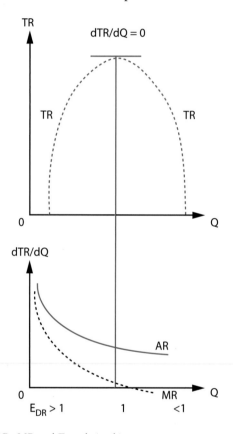

Figure 3.8 *TR, AR, MR and E_{DP} relationships*

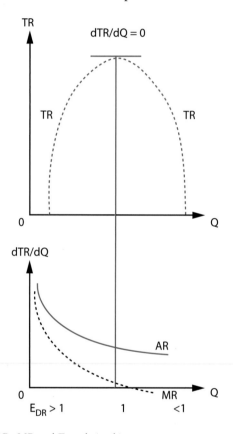

BOX 3.1

Profit-sharing with Labour and Elasticity of Demand

It is easy to demonstrate that under-payment to labour inevitable under monopolistic competition, can be undone in the Islamic system if the workers are given, in addition to market wage rate $\hat{w}$, a proportion σ of profit P that would yield an amount equal to the difference of the value of marginal physical product of labour VMP$_L$, and its marginal revenue product MRP$_L$ multiplied by the number of labour units L used to produce the corresponding output Q$_L$. Here, VMP$_L$ = $\hat{w}$Q$_L$

and $MRP_L = PQ_L$ where P is the price at Q_L output. Under-payment to workers thus equals $PQ_L - \hat{w}Q_L = (P - \hat{w})Q_L$ as $P > \hat{w}$ under monopolistic competition (See Chapter 5). Profit is, as usual, total revenue PQ minus total cost $\hat{w}L$. One can then demonstrate that paying a share σ in profit P to workers, additional to market wage rate, $\hat{w}$ would eliminate the under-payment to them. We state without reproducing proof that:

$$\sigma = \frac{1}{E_{DL\bar{w}}} \cdot \frac{r}{\beta}$$ where, σ is the ratio of profit P for the workers, $E_{DL\hat{w}}$. is elasticity of demand

for labour, p is capital employed per worker, and r is the rate of return on that capital.

It flows that for different price-output combinations, the profit-sharing ratio, σ for labour would vary inversely, within and between firms, with changes in elasticity of demand for labour and β, the amount of capital per unit of labour employed and it would vary directly with changes in the ratio of workers productive contribution to the rate of profit on that capital. Under dynamic conditions, the direction of the net influence would depend on the mutual interaction of the three determinants. The sharing would give the workers $(\hat{w} + \sigma P)$ as compensation for their contribution to production. In practice, there can be difficulties in arriving at the value of σ but that need not negate the significance of sharing obligation and its efficacy. In essence, the scheme advocates for a flexible wage system as a share in profit varying with the performance of business. The assumptions of the scheme that economic agents would behave in accordance with the Islamic norms of the firms, and the management would resist the tempted of enlarging the profit at the workers' cost.

Exercise   3.8

(i) Compare Figures 3.4 and 3.5 with Figure 3.8 and note down the similarities and differences between them.
(ii) $E_{DP} = AR/(AR - MR)$. Given P = 30 in a demand schedule, find E_{DP} if MR were equal to (a) 16, (b) 30 and (c) 40. Assuming that all the output produced is sold, what will be your advice about output increase to the firm you work for as a consultant?

3.4   DETERMINANTS OF EDP

So far we have discussed what price elasticity of demand E_{DP} means and how we can measure it. But an equally important question is why price elasticity of different commodities at the same time or of the same commodity at different times differs? In other words, what factors influence or determine the E_{DP} of a commodity? The main factors in addition to the price of the commodity itself are as below. However, none of them may be the sole determinant of elasticity in a case.

There are many factors that influence elasticity of demand for a commodity including availability of substitutes, the number of uses it can be put to, the type of want— necessity, comfort or luxury—which in general satisfies and the time allowed for adjustments to take place.

1. **Availability of substitutes**: *In general, the larger the number of goods that can be easily used in place of a commodity, the greater the expected price elasticity.* If the price of a commodity X falls, i.e. it becomes cheaper relative to any of its substitutes (Y), the

buyers of its substitute are likely to shift part of the demand for Y to commodity X. Tea and coffee, pen and ballpoint, wheat and rice, and different edible oils come to mind as examples. Substitutability makes their demand elastic. On the other hand, common salt virtually has no substitutes and this is *one* reason, among others, that its demand for domestic use is inelastic. Another good example of inelastic demand is of petroleum. It yet has no viable competitive substitutes. Despite the 2008 phenomenal rise in its price, the producers are under constant pressure to increase production as demand **tends to rise**.

2. **Variety of uses**: *The larger the number of uses a commodity has, the greater its price elasticity and vice versa.* For that reason the demand for electricity, rubber and plastics is, to illustrate, more elastic compared to coffee or bananas.

3. **Nature of wants**: Commodities are demanded to satisfy human wants. We have seen that wants in general can be classified into necessities, comforts and luxuries. As a rule, demand for commodities that meet at a point in time necessities of life such as food, clothing or shelter is inelastic; for comforts elastic, and for luxuries of life such as tourism even more elastic.

4. **Time element**: *In general, demand for goods is more elastic in the long run compared with the short run.* Consumers usually need time to adjust to price changes with reference to their incomes and tastes. Consumers cannot, for example, shift from sea food to meat or vegetables if the widespread damage to fishing industry brought by calamities like the Asian Tsunami raise fish prices suddenly. However, if the rise in fish prices persists over time, adjustment can be smooth. Also, the demand for petroleum products in the short run has been found to be less elastic than in the long run.

3.4.1   Significance of EDP

Knowledge of the elasticity of demand is crucial for business firms—even industries—to decide on pricing policies for their products. Some reasons are as below.

1. **Competitive prices and E_{DP}**: In general, if at the current price–demand is less elastic (< 1) a firm might gain if it raises the price a little but is not likely to gain from its reduction. For example in Table 3.3 above demand is less elastic over price range 1 to 5. Thus, a firm selling the commodity at price 3 per unit will certainly gain in terms of revenue if it raises the price to 5 but would lose if it lowers it to 2. The policy conclusion will be in the opposite direction if demand were price elastic (> 1). The demand for agricultural products, for food-related crops especially, is less elastic. That is one reason why agricultural prices rise at a relatively faster rate during periods of inflation

and tend to crash during recessions. This less elastic nature of demand for agricultural products makes public intervention in the market look reasonable as we saw in Chapter 2 while discussing the fixation of ceiling and floor prices to achieve stability in the markets.

2. **Pricing power and E_{DP}:** Another good example of the usefulness of the concept is the ability of firms to charge in some situations different prices for virtually the same product in different market segments. Total revenue is enlarged by keeping price higher in the segment where demand is less elastic and lower where it is more elastic, if price discrimination were possible. We shall explain this case more fully in a subsequent chapter.

3. **E_{DP} and taxation:** Levying taxes on production, sale, import or export of goods is a major source of public revenue. In all cases, the person whose legal responsibility is to pay the taxes to the government attempts to pass them on to the purchasers of the commodity. Obviously, to the extent he succeeds the tax raises the price of the commodity and reduces its demand. With the reduction in demand, profit of firms is also reduced. Figure 3.9 illustrates what may possibly happen when a seller may attempt to transfer a sales tax forward to the consumers.

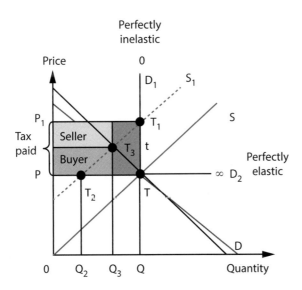

Figure 3.9 *Who bears the sales tax?*

In Figure 3.9, S and D are the initial supply and demand curves crossing each other at mid-point of D. Thus, the elasticity of demand at the intersection point, T, is unity. P and Q are the equilibrium price and quantity bought and sold. Now, suppose the government imposes a per unit sales tax on the commodity measured by t. The legal obligation of paying the tax to the government is of the seller. But as the tax reduces the profit of the seller, he would like to recover the tax amount from the buyer, adding it to his bill. Thus, who finally bears the *money burden* of charge is discussed in economics as the incidence of tax. Who would bear a part or whole of the tax would depend on the elasticity of demand for the commodity. Figure 3.9 makes you understand three cases.

1. Demand is perfectly inelastic (D_1). Here, the buyer needs the commodity irrespective of price. He will pay the whole tax and will buy Q quantity at P_1 price. The profit of the seller would remain unaffected.

2. Demand is perfectly elastic (D_2). If the seller adds tax to the price, the buyer would cut back demand to Q_2. It will be in the interest of the seller to pay the whole tax and continue selling the Q quantity of the commodity at old price P. His profit will of course be reduced by the full amount of tax.

3. In the case of unit elasticity of demand, the consumer would still reduce demand but not beyond Q_3. He will share the tax with the seller allowing 50% tax addition to price. (Why?)

It follows that as we move from 1 towards infinity on the elasticity scale, a larger part of the tax will be paid by the seller. The opposite will happen if the movement is towards zero.

For commodities that have more elastic demand such reductions are more than for those that have less elastic demand. Also, the revenue of the government from the tax is smaller when demand is more elastic. The government has to look into such consequences of a tax.

What is true for different commodities in the same market is also true for the same commodity in different markets. Figure 3.10 illustrates the point from this latter angle.

> Elasticity of demand is of great significance in designing economic policies, especially in matters of competition versus monopoly power taxation and exchange rate fixation.

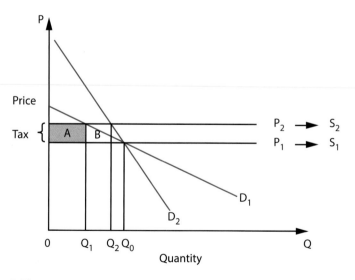

Figure 3.10 *Price elasticity of demand and tax policy*

To neutralize the role of elasticity of supply we have here supply curve P_1S_1 as perfectly elastic, i.e. sellers are willing to supply any quantity of the commodity at the prevailing market price.

The two demand curves are for the same commodity but D_1 is for foreign market and D_2 for the domestic market. Now, the government wants to choose one of these markets for levying a per unit tax on the commodity. The price elasticity of demand helps in making the choice. It is easy to see that demand for the commodity is on the whole more elastic abroad (D_1) than at home (D_2). The figure shows that at P_1 price the quantity bought and sold of the commodity is the same in each of the markets (Q_0). Now, suppose the government wants to know the result of imposing a blanket unit tax P_1P_2 on the commodity. The price would rise by the full amount of tax and push up the supply curve to P_2S_2 position. It is clear that the rise in price would lead to a greater reduction in sales abroad (Q_0Q_1) than at home (Q_0Q_2). Notice also that the tax revenue in the home market with less elastic demand equals A + B area while it is just equal to (A) in the foreign markets with more elastic demand. It follows that domestic market must be the choice for taxation.

To conclude, other things being equal, it is advisable to levy taxes on commodities or in markets where demand for them is relatively less elastic simply because it would arrest the dampening of incentives and will at the same time bring in more revenue to the government.

4. **Currency markets and E_{DP}**: Finally, whether a relatively *high* domestic price of foreign currency, e.g. quoted at RM 3.83 for one US dollar, or a lower one, say RM 3.50, will be more advantageous for the Malaysian economy cannot be decided without reference to the nature of elasticity for its exports and imports. For example, if exports were less price elastic than imports keeping exchange rate on the higher side, if possible, will benefit the country. For example, the 2008 rise in oil prices benefiting the producers handsomely for the demand for oil is not elastic. (Does it mean that price elasticity of demand for oil is less than 1?)

It follows that the price elasticity of demand has operational significance at both the micro and macro levels of an economy. Some interesting policy implications of price elasticity relate to the market for productive resources that we shall have occasion to discuss later when we deal with the pricing of these resources.

| **Exercise** | **3.9** |

In Figure 3.8, who bears the tax, the sellers or the buyers and how much? Give reasons for your answer.

3.5   ELASTICITY OF DEMAND: NON-PRICE CONCEPTS

Elasticity of demand is not considered with reference to the price of the commodity alone; it is also measured with reference to consumers' income and the prices of related goods.

The concept of price elasticity of demand keeps us on the *same* demand curve and discusses what happens to elasticity if we are on one point of it rather than the other. However, in a dynamic practical situation we move from one demand curve to another. Thus, demand increases as we move from a lower to a higher demand curve price remaining unchanged. *Quantity demanded changes here also but not in response to a change in price: it changes because of change in non-price factors.* To refresh your understanding of the factors you may go back to *'causes'* under Section 2.5 in the preceding chapter. Of the factors we have discussed there, two are precisely measurable: (a) the prices of related goods and (b) the income of the buyers. But like E_{DP}, here also the extent of demand response to a change in either case is not often the *same*. Case (a) gives rise to the concept of *cross* elasticity of demand, while (b) to the notion of *income* elasticity of demand. We discuss these below in that order.

3.5.1   Cross Elasticity of Demand

Cross elasticity of demand or E_{DC} is the response of quantity demanded of a commodity to a change not in its own price but in the price of a *related* commodity. The formula for calculation is:

$$E_{DC} = \frac{\text{Proportionate change in quantity demanded of commodity A}}{\text{Proportionate change in price of a related commodity B}}$$

$$= \frac{\Delta Q_A}{\Delta P_B} \cdot \frac{P_B}{Q_A} \tag{3.6}$$

Notice that the formula is of the same form as in equation (3.2). Try to write down all the steps to arrive at the result here.

The relationship between goods can be of two types. They can be competitors for the income of the customers because one can be used in place of the other. Coffee and tea, or apples and oranges easily come to mind as examples. If the price of coffee rises relative to that of tea (recall Figure 2.2), people may demand more of tea as a *substitute* for coffee. Thus, the relationship between change in the price of one and the quantity demanded of the other in the case of substitutes is *positive*.

In contrast, if any two goods are used together, not in isolation of each other, they are complements. Things like pen and ink, car and petrol, kite and string, cup and saucer are a few illustrations. Thus, if the price of one of them, say pens, rises causing a decrease in their demand, the demand for ink will also fall even as its own price remains unchanged. Here the change in the price of one commodity is *inversely* related to the change in quantity demanded of the other. Figure 3.11 illustrate the difference.

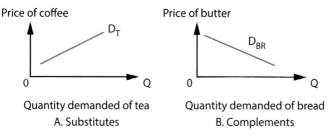

Figure 3.11 *Relationship between price of a commodity with the demand for its substitutes or complements*

Interestingly, cross elasticity of demand has great significance under competitive conditions. After the American led invasion of Iraq, some western firms faced customer aversion in many countries, Muslim especially. To illustrate, a pizza outlet manager in New Delhi reduced prices to retain customer. Another close-by shop famous for their burgers, knew that pizza was a close substitute for its product. So, it also wanted to cut prices to stay afloat. But it thought of two alternatives: (a) reduce the price of burgers or (b) cut the price of the drink it supplied with them. The first focused on neutralizing the possibility of losing market to a substitute, while the second on a cheaper complement to stay in competition. In either case, the question was how much should be the reduction? A knowledge of cross elasticities of demand was needed for appropriate action.

Knowledge of the cross elasticity of a product helps in a competitive market.

Exercise 3.10

Suppose the quantity demanded for good X increases by 10% in response to a 20% rise in the price of good Y, answer the following questions, other things remaining unchanged.
  (i)   Are X and Y substitutes or complements? Give reason for your answer.
  (ii) Make an illustrative figure to show how the demand for X would change.
  (iii) Calculate the cross elasticity of good X with reference to good Y. Is demand elastic?

Exercise 3.11

Suppose the facts supplied to you are:
• The price of air conditioners falls in Lahore from INR 40,000 to INR 30,000 and their demand rises from 200 to 300 units.
• The demand for dessert coolers decreases from 400 to 350 units.
• At the same time, the demand for electricity rises from 1,500 to 2,100 kW.
Answer the following questions assuming that other things remain unchanged:
  (i)   What would be the elasticity of demand for dessert coolers with reference to the change in the price of air conditioners?
  (ii) Would you agree that air conditioners and electricity are not substitutes for one another? Justify your answer.

3.5.2   Income Elasticity of Demand

Variations in prices alone do not cause changes in demand for goods. Incomes too have a great impact on what people buy and how much. In Malaysia, for example, the economy has been expanding over the decades and people are enjoying rising incomes. The prosperity is bringing increased demand for all sorts of goods. But a car dealer may want to know by how much the demand for local cars is likely to rise in future? The answer depends on the nature of income elasticity of demand for local cars. Normally there is a positive relationship between change in income of a buyer and change in his quantity demanded of a commodity, its own price remaining unchanged. We estimate here the proportionate change called the income elasticity of demand or E_{DY}. The formula is:

$$E_{DY} = \frac{\text{Proportionate change in quantity demanded of commodity A}}{\text{Proportionate change in consumers' income Y}}$$

$$= \frac{\dfrac{Q_{1.DA} - Q_{0.DA}}{Q_{0.DA}}}{\dfrac{Y_1 - Y_0}{Y_0}} = \frac{\dfrac{\Delta Q_{DA}}{Q_{0.DA}}}{\dfrac{\Delta Y}{Y_0}}$$

$$= \frac{\Delta Q_{DA}}{P_{0.DY}} \cdot \frac{Y_0}{\Delta Y}$$

$$= \frac{\Delta Q_{DA}}{\Delta Y} \cdot \frac{Y_0}{Q_{0.DA}} \tag{3.7}$$

Notice that in its form, equation 3.5 is identical with equations 3.2 and 3.5. Income elasticity of demand is usually of three types:

1. **Greater than one**: This is the case of *normal* good; demand is income elastic.
2. **Less than one**: This too is the case of a normal good but demand is inelastic.
3. **Less than zero**: This is the case of an *inferior* good. Unlike the first two cases, income elasticity of demand for inferior goods is negative.

Normal goods

> A good remains a normal good so long as it has positive utility for the user.

We had stated earlier that the negative sign of the elasticity coefficient is ignored and there are valid reasons for the same. That statement was true for normal goods. However, in the case of income elasticity, the sign becomes important: it helps us to distinguish between normal goods and the Giffen or inferior goods. For the latter type of goods, income elasticity of demand is always positive. (Why?) Study the following cases.

Cases A and B in Figure 3.12 are of normal goods. These are *by definition* goods whose demand and consumers' income are positively related. The curve has a *positive slope*. In Figure 3.12A, the curve has an *increasing* slope; quantity demanded Q increases faster than the rise in income Y. Demand is income elastic. Air travel, jewellery and perfumes are some of the examples.

In Figure 3.12B, quantity demanded still increases with a rise in income but at a slower rate. The slope of the curve, though positive, *decreases* as income rises: demand is inelastic. Researchers cite demand for necessities of life such as food and clothing, furniture, newspapers and telephones as examples.

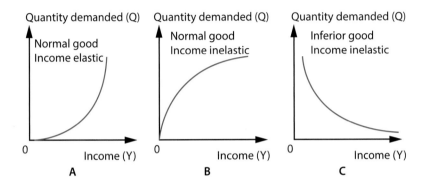

Figure 3.12 *Income elasticity of demand*

Inferior goods

These include commodities that consumers usually purchase less than before when their income rises. Quantity demanded and incomes are *inversely* related: the slope of the demand curve is *negative* and decreasing. (See Figure 3.12C.) In developing economies, course grains, unrefined sugar, long distance bus travel, lower class cinema tickets, used clothing provide some illustrations. You may use line segment ratio to measure elasticity of demand at any point in all three cases.

> In the case of normal goods, if quantity demanded increases at a faster rate than increase in income, demand is income elastic and vice versa. However, in the case of inferior goods, quantity demanded decreases with a rise in income and elasticity of demand tends to be less than one.

Exercise 3.12

Other things remaining unchanged, when the income of Selamah increases by 5%, she decreases the quantity demanded for macaroni by 10% and increases the quantity demanded for mutton by 10%. Given these facts answer the following questions:
Calculate the income elasticities of demand for (a) macaroni and (b) mutton.
  (i)   Is macaroni a normal good or inferior good? Give reasons for your answer.
  (ii) Is mutton an inferior good? Justify your answer.
  (iii) Is demand for mutton income elastic? Support your answer with the results of the calculation.

The income demand function of a commodity for A is $Q = -500 + 0.0025Y^2$. Find for A the income elasticity of demand E_{DY} when his income is RM 1000 a week. Is the demand for the commodity income elastic? (**Hint**: Use first derivative to find slope of the curve at $Y = 1000$. Also, find from the equation the value of Q when Y is 1000.)

3.6 PRICE ELASTICITY OF SUPPLY

The notion of elasticity is as much applicable to supply of commodities as to their demand.

Supply of goods also responds to price changes. The degree of responsiveness gives rise to the concept of price elasticity of supply. We determine this degree or price elasticity of supply E_{SP} by comparing the proportionate change in quantity supplied with proportionate change in price. Proportions can be expressed as percentage if we multiply them by 100. The formula is:

$$E_{DY} = \frac{\text{Proportionate change in quantity supplied}}{\text{Proportionate change in price}}$$

$$= \frac{\dfrac{Q_1 - Q_0}{Q_0}}{\dfrac{P_1 - P_0}{P_0}} = \frac{\dfrac{\Delta Q}{Q}}{\dfrac{\Delta P}{P}} = \frac{\Delta Q}{Q} \cdot \frac{P}{\Delta P}$$

Rearranging the equation we get:

$$= \frac{\Delta Q}{\Delta P} \cdot \frac{P}{Q} \tag{3.8}$$

The common method here is to measure the proportionate change in quantity supplied in relation to proportionate change in price of the commodity. The range and types of elasticity here are the same as in the case of demand.

We may use dQ/dP in place of $\Delta Q/\Delta P$ if we need greater accuracy, given the supply function.

Thus, if the supply function is $QS = -a + bp$, we can find QS for any P given the values for the constants a and b. The slope of the curve is constant, b. E_{SP} can easily be set up as equal to b[P/Q]. The range and types of price elasticity of supply are the same as in the case of price elasticity of demand with the difference that the sign of E_{SP} is invariably positive, not negative. Figure 3.13 explains the various types of price elasticity of supply or E_{SP}.

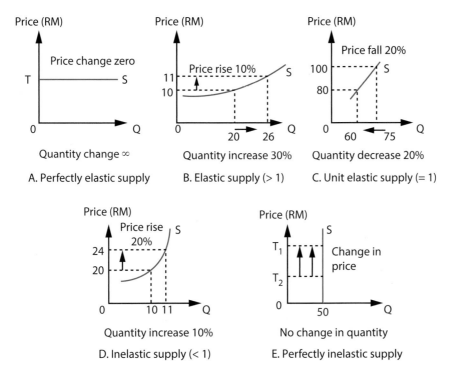

Figure 3.13 *Types of price elasticity of supply*

3.7 **DETERMINANTS OF PRICE ELASTICITY OF SUPPLY**

Why is the supply of certain goods elastic and of others inelastic? Four factors broadly determine the price elasticity of supply: (a) opportunity cost, (b) time element, (c) storability of the commodity and (d) variety of uses.

1. **Opportunity cost**: You are already familiar with the concept of opportunity cost. Since resources are scarce and have alternative uses, the employment of a bundle of resources for producing X commodity would make it unavailable to produce Y commodity. Thus, in a way the quantity of good Y that we forego to produce X would be its opportunity cost. *The smaller is the opportunity cost of producing a commodity the greater is its price elasticity.* An example is of silicon used in making computer chips. Silicon is extracted from sand. The opportunity cost of extraction is tiny and almost constant. So, the supply of silicon is price elastic. In contrast, we cannot convert hotel rooms in Kuala Lumpur into office rooms and vice versa; supply of both is inelastic.

> Opportunity cost of a commodity is the next best alternative you have to forego to have it.

Exercise 3.14

If the price of a commodity rises from $10 a unit to $12 and its quantity supplied increases from 100 to 120 units, calculate the price elasticity of supply over the given range of rice. Is the supply over that range of price elastic or inelastic? Explain.

Exercise 3.15

Suppose the supply function for a producer is $Q = -25 + P^2$. At what price will the supply be zero? Complete the following table.

P	7	8	9	10	11	12	13	14	15	16
P^2	49	–	–	100	–	–	169	–	225	–
Q	24	–	56	–	–	119	–	–	–	231

Construct the supply curve. Calculate and compare price elasticities of supply at prices 8 and 16. Explain the difference.

2. **Time element**: We have seen that supply takes time to adjust to price changes for a variety of reasons. As more time elapses after the price change better adjustment with demand becomes feasible. Thus, more time is allowed for supply to respond to a change in price greater tends to be the elasticity of supply: as time passes price elasticity of supply increases.

3. **Storability**: The supply elasticity of a good that cannot be stored or stored for long is low. Fresh vegetables or fish are examples. Storability of goods increases the staying power of the sellers. They can hold stocks of such goods in expectation of obtaining better prices provided the Islamic injunction against hoarding is not violated. The supply may thus become relatively more elastic.

4. **Variety of uses**: The more are the alternatives for using a commodity, the larger is the size of the market for it: electricity, water, printing presses and video cameras are some of the examples where variety of uses contributes to making their supply more price elastic. Medicines being use specific have less elastic supply.

**BOX
3.2**

Iran: Elasticity and Export of Dates

Iran is one of the producers and exporters in the dates industry, accounting for 34.1 per cent of world production, cultivation area, export quantity and export value, respectively (FAO, 2003). Around 0.09 per cent of non-petroleum export value is realized from dates accounted for about 100 million dollar per year. Dates are major non-oil exportable agri-crops in Iran, with an outstanding historical background. The country enjoys a reputation for its dates export at global levels and has maintained a 1st or 2nd rank in dates export globally. This survey aims at identification and assessment of the impacts of effective factors contributing in dates export development, using theoretical principles in export supply with focus on economic analyzing techniques. Moreover, calculating the elasticity of effective factors on dates export supply, specially the elasticity of price and income, role of relative prices, exchange rate, world dates production and the link in dates export have been examined in this analysis.

Dates are cultivated in Iranian dry regions with low rainfall of nearly 100 mm/year with also extreme geographical climate and temperatures. High salinity level of agricultural water and inadequate irrigation are the main restrictions that farmers are facing. As such, areas are not suitable to produce other crops economically; hence dates plantations remain the only opportunity for farmers.

Dates are one of the major exported produce of the country, so the study of dates export supply, production, export growth and export competitiveness is one of the major areas of research to be covered by the researchers to define the major sources of export changes and to use the appropriate tools in retaining the country's competitiveness in the world market. Review of literature shows that exponential trend equation is widely used for the aim of studying growth patterns computed for the growth rates in area, production and productivity of sweet potatoes in major growing states, estimating the annual compound growth rates in the exports of principal agricultural commodities from India, studying the compound growth rates of pulses in India, while assessing the regional variations in agricultural performance in India, estimating the compound growth rates of area, production and yield of pulses, quantifying trends and growth rates of area, production and yield of fruit crops in Haryana.

Source: Mehdi, S. and Reza, M. (2011), Sources of date export supply and investigating export in Iran, *European Journal of Experimental Biology*, 1(3): p. 80.

3.7.1   Cost Elasticity

In our discussion of elasticity of demand we established its link with total, average and marginal revenues of the firm. However, no effort is usually made in introductory textbooks to link elasticity of supply to cost of production even as the shapes and levels of supply curves are reflections of the total cost incurred in producing the commodities. The discussion of price elasticity of supply will be incomplete unless we get some insights into total cost elasticity with reference to output. The concept is extremely useful for the applications of elasticity notions in real-life situations.

> If we divide the relative change in the cost of production by that in the output of the commodity, we get the cost elasticity of supply.

$$K = \frac{\text{Proportionate change in total cost}}{\text{Proportionate change in output}}$$

$$= \frac{\Delta \Pi}{\Delta Q} \cdot \frac{Q}{\Pi} \text{ where } \Pi \text{ represents total cost of production} \qquad (3.9)$$

In the case of demand, we saw that total revenue curve is bell-shaped. It rises, reaches a maximum and then steadily falls. The story of total cost behaviour is entirely different. Total cost increases for every increase in output and its elasticity is defined and used to deduce properties of average cost. We shall return to cost elasticity in a chapter later.

3.8 ELASTICITY AND ISLAMIC ECONOMICS

The concept of elasticity—demand or supply—is that value is neutral and can be used in Islamic economics as well, despite some confusion in the literature on the topic.

An economic concept essentially is a matter of definition. Even when there is a broad agreement on what a term means, not every one may accept it; recall the discussion in Chapter 1 on the language of economics. The concept of elasticity discussed above is no exception. R. G. Lipsey writes in his textbook that there is no observable tendency for commodities to fall into two groups: one with very low elasticity and one with very high elasticity; yet, he agrees that food and shelter are necessities in the sense that life cannot go on without some minimum quantity of them and it is possibly true that food as a whole would have an inelastic demand albeit individual food items may or may not. Some Muslim writers likewise, feel that the mainstream elasticity concepts do not fully meet the requirements of Islamic economics. However, they never spell out those requirements or show how the mainstream concepts fail to meet them. They talk of elasticity of 'need-based demand' and 'capacity-based supply' but do not provide clear convincing explanations of these notions, their measurement, usefulness or application.

Furthermore, the concept of elasticity of demand or supply belongs essentially to the micro field of economics while need-based demand and capacity-based supply, whatever the terms might imply, tend to transport us to macroeconomic policy frames. It is not that elasticity concept at macro level is non-existent or irrelevant because we do talk of the elasticity of exports and imports of a country as a whole. Also, the discussion presented above is relevant and useful for Islamic economics as well.

Summary

- Elasticity is a measure of expansion or contraction of anything in response to force operating on it. Demand and supply both respond to changes in their determinants: they are elastic in a measure.

- The law of demand indicates that the change in quantity demanded of a commodity in response to a change in its price takes place in the opposite *direction* but it does not tell us anything about the *magnitude* of that change. Elasticity of demand provides us this *additional* and useful information.

- The importance of the concept of elasticity lies in the fact that for any given change in the prices of goods the quantity demanded in each case does not change by the same magnitude.

- Four different methods are available for measuring price elasticity of demand for commodities bought and sold in the market (Figure 3.12).

    (i)   The proportionate change method:

    $$E_{DP} = \frac{\text{Proportionate change in quantity demanded}}{\text{Proportionate change in price}}$$

    $$= \frac{\Delta Q}{\Delta P} \cdot \frac{P}{Q}$$

    (ii) The total outlay method: With a *fall in price* if total outlay (expenditure) on the commodity:

    (a)   Increases, demand is elastic, $E_{DP} > 1$

    (b)   Remains unchanged, $E_{DP} = 1$

    (c)   Decreases, demand is inelastic, $E_{DP} < 1$

    (iii) The line segment rule: If we extend a linear demand curve DD (or a tangent TT to a non-linear curve AA) to meet the axes, then any point C on it (or C the point of tangency) will divide the line (or tangent) in two parts: the lower part and the upper part.

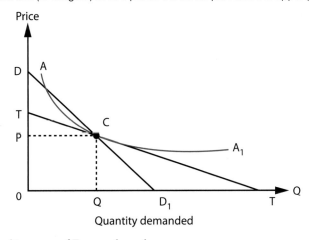

Figure 3.14 *Graphic measure of E_{DP} on a demand curve*

$$E_{DP} = \frac{\text{Lower segment}}{\text{Upper segment}}$$

$$= \frac{CD_1}{TC}, \text{ if DD is the demand curve; or}$$

$$\frac{CT_1}{TC}, \text{ if AA is the demand curve}$$

(iv) The average revenue and marginal revenue relationship: This is a very convenient way to find price elasticity of demand. Price we know, always equals average revenue. So, if we know price and marginal revenue at that price, we can easily calculate price elasticity as:

$$E_{DP} = \frac{AR}{AR - MR}$$

Clearly, if AR = MR, E_{DP} = ∞; if AR > MR, E_{DP} > 1, and if AR < MR, E_{DP} < 0.

- Factors that influence price elasticity of demand include availability of substitutes, variety of uses, nature of wants and time available for demand to adjust to price changes.

- The concept of price elasticity of demand is of great practical significance. In general, if the demand at current price is inelastic, the firm could gain in terms of revenue if it raises the price a little but it is not likely to benefit by a reduction in price. In case the demand is elastic, price reduction may be advisable to expand revenue.

- If a firm has the ability to charge different prices in two segments of a market, it can charge a higher price for its product in the segment where demand is less elastic than where it is more elastic to enlarge total revenue. Publishing the same material in cheap paper backs and costly hard covers, or railways charging different rates and fares from different users are examples.

- Public authorities may reduce tax evasion and collect larger revenues if, other things being equal, taxes are imposed on commodities with less elastic demand. An overvaluation of currency may benefit a country if its exports were less price elastic compared to its imports.

- How elastic would be the demand for a commodity depends not only on its own price but also on the prices of other commodities. This we call as cross elasticity of demand. It is distinct from price elasticity measured on the same demand curve with a change in price; here the movement is from one demand curve for the commodity to another. We go off the demand curve.

- The general formula for estimating cross elasticity of demand is:

$$E_{DC} = \frac{\text{Proportionate change in quantity demanded of commodity A}}{\text{Proportionate change in price of a related commodity B}}$$

$$= \frac{\Delta Q_A}{\Delta P_B} \cdot \frac{P_B}{Q_A}$$

- The good in whose price the change affects the quantity demanded of another commodity can be its substitute or complement. The price of the substitute and quantity demanded of a commodity are positively related while for complements this relationship is negative.

- Income of the purchasers is another non-price factor relevant for the elasticity of demand. The concept is important as economies continue to grow and incomes in general rise. Businesses especially must know how expanding incomes are likely to affect their revenues to pan output ahead of change. The formula linking quantity demanded with income is as follows:

$$E_{Dy} = \frac{\text{Proportionate change in quantity demanded}}{\text{Proportionate change in income}}$$

$$= \frac{\Delta Q}{\Delta y} \cdot \frac{y}{Q}$$

For normal good s, the relationship between quantity demanded and income of the buyers is always positive but if the slope of the income demand curve tends to increases with a rise in incomes; the elasticity is greater than 1, demand is income elastic, but if the slope of the curve is decreasing demand is less responsive to income changes. In the case of inferior goods, however, there is inverse relationship between income of the consumers and quantity demanded. For inferior goods, the income elasticity is less than one.

Supply of goods also responds to price changes. We measure price elasticity of supply as:

$$E_{SP} = \frac{\text{Proportionate change in quantity supplied}}{\text{Proportionate change in price}}$$

$$= \frac{\Delta Q}{\Delta P} \cdot \frac{P}{Q}$$

The types of price elasticity of supply and their interpretation is the same as for price elasticity of demand, the value of E_{SP} too ranges between zero and infinity, but its sign is positive.

- The main factors that affect the supply elasticity of goods with reference to price are the opportunity cost of producing it, time allowed for supply arrangements for adjusting to price change, storability of the commodity and the number of its uses.

- Behind supply curves lies the objective fact of cost of production. In fact, price elasticity of supply reflects its total cost of production elasticity. The total cost elasticity with reference to output is given as:

$$K = \frac{\text{Proportionate change in total cost}}{\text{Proportionate change in output}}$$

$$= \frac{\Delta \Pi}{\Delta Q} \cdot \frac{Q}{\Pi}$$

Where Π represents total cost of production.

Glossary

Cost elasticity of supply Resources being scarce, attempt is made to minimize the cost of producing goods. In this connection, the concept of cost elasticity of supply comes handy. It refers to the measure of change in the output of a commodity in response to a given change in the costs of input combination.

Cross elasticity of demand It is a measure of change in the quantity demanded of a commodity in response to a change in the price of a related commodity—a substitute or a complement—the price of the commodity itself remaining unchanged.

Elasticity This term in economics refers to any measure of the extent of change in a variable in response to a given change in some related variable.

Income elasticity of demand It is the measure of change in the quantity demanded of a commodity in response to a change in the income of the consumer, the price of the commodity remaining unchanged. Income elasticity of normal goods is positive but it is negative in the case of inferior goods.

Inferior goods They are by definition those which consumers tend to demand less—not more—with a rise in their income. They get their income released to for spending on normal (superior) goods which they can now afford to purchase. Second-hand cars and new cars, coarse grains and rice (or wheat) are the examples of the two sorts of goods.

Price elasticity of demand It is the measure of the extent of change in quantity demanded of a commodity in response to a change in its price; demand curve remaining the same.

Price elasticity of supply It is the measure of, like price elasticity of demand, the change in quantity supplied of a commodity in response to a change in its price as in the case of price elasticity of demand.

Concepts for Review

- Complements
- Cost elasticity
- Cross elasticity of demand
- Determinants of price elasticity of demand
- Elastic demand
- Elasticity
- Factors influencing elasticity of supply

- Income elasticity of demand
- Inelastic demand
- Inferior goods
- Normal goods
- Price elasticity of demand
- Price elasticity of supply
- Substitute goods
- Types of elasticity of supply
- Unit elasticity of demand

Case Study   3.1

Indian Railways and Elasticity of Demand

In administration, it is not always the knowledge about the nature of elasticity for a good or service but the pulse feel that may sometimes guide people to what turns out to be a correct hunch. Indian railways had been in the red over the decades, not even able to pay the low dividend to the central government. Railway transport was a troubled ministry. When Laloo Prasad Yadav took over as the minister of railways, his advisors suggested streamlining of the labour force and raising railway fares and freights as apparent remedial actions. But the minister had his own ideas. He indeed surprised all and sundry doing just the opposite; railways lowered fares and freights across the board and did not resort to retrenchment of the work force. The result: In a couple of years, Indian railways cleared their accumulated dividend debt to the government and are sitting pretty on a surplus of over 200 billion rupees. The minister probably never knew what elasticity of demand was about, let alone whether it was high or low for railway transport but his gut reaction to the situation guided him to a policy so successful that he was invited in prestigious universities at home and abroad to explain the miracle.

Case Questions
1. What do you understand by 'pulse feel' and 'gut reaction'? Explain.
2. Why did the policy the ministry implemented prove so successful?
3. Comment on the nature of price elasticity of rail transport in India in the light of the above experience. Does that explain the miracle?

Case Study   3.2

Elasticity of Malaysian Exports and Imports

During the Asian financial crisis (1997–1998), Malaysia pegged the ringgit on September 2, 1998 to US dollar at RM 3.80 compared to RM 2.52 from where the depreciation of the currency had started in July of the preceding year. The official action was informal recognition of about 34% devaluation of the currency the crisis had forced on the country. The measure made her exports cheaper by the same percentage but raised the cost of imports much more: by 51% to be precise. Consequently, Malaysian exports did increase in 1999 by 12%, but imports too expanded by 10%. Imports could not be curtailed as 70% of them were needed to support exports of the country.

Case Questions
1. Calculate the price elasticity for Malaysian exports and imports for 1999. You may use the proportionate change method.
2. Based on your estimation of the elasticities, can you say that devaluation of ringgit benefited Malaysian economy? Give reasons for your answer.

Test Questions

3.1 Define price elasticity of demand. The price of each of the three commodities X, Y and Z falls by 10%, but the change in quantity demanded is X, 8%; Y, 10% and Z, 12%. Find price elasticity of demand for each and explain its significance.

3.2 Reconstruct Figure 3.4 showing E_{DP} in terms of total outlay with a rise in the price of a commodity.

3.3 How does price elasticity of demand differ from income elasticity of demand? Do you stay on the same demand curve in each case? Explain using illustrative diagrams.

3.4 Explain cross elasticity of demand. Distinguish in this context between normal and inferior goods. Give appropriate illustrations.

3.5 The following are the values from a demand schedule. Using the total outlay method, comment on the nature of the curve from the viewpoint of price elasticity of demand.

Price (RM per unit)	P	1	2	3	4	6	9	18	36
Quantity demanded (units)	Q	36	18	12	9	6	4	2	1
Total outlay	PQ	–	–	–	–	–	–	–	–

3.6 In Q3.4, find the elasticity of demand over the price changes from 4 to 6 using (a) proportionate change, (b) Marshall–Edgeworth, and (c) total outlay methods. Which of them do you think gives the correct answer and why?

3.7 In Figure 3.14, point C is common to both the demand curves DD_1 and AA_1. Which of the two demand curves has greater price elasticity at point C and why?

3.8 Explain the main factors that determine price elasticity of demand. Why price elasticity over the same price range is likely to be greater the longer is the time we allow for necessary adjustments?

3.9 What do you understand by cross elasticity of demand? Bring out clearly the effect of substitutes and complements in this context. Support your answer with suitable examples and figures.

3.10 The following table gives imaginary demand schedule of three goods A, B and C. Construct the demand curve for each separately.

Income of the consumer Y (Per thousand units)	0	1	2	3	4	5
1. Quantity demanded Q_A (Units)	50	55	62	71	83	99
2. Quantity demanded Q_B (Units)	50	66	78	87	94	99
3. Quantity demanded Q_C (Units)	99	94	87	78	66	50

Answer the following questions.
(a) Are all cases of normal goods? Explain reasons for your answer.

(b) How does the difference you mention in the first two cases affect the income elasticity?

3.11 Explain the significance of elasticity of demand for business firms and tax policy of government.

3.12 Define price elasticity of supply and explain its various types. Explain the factors that influence price elasticity of supply.

3.13 Explain the meaning and importance of cost elasticity. How does it affect elasticity of supply for a commodity? Explain.

Web Exercise

Search on the Internet for the Indian Economic Journal, Volume 49, No. 1 and see P. 46 to verify your answers to questions in Case Study 3.2.

Forward Link

In this and the preceding chapter you have learnt about the tools of economics demand and supply and the related elasticity concepts. In the following Chapter 4, we shall explain what guides consumers in making decisions to choose what they buy. For it is these decisions that give rise to demand for goods and services sold in the market. We shall also examine why consumers are willing to pay the price for a given commodity?

4 Consumption: Analysis and Behavioural Norms

LEARNING OUTCOMES

This chapter should enable the student to understand:

- Human wants, needs and desires: Distinctions
- Consumer behaviour: Rationality versus morality
- Utility and satisfaction: Their meaning and implications
- The law of diminishing marginal utility
- Maximization of utility: Is it necessarily un-Islamic?
- Consumer surplus: Meaning, measurement and significance
- Value in use versus value in exchange
- Indifference curves: Meaning, properties and uses
- Indifference curves and consumer equilibrium
- Price effect, substitution effect and income effect
- Normal goods and inferior goods: The distinction
- Revealed preference

4.1 ISLAM AND CONSUMPTION

> Man is bipolar by creation: he has wants, material as well as spiritual, and both have to be satisfied.

Man by creation is a combination of dust and divine spirit (Qur'an 32:6). So, he broadly has two types of urges built into his person:

1. Earthly or mundane, i.e. he wants material facilities for living and, therefore, must produce them in abundance.

2. Spiritual, i.e. an environment which allows freedom to work for ideals—moral, ethical and social—and create not only what nature does not provide but beauty in its widest sense including compassion, commitment, justice and cultivation of love expressed in willingness to make sacrifice of the highest order for the cherished ideals.

The two types of urges—mundane and spiritual—may appear conflicting but they are basically interrelated and interact with each other in the unity of human existence. Islam seeks to regulate the urge for acquiring material goods (to consume) so that the two aspects of human living remain harmonized and supportive in a balance. Material progress is an inalienable ingredient of Islamic notion of progress; it is rather inherent in the divine scheme of creation. However, here we shall deal with only the mundane aspect of human existence.

The urge in human beings to acquire goods and services for satisfying their wants is but natural. This urge gives rise to various economic phenomena, a leading one being what we call consumption. The availability of goods and services being limited compared to what the people may want to consume, the economic decisions they make in this context are probably the most consequential. In fact, consumption is regarded as the point where economic activity originates as also the point where it ends. To understand the law of demand discussed in the preceding chapter more fully, we have to understand what guides the behaviour of consumers in making these decisions. This chapter addresses this question, especially with reference to the Islamic behavioural norms. We begin with an explanation of some basic concepts and relationships to fix ideas for utilization in the following discussion.

> In a way, consumption may be seen as the beginning and the end of all economic activity.

4.2   WANTS, NEEDS AND DESIRES

People in general instinctively want to get rid of hardships or seek pleasure, mundane and/or spiritual. This instinct is the essence of human existence and spurs men to work for a better living. You require food if you are hungry and if not, you may like to study or pray or go out for a joyful ride. This sort of inner urges in people are called in mainstream economics a human want, i.e. something people feel lacking. Wants in this sense are unlimited. If we satisfy one want, others crop up to take its place. An individual want may be satiable but his desires tend to come back again and again; we need something to eat more than once in a day and every day. These characteristics of wants pressure man to work to meet them. The pressure has, indeed, been the main spring of human toil to progress ever since Adam set foot on Earth. Even the religious literature, Islam included, takes note of these facts. Man was destined to live in difficulties (Qur'an 90:4). Multiplicity of wants, i.e. their overall insatiability, ingrained in human nature was the source of his difficulties.

> Our wants are those desires for which we have the means to meet and are willing to use them for the purpose.

There has been some confusion in the literature on the distinction between wants and needs that has increased all the more after the advent of Islamic economics on the scene. The mainstream view implies that the notion of a want is rather generic; it refers to the urge for seeking relief from pain or seeking pleasure. On the other hand, needs refer to *specific* goods one prefers to satisfy a want. For example, removal of thirst is a *want* in a balanced way. What drink one would like to have for satisfying it—plain water, orange juice or syrup to name a few—is what he *needs*. Mainstream economics classifies wants—not needs—into necessities, comforts and luxuries. The classification rests on an objective and measurable criterion: the impact of satisfying wants on *work* efficiency of a person. Accordingly, necessities are wants whose non-fulfilment would result in a reduction of work efficiency. Food, clothing, shelter, education and healthcare are some of the examples. Addition of comforts such as air conditioning or better transport facilities is likely to improve the efficiency. Finally, luxuries may have little impact on efficiency, may even reduce it, or even be injurious to health such as liquor, tobacco or drugs. The categories stated need not always have a mutual linkage. Also, the *same* commodity could fall in any of the categories for an individual depending essentially on his judgment about the nature of his particular want. An outsider—an economist, a jurist or the state—cannot normally decide what is a necessity, comfort or luxury for a consumer unless he violates the legal or moral code of the society. The state can, of course, indicate preferential or harmful categories of goods to encourage or curb their production from a social welfare viewpoint; it may guide allocation of resources and initiate policies needed for achieving the declared goals including the *maqaasid* (objectives) of the Shari'ah.

> Want is a generic urge to remove a hardship or get pleasure. To satisfy a want we need specific goods to consume.

Interestingly, the Greek philosophers described *desires* as what we call wants today and made a distinction between *needs* and *desires*. They thought that human needs were natural and moderate but human desires (wants) were unlimited. So, to them, the production of goods to satisfy needs was valid and natural whereas the production of goods for satisfying desires (wants) was unethical. Islamic jurists and economists seem to project in their writings a similar line of thought. They maintain that there is enough on Earth to fulfil the *needs* of all but not the greed of even one. In fact, J. K. Mehta, a noted Indian economist of the yester century, built up the hypothesis that human salvation lies in the minimization of wants, not in their maximization. Islam does not entertain any such notion though, but it does insist on the avoidance of wasteful expenditure (*israf*) and the following of moderation in consumption, preferably restricted to the fulfilment of one's *basic needs*.

> What is wasteful expenditure or *israf* is difficult to determine, especially for an outsider like an economist or a policy maker.

However, it would not always be easy to say where the basic or genuine needs fulfilment stops and *israf* (wasteful consumption) begins in the individual or social behaviour. The classification of needs or wants into *dharooriyyat* (necessities), *hajjiyaat* (comforts) and *tehsinyaat* (luxuries) in economics may be looked at as a generic classification for resource use with a view of promoting human welfare both material and spiritual. It may not be possible to quantify *israf*. To start with a zero *israf* position and then introduce *israf* as a departure from that ideal may be more helpful for better understanding of the point. Figure 4.1 presents a simple model incorporating *israf* in consumer behaviour. The height of the rectangle measures the income of the consumer. Line CC cuts off the consumption of the consumer on the assumption that *israf* is zero. The income above the line is savings. Now, if the consumer indulges in *israf*, spending in the way of God, savings will progressively fall, investment would decrease and his asset growth will suffer. Zero *israf* being the ideal, Islam advises to strike a balance between savings and spending in the way of God.

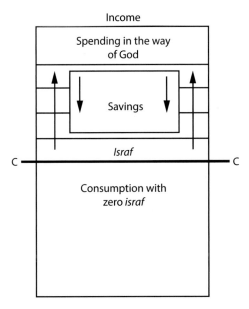

Figure 4.1 *Israf versus savings*

The crucial point here is that no external observer can fix the position of CC in the figure even as our conclusions may remain valid.

4.3   CONSUMER BEHAVIOUR

What regulates the behaviour of a consumer in the want-satisfying process? We start with the presumption that consumer is a rational being in the sense that he seeks to *maximize* his satisfaction from a *given* disposable income *without violating any Islamic norms of behaviour including altruism and benevolence*. With the italicized qualifications, there can hardly be any objection to take advantage of the mainstream maximization postulate to gain insights into the market conduct of consumers. Several approaches such as (a) utility analysis, (b) the indifference curve technique, and (c) the revealed preference hypothesis have been used to explain how consumers can maximize their satisfaction from given resources. These approaches have helped in understanding what underlies the law of demand, i.e. why there normally is an inverse relationship between the price and quantity demanded of a commodity.

We shall find that the indifference curve technique is a refinement and reflection of the initial utility analysis of consumer behaviour. The revealed preference approach is presented as a better alternative to these analyzes but we do not discuss it here because of its advanced level. However, to claim as it does, that consumers prefer to buy what they are seen as buying is a bit tautological. Let us begin with the initial utility approach.

> Utility maximization is assumed to regulate consumer behaviour in economics for price formation analysis. It is needed for the same reason in Islamic economics.

4.3.1 Utility: What It Is and What It Is Not

To understand the notion of utility, you must remember two things:

1. Utility is not the same thing as satisfaction.
2. Utility is not *internal* to commodities.

Utility versus satisfaction

Utility is an *ex ante* concept: it is *expected* satisfaction. It guides consumer behaviour. In contrast, satisfaction is an *ex post* concept: it is *realized* satisfaction.

Utility is the satisfaction one *expects* from having a commodity; it is an *ex ante* concept. It is *expectations* that guide the consumer in allocating his income to various uses, including savings, even charity. Satisfaction, on the other hand, is an *ex post* notion; how one feels after having spent his money for a particular thing. Utility—the *expected* satisfaction—need not equal the *realized* satisfaction. A couple leaving the Golcha cinema hall in New Delhi was overheard commenting on the quality of the movie they had just seen. The husband declared joyfully that the title song itself was worth more than the money they spent on the show while the wife lamented that the film was disappointing. For the husband, satisfaction was much more than the utility of the money spent while his wife thought otherwise. *It is then utility not satisfaction that guides consumers in allocating resources to various uses.*

Where does utility sit?

Utility is not internal to commodities. The seat of utility is the human mind; it is a psychological feeling of satisfaction expected from the consumption of a good. Thus, a glass of water has no utility for a person who is not thirsty. Also, the utility of additional units of water for him would diminish if he gets more and more of water. The intensity of our want measures the utility of a good we need to satisfy that want.

4.3.2 Utility Maximization

Utility maximization would be a needed and valid assumption for Islamic economics as well; we have only to insist further that the consumer does not violate any of the Shari'ah norms in pursuing this goal.

Islamic economists often raise objection to the maximization of utility; its approval, even as a facilitating assumption, is supposed to promote greed and miserliness in the people. This position needs a review. Let us repeat that maximization *per se* is value-free; *what is maximized, with what constraints and for what purpose are the questions to be answered before passing judgment in a case.* For example, why should an administration not attempt maximizing tax revenue within the confines of law? Or, why should we object if a person sticks to the fundamentals of his religion to maximize the pleasure of God? Or, shall a consumer be foolish if he seeks to enhance expected satisfaction as much as possible from a given income once he has fulfilled all his legal and moral obligations? A blanket rejection of the maximization norm in consumption, or in any other area of economics for that matter, is difficult to justify. Scarcity forces maximizing behaviour on economic agents for ensuring efficient use of resources. Maximization underlies the concept of optimality in economics.

But recall that Islam abhors unleashed human conduct including maximization. The overreach no longer means consumption but consumerism which is different from consumption. Consumption is essentially an individuals' act, a process of satisfying their wants using their income. Here, the Islamic position on what to consume and how much is quite clear. (See Box 4.1.) In contrast, consumerism is a market-oriented-greed-fuelling demonstrative competition in having material pleasures that leads to spiritual degradation and impoverishment of the individual instead of his ethical development. The Qur'an had long back denounced consumer gluttony thus: *And those who do kufr, eat like animals; their abode is hell (47:12).*

BOX 4.1

Utility: The Islamic Backbone of Economics

Treatment of utility as a scientific tool of analysis is the scholarly product of most notably al-Ghazali (550 H), Izzaddin Ibn Abdelsalam (or al-Izz) (660 H), Ibn Taimiyah (728 H) and Al-Shatibi (790 H). These scholars discussed the subject in the context of what we describe today as micro and macro branches of economics. Therefore, it is possible to review the salient features of utilities jurisprudence through the macro/micro classification. Al-Ghazali and Al-Shatibi focused mainly on the macro theory of utility.

Al-Izz thought that 'most worldly utilities are recognizable through the [human] mind'. His approach, as of IbnTaimiyah, are the most relevant to microeconomic theories since they both depart from a behavioural concept of utility as a fundamental basis for the macro concept.

In light of the views of these scholars, the goal of Shari'ah is defined to achieve utilities and avert difficulties. This postulate forms a general consensus among Muslim scholars, with the added provision that no contradiction is perceivable between worldly utilities and the hereafter's utilities except through misunderstanding of either. It is the basic jurist provision whereby economics and ethical values are firmly linked in the pursuit of a better economic order.

Source: Paraphrased from Asutay, M. (2009), *An Introduction to Islamic Moral Economy,* International Conference on Moral Values and Financial Markets: Assessing the Resilience of Islamic Finance Against Financial Crisis, Milan, Italy.

4.4 CONSUMER'S EQUILIBRIUM

There are two broad approaches to analyze the behaviour of consumers (i) the utility approach, and (ii) the indifference curves analysis. We shall see that the two are but different ways of saying the same, the latter being more precise and revealing.

4.4.1 Utility Analysis

Utility cannot be measured in itself like time, weight or distances. But the concept has such explanatory value that economists use arbitrary numbers called *utils* for expressing utility. As a consumer buys more and more of a commodity its *total* utility for him increases but at a diminishing rate. What in fact diminishes is *marginal* utility (MU).

Marginal utility can be defined as the addition to total utility of a commodity when one more unit is added to the stock of it the consumer already has.

> Marginal utility of a commodity for a consumer is the addition to its total utility if he acquires one more unit of the commodity. Total utility increases until the falling marginal utility becomes zero. It starts decreasing when marginal utility becomes negative.

Table 4.1 provides an example.

Table 4.1 *Units of commodity, total utility and marginal utility*

Segments		A						B	C	
Units of commodity X	1	2	3	4	5	6	7	8	9	10
Total utility, TU (utils)	20	25	29	32	34	35	35	34	32	29
Marginal utility, MU (utils)	–	5	4	3	2	1	0	–1	–2	–3

Notice that total utility in the table continuously rises so long as MU remains positive even as it diminishes. Figure 4.2 presents visual depiction of the data given in Table 4.1. The height of the rectangles measures the total utility as the consumer takes in more and more units of the commodity while their shaded portions portray the *diminishing* marginal utilities. In segment A, MU remains positive (> 1) and total utility keeps on rising. The consumer has maximum total utility when falling MU reaches zero in segment B. After that, any further acquisition of the commodity becomes inconvenient. Physical constraint may operate: stomachs have, for example, a limit to take in food, however delicious. Or, storing may involve prohibitive cost—how long can one allow old newspapers to pile up in his flat? Space is limited. Additional units of old newspapers have negative utility and total utility thus declines as negative MU rises. This is shown in segment C of the figure.

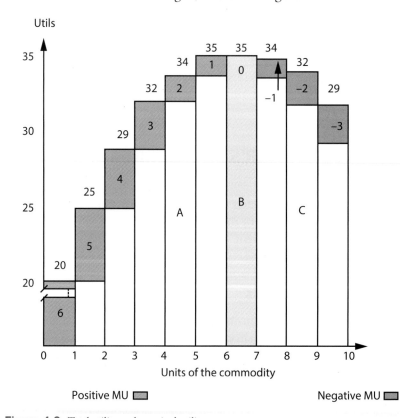

Figure 4.2 *Total utility and marginal utility*

The law of diminishing MU helps us to understand why most demand curves slope downwards. Money with us is limited and has alternative uses. It too has utility for us. As the amount of money we have decreases when we purchase more and more of a commodity, the MU of money tends to rise. But for simplicity economists assume that the MU of money remains constant. The consumer may be willing to buy a commodity so long as he feels that the utility of the commodity for him is more than or at least equal to the utility of as much money as he spends on a unit of it.

Suppose in our example of Table 4.1, the price of the commodity were RM2 per unit and the utility of one ringgit is equal to 1 util. It is easy to see that the consumer will not purchase more than 5 units of the commodity because from 6th unit onwards, its MU for him is less than that of money to be spent on it. But if the price were RM1 per unit, he could have opted to purchase 6 units of the commodity. In case it was RM4 a unit, he would restrict his buying to only 3 units. Thus, there is an inverse relationship between the price and quantity demanded of a commodity. Note that here the MU of a purchase equals its price. Figure 4.3 helps us to understand the relationship between MU of a commodity X and its price.

We measure MU of X on Y-scale as equal to the price at which the consumer would be willing to buy corresponding units of it shown on the X-scale. The utils-price equality makes the MU curve also the demand curve for X. The dotted portion of MU is not part of the demand curve. Interestingly, the figure displays another useful notion in economics—the consumer surplus (CS).

The consumer buys additional units of a commodity at best so long as the falling utility equals its price, i.e. the utility of money he gives for it.

Consumer surplus

A consumer pays the price for a commodity equal to its MU to him. But he pays the same price for all the units he buys; so he gains a surplus utility from all earlier units of his purchase. To illustrate, let us assume that in Table 4.1 above the price of the commodity is RM2 a unit. Thus, the consumer will buy 5 units. (Why?) For the first unit, his want was so intense that he would have paid as much as RM20 to have it, but pays only RM2 as the price. He gains extra utility equal to RM18, i.e. (20 – 2) for the first unit. You may similarly find the surplus he will get for each of the remaining units he purchases. Thus we may define:

The excess of price that a consumer is willing to pay per unit of commodity (RM20) over what he actually pays (RM2) is the economic measure of his gain (RM18). The sum of such gain for all the units purchased is called consumers surplus.

In Figure 4.3, the shaded triangle shows the volume of consumer surplus that arises in our illustration. One usually gets more satisfaction out of a given income in a town than in a village because of the welfare service facilities the town provides. This is one of the reasons of large-scale migration of people from rural areas to urban centres.

The excess of expenditure a consumer would be willing to incur for units of a commodity he buys over what he actually has to incur is the economic measure of the consumer's surplus he enjoys.

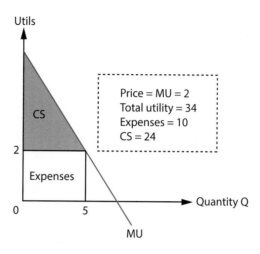

Figure 4.3 *Price, marginal utility and consumer surplus*

Exercise   4.1

Suppose in Table 4.1, the price of the commodity falls to $1 per unit, other data remaining unchanged. How many units of the commodity would the consumer buy? Calculate consumer's surplus per unit and add to find the total consumer surplus.

Fulfilment of necessities of life yields more consumer surplus than luxuries.

The concept of consumer surplus is also related to the price elasticity of demand. There is more consumers' surplus in necessities of life than in luxuries as the demand for the first is comparatively less elastic. How much consumer surplus people will enjoy in a place depends on what Marshall called their *conjuncture*—the sum total of their circumstances: personal, social, political and the development stage of their country.

A Qur'anic verse (30:39) says: *That which you give as interest to increase the peoples' wealth (hoping that you may gain even more out of the loan), such gain increases not with God; but that which you give in zakat for seeking His pleasure, multiplies manifold.* The multiple or the *surplus* one will get in the hereafter.

We shall further elaborate the concept of the surplus in our discussion on consumer's equilibrium later.

Utility and competing claims on income

So far, we have been considered the behaviour of a consumer as if he buys only one commodity. The fact is that he has to satisfy a multitude of wants and his income is never sufficient to meet them all and in full. Naturally, he wants to spend his income on an assortment of goods, which he expects to give him *maximum* satisfaction. The future is uncertain, and available courses of action are many, it is therefore impossible to know for sure if a consumer could ever get maximum satisfaction from spending his income on various goods he chooses to purchase. At the theoretical level, maximization principle suggests only a direction for analysis.

Here is how it guides to a sensible behaviour. Suppose a consumer plans to spend RM100 on three goods A, B and C. The prices of these goods are 10, 20 and 30 ringgit per unit, respectively. Table 4.2 provides the utility measured in utils he may get from units of the three goods. Figures in the MU columns show the marginal utilities of different units of A, B and C, respectively. As the prices of the three goods are different, the consumer estimates *utility per ringgit*, i.e. MU/P, while spending money on any of them. To facilitate comparison, figures in light-shaded columns in the table record this estimate in each case.

For deriving maximum satisfaction out of a given income, the consumer so spends his money on various commodities that the marginal utility and price ratio in each case is the same. In other words, he gets the same marginal utility for a ringgit spent on each commodity.

Table 4.2 *Consumer's preference order for utility maximization*

Units	A MU	A MU/Price	B MU	B MU/Price	C MU	C Mu/Price
1	60	1 6	100	2 5	90	4 3
2	40	3 4	60	5 3	45	1.5
3	30	6 3	50	2.5	30	1
4	10	1	20	1	0	0
5	0	0	10	0.5	−4.5	−1.5

Note: Numbers in the right-hand top of cells show the order of money spending on units of the three commodities: A, B and C.

Clearly, he will start with buying the first unit of commodity A where per ringgit utility (6) is the highest. He will then buy the first unit of B on the same criterion (5) and so on. His spending order on goods and their MU estimate in each case is as given in Table 4.3. The table shows that the consumer will buy three units of A, two units of B and one unit of C with his RM100 budget for them and will get a surplus as given in the last column of the table. The table shows that the consumer will buy three units of A, two of B and one of C to get maximum utility—the sum of the MUs of all units (380).

Table 4.3 *Utility maximization and consumer surplus*

Commodity	MU per $	Unit number	MU	Expenditure (RM)	Consumer surplus
A	6	First	60	10	60 − 10 = 50
B	5	First	100	20	100 − 20 = 80
A	4	Secon	40	10	40 − 10 = 30
C	3	First	90	30	90 − 30 = 60
B	3	Second	60	20	60 − 20 = 40
A	3	Third	30	10	30 − 10 = 20
Total			**380**	**100**	**380 − 100 = 280**

As he pays out RM100 on his purchases, he earns a surplus equivalent to RM280. He cannot gain more than that by any other distribution of RM100 expenditure on buying the three goods, other things remaining unchanged. He is in equilibrium. Notice that the MU per ringgit for the three commodities is identical, i.e. 3.

Thus, under the utility analysis, the consumer is in equilibrium only when:

$$\frac{\text{MU of A}}{\text{Price of A}} = \frac{\text{MU of B}}{\text{Price of B}} \qquad (4.1)$$

which can be rearranged as

$$\frac{\text{MU of A}}{\text{MU of B}} = (\text{Price of A}/\text{Price of B}) \qquad (4.2)$$

Until this equality is established consumer will gain by shifting expenditure from one to another commodity. In reality, none of us makes such fine calculations but we do so subconsciously because we are rational beings.

Value-in-exchange and value-in-use

Why are people usually willing to pay more for a commodity than the price they actually pay for it? In other words, what gives rise to consumer surplus in everyday purchases? Price denotes the value of a commodity in terms of other goods that money spent on it could otherwise buy in the market. Thus, price measures the exchange value of a good. *It has little to do with the intensity of an individual's want for it.* But it is this *intensity* that measures his willingness to pay more than what he actually pays in the form of (money) price. We saw that price of a commodity, or its value-in-exchange, equals its *MU*. On the other hand, intensity of a want finds expression in its *total* utility for the consumer.

Water–diamond paradox

The distinction between value-in-exchange (price) and value-in-use helps explain the famous paradox as to why the market price of diamonds is much more than water even as water is infinitely more useful than diamonds. Figure 4.4 helps us understand this paradox which originated in Adam Smith. The utility of the *initial* units of water for a person dying of thirst is infinite. He may be willing to part even with a truck load of diamonds for a glass of water to save his life; he could well be at a point such as T in the figure. But once he gets a glass or two of water, the MU of water declines very rapidly, may even become zero. The price of water which equals MU, therefore, becomes very low. But as the MU of *initial* units of water is tremendous, its total utility or value-in-use remains incalculable. Diamonds, on the other hand, are not a life-saving commodity and their MU falls only slowly. So, their market price is invariably much higher than the price of water. But the total utility of diamonds compared to water is almost negligible. So, water is more useful than diamonds even as their price is much higher.

Water is more useful than diamond because the *total* utility of water is much more than that of a diamond. (Why?) But the market price of diamond is much higher as its *marginal* utility is much higher than that of water. (Why?)

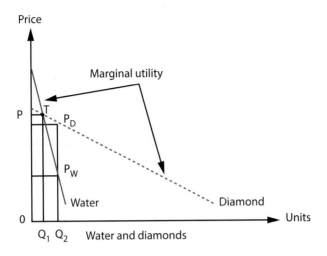

Figure 4.4 *Water–diamond paradox*

Consumers and riba al-fadl

The distinction between exchange value or price of a commodity and its use value calls for review of a formulation concerning justice in the market place. Some Islamic economists argue that in spot transactions where cash payment is made by one party and the commodity or service is delivered by the other, justice and fair play demand that the price and its counter-value must match; anything that is received as extra by either of the parties to the transaction is unjust, for it would constitute *riba al-fadl* that Islam prohibits. *Justice can be rendered only if the two scales of the balance carry the same value of goods.* This is confusing. Unanswerable questions follow. What would be, for instance, the measure of equivalence and who will decide on the matter in millions of transactions taking place every minute in modern markets? Even if that could somehow be done, equivalence will evaporate all consumer surpluses. The distinction between value in exchange and value in use will become meaningless and the gains of inventions and innovations will rarely pass on to the consumers. Surely, there is something amiss in the equivalence notion for a just deal.

'Just price' concept: the confusion.

BOX 4.2

What to Consume and How Much?

The Qur'an instructs:
O mankind, eat from whatever is on earth [that is] lawful and good and do not follow the footsteps of Satan. Indeed, he is to you a clear enemy (Al-Baqarah 2: 168).

Notice that the above verse places lawfulness ahead of goodness. The implication is that it is God-determined lawfulness that defines what is 'good' or wholesome. For example, intoxicants do not fall within the scope of 'goods' as an economist would consider them. In other words, definition and value of 'goods' in Islam is not determined exclusively by market forces such as supply and demand. There is supposed to be no 'supply' produced in the first place, nor is there supposed to be 'demand' either in a community that accepts such injunctions. Failure to observe the divinely-defined lawfulness means 'following the steps of Satan'. As it is forbidden to consume the unlawful, it is also forbidden to restrict the consumption of the lawful without a valid reason; the Qur'an instructs:

Say, who has forbidden the adornment of Allah which He produced for His servants and the good [lawful] things... (Al-A'raf 7: 32).

It follows that the issue of what to consume is settled in Islam by the principle that everything is deemed lawful, unless there is juristic evidence to the contrary. It is not possible to define how much to consume as the needs of various people may genuinely differ, at times considerably. Nevertheless, Islamic guidelines on the issue are quite clear. Moderation in consumption and the avoidance of extravagance (*israf*) is the watch word. Of the true believers, the Qur'an says:

And those who, when they spend, they do so not excessively or sparingly but are ever, between that, [justly] moderate (Al-Furqan 25: 67).

It is not always easy for an external observer to draw a line of demarcation as to where moderation ends and excess in consumption spending in individual cases begins; for them it is largely a matter of self-discipline; a characteristic of true believers. The implications of moderation in consumption are more relevant, as we shall see later, to macroeconomic analysis and policy-making.

Source: The contents of this box have been adopted from Jamal Badawi (March, 2012): *Production and Consumption Ethics in Islam: Part 4*, <http://www.onislam.net/english/index.php>, accessed 29 December 2013.

4.4.2   Indifference Curves and Utility

The indifference curve analysis of consumers' behaviour is better than utility analysis though based on it. Indifference curve technique is based on comparison of utilities not on their *abinitio* measurement.

The main problem with utility analysis of consumers' behaviour was that utility cannot be measured; we do not have a utility metre. However, a consumer can compare the utility of different goods, say of A with B. He may prefer (a) A to B or (b) B to A. A third possibility is that both are equally welcome to him. In the first case, we are saying that the utility of A for the consumer is greater than that of B. In the second case, the utility of B is more than that of A. In the last case, the utility of both goods is equal for him. And this last one is not an imaginary case. Such situations are, in fact, part of our daily lives.

When we have a visitor in the house, it is the Asian tradition to ask what he may like to have, e.g. something hot or cold. People indicate their choice but often one's reply is: 'as you may please; anything will do'. The last answer means that for the visitor, the utility of either of the drinks—hot or cold—is the same. Economists say he is indifferent to a choice between the two. Note that his expression of indifference implies that to him at that moment, the utility of both is the same. But, remember the story of the donkey that got stuck between the two equally attractive stacks of grass!

An indifference schedule

The notion of indifference takes us to what we call the indifference curve technique of analyzing consumer's equilibrium. We may generalize the above example and say that a consumer may face such combinations of two goods that from each of them he expects to derive the same satisfaction. A list of such combinations is called an *indifference schedule*. One such schedule we present in Table 4.4.

In the table, X represents apples and Y oranges. If we plot the A, B, C, D, E and F combinations of the two goods on a graph paper, we shall obtain what is called an indifference curve as shown in Figure 4.5. Even as a consumer moves up and down an indifference curve, his expected satisfaction at each point remains the same.

> It follows that possibly we can think of a number of combinations which may be equally attractive to a consumer. A list of such combinations of two (or more) goods is called his indifference schedule. The graphic depiction of such a schedule gives us indifference curve of the consumer.

Table 4.4 *Indifference schedule*

Combination	Apples (kg) X	Oranges (kg) Y	Marginal rate of substitution of X for Y
A	0	21	–
B	1	15	6
C	2	10	5
D	3	6	4
E	4	3	3
F	5	1	2
G	6	0	1

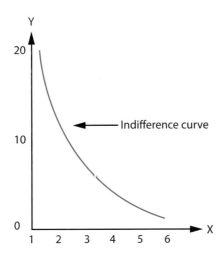

Figure 4.5 *An indifference curve*

Exercise 4.2

Define marginal rate of substitution (MRS) of Y for X, and rewrite the last column of Table 4.4 giving entries of MRS of Y for X. Compare the values with those of the table. What relationship do you find between the two marginal rates of substitution? Explain.

Properties of indifference curves

Some important properties of indifference curves for normal goods are as follows:

> Indifference curves *normally* (not always) slope downwards and are convex to the origin. ▶

1. An indifference curve slopes downwards to the right as in Figure 4.4. This is because the gain in utility due to increase in the quantity of one commodity must be neutralized by the loss of utility through the reduction in the quantity of the other commodity, keeping the total utility of the combination unchanged.

> The marginal rate of substitution of X for Y is the quantity of Y which the consumer is willing to give up for acquiring one more unit of X. This rate diminishes as he acquires more and more of X. ▶

2. The curve is convex to the origin. It means that the marginal rate of substitution (MRS) of one commodity for the other must diminish, e.g. when we are taking in one more *unit* of X, we shall be willing to sacrifice less and less of Y down the curve. As the stock of X with us increases, its MU for us decreases. In contrast, as our stock of Y decreases, its MU rises. Thus, the decreasing gain and increasing loss of utility will exactly neutralize each other when less and less of Y is given up to obtain one more unit of X. The last column of Table 4.4 is in line with this fact. Let us formally define the MRS. *The MRS of X for Y is the quantity of Y that the consumer is willing to give up for having one more unit of X so that his utility from the combination remains unchanged.*

> There are two limiting cases of indifference curve shape: if the two goods are perfect substitutes for one another the curve is a straight line and if the goods are complimentary the curve is L-shaped. ▶

What lies behind the diminishing MRS is the fact that different goods are but *imperfect* substitutes of one another. If the goods were perfect substitutes, we would have a straight line as a limiting case of an indifference curve with a constant MRS equal to the slope of the line. Another limiting case occurs if the two goods are complements, as are cups and saucers. Here, the indifference curve is L-shaped and MRS equals zero. Figure 4.6 illustrates these limiting cases.

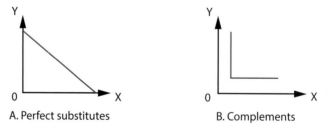

Figure 4.6 *Limiting cases of indifference curves*

> Any two indifference curves of the same consumer could never cross each other on *his* indifference map. (Why?) ▶

3. Two indifference curves cannot cut each other if they belong to the *same* indifference map. The reason is that the two curves will of necessity show two different levels of satisfaction but on the point of intersection as in Figure 4.7 one combination common to both cannot do so. Here, combination Y_0X_0 gives D as a common point. For normal goods, a higher indifference curve shows a higher level of expected satisfaction for a consumer.

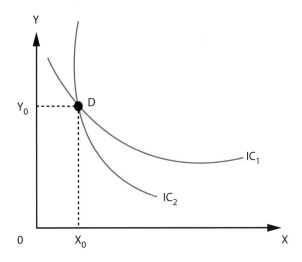

Figure 4.7 *Indifference curves do not cut each other*

Indifference map

Consider the following Table 4.5. Here X and Y columns are the same as in Table 4.4 with two more columns added, i.e. Y_1 and Y_2. Now, it is easy to see that if in the above case, X remains constant but the corresponding Y increases to Y_2 in each combination, the consumer will move to a higher indifference curve with XY_2 combinations. For example, suppose in combination C, the quantity of apples remains 2 kg but of oranges increases to 12 kg. The satisfaction expected from the combination will increase; the consumer shall be on a higher indifference curve. The opposite will happen if oranges in the combination are reduced to 9 kg; he will move to a lower curve showing XY_1 combinations. Figure 4.8 shows such movements of a consumer. Travelling from Y_0 towards Y_1, he will cross indifference curves, showing higher and higher levels of expected satisfaction because X will increase in the combination and vice versa. So will be the case if he climbs up the ladder from X_0 to X_1 or vice versa; this time Y will change in the combination. A collection of such curves of a consumer is called an *indifference* map.

> An indifference map is the collection of indifference curves of a consumer—the higher the curve, the higher the level of satisfaction.

Table 4.5 *Indifference map schedule*

Combination	Oranges (kg) Y_1	Apples (kg) X	Oranges (kg) Y	Oranges (kg) Y_2
A	20	0	21	23
B	14	1	15	17
C	9	2	10	12
D	5	3	6	8
E	2	4	3	5
F	0	5	1	3
G	−1	6	0	2

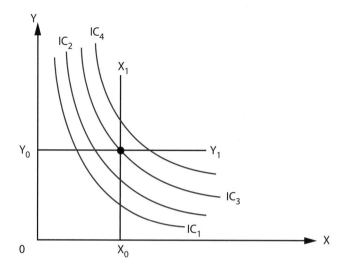

Figure 4.8 *An indifference map*

The equilibrium

We saw that as a consumer moves from a lower to a higher curve on his indifference map as his expected satisfaction increases. Naturally, he would want to move up to a higher curve. But he also has to spend more for what he wants to have. What then limits his movement up to the right on the indifference map? These are (a) his income, and (b) the price of the commodities. Given these two variables, we can construct what is called the *budget constraint* or the *income–price* line for the consumer. Working with the data from Table 4.5, let us assume that:

1. From his income, the consumer decides to spend RM120 per week on apples (A) and bananas (B).
2. The price per kg of apples is RM20.
3. The price per kg of bananas is RM10.

> Given the amount a consumer decides to spend on two commodities X and Y, he will have a budget line extending to the X and Y axes being its slope. On any point of this line he will purchase such quantities of the two commodities as would exhaust all his income. This we call as the budget or the income–price line of the consumer.

Now, if the consumer spends the entire budget RM120 for these items on apples, he can get 6 kg of apples (120/20). Alternatively, if he chooses to spend the entire amount on bananas he can get 12 kg of bananas (120/10). Thus, in the first case, he gets 6 kg of apples and no bananas, in the second no apples but 12 kg of bananas. These two points will of course be on say axes A and B, respectively. The line joining the two points is called the budget or income–price line for the consumer. Prices of the goods remaining unchanged, this budget line will move up to the right if the budget allocation of the consumer for apples and bananas rises and will move downwards to the left if the allocation falls. These budget lines will be parallel to one another. (Can you say why? Is it that the price ratio of the two goods does not change?) Figure 4.9 illustrates the case. Here, the original budget line is (6, 12) then (9, 18) shows its upward shift due to increase in budget allocation (by how much?) and (3, 6) its downward shift if the allocation were reduced to RM60.

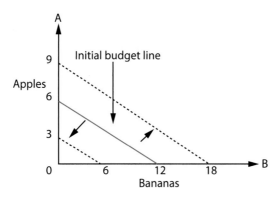

Figure 4.9 *Budget or income–price lines*

Exercise   4.3

The equation for the budget line in our example is $120 = 20\,Q_A + 10\,Q_B$, where $Q_A \leq 6$ and $Q_B \leq 12$. How many kilograms of bananas would the consumer buy if he buys 4 kilograms of apples?

Suppose we construct an indifference map and budget lines on the *same* scale, on two transparencies and superimpose one on the other along the axes, we shall see the result as in Figure 4.10. Given his income and the prices of the two goods, the consumer cannot leave the income–price line which has the same slope as the price ratio of the two goods. (Can you explain why?) To maximize utility from his income, the consumer has to reach the highest curve on his indifference map while remaining on the line. This he does at point T, where the line is tangent to IC_2. Higher curves IC_3 and IC_4 are beyond his reach due to budget constraint.

The consumer is in a state of equilibrium when he obtains maximum utility out of a given sum of money he spends on any two commodities such that his marginal rate of substitution equals the price ratio of the two commodities. Here, his income-price line is tangent to the highest indifference curve he could reach on his indifference map.

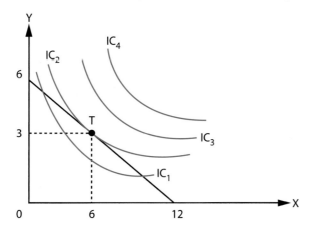

Figure 4.10 *Equilibrium of the consumer*

Even though he can exhaust his given allocation on buying either of the two combinations where the line crosses IC_1, but it would be unwise to do so as he can still move to T for a higher satisfaction level. Islamic economics approves such a movement. At point T, the consumer will be

Utility analysis and the indifference curve technique interface.

in a state of equilibrium, as the condition for utility maximization will be fulfilled. We shall have:

$$\frac{\text{MU of X}}{\text{Price of X}} = \frac{\text{MU of Y}}{\text{Price of Y}}$$

Which can be reset as:

$$\frac{\text{MU of X}}{\text{MU of Y}} = \frac{\text{Price of X}}{\text{Price of Y}}$$

For our example, this gives us:

$$\frac{\text{MU of X}}{\text{MU of Y}} = \frac{10}{20} = 0.5 \text{ the price ratio} \tag{4.2}$$

You may have noted in the above analysis that the indifference curve technique is not free of the utility concept discussed earlier. However, it makes a vast improvement over the utility approach to consumer behaviour. Its merits are:

1. We no more require the cardinal measurement of utility; the equilibrium point T on the indifference map gives us the same result.
2. The law of demand informs us that quantity demanded of a commodity changes inversely in response to a change in its price. The technique makes it possible to break this price effect, we shall see, into its two components: the income and substitution effects. It improves our understanding of the nature of consumer demand.
3. The technique provides a firm basis of distinction between normal goods and inferior goods.
4. It has applications in many areas of economics as a general instrument of analysis.

Exercise 4.4

In Figure 4.10, suppose Hanif is the consumer and he purchases bananas (Y) for a free distribution among children of an orphanage as a good deed to please Gog and apples (X) for his own use. Other things remaining the same, will this change in his attitude make any difference to the equilibrium analysis of the figure? Explain your answer.

We explained above the notion of consumer equilibrium with *given* values of the constraints. One may want to know the *effect* on equilibrium if one or more of these constraints change. This we shall discuss in the following sections.

4.4.3   Income Effect

If the income of the consumer increases or decreases while the prices of goods and his preference scale, i.e. indifference map, remains the same as before, his income–price line will shift as in Figure 4.9. The shift in his equilibrium is shown in Figure 4.11. The solid curve and line shows the initial equilibrium at their point of tangency, T. Here, the consumer purchases Y_0 and X_0 is the quantity of the two goods. As the income of the consumer rises, the tangency point moves upwards to the right: the consumer purchases more of both the goods. The opposite will happen if his income falls. It is possible that the consumer keeps his purchase of one commodity, e.g. Y, constant, and spends his income entirely on buying more of X. In that case, the income–consumption curve will be a straight line parallel to the X-axis. For completion of the argument, we state without explanation that if one of the goods, e.g. Y, is *inferior,* the curve will slope downwards. The three income–consumption paths are shown in Figures 4.11 and 4.12.

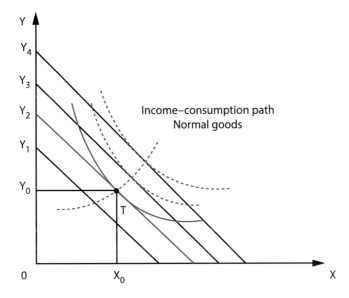

Figure 4.11 *Income–consumption path*

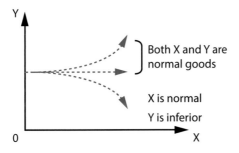

Figure 4.12 *Income–consumption paths for normal and inferior goods differ*

If the income of the consumer remains the same, and the price say of X alone falls—it becomes cheaper relative to Y—he will purchase more of X than before under price effect. One component of this is substitution effect. It means that a part of income may now be shifted from Y for substituting X for it.

4.4.4   Substitution Effect

Let us consider the case where income of the consumer remains unchanged but the relative prices of goods change. In Figure 4.13, the income–price line IP_1 is tangent to the indifference curve IC, and the consumer buys (X_1, Y_1) combination of the two goods. Now, assume the price of Y rises and that of X falls: Y becomes costlier than before and X cheaper for the consumer such that his expected satisfaction from his income remains as before. The income–price line changes to IP_2. Since the expected satisfaction of the consumer has not by assumption changed, his total utility has to remain the same: he cannot leave the IC. For this reason, the price line is now tangent to the same IC at point T_2. Following the law of demand, the consumer buys less of Y and more of X (Y_2 and X_2). He substitutes X_1X_2 for Y_1Y_2. This we call the *substitution effect* of a change in prices.

Exercise 4.5

In Figure 4.11, the income–consumption curve is convex to the X-axis. If we assume that Y represents the income of the consumer, what would Y_0 show: his savings or expenditure on X_0? Give reasons for your answer.

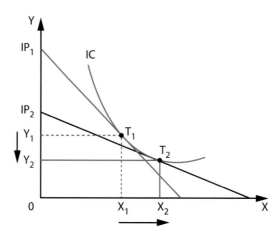

Figure 4.13 *Substitution effect*

4.4.5   Price Effect and Its Components

Normal goods

The two ideas discussed above—income effect and substitution effect—can be isolated as components in what we termed as the *price effect* which the law of demand states. Explaining the law through indifference curves has some merits. Let us assume that we are considering two goods, Y and X, that are substitutes for one another and the price of X alone falls. The consumer can now buy more of X than before, if he spends his entire income on X. This pulls the lower leg of his income–price line outwards and he moves to a higher indifference curve. The satisfaction he expects from his income increases.

Figure 4.14 helps us to explain the price effect and isolate its components, the income and substitution effects. The initial equilibrium position is on IC_0 where the income–price line IP_0 is tangent to it at T_0 and the consumer buys (Y_0, X_0) combination of the two goods in a state of equilibrium. Now, if the price only of X falls, the lower leg of the IP_0 extends as far as X_P. As a result, the consumer moves to a higher indifference curve IC_1 buying less of Y and more of X, i.e. he buys their (Y_1, X_1) combination.

In the case of normal good, for a fall in its price both income effects—income and substitution—are positive. They enhance the price effect.

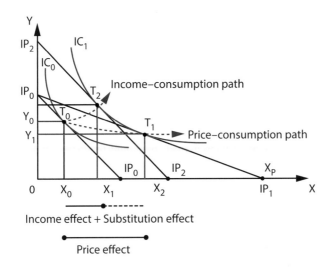

Figure 4.14 *Price effect as combination of income and substitution effects*

The downward sloping curve T_0T_1 traces the path of increasing purchases of X along the indifference map as its price falls. The move from X_0 to X_2 is in accordance with the law of demand and shows the price effect. The merit of the indifference curve technique is that it explains the law not only with reference to X whose price falls and quantity demanded increases, but also in terms of Y, whose price rises *relatively* (what does this mean?) and quantity demanded falls from Y_0 to Y_1.

If the price of X had not fallen, the other way to reach a higher level of consumption could be an increase in the income of the consumer, shifting the position of the income–price line upwards to the right from IP_0 to IP_2 until it is tangent to IC_1 at T_2. The consumer at T_2 would increase his purchase of X from X_0 to X_1. This is the income effect of a fall in the price of X. The remaining part of price effect X_1X_2 arises due to substitution of X for Y that has become costlier relative to X.

Notice that when X and Y are *normal goods*, as assumed above, the income and substitution effects are both positive; each increases the purchase of X as its price falls. An interesting case of consumer equilibrium arises when one of the goods is *inferior*.

Inferior goods

We may begin with the statement that for a *fall* in the price of any good—normal or inferior—the substitution effect is always positive. What separates the normal goods from inferior goods is the behaviour of income effect: it remains positive in the case of normal goods and reinforces the substitution effect, but turns out to be negative if the good is an inferior one. Let us now assume that of the two goods X and Y of our illustration, X is an inferior good.

We use Figure 4.15 to explain the case. The tangency point T_0 of the income–price line IP_0 with IC_0 shows the initial equilibrium of the consumer buying the (X_0, Y_0) combination of the two goods. Subsequently, the price of X falls and the income–price line shifts to IP_1. This takes the consumer to a higher indifference curve IC_1; the positive effect X_2–X_1. But the fall in the price of X induces a negative income effect X_0–X_2. In the process, the substitution effect is reduced by $X_0 - X_2$ to reduce overall price effect to X_2–X_1.

In the case of a normal good, the income and substitution effects reinforce each other, while in the case of an inferior good, they tend to offset each other.

In the case of a non-normal good, with a fall in its price, the substitution effect remains positive but the income effect becomes negative. If the negative income effect is less than the positive substitution effect, price effect will stay positive. Such a good is called 'inferior'. In contrast, if the negative income is stronger than the positive substitution effect, price effect will become negative. Such a good is termed as a Giffen good.

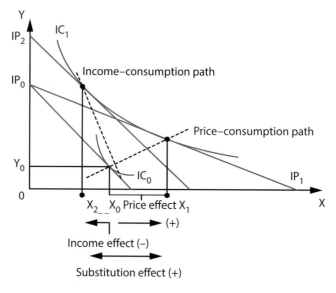

Figure 4.15 *In the case of inferior goods, negative income effect reduces positive substitution effect*

Sometimes the negative income effect is so strong that it more than offsets the positive substitution effect when price falls, making the overall price effect negative. This gives rise to the concept of *Giffen goods* as a category distinct from that of inferior goods.

4.5 INDIFFERENCE CURVES: DIFFERENT SHAPES

The notion of inferior goods is a matter of practical experience but Giffen goods are rarely found in real world situations. However, the ability of indifference curve analysis of consumer behaviour leads us to an understanding of the general nature of these curves. This has helped in extending the application of the technique to numerous other uses in economics and beyond leading to rational propositions. To generalize the technique we introduce into the picture what we call the *negative goods*. A negative good is that whose additional units are unwelcome to the consumer because of their increasing *disutility* as his stock of the good grows beyond a point. Risk, debt, illiquidity, old newspapers, non-mowed grass, uncut nails and hair are easy examples. We may have different sorts of combinations in real world situations of positive normal goods and negative goods. Indifference curves take different shapes depending on the combination.

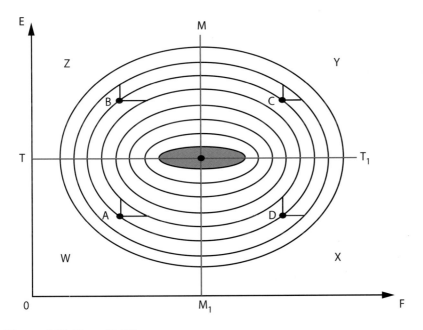

> The shape of the indifference curve depends on whether the two goods X and Y are both either positive or negative, or one of the two is positive and the other is negative.

Figure 4.16 *Types of indifference curves*

Figure 4.16 explains the sort of shapes these combinations can generate. You may imagine having a helicopter view of an upward rising utility pile whose peak—the black area—is the limit one attempts to approach by climbing up the steps around it. Movement from a lower to a higher step increases utility; a climb down reduces it. It remains unchanged so long as one remains on the *same* step. Thus seen, the steps are in the nature of circular sort of indifference curves. The increase or decrease in the stock of either of the two goods E or F along the relevant axis causes the upward, downward or sideward movement on the steps. The two lines TT_1 and MM_1 join the points where steps are parallel to the axes. They divide the figure into four quadrants: W, X, Y and Z giving four sets of steps. Take them as indifference curves because the utility of the consumer remains unchanged if he moves on the *same* step irrespective of where he is.

Let us start with quadrant W. Suppose the consumer is on the step or curve 3 at point A. If he increases his stock of either E or F he reaches a higher curve. His utility increases in each case. E and F are both normal goods. This is the case that we have used in our figures of this chapter. The indifference curves are convex to the origin. Notice that we can have an inferior good in W but not a negative good. (Why?)

In quadrant X we are also on curve 3 at point D. If we increase E, we shall move to a higher curve. E is a normal good such as profit. But if F increases, we slip down to a lower curve. F is a negative good like risk. If you have to construct curves showing trade-off paths between profit and risk such that the firm remains indifferent to a selection of points on it, you may use a set of this sort of indifference curves. Movement on a particular curve would mean that additional risk could be taken only if it promises to bring in a more than proportionate increase in profit. Also, for any *given* profit, you will like to be on a higher not a lower curve. Notice that these curves are convex to F-axis but are concave to E-axis.

If you are at point C in quadrant Y, an increase in either of the goods E or F will take you to a lower curve. Both carry disutility; they are negative goods. Non-performing debts and illiquidity make an appropriate combination for a bank. Good management will want to move down or to the left (or both) so as to reach a higher curve for relief. The case is just opposite to the one we started within quadrant W. The curves here are concave to the origin.

The case in quadrant Z is like the one we dealt with in X above. But the role of the goods reverses. Now, E becomes a negative good: an increase in its quantity takes you to a lower curve. On the other hand, F becomes a positive or normal good. Increase in it takes you to a higher indifference curve. You can also use this sort of curve to construct a profit-risk trade-off as in quadrant X. Only, you have to switch axes between the variables, taking risk on the vertical and profit on the horizontal scale. Here, for a given profit, the firm would like to be on a lower, not a higher, curve. Movement along the same curve would imply that additional risk could only be taken if it promises to bring in more than proportionate profit.

Summary

- Consumption is the beginning and end of all economic activity. Consumers make the most important choices in a market economy.

- Human wants are unlimited while resources to satisfy them are scarce and have alternative uses. Consumption is no exception.

- Wants are classified into necessities, comforts and luxuries on the criterion of their impact on an individual's work efficiency: fulfilment of necessities maintain it, comforts improve it while luxuries make little contribution, may even reduce it if injurious to health.

- Classification of wants is relative to individual perception. An outsider cannot determine what would be necessities, comforts or luxuries for him. State can indicate, if necessary, priorities for the allocation of resources and influence their distribution for various uses from the viewpoint of societal well-being—material and spiritual. Individuals may take some guidance, if they want, from public direction.

- The consumer is a rational being. Rational behaviour includes pursuit of self-interest with constraints of altruism, benevolence, good deeds however perceived, commitment and religious obligations. Given this overall framework, there is no Islamic bar restraining the consumer from maximization of utility from his limited resources.

- The basic tool for a maximizing behaviour of the consumer is the conventional utility analysis. Indifference curve technique is an improvement and extension of utility analysis, not a replacement. This being an introductory book, we have not discussed here advanced tools like revealed preference and beyond.

- The MU of a commodity for a consumer diminishes as he buys more of it. He stops buying it when for him the decreasing MU of the commodity equals that of the money he spends on it as price. This implies that a consumer is willing to pay for earlier units of the commodity more than he in fact pays.

- The total utility for the consumer of units of a commodity he buys measures its *usefulness* to him. However, the money he pays for it is its exchange value. The difference of the two is called consumer's surplus.

- The condition for maximization of utility is:

$$\frac{\text{MU of A}}{\text{Price of A}} = \frac{\text{MU of B}}{\text{Price of B}}$$

- The excess of what a consumer is willing to pay for a commodity over what he actually pays for it is the measure of consumer's surplus.

- An indifference schedule is a list of such combinations of two goods, X and Y, from each of which the consumer expects to derive the *same* satisfaction. The curve showing such a schedule is called an indifference curve. A set of such curves gives us the *indifference map* of a consumer.

- Indifference curves have some important properties. For normal good, an indifference curve slopes downwards to the right. It is convex to the origin. Curves on the indifference map of a consumer do not cross each other. A higher curve in the map indicates a higher level of satisfaction.

- Indifference curves for normal goods slope downwards because reduction in the quantity of one good must be compensated by increase of the other such that the utility of the combination remains the same as before the change.

- An indifference curve is convex to the origin because the MRS of one good for the other to keep utility of the combination unchanged, must diminish. The MRS of X for Y is the quantity of Y the consumer is willing to give up such that his utility from successive combinations remains the same.

- If X and Y are perfect substitutes for one another, the indifference curve will be a downward sloping straight line. If the goods are complements, the curve will be L-shaped. These are limiting cases; most indifference curves fall between these extremes.

- Since a higher curve on the indifference map of the consumer indicates greater utility, he will want to climb up the map *ad infinitum.* However, he is restricted in his movement up the map by two constraints: (i) his income or budget and (ii) prices of the commodities.

- The constraints find summation in what we call income–price or budget line. The ratio of prices of the two goods involved is the slope of this line. The consumer buys such combination of the two goods at each point of the line that his budget is exhausted.

- The consumer attempts to reach the highest curve on his indifference map moving on the Income–price line. The highest curve he can thus reach is the one to which the line is tangent. The consumer is in a state of equilibrium at this point; he can no more increase his satisfaction by shifting expenditure from one to another good.

- If prices of the goods do not change, an increase in income shifts the budget line upwards parallel to the old one and vice versa. The shifting lines are tangent to various curves on the map. The curve joining the tangency points is called the income–consumption curve. The movement along this curve causing changes in the combination of goods is income effect.

- If the income of the consumer remains the same, but prices of the two goods change such that one falls and the other rises, the consumer cannot leave the indifference curve but his point of equilibrium on the curve will change such that he will buy less of the good whose price has risen and more of the good whose price has fallen. The change is called the *substitution effect.* The consumer takes in more of the cheaper good reducing the purchase of the good whose price has gone up.

- If the price of a good falls, the price of the other and the income of the consumer remaining unchanged, the change takes the consumer to a higher indifference curve. The change is described as *price effect.* It is the merit of the indifference curve technique that we can break price effect in two components—income effect and substitution effect.

- For a fall in price, the substitution effect is always positive for all sorts of goods. This is not so for income effect. It is positive in case of normal goods and augments the substitution effect. However, the good is inferior if it attracts a negative income effect and reduces the positive substitution effect.

- If the negative income effect is so strong that it exceeds the positive substitution effect, it gives rise to the notion of Giffen goods.

- Normal goods are positive goods in the sense that increase in the stock of any of them will add to the consumer's satisfaction. But we can come across negative goods also. These are goods whose stock if increases yields, at least after a point, disutility; having more of them reduces our satisfaction. Risk, lack of liquidity and increasing liabilities are examples.

- We can imagine a circular indifference curve if we divide it along the points where it runs parallel to the axes, X and Y. We shall then have four indifference curves, each with its own properties.

Glossary

Consumer surplus This is the difference between the amount that a consumer is willing to pay for a good or service indicated by his MU curve and the amount that he actually pays (the market price times the units of the item purchased). The aggregate of consumer surplus is shown by the area under the demand curve for the commodity and the market price cut-off (as shown in the figure below).

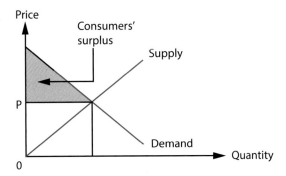

Income–price line It is also called the budget line, of a consumer is the line with its one end on Y-axis and the other on the X-axis. The two points are obtained by dividing the budget amount for the commodities by their respective prices.

Indifference curve An indifference curve sketches the path of such different combinations of two commodities X and Y that from each of them a given consumer is expected to derive the same satisfaction. It is obvious that he will be indifferent as to which of the combinations he opts for; the question of preferring one to the other does not arise.

Indifference map A collection of indifference curves of a consumer is called his indifference map. Even as he is expected to have the same level of satisfaction on each point of a particular curve on the map, movement from a lower to a higher curve shows a higher level of satisfaction and vice versa.

Marginal utility It is not an observable concrete quantity; it is an abstract notion. The utility measure, i.e. utils, which we assign to various commodity units are purely arbitrary, representing only a relative value. Total utility is the aggregate sum of satisfaction or benefit that an individual expects to obtain from consuming a given amount of goods or services. MU is the addition of gain to total utility that each extra unit of consumption is expected to bring in.

Utility It is the satisfaction that one expects to derive from the purchase of a commodity; thus, it is an *ex ante* concept. It is not the same thing as satisfaction we realize after consuming a thing, an *ex post* concept. However, in economic textbooks the two are mostly used interchangeably.

Value-in-use This refers to the satisfaction a consumer actually derives from the consumption of a commodity. Its measure is what he would be willing to pay for it rather than go without it. It expresses the total utility of a commodity for the consumer.

Concepts for Review

- Circular indifference curves
- Complements
- Consumer surplus
- Equilibrium
- Giffen goods
- Income effect
- Income–consumption curve
- Income–price line
- Indifference curve
- Indifference map
- Indifference schedule
- Inferior goods
- Marginal utility
- Maximization

- Needs
- Negative goods
- Normal goods
- Point of inflexion
- Price effect
- Price–consumption curve
- Properties of indifference curves
- Substitutes
- Substitution effect
- Total utility
- Value-in-exchange
- Value-in-use
- Wants

Case Study   4.1

Poverty and Its Impact

1. More than 80 per cent of the world population lives in countries where income differences are widening.
2. The poorest 40 per cent of the world population accounts for 5 percent of global income. The richest 20 percent account for 75 per cent of world income.
3. More than 80 per cent of the word population lives in countries where income differences are widening.
4. In developing countries, 22,000 children die each day due to poverty and 27–28 percent of children there are found to be under weight or stunted, the bulk of them in Pakistan, India and Bangladesh and sub-Saharan Africa.
5. On optimistic estimates, about 72 million children of primary school age in the developing world were not in schools in 2005, 57 percent of them were girls.
6. Nearly a billion people entered the 21st century unable to read a book or sign their names.
7. Less than one per cent of what the world spent every year on weapons was needed to put every child into school by the year 2000 and yet it did not happen.

Note: The above data is provided on the basis of $1.25 per day income and is estimated as equivalent $33 in terms of purchasing power parity.

Source: Anup Shah (2013), *Global issues: Poverty facts and stats*.

Case Questions

1. Calculate the poverty line in terms of annual per capita income. Compare it with the per capita income of your country and comment on the difference with reference to the poverty reduction programme.
2. Do you find the level of literacy in your country satisfactory? Give reasons for your answer.
3. Comment on the statement in point 7 above. Do you find that military expenditure in your country can be reduced to have more resources for the poverty reduction programme?

Case Study 4.2

Table 4.6 *Global priorities in consumption spending (1998)*

Global Priority 1		Global Priority 2	
	$US billion	Estimated additional costs for achieving the universal access to basic social services in all developing countries	
Cosmetics in the United States	8		
Ice cream in Europe	11		
Perfumes in Europe and the United States	12	**Global Priority**	**$US billion**
Pet foods in Europe and the United States	17	Basic education for all	6
Business entertainment in Japan	35	Water and sanitation for all	9
Cigarettes in Europe	50	Reproductive health for all women	12
Alcoholic drinks in Europe	105	Basic health and nutrition	13
Narcotics drugs in the world	400	A mere 15% of global water is used by 88% of the world population of developing countries	
Military spending in the world	780		

Source: Anup Shah (2013), *Global issues: Poverty facts and stats.*

Case Questions

1. The expenditure on various items in section 1 is *israf* (wasteful), which Islam condemns. Do you think that this sort of consumption is taking place in your country? If yes, what public policy would you suggest to reduce it?

2. Consider the military expenditure in the world; it is much more today than it was in 1998. Study the position in your country. Do you think that military expenditure reduces economic welfare? How can this competitive waste be reduced, any suggestions?

3. What possibility do you see of the world living in peace when comparing the consumption expenditure—heads and amounts—in section 1 with those in section 2 of the table? Explain.

Test Questions

4.1 What do you understand by a human want? In what ways are human wants the cause of human toil and progress?

4.2 Discuss the basis of classification of wants into necessities, comforts and luxuries. Is this classification independent of individual perception and can it be decided for him externally?

4.3 Define utility carefully. How does it differ from satisfaction? Explain.

4.4 Distinguish between total utility and MU. Explain the relationship between the two. How does the distinction between them help in resolving the paradox that water is more useful than gold, but the market price of gold is much higher than water.

4.5 State and explain the law of diminishing MU. How is this related to the law of demand? Explain.

4.6   Construct an illustration to show that in the case of two goods, A and B, the consumer will be in a state of equilibrium only when he buys such quantities of both the goods such that the ratio of their marginal utilities equals the ratio of their prices. In other words, the condition is met.

$$\frac{\text{MU of Q}}{\text{MU of B}} = \frac{\text{Price of A}}{\text{Price of B}}$$

4.7   Assume in the case that Table 4.2 illustrates that the income of the consumer is RM120 a week. Reconstruct the table to show the change in the equilibrium of the consumer. Is the equality of ratios condition satisfied as before? If not, what is the reason? Do you think that even if the consumer may want to maximize utility, he may fail to do so in practice? Give reasons for your answer.

4.8   Explain and illustrate the concept of consumer surplus. Calculate consumer surplus in the case of Q4.7. Show how the concept is important for the taxation policy of the government.

4.9   What is an indifference schedule? In the table below, add the following two columns for Y. Also add two more curves (X, Y_1) and (X, Y_2) to the table. Comment on the level of satisfaction in each case compared with the original curve Y.

Table 4.7 *An indifference schedule*

Combinations	A	B	C	D	E	F	G
Y_1	18	12	7	3	0	0	0
Y_2	24	18	13	9	6	4	3

4.10   What do you understand by the MRS of Y for X. Find this rate for Table 4.4. Why should MRS diminish? Explain.

4.11   Explain the properties of indifference curves. In what way is the indifference curve analysis of consumer behaviour an improvement over the initial utility analysis? Explain.

Web Exercise

Search the Internet for literature on consumerism and write a short essay as to how believers in various Muslim countries respond to it.

Forward Link

In this chapter, you studied what lies behind the demand curve for a commodity and why it normally slopes downwards. The focus was the wants of the consumer and his behaviour in a market economy, both mainstream and Islamic. In Chapter 5, you shall learn about the nature and composition of the costs of production that lie behind the supply curve. Naturally, the focus here will be the behaviour and motives of the producers.

5

Production and Cost Functions

LEARNING OUTCOMES

This chapter should enable the student to understand:

- Production and society
- The objectives of business firms
- Factors of production and their classification
- Production function: The input–output relationships
- The isoquant–isocost framework and the laws of returns
- The conversion of physical input–output quantities into money terms.
- Equilibrium of the firm: Revenue, cost and profit
- Technology and efficiency

In Chapter 4, you studied the behaviour of the consumers who operate on the demand side of the market and seek to maximize their satisfaction out of their incomes. This chapter deals with the behaviour of producers or firms operating on the supply side. Firms want to maximize profits, so they have to adjust their production capacity in the short run and the long run to achieve this objective, of course with ethical constraints; firms go about choosing the best input-output combination to maximize profit.

5.1 PRODUCTION: PHILOSOPHICAL AND TECHNICAL ASPECTS

Production issues in economics have two broad aspects: technical and doctrinal. The first is free of values and the second is not.

Production of goods and services is needed to satisfy unending human wants and to sustain the march of civilization to newer and greater heights. The availability of resources being scarce for individuals as well as for nations, poses a basic question: what assortment of goods

Production and doctrines: mainstream versus Islamic.

and services from the available resources should be produced in the face of unending human wants and how are the products to be distributed? Indeed, it is the search to answer this question that has divided mankind into structuring different types of economic systems and even wage wars to establish the superiority of ours over the others. The superiority debate belongs to the politico-philosophical arena. Moreover, it is more an issue for macroeconomics to consider and we shall discuss this in our later chapters. For the present, we assume a market economy observing Islamic norms. For however we may define these norms, market mechanism raises and seeks to resolve some basic technical issues.

5.1.1　　Factors of Production

This chapter focuses only on the technical aspects of production.

To begin with, no matter how large or small a business is or who owns it, all businesses need resource inputs to produce goods and services. These inputs are too numerous to handle. We classify them into several broad categories, which differ from one another with reference to some common characteristics of inputs each group puts together. Interestingly, the number of categories has varied over time with the maximum being five—land, labour, capital, organization and enterprise—and the minimum just two—labour and capital. Let us have a brief look at these changes beginning with the five-fold classification: land.

Land

- Land refers to all resources that Allah has created for His creatures on Earth—below its crust, on it or above it. Water, air, rivers, mines, plants, mountains, plains and oceans are the examples.
- Land is a free gift of nature to mankind as a whole. The Creator is the owner, human beings are the trustees. Property rights and related issues arose from population growth over time and the complexity of social dynamics. The law defines property rights to avoid dispute and strife.
- Fixity and countless variety are dominant characteristics of land.

Labour

- Labour refers to all physical and mental exertions that people undertake to earn a living. Labour can be skilled or unskilled.
- Labour cannot be separated from the worker. So, leisure and work environment become important.
- Labour cannot be stored; it is the most perishable of commodities. The characteristic weakens the bargaining power of the workers and has won the right of collective bargaining.
- The staying power of workers is weak in wage negotiations. It is sought to be improved through fixation of minimum wages and other social security schemes.

Capital

- Capital includes all man-made tools and instruments that save human time and effort in the process of production, promotes division of labour and facilitates mass production.
- Capital facilitates and speeds up division of labour, increases productivity and does what human beings cannot do.
- Capital formation needs savings from wealth; it involves sacrifice of consumption now to consume more in the future.
- Investment in human beings—education, health care and old age security—helps in developing human capital and has gained significance in recent times.

> Initially, economists thought of three factors of production: land, labour and capital. After the industrial revolution, two more were added: enterprise and organization. Today, they usually speak of two factors: labour and capital, merging land with capital, organization with labour. Some place enterprise under capital, others under labour.

Organization

- Until the 19th century, most production was not on a large scale; the management of firms could mostly be run by the owner-operators.
- After the industrial revolution, firm sizes expanded fast and specialized skills were needed to run businesses. Business management schools of all shades began attracting multitudes of students.
- Management got divorced from ownership, especially with the rise of modern gigantic corporations. Organization became a distinct factor of production.

Entrepreneurship

- Business revenue fluctuates, sometimes violently. But most people want sure and stable income. This divides people into hired and un-hired factors. The latter guarantees contractual fixed payments to the former and runs the risk of losing money as revenue may fall short of contractually fixed payments on the whole.
- Owning financial resources is not considered necessary for being an entrepreneur in Islam. The religion had separated entrepreneurship from finance in the seventh century. After much confusion mainstream economics too accepts that ownership of capital is not a necessary condition for being an entrepreneur, having sufficient finance ensured is enough.

> It has become difficult to identify the entrepreneur or his functions in large multinational corporations.

Earlier, the unhired factors were called enterprisers, now they are entrepreneurs. They can also be nurtured through education and training. Some countries have exclusive ministries for the purpose.

The classification of the inputs for production into factors of production was helpful in cost analysis as well. But probably the same reason led later to a reduction of categories. Land and capital were soon merged together on the plea that natural resources require a lot of capital investment before they can be used for production. Organization was considered as specialized sort of labour. Some included enterprise in capital on the plea that an empty-handed person cannot be an entrepreneur, some thought of it as a special sort of labour. Islam too seems to endorse this view. Today economists mostly talk of two factors of production: labour and capital though entrepreneurship is occasionally mentioned as a third entity.

5.1.2   Time and Factor (Input) Classification

An important and more common classification of production factors additional to their hired and unhired categories is with reference to time. A time span is considered short if in its duration, some of the factors can be varied while some others cannot be varied. Thus, a short run by definition is a period in which some factor, usually capital, remains fixed i.e. independent of how much output is produced or even if nothing is produced; the facility remains shutdown. But in the same span of time, other inputs like raw materials and labour can be varied. On the other hand, a period wherein *all* factors can be varied—the distinction between fixed and variable factors—is called the long run.

BOX 5.1

Islamic Ethics in Production

Islamic ethical norms in production essentially belong to macroeconomics; they are broad-based. Allah planted humans on the Earth as His trustees and stocked it with inexhaustible resources for their use. The Quran exhorts people to develop and harness these resources to improve their quality of life so that they could perform their trusteeship role on Earth with ease and comfort. Thus seen, the divine wisdom linked the availability of resources to human effort making labour a primary factor of production. Islam views the search for one's sustenance an obligation only next to prayers. Islam recognizes the right of the weak, young and poor for a minimum level of adequate living, it discourages begging and the abuse of welfare system. Good work never goes unrewarded (Qur'an 18.30). But all work is not good; there are qualifications.

Restrictions on production.

Production of goods and services is governed by trusteeship norms. These norms put the following restrictions on production:

- The product must be lawful and must not violate the limits (Qur'an 2: 229). For example, the production of wines or other intoxicants is is not allowed. Likewise, any activity connected to gambling, prostitution or other 'indecencies' is not permitted.
- The method of production should not cause undue exploitation or overuse of natural resources meant for the benefit of all. The Qur'an calls such exploitation or use as mischief or corruption; it warns time and again against their spread in the land. (Qur'an 2:60, 2:205, 5:46, 7:56).
- Productive resources are not to be left idle in the name of private ownership, especially resources that are crucial to the lives of people. Islam instructs: partake what is legitimate; be a user not the corrupter of resources. Also, do not leave productive resources unutilized over reasonable time.
- The production process should not cause harm to others [e.g. building a noisy factory in the middle of a residential area] as restricted currently by zoning regulations. In situations where some harm is inevitable, a careful weighting of relative harms and benefits should be made. Furthermore, a party that may be harmed must be compensated.

Source: Based on Jamal Badawi (2012), *Production and Consumption Ethics in Islam: Part 4*, <http://www.onislam.net/english/reading-islam/research-studies/islamic-thought/456165-islamic-business-ethics-part-4-.html>, accessed 23 January 2014.

5.2   FIRMS AND THEIR OBJECTIVES

People need goods and services to satisfy their wants. Firms are the institutions that make arrangements for their production. They control vast materials and human resources of the community and organize productive activities at the local and international levels. Firms are not only the source of producing what people need but are also the providers of employment. People receive income for services rendered to firms and spend money on their requirements. Preferences of the buyers guide firms in what they produce but at the same time, firms are also the agents of change in determining individual and societal tastes through aggressive marketing. For these reasons, the success and failure of business firms no longer remain a matter for private concern alone; public interest is involved. The social responsibility aspect of a business is increasingly coming under the public gaze, more so if Islamic norms of honesty and transparency in business are to be emphasized as religious obligation of individuals towards the society. Traders are promised to be raised with prophets and martyrs on the 'Day of Judgment' for the reason that it is very difficult to stay honest in business.

> With the increase in the size of modern firms, the number of workers they employ and the resources they handle in an economy, their failure is no longer viewed as a private matter; it invokes public concern. Private business has societal responsibilities to meet.

In sheer numbers, small owner-operated businesses far exceed corporate organizations, but in matters of control over resources, volume of output, job creation and political influence, the latter plays the major role at the local and international levels. Large corporations dominate trade, industry, commerce, transportation, communication, finance, insurance and in some countries even agriculture. Some multinational corporations, General Motors for example, spend volumes just on advertising each year, more than the annual budget of the government of India.

Individual enterprises operating in real life are usually engaged in producing and selling a variety of products. In many cases, they combine very different lines of production—detergents, chemicals, book publishing, automobiles, communications, transportation, farming and education all under the same interest and control. The Tatas in India are one of the leading examples of such diversification.

In contrast, economics sees the firm as a theoretical construct, an aggregation of assets devoted to the production of a *single* commodity, and run by an individual entrepreneur. Thus, 'firm' in economics is a heuristic notion, far from what you come across and deal with in real life. And yet, it is a useful notion that greatly facilitates the analysis of producers' behaviour in an economy. In the following discussion, our firm is of this design.

> In economics, the firm is a theoretical construct, a heuristic concept coined to facilitate economic analysis. In most (not all) cases, it is viewed as an owner-operated single product entity working for profit.

5.2.1   Maximization and Minimization

Firms wanting to maximize their profits are well-known, but it is not commonly realized that a pre-condition for profit maximization depends on output maximization in the physical sense. Maximization of output has two aspects: (i) to produce maximum output from given resources or, (ii) to produce a given output using minimum resources. It is in the latter way that cost minimization is said to mean profit maximization. But remember, (i) and (ii) do not mean the same thing. Suppose you are a furniture-making firm and have a hundred logs of wood in stock. Your designers' problem would be what items of what size and shape must the firm produce that would result in the least wood wastage. They are aiming at maximizing output, given the material. Alternatively, your firm gets an order of supplying as many tables as possible of a specified shape and dimension. The time line for the order is such that you have to meet it within the present limit of your wood stock—100 logs. It is easy to see that the wastage of wood will not be the same in both cases. (Which case will have more wastage and why?) In other words, the given output, Y_G, need not be equal to the maximum output, Y_M. Figure 5.1 depicts the difference. Here, X_1 and X_2 represent inputs used in making the furniture. Of the second suffix attached to these inputs, 1 is for the given output and 2 is for the maximum output the given resources could produce. The latter is usually the assumption when related to firms.

> As resources have alternative uses, firms employ them where the expected return is more than in any other use. The return in the next best use which is sacrificed is called as the economics or opportunity cost of the current use output. ▼

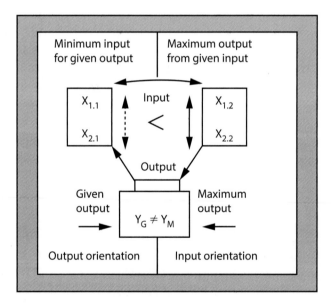

Figure 5.1 *Results need not be identical*

Exercise   5.1

Is it true that maximization of output is the same as minimization of input in the process of production? Elaborate and say if you support the statement. Give reasons for your answer.

5.3 THE PRODUCTION FUNCTION

A production function is a mathematical expression showing the maximum output, Q, of some commodity a firm can produce with given quantities inputs—say, labour, L and capital, K. It summarizes the conversion of inputs into finished products. Production functions are used to study the firms' behaviour in economics. You shall see that the analysis framework is much the same as we would use to analyze the behaviour of consumers. The general form of the function is:

> A production function states the input–output relationship.

$$Q = f(L, K) \tag{5.1}$$

Figure 5.2 provides a bird's eye view of what this function means. Here, K shows that capital is fixed; only labour is a variable.

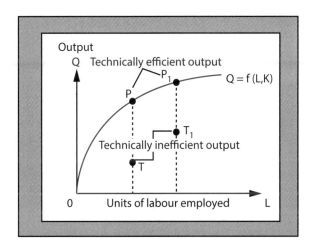

Figure 5.2 *Production function with fixed capital*

Inputs are within limits and substitutes for one another, each possible output such as Ps and Ts in the figure can be produced by different combinations of inputs. More machines can be used for example in place of some workers and vice versa. Computerization of work in offices creates initial unemployment; introduction of automation does the same in industries. The extent of substitution varies between 0-1, i.e. the inputs cannot at all be mutual substitutes at one end or one can fully replace the other on the other end. The degree of possible replacement is called the ***elasticity of input substitution***. We shall revisit this topic in the following example.

Exercise 5.2

In Figure 5.2, the points P and P_1 are labelled as showing technically efficient outputs, while points T and T_1 are declared as inefficient outputs. Is it correct? Give reasons for your answer.

Example 5.1 Consider the data in Table 5.1. It is the input–output matrix of a firm's Production Department presented to the management. Some figures such as 35 and 40 appear indifferent to row–column combinations. The firm is using two inputs, labour and capital, and has the choice of producing the *same* output from their different combinations. Recall the consumers' behaviour analysis to maximize their satisfaction out of a given income based on indifference curves. Firms use the same technique to discover the maximum output they can possibly produce from the given inputs. Here, equal product curves replace the indifference curves and equal cost lines become substitutes for budget lines. The word 'iso' means equal. Thus, here we have equal quantity (product) curves known as **isoquants**. A collection of such curves gives us the **isoquant map**. However, at what isoquant the firm would produce depends on the amount of money it plans to spend on the inputs given the prices of the two inputs, say K and L. The line having the ratio of these prices (P_K/P_L) as its slope, gives us an equal cost curve called the **isocost**. We can generate a family of isocosts by varying the aggregate expenditure on the two inputs. They would also change if the input prices change.

Table 5.1   *Input combinations and possible outputs*

				UNITS OF OUTPUT			
	13	38	**40**	50	53	60	67
	1	**35**	39	47	49	58	65
	9	31	38	**40**	45	55	62
	7	**25**	**35**	38	**40**	48	50
	5	13	**25**	30	**35**	39	**40**
	3	8	11	19	**25**	32	**35**
	1	**4**	**7**	**11**	**15**	**18**	**20**
	0	1	2	3	4	5	6

*(Left vertical axis: UNITS OF CAPITAL; bottom axis: **UNITS OF LABOUR**)*

Now, take note of the following facts in Table 5.1.

1. Factors of production are substitutes for one another, though substitution in most cases is not perfect. It means that, the same quantity of a product can be produced by different factor combinations. For example, from the same piece of land you can grow 100 tons of wheat using either more of capital (machines) and less of labour or using more of labour and less of capital. Notice, the bold-face figure 40 appears in four cells of Table 5.1 and seems to fall on a curve. The same is the case with output 35. Figure 5.3 plots these two cases. It helps to explain some basic concepts. The slope of such curves is determined by what we call the **marginal rate of technical substitution (MRTS)** of say labour for capital. This rate is calculated in marginal terms as follows:

a. $MRTS_L = \Delta K / \Delta L$ (5.2)

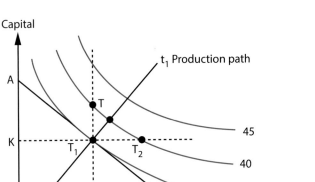

Figure 5.3 *Isoquants and production path*

2. The reason for substitution possibility is that in factor combinations producing an output, the production capacity of one or the other factor invariably remains unutilized. Thus, capital remaining unchanged at K, you can increase output, Q, from 30 to 40 and beyond by employing more workers. This could also be possible if labour is kept constant at L*, not having sufficient tools and implements to make them fully occupied; capital is increased from T_1 to T_2 and beyond.

> If capital K is kept constant, output can be increased by using more labour along the production path.

3. If we bring in factor prices and aggregate expenditure into the picture, an isocost like AB would give us the optimal output for the firm at T_1 showing output at 40 units. For, given the AB constraint, T_1 is the highest point the firm could climb to on its isoquant map.
4. If we pass a line through 0 and T_1, it would pass through the higher isoquant-isocost tangency points. The line traces the growth path of output Q for a given state of technology in time (t_1). The line t_1 can rotate up or down on point 0 showing a technical change in production over time.

5.3.1   Properties of Isoquants

Isoquants have properties similar to those of indifference curves.
1. Isoquants slope downwards. Isoquants show only efficient production, an upward–sloping isoquant is impossible. (Why?)
2. The farther away an isoquant is from the origin, the greater is the level of output—the more inputs a firm uses, the more output it gets if it produces efficiently.
3. Isoquant curves are convex to the origin because of diminishing marginal rate of technical substitution.

> Isoquants are also called equal product curves.

4. Isoquants do not cross each other simply because one input combination cannot produce two different output quantities, say 35 and 40 in our example.

An isoquant map has similar characteristics of the indifference curves that describe utility function.

Exercise 5.3

Compare the equilibrium of the consumer and the producer based on the indifference curve techniques. Explain the impact of technological improvements on growth of output.

5.4 SHORT-RUN PRODUCTION FUNCTION

> Short-run is defined as a period when some of the factors remain fixed while others can be varied.

Focus on the last row in Table 5.1. Capital remains fixed at 1 unit but output can be increased from 4 to 20 by employing more and more labour through better utilization of capital capacity. The following is the production form that depicts this situation. Notice that the return to labour i.e. its marginal physical product, MP_L, first increases, remains constant for a while, and then tends to decrease. This is a short run phenomenon as the firm cannot increase its production capacity. The production function assumes the following form:

$Q = f(L, K)$ where Q is the output, L is labour and K is capital. (K is the fixed input).

The behaviour of MP_L indicates how returns to a factor of production behave in the short run. Figure 5.4 demonstrates the phases of the returns. It shows that eventually the law of *diminishing returns* would dominate the production process of a firm in the short run.

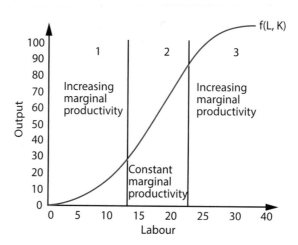

Figure 5.4 *Stages of returns to a factor of production*

Let us now see what happens to the firm's total product, marginal product and average product when it employs more and more of variable inputs. This knowledge is important for making various decisions in a firm. The exact relationship between output (total product) and variable inputs such as labour, can be illustrated by using a production function as above: $Q = f(L, K)$ as in Table 5.1.

5.4.1   Total, Average and Marginal Output

We have seen that in the short run, we have two sorts of factors: fixed and variable. Since fixed factors cannot be changed in the short run by definition, a firm can increase output only by employing more and more of variable factors. A cloth mill, for example, can increase output with the *same* plant capacity by using more of cotton and employing more of labour. Traditionally, we measure the production in physical terms with reference to the variable factor labour, capital remaining fixed. Two concepts emerge: average product and marginal product of labour. Table 5.2 helps us to understand these concepts.

In price theory, short run is defined as the span of time wherein supply of a product is limited by the existing production capacity of the industry. The period could even be so short that supply cannot be more than the stock of the commodity in the market.

Table 5.2 *Total, average and marginal product of labour*

Labour units L	Output produced TP_L	Average product APP_L	Marginal product MP_L
1	400	400	400
2	900	450	500
3	1,500	500	600
4	**2,100**	**525**	**600**
5	2,600	520	500
6	2,994	499	394
7	3,269	467	275
8	3,392	424	123
9	3,447	383	55
10	3,450	345	0
11	3,410	310	− 37

Notice that we define:

$$\text{Marginal product of labour (MPL)} = \frac{\text{Change in total product}}{\text{Change in labour units employed}}$$

$$= \frac{\Delta TP_L}{\Delta L} \qquad (5.3)$$

In the short run, we can obtain average product of labour by dividing physical output by the labour units that produced it. However, if we divide the increase in total output by the additional units of labour needed to produce it, we get the marginal physical product of labour.

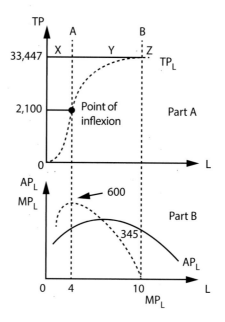

Figure 5.5 *Total, average and marginal product of labour*

Exercise   5.4

We explained above the point of inflexion and the behaviour of the tangent with reference to Part A of Figure 5.5. Explain the same with reference to Part B of the figure. What difference do you see from the two explanations?

Exercise   5.5

(i) Explain the law of diminishing returns. Show how and why it operates in the short run production of output.

(ii) You are a student. Do you think that the law of diminishing returns applies to work effort in studies also? Explain your answer defining fixed and variable factors in this case.

5.5   SHORT-RUN PRODUCTION COSTS

5.5.1   Total Cost

Total cost of production is the sum of total fixed costs and total variable costs for a given output. When divided by the output, we obtain average total cost of production. Note that in the discussion of short-run output behaviour in Section 5.4, we related output to per unit of variable factor, labour, in physical terms. Now, we are relating money costs to units of output. The two components of total cost are:

1. **Fixed costs**: A firm must pay for the factors of production—fixed or variable—that it uses for producing a commodity in the short run. Fixed factor costs for an accounting period include the rental value of its assets, insurance premiums, property taxes, debt servicing and other contractual payments it is obliged to make. Their aggregate is called fixed cost, i.e. it does not vary in the short run no matter the level of output. The average or per unit fixed cost of production continually decreases as output expands. (Why?)

2. **Variable costs**: The money a firm spends on buying raw materials and stores, for paying employees' salaries, energy bills, routine asset maintenance and so on adds up to what we regard as variable costs of production; variable because these costs increase or decrease with a corresponding increase or decrease in output. Total variable costs, when divided by output, gives us the average variable cost.

> In the short run, we have two types of costs: investment and fixed assets. These are also called overheads or sunk costs and represent the capacity of the industry. Others are variable costs, in the sense that they increase (decrease) with an increase (decrease) in output.

Adding total fixed and total variable costs, we obtain the total cost of production. Division of total cost by aggregate output yields average total costs. A final concept in this area is marginal cost. Marginal cost is defined as the addition to total costs if one more unit of the commodity is produced. It can also be thought of as reduction in total cost if output was reduced by one unit.

Table 5.3 presents numerical examples of various cost concepts for understanding their mutual relationships. Note the abbreviation below each sort of cost. Notice that the first column of the table records output in packs of thousand units, for example, 5 in the column means 5,000.

Table 5.3 *Short-run costs of production (amount in RM'000)*

Units produced ('000)	Fixed costs Total TFC	Fixed costs Average AFC	Variable cost Total TVC	Variable cost Average AVC	Total cost TFC + TVC	Total average cost ATC	Marginal cost MC
0	2,520	2,520	–	–	2520	–	–
1	2,520	2,520	4,000	4,000	6,520	6,520	4,000
2	2,520	1,260	7,000	3,500	9,520	4,760	3,000
3	2,520	840	9,000	3,000	11,520	3,840	2,000
4	2,520	630	12,000	3,000	14,520	3,630	3,000
5	2,520	504	16,250	3,250	18,770	3,754	4,250
6	2,520	420	21,000	3,500	23,520	3,920	4,750
7	2,520	360	27,580	3,940	30,100	4,300	6,580
8	2,520	315	36,000	4,500	38,520	4,815	8,420
9	2,520	280	49,500	5,500	52,020	5,780	13,500

In practice, firms usually do not consider increasing output unit by unit as it is mostly not cost effective. They think of increasing the output through a minimum unit of packs. For example, publishers do not reprint a book unless they estimate the potential demand for the work at minimum, say 300 copies. Figure 5.6 brings out the relationship between various costs. These are as follows:

1. Total cost and total variable cost curves run parallel to each other; the distance between them measuring the total fixed costs.

2. The total variable cost first increases at a diminishing rate but after the point of inflexion it increases at an increasing rate. (Proof?) The total cost curve exhibits the same characteristics. (Why?)

3. Marginal cost curve crosses both the AVC and ATC curves at their lowest points.

    Also, notice that the crossing point on ATC occurs at a higher output than AVC.

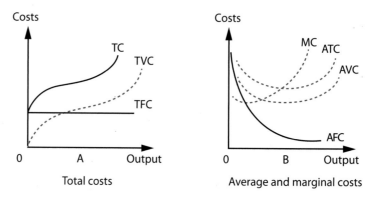

Figure 5.6 *Short-run total, average and marginal cost curves*

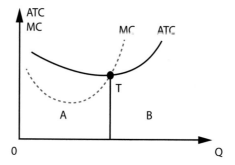

Figure 5.7 *MC and ATC relationship*

4. The relationship between MC and ATC is not so straightforward and needs some elaboration.

Remember it would be wrong to believe that ATC is falling when MC is falling or ATC is rising when MC is rising. *It is the level not the direction of change (rise or fall) in MC that brings about the rise or fall in ATC.*

Put simply, the rules are as follows:

- As long as MC < ATC; the ATC must be falling.
- As long as MC = ATC; the ATC must be constant.
- As long as MC > ATC; the ATC must be rising.

Figure 5.7 helps clarify the point. Note that in section A of the figure, MC starts falling to the left of point T, reaches a minimum and then starts rising but because all along it remains *below* the ATC, ATC continues falling. However, as MC equals ATC at point T, ATC stops falling. But once MC crosses T and becomes *higher* than ATC in section B, ATC starts rising.

> The relationship between marginal and average cost of production is a bit complicated: it is not the rise or fall of the marginal cost but its *level* relative to average cost that determines the rise or fall in the latter.

5.5.2   Output and Costs

We shall see later in the discussion on resource markets that for a given wage rate, employment of labour depends on its marginal productivity MP_L. We can find the output corresponding to a given labour input on the Q-axis by multiplying the AP_L with labour units, L associated with that AP_L. Figure 5.8 clarifies the point assuming that wages alone were the variable cost. Interestingly, the product and cost curves look like mirror images of each other. The highest point on one and the lowest on the other coincide. Short-run costs may shift in any direction depending on changes in its determinants, among them variations in technology used and factor prices are important.

> The physical output and revenue curves are reverse images of one another. (Why?)

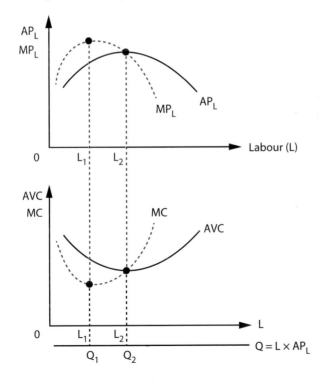

Figure 5.8 *Physical product and corresponding cost curves*

5.6 **LONG-RUN COST CURVES**

Long run is the period in which an industry and its constituent firms both freely make resource adjustments. The short run distinction between fixed and variable factors is that: *all factors become variable*. A firm can change its production capacity; it can erect a larger plant or can go back to a smaller one. Also, the time is long enough for new firms to enter the industry or the old ones to leave it, if they so decide. Here we look at these long run adjustment possibilities from the viewpoint of costs for a firm.

5.6.1 **Firm Size and Costs**

In the long run, the distinction between fixed and variable costs goes: all costs become variable. Here, it is the size of the firm that determines the output and cost behaviour or what we call the returns to scale.

It is obvious that in the long run, a firm will not have fixed cost curves, total or average. It will only have average and marginal cost curves. Also, as plant size increases these curves must become wider and less steep compared to short-run ATCs and MCs. Plant size is increased gradually. The firm passes from smaller to larger size in stages. Each stage has short-run features with a larger capacity. Figure 6.6 shows three curves illustrative of the sort because there can, in fact, be a large family of them. The plant size is increased when production has well crossed its optimal production point on a given size and a bigger plant looks more efficient. Notice that output Q_1 can be produced both by S_1 and S_2 plants. But ATC along S_1 is rising but is falling along S_2. So, for output range Q_1–Q_2 plant S_2 is more economical: it produces more at lower cost. The same argument takes us from S_2 to plant S_3 and so on. If we join the lowest points of all possible short run plants, we shall have the path of long-run average total cost like ATC-L in the figure. It is also called an envelop curve as it laps in all possible short-run curves.

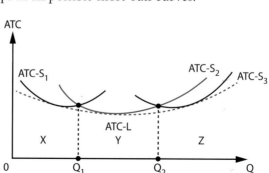

Figure 5.9 *Long-run average total cost curve (ATC-L)*

Interestingly, ATC-L curves are also U-shaped like the short-run curves but for different reasons. In the long run, the scale of production increases. Large scale of operations brings in certain economies that reduce production costs. But some diseconomies also occur that work in the opposite direction. So long as economies are more than diseconomies, overall costs fall. When the two tend to be equal, the firm experiences constant costs. But when diseconomies become more pronounced than the economies, *diminishing returns to scale* set in: ATC-L starts rising. Let us have a look at these economies and diseconomies.

> Increase in size allows a firm some cost-reducing benefits or economies but it also causes on some counts increases in costs or diseconomies of scale. It is the relative measure of economies and diseconomies that determines the net returns to scale.

5.6.2 Economies of Scale

1. **Division of labour and specialization**: As a firm has to expand output because of expanding demand for its product it can divide the work in simpler sub processes and can use more of machines for doing different jobs. Machines work non-stop for long hours and produce better quality goods. Workers with better skills and specialists can be engaged as departmental heads. All this helps in reducing per unit cost of production.

2. **Advantages of bulk buying and bulk selling**: In large-scale production raw materials, spares, stores fuel, etc., can be bought in large quantities from suppliers at cheaper prices. In fact, firms may produce their own raw materials. Tea companies have their own plantations, textile mills their cotton growing fields, flour mills own wheat growing farms and sugar mill sugarcane areas. Also, there are advantages in bulk selling. Money turnover is faster and may save on payments to the financiers. Goodwill may bring in credit on more favourable terms.

3. **Reduction in transportation cost**: Large firms can hire more transport capacity in one transaction. They can get better terms from the shippers, insurers, clearing agents, railroads and truckers. In fact, very large firms may and do have their own transport systems to bring in materials and fuel and distribute their product to the retailers. You must have seen soft drinks trucks distributing filled-in bottles to retailers and collecting back the empty ones from them.

The economies of large-scale productions result in unit cost reduction and the long-run ATC curve slopes downwards as Figure 5.10 shows. However, the trend cannot continue indefinitely: diseconomies of scale in production eventually set in.

> In the beginning, the economies of scale increase faster than the diseconomies and the firm experiences decreasing costs of production.

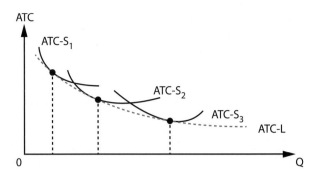

Figure 5.10 *Increasing returns or decreasing costs to scale*

5.6.3   Diseconomies of Scale

As the scale of production increases, it becomes increasingly difficult to maintain efficient coordination and supervision of various processes. After all, the skill of a manager at the top is not infinite. Difficulties of coordination may lead to accumulation of stores and inventories in excess of the requirement, locking in liquid funds. Inabilities of adequate supervision tend to cause wastage of materials, inadequate maintenance of plant and machinery, pilferage, and labour hour losses. Departmental heads tend to become independent and attempt to promote their own interests to the disadvantage of the firm. Cronyism and corruption may start eating into the vitals of the organization.

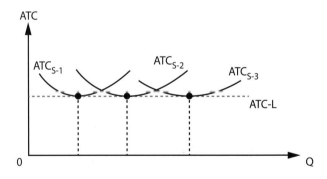

Figure 5.11 *Constant returns or constant costs to scale*

After a point, diseconomies tend to catch up with economies: the two become equal, and for a while the costs or returns tend to become constant over a range of output. Soon, the diseconomies overtake economies and per unit cost of production eventually begins rising.

All this tends to neutralize the economies of scale discussed above. As the economies and diseconomies balance, the firm experiences constant returns to scale as shown in Figure 5.11.

However, with a further increase in the scale of operation the diseconomies overweigh the resulting economies and cause a net rise in production costs. Figure 5.12 shows this result.

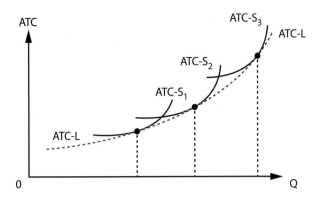

Figure 5.12 *Decreasing returns or increasing costs to scale*

It is clear from Figures 5.9–5.12 that long–run cost curves also tend to be U-shaped. But they are wider and firms in an industry may be producing for quite long along the flatter bottoms at constant average costs. Figure 5.13 puts the three phases of long run costs together.

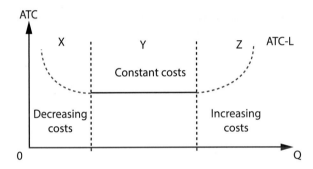

Figure 5.13 *Phases of average total cost in the long run*

We can now summarize the returns to scale discussion using the functional form as shown in Figure 5.14. We did not indicate slope markings for constant returns case as the slope of a straight line is always uniform.

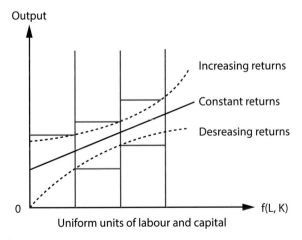

Figure 5.14 *Returns to scale in summary*

Exercise **5.7**

In Figure 5.13 write the cost behaviour against each type of return. Copy the Figure on a new page and try to mark off the slope below and above the top and bottom curves respectively.

5.6.4   Scale, Efficiency and Social Responsibility

Efficiency of production in physical terms means either of the two things: (i) to produce a *given* output with minimum factor use, or (ii) to produce maximum output with *given* stock of inputs. For example, you are in furniture-making industry where wood is the basic raw material. Suppose you have an order for making 100 tables of a particular size and design. The measure of your efficiency lies in how much wood you use to meet the order. The less wood you use, the more efficient you are in the sense of (i). Efficiency will depend essentially on your technical skills.

Alternatively, you have 100 logs of wood and complements for the trade. There is no restriction regarding the size, design or items of furniture you may want to produce and sell. In this case, your efficiency lies in reducing the wastage of wood and other materials. For this you must allocate your resources to various sorts of furniture items that you are able to produce the largest number of marketable item from what you have. You shall then be efficient in sense (ii). Cost of production, sales revenue and profit are reckoned in terms of money. So, you will have to bring together prices of materials and output into the picture and relate them to physical input–output matrix. This creates additional problems in efficiency measurement that we do not discuss in this introductory work.

Remember, whichever criteria of the above you may have to adopt, given the situation, there is always a specific scale of operations working as a reference point. But variations of scale may themselves be an additional and important determinant of efficiency. With scale, the relative weight and impact of economies and diseconomies on costs also changes. An important question then is: Can we find an optimal least unit cost size for a firm in an industry? It remains a much debated and researched question in applied economics. In a dynamic situation, no conclusive or permanent answers can ever be provided. Nonetheless, there is much support these days for enlarging the size of modern firms producing commodities or services with a view to improving their cost-profit efficiency and stability. Today, even the minimal size for a match-cutting machine, a steel factory, a paper mill, electricity generation unit or of a transport system is, indeed, huge. Firms increasingly become, as mentioned earlier, the carriers of a nation's progress, custodian of its resources in men, money and materials. Public interest is involved in their performance. Intellectuals, Islamic economists especially, raise the issues of societal

> Efficiency may be defined as producing maximum output from given input or producing given output from minimum input.

preferences and social responsibility as goals of modern business, not just costs and profits. Concerns are also expressed about monopoly power that size enlargement bestows on bigger firms. The 2006–2007 budget of Pakistan—currently a booming economy—envisages a 35% expansion of the public sector probably as a response to such concerns and anxieties.

Exercise 5.8

Explain the economies and diseconomies of large scale productions and show how their emergence in production makes the long-run cost curves. Are the reasons for which make short-run cost curves U-shaped different? Explain your answer.

BOX 5.2

Capital Productivity, Interest and Profit

In the framework of a business firm, both interest and profit are cost payments for the use of capital in production, yet interest is not allowed in Islam while profit is. Why? Islam recognizes the productive attribute of capital and does not intend to deprive it of its due reward. This is why Islam allows *mudharabah* as a form of business organization. But, to begin with, is interest commensurate with productivity? The level of interest rates is mainly determined by the state of opinion in the market for placements—the stock exchange—and manipulation of monetary policy. Likewise, rate of profit depends on the state of technology and the level of real wages. What has the productivity of capital to do with either of them? Again, all the funds are intermixed in the asset formation of the firm and are, from its viewpoint, equally productive and exposed to the same type of risk and uncertainty in its business. How do the productivity of the borrowed and the equity parts of funds differ? Further—and this is crucial—why should the firm make different payments to capital for identical functions, one at the predetermined rate (interest) and the other (profit) variable with the results of the business operations? Financial expediency need not meet the ends of justice.

The non-symmetry clearly invokes the principle of *gharar*. Market economies are characterized by business fluctuations where interest rates invariably lag behind price variations. The result is that the loan-equity mix in the capital structure of the business firms proves, in general, unjust to the lenders during periods of inflation and hurts the equity holders when the economy is going down the hump. Islam obliterates the inequity by the abolition of interest so that the capital participates in the productive ventures on equal footing—the proportionate sharing of profit.

Source: Hasan, Z. (1983), *Theory of profit: The Islamic Viewpoint*, KAU Journal of Research in Islamic Economics, Volume 1, No. 1.

5.7 EXPLICIT AND IMPLICIT COSTS

We have discussed the various types of costs, but missed one important classification—explicit and implicit costs. Part of the inputs (resources) used in small proprietary businesses for producing commodities usually belong to their owners, others are bought or hired from the market. This fact leads to a splitting of money costs of a business into their explicit and implicit components.

In owner-operated firms, the resources belonging to the owners usually include capital that they bring in, their land and buildings that they commit to business, and the time and energy they spend in running it as managers. The owners can employ these personal resources elsewhere for remuneration. They forego that opportunity when they employ them in their own business. Owners must count these implicit costs—gains lost—also to arrive at the full cost of production. The economic or *full cost* of producing a commodity equals explicit plus implicit costs.

You must remember that explicit costs consist of *actual* payments made to outside suppliers of resources. These may include payments for raw materials, transportation charges, wages and salaries, etc. On the other hand, implicit costs are essentially a matter of estimation both of the value of owned resources and of their returns if employed elsewhere. Nevertheless, the concept creates a gap between the economic and the accounting views of both production costs and profits. For, the accountants record only the explicit costs of business ignoring the implicit costs involved in running it.

> Payments that go into the accounts of a firm constitute explicit costs. On the other hand, costs that do not appear in account books are implicit costs; these are in fact part of the opportunity costs of a firm.

> Implicit costs are not to be ignored in reckoning the true profitability of a firm.

Example 5.2 Suppose you are to open a restaurant. You must have a building large enough to accommodate a kitchen for cooking and storing a variety of items to make dishes for at least, say ten customers, sufficient crockery and a properly set hall with adequate furnishing to accommodate no less than fifty visitors at a time so that they may enjoy their meals in comfort. You also have to employ a manager, a cook and a server, i.e. a minimum of staff is also needed. This arrangement is in anticipation of the number of visitors eventually expanding to fifty at a time to give you ultimately a profit you would consider reasonable with reference to your present circumstances and aspirations. Thus, you decided to start with an arrangement of a minimal capacity to serve fifty visitors at a time. Now, in the beginning, whether one or not fifty visitors comes to your restaurant, your fixed facilities and expenditure on them remains virtually unchanged. But as your business picks up, you will have to increase the purchase of materials—cooking oil, vegetables, spices, meat, etc.—you may have to employ more and more workers as you increase the business hours. For a fuller utilization of the capacity of your establishment, you have to increase the variable factors appropriately as sales pick up.

> Interestingly, the law of diminishing returns was discovered by a Scotland farmer who found that with more and more inputs he uses on his piece of land, total output does increase but tends to diminish per unit of inputs. Thus, Marshall thought that the part which nature plays in production leads to diminishing returns while the part man plays leads to increasing returns.

This example may help you imagine how huge would be the minimal capacity that a railway system, a steel mill, an auto-assembly line and other production units must install to start with. In the beginning, the employment of a variable factor (labour) is in fact not sufficient enough for optimal use of this capacity. The output per additional worker (MP_L) tends to rise. When expansion of employment touches the optimal level, MP_L tends to become constant. Eventually, employment of more and more workers causes shortage of the supporting fixed factors and now the full potential of the variable factor—increasing work force—is not fully utilized: the law of diminishing returns (MP_L) sets in permanently. Study the course of curves in the lower part of Figure 5.4 carefully.

There is another way of looking at the short-run behaviour of output. It is obvious that in a combination of fixed (f) and variable (v) factors the ratio f/v must decline as v increases. The effect of this decline on the behaviour of returns (output) is not uniform. It has three distinct phases, as stated above. In the first phase, when the ratio remains more than one, returns tend to rise. In the second, when the falling ratio hovers around one, returns stay constant for a while, but in the final stage the decreasing ratio runs below one and returns start and continues diminishing. For the behaviour of the ratio f/v, the law of diminishing returns is sometimes called the *law of variable proportions*. You can see the law in its three phases in the sections of Figure 5.13 marked as X, Y and Z. Remember that the law relates to the behaviour of the marginal product of the variable factor (labour) in the short run. It is a fundamental law of economics, independent of the form of economic system and valid, as we shall see, in the long run as well, though for different reasons.

Suppose Halim got RM100,000 as a gift from his father and an empty shop after graduating in Business Management from the International Islamic University of Malaysia. Preferring business as a profession because of his training, Halim uses his money and shop to start a store selling mobile phones and necessary accessories under the name Air Communications. He hires a salesgirl, Aisha, who also assists him in keeping accounts. At the end of the year, Aisha presents to him a summary statement of income and expenditure as in Table 5.4.

> In estimating the profitability of a firm, accountants take note of only explicit costs while economists count, in addition, implicit costs as well.

Table 5.4 *Air communications: summary of accounts for the year ending December 2013 (amount in RM)*

Total sales revenue		106,000
Cost of mobile phones	70,000	
Less		
Value of closing stock	22,000	
Cost of units sold	48,000	
Add		
Aisha's salary	18,000	
Utilities	12,000	
Total cost		78,000
Accounting profit		28,000

Halim was happy with the results thinking that he has made a return of 28% on his investment and narrated the story of his success to an economist friend, Hasan. Hasan, however, was not impressed.

He reminded Halim that the results are based only on explicit costs. If implicit costs were taken into account, he has made a meagre 1% return on his investment. Halim was surprised. Hasan explained to him that Halim could have earned RM6,000 in profit if he had invested his money in Islamic bonds where *average* return was 6%. His shop would have brought him annually RM6,000 as rent if he so wished. Likewise, had he employed himself as a trainee manager with some firm, he could have easily got another RM1,250 as monthly salary. Hasan made the following statement for Halim, showing that he was not in a profitable business. He suggested that Halim should wind up his business, rent out his store, invest his money in Islamic bonds and seek a trainee position in some firm (Table 5.5).

Table 5.5 *Adjusted statement (amount in RM)*

Accounting profit		28,000
Less (implicit costs)		
Foregone profit on Islamic bonds	6,000	
Foregone rent	6,000	
Foregone salary (1,250 × 12)	15,000	27,000
Economic profit		1,000

Exercise 5.9

In the above illustration, Halim did not agree to follow the advice of Hasan. He thought that his business was still new and would pick up in due course. So he decided to wait and see. On a more important note, he felt that freedom of thought and action, innovation and experimentation were important for him. Whom would you agree with, Hasan or Halim, and why?

Exercise 5.10

Suppose you invested your money, unlike Halim, in Islamic bonds, rented out your shop and were working in a firm as a manager. Assuming that the other information in Table 5.5 remain unchanged, would you want to switch over to business establishing and running an Air Communication like store? Give reasons for your answer.

> Normal profit carries an ethical air around it. For, it is the minimum that a firm must earn in the long run to stay in business, and hence just and legitimate. Opportunity cost is a good bench mark for the normal profit estimation.

5.7.1   Normal Profit

The sum of implicit costs is also referred to as normal profit but sometimes a distinction is made between the two. Normal profit is considered as the minimum amount firms must earn *in addition* to implicit costs for encouraging people to provide entrepreneurial services to society. It is treated as an element of the production costs. *Economic or pure profit* is the surplus that remains after deducting from sales revenue both components of economic costs—explicit and implicit including normal profit. We shall come across the concept again in our discussion on profit as a distributive share in Chapter 12.

> Mainstream economics essentially rests on the assumption of harmony between the interests of the individual and the society.

If we add RM1,000 as normal profit to implicit costs in our example (Table 5.4), economic profit will become zero. However, Halim would still be making normal profit of RM1,000 included in implicit costs. He may want to continue in business. Normal profit enables a firm to keep its head above water and wait in the hope of better times. Figure 5.15 explains the relationship among various cost and profit concepts we have just discussed.

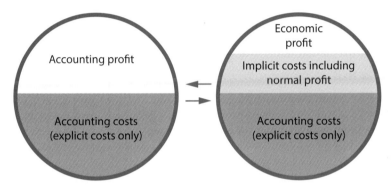

Figure 5.15 *Economic versus accounting profit*

Exercise 5.11

Suppose Anisa starts a retail store under the name Ladies Grace selling head scarves. She employs Shama as her assistant to keep the accounts. The transaction record for the first month is as follows. Cost of scarves made Riyal 20,000, salary of Shama, Riyal 9,000, value of unsold stock Riyal 4,000 and other expenses, Riyal 3,000. The sales revenue earned for the month is Riyal 60,000. Draw the profit statement Shama will present to Anisa for the month.

Exercise 5.12

Anisa knows that she has invested in her business Riyal 100,000 which would bring her Riyal 500 a month in a safe Islamic Unit Trust investment. She is also using an outroom of her residence to run the store for which she can get a monthly rent of Riyal 100. Also, she had left a job with a salary of Riyal 500 a month to run a business as she wanted to be her own boss. For uncertainties of business, she expected a monthly entrepreneurial income of no less than Riyal 1000. Do you think she should be happy with her decision to leave the job for business, taking her implicit costs into consideration?

| 5.8 | COBB-DOUGLAS PRODUCTION FUNCTION AND RETURNS |

In the foregoing discussion, we have used a general form of production function, i.e. $Q = Af(K, L)$. But the function can assume various forms depending on the treatment of the variables K and L. An important form that has many variants is Cobb-Douglas' formulation of the function that assigns coefficients to the variable K and L as follows:

$$Q = f(AK^{\alpha}L^{\beta}) \tag{5.4}$$

Here, Q is output and A is a constant as usual but α and β are the powers or coefficients assigned to K and L respectively. In the present context, this function helps to easily find the returns to scale. The sum of the two coefficients provides the relevant information as follows:

$$
\left.
\begin{array}{l}
\text{If } (\alpha + \beta) < 1 \text{ returns to scale are decreasing} \\
\text{If } (\alpha + \beta) = 1 \text{ returns to scale are constant} \\
\text{If } (\alpha + \beta) > 1 \text{ returns to scale are increasing}
\end{array}
\right\} \tag{5.5}
$$

Example 5.3 Let us assume that $A = 20$, K_1 and $L_1 = 10, 10$; and K_2 and $L_2 = 20, 20$; both being doubled to increase the scale of operation. But we vary the values assigned to $(\alpha + \beta)$ as (i) $0.3 + 0.5 = 0.8 < 1$; (ii) $0.4 + 0.6 = 1$, and (iii) $0.5 + 0.7 > 1$. Substituting the values in the formula, we generate the following Table 5.6.

Table 5.6 *Cobb-Douglas production function and returns to scale (when both K and L are doubled)*

Case number	$\alpha + \beta$	Q_1	Q_2	Increase in Q	Returns to scale
(i)	0.3 + 0.5	126	220	74.6%	Decreased
(ii)	0.5 + 0.5	200	400	100%	Remained constant
(iii)	0.5 + 0.7	317	728	130%	Increased

| BOX 5.3 | |

World Bank Regulates African Mineral Policy

Many African countries in the early 1980s were severely indebted, leading the World Bank to become increasingly involved in designing reforms that were introduced into Africa's mining industry. The key elements of African mineral policies that emerged in the late 1980s and in the 1990s, based on World Bank prescriptions, may be summarized as follows. African governments:

- Reduced or eliminated state participation in mining enterprises.

- Provided a wide range of incentives, causing foreign direct investment (FDI) into the industry to surge.
- Made tax regimes more competitive relative to those in other developing regions, particularly Latin America.
- Liberalized exchange controls and exchange rate policy.
- Introduced investment protection assurances, including those on the stability of the fiscal regime for a specified length of time (the 'stabilization period'),dividend repatriation and non-expropriation.

Although the extensive reforms of regulatory and legal frameworks thus introduced helped to create a more favourable environment for foreign investment in African mining, their contribution to social and economic development objectives has been farless certain—even contested in many countries. Within the past decade a very visible civil society movement, protesting about the costs and revitalized

Source: Report of the International Study Group on Africa's Mineral Regimes December 2011, Chap. 3, <http://www.au.int/en/sites/default/files/Overview%20of%20the%20ISG%20Report.pdf>, accessed 1 February 2014.

Summary

- People need goods and services to satisfy their wants. They buy these goods from business firms in the market for money. With the passage of time, the size of the firms become larger and larger; they have become the carriers of progress and custodians of the material and human resources of modern economies. This has added a social dimension to their performance.
- Productive resources were initially divided in five categories: land, labour, capital, organization and enterprise. These categories have been merged together over time into two broad divisions: labour and capital. Enterprise continues to move in and out of these divisions.
- Resources being scarce, we have to sacrifice in part or in full, the production of something to have what we may prefer to have. What we sacrifice to have a commodity we want is the opportunity cost of the latter.
- Costs of production can be explicit or implicit. Explicit costs are those that firms pay outsiders for supplying resources to producing commodities. Implicit costs refer to the income foregone by the owners which their resources contributed to the firm could earn elsewhere outside the firm.
- Accountants include payments made to outsiders alone in total costs, while economists include implicit costs to find the true or full costs of production. Broadly, implicit costs are known as the opportunity cost of a firm's own resources employed in its business. In the aggregate, these implicit costs are often termed as *normal profit*. Normal profit is the minimum that firms must earn for survival in the long run.
- Supply takes time to adjust to changes in demand. For this reason, we study the behaviour of costs with reference to time. Broadly, two periods are distinguished: short run and long run. But remember, the categories are essentially a matter of *definition*, not of time.

- The stream of resources that production processes convert into consumable goods includes items such as machines and buildings that move very slowly and can be seen being used over long stretches of time. In contrast, there are items that disappear at a fast pace: labour hours, lubricants, raw materials, energy and the like are examples. With reference to a given time span, the slow moving items are referred to as fixed factors and the fast-moving ones as variables.

- The short run is *defined* as a span of time when factors in a firm can be identified as fixed, i.e. not yet fully consumed in the production process, and those such as labour and raw materials that are fast used up in making finished products; they can no longer be used again. The time is so short that new firms cannot enter the industry nor can the old ones leave it. On the other hand, the long run is defined as the span of time that is enough to vary all factors of production; the distinction between fixed and variable factors. The long run is such that all factors become variable. Entry of firms to and exit from industry now becomes free.

- The behaviour of output in the short run passes through three phases with reference to the variable factor, e.g. labour. First, to increase production more labour is employed. There is better utilization of the capacity of fixed factors. Output per worker AP_L increases at a faster rate compared to labour hours. But as better and fuller utilization of fixed factors approaches, average production increases at a constant rate. Employment of additional workers would find less and less fixed factors for keeping them fully occupied. AP_L would start falling and *the law of diminishing returns would set in*.

- The behaviour of marginal physical product of labour MP_L follows a course similar to that of AP_L. Total output is at maximum when MP_L reaches zero and falls as MP_L becomes negative. MP_L curve crosses AP_L at its highest point.

- As costs are expressed with reference to output, it is possible to convert TP_L, AP_L and MP_L curves into cost curves and the two curve sets will look like the mirror image of one another.

- For studying the nature and behaviour of costs also we use the short- and long-run concepts as explained above. We have short-run costs and long-run costs. Both follow the same laws and patterns of behaviour as output but for different reasons.

- In the short run, total costs TC are the sum of total fixed costs TFC and total variable costs TVC incurred to produce a given output Q. Fixed costs remain the same within the capacity range of fixed factors of production. Payments made to variable factors for their contribution to output constitute variable costs. If we divide fixed cost TFC by the output Q, we get average fixed cost AFC which tends to fall as output increases. We can derive the average variable cost AVC if we divide total variable cost TVC by total output Q. AFC + AVC = ATC. Marginal cost of production is the cost of producing one more unit of output: $MC = TC_{t+1} - TC_t$.

- Short-run ATC, AVC and MC are all U-shaped because of the application of the law of variable proportions more commonly known as the law of diminishing returns or increasing costs.

- The relationship between ATC and MC is as follows: so long as MC is smaller than ATC, ATC must be falling. So long as MC is equal to ATC, ATC must remain constant. Finally, so long as MC is greater than ATC, ATC must be rising. These relationships between ATC and MC are valid both in the short run and in the long run.

- The economies and diseconomies of scale make long-run cost curves also U-shaped. So long as economies of scale remain larger than diseconomies the expanding firm experiences increasing returns to scale or decreasing average cost of production. When economies and diseconomies tend to balance each other constant returns or constant average costs operate. But ultimately, diseconomies overtake economies, returns to scale diminish and costs per unit start increasing.

- In the long run, all costs becoming variable use of the term average total cost does not make sense; we can more appropriately say average cost or AC in the long-run cases. But we have retained ATC in the text for the long run as well to save you from confusion.

- Due to the very large size of firms in modern times, their success or failure is no longer a matter of private concern; social and national interests are related to their performance. As such, social responsibility of business firms is on the rise in modern societies, more so in an Islamic economic perception.

Glossary

Cost efficiency Efficiency in cost is looked at from two angles: (a) to produce maximum output from a given set of inputs, or (b) to produce a given output with the minimal input use. The two approaches are different; they do not reciprocate. Efficiency has several interrelated variants but in the ultimate analysis all centre around costs of production. Recently, the concept is being extended to include environmental damage also into the concept of costs.

Firm A firm is an economic entity that transforms input services into output with a view of earning profit for its owners. It is a dynamic social institution operating in any sector of the economy, public or private. In price theory, firm is conceived of as a single product entity and is in that a heuristic concept meant to facilitate economic analysis. In recent times, firms are supposed to address some societal needs in addition to earning profits. Their success and failure is no longer considered a purely private affair, more so in Islamic economics.

Law of diminishing returns It is a fundamental law of economics. It says that other things remaining unchanged, if variable factors work with some fixed factors, total output increases as more and more variable factors are employed but at a diminishing rate beyond a point. The tendency was first experienced by a farmer in Scotland. Alfred Marshall economists thought that the part which nature (land) plays in production leads to diminishing returns, while the part that man plays (technology) results in increasing returns. But this bifurcation is no longer emphasized. Law of diminishing returns eventually pervades all fields of production. The valid distinction to be made is between the short and the long run because the causes are different. In the short run, it is the division of factors into fixed and variable; in the long run, it is the diseconomies of large–scale production overtaking its economies.

Normal profit It is the sum of returns which the factors contributed by the owners to a firm could earn in their next best use, i.e. the sum of their transfer earnings. Normal profit constitutes the implicit costs of doing business; it is an element of the total costs of production. If price of a product covers no more than the total cost, economic profit is zero. Firms tend to earn only normal profit under perfect competition that is just enough to keep their heads above water. The concept thus carries an ethical air around it. It is akin to just or fair profit of the Islamic vintage. The difficulty is that competition seldom remains perfect.

Social responsibility of business Corporate form of organization dominates modern business. Corporations are the main carriers of economic activity. They have control over the vast resources of an economy in men, money and materials. Their success or failure is a matter of public interest and concern. They depend in a large measure on public funds and support. So, they have—apart from profit making—social responsibilities in conducting business, more so in Islam. Corporate social responsibility is fast coming up as an academic discipline.

Concepts for Review

- Accounting profit
- Diseconomies of large-scale production
- Economic costs
- Economic profit
- Economies of large-scale production
- Efficiency
- Explicit costs
- Factors of production
- Firm
- Fixed and variable costs

- Implicit costs
- Law of diminishing returns
- Long run
- Marginal cost
- Normal profit
- Productivity and costs
- Short run
- Short-run production costs
- Size of the firm and costs
- Social responsibility of business
- Total costs and average costs

Case Study   5.1

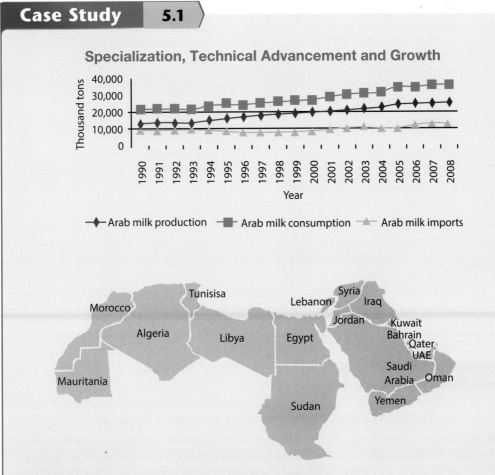

Specialization, Technical Advancement and Growth

−◆− Arab milk production   −■− Arab milk consumption   −▲− Arab milk imports

Figure 5.16 *Milk production, consumption, and import in MENA*

Case Questions

1. What are the sources of local milk production in the Middle East and North Africa (MENA) region? Find out.

2. Have a careful look at Figure 5.16. Which is increasing faster—milk consumption or production? Find what are the sources of milk import for the region.

Case Study   5.2

Kuwait Economy: Some Aspects

Kuwait is one of the richest Arab nations. It is a constitutional monarchy but is having elections and a parliament since the 'Arab Spring' of 2011. Kuwait controls roughly 7 per cent of the world's oil reserves. Oil accounts for nearly 50 per cent of GDP and 95 per cent of export revenues. The country has no individual income tax. Foreign-owned companies pay a 15 per cent corporate tax on net profits, but there are also exemptions for foreign investment in certain areas. Most other revenue is collected from the state's sovereign wealth fund. The overall tax burden is less than one per cent of GDP. Government expenditures are 39 per cent of gross domestic output. Public debt is relatively low, at about seven per cent of GDP. Average tariff rate is low at 4.1 per cent but there are restrictions on imported meat, used vehicles, and other products. Foreign ownership levels in some sectors of the economy have limits. The financial sector continues to evolve. With non-performing loans declining, the banking sector remains well capitalized.

Kuwait's economic freedom score is 62.3, making its economy the 76th freest in the 2014 Index. Some of the components are as follows:

Regulatory Efficiency
Trade Freedom 76.7;
Investment Freedom 55.0;
Financial Freedom 50.0;

Open Markets
Business Freedom 57.7
Labour Freedom 63.6
Monetary Freedom 73.2

Source: Compiled from World Bank Report 2014

Case Questions

1. Comment on the impact of low tariff rate on the imports and exports of the country. Would low rates attract foreign capital flow into the country? Argue your case.

2. Comment on the freedom score and its components in Kuwait. Can these indexes be relied upon to measure what they purportedly measure?

Case Study   5.3

Trend in Global Demand for Resources – Minerals

With the rising demand for recourses to boost domestic development, their suppliers can no longer in a position to maintain exports to the developed countries as during the colonial era. This has given rise to new trends and challenges in resource demand and supply patterns. The following passage regarding minerals is a mini-illustration of the emerging global trends and challenges.

'Following a long period of decline, mineral commodity prices and investment experienced a boom that began in 2003 and is projected to continue for some years yet. Unprecedented demand driven by large developing country industrialization, particularly China, has created an anxious global environment over security and reliability of mineral supply. The historic mineral importing countries in Europe, Japan and the United States, alongside newcomers China and India, have begun to focus—in competition—on ensuring access and security of supply for strategic mineral resources. Many governments have politically and financially backed investment in mineral resources globally, including those in Africa. The capital cycle is showing an upward trend, with multinational mining companies making large investments in new and existing capacity'.

Source: Report of the International Study Group on Africa's Mineral Regimes December 2011, <http://www.au.int/en/sites/default/files/Overview%20of%20the%20ISG%20Report.pdf>, accessed 1 February 2014.

Case Questions

1. The passage says that the entry of China as mineral importer has created an 'anxious global environment over security and reliability of mineral supply'. Can you say why? Elaborate your answer.

2. Until 2003, African countries could not convert their minerals into finished products, though they could pursue an export curtailment policy in case of some important raw materials for local processing. Why? See Box 5.3 for help.

Test Questions

5.1 Write a note on the concept of a firm in economics. How are the firms, as we find them in actual life, different from this theoretical concept? Do you think that modern firms have social responsibilities to meet? Explain your reasons.

5.2 What are factors of production? Originally economists used to discuss five factors of production. Name them. Now we usually mention two —labour and capital, how and why?

5.3 Distinguish between accounting and economic profit using the concepts of explicit and implicit costs of production. Explain the importance of the distinction.

5.4 Aamir is running an electronic goods sale cum servicing centre under the name Electronik Marvels. He bought a shop for his business and invested INR 200,000 in stores and equipment. He employs Asma a technician and Noor an accounts clerk to assist him in his work. He pays Asma INR 5000 and Noor INR 3000 each month as remuneration. Aamir had to leave a technician's job to start his business where he was getting INR 8000 as monthly salary. On 31 December 2005, Aamir found that during the year he bought from manufactures different electronic items for INR 300,000 and sold part of them for INR 400,000. The remaining stock he values at cost price worth INR 150,000. Apart from the salaries of Asma and Noor, he spent another INR 50,000 on utilities. He earned another INR 100,000 from repair and servicing. He found that he could have earned INR 5000 on his INR 200,000 in a safe Islamic unit trust investment. The monthly rental for shops in the area of the size he had was INR 1000. Do you think Aamir made a right decision to leave his job and enter business? Give reasons for your answer.

5.5 Why is behaviour of output and costs studied with reference to some time frame? Carefully define short run and long run in this context and bring out their differences with reference to production and cost functions of a firm.

5.6 Using the information of Table 5.4, construct a figure showing the ATC and MC curves of the firm and explain the relationship between them.

5.7 Construct a production curve from Table 5.5, taking output Q on the Y-axis and labour L on the X-axis. Mark the point (Q, L) below which the firm gets increasing returns to the variable factor labour L and beyond which diminishing returns apply to it. At what level of employment maximum output is produced?

5.8 Why does the short-run MC curve cut both the short-run ATC and AVC curves at their lowest points? Explain.

5.9 Fill in the missing information in Table 5.7. Labour units are measured in a working day of 8 hours. Output is in tons of butter, total fixed costs are in thousand dollars.

Table 5.7 *Short-run costs of production (amount in RM)*

L	Q	FC	VC	TC	AFC	AVC	ATC	MC
0	0	50	0	–	–	–	–	–
1	5	–	20	–	–	–	–	–
2	15	–	40	–	–	–	–	–
3	28	–	60	–	–	–	–	–
4	44	–	80	–	–	–	–	–
5	55	–	100	–	–	–	–	–
6	73	–	120	–	–	–	–	–
7	82	–	140	–	–	–	–	–
8	85	–	160	–	–	–	–	–

5.10 When the average product of labour is the same as the marginal product of labour, will AVC and MC be equal or different? Justify your answer.

5.11 The production function of a firm is where K and L denote its capital and labour inputs, respectively. If the price of labour were $1 and capital $4 a unit, what quantities of capital (K) and labour (L) should be employed if the firm wants to produce 6 units of output at minimum cost? What shall be the cost per unit of output (Table 5.8)?

Table 5.8 *Least cost combination for Q = 6 (factor prices per unit: L = $1 and K = $4)*

Factor units		Costs of production		
Labour L	Capital K	Cost of L	Cost of K	Total (TC)
1	36	1	144	145
2	18	2	–	74
3	12	3	–	–
4	9	4	36	–
6	6	6	–	–
9	4	9	–	–
12	3	12	–	24
18	2	18	8	–
36	1	36	4	40

[**Hint**: Square both sides of the production function. You get Q2 = K × L. Put Q = 6 in the output to be produced and get the value of L in terms of K. Now, write down the total cost function: TC (Q) = L + 4K. In this function, replace L with its value expressed in terms of K that you already know. You will have TC (Q) = 36/K + 4K. Find the first derivative of this function and equate it to zero to find the required value of K. The value of L for the least cost combination for Q = 6 can then be easily found. Verify if the per unit cost is $4.]

5.12 The production curve of the firm in Q5.11 is expressed as 36 = K × L. Using the information about the prices of K and L in that question, fill in the missing values in the following table and indicate the least cost combination for Q = 6. Plot the total cost curve on a graph paper taking K on the Y-axis and L on the X-axis. At each point of this curve, the output produced is the same, i.e. 6 units. It is called the equal product curve. It is akin to the indifference curve of the consumer. Also, draw the budget line of the firm if it has to spend no more than $24 on producing the output. Mark the values of units of labour and capital employed where the line is tangent to the equal product curve.

5.13 Explain the economies and diseconomies of scale. What impact do they have on long-run cost curves of a firm?

5.14 The long-run total cost curve of a firm is a straight line passing through the origin with capital K measured on Y-axis and labour L on X-axis. The firm employs 2 units of labour and 3 units of capital to produce 5 units of output. What units of K and L will it use when its long-run total cost equals 70?

Web Exercise

Search the Internet and write a note on the concept of an entrepreneur in economic theory from Islamic perspective.

Forward Link

You have learnt what lies behind the forces of demand and supply, i.e. why people are willing to pay the price which they pay for a commodity as well as why they have to pay that price. In the next three chapters, we explain how the prices that people are willing to pay and have to pay for commodities are formed under varying market conditions, the demand and supply tools remaining operative. The two market structures at the extremes are benchmark cases; what lies between them is closer to reality. In the following chapter, we will discuss one of the benchmark cases: the dreamland of perfect competition.

Perfect Competition

LEARNING OUTCOMES

This chapter should enable the student to understand:

- What gives rise to different market structures
- Profit maximization: Short- and long-run concepts
- Profit maximization: The total revenue–total cost approach
- Profit maximization: The marginal cost and marginal revenue approach
- Cost types and their interrelationship
- Cost efficiency: Concepts and measurement
- Profit maximization in the long run
- What is producers' surplus
- Unit tax on output and its effects

6.1 MARKET STRUCTURES

In the preceding chapters, we have explained the concept of markets, the nature of demand and supply of goods and services, the laws that govern them and their relationship with price. We saw that utility operates behind the demand for goods and services consumers are *willing* to pay for in the market to satisfy their wants. They *have* to pay for goods and services required because resources needed to produce them are scarce and have competing uses. Thus, production of a commodity involves costs that constitute the minimum a buyer has to pay to the seller as he may not be willing to sell it for anything less than that. In other words, the price of a commodity as Figure 6.1 shows, is determined by the forces of demand and supply somewhere between the maximum a buyer is willing to pay for a commodity and the minimum below which the seller is not willing to accept. Free competition between the buyers and sellers in an open market would also would also result it is claimed efficient allocation of resources to various uses but also a just distribution of wealth in the society.

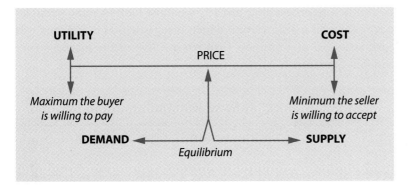

Figure 6.1 *Determinants of market price*

Islam too supports free markets and is not averse to competitive effort for acquiring wealth. However, there is evidence that unrestrained competition in production tends to benefit the rich more at the expense of the poor. For this reason, Islam regards c ooperation as the more important aspect of the production activity and advocates for state regulation to keep competition fair and gainful. But the problem is that in modern times the rich are mostly able to dominate the legislature and use political power to their advantage.

We cannot pursue further the Islamic notion of fair play here and go back to the point that price is determined by the forces of demand and supply. As different firms producing the same commodity mostly do not have identical costs of production, two important issues arise in price formation. These are as follows:

1. If the products of various sellers are identical in the eyes of buyers and for that reason they cannot charge different prices despite differences in production costs, how a single price for them all is determined in the market?
2. If any of the seller wants to charge a price for his product different from what others are charging, he wants to have pricing power, could he and if yes how?

The answers to these questions lie at the heart of price theories in economics. These theories describe the market structures wherein pricing of the commodities takes place. We may put these structures on a straight line as in Figure 6.2. They differ from one another with reference to the *degree of pricing power* firms are able to acquire in a particular case. In perfect competition, at one end of the scale, no firm has any pricing power, while in monopoly, at the other end of the scale such power with the firm is substantive. Thus, as we move from left to right on the scale we meet rather gentle increase in pricing power the firms exercise in the market reaching the other end without climbing a fence or jumping across a ditch. In this chapter, we shall discuss pricing issues under perfect competition. The discussion is largely a response to the first of the questions we raised above: single price with different

Two basic questions in price formation are (a) how a single price for identical commodities is formed as production costs of producing it are not the same for different firms and (b) how can a firm charge a price different from others for its product if it so wants? Answers to these questions lead us to market structures.

costs. But before proceeding further, we must look in some detail at the question of profit maximization which is regarded, as mentioned earlier, the primary goal of a business firm irrespective of the market structure in which it operates.

Figure 6.2 *Market structures differ with reference to the degree of pricing power the firms have in each case*

BOX 6.1

Free Markets: Adam Smith versus Karl Marx

Adam Smith is famous for his view that individuals' pursuit of their own interest invokes in them a sort of self-discipline enabling markets to regulate their behaviour through completion so as to maximise their benefit and of the society as well. Markets produce this ideal result automatically and we should therefore leave them free; public intervention in their working is not advisable. The passage from Smith's *Wealth of Nations* regarding self-interest—the invisible hand—and market freedom reads as follows:

...Every individual necessarily labours to render the annual revenue of the society as great as he can. He generally, indeed, neither intends to promote the public interest, nor knows how much he is promoting it. By preferring the support of domestic to that of foreign industry, he intends only his own security; and by directing that industry in such a manner as its produce may be of the greatest value, he intends only his own gain, and he is in this, as in many other cases, led by an invisible hand to promote an end which was no part of his intention. Nor is it always the worse for the society that it was no part of it. By pursuing his own interest, he frequently promotes that of the society more effectually than when he really intends to promote it. I have never known much good done by those who affected trade for the public good.

Smith was deeply religious, and saw the 'invisible hand' as the mechanism by which a benevolent God administered a universe in which human happiness was maximized. He made it clear in his writings that quite considerable structure was required in society before the invisible hand mechanism could work efficiently.

In contrast, for Karl Marx—a keen reader of Smith—production under capitalism creates great trouble. He demonstrated that a capitalist society worked in a way that the rich factory owner benefited and the poor factory workers lost. In his view, the capitalist system was inherently meant to benefit the rich and exploit the poor; he believed that free markets helped the system achieve this end. He wrote:

All the bourgeois economists are aware of is that production can be carried on better under the modern police...on the principle of might makes right. They forget only that this principle is also a legal relation, and that the right of the stronger prevails in their 'constitutional republics' as well, only in another form.

Marx saw the suffering workers eventually rising in revolt and capture political power to demolish the capitalism and its exploitative institutions.

Smith and Marx belonged to the same classical school of thought. That their views on market capitalism are poles apart is the result of difference in time and space. Smith wrote his theoretical dissertation in an era when great scientific discoveries and inventions were taking place. An elated William Godwin wrote in his *Political Justice* that man will no doubt never become immortal, but it is possible that the span of life may be lengthened indefinitely. A major technological breakthrough was around the corner. Smith saw industrial revolution knocking at the doors of England. Naturalism and optimism filled his *Wealth of Nations* (read England) in the hope of a coming paradise.

In contrast, Marx saw the phenomenon after it had unfolded the misery it brought in its train for the toiling masses, paradise though was there for the rich. The tyranny of unregulated markets was widening the gulf between the haves and have-nots. More so in the Marx era, Germany was lagging far behind England in the industrialization race.

The difference between Smith and Marx is largely accounted by who saw market capitalism unfolding when and from where.

6.2   PROFIT MAXIMIZATION

Profit maximization as a business goal has two aspects. First is the motivational aspect: do firms really want to maximize their profits? The other is the operational aspect: can firms maximize their profits if they so desire? For, desire does not ensure success. (Remember that we are talking of economic profit (EP) because normal profit is part of production costs.)

On the motivational plane, the pursuit of maximum profit tends to raise visions of greed and is often questioned on ethical grounds, more so in Islamic economics. To erase such impressions, claims in mainstream economics abound since long; that firms neither aim nor attempt at maximizing their profit and for two reasons. First, there has been a separation of ownership from management with the rise of corporations as the dominant form of business organization. The number of corporate shareholders is often very large and widely dispersed. They neither have the desire for nor the means of knowing if the profits of their firm are in fact being maximized. What keeps shareholders happy is a *satisfactory* not a *maximum* dividend. Again, corporate managers are professionals working for their own compensation packages. They are interested in their reputation and continuation in the job. They attempt to maintain profits of their firm at levels that would keep them secure. Security, it is argued, need not lie in maximizing profit. Promotion of goodwill, non-provocation of rivals, share of the market and sales maximization, among others, seem to have replaced profit maximization as the business management goals.

There may be a measure of truth in such claims but they do not clinch the point against profit maximization simply because such large-sized corporations do not constitute the model of a firm that lies behind and explains price theory in general, rather the notion of a firm is *heuristic* as described earlier.

Second, *ex post* (realized) profit cannot be changed. The notion of maximization is relevant only to *ex ante* (future or planned) profit—profit functions extend into the future—they are imprecise and overlapping.

In the face of resource scarcity, maximization of profit an imperative for efficient performance as it implies minimization of costs. The assumption can be retained in Islamic economics subject to the provision that prescribed norms of behaviour are not violated.

Maximization concept is applicable only to *ante* profit which is an uncertain entity. Thus, it is directional only: *ex post* profit cannot be proved to be the maximum that could be earned. Desire does not ensure results.

Future *ex ante* profit being vague and uncertain, its maximization cannot be made *operational* even if it were having primacy among the business goals. However, non-operability is in no way unique to profit maximization. In fact, the position, at times even the shape, of the curves that you come across in economics textbooks, including the one you are reading, cannot be fixed on a diagram if we are so mindful of the uncertainties in economics. But we do so with an air of authority because these diagrams are merely explanatory tools based on abstractions. Uncertainty can make most sensible decisions look idiotic if expectations fail, but that does not make efforts of peeping into the future meaningless. If the results of human effort, including one at profit maximization, were entirely and always at the mercy of chance, intelligence would hardly have any role in human life. Decision-making ability productive of results becomes scarce and hence valuable only under uncertain conditions.

Mainstream economics has some good reasons for retaining profit maximization as an analytical assumption. Price theory, the core of economic science, cannot stand erect if its profit maximization assumption were removed. All concepts of efficient resource allocation and performance will become shaky and imprecise. The critics of the assumption, Islamic in particular, have not so far been able to offer an alternative behavioural rule for the firm with the same, if not superior, predictive value and ability to lead empirical research for testing theoretical conclusions.

Islamic economics also need not throw away the baby with the bath water. As indicated in Chapter 4, the notion of maximization per se is value neutral: what is maximized, how and to what extent are the decisive questions. More important is that maximization is only a *directional* concept. Under dynamic uncertain conditions, no firm can say for sure what the maximum amount of profit it would like to obtain is. Remember that, the notion of fair profit Islamic economists advocate for replacing that of the maximum is no less vague. Interestingly, fair profit, could well be the attainable maximum under perfect competition.

> Despite some scathing criticisms, mainstream economics has retained the profit maximization assumption, for it has a predictive value and no better behavioural norm is available to replace it for erecting price theory. Islamic economics also need not throw away the assumption for the same reasons: it can be made to operate within the confines of Shari'ah.

BOX 6.2

Markets and Islam

Islam places legitimate business in *real* goods and services, in its widest sense, among the most beneficial and the noblest of vocations for earning a living and acquiring wealth. Markets and their performance have always been a focal point in Islamic writings. For instance, in his letter appointing al-Ashtar as the governor of Egypt, Caliph Hazrat Ali wrote:

> *...And all of these (soldiers, taxpayers, judges, administrators and secretaries) have no support but the merchants and the craftsmen through the goods which they bring together and the markets which they set up. These provide for the needs of (these) classes by acquiring with their own hands goods to which the resources of do not attain ... then make merchants and craftsmen your own concern and urge others to do so, for they are the basis of benefits and the means of attaining convenience* (Tabatabai, 1982).

Business in the Islamic system has added esteem for two reasons. First, Islam sees business as *fard kafaya*, i.e. a duty whose performance is obligatory for all Muslims in general, but when performed by some of them, absolves others from their responsibility in the matter. The requirements of the community as for the soldiers, doctors, teachers, jurists, and administrators are some of the examples of this category of obligations. The application of the principle to business implies the achieving of a self-reliant economy. Thus, those joining business, fulfil religious obligation in a significant and risky sector. Second, Islam accords respect only to *honest* traders; for there is presumably the greatest temptation to ignore demands of honesty for increased earnings in business. The Qur'an refers time and again to greed and love for worldly gains among the weaknesses of humans. Thus, Ghazali pertinently remarks:

Profit cannot but be fair if business follows the (religious) instructions. But the trouble is that people do not remain content with relatively small (profit) and they cannot earn more without violating the injunctions (Ghazali 1955; 92).

The mundane being in man tends to overpower his moral self, more so in business than elsewhere. The moral code of Islam for market behaviour focuses mainly on protecting the consumer. Modern economies are of course not oblivious to consumer protection, but there are significant differences in approach and attitude. Broadly speaking, moral conduct of Islamic vintage is part of developing *human personality*; piety has to grow *within* believers, rather than enforced from outside. In fact, moral norms are no part of mainstream economic theory. However, if Islamic norms of behaviour are not imbibed by the believers, their markets would rarely have features productive of distinctive results. The main elements of an Islamic market conduct are as follows.

1 Islam imposes a number of obligations on the sellers with regard to measurements, quality of goods, their prices and provision of information to the buyer (Ghazali, 1955). *Scales are the symbol of justice* (Qur'an 27:25). The traders are required to keep standard weights and measures, and use them scrupulously. It is better to error on the side of giving more while selling and prefer to accept a little less when purchasing to avoid harming the other party, even unknowingly. Ghazali derived this rule presumably from the following verses of the Scripture: *Woe to those who deal in fraud, those who when they have to receive by measure from me take full measure but when they have to give by measure or weight to men give less than that* (Qur'an, 83: 1-3).

2 Goods sold must conform to declared quality or description; they must be suitable for meeting the purpose stated by the buyer if he relies on the seller in that matter.

3 The price a seller charges for a commodity should not be more than what rules the market (Ghazali, 1955). The Shari'ah condemns any attempt at raising prices by creating artificial scarcities e.g. through hoarding or cornering the supplies. If markups were to be used, the addition over costs, some jurists hold, should be within one-third of spot price. Others prefer to leave the margin to the sellers' discretion presumably because compulsion may not always be the best course to make sellers charge reasonable prices. It is better, they feel, to invoke in traders an urge for compassion.

4 As a distinct departure from the mainstream, Islam insists that not only should the seller desist from undue praise of his wares, he is under obligation to reveal to the prospective buyer defects, latent or patent, if any, in the goods offered for sale. From Ghazali's explanation, of this norm, two implications of major import follow in my opinion.

   a) First, the provision requires the producers to implement strict quality control norms for their products and urges the sellers to accept from the suppliers only such of the goods as are free from defects. Despite adequate care, if any of them—manufacturer or distributor—fails in his responsibility, he alone must bear the consequences in the form of, say, reduced price, or even loss.

   b) Second, the provision sets some norms for 'sales management' which today tends to become over glamorous, diversionary, wasteful of resources, manipulative of consumer preferences, aggressive and even deceitful. The Islamic norm seeks to keep the sales management sublime, purposeful, informative and socially beneficial transportation and communication.

5 In principle, Islam stands for free markets requiring the government to merely oversee if the tenets of the Shari'ah are being observed in letter and spirit. A leading Islamic jurist writes:

If people are selling their goods according to commonly accepted manner without any injustice on their part and the price rises due to the decrease of the commodity [qillat-al-shay] or due to increase in population [kathrat-al-khalq] then this is due to Allah [no intervention is required] (Ibn Taymiyyah 1976, 24; (parenthesis content is interpretive, non-textual).

Similar opinions are expressed in the writings of Abu Yusuf and Ibn Khaldun. However, non-intervention in the market in case the fluctuations in the demand and supply of a commodity are the result of natural factors is a tiny, though important, part of the story. *If we assume that an Islamic economy is in operation*, the involvement of the government in the market would not be occasional or temporary. The fuller picture of an Islamic system shows the government co-existing in the market with the private sector on a permanent and stable basis. It can be seen as a planner, supervisor, producer and consumer. What follows is based on this sort of perception but much of it may be found relevant to mainstream economics as well.

6 Even as Islam upholds freedom of markets but state regulation is not ruled out for legitimate reasons. The following are a few examples.

 (i) To oversee the performance of markets so that the violation of Shari'ah principles, norms and standards are adequately observed

 (ii) To ensure that provision for public goods and, especially adequate availability of goods for meeting the basic needs of the masses—food, clothing, shelter education and health care are available.

 (iii) Environmental care is being observed as per the Shari'ah norms. The social well-being is not compromised for private gain the well-known market failures are mostly absent from the economy. Poverty is reduced and markets do not aggravate income and wealth inequalities.

Source: Zubair Hasan, Markets and the role of government in an economy from Islamic perspective, *Islamic Economics Encyclopaedia,* Part 3 – Islamic Foundation, UK.

6.3 PERFECT COMPETITION

Mainstream economic principles have mostly been led by ground realities. The industry in England was dominated until the close of the 19th century by tiny owner operated business firms. The scenario inspired what came to be known as, the perfect competition model in price formation theory.

Adam Smith (1776) argued that the pursuit of self-interest was not likely to create a conflict between the individual and social interest. He thought that competition among the sellers and the buyers in the market would keep prices in reasonable relationship with production costs and would act as an effective check on excessive business profits. He also believed that a system that promotes the individual interest would automatically promote that of the society because society is but an aggregation of individuals. The business scene around Smith shaped and largely justified his belief.

In his times, industries in England and elsewhere were dominated by tiny owner-operated firms mostly producing a single commodity in a rather 'open' industry. Individual proprietorship was the dominant form of business organization though partnerships were not rare. Even Alfred Marshall, in the first edition of his *Principles* (1898), likened industry to a forest where firms, like trees, competed for survival and growth. The owner-manager invested mainly his own money, energy and assets in business took all the risks and managed it for personal gain. Competition was intense and profits were not large. It was this early model of business that gave economics the concepts of firm, entrepreneur, managerial skills, opportunity costs and normal profit.

6.3.1   The Model

Early writers on the subject did talk of competition and indicated its implications but it was much later that economists constructed the *formal* perfect competition model to analyse the pricing of goods and services. The hallmark of theoretical models is their ability to predict however roughly the behaviour of economic agents. The model of perfect competition has been developed to predict how much output a competitive firm is likely to produce. The model is a purely theoretical structure—a sort of benchmark to assess reality but itself having no real content. It rests on the following assumptions. There is no apparent reason why the model cannot be used in Islamic economics as a tool for the same purpose.

1. **Firms produce a standardized product**: In a perfectly competitive market, all firms are supposed to produce an *identical* product such that the product of one is a perfect substitute in the eyes of the consumers for the product of others. Wheat and cucumber are the examples. This is a stringent condition rarely satisfied in actual markets. Mannerism and appearance of sellers may make their product look different from others. All shirts can be of the same cloth, colour or design and yet could be different in stitching. Sugar could be white and sweet but the crystal size may differ. *The assumption essentially means that buyers will not have any preference for the product of one firm to the exclusion of others except for difference in price.*

2. **Individual firms cannot influence price**: Each firm produces such a tiny proportion of total output that it cannot influence the market price by its own *individual* action. It must believe that market price will not be affected however small or large output it may produce. This can be a realistic condition if the number of firms producing the commodity is very large. Thousands of farmers produce wheat in Pakistan. If in a particular year, anyone of them decides not to cultivate wheat at all or doubles the acreage under that crop, his action alone will not change the price of wheat in the market. The assumption means that *firms in a perfectly competitive market are price takers; they have no pricing power.*

3. **Perfect mobility of production factors**: Capital and labour can be shifted between uses without any hindrance. The implication is that if there is opportunity in the opinion of a firm to earn a higher profit in another line of production, it can

exit from the present industry and enter the one it thinks is more profitable. The assumption sees the movement of firms in pursuit of profit as unrestricted between industries. The assumption is not very realistic, though it could be a bit more operational in the long run. Nowadays, it is not always necessary for workers to move out in search of jobs to new locations. Multinational firms move out to where cheap labour is available. This is one reason why multinational corporations move to developing countries so often. But such firms are no part of a perfect competition model.

4. **Perfect knowledge of the market**: A firm can leave an industry only if it knows that there are opportunities to earn higher profits elsewhere. Likewise, a consumer will not buy from a seller if he is aware that he can get the same thing for lower price from another. Transportation costs could still create price differences between localities. Perfect competition model assumes away the existence of such costs. Buyers and sellers must also have complete knowledge of the market. This is a difficult condition. Some like to interpret it more liberally: to them, it means that sellers and buyers have easy ways to gain adequate information for choice making. However, even in this sense the assumption may create problems.

> The perfect competition model is a heuristic model; away from reality. It serves as an ideal benchmark to measure the departure of reality from the ideal. It is based on some very stringent assumptions with the result that firms have no pricing power: they are price takers, not price makers.

6.3.2 Pure Competition

Pure competition is a somewhat realistic reduction of the perfect competition model.

It is felt that the assumptions of that model, especially the requirements of perfect factor mobility, and complete market knowledge on the part of buyers and sellers make it grossly unrealistic. So, economists, especially in the US, tend to relax these assumptions for converting the model into what is called *pure competition*. It retains the assumptions of a very large number of buyers and sellers in the market, a standardized product, sellers being price takers and free entry–exit facility for the firms. However, we shall see later that the purification effort reduces the utility of the model as an analytical tool in the case of input pricing, labour especially.

> The pure competition model is closer to real world situations as it does away with some of the very strict assumptions of perfect competition.

Perfect (or pure) competition model is a *limiting case* of market structures where assumptions reduce the pricing power of individual firms to zero. Even though imaginary, the model provides useful insights into the output policies the firms pursue for achieving their profit maximization goal.

Under perfect competition, a firm has no pricing power. Price is handed down to it by the market. It has only to decide how much it will produce and sell at that price in the short run, and is that price from the long-run viewpoint attractive enough for it to continue in the present industry or it must shift to some other line of production. Let us have a look at the short run choices of a firm working in a perfectly competitive industry.

The assumptions on which the perfect competition model rests are grossly unrealistic. But that is characteristic of most models which attempt to simplify real world complexities to focus on certain specific relationships. The major difficulty with the model is that under it a firm can produce *without limit* at the given market price. Logically, some firm must sooner or later grow large enough to acquire pricing power against the presumption of the model. Thus viewed, the model tends to (and does) collapse under its own weight.

6.4   PROFIT MAXIMIZATION IN THE SHORT RUN

6.4.1   Total Revenue–Total Cost Approach

We may begin with an example. Mohammad Noor Alam is a Bangladeshi artisan. He produces, as others in the trade, coir cushions of a standard design. These are sold in the market at Taka 500 a piece. Table 6.1 presents his weekly statement of output, costs and revenues. You can see that his profit is maximized when he produces six cushions a week. The breakeven point—revenue *first* time equals full cost—occurs when the output is 4 units a week. We show these facts in Figure 6.3. Here, the TR curve of Noor's firm working under perfect competition is a straight line. (Why?) It informs us that P_1 is the breakeven point of the firm. (Why not P_3?) The firm earns maximum profit when the output is 6 units, i.e. where the tangent to the total cost curve is parallel to TR, the total revenue line.

> As short run by definition is a time span where in a firm the capacity of some of the factors is not fully utilized, factors and costs both get divided into fixed and variable. One course a firm may take for profit maximization is to focus on total costs in relation to total revenue.

Table 6.1 *Noor's input, output and cost statement for a week (amount in RM)*

Output	Total fixed cost	Total variable cost	Total cost (TC = FC + VC)	Total revenue	Economic profit
(Q)	(FC)	(VC)		(TR)	(EP)
1	1,260	1,240	2,500	500	–2,000
2	1,260	2,240	3,500	1,000	–2,500
3	1,260	1,740	3,000	1,500	–1,500
4	1,260	740	2,000	2,000	000
5	1,260	40	1,300	2,500	1,200
6	**1,260**	**260**	**1,520**	**3,000**	**1,480**
7	1,260	1,050	2,310	3,500	1,190
8	1,260	2,740	4,000	4,000	000
9	1,260	4,490	5,750	4,500	–1,250
10	1,260	6,280	7,540	5,000	–2,540

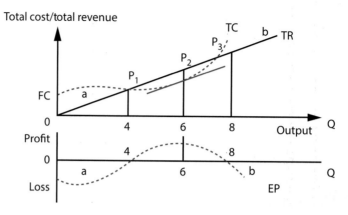

Figure 6.3 *Revenue, cost and profit*

Exercise 6.1

Notice that in Figure 6.3, the EP curve looks like the inverse image of TC. This is so as the TR is a straight line. Elaborate.

Exercise 6.2

The area between the TR and TC curves over the 4 to 8 unit's range of output is the profit zone. What do the areas before and after this zone show? Explain your answer.

Exercise 6.3

In the top panel of Figure 6.3, TC first rises then falls before it starts rising again. Can you say how the returns to the variable factor labour must be behaving in Noor's firm with an increase in employment?

Exercise 6.4

From Table 6.1, mark on the following ray, the level of output at which each of MC, AVC and ATC is the lowest on a 0 to 10 scale. For unit 10, the MC has fallen but ATC continued to rise, why?

MC   AVC   ATC

0   1   2   3   4   5   6   7   8   9   10   Output

Note: The student has to find MC from the total cost column

Exercise 6.5

$TC = (X^3 + 10X^2 + 50X) + 100$ is a total cost function where X stands for output. Find the fixed cost, variable cost, total cost, average fixed cost, average variable cost, average total cost and marginal cost. Take the range of output (X) from 1 to 10 and fill the data in the following table:

	0	1	2	3	4	5	6	7	8	9	10
X											
X											
X											
Variable cost (VC)											
Fixed cost (FC)											
Total cost (TC)											
Marginal cost (MC)											
Average variable cost (AVC)											
Average fixed cost (AFC)											
Average total cost (ATC)											

6.4.2   Marginal Cost–Marginal Revenue Approach

The profit maximization process for the firm is easier to explain and reveals more information if we use average revenue, marginal revenue, average total cost (ATC) and marginal cost (MC) concepts instead of the aggregative approach that we have just explained. Table 6.2 below gives the weekly data of Khurshid & Co. of Karachi who produce electric fans of a type that sell at PKR 1,000 a piece in the market.

Table 6.2 *Average and marginal revenues and costs (amount in PKR)*

Output	Fixed cost	Total variable cost	Total cost TC1VC	Average fixed cost	Average variable cost	Average total cost	Average revenue marginal revenue	Marginal cost
(Q)	(FC)	(VC)	(TC)	(AFC)	(AVC)	(ATC)	(AR=MR)	(MC)
0	2,520	0	2,520	–	–	–	–	–
1	2,520	500	3,020	2,520	500	3,020	1,000	500
2	2,520	980	3,500	1,260	490	1,750	1,000	480
3	2,520	1,420	3,940	840	473	1,313	1,000	440
4	2,520	1,910	4,430	630	477	1,107	1,000	490
5	2,520	2,490	5,010	504	498	1,002	1,000	580
6	2,520	3,490	6,010	420	582	1,002	1,000	1,000
7	2,520	4,790	7,310	360	684	1,044	1,000	1,300
8	2,520	6,429	8,949	315	804	1,119	1,000	1,639
9	2,520	8,213	10,733	280	913	1,193	1,000	1,784
10	2,520	10,013	12,533	252	1,001	1,253	1,000	1,800

Note: You may notice some minor discrepancies as fractions have been rounded up to 0 or 1.

We can use the information contained in Table 6.2 to explain the profit maximization or equilibrium position of a perfectly competitive firm in the short run. If we plot the data of the table on a graph paper, we will create a diagram close to Figure 6.4. Here, MC cuts both AVC and ATC from below at their lowest points and the $T_0 T_1 T_2 P$ the shaded rectangle shows the short-run EP of the firm when output is 6 units. Notice that MC equals MR not only at T_2 but at T as well. But T does not give us the equilibrium point. It is the breakeven point. (Why?)

However, in the short run, several other possible cases of a firm's equilibrium may arise under perfect competition. Consider, for example, the situation if the market price of the fans in Table 6.2 were (i) 477 or (ii) 450 instead of 1,000 a piece. Recall also that in the short run, a firm cannot by definition leave the industry. Its only choice is either to continue production at the current price or to shutdown in expectation of better times to return soon.

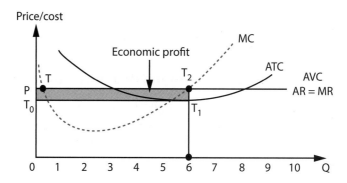

Figure 6.4 *Profit maximization using average and marginal revenue and cost curves*

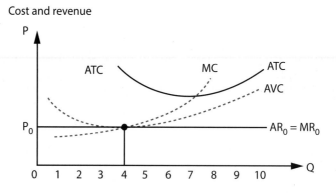

Figure 6.5 *A no-shutdown position*

In case (i), the market price of the fan at 477 just equals the average variable cost. Figure 6.5 depicts such a situation where the firm is losing only fixed cost. It will continue in business and keep its clientele intact. But in case (ii) with the market price at 450, even the variable costs are not covered (Figure 6.6). The best course of action for the firm to minimize losses is to close down until the situation becomes favourable.

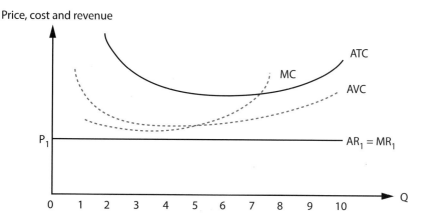

Price, cost and revenue

Figure 6.6 *Shutdown position*

6.4.3   Relationship between MP, AP, MC and AVC

In Chapter 5, we talked about the relationship between productivity and costs assuming labour alone as the variable factor. The relationship is precise and must be clearly understood. In Figure 5.8, we saw that the marginal product (MP_L) curve cuts the average product curve (AP_L) from above at its highest point whereas the MC crosses the ATC curve at its lowest point from below. The explanation is as follows. Notice that by definition we have:

We may link various types of costs to labour productivity.

$MC = \dfrac{w\Delta L}{\Delta Q}$, where w is the wage rate, L is the increase in labour and Q is the increase in output.

We know that $MP_L = \dfrac{\Delta Q}{\Delta L}$

Therefore, $\dfrac{1}{MP_L} = \dfrac{\Delta L}{\Delta Q}$

Thus, we also have $MC = \dfrac{w}{MP_L}$ $\qquad\qquad$ (6.1)

Likewise, $AVC = \dfrac{VC}{Q} = \dfrac{wL}{Q}$

And since $\dfrac{L}{Q} = \dfrac{1}{AP_L}$, we have $AVC = \dfrac{w}{AP_L}$ $\qquad\qquad$ (6.2)

Thus, from the definition of MC we get equation 6.1. We find that the minimum value of MC corresponds to the maximum value of MP_L. In the same way, equation 6.2 tells us that the minimum value of AVC equals the maximum value of AP. Recall in Chapter 5, the upper panel of Figure 5.8 plots the MP_L and AP_L curves as functions of labour (L), while its lower panel presents MC and AVC values as functions of output (Q) and the two curve sets look like the inverse images of one another.

Exercise 6.6

The total cost curve for a process in a ready-made garments factory is given as:

$$TC\ (Q) = 8 + 2Q$$

If output Q_1 is 4, verify that AFC = 2, AVC = 2 and ATC = 4. What shall be the value of MC if Q_1 is also the least cost output?

Exercise 6.7

There is a level of output from a production function at which the MP is lower than the average product, AP. For the same level of output, will MC be smaller or greater than the average cost of production? Give reasons for your answer.

Exercise 6.8

We stated above that MC = $\Delta VC/\Delta Q$. Verify this relationship from the data given in Table 6.2.

6.4.4   Cost Efficiency Again

Minimization of the cost of production is necessary in all circumstances, more so for a firm operating in a perfect competition market where it has no pricing power. Minimization of cost can alone maximize its profit. The firm faces the same sort of problem as the consumer faces in allocating income to various uses. The solution for a firm is also along similar lines. We discussed this in Chapter 5. Here we present an illustration of efficient resource allocation between distinct but interrelated processes of a firm.

Suppose the firm produces cloth and production has two distinct processes, spinning and weaving. It has to decide how a given quantity of cloth Q can be produced at the minimum cost of production. The objective can be achieved if it so allocates the monetary cost of resources to the two processes weaving (w) and spinning (s) that equates their MCs.

Now, suppose that:

$$MC_W = 12Q_W \tag{6.3}$$

$$MC_S = 4Q_S \tag{6.4}$$

$$Q_W + Q_S = 40 \tag{6.5}$$

Equating MCs we have,

$$12Q_W = 4Q_S \qquad\qquad (6.6)$$

Substituting from equation 6.5, $Q_W = 40 - Q_S$ into equation 6.6 we have,

$$12(40 - Q_S) = 4Q_S$$
$$480 - 12Q_S = 4Q_S$$

This gives us $Q_S = 30$

Inserting the value of Q_S into equation 6.6, we get:

$$Q_W = 10$$

And in both cases,

$$MC = 120$$

Figure 6.7 maps the results.

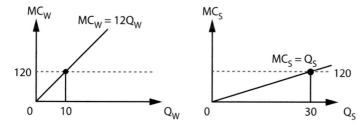

Figure 6.7 *Allocation of total output to minimize cost*

Exercise 6.9

In the example that Figure 6.7 demonstrates, nothing changes except that the total output is reduced from 40 to 24. Find out relevant values and construct a figure to show the adjustments.

This inter process allocation of resources leaves out the issue of their technical efficiency *within* each process. To illustrate, let us assume that two factors, labour (L) and capital (K), are used in both weaving and spinning. How shall the firm minimize their use in each of them? The rule is that the firm must equate the ratios of MP of each factor to its price (P) with others. If the ratio for one factor, say labour, is greater than the other, say capital, it is cheaper. (Why?) The firm will reduce total cost for the *same* output if it relates MP of each factor to its price (P) so that we have:

> Resources between users are efficiently allocated if the ratio of the marginal product of each factor to its price becomes the same.

$$\frac{\text{MP of labour}}{\text{Price of labour}} = \frac{\text{MP of capital}}{\text{Price of capital}} \qquad\qquad (6.7)$$

If the ratio for one factor, say, labour is greater than that for capital, labour is relatively cheaper. (Why?) The firm will reduce total cost for the *same* output if it substitutes labour for capital until the equality of the ratios is restored.

6.4.5 Profit Maximization in the Long Run

Industry and the firms

The foregoing discussion was based on the fact that firms under perfect competition are price takers. The price for them is determined by the overall demand and supply conditions prevailing in the market. The reason for this unidirectional relationship was that by assumption the time allowed for adjustment was not enough for individual firms to leave or enter the industry. However, in the long run entry or exit is possible, and the behaviour of firms may cause market price to increase or decrease. The relationship between the firms and the industry becomes bidirectional. It passes through an adjustment process as shown in Figure 6.8. The figure has two panels: one for the industry and the other for the firms.

> Change in supply demand remaining constant.

The output of the industry is shown in million units and for the firms it is measured in thousand units. We may start with a position where the product price in the market is P_1 and the output of the industry is Q_1 million units, that includes the output of firm A and B as the third firm C is in a shutdown position. (Why?) Now, this short run position melts into the long run adjustment process as we lift the entry–exit restriction.

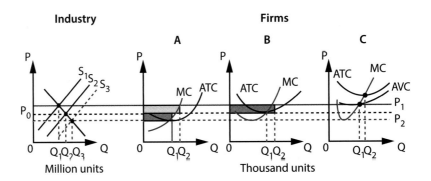

Figure 6.8 *Industry–firm interrelation, long-run dynamics*

As soon as the restriction is lifted, firms which were losing like C, have their fixed costs move out of the industry. Their action will have no impact on the market price (P_1) as they were not contributing to the industry's supply (Q_1). But since firms like A that are still making large economic profit (EP), might tempt *new* firms to enter the industry until supply increases to S_2 and the market price falls to P_2. The EP of A that the two shaded areas show will fall by the light-shaded area as the price slides down to P_0 and B's shaded EP will be wiped out completely. When the price touches the P_2 level as new entrants push up supply, A will only be earning normal profit and make firms like B which are earning only normal profit at P_1 to go bankrupt. That must make them all exit the industry in due time. Since such firms together may possibly

> Long-run equilibrium can be thought of in two ways: demand remains constant while there is change in supply or vice versa.

be contributing substantial quantity of the industry's output, their exit is likely to start contraction of overall supply towards S_0, pushing up the market price to P_0, where firms like C will be recovering their variable costs to mark time. In short, a reversal of the fall in price may be set in motion and a whole new round of entry and exit may well start afresh. Thus, it is highly unlikely that all firms in the long run will only be making normal profit in an industry. This could happen, if at all, only momentarily. All sorts of firms making EP, normal profit or winding up their businesses may exist in an industry in the long run.

Even though the long-run market price is determined by the forces of aggregate demand and aggregate supply, will not that price be corresponding during the adjustment process to the production cost of any individual firm?

Let us begin with a look at Figure 6.9 in search for an answer to this question. It is assumed that diminishing returns or increasing costs to scale operate in the industry; it rises with the passage of time. Thus, the supply curve in the industry panel of the figure is kept fixed and sloping upwards while demand rises through D_1, D_2 and D_3.

> Change in demand supply remaining constant.

The firms' panel contains three illustrative cases. Firms operating in any industry would be a replica of any one of them. To begin with, let the demand for the commodity be D_1 so that the market price is P_1 corresponding to the industry output, Q_1; all firms in the industry are obliged to sell their output at that price. Moving along the P_1 price line, we find that some firms would be making EP as A producing Q_1 output. (Can you identify the profit?) Some firms as B would be earning only normal profit with Q_1 output. C-type firms, where the price, P_1, does not cover even the variable cost, might be in the process of leaving the industry.

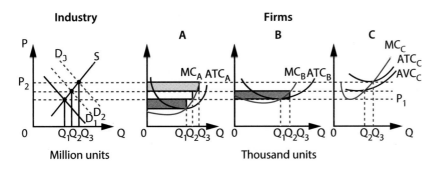

Figure 6.9 *Marginal firm: cost and market price adjustment*

Now, the demand for the commodity rises with the passage of time from D_1 to D_2, pushing up the market price to P_2. At this price, the output of A increases to Q_2 and its profit by the white area. For firm B, the higher price brings in EP as its output rises to Q_2. Price P_2 now covers the average variable costs of C and the firm may slow down its liquidation process. The output of the industry will rise to $Q_2 = Q_{A2} +$

$Q_{B2} + Q_{C1}$. As pressure of demand increases, price must rise further, say to P_3, so that the production costs of firms like C is also covered. The rise would push the output of the industry to meet demand at Q_3, the sum of increased output of the three firms, $Q_{A3} + Q_{B3} + Q_{C2}$. The profit of firms such as A and B will increase further by the black and white areas, respectively, while C will now be having normal profit included in its costs the price now covers.

It follows from the above discussion that if diminishing returns operate in an industry, long run is no different from short run; in either case the society has to cover in price the costs of the *marginal firms* like C until output rises sufficiently to meet societal demand Q_3. However, things are not so easy to explain in the long run if increasing returns to scale or decreasing costs phenomenon characterizes an industry. In such cases, more so under dynamic conditions, it is difficult to identify the firm whose costs the price must equal. Economists, therefore, make some additional simplifying assumptions to explain precisely the long-run industry–firm relationship. These are:

Determination of equilibrium in the short and long runs is not much different in industries where diminishing returns apply but difficulties arise when increasing returns to scale are involved.

1. All short-run adjustments are ignored in order to focus on the effects of long run adjustments. But the free entry–free exit provision is retained.

2. Individual firms in the industry have identical cost curves. This assumption enables us to avoid the difficult issue of identifying an average or a representative firm for explaining the equilibrium conditions.

3. The entry–exit provision for firms does not affect input prices, i.e. the location of the average-total-cost curves of individual firms does not change.

Some more assumptions are added to make the perfect competition model further unrealistic for explaining long-run equilibrium of an industry. The effort essence is to show that firms even here would earn only normal profit.

These assumptions further add to the already unrealistic and complicated nature of the perfect competition model. Its heuristic character sharpens. Figure 6.10 depicts the industry–firm relationship the model contains. The message of the figure is that EPs are a temporary phenomenon; competition ensures that in the long-run profits are but *normal* and *fair*. Plant utilizationis also optimal (at point T). Goods are produced at the least cost: *P = Minimum ATC*. So, consumers gain. At T, we also have P = MC, implying that competition ensures allocative efficiency as well (recall Figure 6.9 and the related discussion). In short, the long-run model shows capitalism as an efficient and just system. It is seldom mentioned though that these claims are no more realistic than the assumptions on which perfect competition model is based. Finally, what puts the question mark on these claims is the incompatibility of the constant or increasing returns with the notion of perfect competition: some firms may grow fast to acquire pricing power to make competition imperfect. Figure 6.10 has no more than a directional message. Interestingly, 'pure' models for deriving the principles of Islamic economics are rarely treated with such understanding. They are often brushed aside as resting on norms that are seldom put into practice.

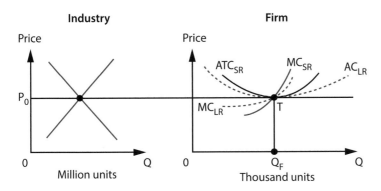

Figure 6.10 *Eventual long-run equilibrium*

6.5 PRODUCERS' SURPLUS

In Chapter 4, we had discussed the concept of consumers' surplus. That surplus is, in fact, one part of social surplus that growth of output continues to generate and enhance at a greater pace in modern societies. The other part of this surplus is that goes to the producers of goods and services. Price equals the maximum MC that the society has to pay in the form of price if it has no option but to buy that unit of the product. As all units prior to the marginal one would be sold at this price, a surplus over cost appears on them. In market equilibrium, the same unit is also the marginal unit for the consumers as its marginal utility equals price. Recall that the law of diminishing marginal utility governs consumer's behaviour, all units prior to the marginal unit yield to them a surplus of utility or consumers' surplus. Table 6.3 illustrates the emergence of both the surpluses. Here, corresponding changes in marginal utility and MC are kept identical in value, i.e. −100 and +100. So, the social surplus is evenly divided on either side of the price line. Figure 6.11 shows this division. As usual, the market price is determined by the aggregate demand and aggregate supply of the product in the industry panel. For firms A and B, the marginal utility curve remains the same as it is the average for all buyers. The relative share of the consumers and the producers in the social surplus would, therefore, depend on the slope of their original cost (MC) curve relative to the slope of MU curve. Thus, in the case of industry where the slopes of the two curves are kept equal, one surplus equals the other. However, for firm A, the slope of MC being greater than the slope of the MU, producers' surplus is larger. In contrast, for firm B, slope of MU is sharper and so the producer surplus is smaller. Notice that areas marked as 'a' in the figure beyond the point of equilibrium show negative producer surplus while areas marked as 'b' indicate negative consumer surplus. The sum of the two, i.e. the social surplus, will be negative.

As price equals marginal cost under perfect completion, producers earn under diminishing returns a surplus. Indeed, we have a social surplus divided between the consumers and the producers. Who will have a larger share would depend on the relative elasticity of demand and supply.

Table 6.3 *Social surplus under perfect competition (amount in RM)*

Marginal units of output	(1)	1	2	3	4	5	6	7	8	9
Marginal utility	(2)	1,000	900	8,000	700	600	500	400	300	200
Marginal cost of production	(3)	200	300	400	500	600	700	800	900	1,000
Price per unit	(4)	600	600	600	600	600	600	600	600	600
Consumer's surplus (5) = (2) – (4)		400	300	200	100	0	–100	–200	–300	–400
Producer's surplus (6) = (4) – (3)		400	300	200	100	0	–100	–200	–300	–400
Total surplus (8) = (5) + (6)		800	600	400	200	0	–200	–400	–600	–800

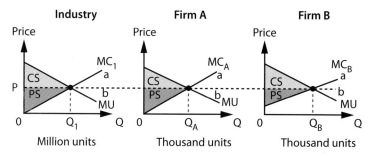

Figure 6.11 *Division of social surplus between consumers and producers*

Necessities of life have steeper MU curves; they generate more consumer surplus than comforts and luxuries. This presumably is one reason for Islam putting explicit emphasis on the fulfilment of basic necessities of life, and abhors expressions and display of one's riches. On the other hand, arms supply curves are steeper than of sewing machines; so, arms sales bring in more producer surplus. Nations may be tempted to produce more guns than butter!

6.6   EFFECT OF A PER UNIT TAX ON OUTPUT

A per unit tax on output raises price, results in dead weight and reduces social surplus.

Public authorities often impose a per unit tax on the sale of goods to raise revenue or curb the consumption of harmful things such as cigarettes. What is the impact of such a tax on the price of a commodity? The common perception is that price rises by the full amount of tax. Economists do not agree and show that the amount is split between the sellers and the buyers. Figure 6.12 explains their position. Here, $P_0 Q_0$ represents the equilibrium price and quantity bought and sold before the imposition of tax. When the unit tax $T_1 T_2$ is levied, the supply curve moves up parallel to the initial supply curve SS by the amount of tax to S + t position. Price rises from P_0 to P^*, i.e. not by the full amount of tax. Government gets B + S amount as tax but of this, B is borne by the buyers and S by the sellers. Area (a + b) represents dead weight loss; that no one benefits from the imposition of the tax.

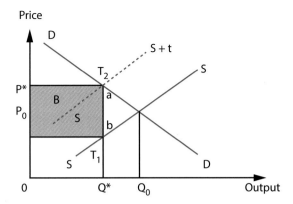

Figure 6.12 *Effect of tax per unit of output on price*

However, things are not as simple as the figure shows. The relative elasticity of demand and supply and the law of returns complicate the situation. For example, it is easy to see that if demand for a commodity were totally inelastic, it would be possible for the sellers to pass the entire tax amount to the buyers. The discussion of the complexities involved falls outside the scope of this introductory book.

Summary

- Market structures mainly differ with reference to two issues. First, if firms have no pricing power how do they maximize their profits? Second, if firms desire to have pricing power how can they obtain it? Here we deal with the first of these questions. The answer refers to a perfectly competitive market.

- The perfect competition model is a purely theoretical construct. It rests on the assumption that all firms in an industry produce a single standardized product such as wheat or cucumbers, they cannot influence price by their individual action, factors of production are perfectly mobile among alternative uses in the long run and parties to a contract have perfect knowledge of the market. There is no restriction on the entry into or exit from the market.

- The assumptions of perfect competition model are too unrealistic, especially its insistence on perfect factor mobility among alternative uses and complete market knowledge on the part of buyers and sellers. If we drop these two assumptions, we have what is described as pure competition.

- Profit maximization process in the short run is quite different to what the firms do in the long run. Profit maximization in the short run has two approaches: we may use the total cost-total revenue tools or the MC-marginal revenue apparatus for the purpose.

- In the short run, firms produce an output determined by the equality of marginal revenue and MC both equalling price. The difference of P = AR and ATC gives per unit profit. This multiplied by output Q gives us the maximum total profit the firm could earn. If the difference is zero, the firm would only be making normal profit included in the costs of production. However, the difference could be negative as well. In that case if the difference is equal to fixed cost only the firm will continue production, and if it is more than the fixed cost the firm will shutdown to minimize losses.

- If labour alone is the variable factor in the short run it can be shown that MC = w/MP and AVC = w/AP (MP and AP are both physical quantities of output). This shows that the set of AC and MC curves would be an inverse image of the AP and MP curves' set (see Figure 6.5).

- Firms can achieve cost efficiency in the short run if they so allocate the money expenditure on inputs between different processes that the MC in each process is the same (see Figure 6.6).

- In the long run, the distinction between variable and fixed factors of production ends. All factors become variable. Therefore, the distinction between fixed and variable costs also goes; all costs too become variable.

- In the long run, the possibility of new firms entering the industry and the old ones being able to leave it are of significance. Removal of the entry–exit restriction creates a two-way relationship between the firms and the industry. This relationship can be looked at in two ways: from the supply side assuming that the demand does not change and from the demand side assuming that supply remains constant.

- In a diminishing returns industry, as the short run melts into the long run, the firms in a shutdown state are first to leave the industry. But their exit does not affect either the market price of the commodity or the aggregate supply as they were not making any contribution to the aggregate output.

- Firms, for whom the price covered only the variable costs and were staying in the industry for a favourable turn in the situation, would now also leave. As such firms were contributing to the total output of the industry their exit is most likely to reduce total supply causing the price to rise.

- The rise in price would make EP appear for firms that were making just normal profits, and would enhance the profits of firms that were already making EPs. This would attract new firms into the industry, supply would increase, price would fall and the whole process would repeat itself but not necessarily along the old path.

- Another question in the context of industry–firm long-run relationship is: will the market price of the commodity not correspond to the production costs of any individual firm during the transition period? The search for an answer to this question leads us to look at the matter from the demand side of the market.

- With supply remaining constant, if the demand for the commodity rises price has to rise until the MC of the firm whose output is needed to meet the increased demand is covered. Such a firm we call as the marginal firm and it makes only normal profit in the long run. Other things remaining the same, the pressure of demand continues to raise price, extending the marginal firms and raising profit for other firms. New firms will be attracted to the industry pushing price and profits down. Further increases in demand would restart the adjustment process once again.

- There is no precise answer to the question of identifying such a representative firm under increasing returns to scale. To see that the perfect competition model remains meaningful some additional assumption are made: these include ignoring all short-run adjustments except the free entry and exit provision, holding that the cost curves of individual firms are identical, and the industry operates under the law of constant returns to scale.

- These assumptions help us show that in the long run all firms under perfect competition would only be making normal profits. The demonstration though complicated helps in showing that capitalism is both an efficient and equitable system.

- Since price must equal the marginal (average) cost of production of the least efficient firm whose output is needed to meet the societal demand and because all units of the product prior to the marginal must be sold at that price, a surplus over costs emerges on all prior to the marginal units. This is called the producers' surplus. This surplus added to the consumers' surplus gives us what we call the social surplus.

Glossary

Cost efficiency Efficiency in costs refers to either of these two things: firms produce maximum output with given resources or they use minimum resources to produce a given volume of output. Either approach leads to the minimization of production costs. Cost efficiency presupposes what we call allocative efficiency, i.e. scarce resources must be distributed among different uses that output ratios correspond to price ratios of resources. If the norms of both cost and allocative efficiency are met we obtain overall or economic efficiency in production. The concept of efficiency is now sought to be extended further by including value of environmental goods in production costs.

Market structure This refers to the extent of power each seller has to charge a price from the buyers different from the competitors for virtually the same product.

Perfect competition It is a hypothetical market design where all sellers of a commodity sell its identical units and their number (as also of buyers) is so large that none of them is able to influence its market price by his individual action, they are price taker, not price makers. Price of the commodity is determined by its aggregate demand and aggregate supply. The choice of the individual firm is whether to produce and sell at that price and if yes, how much.

Profit maximization This is an assumption guiding firms' behaviour in a free enterprise economy. This is an unrealistic proposition but guides price theory formation along realistic lines. An ex ante view of profit underlies the assumption. Therefore, from practical viewpoint it only means that the firm does not miss if it sees an opportunity to earn more from its given resources. Islamic economics need not have any reservations to the use of this analytical tool if the producers do not violate any Shari'ah norms of conducting business.

Concepts for Review

- Allocative efficiency
- Cost efficiency
- Cost–revenue relationships
- Market structure
- Perfect competition
- Pricing power
- Producers' surplus

- Profit maximization in the long run: industry–firm relationships
- Profit maximization: total cost-total revenue approach and MC marginal revenue approach
- Pure competition

Case Study 6.1

Profit Maximization versus Social Responsibility

Share capital is the foundation of a company. If shareholders well-being is not taken care of, the company may run into liquidation. Milton Friedman argued that 'the sole purpose of a business is to earn profit for its shareholders'. By implication, profit maximization is then justified for risks the investors take.

A company may earn huge profits for its shareholders, but it has a social responsibility of contributing to people's well-being. It lives in a social web and its success and failure have become matters of public concern. Theodore Leavin says '…today's profits must be merely adequate, not maximum. Businesses exist to serve the public'.

Source: 2008 Proceedings of the Academy of Business Economics.

Case Questions
1. Which of the above opinions would you support and why?
2. Is profit maximization assumption needed in the price theory formation from an Islamic perspective? If yes, with what constraints?

Case Study 6.2

Economies of Scale: Grameen Shakti

Grameen Shakti (meaning 'village power' in Bengali), established in July 1996 by Grameen Bank, aims to support this bank's poverty reduction mission by developing and delivering systems to rural households and businesses in Bangladesh. While the focus was on solar pv programmes, Grameen Shakti also supported wind and biomass projects, though on a much lesser scale. Grameen Shakti has been mandated to help connect rural areas to the world through (solar-powered) information technology. Although registered as an NGO, it is run, for the most part, as a for-profit enterprise. The company's solar pv programme represents its largest business line, purchasing solar pv panels and other systems components (i.e. batteries) from a range of foreign and local suppliers; and assembling, selling, installing, and, where necessary, financing them. The company expansion with reduction in per unit cost has been a manifestation of economies of scale.

To date, Grameen Shakti has installed over 77,000 solar pv systems, with a total installed capacity of 3.85mw (a power generation capacity of 16mw per hour). This has considerably improved lives and has provided cleaner energy to 700,000 Bangladeshis. As rural communities have become electrified, the company has been able to work toward achieving its secondary objective, that of connecting the rural areas of Bangladesh with the rest of the world through the service of information and communication technology. Computer education and Internet access provided by engineers at solar powered computer based education includes applications such as Microsoft's new technology and graphic design, as well as hardware installation and computer language. This successful company has diversified its operations to include the construction of 500 biogas plants to provide improved energy solutions to cooking.

(See the table below for a summary of Grameen Shakti's achievements.)
Grameen Shakti at a glance, 2007

Number of villages covered 25,000	Total beneficiaries more than 700,000 people
Unit office 227	Total employees 1135
Total installation of SHS 77,000	Installed power capacity 3.85 MW
Daily power generation 16 MW-hr	Installation of microutility system 1000 system
Installation rate Over 2000 SHS/ month system	Installation of biogas plant 500 (up to October 2006)

Source: Selling solar part II case studies.

Case Questions

1. Explain what you understand by economies of scale. Do you think that such economies will further reduce the per unit energy cost in Bangladesh?
2. What are biogas plants? Why rural areas are ideal place for developing this source of energy? Can you point out some of its uses?

Test Questions

6.1 One basic assumption of the price theory is that firms aim at maximizing their profits. Do you agree? Give reasons for your answer. Discuss in this context the motivational and practical aspects of the assumption.

6.2 State briefly the basic assumptions of perfect competition. Which of these assumptions are dropped and why to define pure competition? In your opinion, will the consequences of perfect competition and pure competition be identical? Explain your answer.

6.3 Explain what you understand by short run and long run in the price theory. Is it true that the distinction between the two is a matter of definition not of time span? Illustrate your answer.

6.4 Fill in the blanks in the following table:

Product price	Quantity demanded	Revenue		Costs of production (amount in RM)				
		Total	Marginal	Fixed	Variable	Total	Average	Marginal
4	0			8.4		8.4		
4	1			8.4		9.6		
4	2			8.4		10.6		
4	3			8.4		11.4		
4	4			8.4		13.2		
4	5			8.4		17.2		
4	6			8.4		24.0		
4	7			8.4		33.7		
4	8			8.4		48.0		

6.5 Using the price, output, total revenue and total cost data of the table above (Q6.4), construct a diagram showing the profit maximising output of the firm and also mark on it the breakeven point, total profit and loss areas on the same pattern as Figure 6.2.

6.6 Again, using the information provided in the table above (Q7.4) draw a diagram showing the equilibrium of the firm employing marginal revenue-MC approach as in Figure 6.3. What shall the firm do if the price of the product falls to 3? Explain your answer.

6.7 A transport company in Kuala Lumpur plies in the city both buses and taxies. Both are equally profitable. It has a budget of RM480,000 for the year 2006 to renovate its fleet. Based on past data, the management finds that the marginal renovation cost for buses B is $MC_B = 10\ Q_b$, and for taxies $MC_T = 15\ Q_T$. It is also known that MCs are constant and the fleet has 40 buses plus taxis. The company consults you on how to allocate the budget between the two services. Write a report for the company regarding the allocation including an explanatory diagram.

6.8 Write explanatory notes on the following:
(i) Conditions that would make all firms under perfect competition only earn normal profit in the long run.
(ii) Social surplus generated by an industry equals consumers' surplus plus the producers' surplus showing what would determine the division between the two groups.

6.9 Perfect competition is an economic fiction. Reality has nothing to do with it. Is this true? Give reasons for your answer. If you agree with the statement then why should we study price formation under perfect competition?

6.10 Assuming that labour alone is the variable factor in a production line, show that if MP of labour is rising, the marginal labour cost of production must be rising.

Web Exercise

Collect material on the concept of efficiency and its types in economics and write a note on the subject.

Forward Link

In this chapter we have discussed the market model and its implications at the end of perfect competition. It is a limiting model for measuring the departure in the actual life from the benchmark capitalist ideal. In the next chapter we shall introduce you to the other extreme case of market structure: the monopoly. This theoretical structure is almost as unrealistic as the model of perfect competition. But it is also useful as a guide to action.

CHAPTER 7

Monopoly and Pricing Power

LEARNING OUTCOMES

This chapter should enable the student to understand:

- The meaning of monopoly: A limiting market situation
- Monopoly and perfect competition differences
- The nature of pricing power a monopolist has
- Reasons that give rise to monopolies and Islamic view
- What profit maximization means to a monopolist
- Factors influencing monopoly pricing decisions
- Price discrimination: Meaning and requirements
- Markup pricing as a guide for Islamic finance
- Whether monopolies are always undesirable

Islam prohibits *iktinaz*, i.e. the hoarding of wealth for its own sake, especially without paying *zakat* on it (Qur'an 34:9; 59:7). It also condemns *ihtikar* or the cornering of goods—food stuffs especially—with a view to raise prices for enlarging profit. Both acts are exploitative of people and violate the Islamic norms of fair play. Islamic economists often read in these prohibitions a generic overall condemnation of monopoly in modern economies. This interpretation of the Arabic terms looks stretchy for monopoly as we know it today, appeared on the scene after the industrial revolution; about 1400 years after the Islamic prohibitions were announced. Mainstream economics also does not in principle support monopolies though allows them where needed. We present here an objective discussion on the subject.

7.1 THE OTHER LIMIT

In the preceding Chapter, Figure 6.1 on market structures showed perfect competition on the one end of the scale and monopoly on the other as the two limiting cases. You have learnt about perfect competition in the preceding chapter. Now, we discuss monopoly, the structure on the other end of the scale. A monopoly is a situation where a firm has sufficient control over the supply of a particular commodity to determine the terms and price for which others can have it. Monopolies face little competition in the market for what they provide. *Monopolization* refers to the process by which firms persistently acquire greater market share than what one could acquire under competitive conditions.

Even though monopoly is opposite of competition, it does not mean that the two have nothing in common. We shall see that economists in both cases use the same tools for analysis; firms in both have the same sort of goals and exhibit similar behavioural patterns in the market.

In monopoly, as in perfect competition, the logic of cost-benefit analysis provides the basic framework to investigate firms' decisions on the desirability of altering their current course of action. Also, maximization of profit remains the prime business objective in either case. However, the differences between the two structures are no less marked than are similarities and have different policy implications.

7.2 NATURE OF MONOPOLY POWER

Monopoly is opposite of competition. A monopolist has no rivals: he is not only the firm but the industry as well.

A monopoly in the *pure* sense is a situation in which there is a single seller of a product in the market having no *close* substitutes. There is, what Doel Jean once called, 'a gap in the chain of substitutions'. Notice that in monopoly, the distinction between the firm and the industry under perfect competition is that *the firm is also the industry*. There may, however, be many buyers for its product in the market.

This view of a monopoly is quite simple and straightforward. However, it is rare to find *pure* monopolies operating in practice. There may be only one cinema hall in a small town showing a particular movie. Again, there may just be one company allowed to sell mobile phones in a metropolis like Jeddah. Shall we call cases like these as examples of monopoly? The answer essentially lies in what one may regard a 'close' substitute in a particular case. The cinema hall could well be in competition with musical concerts or theatricals staged in the town as alternative sources of entertainment. Likewise, land lines may offer tough competition to mobile phones.

The key element that distinguishes a monopoly from a perfect competition firm is the slope of demand curve each faces. We have seen that a firm under perfect competition is powerless to influence price by its individual action. At a given market price it can sell as much as it may want; it has no incentive to reduce the price. If it charges more than the market it would lose all its customers to the competing sellers. Thus, the slope of the demand curve the firm faces is infinity.

The outputs that firms are willing to produce at various prices when added together horizontally provide us the supply curve for the industry which, in interaction with the demand curve, determines the price of the commodity. All firms in the industry have to sell their product at this price: they are price takers. On the other hand, the demand curve of a monopolist, like that of an industry, is downward sloping: it has a negative slope. The implication is that while a firm under perfect competition has no pricing power, a monopoly firm has. Nevertheless, the pricing power of a monopolist is restricted by the law of demand: he can sell more only by lowering the price of his product but he cannot raise the price without a reduction in sales. Figure 7.1 shows the comparative position.

In perfect competition, the demand curve a firm faces is horizontal, its elasticity being infinite. Monopoly, on the other hand, has a downward sloping demand curve; it can sell more only at a lower price.

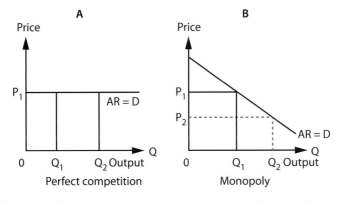

Figure 7.1 *Demand curve of a firm under competition and monopoly compared*

7.2.1   Measuring Monopoly Power

It is useful if one can know how strong or weak the pricing power of a monopolist is in a particular case. One way to measure the extent of this power is to look at the *potential* competitors to the monopoly product. One way often recommended is to measure the cross price elasticity of demand vis-à-vis the available substitutes for the monopoly product. A good illustration often quoted on the efficacy of the tool is the case of DuPont Corporation of USA. It was charged under the antitrust laws for having an effective monopoly in the selling of cellophane with 80% share of the market. The corporation argued that the coefficients of cross price elasticity between cellophane and its close substitutes—waxed paper and aluminum foil in particular—were sufficiently high to justify treating all wrap products as constituents of a single market. In the market so defined, the share of DuPont was even less than 20%. On that demonstration, the corporation was let off the hook: it was not a monopoly.

In fact, single firm monopolies are rare in modern economies, mostly there are firms scattered throughout the market with varying degrees of monopoly power.

The essence of monopoly lies in the ability of the firm to control the price of its product; it has pricing power. Its objective is not to charge a high or low price, but one that would make its revenue the largest.

7.3   SOURCES OF MONOPOLY POWER

What enables a firm to acquire monopoly position in the market? Four factors are often indicated; any one of them alone or in combination with the other(s) can result in the emergence of a monopoly firm in the market. The sources could be natural or legal or economic.

7.3.1   Natural Monopolies

Monopolies come into existence for a variety of reasons. An important source is control over the source of natural materials needed by the industry.

Exclusive control of a firm over the source of important raw material may give rise to a natural monopoly. An oft quoted example is the DeBeers Diamond Mines of South Africa. The company has almost an exclusive control over the supply of raw diamonds of the world. Synthetic diamonds have emerged on the scene and their quality has improved so much that even the experienced jewellers at times fail to distinguish them from the real. Still, many buyers who have no idea of the quality of a gem prefer a stone from the earth and they believe that DeBeers alone can supply it to them.

The water of some falls, springs and lakes in the world is believed to have unique curative properties or carry religious significance. But the public authorities controlling them do not charge a price for the use of their waters; it remains a free gift of nature. Cases of natural monopolies tend to become scarcer with the advance of science and technology. Appearance on the scene of cultured pearls, artificial diamonds and rolled gold has, for example, had over time a loosening effect on the monopoly prices of these commodities.

7.3.2   Legal Monopolies

Public authorities establish or permit private monopolies in utilities to avoid wasteful duplication of overheads which are often heavy and involve high risks.

In cases where fixed costs are very large and constitute the bulk of the total expenses needed to produce a commodity or provide a service, the granting of legal rights to a single firm for doing the job has often been the practice. We have legal monopolies in many countries in areas such as shipbuilding, aeronautics, electricity generation and supply, sewage disposal in metropolitan towns, air transport and the like. Creation of legal monopolies aims at avoiding duplication of facilities and wastage of resources. Imagine what would happen to the streets if two or three companies competed to lay and manage the parallel sewer systems in a town or railway services between two cities in the same corridor. Legal monopolies are often used in the area of public utilities or projects of national importance involving heavy overhead costs.

7.3.3   Scale and Monopolies

Heavy overhead costs often warrant monopoly creation for some other reason in addition to those stated above. Some lines of production such as steel making, paper manufacturing or match cutting have to be installed with a minimal capacity to be *economical*. Sometimes this capacity to be cost effective is so large, especially if the local market for the product is not large enough, that a single plant can produce sufficient or more than a country requires. As output expands such industries tend to experience economies of scale and decreasing cost of production allows availability of goods to society at falling prices. Thus, economies of scale may enhance social well-being.

Some industries prove economical only if organized on a very large scale. Here, competition cannot be enforced to take advantage of scale.

7.3.4   Islam and Monopolies

It is commonly believed that monopolies are always exploitative. Islamic economists in particular tend to have such a view. This is not correct. We noted earlier that Islam condemns hoarding (*iktinaz*) or cornering (*ihtikar*) of goods in the market with the intention to stifle competition and raise prices. We find nothing specific in the Scripture going against modern sort of monopolies Presumably, It is not perhaps feasible to derive from the Shari'ah an unequivocal condemnation of modern monopolies. Threat from monopolies essentially arises from the *misuse* of pricing power they tend to acquire, not from their big size *per se*. At times, a large size may be an imperative, as we saw, for efficient use of resources and the avoidance of their wasteful duplication. The recent US–Saudi tie-up to establish an aluminium industry complex in the kingdom involving multibillion dollar investment and slated for completion not before 2013 is a case in point. Of course, there cannot be a blanket support for monopolies. If they indulge in misdeeds and socially harmful activities, there is a need to curb them and legal frameworks are in place to address such situations.

Monopolies emerged on the economic scene after the industrial revolution. There is nothing in Islamic jurisprudence to justify an indiscreet condemnation of modern monopoly structures. Sometimes we need them in social interest. Also, we can take action if monopolies misuse their powers against social interests.

7.4   MONOPOLY AND PROFIT MAXIMIZATION

The assumption of profit maximization is also as relevant, though less compelling, in the case of a monopoly as it is in the case of firms operating under competition. In either case, firms attempt to earn as much economic profit as possible. However, this profit is in the long-run zero for a competitive firm but so is not the case with a monopoly. Monopoly profits are of a relatively durable sort.

Note that although a monopolist has pricing power, it is limited in the sense that market demand is independent of his decisions. Thus, he can fix the price (P) for his product or decide what quantity (Q) of it he may want to sell. He cannot fix both P and Q at the same time. If he determines one, the other is determined by the demand side of the market. Thus, a monopolist is always in search of a price–output combination that would maximize his profit.

A monopolist can raise the price of his product but will sell less and vice versa. So, the firm is not interested in price levels per se. Rather, it wants to arrive by trial and error at the price–output combination that would give it maximum revenue. Whether price in this combination will relatively be low and output high, or just the reverse, would depend on the nature of elasticity of demand for the product.

To understand the profit maximization process in a monopoly, let us imagine that Yawar found 10 coins of the 8th century when the foundation for his house was being dug. These coins, which only he possesses, have artefact value. No other person has such coins. As a monopolist, he wants to arrive at a price–quantity combination that would give him maximum monopoly revenue. Let us assume that his demand schedule is as given in Table 7.1. Figure 7.2 supplements the table. It shows marginal revenue (MR) and marginal cost (MC) curves. (Where?) Both are equal to zero along the X-axis. Thus, in equilibrium MR = MC = 0. The sale of six coins maximizes monopoly revenue; four coins remain unsold. The figure shows alternative revenue possibilities at a point in time, not over time. He may sell the remaining coins later in another place.

Table 7.1 *Monopoly revenue of Yawar*

Price (RM'000) P	Number of coins demanded Q	Total revenue (RM'000) TR = P × Q	Marginal revenue MR
10	1	10	10
9	2	18	8
8	3	24	6
7	4	28	4
6	5	30	2
5	6	30	0
4	7	28	−2
3	8	24	−4
2	9	18	−6
1	10	10	−8

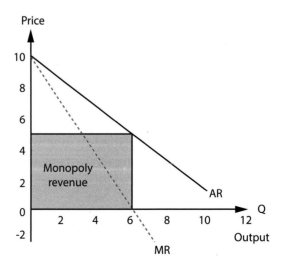

Figure 7.2 *Monopoly price, output and revenue*

Example 7.1 However, monopolies without production costs, like the one in the above example, seldom exist. Let us, therefore, see how monopoly works when costs are involved. Consider the case where the demand curve of the monopolist is as follows.

P = 100 − Q and his total cost, TC = 640 + 20 Q. What shall be his revenue maximizing price–output combination?

We shall have his total revenue equation as:

$$PQ = (100 − Q) × Q$$
$$TR = 100Q − Q^2$$

His MR equation will be:

$$MR = dTR/dQ$$
$$= 100 − 2Q$$

Likewise, from his total cost function, TC = 640 + 20Q, we get his MC:

$$MC = dTC/dQ$$
$$= 20 \text{ (a constant)}$$

In equilibrium,
$$MR = MC$$
$$100 − 2Q = 20$$

Therefore, equilibrium output, Q = 40. By inserting the value of equilibrium output (Q) in the demand equation P = 100 − Q, we have equilibrium price, P = 60.

The maximum revenue the monopolist can get is:

TR − TC when Q = 40
$$(60 × 40) − (640 + 20 × 40) = (2{,}400 − 1{,}440)$$
$$= 960$$

Table 7.2 provides a verification of the above results and Figure 7.3 helps us with a diagrammatic explanation of the illustration.

> The tools for arriving at and the conditions for reaching the revenue maximizing output combination remain the same as under competition MR = MC after crossing the breakeven point. In competition, this equality takes place at optimal capacity utilization; in monopoly before that. Thus, in monopoly price is higher and output lower than in competition.

Table 7.2 *Verification of the results (amount in RM)*

Price	P = 100 − Q	10	20	30	40	50	**60**	70	80	90	100
Quantity	Q = 100 − P	90	80	70	60	50	**40**	30	20	10	0
Total revenue	TR = P × Q	900	1,600	2,100	2,400	2,500	**2,400**	2,100	1,600	900	0
Total cost	TC = 640 + 20 Q	2,440	2,240	2,040	1,840	1,640	**1,440**	1,240	1,040	840	640
Profit	PR = TR − TC	−1,540	− 640	60	560	860	**960**	860	560	60	−640
Marginal revenue	MR	−80	−60	−40	−20	0	**20**	40	60	80	100
Marginal cost	MC	20	20	20	20	20	**20**	20	20	20	20
Average total cost	ATC = TC/Q	27	28	29	31	33	**36**	41	52	84	–

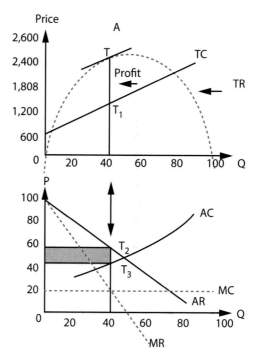

Figure 7.3 *Profit maximization under monopoly*

Exercise   7.1

Using the data in Table 7.1, construct a diagram on the same pattern as Figure 7.3 to show the relationship of total revenue with average revenue and MR. Show when elasticity of demand is 1.

Exercise   7.2

The demand function of a monopolist is given as $P = 200 - 2Q$. Construct his demand curve and total revenue curve showing their linkage. At what price is the revenue PQ maximized?

Exercise   7.3

Using the demand and cost functions of a firm given as $P = 50 - 0.5Q$ and $TC = 20 + 10Q$, construct a table showing the data for the average revenue, marginal revenue, average cost and marginal cost of the monopolist. Put output Q as 10, 15, 20, 25, 30, 35, 40, 45 and 50. Construct a table showing your results.

(***Hint***: Use the structure of Table 7.2).

A monopolist differs in another important way from a producer operating in a competitive market. With a rise in the demand for a product its price also moves up. In a competitive industry operating under diminishing returns, the MC of production climbs up with expansion in output. The long-run price has to cover the rising cost. Output expands while firms can earn only normal profits. This is not so with a monopoly firm: it can raise price with an increase in demand even when there is no rise in cost compulsion: the MC may stay unchanged. Figure 7.4 helps explain the point.

> The distinction between the firm and the industry is exemplified in the case of a monopolist. His firm is also the industry.

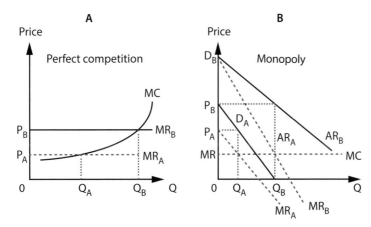

Figure 7.4 *With a shift in demand, the same marginal cost may equal different prices under monopoly but not under perfect competition*

Note that in panel A of the figure the price for individual firm rises from P_A to P_B as the increase in aggregate demand for the product pushes it up to that level in the market. The equilibrium output of the firm rises from Q_A to Q_B but MC (= MR) also becomes higher; it does not remain the same. In contrast, in panel B, marginal cost equals to marginal revenue (MC = MR) may remain the same as demand shifts upwards from D_A to D_B in monopoly, even as both price and output rise from P_A to P_B and Q_A to Q_B, respectively. We shall see that this difference between the two sorts of firms helps explain, among other things, why the monopolist may charge different prices for his product from customers in different market segments.

Exercise   7.4

Suppose the total cost and demand functions of a monopolist are:
$$TC = 50 + Q^2$$
$$P = 40 - Q$$
(i) Construct a table like Table 7.2 using the above cost and price functions. Also, construct a diagram like Figure 7.3.
(ii) Find its MC and MR functions. With MR = MC, verify that profit is maximized when Q = 10. What is the price and profit at that level of output?

7.5   FACTORS INFLUENCING PRICING DECISION

Contrary to common perception, the monopolist is not interested in charging a high price. He is in search of a price–output combination which will maximize his profit. It can be as much a high price small output combination as a relatively low price and large output combination. The choice between the two depends on the following factors.

1. **Price elasticity of demand**: For simplification, assume that the law of constant returns applies in production. We state that (a) the greater is the price elasticity of demand for the product of the monopolist the lower will be his price and larger the output. In contrast, (b) smaller is the elasticity of demand, higher will be his price and smaller the output. Figure 7.5 puts the two cases A and B side by side for comparison. The firms are assumed producing under constant returns, i.e. MC = AC so that the figure could highlight the consequences of difference in the elasticity. It is easy to see that the demand curve, $D_A = AR_A$ is less elastic than $D_B = AR_B$. (How?) Therefore, $P_A > P_B$ and $Q_A < Q_B$.

Exercise   7.5

In Figure 7.5, indicate the profit the monopolist will be making if the demand for his product is (a) elastic and (b) less elastic. Also, specify how much profit he would earn in each case, shading the relevant areas in the figure.

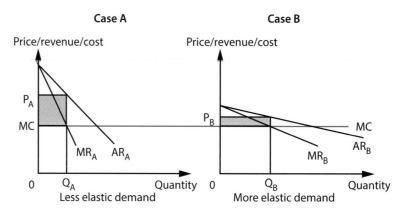

Figure 7.5 *Monopoly price–output combination and elasticity of demand*

2. **Nature of return**: In case the law of constant returns applies to production of a monopolist it will not affect his price–output decision: elasticity of demand as shown in Figure 7.5 will alone be the deciding factor. If the monopolist is operating under conditions of diminishing returns his output will be smaller

and price higher than that under constant returns. The reason is that a rising marginal cost curve will catch up faster with a falling marginal revenue curve than with a horizontal one. Figure 7.6 sketches the comparison. If diminishing returns apply in production, MC_{CR} rotates, so to say, upwards to become MC_{DR} and separates from AC_{DR} that now runs below it. Output contacts from Q_{CR} to Q_{DR} and price rises from P_{CR} to P_{DR}. Profit $_{CR}$ measured by $(P_{CR} - AC_{CR})Q_{CR}$ reduces to Profit $_{DR}$, as the shaded area shows.

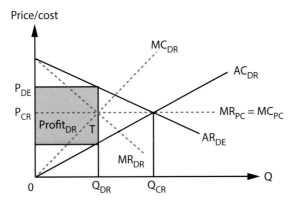

Figure 7.6 *Comparison of monopoly price, output and profit under diminishing returns (DR) and constant returns (CR)*

If a monopolist experiences increasing returns in production, due to economies of scale, he will sell relatively large quantity at a lower price to maximize his profit—lower than even under constant return. Figure 7.7 illustrates the case. Here, MR falls at a faster rate than MC; thus, the curves intersect one another at T and Q_0 specifies the equilibrium output. Intuitively, these results in general are likely to promote welfare more than those obtained under competitive conditions. Under such circumstances, monopoly is to be encouraged provided the benefit of cost reduction through output extension is passed to the consumers. This may call for a regulation of monopoly power or its installation in the public sector, more so in an Islamic economy.

The factors that influence the choice of price–output combination for revenue maximization are mainly two: elasticity of demand and the law of returns operating in the monopoly industry.

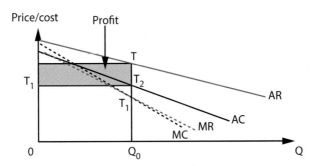

Figure 7.7 *Equilibrium of the monopolist under increasing returns*

7.6   PRICE DISCRIMINATION

We have shown in Figure 7.4 that an important feature of monopoly is that the same MC can be associated with different prices. This may tempt the monopolist to discriminate among the buyers of his commodity with reference to the price of virtually the same commodity if it promises to increase his profit. Railways charging different fares from passengers and different freights from goods, air transport charging economy class, executive and business class fares for the same distance, hard cover and paperbacks of the same book in publishing and so on are a few examples. Remember, however, that a monopolist can exercise price discrimination only if following conditions obtain in the market.

1. The market has buyer segments such that the price elasticity of demand for the monopoly product in one segment is greater than in the other. For example, hard covers target libraries that can afford to pay higher price for a book and need greater durability to hold it on the shelf over a long period of time for the use of its members. On the other hand, students need the book at a lower price; their object often not being to build up collection. Publishers know that more copies of a book can be sold at a relatively lower price.

2. It is not possible to transfer the commodity from one segment of the market to the other for resale assuming that transport cost between the segments equal zero. Note that in railway transport passengers classify themselves into various classes through purchase of tickets, while goods are classified into categories for charging different freights by the railways. (Why?)

A monopoly firm can charge different prices from sets of customers for virtually the same product if (a) it can segment the market on the basis of differences in the elasticity of demand and (b) it can ensure that the commodity cannot be transferred from one segment of the market to another.

Example 7.2 If these conditions are fulfilled, as they usually are in cases such as the one mentioned above, a monopolist can charge a higher price of his product in the market segment where the demand for it is relatively less elastic to enlarge his profit. To illustrate, consider the case where the demand function (D) of a monopolist in segment A of the market is $P_A = 120 - 0.75Q$ and in segment B is $P_B = 100 - 0.55Q$. His total cost function is $TC = 45Q$. The slope of D_A (0.75) being greater than of D_B (0.55), D_A is clearly less elastic than D_B over the same price range. We derive the two MR functions and verify that they are $MR_A = 120 - 1.5Q$ and $MR_B = 100 - 1.1Q$. The MC function will be $MC = 45$ and $AC = TC/Q$.

On the basis of this information, we construct Table 7.3 showing the equilibrium of the monopolist. Note that the bold figures show the profit maximization path: the MR in both segments of the market must be equal otherwise the monopolist will transfer units of product for sale from where it is low to where it is high to increase his profit. Thus, the monopolist sells 50 units of the commodity in segment A of the market at a price of 82.5 and 50 units in segment B where elasticity of demand is higher at a price of 72.5. Figure 7.8 highlights these facts. The thick broken line in the Q_{A+B} panel shows the preference for one curve on the other where it yields a larger profit.

Table 7.3 *Discriminating prices in monopoly enlarge profits*

Output	Market segment A				Common	Market segment B				Output
	10	20	30	40	50	40	30	20	10	
MR_A	105	90	75	60	**45**	56	67	78	89	MR_B
MC	45	45	45	45	**45**	45	45	45	45	MC

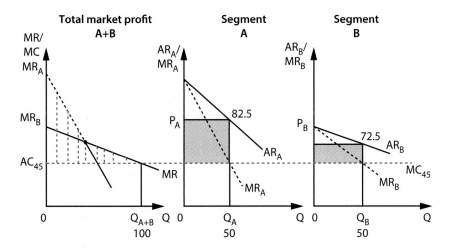

Figure 7.8 *Price discrimination under monopoly*

> Discrimination increases aggregate monopoly revenue.

Exercise 7.6

(i) A railway company provides transport services between Imaginepur and Khyalabad, running between them a Popular Express consisting of only lower class compartments with uniform facilities. Its demand function is stable at $P = 1250 - Q$ while its total cost $TC = 25Q + 0.5Q2$. The carrying capacity of the Express at 750 passengers per trip is always fully booked. Is the profit the company earns per trip equal to 75,000 money units? Verify.

(ii) The Popular Express intends to introduce upper class coaches in the train, keeping its carrying capacity unaltered. The change is expected to involve an additional fixed cost of 25 per passenger. The company expects that the number of upper class travellers will soon be around half of the capacity at a price 1.5 times the current fare. The lower class charges will remain the same as before. Will price discrimination benefit the company? If yes, by how much?

7.7   RULES FOR INITIAL PRICE FIXATION

An initial tool to start the trial for finding the most likely price–output combination is provided by a revenue-based measure of elasticity of demand given the marginal cost function of the monopoly firm.

Price elasticity of demand E_{DP} plays a crucial role not only in allowing price discrimination to enlarge profit, but also in providing a basic operational rule for the initial fixation of a profit maximizing price–output combination. Most firm managers have scant knowledge of the average and MR curves. Likewise, the information about the MC is also not available except over a narrow range of output. Economists have, therefore, formulated a rough and ready rule using the marginal concepts; it is of great practical utility.

For our purpose, let us recall the simple expression that defines MR:

$$MR = \frac{\Delta TR}{\Delta Q} = \frac{\Delta (PQ)}{\Delta Q} \tag{7.1}$$

It is clear that the additional revenue for an incremental unit of output has two elements: price (P) and quantity (Q). But in PQ, if increase in Q adds to revenue, the corresponding fall in P reduces it in some measure as the monopolist faces a falling demand curve. The reduction in price is not merely for selling the additional unit but also on all prior units. The net effect of the process on total revenue of selling an additional unit is measured as: [New price − (Old price − New price) preceding Q]. For example, if the monopolist could sell 10 units at 20 a piece but sells 11 units at 19 only, the increase in his revenue will be [19 − (20 − 19)10] = 9. This is because with a change in price, the elasticity of demand usually changes. One advantage of bringing elasticity of demand into the picture for monopoly price fixation is that even when we do not know the entire demand schedule, the effect on revenue of a shift in demand may still be measured. So, let us look more closely at the relationship between price, marginal revenue and E_{DP}. We shall be using elementary calculus for the purpose.

Example 7.3 Under normal demand conditions, we have:

TR = PQ

The first derivative gives us:

$$\frac{dTR}{dQ} = P + Q\frac{dP}{dQ} \qquad \text{(by product rule)}$$

But, $\dfrac{dTR}{dQ} = MR$

Rearranging the equation we get:

$$MR = P\left(1 + \frac{QdP}{PdQ}\right) \tag{7.2}$$

We know that elasticity of demand, $E_{dp} = -\dfrac{P}{Q} \cdot \dfrac{dQ}{dP}$

Thus, we get:

$$\frac{1}{E_{DP}} = -\left(\frac{Q}{P} \cdot \frac{dP}{dQ}\right)$$

As MC = MR, we can set up monopoly equilibrium as:

$$MC = \left(P - \frac{P}{E_{DP}}\right) = MR$$

Rearranging the equation we get:

$$MC.E_{DP} = (P.E_{DP} - 1)$$

Finally, we have the equilibrium price:

$$P = \left|\frac{MC}{1 - \dfrac{1}{E_{DP}}}\right| \tag{7.3}$$

Exercise 7.7

(i) Using the result in equation 7.2, show that $E_{DP} = \frac{AR}{AR-MR}$. Find MR, if EDP = 1, Price = 5.

(ii) Given, P = 120 − 0.75Q. Find elasticity of demand when Q = 50. (Insert Q = 50 into the equation to find P.) Use the inverse function rule to find dQ/dP = 1/0.75. Verify if EDP = 2.2.

(iii) Using the information in Example 7.2 on discriminating monopoly, find the elasticity of demand for segments A and B of the market separately. Also, calculate the total economic profit of the monopolist. Is it 3,250?

It follows from equation 7.3 that given MC and E_{DP}, the monopolist has an initial rule for fixing the price of his product. For example, in Example 7.2 we find the E_{DP} for the market segment, A = 2.2 in the state of equilibrium when P = 82.5, Q = 50 and the slope of the demand curve = 1/0.75. (Why?) We can easily verify that the price should be 82.5; by inserting values of E_{DP} and MC = MR = 45 into equation 7.3, as shown below.

$$P = \left|\frac{MC}{1 - \dfrac{1}{E_{DP}}}\right|$$

$$P = \left|\frac{45}{1 - \dfrac{1}{2.2}}\right|$$

$$P = 82.5$$

7.8 MARKUP PRICING AND ISLAMIC BANKS

Markup is the amount a seller adds to the cost price of a commodity to cover the overheads and possible profit. Monopoly power allows firms to use markup pricing. One recent illustration is the use of the device by Islamic banks under the broad category of *murabahah* or 'cost plus' transactions. These banks are not monopolies in the strict sense of the term, but they do enjoy some such power and use markups in most of their transactions. Markups are main contributors to their income.

It is not very clear what rules guide Islamic banks in deciding the markup for their cost plus charge in financing the deferred payment transactions. However, if a bank could have an estimate of the elasticity of demand for the products it sells, it may get some idea of its monopoly power in the matter. Lerner's index $(1/E_{DP})$ tells us that the larger is the elasticity of demand the lesser is this power. Thus, if a bank finds this power small, small shall be the markup it could use and vice versa.

The revenue-based elasticity of demand concept can come handy to Islamic banks in fixing the markup in murabahah *contracts widely used in Islamic banking.*

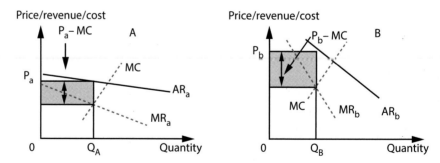

Figure 7.9 *Markup pricing and elasticity of demand*

Figure 7.9 provides a comparison of the two cases. In panel A of the figure demand being more elastic the markup (P_a − MC) is small compared to one in panel B where markup is larger because the elasticity of demand is relatively small.

To determine for an individual firm the price elasticity of demand for a commodity, say computers, an Islamic bank for example, seeks to finance under its deferred payment scheme may be much more difficult than determining the same for the market as a whole. Product specific sample surveys may be conducted to collect the needed data for specific products to determine the price elasticity of their demand. Individual banks can then use the information for determining the mark-ups. An illustration may help understand the markup pricing technique.

Suppose there are branches of several Islamic banks scattered over areas of a metropolitan town like Karachi. The price elasticity for the computer industry as a whole is estimated to be as 10. An individual bank would in all probability have a higher elasticity. So, if it uses a larger mark-up than others it is most likely to lose business to its competitors. We assume that the MC of the Bank Islam is PKR 45. Let us insert the available information into equation 7.3. We have:

$$P = \left(\frac{45}{1 - \frac{1}{10}}\right) = \frac{45}{0.9} = 50$$

Thus, Bank Islam may well be advised not to have a markup greater than (P − MC) = (50 − 45) = 5 that is not more than 10% in financing the deferred payment transactions. Markup will vary directly with MC of the bank, but a higher MC would be a competitive disadvantage. Notice that the price rises more than the tax amount.

7.9   MONOPOLY AND TAXATION

The money burden of a tax usually falls partly on the consumers and partly on the sellers. The share of each under all market structures depends on the shapes of the market demand and supply curves and in particular on their relative elasticity.

We saw in the previous chapter that under perfect competition the seller shares a unit tax on output with his customers and for that reason the price of the commodity increases by less than the full amount of tax. The case of monopoly is different: the price of the commodity *may* rise by more than the amount of tax depending on the demand and supply conditions. Figure 7.10 provides an illustration.

Impact of tax per unit of production.

We considered above the effect of a unit tax on output to keep matters simple, but there are other tax forms as well. A leading example is of an *ad valorem* tax that is a proportional tax on *value* of the product. Examples are state sales tax on cigarettes or T-shirts. The analysis of an *ad valorem* tax is roughly the same as of a per unit tax on production and leads to the same qualitative results.

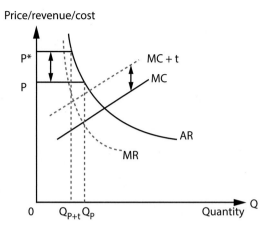

Figure 7.10 *Effect of a unit tax on monopoly*

7.10   MONOPOLY AND SOCIAL WELFARE

Market price equals average revenue of the firm. In perfect competition, average revenue equals MR which in turn equals MC. Thus, under competition price equals MC. It implies that the society pays for an extra unit of output the minimum it must, if it needs to have that unit. The rule price-equal-to-marginal-cost, therefore, constitutes a social welfare norm in economics. As monopoly power results in higher price and lower output relative to a competitive market, we expect it to make producers better off at the expense of consumers. But does monopoly power makes them better off in the *aggregate* is all the more important question from the social viewpoint?

We search for an answer to this question. To keep our discussion free of complications, we assume as under.

Monopolies may be a boon or bane for social well-being.

1. The monopoly is created through the purchase of competitive firms to merge them into a single entity.
2. The long-run average and MC curves of the monopolist remain the same as the competitive industry had before the merger.

Figure 7.11 compares the welfare position before and after the acquisition. Here subscript $_{(M)}$ indicates monopoly and $_{(C)}$ competition. We find that after merger, the price of the monopoly, P_M is higher than was the competitive price, P_C and output, Q_M is smaller than Q_C. Consumers' surplus is reduced as measured by the dark rectangle, $P_M T_1 T_2 T_3$. In addition, area $T_3 T_4 T_5$ shows the dead weight loss that monopoly creation inflicts on society. Thus, apparently monopoly structures do not seem to bring any improvement in the overall social welfare. However, let us examine if monopolies are invariably harmful to public interest or there could be situations for allowing them.

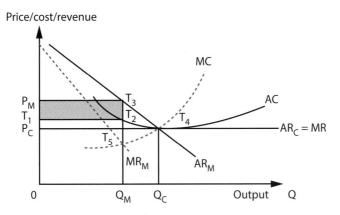

Figure 7.11 *Monopoly, competition and social welfare*

7.11 WHY DO MONOPOLIES EXIST?

Apart from natural or legal factors, monopolies come into being for a variety of reasons.

1. Perfect competition is an ideal model constructed to assess the departure of reality from the norm. In fact, it tends to hang itself by the noose of its own making. The demand curve facing individual firms being horizontal, they can expand output ad infinitum. Thus, some of the firms may become in course of time large enough to acquire monopoly muscles.

2. In an economy, firms are go-between two sets of market prices: one at which they sell their products to earn revenues and the other at which they incur costs to acquire their inputs. The gap between the revenues and costs is their profit. Competition is the force of discipline that tends to restrict their long-run profit to be no more than normal. So the firms are tempted to attack competition for enlarging their profit. Markets are left only with as much of competition as the firms have not been able to eliminate. Propensity to monopolize dominates the market scene.

3. We have discussed above in Section 7.3 on sources of monopoly power that technological progress has continually enlarged the minimal size of production capacity of plants to be economical or cost effective. In many cases, cost considerations leave little scope for a large number of firms to remain viable. Allowing monopoly power to emerge and flourish has long become a societal compulsion.

   > Monopolies in modern economies exist for a variety of reasons, especially because efficiency is often associated with economies of scale.

4. Large firms have been found more competent to withstand economic booms and depressions; empirical studies showed firms beyond a particular size measured in terms of paid up capital making profits even at the bottom of 1930s Great Depression. During the Asian financial crisis of 1998, bigger banks could face the trouble more successfully. Merger of banks—even forced—

has since been a distinct trend in some countries including Malaysia. The danger of monopoly power does not reside in the mere bigness of size; it flows from the *misuse* of that power. Some Islamic economists believe that Shari'ah is opposed to the presence of monopoly power in the economy. What the Islamic notion of *ihtikar* refers is the cornering of goods to artificially raise their prices, especially of food grains. It can hardly be interpreted as a barring of the existence of monopoly power of the modern sort.

BOX 7.1

Monopoly in Classical Islamic *Fiqh*

Numerous prophetic traditions proscribe monopoly. One of them was authenticated by Muslim (r.a.) in two versions: 'He who monopolizes is a wrongdoer' and 'only a wrongdoer monopolizes'. No legal text however defines outlawed monopoly, leaving the matter to juristic efforts of the Companions and later scholars.

A survey of jurists' views unveils two main tendencies with regard to monopoly. First, the majority of jurists, restricts the scope of outlawed monopoly. This may be referred to as the restrictive or the main view. The second is the view of the minority; it advocates a wider scope for actions and situations that fall under outlawed monopoly.

All classical jurists seem intensely aware of the fact that both 'legitimate trade and productive activity', and 'outlawed monopoly', involve a similar buy-keep-sell cycle. Understandably, they went to great pains to distinguish what they deem 'outlawed monopoly', lest they prohibit legitimate trading activities that Shari'ah not only permits but clearly encourages.

Mainstream jurists take a narrow restrictive view of 'outlawed monopoly'. They include the three schools of Hanafis, Shafi'is and Hanbalis. Their posture is well expressed in the Hanbalis' definition of monopoly as the buying of victuals and withholding them (from the market) in anticipation of selling at higher prices. In explaining this definition, jurists emphasize that:

  i. The term victuals (supplies) is more specific than food and is confined to basic essential items which can sustain humans for extended periods. Fruits and non-essential foods are not victuals.
  ii. Buying victuals for own consumption is not monopolistic, unlike buying for trade when prices are high.
  iii. The definition also stipulates *buying* as a requisite for monopolistic behaviour. Thus, saving the crops of one's own farm is not monopolistic.
  iv. Importing victuals from outside and withholding them for selling at higher prices is not monopolistic. This stands to reason; for a sinful monopolist buys from the local market thus putting town people in a straitened situation, while an importer increases local supply if he sells, and does not reduce it if he withholds.

Jurists versus economists: Classical jurists observed more than ten centuries ago, a world where productive units were small, numerous and generally competitive. Monopoly then was largely the result of local commercial behaviour, within regular commercial activity. The industrial revolution in the 18th century brought economies of scale, mass production, and persistent innovation, all connected with production, giving rise to the non-competitive market structures analyzed by modern economists. Whereas classical jurists focused on commercial monopolistic actions directed at socially important products, modern economists focused on market structures that motivate and facilitate monopolistic producer behaviour in many kinds of product.

Source: Muhammad Anas Al-Zarqa (2009), *Encyclopedia of Islamic Economics*, (Eds) Abdel Hamid Brahimi and Khurshid Ahmad, London, p. 97–105 (shortened).

7.12   REGULATION OF PRICE

Though monopolies have valid reasons to come into being and may have social welfare aspects, their pricing power can and is often used to the disadvantage of the ordinary consumers. The legal framework in many countries attempts in the first place to prevent the emergence of monopoly, tries to break it, if it emerges, or provides for price regulation to curb its exploitative potential. Here we shall discuss the need for regulating monopoly prices and its likely consequences only.

Price regulation implies that the state fixes a price for the monopoly product *lower* than what the monopolist would otherwise charge. We have seen that price regulation under perfect competition would result in a dead weight loss. Interestingly, this is not the case when regulatory law is applied to a monopoly. Figure 7.12 helps clarify the point. The figure assumes that the law of diminishing return would apply in both monopoly and the competitive industry, if each alternative produces the same commodity.

> Apparatus for price regulation in case of monopolies is always kept in place so that they may not use their pricing power against wider societal interests.

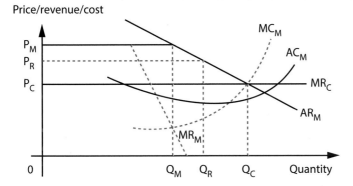

Figure 7.12 *Monopoly price regulation and competition compared*

In this figure, subscript M indicates variables under monopoly, R under regulation and C under perfect competition. We see that $P_M > P_R > P_C$. Accordingly, $Q_M < Q_R < Q_C$. Note that there is no dead weight loss when regulation lowers price from P_M to P_R. Natural monopolies receive special treatment in regulation schemes. It is often argued that they should be allowed to operate with their profit maximizing price–output schemes but the government should tax away their profits and distribute them to the consumers in proportion to their purchases of the monopoly product. The suggestion may attract the attention of the Islamic economists.

Exercise   7.9

What do you understand by the term dead weight loss? Explain why Figure 7.12 does not show any dead weight loss under price regulation. Mark in the figure, the area showing dead weight loss in consumption if price were raised from PC to PR per ton of sugarcane in India to benefit the farmers.

Summary

- Monopoly is a much different market structure than competition but both use the same tools of analysis and pursue profit maximization as their primary goal.
- A monopoly is a single firm producing a commodity that has no close substitutes. The firm is also the industry; the distinction between the two vanishes.
- It is difficult to apply the concept of monopoly in practice because the precise definition of a 'close substitute' is difficult to provide. In the ultimate analysis, all goods—even such diverse products as chocolates and detergents—compete for the consumer's income.
- The main distinction between monopoly and competition lies in the slope of the demand curve each faces. A competitive firm has a perfectly elastic demand curve, its slope being infinity. It has no power to influence the price of the product it sells; it is a price taker. On the other hand, monopoly is an industry, its demand curve slopes downwards to the right and it has power to alter the price at which it would sell its product.
- Several factors may be responsible for the emergence of monopolies in an economy. These include exclusive control of the firm over a crucial raw material needed for the product, entry into industry blocked by law and economies of large-scale production.
- A monopolist can charge different prices for the same product in various segments of the market to enlarge his revenue if two conditions are met: (a) the elasticity of demand for the product is not the same in different segments of the market and (b) it is not possible for the buyers to tran sfer it from one segment to another for earning profit.
- A monopolist usually adopts a cost plus or markup principle to fix the initial price for his product. The principle for deciding the markup value requires the information about the marginal cost of the product and the elasticity of demand for it. Given this information, we estimate the price P as:

$$P = \left(\frac{MC}{1 - \dfrac{1}{E_{DP}}} \right)$$

- The value of the markup then is P – MC.
- A tax levied per unit of output under diminishing returns is usually shared by the buyers and sellers of the commodity. In competition, the price of the commodity rises by less than the amount of tax but in monopoly it can, under certain conditions, rise by a larger than the amount of tax.
- The pricing power the monopolies may be used against the social welfare norms. So, regulation of monopoly power is often advocated and put into operation in modern economies. However, unlike completion, there is no deadweight loss of consumers' surplus.
- Monopoly by itself is neither good nor bad. Its merits and demerits in particular case have to be evaluated before passing judgment.

Glossary

Dead weight loss If a firm restricts as in monopoly the output of a commodity to less than the optimal utilization of plant capacity, the unused capacity constitutes the loss of productive resources locked in the production line. This loss is measured by the loss of potential output; it is called dead weight loss because under utilization of resources does not benefit anyone in the society except that it brings in and enlarges gains for the owners of the firm.

Ihtikar The Arabic term refers to the attempt of sellers to corner supplies of a scarce commodity for the time being with a view to raising its price for profiteering. Islam unequivocally condemns such efforts.

Iktinaz This Arabic word refers to the temptation of sellers to hoard goods in short supply to take advantage of the market for enhancing profits. Islam requires sellers to resist such temptations, especially in case of essential goods such as food stuffs.

Markup pricing When a firm has monopoly power it can raise the price of the product above for what it costs by adding a profit margin revealed and agreed to by the customers. Islamic banking is thriving currently on markup business.

Monopoly power This refers to the ability of a firm to raise or reduce the price of its product in the market along its downward sloping demand curve. It is not necessary that such a firm should always be the sole producer of the commodity in the market. Monopoly power of a firm varies inversely with the price elasticity for its product.

Price discrimination It means the ability of a firm to charge different prices for essentially the same commodity or service from different buyers. This can be done if the market for the commodity or service could be segmented such that the elasticity for the product is different in the segments and the product cannot be transferred from the segment with lower price to one where it is higher because of legal restrictions or prohibitive transfer costs.

Concepts for Review

- Dead weight loss in monopoly
- Efficacy of monopoly
- Markup pricing
- Monopoly and taxation
- Monopoly power

- Price discrimination
- Regulation of monopolies
- Social welfare loss
- Sources of monopoly

Case Study   7.1

Tata Steel

Tata Steel formerly known as TISCO and Tata Iron and Steel Company Limited (established in 1907) is the world's sixth largest steel company, with an annual crude steel capacity of 31 million tons. It is the largest private sector steel company in India in terms of domestic production. Tata Steel is India's second largest and second most profitable company in the private sector, with consolidated revenues of INR 1,321 billion and net profit of over INR 123 billion during the year ended 31 March 2008. Its main plant is located in Jamshedpur in Jharkhand state. With its recent acquisitions, the company has become a multinational with operations in various countries.

Tata Steel annually produces 18 million tons of steel in India and 52.32 million tons overseas, making it the fifth largest steel producer in the world. It produced a record-breaking 10.32 million tons of saleable steel in its Jamshedpur works in 2009–2010. The company's gross revenue in that financial reporting year was INR 20,196.24 crores. Its profit before tax (PBT) was INR 6,21,261.65 crores and profit after tax (PAT) was INR 4,22,212.15 crores in the same year.

Tata Steel introduced an 8-hour workday as early as 1912 when only a 12-hour workday was the legal requirement in Britain. It introduced leave-with-pay in 1920, a practice that became legally binding upon employers in India only in 1945. Similarly, Tata Steel started a Provident Fund for its employees as early as 1920, which became a law for all employers under the *Provident Fund Act* in 1952. Tata Steel's furnaces have never been disrupted on account of a labour strike and this is an enviable record.

Case Questions

1. India has five steel mills in the public sector. In what sense then can Tata Steel constitute a monopoly? Explain.
2. What labour welfare measures were introduced by Tata Steel in India? Comment.

Case Study   7.2

Nippon Steel Corporation

Nippon Steel Corporation was formed in 1970. It was created by the merger of two giants, Yawata Iron & Steel and Fuji Iron & Steel into a juggernaut. Today, Nippon Steel is the world's second largest steel producer in volume terms and the second most profitable steel company in the world.

In 2005, the Nippon Steel Corporation made a plan to step up its capacity for recycling waste plastics into coke by 30%. Coke is a main resource in steel production. To manage the load they have invested 4 billion yen (about $38.2 million) to install equipment at Oita Mill and set up a second furnace at Kyushu facility.

In 2006, Nippon Steel and Mitsubishi Heavy Industries Ltd (MHI) jointly created a high tensile strength steel. The first application this steel was used for was the hulls of container ships. This steel allowed the ships to be just as strong without the thick steel that was for required for their size. The slimmer thickness allowed the ships to attain greater fuel efficiency, cutting down on the environmental load of the ships.

Nippon Steel announced a pilot project to process food waste into ethanol in 2006. It has tasked Kitakyushu City with collecting and sorting the food waste and Nishihara Co, a waste management company, with developing new technologies to implement the sorted collecting system. To minimize costs, they will use waste heat from an existing incineration facility that had not been effectively utilized, and the residue left after ethanol recovery will be burned in this incinerator.

Case Questions
1. What process has enabled Nippon Steel Corporation to become the second largest steel producer? What are its main achievements?
2. Japan has neither coal nor iron mines. How did it develop its steel industry, which is so cost efficient?
3. Explain the environment-friendly measures Nippon Steel has introduced in their production strategy. Should others adopt similar measures? Elaborate.

Test Questions

7.1 What does monopoly mean as a form of market structure? Explain the main sources that may give rise to monopolies in an economy.

7.2 Produce appropriate diagrams to explain how monopoly price is determined under diminishing returns using (a) total cost and total revenue curves, and (b) MR and MC curves.

7.3 Suppose the following are the total cost (TC) and total revenue functions of a monopolist. Find the price–output combination that would maximize his profit. Also indicate the profit he would earn.
$$TC = 60 + Q^2$$
$$TR = 40Q \quad Q^2 \quad Q < 40$$
Present also in a table, the average revenue, marginal revenue, average cost and marginal cost of the monopolist.

7.4 Explain and illustrate how elasticity of demand and the laws of return affect the pricing decisions of a monopolist.

7.5 What does price discrimination under monopoly mean? Give suitable examples. Explain briefly the conditions for successful price discrimination. Is price discrimination beneficial to the consumers? Give reasons for your answer.

7.6 What do you understand by markup pricing? Is markup pricing beneficial to the society? Give reasons for your answer. Do you think it is valid for Islamic banking to use the system for earning profit? Explain your answer adequately.

7.7 Do you think it is necessary to regulate monopoly prices? Why or why not? Can the regulation be successful in your opinion? Give reasons for your answer.

7.8 A monopolist has the total cost function TC = 10Q. He sells his goods in two markets X and Y. His demand curve for market A is $Q_A = 100 - P_A$, and market B is $Q_B = 100 - 2P_B$. Assuming that goods from one market cannot be transferred to the other market, answer the following questions.
   (a) What quantity of output should the monopolist produce and what price should he charge in each market?
   (b) At what price will he sell the product in each market, and why?
   (c) What shall his total profit be?

7.9 In regard to resource allocation, the interest of the sellers and the society coincides in pure competition but clashes in pure monopoly market. Explain using a suitable diagram.

7.10 Critically examine the following statements.
   (a) The larger the profit of a firm, the greater its monopoly power.
   (b) The monopolist has a pricing policy to follow, but a producer in a perfect competition has none.
   (c) In the case of natural monopolies, it would be Islamic if their profits are taxed by the government for spending on the provision of social welfare services.

Web Exercise

Collect information from the Internet about Tata Group of industries. On the basis of that information, can you say that the Tatas of India constitute a monopoly? Give reasons for your answer.

Forward Link

In the preceding chapter and the present one, we discussed the two limiting market structures—pure competition and pure monopoly—located at the opposite ends of the scale. These cases provide the benchmarks to measure the departure of the actual market situations from the extremes. Economists did not probe the real world market structures in a formal and systematic way until the 1930s. The following chapter sketches what exists between the two purely theoretical models. You may find it more interesting as it is closer to what you may experience in the market place.

8

Monopolistic Competition and Oligopoly

LEARNING OUTCOMES

This chapter should enable the student to understand:

- If perfect competition and pure monopoly are limiting cases, what lies in between
- Distinctive features of monopolistic competition
- The relationship between the pricing power the firm has and the competition
- How firms acquire monopoly power and how they retain it
- The role of advertising in monopolistic competition
- Salient features of oligopoly
- Firms' behaviour in oligopoly and the models followed

A. MONOPOLISTIC COMPETITION

8.1   NEW STRUCTURES

Advent of new market structures.

In the last two chapters, we talked about two limiting market structures—pure competition and pure monopoly—located at the opposite ends of the scale. Economists invariably confined their discussions on price formation to these theoretical models for drawing inferences concerning market performance until the early 1930s when the work of Mrs Joan Robinson, *Theory of Imperfect Competition* in England, and of Edward Chamberlin *Monopolistic Competition* in the US made their appearance on the scene. These researchers covered the vast, unattended grey area lying between competition and monopoly, and their analyses led to a similar sort of output, differences though there have been.

Initially, in textbooks of economics both names—imperfect competition and monopolistic competition—appeared depending on where the publication came from, England or the US. Modern textbooks invariably discuss the area under the title 'monopolistic competition' and we use the same term here. Monopolistic competition has some features of pure competition and some of pure monopoly. This fact also distinguishes it from them both.

8.2   DISTINCTIVE FEATURES

Important features:
Small number of sellers, product differentiation, advertising and entry–exit difficulties.

1. **Number of sellers**: The number of sellers in monopolistic competition is relatively smaller than pure competition, but is still large enough to make them compete and eliminate the possibilities of their collusion to influence the commodity price or output. Each seller acts independently and enjoys the power to cut price for attracting customers away from other sellers. In fact, the emergence of monopolistic competition on the stage has done much in changing the view of a monopolist as the 'sole seller of some product' to firms that have discretion in the pricing of their products and may capture a small or large share of the market. The interesting question is not who is or who is not a monopolist, but rather under what circumstances is a monopoly strong and in what circumstances is it weak.

Product differentiation means to make consumers believe that the brand sold is better than the competitors'.

2. **Product differentiation**: In pure competition, all firms sell identical products, for example wheat of a particular grade or cloth of the same quality. They have to remain contented with profit which is no more than normal in the long run. They may earn more only by reducing competition they face in the market. To that end, firms attempt to distinguish their product from those of their competitors. Brand names, trademarks, designs, models, packaging, after-sale services and location are some of the major devices modern firms use to *differentiate* their product from those of their rivals. The differences could possibly be in physical features and/or qualitative aspects of the product. Differences in the materials used or packaging may also give the products a different look. After providing the product some distinctive features, a marketing strategy is evolved, highlighting such features to convince buyers that what the firm is selling is different and by implication superior to that of the competitors. The differences may be real or perceptive, as created by the selling effort of firms.

3. **Advertising**: To convince buyers of the comparative superiority of their product, firms spend astronomical amounts of money on advertising. For example, the expenditure of General Motors on advertising in 2002 was 3.65 trillion US dollars, much more

than the purchasing power parity-based gross national income of India. The bulk of the expenditure on advertising is competitive, self-cancelling and wasteful. Whether we are aware of it or not, advertising is thrusting one or the other product upon us every moment, everywhere: on the streets and highways, on the radio, TV and the Internet, on bags we carry and even on shirts we wear. We shall revert to this topic later in the discussion.

4. **Pricing power**: Product differentiation has psychic appeal and tends to subdivide the market for a commodity among its various brands. For example, everyone knows what soap is and what it does, but there are strong buyer preferences for Maharani, Sandal, Jai, Lux and others in India. Product differentiation in automobiles, television sets, music systems, mobile phones and so on has fragmented the markets between brands of the same commodity. The number of firms in an industry does not remain large enough to keep competition perfect and profit normal as products of various firms are imperfect substitutes for one another. The seller of each brand has a downward sloping demand curve. Under monopolistic competition, the firms do not remain price takers: they tend to acquire pricing power.

> Product differentiation and advertising separates markets of different brands and gives some pricing power to the individual producers. Each can vary the price of the product within limits.

5. **Entry–exit conditions**: Conditions for entry into industries under monopolistic competition are much relaxed compared to pure monopoly or oligopoly. There are several reasons. The firms are relatively small in size, overheads are not heavy and much economies of scale are not available as incentive to expand. On the other hand, firms here need more finance for product development and advertising. But entry into industry is more difficult than it is in pure competition. Exit from the industry is, of course, no problem. No one stops a monopolistic competitor from leaving the industry, if it so decides.

8.3   PRICE AND OUTPUT

Price–output decisions of a firm operating under monopolistic competition may be studied, as in pure competition, with reference to (i) short run, and (ii) long run. In the short run, the firms cannot change their production capacity and entry–exit facilities are by definition not available. In the long run, both these inabilities do not operate; firms can alter production capacity and can enter or leave an industry.

We shall ignore in the following discussion the advertising cost firms incur for selling the products. Later, we shall examine what happens if this cost element is taken into account. As the firms have downward sloping demand curves, their average and marginal revenue curves and their relationship with the price elasticity of demand are the same as pure monopoly.

8.3.1 Short-run Equilibrium

In the short run, individual firms may be making economic profits or incurring losses. Figure 8.1 explains the determination of equilibrium price and output in each case. Firm A earns economic profit shown by the horizontal line area (shown in the form of a rectangle in the figure). On the other hand, firm B suffers a loss, depicted by the vertical line area. Note that the two firms are not selling at the same price as the firms in pure competition are compelled to do.

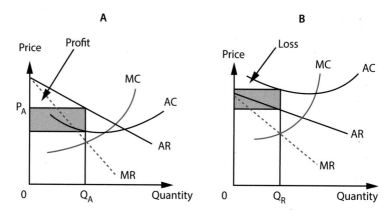

Figure 8.1 *Monopolistic competition: short-term equilibrium of firms*

8.3.2 Long-run Equilibrium

If the firms are seen making economic profits, as A in the figure, for quite some time, new firms may, in the long run, enter the industry. Their output will increase supply of the commodity. The process must lower the overall level of prices in the industry until economic profits are wiped out. If some firms continue making losses, as B in the figure, they would wind up and leave the industry. The resulting reduction in output would make prices on the whole remunerative for the remaining firms ensuring normal profits. Figure 8.2 shows the long-run equilibrium typical of a firm operating under monopolistic competition. Here, price, P and output, Q are the equilibrium values. Average revenue is equal to average cost of production, allowing firms only normal profit in the long run.

The entry of the new firms into the industry results in a leftward shift of demand curve of the existing firms. The reason is that each firm is assumed to compete on an equal footing for a share in the total market demand; the entry of new firms thus causes, it is believed, a proportionate reduction in what each firm can sell in the market at a given price. As each firm is assumed to claim an equal portion of the industry's demand, this share must obviously decline as more firms enter the industry. The leftward shift of the demand curves continues until each become tangent to the relevant average cost curve, profits become normal and fresh entry into the industry stops.

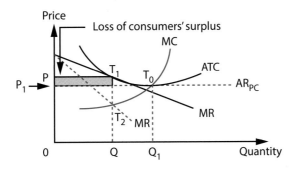

Figure 8.2 *Long-run equilibrium of the firm under monopolistic competition*

Efficiency notion as derived from the benchmark perfect competition model requires three-way equality: $P = MC =$ Minimum ATC. We saw in Chapter 6 that the equality of price and marginal cost is the criterion for efficiency in resource allocation. Equality of price and minimum average total cost ensure efficiency in production or factor use; expenditure on inputs is minimized. What producers get as profit is just normal and, therefore, legitimate (and Islamic also?).

Imperfect model is inefficient because price is not equal to marginal cost.

Under the notion, firms operating in monopolistic competition become inefficient to both counts. In Figure 8.2, the long-run marginal cost and marginal revenue curves of the firm meet at T_2. The point determines the equilibrium output of the firm as Q at price P where MR is tangent to ATC. The firm is just earning normal profit.

Now, suppose AR_{PC} is the average revenue curve under pure competition and is the same as the marginal revenue curve of the firm. It is tangent to ATC at T_0, as it would be in pure competition. The tangency point occurs where MC just crosses the ATC giving P_1 price and Q_1 as the *optimal* output. A comparison of alternative equilibrium positions at T_1 and T_2 shows that the firm under monopolistic competition does not make the best use of its production capacity: $(Q < Q_1)$, i.e. it lacks in productive efficiency or in using resources. Again, P is more than MC in equilibrium, thus there is inefficiency also in allocating resources.

There is loss of consumers' surplus as well. This loss is shown by the white shaded area in the figure. In that, monopolistic competition reduces social welfare. We shall show in the later chapter that, given pure competition in the labour market, wage rate equals both the average and marginal revenue product of the firm: labour receives full value of its contribution to output. However, the figure here shows that in monopolistic competition, workers do not get the full value of their contribution to output: $T_2Q < T_1Q$ or MR is less than AR.

Price is higher and output is smaller than under perfect competition.

It comes about that in monopolistic competition, full plant capacity is not utilized; there is wastage of resources. Consumers suffer and social welfare is reduced. Labour does not get the full value of its contribution to output; it is exploited even though long run profits are normal. Is not the situation rather peculiar: to whose benefit does the system operate?

8.5   THE VARIETY ISSUE

It is often argued that the picture Figure 8.2 presents is a still photograph, not a movie of the market. Economic activity is not static; it is dynamic. A firm in monopolistic competition as shown in Figure 8.2 does not stand idle and watch competitors imitate its product and selling techniques to eliminate its economic profit. It continually attempts to keep its product distinct from its imitators and other rivals through design change, improved services and more vigorous advertising. Firms in monopolistic competition are in a race, each striving to surge ahead of the competitors. They hope to succeed, as human beings instinctively desire variety in consumption—manna stopped falling from the heavens when Israelites insisted to have a change. They had to search for variety—the spice of life—in the land of God.

The real issue is not the desire for variety; it is how much variety do we need? Are not brands for the same product too many? Is not the change in designs and models too frequent? Do benefits of increased variety always outweigh the costs involved? Can the expenditure for variety in some way be related to the stage of economic development of a nation? Much controversy and honest difference of opinion may surround such questions, and yet these *are* the questions worth billions of dollars, more so in the poor developing economies.

> Provide more variety but social cost is higher than satisfaction.

8.5.1   Islamic Angle

> Too much variety is a waste of resources. Presumably, it works against the Islamic notion of simple living and moderation in consumption.

There is also an Islamic angle to the question. Islamic advocacy for simple living intends to curb demonstrative instinct in human beings and may imply restrain on variety seeking in consumption. Variety is a luxury of life, not a necessity. Poverty, income inequalities and the need to free resources for growth seem to endorse the viewpoint for developing economies. A vivid illustration comes from China's recent past. In the early years of the communist revolution there, the president and his chauffeur wore the garments made from the same blue cloth; indeed, the material remained for decades the trademark of the Chinese dress culture.

8.6   ADVERTISING AGAIN

A more complex issue in monopolistic competition is the place of advertising that, we saw, involves huge expenditures. Broadly, advertising plays two roles in modern societies: informative and persuasive. To an extent, advertising brings new goods, to the knowledge of the people, their uses and prices perform a welcome social function. It is in line with the Islamic norms if information provided is complete, transparent and free of rhetoric, to paraphrase Ghazali, the jurist.

The real problem is with persuasive advertising. The goods that satisfy basic physical needs of human beings do not offer much scope for persuasive advertising as demand for them is not much price elastic. It is in the area of *psychic* needs, luxuries especially, that persuasion finds its natural terrain. Here, it does not remain merely informative. The high price elasticity of comforts and luxuries tempts for persuasive advertising: it promises to beat competitors and enlarge profits. Persuasive advertising tends to overpower consumers' sovereignty and makes them feel they really need the commodity. Thus, instead of instructions going from consumers to the market for what to produce, they flow today from the market to the consumers as to what they should buy in their own interest. There is a *reversal* of instructional direction between them and the market.

John Kenneth Galbraith called the reversal as the 'revised sequence'. Corporate 'management of demand' is needed, he thought, because corporations control vast resources of the community in terms of men, money and materials. For an efficient use of these resources, corporations must be allowed action to ensure the demand for their products. To the extent advertising is able to provide such assurance; it promotes stability in the market. Advertising enlarges *ipso facto* the size of the market and, therefore, contributes to national wealth.

> Advertising if informative, serves social interests but persuasive advertising tends to overpower consumers' preferences.

However, increase in wealth alone need not always be an indicator of societal well-being. In what sector of the economy this increase takes place and to what effect is no less important. Modern advertising increases mostly the production of luxury goods. More than that, it tends to pitch psychic needs in demand for resources against social priorities such as provision of food, shelter, medical facilities and education for the poor. Islamic norms require putting of restrictions on such a consequence of advertising to improve the provision of basic needs to the masses in developing economies. It is worth noting that high-value industries are first to collapse in times of adversity like the sort of current global turmoil and presumably contribute to their intensity and duration.

Exercise 8.1

Compare and contrast monopolistic competition with (i) pure competition, and (ii) pure monopoly with regard to their main characteristics. Firms in monopolistic competition too earn only normal profit in the long run, but utilize less than their optimal production capacity, why? Who benefits from this and how?

BOX 8.1

Ruling on Commercial Advertising

Advertising in order to attract business is one of the modern ideas that cannot be regarded as being exempt from the general Islamic principles governing transactions. But because, in many cases, this method of attracting business has gone too far, we have to mention these general principles in detail, paying special attention to the aims of Shari'ah and correct etiquette. This includes the following points:

1   The businessman must have a good intention when advertising, i.e. his intention should be to acquaint people with the advantages of his goods or services, to draw their attention to things they did not know about them, and to provide other information that they may need about them.

2   He must always be honest in his advertising; what he says must reflect the reality of the product or service. Honesty is an essential fundamental in all dealings, but especially in selling. The Prophet (pbuh) said: 'The two parties engaged in a transaction have the choice of either going ahead with the transaction or canceling it, until they part. If they are open and honest, their transaction will be blessed for them, but if they conceal things and tell lies that will destroy the *barakah* (blessing) of their transaction' (narrated by Al-Bukhaari, no. 2079 (2/82-83) and by Muslim, 1532 (3/162), from the hadeeth of Hakeem Ibn Hizaam).

3   One of the essential means of being honest is to avoid over-praising a product or service or exaggerating about it, for this could go beyond the bounds of being open and honest. The Prophet (pbuh) said: 'Try not to praise products to one another' (Al-Tirmidhi, no. 1268), i.e. the vendor should not praise it in order to encourage the one who hears him to buy it, so that the only reason he buys it is what the vendor says. Some of the scholars counted praise of a product for what it is as a kind of insane or senseless speech from which people should refrain. The guideline here is that the vendor should refrain from saying anything which could later result in regret on the part of the purchaser.

4   The vendor should avoid any kind of cheating and deception in his advertising; i.e. he should not make the product appear more attractive than it is, or conceal its faults, or praise it in terms of characteristics and features that it does not have. All of this is *haram*.

5   A vendor's advertising should not include any condemnation or belittling of any other person's products or services, and it should not try to cause harm unjustly to others. The Prophet (pbuh) said: 'None of you truly believes until he wants for his brother what he wants for himself' (narrated by Al-Bukhaari, no. 13 (1/2) and by Muslim, no. 45 (1/67), from the hadeeth of Anas Ibn Maalik). The guideline here is that if something would cause him distress, if it were done to him, he should not do it to others. The Prophet (pbuh) said: 'There should be no harm and no reciprocating of harm' (narrated by Ahmad; 5/326-327, 313 and by Ibn Maajah, no. 2340-2341, from the hadeeth of Ubaadah Ibn Saamit).

6   The advertising should contain nothing that calls people to be extravagant or to spend too much, because these are things that are forbidden in Islam. Allah says (interpretation of the meaning):

   … And waste not by extravagance. Verily, He likes not al-Musrifoon (those who waste by extravagance)… [Al-An'aam 6:141].

   …But spend not wastefully (your wealth) in the manner of a spendthrift. Verily, the spendthrifts are brothers of the Shayaateen (devils)… [Al-Israa' 17:26-27].

7   The advertising should contain nothing that violates the sanctity of the pure Shari'ah, such as advertising *haram* things or being accompanied by things that are not allowed, such as music and singing, or showing women, and so on.

8   The advertising should not be so expensive that the consumer has to pay towards the cost of the advertising. It should be brief and to the point, concisely describing the product or service without going to extremes that may cause the price to be raised.

Source: Khaalid Ibn Abd-Allah Al-Muslih, *Al-Hawaafiz Al-Tijaariyyah Al-Tasweeqiyyah*, p. 209 < http://islamqa.info/en/7834>, accessed 4 March 2014.

B. OLIGOPOLY

We saw that a monopolist has virtually no rivals but firms in monopolistic competition have. It is also to be noted that the price and output strategies of individual firms under competition do not invoke any reaction among the rivals. However, we now examine a market structure where *strategic action and reaction* among the rival firms occupy the centre stage in the market. This structure is an *oligopoly*. Here, the industry has only a few large-sized firms, say, six or seven in number. If the number of firms in an industry is just two, the structure is called a *duopoly*.

Concern about rivals' reaction.

8.7   SALIENT FEATURES

As the number of firms is small in oligopoly, each has greater control relative to competitive positions on the price of the product it sells. The main features of an oligopoly are as under.

1. **Product type**: We saw that in pure competition, the firms sell a homogenous product but for monopolistic competition, product differentiation is a basic characteristic of an industry's output. In oligopoly, however, what the firms are selling may either be (a) a homogenous or (b) a differentiated product. For example, firms in industries such as steel, copper and cement sell homogenous products, while producers of automobiles, tires, household appliances and so on deal in differentiated goods.

2. **Control over price**: Being large in size and few in number, firms in oligopoly usually have substantial control over the price of their products; they are not 'price takers' as in pure competition. Each firm is in search of a price–output combination that would maximize its profits. But even though it has pricing power, the firm, unlike monopoly, has its rivals and cannot ignore their reactions to what it does. Firms here must have a strategy of dealing with the possible reaction of rivals to what they individually do. *Strategic behaviour* is the demand of interdependence among them. The profit of each firm in the industry depends not merely on its own price–output policy but also on how others would respond to that policy and variations in it. For example in India, the Maruti can no longer ignore the possible reaction of the Tatas and other car makers in deciding on a revision of its prices.

3. **Entry restrictions**: Erecting the same sort of entry restrictions as a monopolist uses also helps the creation of oligopolies. Economies of scale constitute important hindrance to entry in such industries as oil exploration, copper, rubber, ship-building or aircraft manufacturing. In such industries, not more than

three or four firms can realize these in full depending on the size of the market. After the 1997–1998 financial crisis, to have fewer banks of larger size in Malaysia was considered expedient to avoid the recurrence of the trouble in future. The reorganization scheme considered it advisable to merge commercial banks in no more than six units for the economy.

4. **Mergers**: Oligopolies emerge at times because some firms become *dominant* in an industry. Smaller firms find it difficult to stay in competition and merge with larger units. Chewing gum and candy bars from the USA, and the proposed merger of Sahara and Jet Airlines from India are the recent illustrations. Sometimes the state may persuade existing companies to merge because bigger units can resist or meet crises better. Prospects of increased pricing power reinforce the urge to merge.

8.8 CONCENTRATION MEASUREMENTS

The percentage of total output produced by the largest firms gives us a measure of oligopoly concentration in an industry. However, concentration ratios have several limitations.

1. Concentration ratios relate to the country as a whole, while the markets for some products could be highly localized due to high transport costs.

2. The definition of an industry is often loose and infirm. Attention then has to be paid to inter-industry competition in determining a concentration ratio.

3. Concentration ratios take into account the domestic output of an industry but imports might be keeping the market fairly competitive.

8.9 FIRMS' BEHAVIOUR

Pricing behaviour of a firm in oligopoly, as noted above, is much influenced by how others are expected to respond to its policy initiatives. In other words, firms pattern their actions according to the actions of their rivals. Economists pattern such conduct as of players in a game of chess, poker or bridge. The *games theory* is now widely used to solve strategy problems in economics including the behaviour of firms in an oligopoly market. Bluff and cheating are admitted as important variables in determining their strategies. Since Islam does not approve such immoral conduct including business, games theory is not in much use in Islamic economics.

Firms in oligopoly situations—in Islamic economics as well—can influence their rivals' profits by varying their pricing strategies. The profit of each firm depends on what it does plus on what others will do. Mutual interdependence is a more positive element in oligopoly than competition; firms can often benefit more from collusion, i.e. cooperation with rivals. Cooperation is hailed by Islam if it were not aimed at the exploitation of consumers. But collusions seldom have consumers' interest in the forefront of their motives or policies.

8.10 MODELS

In our discussion of other market structure—pure competition, monopoly and monopolistic competition—we used a single model to describe the price–output behaviour of the firms. The case of oligopoly is different and for two reasons.

1. **Diversity**: Compared with other markets, oligopoly structures have much greater diversity. There are *tight* oligopolies where three or four firms dominate the market scene, and there are *loose* oligopolies where, say, seven to eight firms compete as rivals. These firms may share 70 or 80% of the market for example, while smaller firms compete at its outer fringe. It is a situation wherein firms may be selling a standardized or a differentiated product; they may be operating independently or in collusion with one another.

2. **Interdependence complications**: Mutual dependence does not enable individual firms to predict the reaction of rivals with reference to their policies. They find it hard to estimate their own demand and marginal revenue precisely. There is much of uncertainty and a lot of groping in the dark.

For these reasons, a number of models are used to explain the behaviour of firms operating in an oligopoly. Of these, we shall discuss three: (i) the kinked demand theory that assumes a non-collusive setting, (ii) collusive pricing, and (iii) price leadership.

8.10.1   The Kinked Demand Theory

Our discussion of the theory is based on the following assumptions.

1. There are three imaginary firms A, B and C in the market sharing it in equal measure.

2. The firms are independent in the sense that they do not engage in collusive price changes.

3. The going price for the product of A is P_A and its current output is Q_A as shown in Figure 8.3.

Assumptions of theory.

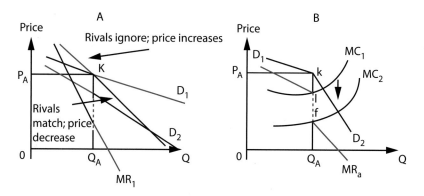

Figure 8.3 *Oligopoly: the kinked demand curve model*

Figure 8.3A shows that A can raise the price of the product along his demand curve D_A from point K upwards without inviting reaction from the rivals B and C because in the process it would only lose to them sales from its share of the market. But if A lowers the price beyond P_A along D_1, it will invite competitive price cutting from B and C, the rivals. The portion of D_1 downwards from K will rotate to D_2, making sales at price lower than P_A unattractive due to demand becoming much less elastic. Rivals' reaction will make the firm stick to P_A, selling Q_A quantity of the product. Point K constitutes the kink in A's demand curve.

Figure 8.3B shows that the rivals' reaction to a decrease in P_A but not to an increase makes the demand curve of A kinked at point k, it becomes D_1kD_2. It also causes the marginal revenue curve to have a vertical break. In case, there is any shift in the marginal cost curve between MC_1 and MC_2, it will cut this vertical segment of the marginal revenue curve resulting in no change in the price P_A or output Q_A of the firm.

Evaluation of the theory

The kinked demand curve analysis of oligopoly firms' behaviour is valid in that it focuses on the interdependence of their behaviour and the nature of rivalry among them. However, it has a few notable limitations.

Limitations: The theory fails to explain how the initial kink is formed or what causes it to shift and to what extent.

1. It explains well the cause of price rigidity but not of it being what it is. It fails to explain how the price P_A is determined in the first place. In other words, how and why is the kink formed at point K, not elsewhere? One possible answer could be that the kink is likely to be formed at the point where the price elasticity E_{DP} on the demand curve equals one. (Why?)

2. There is empirical evidence that oligopoly prices in practice have not remained rigid during the cyclical fluctuations in many economies. Firms have increased their prices unabated and substantially during periods of inflation. They have also cut prices during the downturn of the economic cycles. In fact, competitive price cuts have at times proved ruinous to industries dominated by oligopolies.

8.10.2   Collusion: Motivations

Games theory suggests that rivals can at times gain more through collusion than they can through competition. Collusion among firms in an industry takes place when they enter into an agreement to (a) fix prices and (b) divide the market among themselves, or (c) restrict mutual competition in any other way. The agreement need not always be formal and can be hammered out at an occasional meeting or dinner of the managers. Collusive agreements, formal or informal, may result in the formation of cartels. A cartel is the most comprehensive form of collusion. The Organization of Petroleum Exporting Countries (OPEC) consisting of eleven members with about 40% of the market share is considered as one of the leading examples of a formal cartel assembled to look after the prices and output interests of the member countries. Some do not subscribe to this description of the OPEC on the plea that the number of countries is large, their combined share of the market is small and they are in potential competition with alternative sources of energy. Forming cartels is illegal in the USA; any collusion that exists in that country is covert or secret; still there are many in subtle forms or based on tacit understandings.

Collusive agreements usually take place during periods of economic recessions when ruinous price cutting tends to dominate the scene. Every firm becomes worried as goods pile up on its shelves, profits fall and excess capacity mounts. The downturn can attempt new firms to break through the entry barriers and indulge in aggressive price cutting to gain a foothold in the market for future gains.

Collusion appears as the remedy to surmount recession difficulties. It promises the firms in oligopoly a reduction in uncertainty, increase in profits and safer barriers against entry. Finally, the tendency of prices to remain rigid, as the kinky demand curve model suggests, may cut into profits if production cost tends to rise under inflationary pressures. Collusion helps resist such temptations.

> Competition often leads to price cutting resulting to losses. So, oligopolies often tend to collude which can assume several forms, from a merger to a gentleman's agreement.

Collusion: price–output policies

But we have to demonstrate that collusion *alone* would give each of our three firms A, B and C the maximum profit. For this, we change our assumptions listed in Section 8.10.1 to:

1. The three firms produce a *homogenous product* and have identical cost curves.
2. The demand curve of each firm is *indeterminate* unless it knows for certain the reaction of the rivals to any price change it initiates.
3. Each firm believes that its two rivals will match any increase or decrease in price it may introduce.

> Collusion may be on price–output policies. It can also result in policies restrictive of the entry of new firms into the industry.

Given these assumptions, firm A will behave as does a monopolist to have its profit maximizing price–output combination as shown in Figure 8.4. Price P_A and output Q_A are, respectively, the equilibrium price and output values for the firm giving it the maximum profit indicated by the shaded area. If the assumption of the firm that its rivals will match its actions turns out to be correct, the figure would depict the position of firms B and C also as the revenue and cost curves of the three firms and their market shares are by assumption identical.

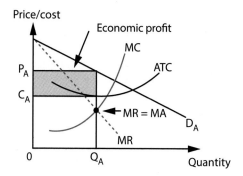

Figure 8.4 *Price and output in collusive oligopoly*

However, what will happen if A's assumption of rival matching its behaviour is incorrect? Firms B and C will not set for the product a price higher than P_A as they will lose their market share to firm A. But if they choose to set a lower price, the consequences for firm A will be disastrous. Its demand curve will drastically shift to the left and profit will shrink; even losses may occur. However, in retaliation firm A may start under cutting the rivals B and C. A price war might start and eventually all may come to grief. So, for each of them collusion will be the preferred policy with a common price, and corresponding output. The same figure as 8.4 would then show the position of any of the three firms.

Exercise 8.2

There are six firms in the iron and steel industry of a country. They are in an informal collusion to fix steel prices by mutual agreement. An economic consultant advises the government to declare such price fixing illegal but allows price leadership if the firms so choose. Will you agree with him? Give reasons for your answer.

Obstacle to collusion

It is usually difficult to make and sustain cartels and collusive agreements for the following reasons.

1.   There often are differences in demand and costs among oligopoly firms that make it difficult to arrive at a mutual agreement concerning price, especially in lines of production

such as automobiles and electronics where changes in design and accompanying services are the vital and frequently changing features of the commodity.

2. The larger the number of firms in an industry and the smaller the market share of each, the more difficult it is for them to enter into a collusive agreement about the price and output targets.

3. There invariably is a temptation for the firms in collusion to violate the agreement and enter secret deals with customers to cut prices for enlarging individual profits. Such cheating when discovered invariably leads to the breakup of the collusion.

4. It is difficult to maintain collusion during periods of recession in the economy, more so if the downturn is long and sticky. Excess production capacities, waning sales, rising per unit overheads and evaporating profits make firms invariably perceive that they could curtail profit falls or losses through price cuts at the expense of their rivals.

5. Larger profits resulting from collusion may attract new entrants to the industry. Increased competition may lead to the breakup of the collusions.

> Collusion is not easy to form. It is even more difficult to sustain it.

8.10.3 Price Leadership

One important obstacle to informal collusion is that firms find it difficult to agree without talking to each other as to what the appropriate price could be. More so, when demand and cost conditions tend to change fast and make the notion of a 'correct' price further indeterminate. *Price leadership* is a form of tacit collusion that helps go around the difficulty.

> Circumstances may automatically create leader–follower relationship.

Under price leadership one firm sets the price and the other firms follow suit. A leader–follower relationship thus emerges without any explicit agreement. The followers just change what and when the leader changes. In India, the Tatas continued to play that role in the iron and steel industry for a couple of decades even after independence of the country from the British rule.

However, the question remains: what price would the leader set? This depends on any of the two factors: the 'follower firms' not only follow the leader on the price front but keep, in addition, production within limits of their market shares; they are not supposed to cross the line even if the matching price were raised. Alternatively, the leader firm must be so *dominant* that it can set a price to maximize its own profit without bothering what other firms produce and sell at that price.

Figure 8.5 sketches the leader–follower process. It has three sections. Section L shows that the dominant firm would determine its price (P_L) and output (Q_L) levels to have the maximum profit, as the lined rectangle shows, behaving as if it were a monopoly. In Section F, the follower is a price taker and can sell as much as he must at P_A to maximize his profit. His output is determined where his marginal revenue equals his marginal cost.

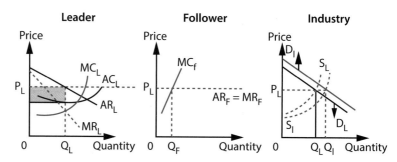

Figure 8.5 *Leader—follower model in oligopoly*

Finally, we integrate the two Sections L and F in I to show the overall equilibrium of the industry. Given the assumptions of the model, the demand and supply curves for the industry would cross at P_L and the combined output of the firms ($Q_L + Q_F = Q_I$) would be cleared at that price.

The price leader invariably informs the other players of any impending price alterations. The method is usually subtle and indirect: speeches, interviews or press releases of the higher executives of the leader company are often used as the means of communication. A common way is to pronounce that there is a 'need to raise price in view of the rising cost', say, of energy as at present.

BOX 8.2

OPEC is an Oligopoly?

The Organization of the Petroleum Exporting Countries (OPEC) is a permanent intergovernmental organization, currently consisting of 12 oil producing and exporting countries, spread across three continents America, Asia and Africa. The members are Algeria, Angola, Ecuador, the Islamic Republic of Iran, Iraq, Kuwait, the Socialist People's Libyan Arab Jamahiriya, Nigeria, Qatar, Saudi Arabia, United Arab Emirates & Venezuela. The organization's principal objectives are: 1. to co-ordinate and unify the petroleum policies of the member countries and to determine the best means for safeguarding their individual and collective interests; 2. to seek ways and means of ensuring the stabilization of prices in international oil markets, with a view to eliminating harmful and unnecessary fluctuations; and 3. to provide an efficient economic and regular supply of petroleum to consuming nations and a fair return on capital to those investing in the petroleum industry.

Source: <http://www.slideshare.net/mattbentley34/oligopoly-an-introduction>, accessed 4 March 2014.

8.11   EFFICIENCY VIS-A-VIS OLIGOPOLY

Monopoly and oligopoly are both inefficient in using and allocating resources. Figure 8.5 is applicable to both of them. None meets the triple equality: P = MC = Minimum ATC = P we referred to earlier. However, opinion differs on which is less welcome—oligopoly or monopoly—from the viewpoint of social welfare? The observers of the US scene find oligopoly less desirable than monopoly. The reason they advance is that the state may find it more convenient to frame regulatory laws and implement them in the latter case. Firms in an oligopoly can enter into informal collusion and escape regulation. However, others have reservations. They find oligopoly less harmful to social welfare than monopoly. They argue that in the modern era of globalization, foreign competition tends to eliminate arrangements like price leadership or limit pricing to an agreed level. On the positive side, they feel that oligopolies may, in the long run, promote faster growth through innovations and technical improvements compared to pure structures—competitive or monopolistic.

Be it as it may, the debate is not of much significance to the developing countries. Oligopolies or monopolies are not common features of their markets. But they do not always find conducive to the national interest the sort of competition domestic industries face from foreign companies which tends to assume monopolistic patterns in the local markets.

> There is argument that oligopoly is more wasteful of resources than monopoly and it is also easier to control one firm rather than a number of them as in oligopoly.

Summary

- Monopolistic competition covers the vast area of varying shades between the limiting pure models of competition and monopoly. It provides treatment of more realistic market situations.

- The distinctive features of a monopolistic market structure are: (i) a large number of sellers but fewer than in pure competition, (ii) firms selling 'differentiated' products, (iii) advertising to convince buyers of the distinctive and better features of the product, (iv) firms having pricing power, (v) easy entry into and exit from the industry, therefore (v) the demand curve of each firm slopes downwards and MR < AR.

- The equilibrium output of each firm is determined where MR = MC while the price for that output must equal AR.

- In the short run, firms may earn economic profit or suffer losses. In the long run, the free entry and exit feature of the industry allows individual firms no more than normal profit.

- Firms operating under monopolistic competition lack efficiency in factor allocation and their use while pure competition ensures both.

- Consumers must have variety but society pays for it in terms of investment locked in excess unused capacities of the firms even in the long run. The question therefore remains how much variety do we need? There is perhaps a case for reduction in variety in developing economies and certainly in an Islamic economy.

- Advertising has advantages. It brings better and improved goods to the knowledge of the people, enlarges the size of the market and helps in wealth creation in the economy. On the other hand, much of the expenditure on modern advertising is a competitive waste.

- Advertising tends to overpower consumers choice in favour of psychic needs distorting their preferences in the process. In developing economies, it may divert the meagre resources from the production of goods to meet the basic needs of the masses to the production of non-essential luxuries.

- An oligopoly is a market structure where several large firms producing a homogenous or differentiated product constitute an industry such that the price–output policy of one invokes reaction among the others.

- The proportion of total output produced by the few largest firms gives us a measure of oligopoly concentration in an industry. High transportation costs, infirm definition of industry and non-inclusion in the calculation of foreign trade component reduce the value of concentration ratios.

- Diversity of market and mutual dependency complications have resulted in several models for describing the behaviour of firms in an oligopoly; only three of them are discussed here: kinked demand curve, collusion and price leadership.

- The kinked demand theory says that up to a certain point, the firm in an oligopoly does not invoke rivals' retaliation if it raises the price of its product but beyond that point, a reduction in price provokes them to competitive price cutting. The demand curve is kinked at such a price.

- The kinked demand curve model fails to explain why and how the kink is formed at a particular price in the first place. Also, the price remains rigid; how it would adjust to cyclical fluctuations in the economy is unclear.

- Collusion among firms producing a homogenous product in an industry takes place to avoid ruinous competition, especially in periods of economic recession, to have an agreed common price or divide the market for sales.

- If firms in collusion agree to have a common price, the match price changes if any and adjust their output to maximize profit given the price. If they divide the market, they take price–output decisions in their area as a monopolist would to maximize profit.

- Differences in demand and costs, a large number of firms, temptation to violate agreement secretly to enhance profit, possible entry of new firms into the industry and business downturns make it difficult to enter into or maintain collusion.

- An important obstacle to collusion is that firms feel uncomfortable about talking to one another as to what could be an appropriate common price for the product. Price leadership is a form of collusion to overcome the difficulty.

- How the leader would determine the price of the commodity broadly depends on either the follower firms honestly following the leader or the leader firm is dominant enough to ignore the reaction of the rivals to its price setting.

- In a leader–follower model of oligopoly, the dominant firm behaves like a monopolist in fixing the price for its product. The followers operate like firms in pure competition, as takers of this price. The industry adjusts its demand and supply such that the price of the commodity remains unaltered.

- Oligopolies are not efficient either in factor allocation or in their use but they are considered better than pure monopolies with reference to social welfare.

Glossary

Duopoly It is a market situation where only two firms control the production and/or sale of a particular commodity or service. Duopoly is quite similar to monopoly as the firms often strike an understanding about the quality, price and division of the market between them.

Oligopoly An oligopoly is a market position dominated by a small number of large firms supplying a commodity—standardized or differentiated. The word is derived from the Greek language meaning a few entities with the right to sell. Because there are few firms in this market, each oligopolist is aware of the actions of the others. The decisions of one firm influence, and are influenced by, the decisions of rivals. Strategic planning the keyword in describing this sort of market as oligopolists always take into consideration the likely responses of the other market players. This causes oligopolistic markets and industries to get involved in collusive action open or hidden not to the advantage of their clients.

Product differentiation This is the process firms use for making their product offerings look more attractive than that of rivals to buyers in the market. In economic parlance, it makes competition imperfect or monopolistic. Brand names and trademarks are used for the purpose and a sales strategy is developed around them to win over the clients. Advertising plays a key role in the process. Differences are created in quality, design, functional features, after-sale services and packaging to name some. Price differences accompany product differences.

Product differentiation is a tool for non-price competition. It targets human longing for variety but also raises the vital question: how much variety do we need because we as individuals and society have to pay perhaps too much for it as qualitative differences between products may be meagre; product differentiation largely involves psychic manipulations.

Concepts for Review

- Collusive oligopoly
- Duopoly
- Kinked demand curve
- Monopolistic competition
- Oligopoly

- Persuasive advertising
- Price leadership
- Product differentiation
- Wastes of monopolistic competition

Case Study 8.1

Market Structure—Oligopoly

In studying market structures, one of the most commonly used case study examples explore oligopolies; the reason is because they are so predominant in modern business. Oligopolies refer to a market structure where an industry is denominated by a small number of large sellers. The following are some good examples of oligopolistic markets structures.

Fast food outlets: McDonalds; Burger King; KFC
Banks: Barclays; HSBC; Lloyds; TSB
Electrical goods: Sony; Hitachi; Panasonic; Canon; Fuji
Bookstores: Amazon; Borders; Blackwell; Waterstones

Case Questions

1. What factors give rise to oligopolistic market structures? Explain.
2. In what industry does each of the following firms fall in the oligopoly structure: Unilever, HMV and Orange.

(Check your answers from the Web source for this case study.)

Case Study 8.2

Oligopoly in the Air: The Middle East Scenario

Dubai, Doha and Abu Dhabi are locked in a multi-billion dollar race to build the biggest, swankiest airport in the Middle East. They are hoping to leverage their location—all three cities are around six hours away from two-third's of the world's population—by building global travel hubs that boost revenues for their national carriers, tourism and real estate developments.

The Dubai international airport is the cornerstone of the Emirate's efforts to build a travel, tourism and retail hub. After handling just 18 million passengers in 2003, the airport attended to 57 million fliers in 2012. This year, it surpassed Paris's Charles de Gaulle airport as the second busiest airport in the world, and is slated to overtake London's Heathrow Airport in 2015 as the airport with the most international traffic. The airport's success helped spawn a retail and hospitality industry centered around it and turned Dubai-based Emirates Airlines into the world's third biggest airline. Government-owned Dubai Duty Free, which operates stores in the airport, is expected to rake in $1.8 billion in revenue this year. Rents in a logistics and business zone surrounding the airport are at a 60% premium to other industrial districts in the region.

The success has made Dubai more ambitious. The airport has embarked on a $7.8 billion expansion programme to boost capacity from the current 60 million to 90 million passengers per year by 2018. The prize that Dubai is eyeing is not just the bragging rights for having the most popular airport in the world. The airport is expected to generate around 22% of the total employment and 32% of the emirate's GDP by 2020, according to the Dubai Airport Strategic Plan 2020 of the civil aviation authority.

Dubai's rivals are anxious to replicate its success. Qatar's $15.5 billion Hamad International airport, whose opening in Doha was scheduled earlier this year but has been delayed, will more than double the city of Doha's capacity to 55 million passengers a year. (Doha is already home to Doha International Airport.) Hamad is two-thirds the size of the metropolitan Doha area and will have 270,000 square feet of retail space and a 100-room hotel. The airport will also boast its own monorail network and a residential district that will house 200,000 workers.

The newest entrant in this airport arms race, Abu Dhabi, has started work on a $3 billion international terminal that will triple its capacity to 40 million passengers by 2017. The new terminal is an integral part of Plan Abu Dhabi 2030, an Emirate-wide strategy to diversify the economy away from oil by focusing on business and tourism growth. The terminal is also crucial to the fate of the national carrier Etihad, which trails regional rivals Emirates and Qatar Airways. The airline has been aggressively expanding its network through partnerships and minority stake investments, and is now betting on the new terminal attracting a bigger share of the passengers who pass through the region during international travel.

But aviation experts caution that this hectic expansion could lead to a capacity glut. Traffic on the main route between Europe and Asia that these three cities prize is expected to rise only by 120 million passengers annually by 2031, well short of the planned capacity expansion. An economic slowdown or an increase in airline fuel costs could further upset calculations. On the other hand, if traffic picks up, there is the issue of congestion. For instance, the Dubai airport is only two hours by road from the one in Abu Dhabi. Increasing the number of aircrafts in that confined space could lead to delays, and reduce the region's appeal as a hub for transit traffic.

Source: Nandagopal, J. (2013), *The Economist* – September 14th 2013 (edited).

Case Questions

1. Is there an oligopolistic structure in the air traffic of the Middle East or is it likely to emerge? Substantiate your opinion.
2. The last paragraph of the case expresses concern about the possible excessive airport capacity contraction resulting in intense competition and causing losses. Do you share this apprehension? Give reasons for your answer.

Case Study   8.3

Cracking the Oligopoly?

For more than a decade, competition regulators have worried that Britain's banking oligopoly is ripping off customers, mainly by stinging them with high fees for overdrafts or late payments. In 2000 a government appointed review found evidence of 'excessive prices and profits' in British banking because of insufficient competition. Promises by the government and industry to improve matters have yielded little. Worse still, Britain's banking market has become more concentrated since the financial crisis. In mid-2008—just before the near-collapse of the global banking system—regulators worried that Britain's four biggest banks had about 65% of the retail-banking market.

Now, the resurrection of TSB Bank on September 9th carved out Lloyds promises to inject competition into a market which is among the most concentrated one among the rich of the world. The dis-investment by Lloyds was forced on it by the European Commission after it was bailed out by the British government five years ago in the midst of the financial crisis.

Any challenger to the current oligopoly needs to jump two big hurdles. The first is scale. Although TSB has enough branches to have a national presence (it claims that most Britons live within a few miles of at least one), it may struggle to win much new business because its branches are thinly spread. This is because of an intriguing characteristic of scale in retail banking; in places where banks have many branches near to one another, they gain a share of customers that is even higher than their scale suggests.

Source: Nandagopal, J. (2013), *The Economist* – September 14th 2013 (edited).

Case Questions

1. Explain in what sense does the banking industry in England exhibit the features of an oligopoly. Comment on the consequences of the structure being oligarchic.
2. Do you think that the reorganization of Lloyds-TSB would succeed in breaking the oligopoly in the British banking industry and restore fruitful completion, its primary object? Give reasons for your answer.
3. The Consumers' Association of Penang (CAP), an NGO, has recently charged that Islamic banks are ripping off customers in Malaysia. Do you agree with this charge? Give reasons for your answer.

Test Questions

8.1 In the long run, monopolistic competition allows firms to monopolize price but not profit. Which of the two—collusive price fixing or price leadership—is better in your opinion from the social welfare viewpoint and why?

8.2 State the assumptions that underlie the kinked demand curve theory. What causes a gap in the marginal revenue curve of the firm in this case? Examine the shortcomings of the kinked demand curve model.

8.3 Much of the expenditure on advertising in monopolistic competition and oligopoly is competitive and self-cancelling; it is a sheer waste of resources serving no social ends. Comment on the statement. Would you advocate some social control on advertising in an Islamic economy? Explain.

8.4 A firm in monopolistic competition has the demand function as $P = 20 - Q$. Its total cost function is $40 + 4Q$. Find the price–output combination that would maximize its profit. Show when the firm would be making optimal use of its production capacity. Verify that $Q = 13$ and $P = 7$ will do so.

Web Exercise

Collect information about the structure of OPEC to assess whether it is a collusive oligopoly or a loose organization, to discuss production and pricing of policies in view of the changing demand and supply conditions of petroleum internationally.

Forward Link

You have so far covered in this course the areas including the nature and scope of microeconomics, consumption, production and exchange of goods and services. Onwards, you enter a new area of economics—the issues concerning income distribution. It is a difficult and controversial area. In production we talk of cooperation, mutual support and harmony. But when it comes to the distribution of the cake among those who contribute or even did not contribute for valid reasons, we are confronted with the questions of justice and injustice where opinions, perceptions and pressures all play their role. Conflicts of interest and social issues tend to occupy the centre of the stage.

In the next chapter, we shall be introduced to the mainstream theory of income distribution, the distributional forms and related issues. Here, we will see that there is much to say from an Islamic perspective.

Factor Pricing and Equity

LEARNING OUTCOMES

This chapter should enable the student to understand:

- The types of income distribution and their importance
- The criteria for a just distribution of income
- Marginal productivity theory of income distribution
- How far we can rely on that theory
- Islam and income distribution
- The notion of *amanah* and its implications
- Islamic redistributive measurers

9.1 FROM PRODUCTION TO DISTRIBUTION

> The process of determining production prices determines in a large measure the structure of income and wealth distribution simultaneously. This lends importance to the how factor.

In Chapters 6, 7 and 8, we discussed how the prices of real commodities and services are determined under different market conditions. However, firms use various sorts of resources or inputs for producing them. These resources are called the factors of production. Factor pricing refers to the determination of payments that firms make to factor owners for their services needed to produce goods. These payments add up to production costs for the firms. We talked about the types, nature and behaviour of these costs with reference to time in Chapter 5 but we did not show how inputs are priced in the factor markets. The present chapter and the two that follow address this question. Thus, we move from the production side of the economy to its income distribution. For what are costs to the firms become their incomes in the hands of input suppliers. Input suppliers are too numerous. We classify factors of production as indicated earlier into broad categories on the basis of some common characteristics.

To reiterate, initially economists used to talk of five factors of production: land, labour, capital, organization and enterprise. But later on, land came to be merged with capital as in most cases substantial investment was needed for levelling, fencing and fertilizing land to make it usable for cultivation or other purposes. Organization was specialized, professional skill; it was merged with labour. The position of enterprise, however, remained unclear. Some merge it with capital, others with labour. Thus, many books on economics usually deal with only labour and capital for discussing their pricing in the market. However, we shall treat land too as a distinct factor separate from capital for that purpose. But it has to be kept in mind that any classification of resources into two or more categories involves a high degree of generalization; each category has to put together many sorts of diverse and non-competing elements in the same container. Still, such categorization is needed to facilitate economic analysis.

The nature and significance of factor pricing is much different from that of pricing the output they produce. In market economies the processes of creating wealth and distributing it among the factors of production are simultaneous. Factor pricing is a dynamic link between the two. Distribution is a more important and complex issue than pricing of products. The reasons are;

1. **Income distribution**: In the circular flow of money income and expenditure between the firms and the households in an economy (see Figure 1.2), the income side of the flow shows the payments firms make to the households in the form of wages, interest, profit and rent for the services they provide for producing goods. This money flow determines the *functional* distribution of incomes in the economy. Usually, a person earns his income from more than one source. The sum of money he receives from different sources is called his *personal* income. Personal income distribution is largely the function of preproduction asset distribution in a society. Still, it is much influenced by the functional distribution of income and, therefore, by how the factor prices are determined in the market. Table 9.1 shows the connection between the two sorts of income distributions, personal and functional.

Income distribution can be viewed as personal or functional.

Table 9.1 *Functional and personal income distributions (amount in INR'000)*

Households	Payments made as				Personal income distribution
	Wages	Rent	Interest	Profit	
A	–	13	12	100	125
B	9	5	1	10	25
C	–	10	5	8	23
D	10	–	–	5	15
E	6	2	2	2	12
Functional income distribution	25	30	20	125	200

The issue of a just distribution of incomes is basically related to personal income. But personal income distribution is much affected by functional income distribution. Microeconomics deals with the first.

2. **Allocative role**: Prices of factors allocate them to various firms operating in various lines of production. Modern economies are dynamic and technologies change quite often. There are also shifts in consumer demands. Factor prices play a role in shifting them from one use to another in response to such shifts. Consequently patterns of income distribution also change. In fact, factor prices, their allocation to various uses and income distributions are locked together in causal relationships—they intimately affect each other.

3. **Policy demands**: Laws of production are quite natural and simple. This is not so with the principles of distribution. They are the results of conventions, legal frameworks and public policies. They raise a host of issues including those of justice and injustice, entitlements and opportunities, of basic needs, poverty and inequalities that have not only economic but also moral social and political implications. Fixation of minimum wages, collective bargaining, property rights, economic controls, taxation and subsidies, monetary management, environmental care all raise issues that urge for appropriate policy response promotive of individual freedom and social well-being; the role of the state assumes importance.

However, the important question here is how much each factor must get from the wealth it helps to generate and on what basis? The question is difficult to answer. Yet it is *the* question that has to be answered. *Justice is the essence of Islamic ethics* (Qur'an 2:188; 4:29 and 16:90). There is no amount of juristic (*fiqh*) analysis of contract forms that will help you determine whether or not there is injustice in the exchange. Nevertheless, the criteria must conform to some ethical norm. The principle that one should get what one contributes to the total output of a firm is widely held as a fair and logical basis for division despite some limitations. Islamic economics also endorses it as valid: to each his due, says the Qur'an. See also the following verse:

God created the heaven and the earth for just ends and in order that each soul may find the recompense of what it has earned (45:22).

The issue then is: can we take the market determined price of a resource as the measure of its contribution? Let us explain how mainstream economics seeks to resolve the issue and how appropriate is the solution.

Marginal productivity theory of income distribution was developed by J. B. Clark, an American economist, to show that capitalism is not only an efficient economic system but also ensures a fair distribution of income. It gives every factor what it contributes to total output.

9.2   MARGINAL PRODUCTIVITY AND DISTRIBUTION: THE THEORY

John Bortes Clark, an American economist (1847–1938), presented in *The Distribution of Wealth* his theory of marginal productivity as an answer to the equity question in distribution. The theory was hailed as a response to the growing criticism of capitalism as an unjust system and the spread of socialistic ideas. Many saw ethical statements of Clark on marginal productivity as reaction to the views of Henry George and Karl Marx. George pleaded for nationalization of land as, to him, rent was but an unearned income, while Marx demonstrated that exploitation of labour was inevitable in the capitalist system of production. Ibn Khaldun had seen centuries earlier that labour was the source of all creation.

The theory of marginal productivity, in contrast, aimed at proving that the capitalist system was both efficient and equitable; it gave each factor what it contributed to total output. Let us examine the basis for this claim. To begin with, let us note that unlike commodities the demand for resources is not for its own sake. It comes from the demand for finished products, more land, for example, may be needed to increase food production with an increase in population. In other words, the demand for resources is not a thing by itself; it depends on the demand for various types of goods and services it can help produce in the economy; it is so to say a *derived* demand.

Taking the supply side of the factor market as given, the marginal productivity theory seeks to provide an answer to the distribution question from the side of factor demand. It rests on the assumption that firms sell their goods and buy factor inputs in *competitive* markets. One important implication of the assumption is that in the long run constant returns to scale operate in the product markets as well as in the markets for factor inputs. The firm is a price taker in either case: it can sell as much or as little of its product as it may choose without affecting the price of the commodity. Likewise, it can hire any amount of a factor at the going price, for example, as much of labour hours as it may want at the current wage rate.

To explain the theory, let us assume that there are only two factors—labour and land—that firms use for producing wheat in the agricultural sector of an economy. (See Table 9.2.)

A firm will hire labour until the dollar value of labour's marginal product (MP_L) equals the current wage rate, say $240 a week. The $$MP_L$ is the product of the price of wheat (P) in the market and the tons of wheat (Q) the marginal unit of labour produces. The farm land area the firm has hired remaining fixed; the law of diminishing returns must apply to labour's contribution to output in the firm. Table 9.2 illustrates the case assuming the price of wheat as $12 per ton. The average and marginal revenue values of the table can be used to draw the respective curves that will resemble in shape to those in Figure 9.1. Using the table values, we find that the wage level WW at $240 per week corresponds to employment of 6 units of labour. If the firm employs more labour than 6 units at the going in a competitive labour market wage rate, ARP_L would fall reducing the profit of the firm. On the other hand, if it employs less than 6 labour units, it would lose the opportunity to earn more. The rectangle 0WTL in the figure shows the total wage bill at W × L = $1,440. If the firm employs 9 labour units, the marginal revenue product would fall to almost zero (point f), with average revenue product being

The theory assumes perfect competition in commodity and factor markets. It takes the factor supply as given and argues equity from the side of demand for the factor.

Mostly a two-factor model (labour and capital) is used to explain the *modus operandi* and the merits of the theory.

$192 (point j). Employing labour units beyond 9 would make the marginal revenue product negative. The falling portion of MRP_L represents for a firm the demand curve for labour. The horizontal summation of such curves of firms gives us the labour demand curve for the industry.

Table 9.2 *Physical product and revenue product of labour per month, land remaining fixed (amount in USD)*

Units of labour employed per week	Price of wheat per ton ($)	Physical product of labour (Q)			Revenue product of labour (MRP_L is per unit of MP_L)		
		Total product (tons of wheat) (TP$_L$)	Average product (tons of wheat) (AP$_L$)	Marginal product (tons of wheat) (MP$_L$)	Total revenue product of labour (TRP$_L$)	Average revenue product of labour (ARP$_L$)	Marginal revenue product of labour (MRP$_L$)
L	P	TQ	TQ/L	Δ TQ	P×TQ	P(TQ/L)	P(MPL)
0	240	0	0	0	0	0	0
1	240	10	10	10	2,400	2,400	2,400
2	240	22	11	12	5,280	2,640	2,880
3	240	39	13	17	9,360	3,120	4,080
4	240	64	16	25	15,360	3,840	6,000
5	240	100	20	36	24,000	4,800	8,640
6	**240**	**120**	**20**	**20**	**28,800**	4,800	**4,800**
7	240	133	19	13	31,920	4,560	3,120
8	240	144	18	11	34,560	4,320	2,640
9	240	144	16	0	34,560	3,840	0
10	240	140	14	−4	−960	3,360	−35,520

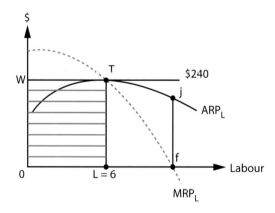

Figure 9.1 *Long-run equilibrium of the firm in a competitive labour market*

We may construct in the same way the revenue product curves for any of the factors combinations. Figure 9.2 puts the cases of labour and land side by side. In panel A, the curve MRP_L is the marginal revenue product of labour obtained as the multiplication of its physical product MP_L and the dollar price of wheat at \$12 a ton in the market. The price will be constant for the firm as competition in the wheat market is by assumption perfect. In panel A of the figure, MRP_L is the marginal revenue product curve of labour and W is the wage rate prevailing in the labour market. The firm will continue hiring workers until W equals the MRP_L in point T. Thus, it would employ L units of labour to produce Q tons of wheat at the minimum labour costs per ton. The total wage bill (W × L = \$1,440) is shown by the lined rectangle 0WTL. The remaining portion of total dollar product, i.e. the area of the triangle D_LWT, is rent for the farm land, the fixed factor.

<aside>In a two-factor model, if the share of one factor in output is proven as just, the share of the other becomes automatically just.</aside>

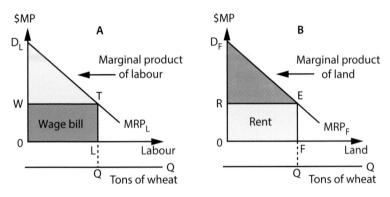

Figure 9.2 *Wages as rent and rent as wages*

We apply the same procedure in panel B as in A to determine the payment of rent. MRP_F is the marginal revenue product of the farm land, now the number of labour units employed remaining constant. Here, the white rectangle OREF gives the total amount of rent paid to land owners. The remaining area under the MRP_F curve, i.e. D_FRE, represents wages. Thus, it follows that in terms of the marginal productivity theory; wages can be depicted as rent and rent as wage. *The theory is involved in a circular reasoning.*

Even so, the theory is considered elegant in showing that the sum of factor rewards equals the total revenue product of the firm. In Figure 9.2, the sum of marginal revenue product of labour multiplied by its units employed (L) plus the marginal revenue product of land multiplied by its units (F) used in production equals the dollar value of its total output Q. In physical terms, we have.

$$Q = \frac{dQ}{dL} + \frac{dQ}{dF} \tag{9.1}$$

This means, given the market price (P) of the product, we shall get:

PQ = P. MP_L L + P. MP_F. F

TR = MRPL .L + MRP_F.F   (9.2)

Note that in the long-run equilibrium, PQ also represents the total production cost to the firm including normal profit. The sum of the shaded areas showing wages and rent in Figure 9.2 exhausts the total revenue product PQ. Under perfect competition in the market, each factor of production would receive a return equal to the value of its marginal product. The return measures the contribution of a factor to both the output of the commodity produced and to the society. (Why?) The return to capital is justified by the fact that capital too is productive. Competitive profits being normal, the return is fair and just as well. The return to land is likewise not an unearned income, but a return for the productivity of land. The same applies to the return to labour. Thus, the marginal productivity theory demonstrates, it is claimed, that capitalism is a just economic system. Theories of exploitation and unearned income are erroneous; they fail to understand the working of freely competitive markets. We must have a look at the logical and ethical aspects of these claims

> The theory is static not dynamic. In the real world, its assumptions may not hold and the sum of the parts may not be equal to the whole.

9.3 EVALUATION OF THE THEORY

Marginal productivity theory has attracted a lot of criticism from its very inception, and much of this criticism remains valid. The earlier critics were unsure whether the theory applied to labour, capital or land because of circular nature of its reasoning indicated above. Special problems arose when attempts were made to determine profits and interest in terms of marginal productivity. We shall discuss these problems in the following chapter. For now, we examine the difficulties in its general application. The main points raised are as under.

> The theory has many weaknesses within its own framework. The concept of marginal productivity is indeterminate.

The final output of a firm, industry or economy is the result of a combinative effort of land, labour, capita and enterprise; it is impossible to separate their individual contributions to the aggregate. In the simple process of driving nails in the wooden panels in the furniture industry, how can one separate the productivity of labour from the productivity of the hammer, the capital? Again, if one hammer alone were added to the stock, what shall be its marginal productivity until a worker is also added to use it? When a farmer and his worker sow and reap a field for tomatoes, how is it possible to determine the quantity each has grown? Or, how will one find the marginal productivity of a teacher in a university department?

The money value of the marginal product of labour is its marginal physical product multiplied by the price of the good. Wages are costs for the firms, but at the same time they are also the income of the workers. During the depression of 1930s, the American economists with their strong *laissez faire* orientation and belief in the marginal productivity theory, suggested to keep the government out of economic matters and let the market find its way for wage reduction. This was their basic difference with Keynes, who agreed that a wage reduction could lower the production costs and help the firms slow the spread of unemployment.

But on a more important side, it would also lower, he argued, the income of the workers. This would increase the contraction of demand for goods leading to a further fall in prices. Reliance on market could not stem the rot. Wages were averse to downward adjustment for a variety of reasons. So, he prescribed increased public expenditure to revive demand through deficit financing, and it did work.

The demonstration that under perfect competition a factor is paid equal to the value of its contribution to output does not by itself *prove* that marginal product *determines* that payment because it is not the contribution of a factor to output but its scarcity relative to other factors that determines both its marginal product and return.

Even if we concede for a moment that perfect markets equate payment to contribution, we cannot draw an ethical conclusion from an ethically neutral analysis. For, what a person *actually* earns need not be equal to what he *should* earn. His actual earning may, for example, equal his contribution to output, but it may not equal the minimum he should get to meet his basic needs. Also, even when there are visible differences in the productivity of workers in a *pay scale*, they are paid the same amount on each point in it. Pay scales in practice rarely exhibit what the marginal productivity theory predicts.

It is valid that we have production functions that yield constant returns to scale but it is wrong to believe, as the theory implies, that all production functions are of that type. Once the function form is different the theory has no legs to stand on.

We cannot derive long-run conclusions from a short-run analysis, if the conditions imposed do not remain intact over time. Take, for example, equations 9.1 and 9.2. The argument based on them assumes the division of factors into fixed and variable, a short-run imperative. But the distinction would not hold good in the long run. Also, returns to a factor in the short run are not the same thing as returns to scale in the long run. What can be shown as valid for the first case may not be applicable to the second. This knocks out the very base of the marginal productivity theory.

Finally, the addition of an individual would depend on the price of the factors in the market and the quantity of *them* that he sells in the market. Individuals owning land and capital would get income from these sources in addition to wages if they work. Equity in *factor* payments, even if achieved, does not ensure equity *in personal* income distribution as well.

> The fact that the marginal revenue product equals its price does not by itself prove that it determines price. Marginal uses and costs do not govern price but are themselves governed together with price by the general forces of demand and supply.

9.4 FACTOR RETURNS IN MONOPOLISTIC MARKETS

Any merits one may possibly claim for the theory flow from the assumption that perfect competition prevails in the product and factor markets. However, we cannot take a system rewarding factors in a fair and just way without scrutiny, if such competition nowhere exists. One step outside the dreamland of perfections and you would find the realities of economic life so different from the productivity model that it would look entirely naïve and misleading.

An important feature of perfect competition in the long-run equilibrium is that average revenue equals marginal revenue. Thus, the equality of price to marginal revenue implies that price also equals average revenue. On the other hand, under monopolistic competition, the marginal revenue is less than average revenue. If the wage rate remains equal to marginal revenue product of labour, it falls short of labour's average revenue product. The gap between ARP_L and MRP_L is a measure of labour's exploitation under monopolistic competition as per Joan Robinson. To illustrate, if we have $9.0 a week as the market wage rate for Table 9.2, the rate of labour exploitation will be dollar $14 - 9 = 5$ per worker employed. Figure 9.3 sketches the position both for the firm and industry. In the Industry Panel, ARP_{LI} and MRP_{LI} represent the horizontal summation of them for individual firms. MRP_{LI}, the demand for labour, is also the marginal cost curve for the industry. It cuts the labour supply curve S_L in point N, determining the full value of workers contribution to output at T. The wage rate would have been higher at W_1 and employment equal to W_1E. (How?) Thus, the wage rate W_0 falls short of a just level on the contribution criterion by $(W_1 - W_0)$. The gap measures the monopolistic exploitation of labour.

While we assumed monopolistic competition in the product market, we retain the assumption of perfect competition in the labour market. Thus, the individual firms in the industry have to be price (wage) takers. For this reason in the firm panel of Figure 9.3 the supply of labour curve W_0K is perfectly elastic. The firm can hire any number of labour units, large or small, at the current wage rate. W_0K cuts the firm's demand for labour curve MRP_{LF} in point H and hires L_F labour units. The gap between ARP_{LF} and MRP_{LF} curves for that number of labour units measures the monopolistic exploitation of workers at the firm level. If at the going rate W_0 the firm could employ labour units up to point K, such exploitation would not exist. (Why?)

> Under monopolistic competition, in equilibrium, the marginal revenue product of labour is invariably less than its average revenue product. Thus, a wage rate equal to marginal revenue product would be unfair to workers.

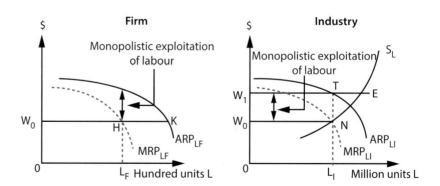

Figure 9.3 *Exploitation of labour in monopolistic competition*

Exercise 9.2

Place Figure 9.1 and the Firm Panel of the table given in Exercise 9.3 side by side. Compare and contrast the two figures in all possible details.

Exercise 9.3

The following is a production function $Q = 10 \, L^{1/2} . \, K^{1/2}$
Fill in the blanks in the following table:

Units of labour	(L)	10	15	20	25	30	35	40	45	50	55
Units of capital	(K)	200	300	400	500	600	700	800	900	1000	1100
Output	(Q)	–	–	–	–	–	–	–	–	–	–

find that the marginal productivity theory cannot apportion the fruits of factors' combinational effort on contribution basis, and functional income distribution, even if equitable, may not ensure fairness in personal income distribution. The issue of the just factor rewards and equitable distribution in economics remains unresolved. Where do we go from here? Islamic economists claim that their religion contains guidelines that may help resolve the problem. Their argument needs attention.

BOX 9.1

Income Inequalities: Muslim Countries versus the Rest of the World

With an overall rising growth rate of global GDP in recent decades the inequalities in income distribution have also been on the rise across countries. However it is interesting to find that inequalities have been smaller in Muslim countries than the rest of the world as the following Figure 9.4 unmistakably shows. The figure is based on Gini coefficients available for 27 Muslim countries and 116 other countries obtained from country surveys conducted in any year during 2004–2008. What could be the reasons?

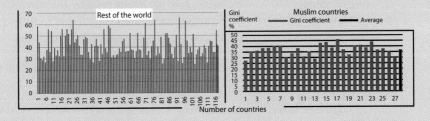

Figure 9.4 *Income inequalities in Muslim countries are in general smaller than in the rest of the world*

9.5 ISLAM AND INCOME DISTRIBUTION

Islamic economics, like its mainstream counterpart, also casts its distribution theory in a *puritan* framework. Assuming that a performing Muslim community is in existence, it seeks to show that:

1. The guiding principles and the institutional arrangements of Islam are such that under their operation the problem of an unjust income distribution would rarely arise.
2. If in spite of the in-built safeguards of the system, distribution tends to become inequitable, the model has corrective measures ready at hand to rectify the situation.

The assumption of a performing community of the believers being in existence in the present era may look unrealistic but it is not more—if not less—unrealistic that the assumption of perfect competition that has largely been the foundation of what looks good and valuable in mainstream economic theory. In any case, pure models—mainstream or Islamic—have utility. They help identify the path to reach specified destinations, provide the needed attitudinal orientation and make easy the choice of the variables relevant to guide policy.

9.5.1 Equity Criteria

Perfect equality in personal incomes would be no less unjust and undesirable as the present inequalities. It will reward hard work and laziness or intelligence and lack of it at the same rate and will adversely affect work incentive. Islam not only allows for income differences, it advises people not to grudge the same (Qur'an 4:32). We pointed out earlier that Islam approves payments according to a factor's contribution to output. But the criterion leaves out high and dry large chunks of population—children, the unemployed, the infirm and the old, victims of war such as those in Afghanistan and Iraq because of America-led invasion, sufferers of natural calamities such as the tsunami in Japan or the 2009 earthquake in Kashmir. Hence, in addition to factor payments being according to contribution, Islam adds the help for the needy to its notion of economic justice. In other words, the Islamic norm of distributive justice is: *Give each according to his contribution but help the poor and the needy as an obligation.* This obligation follows from the all-pervading concept of *amanah* (trusteeship) in Islam we now discuss.

Amanah (trusteeship): the foundation of distributive justice

The concept of *amanah* or trusteeship makes the Islamic approach to the issue of equity in distribution qualitatively different from that in mainstream economics. It lends an edge to the preventive prescriptions of Islam rather than treating the malady after its emergence. Let us explain the notion briefly.

Amanah is fundamental to Islam even as other religions also talk of the notion. *Amanah* in Islam seeks to convert the mundane *ends* of man into the *means* for attaining spiritual heights—his eventual goal. The Qur'an instructs the believers:

But seek with the wealth which God has bestowed on thee the home of the hereafter and forget not thy portion of this world (20:77)

The notion of *amanah* inspires the entire socio-economic philosophy of Islam and encompasses its program for individuals and the community in their relationship with God. The end part of the verse reinforces the oft repeated Qura'nic position that Islam is not an ascetic religion concerned—like other religions—only with the spiritual aspect of human existence.

Amanah may mean different things to different people. Commonly, the word refers to something tangible that a person entrusts to another in good faith for safe keeping, and returns it to the giver, when asked for, in as far as possible the same condition as it was given to the keeper. The fulfilment of *amanah* obligations has always been regarded among the noblest of human traits in civilized societies. Islam regards this common view of *amanah* as a tiny, though important, element of a much wider relationship: the relationship between man and his Creator.

All things in heaven and earth belong to God (Qur'an 31:26; 42:2). He handed over the earth with all its treasures to man, gave him intellect and the ability to understand, subdue, tame and harness resources of nature for his use. He made His bounties flow to him in vast measure (Qur'an 31:20). The reason was that man alone agreed, rather in foolishness, to run affairs on the planet earth as His trust-keeper (Qur'an 33:72). 'In foolishness' because man could not realize how great a responsibility he was accepting in becoming God's vicegerent and co-worker. The source of difficulty, according to Rumi, was that God granted man free will as well. And, it is this grant of *free will* to him that lends meaning and dimension to the Islamic concept of *amanah*.

The concept implies that the Creator of the trust expects man—the trustee—to manage it according to His instructions and not otherwise. He granted man freedom of action but also laid down for him obligation to fulfil so that he may remain on the right path. Broadly, these obligations relate to God, to fellow human beings, and even to one's ownself. Obligations of one person become the rights of others. Islamic *Shari'ah* (law) is essentially an aggregation of these rights and obligations; it is a code of conduct prescribed for man by the Almighty for running the show according to His will. Islam is nothing but a total submission to this will. Thus seen, the entire religion becomes an *amanah* with the believers. Free will granted to people means that they may choose to meet their obligations or ignore them; if they meet they will be rewarded, but if they do not they will be punished. Shari'ah spells outs a system of such rewards and punishments.

Amanah is an all-embracing concept. Here, we take a brief look at its economic content only. God's aim in creating various things was to provide for the needs of all his creatures, mankind in particular. The Qur'an which addresses all humanity without distinction says:

He is Who created for you all that is in the earth (2:29)

According to this divine proclamation, all things in the universe are the common property of Adam's progeny; there is no reason in the origin of resources as to why must anything belong to a particular person or a group; even the produced wealth may be deemed in the light of the above verse as accruing in the first instance to the entire human society. It is to avoid disputes and motivate individuals to produce for better living that the acquisition of resources through permitted means is allowed and recognized. As long as one is in legal and safe possession of something no one else can deprive the owner of its rightful use and enjoyment (Qur'an 4:29). If property still remains a cause of dispute among people it is not because the right to own property is in principle disputed, but because people have different perceptions about the *actual* and the *ideal* distribution of property and the gap between the two.

Since wealth in origin is common to all, it must not remain concentrated in few hands (Qur'an 59:7). The possessor himself should not hold what he perceives as being in excess of his legitimate requirements. He must voluntarily surrender the surplus in favour of the less fortunate members of the community; for, to that extent their rights are clearly invoked in his wealth. The surplus belongs to them; he holds it as their trustee. This is why he is not permitted to indulge in frivolous expenditure or keep wealth in idle hoards. The Shari'ah confronts the holder with a serious trial (Qur'an 26:151; 70:18; 64:15). The Qur'an reminds people time and again of those powerful men who blinded by their riches defied the divine instructions only to meet their total destruction.

The view of property rights in pure *amanah* model is much different from their notion under capitalism. There are, of course, restrictions on private property rights in capitalism as well. For example, a car owner must observe speed limits, cannot jump over stop traffic signals or park anywhere he may please. These sort of restrictions are not, however, the essence of Islamic position. It is rather the explicit *right* Islam grants to the weak and deprived in the wealth of the rich. The Shari'ah insists that one must honour these rights: the excess wealth with a person belongs to others after his own legitimate requirements have been met.

> **Property rights in Islam are not absolute or exclusive.**

What the 'legitimate' needs of a person are and how much excess wealth he has are matters for his own moral perceptions; their external determination is very difficult. *Amanah* is an attitude of mind, a sort of self-discipline. It promotes in man the feeling that he is at the centre of an oceanic circle which consists of a family, a neighbourhood, a group, a community, a nation and humanity at large. We cannot be as we are not pure individualists. We are tied together in a social web: we cannot be completely independent of or non-responsible to one another. The Qur'an says:

…Conduct yourself with beneficence towards parents, and toward kindred and orphans, and the needy and toward the neighbour who is the kindred and the

*neighbour who is a stranger, and the companions by your side, and the wayfarer,
and those who work for you. Surely, God loves not the proud and the boastful that
are niggardly and enjoin others to niggardliness (4:37–38).*

Amanah is not an isolated idea. It is the soul of religion. Without this
base, many Islamic principles would not fit into a pattern as neatly as they
do without conflict or contradiction. On this foundation is raised the
superstructure of Islamic economics.

In-built measures

The extent of departure of *actual* income distribution in a society from
its view of the *ideal* would broadly depend on the place of wealth in its
value system, factor return norms in production and the redistributive
institutions it has in place. Let us briefly examine the Islamic position on
the three.

1. **Attitude towards wealth**: The notion of *amanah* tends to bring
    about a harmony between the individual interest and societal
    concerns in the pursuit of wealth because without that the
    freedom of enterprise which Islam encourages can rarely work
    as an instrument for improving the lot of the masses.

    > Redistributive measures in Islam follow from its all-pervading notion of *amanah*.

    Amanah adds a social dimension to personal gain. It refines
    one's attitude towards material pursuits. Once man takes in the
    idea that he has little moral claim on the wealth he has after his
    legitimate needs have been met, he can more easily accept the
    Islamic advice that he should be moderate in his ambition for
    wealth, that the means to acquire it must be honest and that if
    there is a conflict between wealth and virtue he ought to be
    content with what can rightfully be obtained even if it were
    little (Qur'an 5:103).

    Western rationalistic concepts are atomistic; they are based on
    a split view of human personality pitching the individual against
    society. Islam projects a different vision of man. It focuses on his
    self developmental qualities wherein his social economic, political
    and moral activities are all fused together for achieving a balance
    between his inward ambitions and external obligations. The pursuit
    of self-interest is allowed, but it does not operate as the sole driving
    force of human conduct. Amassing wealth no longer remains the
    primary objective of life. The temptation to become rich through
    deceit, corruption or exploitation is dampened.

2. **Factor returns**: The notion of *amanah* leads to the Islamic
    norm of *Al-adl* or justice and fair play. It has wide implications
    for dividing among the factors of production the fruits of their
    combined effort. We have already noted that Islam regards as just
    the payment made to each factor according to its contribution to
    total output. The Qur'an says:

    > *(Give) to each his due (2:279; 11:85; and 26:183) and,*
    >
    > *God created the heaven and the earth for just ends and each soul will
    > get the recompense of what it has earned (45:22).*

We have seen that the marginal productivity theory fails to answer the question how returns to factors according to contribution could be ensured. We shall discuss in the next chapter as to how Islam addresses the issue through a price-plus-sharing scheme.

3. **Redistributive measures**: Because surplus wealth with the rich is viewed as held in *amanah* for others in Islam, it introduces into the picture a number of redistributive measures. The main ones are as under.

    (i) *Infaq*: It is a general Islamic principle; it seeks to make the notion of *amanah* operational. *Infaq* refers to all spending the rich may make in the way of God for helping the deprived, especially the needy and the poor, to seek the pleasure of God (Qur'an 3:86). Broadly, it starts from one's ownself at the centre of the circle moving out in a ripple effect, covering the family, the relatives, the neighbours and the community on the way until it reaches humanity on the circumference.

    It may be noted that the Qur'an uses the words *infaq*, *sadaqaat* and zakat as substitutes for one another. Its unceasing mention of the three is not a mere persuasion for the pious act of generosity; it is an element of worship that ranks third among the five fundamentals of Islam. Such is its significance in the Islamic system that the divine wisdom could not leave *infaq* entirely to individuals' taste and discretion. God instructed the prophet (pbuh) to extract one *sadaqaah* (payment in the way of God) from peoples' material possessions (Qur'an 9:103).This *obligatory* payment is since known as *zakat* meant for some specified expenditures. It is treated as distinct from *infaq* and *sadaqaat* which fall in the category of *voluntary* spending.

    (ii) *Zakat*: The determination of the minimum limits (*nisab*) beyond which *zakat* would be payable on different categories of wealth and its corresponding rate were left to the discretion of the prophet (pbuh). The system of *zakat* he (pbuh) designed is unalterable on matters of *nisab* and rates. A few characteristics of this obligatory payment may well be noted.

    * The coverage of *zakat* is vast. It applies to both the incomes of certain types such as agricultural earnings and the wealth of the rich. It covers cash in hand, in the bank or on loan; gold, silver or their ornaments, all properties save residential buildings even if under dispute, mortgaged or on auction, insurance, provided funds; agricultural produce, animal husbandry, manufactures, goods for trade, minerals including crude; buried treasures as and

when found; goods on hire; and so on with well laid out exemptions. Even this incomplete list is quite formidable. Thus, in spite of various allowances (not listed here) and low rates the collections would be sizable for the purposes they are meant.

- *Zakat* is not a tax. True, it is a compulsory payment like a tax without any direct and visible benefit accruing to the payer, but the similarity ends there. A tax comes into existence through a decision of the government. Its rates and exemptions can be modified; it can be abolished at will. The money raised through a tax can be spent on any head of the government budget. None of these features applies to *zakat:* it cannot be abolished by an act of the state; its rates or *nisab* cannot be altered; its coverage has little scope for modification. The amount collected cannot be spent except on specified heads. Being part of the Islamic system of worship, it need not arouse, like a tax, the temptation to evade or avoid its payment. *Zakat* is not charity either; it is the *right* of the poor and the needy to a share in the wealth of the rich that they have to part with as believers.

- Finally, *amanah* operating through *infaq, sadaqah* and *zakat* promotes a culture, a way of living imbued with the spirit of fellow-being, mutual support, sacrifice, cooperation, justice and fair play in contrast to rank individualism, self-centredness, competition, avarice, injustice and exploitation of the modern age.

(iii) **Awqaf:** *Awqaf* or public trusts are welfare institutions established voluntarily by the members of the community; they transfer wealth from private ownership to social custody for promoting collective welfare. Islam encourages people to establish *awqaf* and Muslims have responded to this noble call of their religion whole heartedly from its very inception. Inns, wells and rest houses along the highways, schools, colleges, hospital, mosques, burial grounds, agricultural land and manufacturing units have all dotted the Muslim lands in the form of *awqaf* throughout era of Muslim glory in history, and beyond.

Awqaf have played a significant role in promoting the welfare of the weaker sections of the community over the ages. Attempts are underway not only in Muslim countries to revive this grand Islamic institution and improve the management of the existing trusts but also in Muslim minority countries; major changes have for example been made in the *Awqaf* (Amendment) Act 2013, India, to revamp the institution.

System of inheritance

The Islamic system of inheritance was also revolutionary when it first appeared on the scene. Until then, the eldest son inherited almost everything the father left behind after his death. The practice is prevalent even today in some societies. It leads to the concentration of wealth in fewer hands and works against redistributive norms. In contrast, the Islamic system leads to the multiplication of heirs. It does not allow a transfer of more than one-third of property as bequest or through the will to any of the heirs. The system distributes wealth in a wider circle and tends to reduce its concentration even as it increases the spread of wealth in the same social class, not across classes.

9.6   ROLE OF THE STATE

Islam recognizes the merits of free enterprise and does not want to curb individual initiative in the economic field. Nevertheless, it is aware of peoples' nature showing violent love for material gains, as also of their avarice and miserliness (Qur'an 4:18; 17:100; 100:8). They are prone to acquiring wealth through unfair means and tend to ignore their *amanah* obligations. Thus, Islam makes it obligatory for the state to intervene in economic matters if social interest so demands, i.e. economic working of the community is seen leaving the right path. Following are some of the obligatory measures the state has to enforce for reducing poverty and improve distributive equalities in the society.

1. The abolition of interest for establishing an exploitation free financial system.

2. Guaranteeing the fulfilment of the basic needs of all its nationals irrespective of colour, caste, creed or religion. For example, the Iranian constitution provides such a guarantee to its citizens.

3. Regulation of resource allocation to priority uses and regions, if market fails to meet the national priorities.
    (i) Manage the collection and disbursement of *zakat* funds.
    (ii) Do things to promote all that is needed to promote the objectives (*maqasid*) of Shari'ah to the extent private sector is negligent or deficient in the matter.

4. **Growth versus equity**: The issue of distributive justice has usually been discussed with an implicit assumption of a given income that has to be distributed among individuals within and between social groups so as to converge to some perceived 'ideal' division. However, total income of a community is not fixed; it grows. In a dynamic situation, the economic objectives of growth and equity often tend to clash for some valid reasons. As such, we have to build bridges between the ideal and the

Islam allows freedom of enterprise but it is not averse to state intervention in economic matters of social interest.

actual income distributions on the one hand and evolve trade-offs between distribution and growth on the other. It is a highly complex and difficult task. The reconciliation between growth and equity remains an unresolved issue in economics even at the theoretical level.

However, in a pure Islamic model the conflict between growth and equity may not probably be as sharp as elsewhere because of the in-built safeguards of the Islamic system against the emergence of the malady, and the provision of the corrective measures if it does. In any case, the Islamic system would presumably opt in general for a relatively slower rate of growth if that alone can work better for promoting distributive justice compared to a position where faster growth could be ensured only with a worsening of the situation.

Summary

- Factor pricing refers to the determination of payments that firms make to resource owners for the inputs they need to produce the goods they sell. These payments are production costs for firms but accrue to the factors of production as incomes.

- The classification of the factors of production has been changing over time. We shall deal with a fourfold classification: (a) land, (b) capital, (c) labour and (d) enterprise, merging them at times into two—labour (c + d) and capital (a + b).

- In modern economies, the process of wealth creation and its distribution among the factors of production run parallel to one another. Functional income distribution therefore becomes important for personal income distribution in addition to allocation of resources and public policy issues.

- It is agreed, in Islamic economics also, that the payment to a factor of production to be fair must, in principle, equal the value of its contribution to total output. The crucial issue is: how the total output of the factors' combined effort can justly be apportioned among them?

- Mainstream economics continues to maintain that market payments to the factors meet the ends of justice because each factor gets the value of its marginal product to total output. The view has attracted much criticism from its very inception.

- The main points in the criticism of the marginal productivity theory are as under:

  (i) The theory is based on the unrealistic assumptions of perfect competition in the markets including the constant returns to scale in the long run. These assumptions are static. They do not operate in the real dynamic economic situations. So, the theory loses its relevance.

  (ii) Factors complement each other in production. The productivity of each depends on the productivity of others. The theory is caught in circular reasoning.

  (iii) Even on its own terms, the theory is illogical. It is not the contribution of a factor to output but its scarcity relative to other factors that determines both its marginal product and return. The equality of payment to a factor and the value of its contribution do not by itself prove that it is productivity that determines the payment.

- The issue of distribution focuses on personal incomes which may remain unduly unequal even if contribution basis for factor payments holds. This is, for example, possible, if distribution of opportunities and ownership of resources remains unjust.

- Islamic economics presents a model of income distribution including the determination of factor returns. It is cast in a pure Islamic setting like the perfect competition based marginal productivity theory. Assuming that a *performing* Muslim community exists, it shows that the guiding principles of Islam are such that undesirable inequalities in incomes need not arise in the first place. If and when they do arise, the system has a set of corrective measures to bring it back on the right path.

- The Islamic view of distributive justice includes payment to factors according to contribution plus obligatory help for the needy and the poor. The scheme to achieve the norm follows from its notion of *amanah or* trusteeship.

- *Amanah* is a foundational concept of Islam. It is based on the fact that God created resources for all His creatures. So, no one has in principle any exclusive property rights. There is the share in a rich person's wealth of the poor and the needy, and this share must be given to them.

- In distribution, *amanah* seeks to convert the mundane wealth of man into a means for attaining spiritual peace through spending in the way of God. Islamic prescriptions to attain distributive justice are all inspired by this basic concept.

- *Amanah* changes one's temptations to acquire wealth through incorrect means. It adds a social dimension to man's worldly ambitions. It implies a sharing of profit with labour to compensate for their exploitation under the market system.

- *Amanah* lends meaning to *infaq*, *sadaqah* and *zakat* as transfer instruments, especially for the fulfilment of people's basic needs. It encourages the rich for voluntary establishment of *awqaf* with a view to improving the conditions of the weaker sections of the community,

- Islam makes is obligatory for the state to intervene in the working of the markets if its distributive ends are not being met by the system. It may even prefer slowing down growth if that alone could promise a fairer distribution of incomes.

Glossary

***Amanah* (trusteeship)** The concept of *amanah* is the soul of Islamic religion. It follows from man's acceptance to run affairs on the planet earth as the trustee of God the Almighty. But man was also granted freedom of thought and action. So, the Shari'ah lays down the rules of conduct for managing that trust or *amanah*. If man would follow the rules to stay on the right path God will reward him, if not he will be punished by the same law.

Awqaf It is the plural of *waqf* and is Turkish in origin. *Waqf* is an inalienable religious endowment in Islam usually earmarking a building or plot of land to promote Muslim welfare, general or specific. It seems to have inspired the concept of a common law trust. The idea of cash *waqf* is of recent origin and is gaining ground.

Derived demand In general, derived demand refers to the demand for a product resulting from the demand for some other product. For example, demand for petrol is derived from the demand for automobiles. However, in this sense demand for any product can be shown as a derived demand. Therefore, in economics the demand of products for final consumption is regarded as primary; it gives rise to the demand for factors of production which is treated as derived because it arises from primary demand for the output that the factors are used to produce.

Distributional equity Equity refers to fairness concerning the way income and wealth is distributed among members of a society. It essentially is a perceptive concept and therefore controversial. In Islamic economics also it varies how one defines fairness. Still, it is the foundation of morality in economics

Pure models They can be thought of as those that rest on assumptions rarely touching reality. Rather they tend to idealize situations to serve as bench marks for assessing the departures of reality from the desirable so that corrective measures could be taken to minimize the gap. In mainstream economics perfect competition is one such model. In Islamic economics, it is the assumption of a performing community of Muslims being in existence.

Zakat It is a portion of a believer's wealth beyond a limit that he is obliged to give to the poor or for other specified purposes. Literally it means purifying or cleansing. Thus, paying it is a way of purifying one's wealth. It is not charity because it is the appointed right (*haq*) of others in your wealth. Also, it is not tax, though payment is compulsory because it is not subject to parliamentary manipulation; it cannot be abolished nor its structure or expenditure heads be altered. *Zakat* is the third pillar of Islam; an important element in its system of worship.

Concepts for Review

- Assumptions of Islamic distribution model
- Average revenue product
- Awqaf state and income distribution
- Concept of amanah
- Cost income relation
- Criterion for just factor payments
- Derived demand
- Factor pricing

- Marginal productivity theory
- Marginal revenue product
- Nature of *zakat*
- Personal and functional income distributions
- Productivity concepts: physical and monetary
- Pure models
- Trade-off between growth and equity

Case Study 9.1

Efficiency versus Equity in Welfare Economics

Evaluation of public policy is the main task of applied welfare economics. It is obvious that the result of this process heavily depends on the underlying principles of evaluation. Usually two important social criteria, namely economic efficiency and equity, are employed. It is well-known that realizing both objectives at the same time is often impossible and that there is a trade-off between them. A decision criterion must take into account both objectives that raise the issue of assigning them relative weights.

Source: Based on Ebber, U. Bonn, F.R.G. (1986), 'Equity and Distribution in Cost Benefit Analysis', *Journal of Economics*, p. 67.

Case Questions

1. Explain what you understand by efficiency and equity in economics.
2. Why is there a clash between efficiency and equity?
3. If the choice is between (a) faster economic growth with larger inequalities in the distribution of incomes and (b) slower growth of the economy but lesser inequalities in personal incomes, which one would you prefer in an Islamic economic order, (a) or (b)? Give reasons for your answer.

Test Questions

9.1 What do you understand by the term factors of production? In staging the 1982 Asian games in New Delhi, the Games Organizing Authority:
  (i) Borrowed money and sold sponsorships,
  (ii) Built a games village to house the participants,
  (iii) Hired and trained security guards,
  (iv) Employed assistants and ushers, and
  (v) Set up audio–video arrangements for live broadcast of the games.

  Classify this information into land, labour, capital—physical and human—and enterprise.

9.2 What is meant by factor pricing? How does it differ from pricing of the commodities? Explain the implications of these differences.

9.3 Why and how is factor pricing related to distribution of incomes in a market economy? What in your opinion should be the criterion for judging the fairness of a factor price? Give reasons for your answer.

9.4 Distinguish between personal and functional distribution of incomes. Give an example in support of your answer. Do you see a link between the two versions of income distribution? Explain.

9.5 Improvement in functional income distribution is a necessary but not a sufficient condition for a just personal distribution of incomes. Do you agree? Give reasons for your answer.

9.6 What do you understand by the marginal revenue product of a factor of production? Explain how the marginal revenue product of a factor determines the return it gets. Use appropriate diagrams to explain your answer.

9.7 Two factors, labour (L) and capital (K) are used to produce TV sets of a uniform design in an industry where perfect competition prevails. Individual firms can sell whatever output they may want at the market determined price of INR 5,000 a piece. The production function of Saadaf Electronics is as below.

$$Q = 2.75 + 5L^{1/2}$$

The capital stock of the firm is fixed. Find the total, average and marginal revenue product of labour for the firm. You may use Table 9.2 as format for your work. Verify that the number of workers the firm employs is 6. (Why?)

9.8 What is meant by the exploitation of labour? How can we measure such exploitation in monopolistic markets in (a) an industry and (b) a firm? Explain using suitable diagrams.

9.9 Explain the concept of *amanah* in Islamic economics. How does this concept influence human behaviour towards fair play in the treatment of productive factors? Illustrate using examples of the redistributive measures Islam employs.

9.10 There is a clash between promoting growth and reducing income inequalities as goals of economic policy. Why? How should Islamic economics deal with the issue in your opinion?

9.11 Write explanatory notes on the following:
   (i)   Marginal productivity theory and employment,
   (ii) Public policy and distributive justice, and
   (iii) Pure theoretical models and economic reality.

Web Exercise

Search Islamic literature on *zakat* and *awqaf*. Write a note on each based on your findings.

Forward Link

Having discussed the some general issues concerning income distribution, we shall turn to the determination of rewards for various factors individually. In the following chapter, we will discuss the determination of wages and a few related issues.

10

Wages of Labour

LEARNING OUTCOMES

This chapter should enable the student to understand:

- The nature of labour and labour market
- Demand for labour and changes therein
- Supply of labour and its determinants
- Equilibrium in the labour market
- The Islamic approach to labour and wages
- Other labour issues such as minimum wages
- Trade unionism through the Islamic perspective

10.1 LABOUR AND ITS PECULIARITIES

Labour refers to the work effort of people to earn a living. Labour market is the area in which job seekers and those who seek their services are in such effective communication that the wage rate tends to be just and equal. The wage rate is the price of a labour unit expressed per period of time or the quantity of work done; paid mostly in terms of money. Wages are quoted as Riyal per loading or per hour, day or week (month or year). A long–run service contract with a firm or institution is called a job.

> Labour is the most perishable of commodities; it cannot be stored. The bargaining power of workers on wages and related issues is therefore weak vis-á-vis their employers.

All workers have a fixed and equal amount of time, but individual capacity, talent and skills differ because all human beings are not created equal. In addition to natural endowments, labour requires education, training and experience to perform a service. Expenditure incurred on these heads is investment in human beings. More of education, better training and longer experience in addition to food, clothing and shelter increase labour productivity resulting in more human capital. Islam emphasizes on the fulfilment of basic needs covering all these heads; it emphasizes on building human capital with moral values. Variations in human capital largely accounts for wage differences in a society.

In mainstream economics, Labour is conceived as a commodity and wage rate is its price, which is determined by the impersonal forces of demand and supply in the market. But labour is not like lifeless commodities; it is embodied in living beings. In Islamic economics, the worker is first of all a human being and is to be treated by the employers with understanding sympathy and benevolence. Labour is different from other factors of production on several counts. For example, labour is the most perishable commodity; it cannot be stored. Also, labour cannot be separated from the labourer. For these reasons, the position of workers gets relatively weak in wage bargains. On the other hand, employers are fewer than job-seeking workers. They can easily join hands to strengthen their bargaining position. The law permits their associations but mostly hinders the formation of labour unions. There often are legislative acts against raising wages but rarely any against lowering them or curbing profits. Finally, employers have ample resources to enable them live even if they employ no workers during a strike or lockout. In contrast, not many workers can subsist a week, or a month and fewer, if at all, a year. A basic assumption in wage determination is the *uniformity* of labour units traded in the market or in its subdivisions.

> Market distributes output revenue among factors proportionate to their bargaining strength and goods to consumers proportionate to purchasing power.

The weak bargaining position of the workers deflates the case for beneficent working of the market forces; even claims of fair play under perfect competition may seem suspect. In this context, the Islamic norms of treating workers with kindness, paying them fair wages and not burdening them with tasks beyond their capacities assume importance. However, this does not reduce the need to study the working of the demand and supply apparatus for the market determination of wages. It is well to remember that labour units are all treated as of uniform quality in explaining wages in general.

Our discussion on the marginal productivity theory and its criticism in the previous chapter, used labour as an illustrative case. We talked of wage determination in competitive markets both perfect and monopolistic, assuming that the supply of labour remains fixed. That makes our task easier and shorter here. We shall complete our discussion concerning the demand for labour and explain the factors that operate on the supply side of the labour market.

10.2 DEMAND FOR LABOUR

We retain for simplicity our earlier assumption that there is perfect competition in both the product and labour markets and constant returns to scale continue to operate in the industry. However, individual firms are taken as working in a short-run frame and their demand for labour is, therefore, seen with reference to the fixity of capital stock. Finally, individual firms operate under the law of diminishing returns to a variable factor, labour.

How many labour units a firm will demand under the above assumptions? It has to pay a market determined wage per unit irrespective of how many units of labour it employs. Likewise, it has to sell its product at the going market price whether it sells more or little. Under the circumstance, a firm will ask what shall be the additional output it will have if one more unit of labour is hired, how much extra revenue that unit will bring in and will that revenue be more than the wage the firm will have to pay for the additional labour unit? Note that here the words 'additional', 'one more' and 'extra' all imply marginal concepts. Clearly, the firm will add to its profit until the 'extra' revenue the employment of one more labour unit brings in is more than or at least equal to the market wage rate it has to pay. To refresh your memory on the point, you may refer back to Section 9.2 of Chapter 9, even as we present below a fresh illustration.

Example 10.1 Mehmood runs a car wash station in Kuala Lumpur. His carwash schedule for labour is as in Table 10.1. Now, if the market price of the carwash were RM1 a wash, column 4 of the table would also be the column for marginal revenue product (MRP) of labour. However, if the price is RM3 per wash, column 5 will show the relevant MRP values. Figure 10.1 sketches the MRP of labour for the carwash station.

Table 10.1 *Car wash station: value of the marginal product of labour (amount in RM)*

Alternatives	Labour hours hired	Total product (car washes per hour)	Marginal product (car washes per labour hour)	Marginal revenue product (column 4 × price per car wash)
(1)	(2)	(3)	(4)	(5)
A	0	0	–	–
B	1	5	$(5 - 0) = 5$	15
C	2	9	$(9 - 5) = 4$	12
D	3	**12**	**$(12 - 9) = 3$**	9
E	4	14	$(14 - 12) = 2$	6
F	5	15	$(15 - 14) = 1$	3

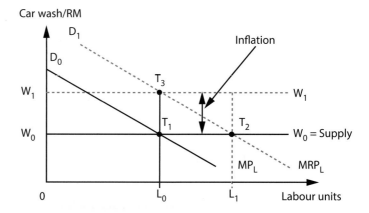

Figure 10.1 *Marginal revenue product of labour*

Here, the horizontal axis measures the units of labour, while the vertical axis shows physical product of labour as well as its money value. When the price of a car wash is RM1, the MP_L curve represents *both* the MP_L and the corresponding MRP_L of labour units (column 4 of the Table 10.1). At wage level $W_0 - W_0 = 1$, the firm employs $L_0 = 3$ workers. Suppose the price of a car wash rises from RM1 to RM3. The station can now employ two more workers ($L_1 = 5$) to increase its profit by area of the $\Delta\, T_1 T_2 T_3$, the wage rate and price level both remaining unchanged. Real wages will remain intact and the equilibrium would move from T_1 to T_2.

However, if the increase in the car wash price were an indicator of an inflationary trend in the economy, i.e. a general rise in prices, it would be unfair to a labour if the wage rate stays at RM1 an hour because real wage rate will then be lower irrespective of the number of labour units, 3 or 5, the station employs. The distance between the two wage lines $W_0 - W_0$ and $W_1 - W_1$ would indicate the fall in the real wage rate of workers due to inflation until the gap is closed through a rise in the money wages making wage rate $W_0 - W_0$ rise to $W_1 - W_1$ equalling RM3 an hour. This mostly does not happen and to that extent wages are eroded during periods of rising prices to the advantage of business. Economists often plead for indexation of wages to meet the norms of fair play and for keeping the growing income inequalities in check. The measure operates in many countries granting periodic dearness allowance as a partial offset of the inflationary impact on wages.

10.2.1   Factors Affecting Demand for Labour

The demand of a firm for labour may undergo changes due to the following factors.

1. **The price of product**: The higher is the price of a firm's product relative to wages the greater will be its demand for labour. The effect operates through the increase in the value of its MRP. We have seen this in our carwash illustration above. The increase in the demand for labour would be larger, the greater is the lag between wage rates the price of the product over time due to a faster increase in the profit of the firm.

2. **Prices of other factors**: Recall that we had noted in Chapter 7 that a profit maximizing firm will so use resources in a production process that the ratio of the marginal product to price in each case will be the same. For example,

$$\frac{MP_L}{P_L} = \frac{MP_k}{P_k}$$

Now, suppose we have the above ratio as $\frac{20}{5} = \frac{28}{7}$ then the price of K falls from 7 to 5, that is, capital becomes cheaper relative to labour. An additional dollar spend on capital adds to output $28/5 = 5.6$ units compared to labour's $20/5 = 4$.

> The factors that affect the demand for labour in the market include the price of the product, the prices of complementary factors, the nature of hazard involved in the work and the technology used in production.

Clearly, it will benefit the firm to shift one dollar from expenditure on labour to capital to have more of it. However, reduction in labour will raise its marginal product while addition to capital will reduce its marginal product, the substitution process ending when the parity of ratios is again restored. (Recall arguments against marginal productivity theory in the preceding chapter.)

3. **Technology**: Technological innovations and improvements may reduce the demand for labour and may also shift it from one sort of labour to another. For example, when power looms replaced handlooms many of the weavers in Indian textiles became unemployed and took time to adjust to the change. The industry again experienced technological employment shift when automatic looms ousted power looms. New technologies need new types of trainings. In more recent years, computers are replacing middle-level workers in most office work and system development.

4. **Trust and efficiency**: Islam encourages preference for trustworthiness and efficiency on the demand side of the market. One of the Shoaib's daughters said to him of a person, *O' my father, employ him; surely the best of men for you to employ are those who are strong and trustworthy* (28:26). Modern markets put a premium on these qualities.

Exercise 10.1

Asma has a workshop producing umbrellas. There is perfect competition in both the product and labour markets. The price for an umbrella is INR 100 and the wage rate for a day's work is INR 1000. The total output schedule for labour in a day is given below.

Table 10.2 *Total output of umbrellas in Asma's workshop*

Workers	1	2	3	4	5	6
Total output (umbrellas)	6	20	32	42	50	54

(i) Calculate the marginal product of hiring the fourth worker.
(ii) How many umbrellas will Asma produce a day to maximize her profit?
(iii) Calculate her maximum profit.
(iv) If the price of an umbrella rises to INR 125, how many workers will Asma hire?

10.3 SUPPLY OF LABOUR

For a vast majority of people labour market is the main, if not the only, source of income. They work and earn a wage. What determines the amount of labour time they supply as there are only 24 hours in a day? There are numerous demands on the limited time people have at their disposal. Many factors, therefore, influence the number of hours they may be *willing* to work for earning a living. One main factor is the wage rate they can get in the market.

The relationship between the wage rate and labour supply is not unidirectional: low wages may force people to work for longer hours to make the two ends meet. This was the case during the early phase of industrial revolution in now developed economies and this still is the case in many unregulated sectors in the developing world. Likewise, high wage rates need not always make people reduce labour supply as they can earn enough for a comfortable living by working fewer hours. The ambition to amass wealth in people is quite strong, if not limitless. However, economists see as a rule a typical labour response to levels of the wage rate; work competing with leisure in demand on their limited time. Table 10.3 provides a typical labour supply schedule relating wage rate change to a worker's responses.

The relationship between wage levels and supply of labour is circular: each influences the other.

Table 10.3 *Labour supply schedule of an individual worker*

Point	A	B	C	D	E	F	G	H
Wage rate per hour (RM)	50	45	40	35	30	25	20	15
Labour hours (per week)	40	45	48	50	48	45	40	0

Figure 10.2 presents the labour supply curve (LSC) based on the data given in the table. If we add up such individual supply of labour curves horizontally, we can get aggregate supply curves for the firm, the industry or the market in general.

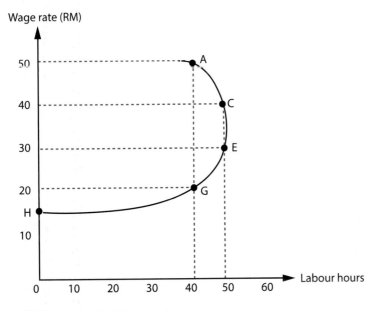

Figure 10.2 *An individual labour supply curve*

The reasons are that (a) all individual schedules are not identical, (b) they do not begin at the same level of wages, and (c) they do not all bend backwards at the same wage level. In the aggregation process, they may make up and neutralise each other's bulge and depressions. A market supply curve for labour we, therefore, take as continually upward. Note that the labour supply curve for the market may not necessarily turn backwards.

It normally would look like, say, for the car wash stations in Kuala Lumpur, as the one shown in Figure 10.3.

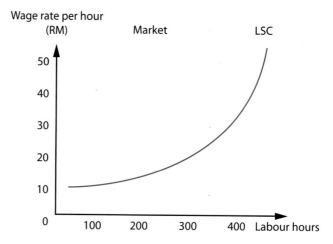

Figure 10.3 *Car wash labour supply curve*

10.3.1   Changes in Labour Supply

> Labour is measured in working hours and not in terms of workers employed.

The supply of labour in the market changes when the amount of labour offered changes due to factors other than the market wage rate. This finds expression in the shifting of the labour supply curve. An increase in the supply of labour takes place when:

1. More labour hours are offered on the *same* wage rate as before, or
2. Labour hours supplied remain the *same* even when the wage rate falls.

Figure 10.4 uses linear labour supply curves to explain the definition. The broken line in the figure shows a shift of the LS curve down to the right indicating an increase in the supply of labour. The movement from L to L_1 takes place while the wage rate at W remains unchanged. On the other hand, even when the wage rate falls from W to W_1, the supply of labour remains unchanged at L.

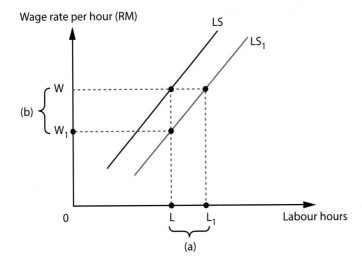

Figure 10.4 *Increase in labour supply*

Exercise 10.2

Define a decrease in the market supply of labour on the same pattern as we have defined an increase in it above. Also, draw an illustrative diagram.

10.3.2   Factors Influencing Labour Supply

Changes in labour supply are influenced by the proportion of people in the working age group in the population of a country, social preferences, time and money spent on education and training.

1. **Population growth**: Increase in population unless accompanied by faster economic growth may increase labour supply; more people may be willing to work though wage rates remain static, even fall. Many developing economies are facing this sort of problems. Liberal import of labour increases a country's work force and keeps prices competitive. This is today a common feature of labour markets not only in most developed countries but also in developing economies of the Middle East, Malaysia and Singapore to name a few.

2. **Population policies**: An increase in the adult population causes an increase in labour supply. The increase may occur due to increase in birth rate over the death rate. Rigorous birth control may make the population structure top heavy reducing the working population of the country. Many of the developed countries such as Russia, and more recently even the developing China are facing this problem and providing incentives to people to have more children in a reversal of the restrictive policies of the past. It helps keep labour cheap and prices competitive in

> Natural talent, education, training, experience, population growth and individual preferences are some of the main factors that influence labour supply in an economy.

globalizing economies. Islam in general does not approve family planning as a *public policy*, though individuals have discretion in the matter subject to certain conditions.

3. **Individual preferences**: Social change brings about alteration in attitudes and preferences for work. In developed nations, the share of working women in employment is much higher compared with many developing economies. In Muslim countries, it is all the more lower due to lower literacy rates and cultural patterns. But the proportion of female workers tends to rise in Muslim countries, as they open up to modernization within Islamic norms. At present, Morocco, Tunisia, Indonesia and Malaysia lead the table.

4. **Education and training**: Cost of education and training both in terms of time and money matter. Both are needed to produce efficient workers and professionals of quality. In developed countries not only the size of GNP is very large they spend a larger proportion, 5 to 6%, of it on education, research and training. In developing countries, the income base is small yet generally education remains a less attended head of public expenditure. Expenditure on armies is more in many cases, especially in Muslim countries. In Muslim countries, from a low of 1.5% of GNP in Indonesia to a high of about 5% in Morocco was the range of expenditure on education in the late 1990s. Of late, both expenditures on education and enrolment in schools colleges and universities are rising notably in these countries.

> Expenditure on education and training is deemed as investment for human capital formation.

10.4 LABOUR MARKET EQUILIBRIUM

The equilibrium of the labour market, like other markets, is determined by the forces of demand for and supply of labour. Figure 10.5 shows such equilibrium, say, for the automobile industry of country A. DL and DS are the demand and supply curves, respectively. Demand and supply for labour are equal when L hours of work a week are hired in the industry.

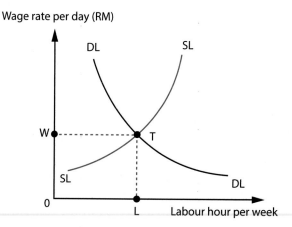

Figure 10.5 *Labour market equilibrium*

Exercise | **10.3**

Pizza Hut in Friends Colony of New Delhi employs both teenagers and retirees for work. The following events take place in the neighbourhood.

(i) In a marketing complex, three just completed cinema halls have started operations.

(ii) Karim Nemat Kedah, a famous eatery of Delhi, opens a branch in the complex and becomes popular with the residents in the area.

(iii) The demand for pizzas decreases and as a consequence, their prices had to be reduced.

Explain the effect of these events on the market for fast food workers in the area, other things remaining unchanged.

10.5   MONOPSONY

We have discussed wage determination so far with the tacit assumption that labour markets are perfectly competitive. In other words, no firm can alter the market wage rate by its individual action; it is a wage taker. In contrast, a *monopsony* is a market situation where a single employer alone hires labour. Such a situation is unusual but at times does exist. Technological progress has vastly enlarged the minimal cost effective size of industrial plants, transportation systems, insurance, banking, advertising and packaging service units in the modern era, and the trend continues. For example, large manufacturing plants such as iron and steel, paper mills, car making, ship building, aeronautics, oil refining and even coal mining are the major employers in developed countries, and in some regions, or places in the developing nations as well.

> Monopsony is a market situation where there is only one employer and many people seeking jobs.

A monopsonic employer decides how much labour to hire, and on what terms. He attempts at paying the minimum wage that can bring in the required amount of labour for work. A monopsony makes a larger profit compared to a group of competing firms in the labour market. Let us examine how it is done.

We have seen that in a perfectly competitive market, the value of the marginal product curve, or for short the MRP curve, shows an individual firm's demand for labour. In contrast, a monopsonist has no such demand curve. For comparison, we shall retain the MRP curve in our diagram with a subscript c for perfectly competitive market. SS is the usual supply curve of labour as discussed above. Figure 10.6 depicts the monopsonistic wage and employment policy. The competitive equilibrium is at point T_C, the intersection of the usual demand and supply curves of labour. However, ML is the monopsonic view of labour demand. For this gives him the required amount of labour L_M for which he has to pay W_M wage rate which is higher than the competitive rate W_C. Thus, the disadvantage of a monopsonic employer for the economy lies in the curtailment of jobs; he makes larger profit through substituting capital for labour. Monopsonistic markets are largely the feature of rich developed economies but their multinational corporations now invading developing economies under expanding globalization also bring in the problem with them here.

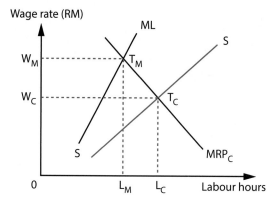

Figure 10.6 *Monopsonic wage and employment*

10.6   SOME OTHER ISSUES

Labour is the most important factor of production; for humans are living beings. Workers constitute the masses. Historically, two most important issues concerning labour have been of their independence of choosing for whom they will work and what shall be a fair wage for the work they will do. Prior to Islam, slaves were the primary source of organized work force and the formal setting up of markets for their sale and purchase was not uncommon until the end of 14th century.

10.6.1   Islam and Labour

Still, it is at times asked with some curiosity as to why Islam—progressive and humanitarian religion as it was—did not formally announce the abolition of slave labour as it did, for example, in the case of drinking wine, gambling and interest? The reason presumably was that slavery at that time was, as alluded to above, a powerful social and economic institution. Its abrupt abolition could have caused chaos and disruption in the socioeconomic life of the community. Divine wisdom thought it is expedient to adopt persuasion rather than compulsion to achieve the objective. The prophet (pbuh) asked people to treat slaves with kindness, better set them free. The Qur'an allowed expenditure on buying and freeing slaves out of the *zakat* funds (9:60 and elsewhere) to make explicit its intentions concerning slavery and speed up its abolition. The spirit and the intention of Islam thus being clear, it is no wonder that the Muslim lands were among the first where slavery as a social institution ended much earlier than elsewhere. Informally though, it continues even today in some places. (See Box 10.1.)

Fairness of wages and treatment of workers are sensitive issues. They involve not only economic but moral, social and political considerations as well. Their source primarily is the weak bargaining ability of the workers across the negotiation table. Questions of human rights, justice and morality confront a social order to stay in order. A satisfied work force is essential for smooth economic progress and prosperity in a society. Therefore, attention has to be paid to matters concerning the work force that remain controversial even in the modern age. We briefly discuss a few of them below.

10.6.2   Minimum Wage

A minimum wage is the amount of money below which the payment for hiring labour is made illegal. The firms may pay a wage in excess of the minimum so fixed, but are liable to prosecution if they pay less. A minimum wage constitutes a sort of *price floor*. It is of little value to the workers if the amount set is smaller than the market wage rate.

The minimum wage will have importance only if it were more than what the market would pay. Economists had mostly not supported the minimum wage legislation until recently, on the grounds that even though the government may set a minimum wage, it cannot tell firms

BOX 10.1

Labour Rights and Islam

Islam projects a vision of labour rights that goes beyond the most progressive views on the subject. Islam sees the relationship between employers and employees in a *brotherhood* framework, It is not a paternalistic relationship nor a patron-client relationship, but one of *equals*, where each has responsibilities to the other. The Prophet Muhammad (pbuh) reportedly said:

Your employees are your brothers upon whom Allah has given you authority, so if a Muslim has another person under his control, he/she should feed them with the like of what one eats and clothe them with the like of what one wears and you should not overburden them with what they cannot bear and if you do so, help them in their jobs.

In return, employees must provide employers with hard work, diligence, and honesty. Muhammad (pbuh) was also very clear that workers must be paid wages on time, and the wages must be fair. He reportedly said that employees must be paid before their sweat dries up. Furthermore, *Islamic juristic discourses suggest that [wages] should be at least at a level that would enable employees to fulfill all their and their families' essential needs in a humane manner.*

Shari'ah law also places strict restrictions on child labour and insists that employers respect their employees' religious beliefs, regardless of their faith. The law and the Qur'an also require that workers be offered adequate sick leave and compensation. And, Islam *candidly forbids human trafficking* i.e. buying and selling people for money to work as slaves.

These attitudes towards labour and worker's rights have been adapted to policy prescriptions in many of the OIC member countries. For example, Egyptian labour law decrees that female employees be entitled to 90 days of paid maternity leave. Women are also guaranteed two breastfeeding breaks every day for up to two years after childbirth. And all workplaces that employ at least 100 women must provide childcare. Similar principles are also enshrined in the Cairo Declaration on Human Rights in Islam, passed by OIC grouping in 1990, based on Shari'ah principles. The declaration reads:

[All workers] shall be entitled—without any discrimination between males and females—to fair wages for his work without delay, as well as to the holiday allowances and promotions which he deserves. On his part, he shall be required to be dedicated and meticulous in his work.

Similarly, the League of Arab States' Arab Charter on Human Rights reads:

The right to work is a natural right of every citizen. The State shall endeavour to provide, to the extent possible, a job for the largest number of those willing to work, while ensuring production, the freedom to choose one's work and equality of opportunity without discrimination of any kind on grounds of race, colour, sex, religion, language, political opinion, membership in a union, national origin, social origin, disability or any other situation.

Despite such pious declarations, some countries however remain notorious for their poor working conditions for immigrant workers. But it should be noted that such exploitation is often the result of individual recruitment and employment agencies, rather than national policies. Even in these countries, working conditions are improving as per latest human rights reports.

Overall it seems pretty clear that Islamic doctrine promotes and protects labour rights. We hear a lot about the important role Christian and Jewish groups in international labour movements. It is about time Muslims were recognized as well.

Source: Adapted from Inside Islam – Dialogue and debates, <http://insideislam.wisc.edu/2012/07/islam-and-labour>, accessed 21 April 2014.

what number of workers to hire at that wage. Fixation of a minimum wage tends to cause unemployment they argued. Figure 10.7 illustrates their argument. Here, we have W_{Mar} as the market wage rate and L_0 is the employment level determined by the intersection of the labour demand (D_L) and supply (S_L) curves at point T_0. Now, if the minimum wage is fixed above the market rate at W_{Min}, supply of labour will exceed the market rate at W_{Min}, supply of labour will exceed the demand for it by $L_1 - L_2$ units, but note that employment from the *previous* level will not fall to that extent; it will decline by only $L_1 - L_0$.

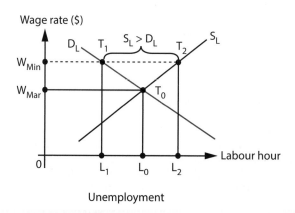

Figure 10.7 *Minimum wage law creates unemployment*

Thus, minimum wage fixation will apparently benefit only those who are able to retain their jobs. Those not able to do so may possibly accept to work even at lower than W_{Mar}, outside the legal frame. The implication is that minimum wage legislation may not benefit the workers as a group. Furthermore, minimum wage may weaken the competitive position of the country in the export markets vis-à-vis those nations where minimum wages are lower or do not just exist.

Evaluation

It may, however, be mentioned that explanatory exercises in economic theory, like the one Figure 11.4 presents, are to be taken with caution. We must clearly understand their nature and limitations. These diagrams do not carry any *factual* information. The relationships they portray are very complex and few lines in a plane can rarely capture their complexity. Diagrams oversimplify real world situations. *They are an aid to think, not the thought; a means to follow an argument, not the argument itself.* They state relationships in a *static* frame and fail to grasp the dynamism of social change affecting economic variables, especially in the realm of factor pricing.

> Islam is not opposed to the fixation of minimum wages. This follows from the Islamic insistence on the fulfilment of the basic needs of everyone living within a country.

Furthermore, diagrams show variable values on their X and Y axes, but do not automatically define the relationship between them; it is a matter of external argument and interpretation. Also, a change, like a minimum wage imposition, though takes place at a *moment*, its consequence run forward in time beyond the boundaries of the diagram; they are difficult to predict. To explain such a change, we need a third-dimension—the time—mostly missing in microeconomic diagrams.

Though there has been unceasing reproduction of figures, the support for minimum wages in modern societies is on the rise. The argument that minimum wage will lead to employment at lower illegal rates has not cut much ice. *Violation of laws cannot be a justification for not having laws.* In fact, there is a consensus that countries must provide to their workers, for reasons economic or non-economic, a minimum 'living' wage, even if that term remains ambiguous. Opinions differ only on the question whether the minimum wage tool can achieve the agreed ends. It depends on what impact one believes the instrument would have on the long-run productivity and poverty situations in a country. The supporters of the measure say it will ameliorate the lot of the workers; opponents argue that the measure would reduce their well-being. Be that as it may, a minimum wage is already in place and has come to stay in most of the countries of the world, developed or developing.

Islam and minimum wages

In Islamic economics, the idea of a minimum wage was probably first formally discussed by the author in a journal article *Theory of Profit: The Islamic Viewpoint* (1983), and has since found support in the literature. The basis for support for it lies in the Shari'ah itself. The Qur'an reminds people time and again that even though people may differ in regard to the *quantum* of *rizq* (sustenance) granted to them, they are *equal in the right for a livelihood from the inexhaustible resources God has provided in the Earth and heavens* (15:20; 41:10). It follows, as mentioned earlier, that a prime consideration governing income distribution in Islam is the fulfilment of the *basic needs* of all members of the community. These needs include, according to Ibn Hazm and others, the minimal requirements for food, clothing and shelter. We may also add education and health care to the list. A minimum wage must cover the cost of providing these needs for an average-sized family. Note that a concept of basic needs has to be flexible. Their range and quality would have to be periodically spelled out in the light of the level and pace of economic progress in a country; minimum wage would need periodic review.

Thus, in 1997, the US Federal Fair Labour Standards Act revised the minimum wage upwards to $5.15 an hour. A further review in 2000 increased the amount by one more dollar for the next 2 years. At the same time, businesses were granted tax relief to cushion the cost increase. In Malaysia, the minimum wage has more than doubled since 1990.

Exercise 10.4

Organize in your class, group discussions on the following statements:
  (i)   Fixation of a minimum wage need not cause much unemployment as the demand curve for labour is not elastic.
  (ii) Minimum wage must be abolished as it leads to the development of black market in hiring labour on wage rates lower than the law requires to be paid.
  (iii) A rise in minimum wages would make the management of firms work for achieving higher efficiency targets to keep costs rise in check.
  (iv) The Bush administration argued after the upward revision of the minimum wage rate in 2000 that the minimum wage has to be uniform for all countries for reasons of international equity in competition.
  (v)   Minimum wage is opposed as it adds to unemployment in labour surplus countries. I shall argue that governments in these countries must push wage rates down even below the market rate to increase employment.
  (vi) In Islam, the responsibility for peoples' basic needs is of the individual, his relatives, society and finally of the state. Zakat funds can take care of the issue. Shari'ah does not make it obligatory for an employer to meet the basic needs of his workers. Fixation of a minimum wage is, therefore, redundant for Muslim countries.

10.6.3   Collective Bargaining

In principle, Islam does not place labour and capital in two hostile camps working against the interest of each other. They have to supplement each other in the process of production for the common good i.e. increase in social prosperity. Some of the very simple, yet fundamental concepts of Islam encourage and hail cooperation among them. The seeds of antagonism between the two were sown and nourished by the perennial suppression and exploitation of the weak by the strong with the dawn of mass production. The situation now is that not only the need for a legal minimum wage but also the workers' insistence to allow them organize into unions for bargaining with their employers collectively on service conditions has become widespread. Even today, workers of all categories have to sign on dotted lines in job contracts prepared by their employers. Thus, labour fought for long and eventually won legal rights in most countries to form labour unions. Millions of workers and their supporters including some student groups participated in the recent French labour strike (April 2006) to oppose the proposed liberalization of the hiring and firing labour laws of the country. In Islam, there seems to be no apparent support or opposition to collective bargaining or union activity and the issue remains unresolved.

Minimum wage legislation is a living reality in most of the modern societies. Here, political considerations have superseded economic concerns.ç

Union objectives

A labour union is an organized group of workers to obtain fair wage deals and influence other employment conditions for their members. The unions may be organized (a) industry-wise, or (b) for all industries in an area, or (c) on the basis of a particular trade such as the union of shop assistants in a metropolitan town.

The *objectives* trade unions work for are broadly as follows:

1. To obtain what they consider as a fair wage for the workers.
2. To get the improvement in their compensation package.
3. To obtain an increase in job opportunities in the trade.

Each of these objectives may have sub-goals. For example, improvement in compensation package may include fight for better wage rates, more fringe benefits, appropriate retirement age, grant of bonuses, health care facilities, safety measures and abatement of environmental pollution in work places. The ability of a union for achieving these objectives depends on the following two factors.

Workers organize into trade unions to strengthen their bargaining position and to promote their welfare through other activities. The law recognizes their right to collective bargaining.

1. The extent to which it can stop non-union workers from supplying their labour to the market the union workers serve. It may not be easy for unions to restrict entry successfully in markets where abundant labour is willing to work at wage rates lower than the union demands. The professional associations like those of dentists and nurses are better equipped to restrict competition from non-union unqualified workers than the union of semi-skilled or unskilled workers.

2. We have seen that labour demand curves slope downwards. Any union effort that succeeds in raising the current wage rates may induce employers to adopt restrictive employment policies. Thus, a trade-off between wage increase and employment level has to be struck. This is not an easy task. Unions, therefore, must and do try to enhance the productivity of their members through education and training as long-run goals. Also, they often work for the enforcement of minimum wages, call for imposing restrictions on imports and support restrictions on immigrant entry.

BOX 10.2

EU Must Push for Fundamental Rights in Bangladesh Garment Sector

The recent accidents, fires, collapses of buildings and hundreds of killed or injured workers as a result, increased the urgency for the European Union to act regarding the situation in the garment sector in Bangladesh. 'IndustriAll European Trade Union insists that the European Commission use all means, including the possibilities available under the Global System of Preferences, to increase the pressure on the Bangladeshi government', said Luc Triangle, Deputy General Secretary during the most recent IndustriAll Europe Sector Committee meeting for the Textiles, Clothing and Leather sector. 'We insist on clear regulations for credible fire and security legislation, a guarantee for the respect of basic labour rights and the introduction and implementation of a decent living wage. Companies that are producing in this region, or buying garment products from this region, have a huge responsibility for the welfare and working conditions of these workers. Together with our brothers and sisters from IndustriALL Global Union, ITUC, ETUC and UNI', IndustriAll European Trade Union issued a press release yesterday.

The global union movement has welcomed the European Commission's commitment to press Bangladesh to meet international labour standards. European Commissioners, Catherine Ashton and Karel De Gucht, made the pledge in a joint statement following the horrific building collapse in Savar, Bangladesh that has claimed some 600 lives and left many more seriously injured in one of the world's worst industrial disasters. The threat of EU action under the Generalized System of Preferences (GSP), rarely invoked such concern.

Source: <http://www.industriall-europe.eu/news/list2.asp?stid=10>, accessed 21 April 2014.

10.6.4 Wage Differences

Workers are not entirely alike. They differ in their mental and physical capabilities, and in education and training. Labour is perforce made of numerous *non-competing groups*. The groups often have smaller subdivisions. Wages differ within and among groups. Some of the reasons of wage differences are as under.

1. **Natural talent or human capital**: Not many people have the aptitude or intelligence to become, for example, brain surgeons, top grade musicians, painters, artists, cricketers or athletes. Since the supply of their types is much limited relative to demand, they command very high price (wages) in the market. The members of such professions do not compete across groups: the surgeon

does not compete with the economist or the economist with a film dancer. But competition among members of the same group—surgeons, economists or dancers—is often intense.

2. **Education and training**: Investment in human capital in terms of education and training improves its earning capacity. But investment involves cost. This cost varies in terms of money and time involved with the sort of education and training one opts for. Cost differences reflect themselves in wage differences. The latter, however, need not be commensurate with skill or productivity differences.

3. **Compensating differences**: Many jobs such as coal mining, working on high seas on oil platforms, building construction, nuclear plants are tiresome and involve risk to limbs and life compared to those working as clerks or teachers in air-conditioned work places. Wage differences arise to compensate for differences in hazard, risk and disagreeableness involved in jobs.

4. **Market imperfections**: Perfect labour markets tend to equate wages for identical jobs. However, markets lack perfection. So, factors such as incomplete information, spatial immobility and entry restrictions due to union or state action give rise to wage differences. Discrimination on grounds such as gender, race or religion may be other contributory factors.

5. **Performance linkage**: Wages may be paid hourly, weekly or monthly, but some fringe benefits such as health insurance, gratuity, paid holidays, free education of children, medical care, housing and professional allowances are often attached to the basic remuneration. These benefits are not the same for all employees; they differ with pay scales. An important element resulting in wage differences are the payment plans designed to obtain a desired level of performance from the employees. The owners of firms need workers to help produce goods that they can sell to earn profit. It is in the interest of both that firms survive and prosper. The prosperity will ensure profits for the owners and workers will remain in employment.

> Wages across industries differ for a variety of reasons. They are almost the same as they influence labour supply at the industry level. We have already referred to them above with some additions.

But the interests of the owners and the workers are not identical. Workers may seek to increase their utility by shirking on the job, by putting in less than the effort expected of them under the contract or by taking unauthorized breaks. They may increase their leisure by sitting idle or engaged in gossip during the paid working hours. The net effect of all this is a rise in per unit cost of production and reduction in profits. As a check, Islam insists that workers must be hardworking, skilled in their job and trustworthy. To the employers who want to take as much work as possible from their labour force, Islam instructs not to burden workers with tasks they cannot perform and treat them with kindness.

One way to make workers put in the required effort is their increased supervision. But this may prove costly. Supervisors may possibly need supervision. An alternative way to resolve the problem is to have some sort of *incentive payment plan* that links wage rates to some agreed performance norms. Some incentive payment schemes are piece rates, commissions, bonuses, stock options and profit sharing.

Piece rates are payments made per unit of work done. Firms in ready-made garments industry may, for example, pay holes and buttons done per T-shirt or tea gardens can pay per kilogram of leaves plucked. Firms may tie commission to the value of sales. Insurance agents, stock brokers and property dealers receive a percentage of the money value of the services rendered. Artists and authors are paid royalties per unit of the net money value of their work sold.

Bonuses are payments made to an employee in addition to his salary linked to the performance of individual workers or a group of them. **Stock options** allow top management officers to buy the shares of the firm they work for a lower price when the stock prices are raised. **Efficiency payments** may also be made to them. Profit sharing is discussed below in a separate section because of its importance and wider implications.

10.7   PROFIT-SHARING

We have argued earlier that the marginal productivity system cannot ensure just wages for workers. John Rawls, a Harvard moral philosopher, finds that the system rather aggravates distributional inequality in the market economies. Those who do well in the market get vastly more than they can spend, while those who fail often find it difficult to meet even their basic needs. It is important to note that such inequality is not strictly the result of talent differences. Talent plays an important role in the earning effort of a person; but having talent is purely a matter of luck. Even so, abundance of talent is no guarantee for success; one must have the *right* talent, i.e. saleable in the market. To overcome the deficiencies of the marginal productivity system and keep workers satisfied, labour participation in profit of the firms has increasingly become a norm in modern large-scale production. Factors such as fear of unemployment and external competition are making managements and unions equally willing to welcome cooperation as a means for survival. Profit sharing is the key element in schemes meant to promote workers' cooperation, loyalty and commitment for industrial peace and progress. Periodic bonus payments out of current profits, in cash or kind, are common features of company management today.

Granting a share to labour in profits in addition to market wage can be used for bringing workers' remuneration closer to the value of their contribution to output. The great potential profit sharing has for promoting growth, equity and stability in an economy is now well recognized. The idea is not averse to the content and spirit of the Shari'ah norms of unity, harmony, trust and fair play.

Sharing profits with their workers has now become a norm with modern firms to maintain industrial peace and win workers' loyalty.

Summary

- A collection of job seekers and employers who are trading labour services is called a labour market. The price of these services is called the wage rate which is determined by the forces of demand and supply.

- The bargaining power of workers is weak for a variety of reasons: employers are fewer than workers and can easily combine, the law hinders formation of labour unions and employers have much more resources that the workers to fall back upon during strikes or lock-outs.

- To understand the workings of a labour market, we assume perfect competition both in the product and in the job markets. Constant returns to scale operate in industry in the long run but individual firms operate in a short-run framework. This means that capital remains fixed and marginal returns to labour diminish: the demand curve for labour slopes downwards.

- We may think of the contribution of labour to output—total, average or marginal—in physical terms such as so many tons of coal, yards of cloth, loaves of bread, etc., or we may obtain their revenue versions through multiplying physical quantities by the market price of the product.

- Revenue concepts are of greater use in economic analysis than physical values. To facilitate analysis, we may readily treat physical quantities as their revenue equivalents if we assume the price of the product equal to one unit of money. For then $Q = Q \times P = Q \times 1 = Q$.

- If wages rise slower than prices during periods of inflation, workers lose in real terms. This makes a case for linking wages to cost of living or compensating bonus payments to maintain workers at a stable living standard.

- The demand for labour is affected by factors such as price level of the product, prices of other goods, price of other factors and technology. A change in any of these factors may bring about a change in the demand for labour.

- An individual's supply of labour is a function of his choice between work and leisure at different wage rates. The relationship between labour hours and wage rate remains positive up to a point but tends to become negative thereafter for higher rates. In other words, the labour supply curve of an individual is seen as sloping backwards.

- The market supply of labour curve is obtained by a horizontal summation of individual supply curves. Interestingly, this aggregative curve is continuously upward sloping because the bulges, if any, in individual curves do not all occur over the same range of wage rates.

- Factors that affect supply of labour in the market include population growth, proportion of people in the working age group, individual work preferences, and the education and training levels needed for various jobs.

- The market wage rate is determined at a level that equates the labour supply with its demand.

- A monopsony is a market situation wherein there is just one employer who hires the workers. Technological efficiency requirements, and economies of production associated with mass production and bulk handling of goods may at times give rise to monopsonic market structures in the economy.

- Monopsony usually results in the curtailment of jobs and substitution of capital for labour in the processes of production.

- The arguments for minimum wages extend beyond economic logic; the legislation on the subject is pervasive and has come to stay for social, moral and political reasons. Static economic diagrams showing the inefficacy of minimum wages fail to capture the complexity of the social dynamics.

- The support for minimum wage fixation in Islamic economics follows from the Shari'ah requirement of ensuring the fulfilment of basic needs of all its nationals and to pay just wages to the workers. There is certainly no opposition in Islam to the adoption of the notion.

- As individual workers have less power vis-à-vis their employers to negotiate over wage rates and other service conditions in the market, they have won the right in civilized societies to form their unions for collective bargaining. Labour unions aim at obtaining a fair wage including a minimum floor and better service conditions for their members within the prescribed legal framework.

- We come across varying differences within and across occupations. Doctors as a group are paid higher than teachers, and professors get more than lecturers in universities. The reasons for wage differences are not far to seek; they include differences in talent, investment in education and training, and job risks and unpleasantness. Market imperfections of various sorts also cause differences in wages.

- Profit sharing with labour is gaining currency in recent times. It is perceived to narrow the gap between market wage rates and the value of labour's contribution to output, tends to keep workers satisfied, loyal to the firm and cooperative. It is in line with the Islamic norms of fair play, unity and hard work.

Glossary

Collective bargaining This is the mechanism workers used to organize, meet, discuss and negotiate with their employers issues concerning wage rates, bonuses, overtime payments, leave retirement benefits and overall work environment. This has over time won social and legal approval. In essence collective bargaining strengthens the weak position of workers vis-à-vis their employers.

Inflation It has presumably been the most familiar term with the common man since the mid-nineties but what it exactly mean even the experts do not seem to bother about. It is a situation in which prices, functional incomes, money supply and output are all found chasing one another in an upward spiral. The important thing is not that general level of prices tends to pace up. If all prices during inflation would rise by identical proportion, no one would probably bother about it. The trouble is that inflation changes the relative price structure making income distribution more and more skewed in favour of the rich. In that, it is a sort of robbery that law permits.

Minimum wage A minimum wage is the lowest amount of money the employers may legally have to pay their employees for a specified unit of time. Although minimum wage laws are in effect in many countries, there are differences of opinion about the benefits and drawbacks of the system. Minimum wages differ from country to country but show strong correlation with the levels of economic development within and between countries. Until the 1990s, economists generally agreed that raising the minimum wage reduced employment, but this opinion is fast losing ground over the past 50 years. If nothing else minimum wage has a strong social appeal and political consequences. In Islamic economics, the concepts of basic needs fulfilment amanah and fair play support the notion.

Monopsony Greek in its root, monopsony refers to a market situation on the reverse side of monopoly. We saw that monopoly refers to a single seller of a product. In contrast, in monopsony there is only one buyer of a product. In some cases, a monopolist in the product market may become a monopsonist in the input market. For example, a large corporation may be the only employer of workers in a small town or buyer of a raw material.

Revenue product The physical output of a commodity multiplied by its price is called revenue product which is the same thing as value product. Usually the concept is mostly expressed in marginal terms. MRP is defined as the addition to total revenue resulting from a unit change in an input, other inputs remaining unchanged.

Concepts for Review

- Backward sloping supply of labour curve
- Causes for wage differences
- Changes in supply of labour
- Collective bargaining
- Demand for labour
- Efficiency in resource allocation
- Factors influencing labour supply
- Inflation and wages
- Labour market
- Labour unions
- Marginal concepts
- Minimum wage and Islamic economics
- Minimum wages
- Monopsony
- Non-competing groups of workers
- Physical product
- Profit sharing and labour
- Revenue product
- Supply of labour

Case Study   10.1

Labour Unrest at Honda Motorcycle and Scooter India (Private) Limited

On 25 July 2005, the management of the Honda Motorcycle and Scooter India (Private) Limited (HMSI), a wholly owned subsidiary of Honda Motor Company Limited (HMCL), encountered violent protests from workers that disrupted production at their plant in Gurgaon.

HMSI workers were severely beaten up by the police, and newspapers and TV channels gave wide coverage to the violence of the action. The protest followed six months of simmering labour unrest at the HMSI factory in which the workers also resorted to job slowdown since December 2004 when the workers' demand for an increase in wages was rejected by the HMSI management.

Labour strife and the management's inability to deal with it effectively had resulted in huge losses for the company due to the fall in the production level at the plant. In addition to this, the company also received a lot of negative publicity as newspapers and TV channels gave wide coverage to the violence of the action.

The case highlights the growing number of instances of clashes between the employees and the management of companies in India, which is often guided by external parties such as trade unions and political parties.

Source: <http://www.icmrindia.org/casestudies/catalogue/Human%20Resource%20and%20Organization%20Behavior/HROB104.html>, accessed 18 February 2011.

Case Questions

1. Why do disputes between workers and the management of a company arise? List at least three reasons.
2. Do you think that the reasons for dispute are always economic and internal to a firm? Support your answer with examples.
3. What sort of losses would workers suffer in a dispute? Does the company also suffer? If yes, in what way? Illustrate.

Case Study   10.2

Aminul Islam and Trade Unions (1973–2012)

Aminul Islam was a labour leader in Bangladesh. He was vocal in advocating for improved working conditions and higher wages. In 2010, the union led protests to push for a larger increase in the minimum wage for garment workers. Islam, as well as other labour leaders, had been arrested in connection with these protests. During his prison period, he was physically tortured by officers of the National Security Intelligence.

Recently, Islam was working to organize workers in factories belonging to the Shanta Group, which produces clothing for multiple American companies including Tommy Hilfiger, Nike, and Ralph Lauren. He had also assisted ABC News in setting up interviews with survivors of a recent factory fire in Bangladesh.

The 6 April 2012 issue of the Bangali language newspaper, Amar Desh, carried photograph of a man whose identity was unknown at the time and whose dead body had been found by the Tangail police. From the photo in the paper, Islam's family was able to recognize him.

Islam's body was found on 5 April 2012 next to a road near Ghatail, Bangladesh, sixty-one miles north of Dhaka. His body bore marks of torture. He had last been seen alive in a centre of the garment industry near Dhaka. It is suspected that he was murdered because of he was involved in seeking justice for the general worker of garment sector of Bangladesh. Islam's murder is still unsolved, but his case gained international attention from AFL-CIO and the US State Department.

Source: <http://en.wikipedia.org/wiki/Aminul_Islam_(trade_unionist)>, accessed 21 April 2014.

Case Questions

1. Do you think Islam supports collective bargaining and trade union activities? Give reasons in support of your position.
2. The case of Aminul Islam has reportedly attracted international attention. What impact do you think it will have on the resolution of the case?
3. The garment industry is the second largest contributor ($18b. yearly) to the national income of Bangladesh. What impact, if any, the recent fire and collapse of a garment factory is likely to have on the exports of the country? Explain.

Test Questions

10.1 (a) Define labour. Explain why the bargaining power of the workers is weak vis-à-vis their employers.

(b) What is a labour union? State briefly the objectives of such unions. Can unions improve the bargaining power of the workers in an industry? Give reasons for your answer.

10.2 (a) An industry is operating under constant returns to scale. Why should the short run demand for labour curve of an individual firm in such an industry slope downwards? Explain and illustrate your answer.

(b) Fatimah runs a beauty parlour in Lahore for bridal makeup. There is perfect competition in the market for such makeup. The price charged is INR 1,500 for one makeup. The labour market is also competitive, the going wage rate being INR 3,000 a week per worker. Table 10.4 shows the total number of brides served by the parlour.

Table 10.4 *Number of workers employed and the corresponding number of brides served*

Alternatives	A	B	C	D	E	F
Workers employed	1	2	3	4	5	6
No. of brides served	6	20	32	42	52	55

Construct a table showing (a) total revenue product, (b) MRP and (c) total cost for each alternative. Which of the alternatives will maximize profit?

How much will that profit be?

10.3   What may cause the labour supply curve of an individual worker to slope backwards? Do you expect the market supply curve of labour also to have the same shape? Give reasons for your answer.

10.4   What factors cause differences in individual earnings? How large should such differences be in your opinion and why? How will you justify the following?

(a) Men earn more than women.

(b) College graduates get more wages than matriculates.

(c) Americans get higher remuneration than Asians in the Middle East for identical jobs.

(d) White workers earn more than blacks in the USA.

10.5   Figure 10.8 gives the market equilibrium for untrained primary school teachers in country A. If these teachers opt to undergo short-term training courses, their skills will improve and they will have at each level of employment a marginal product twice as high as it is at present. The cost of training will add $2 an hour to the wage rate.

(a) Show how the demand and supply curves will shift in the above figure because of training?

(b) Will it be worthwhile to undergo the training?

(c) Show the equilibrium wage rate and level of employment before and after the training.

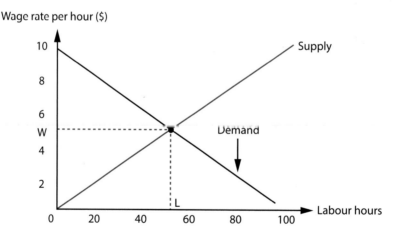

Figure 10.8 *Labour market in equilibrium*

10.6   What do you understand by monopsony? Compare the hiring of labour choices of a monopsonist and a competitive employer. Which of the two will employ more workers and pay higher wages? Give a diagram to explain your answer.

10.7 The price of oil has been rising since the American-led invasion of Iraq. What impact the rise might be having on the employment of workers in the car-making industry? Give reasons for your answer.

10.8 Firm A hires workers at RM1/hour for a standard 8 hour day. It pays over time beyond 8 hour work at RM2.5/hour. On the other hand, firm B pays a uniform rate of RM1.30/hour irrespective of the number of hours you choose to work. Other things being equal, which firm Ahmad will choose for employment if he intends to work (a) 10 hours a day or (b) 12 hours a day? Explain your answer.

10.9 Will you support a share in profit for labour? Give reasons for your answer. Explain the position on this issue in Islamic economics.

Web Exercise

Search the Internet for views of Ibn Khuldun on labour and value, and write a note on the topic.

Forward Link

In the following chapter, we shall continue the discussion on how factor rewards are determined with reference to land and capital. We shall be discussing the determination of rent and several related issues and the Islamic rationale for the abolition of interest.

CHAPTER 11

Rent, Interest and Profit

LEARNING OUTCOMES

This chapter should enable the student to understand:

- What is common in the three distributive shares; rent, interest and profit and why we discuss them separately
- How rent of land is determined and how it is related to prices of goods land produces
- Why tax treatment of rent is different from wages of labour
- The extension of rent concept to other production factors
- What is the source of capital formation
- Why interest is paid and why Islam prohibits it
- What sort of income is profit
- How profit rises and why must labour have a share in it

The three distributive shares—rent, interest and profit—have their ultimate source in the ownership of or control over property. Also, the three income shares largely go to the same social class, the capitalists, in free enterprise economies. This is one reason, as hinted earlier as to why economists now classify factors of production only into labour and capital. However, the three shares are quite distinct in their emergence, nature and role as the same are determined, like all other prices, by the forces of demand and supply in the market. We discuss them separately.

A. RENT

11.1 THE CONCEPT AND THEORY

To the common man, rent means the payment made to the owner of a piece of land for cultivation, an apartment, house or room for its use. Business firms refer to rent as the amount they pay for using a factory building, machinery or storage facility. Such definitions of rent lack purity. For example, rent for an apartment or house may also include the charges for things other than land on which the building stands, for example, expenses on leveling, interest on money borrowed for the construction, and expenditure incurred on its maintenance, insurance and security. Rent paid to the owners is in fact *gross rent*. If we take out from gross rent these other expenses, we get what we call *pure* or *economic rent*. Technically, the definition of economic rent is restricted to the price paid for the use of land including all natural resources that God has provided to mankind as a whole, free of charge. The ownership of land as we find it today at the individual level, is the result of population growth, social conventions and legal frameworks that evolved over time in different societies. However, property rights do not change the fact that landowners never *produced* land.

> Rent is restricted to the price paid for the use of land including all natural resources that God has provided to mankind as a whole, free of charge.

11.2 RICARDO ON RENT

David Ricardo (1772–1823) defined rent as the payment made to the landlord for the *original and indestructible* qualities of soil. He argued that rent arises because land is of *different* quality. We have to cultivate land of lower and lower fertility to meet the expanding demand for food products, say corn, as population grows. The land of the lowest fertility in a point of time that we are obliged to cultivate is called the *marginal* land. The cost of growing corn on this land is higher than on all relatively superior lands. If the society does need the output of the marginal land, it *must* pay a price for corn that would cover this cost. Owners of the marginal land get no rent as cost (including normal profit) equals price. However, it is not the output of the marginal land alone that will sell at that price. The corn raised on lands better than the marginal land shall also get the same price. Their production cost being lower, they will have an excess of price over cost: an *economic* rent. Table 11.1 illustrates how differential rent arises as lower grade land is progressively brought under cultivation as population increases. Figure 11.1 helps us to understand the process of rent appearing and increasing in the economy under the pressure of want and scarcity. The numbers in the grade cells show the rent and its enhancement with the rise in corn price. Table 11.1 puts the process in focus.

> Ricardo thought of rent arising because of differences in the quality of land. The price of corn must cover the cost of production on the least fertile land. The cost of production on superior land being less than the price, the difference is economic rent.

Table 11.1 *Price, marginal land and economic rent*

Grades of land	Price				
	P₁	P₂	P₃	P₄	P₅
A	0	1	1 + 3	1 + 3 + 6	1 + 3 + 6 + 10
B		0	2	2 + 5	2 + 5 + 9
C			0	4	4 + 8
D				0	7
E					0
Cultivation stage	1	2	3	4	5
Marginal land	A	B	C	D	E

Note that the numbers in the cells mark the additional rent that goes to each piece of land with every rise in price. Zero in a cell identifies the marginal piece of land at a particular price, P. The total rent for a grade of land is the sum of the numbered areas in Figure 11.1 at any of the prices.

As margin of cultivation is pushed forward, rent on the preceding non-rent land emerges and on others increases.

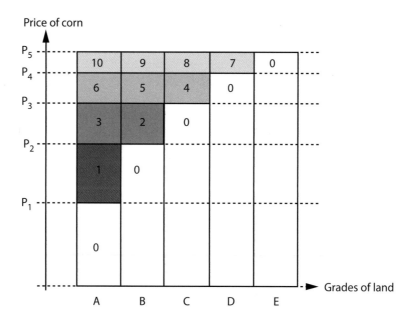

Figure 11.1 *As the margin of cultivation expands, the price of corn increases; raising the rent on super-marginal lands*

11.2.1 Criticism of the Theory Examined

Critics point out the following weaknesses in Ricardo's theory of rent.

1. It is argued that land in its *original* form is not mostly usable. It has to be first cleared, levelled and fenced. This involves cost that rent of land covers in practice. But, this is not a valid objection if we remember the distinction between gross and *pure* rent indicated above. Ricardo limits himself to the explanation of pure or economic rent.

2. People need not always cultivate the most fertile land in a country. Nearness to population is important. However, Ricardo did include location in his notion of fertility. In any case that is merely an explanatory assumption, not the essence of his theory.

3. It is also pointed out that the theory relies on *differential* aspect of land. If all land were of the same quality, will rent not be paid? Supporters of Ricardo explain that his theory is valid even if all land were homogenous in quality as the law of diminishing returns applies in cultivation. The available fertility of land cooperating with other factors in cultivation does not remain the same as we attempt to grow more and more corn from the same field. Price of corn must rise to cover the cost of *marginal* output. Rent arises on earlier units of the variable factors, labour and capital. It is then called *scarcity* rent. Assuming perfect competition, Figure 11.2 explains the point. It shows marginal cost curve MC rising as more and more labour and capital units are applied to the land of uniform quality to raise output under the pressure of increasing demand for corn as population rises. Output is measured along X-axis in tons; Y-axis shows price of corn and marginal cost of labour–capital units used. Price increase to cover the rising marginal cost is made explicit by the rising height of the broken portions of vertical lines. Notice that as price rises, marginal rent falls but aggregate rent increases. (Verify from Figure 11.1.) Rent is maximized with output at 7. Here, MC equals MR while cutting it from below. Further expansion of output is not required, assuming that supply is enough to meet the entire demand at the going price (P).

> Ricardo's theory has been criticized on several grounds: in essence it only says that a better commodity will command a higher price.

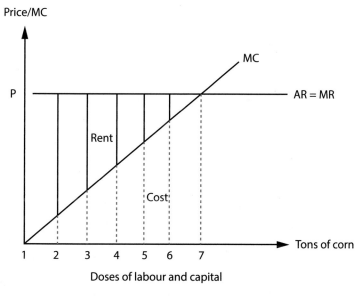

Figure 11.2 *Ricardo's theory applies even if prices of land were of uniform quality*

Scarcity rent increases as the price of corn rises. The supply of land uniform in quality will eventually be fixed; increase in rent will not bring more land into existence. Thus, high rents for landowners are likely to persist.

4. In the final analysis, what Ricardo says is that superior land will receive more rent, the inferior land less. But does it not boil down to saying that a better article will always fetch a better price? Nevertheless, his focus on the marginal land to explain the emergence of rent proved later a fore runner of marginal analysis in economics and helped identify a unique element that most incomes may contain.

Exercise 11.1

The population of country A is growing quite rapidly and it is forced to cultivate wheat on less and less fertile land each year. The agricultural department records contain the following information regarding cost of growing wheat on five large farms, one added to cultivation each year.

Year	2002	2003	2004	2005	2006
Farms	O	P	Q	R	S
Production costs per ton	30	40	50	60	70

Assuming that there is perfect competition in the wheat market, calculate per ton rent paid to each farm owner during the period. You may use the following table as help.

	Rent per ton				
Farm Year	O	P	Q	R	S
2002					
2003					
2004					
2005					
2006					

11.2.2   Rent and Price

Ricardo argued that price equals the cost of producing corn on the marginal land, but marginal land gets no rent. So, rent does not enter price: *rent is high because corn is high; corn is not high because rent is high*. This seems correct if we treat land as a single unit for the economy as a whole; in that sense the supply of land is totally fixed and inelastic. Increase in demand would then raise price and therefore, rent.

Figure 11.3 clarifies the point. Its underlying assumptions are (a) that there is perfect completion in the corn market, (b) that land supply S_0 is fixed, it can produce only Q_0 tons of corn with the given technology, and (c) that the price P_1 covers only the cost of labour and capital employed in production, it yields no rent. As demand for corn rises to D_2, price increases to P_2. Cost of producing Q_0 of corn remaining unchanged, i.e. equal to P_1, a surplus $P_1T_1T_2P_2$ or rent emerges for the landowners. This rent is enhanced if the price rises further to P_3 by the amount the rectangle $P_2T_2T_3P_3$ shows. Rent will continue to rise so long as the demand for corn keeps rising without price rise being the measure.

A rise in price of corn brings in less fertile land under cultivation and raises rent on all superior land.

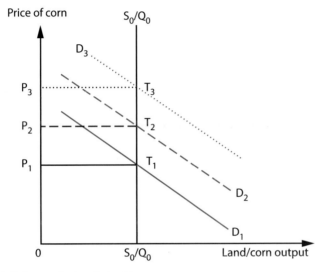

Figure 11.3 *Rent and price relationship*

However, the use of land is not restricted to the production of corn alone. There are many economic activities that compete for the use of land in an economy. The supply of land for a single use does not remain entirely inelastic. More land can be attracted away from its other uses. Interestingly, the possibility also sets a condition for retaining land in its current use: it must earn here at least equal to what it can earn (including rent) elsewhere. Therefore, rent enters price.

11.3   MODERN THEORY

It is pointed out that land is not used just for growing corn; it has a variety of uses. The supply of land for a particular use is not perfectly inelastic. If rent arises in the cultivation of wheat relative to growing rice, there will be a transfer of land from the production of rice to the production of wheat. In wheat, the earnings must at least cover what it was in growing rice, i.e. equal to its *transfer earnings*. What it earns more than that in growing wheat is *economic rent*. The modern view of rent is an extension of this idea. It does not keep rent restricted to land. Rent can be an element in the payment made to any resource—machine, man or

Modern theory of rent does not highlight the differential aspect of land. It measures rent as a difference between the returns land gets over its transfer earnings.

material—for its services if and to the extent that payment is more than what is required to retain the resource in its current use.

The supply of any of the factors, say machines, may at times fall short of its demand at the current price. It may then sell in the short run at a price in excess of its production costs. The *excess* is economic rent. Like machines, if workers in an industry get higher wages than their transfer earnings or opportunity cost, the excess is economic rent. Figure 11.4 is self-explanatory on the point.

In equilibrium, wages equal economic rent plus transfer earnings.

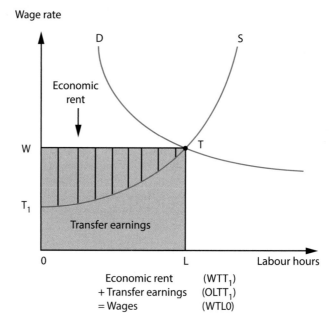

Figure 11.4 *Economic rent as an element in wages*

Today in many countries, workers in the information industry are in short supply and earning handsome scarcity rents wrapped in their compensation packages. Politicians, top business executives and bureaucrats are even more glaring cases. Their high incomes can be understood only if we bear in mind that they are often in a position to fix their own remuneration. Neither supply nor demand takes us far, nor does the concept of productive contribution. Here, power is a more enlightening term than the market forces. In a generic sense, they all seek rent: an economic advantage in addition to their transfer earnings.

Exercise 11.2

(i) A lecturer in a small town college was getting INR 2,000 per month as salary. He shifted to a college in Delhi on a salary of INR 3,500 per month. INR 1,000 is the cost of living compensation in the new pay. Do you see any rent element in the salary he gets in Delhi? If yes, how much?

(ii) What are transfer earnings? Are any transfer earnings involved in your answer to part (i) above?

It comes about that 'the rent of land is not a thing by itself; it is leading species of a large genus'. In the case of land, the scarcity is more apparent, durable and persistent. Other resources are man-made. They may become scarcer temporarily and earn rent. But in course of time, supply is augmented and the rent element in their payments eliminated. This element in factor payments being of a temporary nature is called the *quasi-rent,* following Alfred Marshall.

11.3.1   Some Implications

Even though modern economists have generalized the Ricardian theory of rent, the sues concerning landownership and the rent payable to landowners have all along been the source of conflict and confusion in human history, Islamic included. Opposition of landlords has invariably been a dominant undercurrent of the debate and controversy. Adam Smith thought of them as reaping where they never sow. Ricardo demonstrated that rent is an unearned income: the landlords receive it without doing anything to generate it. Rents have an ever-rising trend due to relatively inelastic supply of land leading to social hardships and distributional inequalities. Henry George in USA proposed the nationalization of land so that the farm surplus may benefit society at large instead of going to a sterile social class for undeserved enjoyment. The proposal for a single tax on land also remained in circulation there for some time. In India, landlordism was abolished after the country won independence in 1947. Land is now mostly with the tillers of it as owners.

BOX 11.1

Agricultural Land and Share-cropping

One of the options available to the Muslim landowner that we discuss here is to lease the land to the cultivator for a fixed amount of money, gold, or silver. Some well-known jurists have declared this to be permissible, while others consider it *haram* on the basis of sound *ahadith*, which disallows renting out land for money. Among the narrators of these *ahadith* are two companions who participated in the Battle of Badr, as well as Raf'i bin Khadij, Jabir, Abu Sa'id, Abu Hurairah, and Ibn 'Umar; all of them report that the Prophet (pbuh) absolutely prohibited the renting of agricultural land for money. (See *Al-muhallah*, Vol. 8, p. 212.)

Exempted from this prohibition is share-cropping for a specified proportion of the total yield, as is demonstrated by the Prophet's transaction with the people of Khayber. He turned land over to them to cultivate for one-half the total yield and continued to do this until his death; after his death, the rightly guided caliphs continued to practice share-cropping on a proportionate basis.

The student of the legislative development of this problem comes across a clear exposition by Ibn Hazm, who stated: When the Prophet (pbuh) arrived in Madinah, the people used to lease their farms, as is reported by Raf'i and others. This practice had undoubtedly been common among them before the time of the Prophet (pbuh), and it continued after he became the Messenger; it is not permissible for any sane person to doubt this fact. Then, as is authentically transmitted by Jabir, Abu Hurairah, Abu Sa'id, Zahir al-Badri and Ibn 'Umar, the Prophet (pbuh) totally prohibited the leasing of land, thus nullifying this practice; this is certainly correct and there is no doubt concerning the matter. He who asserts that what was nullified (i.e. the leasing of land) has been restored and that the certainty of nullification is not established is a liar and denies the veracity of others saying what he does not know. According to the Qur'an, making such an assertion is *haram* unless one brings proof for it. And he can never find a proof for it except in the instance in which the land is let for a given proportion (such as one third or one-fourth) of the total yield, as it is authentically reported that the Prophet (pbuh) did this with the people of Khayber after prohibiting it for several years, and he continued to give them land on a share-cropping basis until his death. (*Al-muhallah,* vol. 8, p. 224.)

Ample and strong analogical reasoning based on Islamic principles and supported by clear texts is produced to show that leasing of cultivable land for money is *haram*.

Source: Extract from 4. Renting the Land for Money - Young Muslims <web.youngmuslims.ca/online_library/.../the...islam/ch4s2p21-4.html> accessed 29 April 2014 (edited).

11.4 RENT IN ISLAMIC ECONOMICS

In Islamic economics, the treatment of rent has been quite confused and diverse. In essence, it is better for one if he has surplus land to give it to a landless brother free of charge for cultivation but if rent is to be taken, share cropping is preferable to cash rent.

Islamic economics does not present any *theory* of rent. It discusses the issue as it was tackled over time and space in the Muslim history. The discussion centres around issues of landownership and rent that remained intertwined during the rise and fall of the Muslim civilization. Opinions on both remain unclear and inconclusive. Those who allow ownership of land by non-cultivators are in majority compared to those who do not support absentee landlordism. However, the former remains divided over the fixation of rent. It is agreed that the best course for a person owning land in excess of what he uses is to give it to his landless brother free of charge for cultivation. Alternatively, if rent were to be taken, there is no consensus regarding its form. Some permit only cash rent, some only share cropping, i.e. *muzara'ah*, and there are still others who allow both.

The outcome of cultivation being uncertain, predetermined rent would only be interest in disguise that Islam prohibits. Fixed rent may turn out to be unjust to either of the parties, landowner or the tenant cultivator, when the crop matures for sale. The difficulty can be overcome if rent is settled as some proportion of the output or of its sale proceeds. In other words, share cropping or *muzara'ah* is considered as the best solution to the problem. However, the issue of determining the sharing ratio still remains. Also, there is no general agreement among the *fiqh* scholars on this.

B. INTEREST

11.5   WHAT IS INTEREST?

Interest has been variously viewed in the economics literature. The classical writers thought of interest as return to capital and its marginal productivity was regarded as the rate of interest. However, they also made a distinction between the natural or real rate of interest on the one hand, and the nominal and market rate of interest on the other. The nominal rate was at which funds could be borrowed, while real rate was the return on investment measured by its marginal productivity.

Modern economists restrict the use of the term interest only for payment made for the use of *money*. The issue of return on investment they treat separately maintaining its link, we shall see, with productivity. However, money as commodity these days is not even worth the paper on which it is printed nor can it produce anything by itself—not even a blade of grass. Why must then its use command a price, a rate of interest per unit? Also, if it must, how this price is determined?

> In classical writings, interest was regarded as the payment to the lender for the use of borrowed money. The rate of interest charged is called the nominal rate of interest. In contrast, the real rate of interest was the return on investment measured by its marginal productivity, prices remaining constant. Modern economics sticks to the old view of nominal interest but they do not establish its link with productivity for defining the real rate; instead nominal rate deflated by price index is treated as the real rate of interest.

11.5.1   Why Pay Interest?

Several theories are available as answer to the first question: why should interest be paid? We need not go into their details as they all boil down to mean that money has a time value. Consider a simple example. Suppose Anil deposits INR 240,000 in a bank for a year and the bank does not pay any interest to him on the amount. Instead, it buys a house with the money and rents it out for INR 1,400 a month. The amount becomes INR 256,800 after a year. (How?) The bank then sells the house at cost price and returns to Anil his money. Thus, the bank earns INR 16,800 or 7% on Anil's money. But the same option was open to Anil also. He could have bought the house himself and earn a return of 7% a year. Why should he give this opportunity to the bank unless the bank compensates him for the same? Perhaps Anil would accept an interest of 5% or INR 12,000 from the bank as it will save him of the trouble of searching a suitable house, find a reliable tenant and pay for the legal work involved in buying and renting the house. The bank will keep the remaining amount INR 4,800 for taking all that trouble for Anil. Thus seen, money has an opportunity cost. Interest is the payment a lender gets for transferring the opportunity of using money to the borrower. He has to wait and postpone his enjoyment over the loan period. The relationship between banks and their customers is indeed a two-way lender–borrower relationship.

The concept of opportunity cost is quite simple, but it is one of the most important ideas in microeconomics. The pitfall in applying the concept correctly lies in the inability to recognize the best of alternatives lost from the earnings viewpoint in the pursuit of an activity. A leading case is of treating *sunk* costs as opportunity costs. Suppose for making a round trip from Kuala Lumpur to Penang, you were to choose from using the bus service or your own car, you should not count for comparison the road tax or the insurance premium you pay in estimating the expenses for travelling by your car. These two expenditures are *sunk* costs, i.e. they have nothing to do with your decision to use or not to use your own car for the trip. Count only expenditure on fuel and maintenance, if you are otherwise indifferent between the two modes of transportation. The opportunity cost concept with reference to interest is relevant only for the amount of this expenditure, not for sunk costs.

If interest is just a compensation for the lost opportunity, however measured, why many people still consider the lending of money on interest a distasteful business? Why of late, is interest free banking in the Islamic mould making rapid strides in conventional economies as well? These questions are both interesting and important. But we shall turn to them later. For now, let us take up the second of the issues we raised above: if interest were an acceptable payment for the use of money, what determines its price, the rate of interest?

11.5.2   Interest Rate Determination

Loanable funds theory

Like all prices, interest rates are determined by the intersection of the demand and supply curves for loanable funds. Since money capital is minutely divisible, the market for these funds is an ideal example of trading in an entirely homogeneous standardized product. The result is that we have not only national but international, market for loanable funds. Thus, the interest rates for a specific sort of borrowing rapidly tend to equality over time and space.

Demand for loanable funds

Business firms demand money to meet different types of capital needs, broadly long and short terms. Long-term requirements are for fixed assets such as plant and machinery or buildings which they meet largely by selling equity and debenture in the stock market. In addition, they need money to finance inventories and make various payments until the production process is completed; they need this sort of working capital for short duration. This part of financing they meet essentially through borrowing from the banking institutions. The aggregate of individual firms' demand for funds makes the demand of an industry for funds.

Apart from firms, individuals need money for current consumption and to purchase durables such as houses, refrigerators, automobiles, computers and other requirements. People also want to keep some money with them to meet day-to-day expenditure and emergencies. Governments require money to construct roads, railway systems, hospitals schools and other public works. The demand for funds in the market is the horizontal summation of the demand for various categories we have mentioned.

Supply of loanable funds

Multiple sources also operate on the supply side of the market. Consumers' savings augment the funds. Business firms save to replace assets, write off bad debts, expand capacity and equalize dividends over time. Public authorities at various levels may also save. Insurance companies, unit trusts and pension funds are important sources of national savings. Creation of new money or activating hoards may also increase loanable funds.

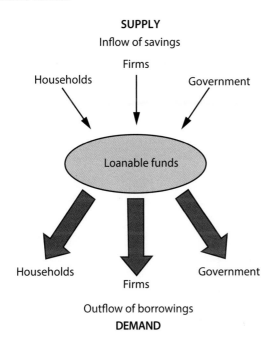

Figure 11.5 *Demand and supply of loanable funds*

Banks are the main intermediaries between the borrowers and suppliers of funds. Figure 11.5 sees capital market as a big lake of loanable funds where small and big streams of savings enter from one side, and mighty rivers of finance flow out from the other to turn the wheels of trade, industry and commerce. If the inflow is more than the outflow, the level of the lake rises and the rate of interest falls to increase the outflow and reduce the inflow to adjust the level. Opposite happens if outflow is more than the inflow; the rate of interest rises to restore the equilibrium of the lake. We shall expand the figure in Chapter 20.

Figure 11.6 shows how the demand and supply of loanable funds determine the equilibrium rate of interest. S_L represents the aggregate supply of funds from various sources of savings, while D_L shows the demand for funds from various sorts of borrowers. The point of intersection of these two curves gives us R and L respectively, as the

> Loanable funds theory is the application of demand and supply tools to the money market for determining the equilibrium rate of interest.

equilibrium rate of interest and amount of funds lent and borrowed at that rate.

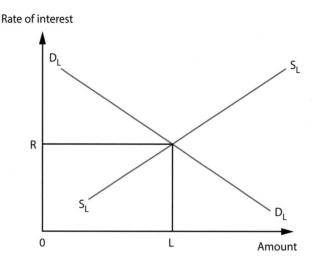

Figure 11.6 *Demand and supply of loanable funds determine the rate of interest*

Following are the demand and supply schedules of loanable funds. Draw a diagram to show the equilibrium rate of interest and the amount transacted as loans.

Rate of interest %	1.5	3.5	5.0	6.5	8.0	9.5
Demand for loans (RM million)	50	45	39	31	19	4
Supply of loans (million)	10	20	35	41	58	80

Evaluation of the theory

The loanable funds theory is more logical and comprehensive compared to the classical viewpoint on interest. It keeps finance separate from real investment, limiting the payment of interest to the former alone. Also, the theory improves our understanding of the factors that play a role in the determination of interest on the demand as well as supply side of the market. It focuses on such wide-ranging factors influencing the rate of interest as savings resulting from thrift, investment demand, hoarding and bank credit. However, Keynes pointed out some weaknesses in the theory including the following.

> Loanable funds theory of interest is more sensible than the classical views on the subject as it keeps finance separate from investment.

1.   The notion of hoarding in the theory is unclear. Hoarding implies reduced investment that may hurt the economy, unless the quantity of money is increased.

2.   The theory is based on the assumption of full employment of resources which does not hold good in the real world.

Rejecting the loanable funds theory of interest, Keynes put forth his own explanation for the payment of interest. His theory rests on why people want to keep money with them rather than have it in circulation through spending. Let us examine his theory; in the process, we shall also evaluate his charges against the loanable funds theory.

Liquidity preference theory

Keynes presented a new view of interest in his epoch making book *The General theory of Employment Interest and Money.* He based it on the store of value function of money. People want to keep money with them because it is the most *liquid* form of wealth in the sense that it can *readily* be converted into any other asset as everyone accepts money in exchange of his valuable goods and services without any special inquiry. Such acceptance is a social convention. Keynes, therefore, defined interest as the *reward for parting with liquidity for a period: the reward for not hoarding.* This might look strange. For money sitting idle in your safe does not provide you any income; its investment can. Why should then people *demand* money to hold as a liquid asset? There are broadly three motives, according to Keynes, for *liquidity preference.*

> Liquidity preference theory is based on the store of value function of money: what motivates people to keep money with them rather than invest it?

1. **The transaction motive**: It refers to the demand for money that is the need for cash to meet current expenditure. Individuals hold cash to bridge the interval between the receipt of income and its expenditure. People mostly receive their incomes once in a month or week, while their expenditure goes on day by day. A certain amount of money has, therefore, to be kept ready at hand for current transactions. The amount needed for the purpose would depend on the size of individual income and the time interval involved between its receipts.

    a. Business firms also have to keep part of their resources in the form of ready cash for meeting current needs including payment of wages and salaries, purchase of raw materials, and make transportation arrangements during an accounting period. The amount needed for the purpose would vary directly with the volume of business conducted: the more is the turnover the greater will be the need for holding cash.

    b. Government bodies, private and public institutions, and other economic units all need to hold some cash because their expenditure does not synchronize with the receipts of income.

2. **The precautionary motives**: The precautionary motive for holding money refers to the desire of the people to hold cash balances for the rainy day, i.e. for unforeseen contingencies such as expenditures arising due to accidents, sickness, disability, loss of income and so on. The amount to be held under this head would depend on the temperament of the individual, living conditions around him and social security network operating in a country.

3. **The speculative motive**: The idea that people hold money also for speculative purposes was among the original contributions

of Keynes to economics. He saw it in the desire of people to earn profit or avoid loss from fluctuations they expect in the rate of interest over time. For simplicity, it is assumed that the only alternative people have to the holding of money is to invest it in bonds carrying fixed rates of interest. When rates of interest are expected to rise, bonds fall in value on the market. People are spurred to sell existing bonds to and have money to avoid possible capital losses. On the contrary, if interest rates are expected to fall, bond prices climb up. People move out of money; they purchase bonds. It follows that there is an inverse relationship between the expected rate of interest and the speculative demand for money M_D via the bond market. If the rates of interest rise demand for money would fall, and if the interest rates fall the demand for money would increase. But to what level may the rate of interest fall? The liquidity preference theory says that interest rate cannot fall beyond a level even if the supply of money is kept increasing, but why? The answer to the question is not far to seek.

> Assuming money supply as given in the short run, interest is defined as reward to people for parting with liquidity (cash with them) as loan to others.

Money supply, interest and liquidity

Supply of money depends on the policies of the government and the central bank of a country. It includes coins, currency notes and bank deposits—both cash and credit. All valuable things in a society carry a price tag. So long as money can buy goods and services in a society, it is valuable, it must command a price. Also interest is the price for using money; it cannot fall to zero. Up to a point it will fall with an increase in the supply of money demand remaining unchanged. Beyond that, any increase in money supply will fall into the trap of idle cash holdings with the people. The rate of interest will cease to decrease. Figure 11.7 illustrates how liquidity trap operates. Here, M_D is the demand schedule for resources people prefer to keep with them during a period in liquid form that is in money holdings at various rates of interest R. It slopes downwards to express the inverse relationship between interest rate and liquidity preference. Thus, when the rate of interest is relatively high such as R_1 people may want to keep less money (liquidity) with them. But as the rate of interest falls, liquidity preference increases along the curve such that it extends to L_2 to equal the money supply fixed at S. This is the limit; the rate of interest cannot fall beyond R_2 even if the monetary authority increases money supply. People will not use additional money put in circulation hoping a reversal of the trend soon. At R_2 rate of interest M_D will become perfectly elastic beyond L_2. The implication of the trap is that monetary policy alone cannot pull the economy out from the mire of depression.

> Demand for money is the urge for retaining it in the pockets. This desire varies inversely with the rate of interest. An increase in money supply may lower interest rate but not beyond a point; the point where the MD curve tends to become parallel to liquidity axis. Beyond this point, additional money supply is hoarded; rate of interest is trapped by liquidity. In simple logic, rate of interest is the price for the use of money; money being scarce, its price cannot fall to zero.

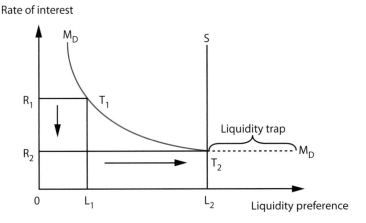

Figure 11.7 *Interest rate falls as money supply increases but not beyond R_0 as all additional money supply people hold*

Change in money demand and interest

We have seen that liquidity preference explains the demand side of the story and a demand for money schedule was used in our explanation of the liquidity trap concept in Keynes. Let us now turn to the relationship between interest rate and a change in demand for money, its supply remaining constant. Figure 11.8 helps explain the position.

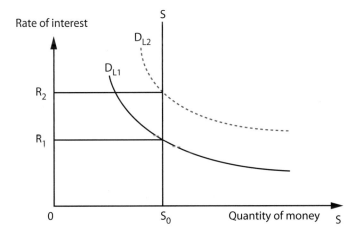

Figure 11.8 *Change in money demand and interest are positively related, supply of money remaining unchanged*

Given the supply of money fixed at S, the initial demand for liquidity D sets the equilibrium rate of interest at R. If the demand increases to D, the rate of interest too moves up to R. Thus, there is a positive relationship between the changes in the demand for money and the rate of interest.

Given the supply of money, interest rate will rise with an increase in liquidity preference, i.e. if the MD curve bodily shifts upwards and vice versa.

Critical appraisal of the theory

We noted earlier that the liquidity preference analysis looks at the demand for money arising from its store of value function. It is an advantage; it helps explain why increase in money supply could not be a cure for unemployment during the 1930s depression. The increase could not raise effective demand that would have cleared the market; it was sucked in by the *liquidity trap*. However, the theory is not without weaknesses. The main ones are as explained below.

1. Motives for liquidity preference may well be operative at the lower income levels. For top income brackets, it has little significance. Interest for a very rich person may be no more than the payment to forego the pleasure of seeing and touching his wealth as and when he pleases.

2. The speculation demand for money does not depend on the existing rate of interest; it rather depends on the *expectations* of a change in that rate in the future. If there is a change in the expectation regarding the future rates of interest, the entire liquidity preference schedule, especially because of it speculative part, will change. Thus, if people on balance expect the interest rate to rise in future (prices of existing bonds to fall), they are likely to sell bonds now to avoid possible losses and have liquid funds ready at hand to take advantage of lower bond prices in days ahead. Liquidity preference would increase and the schedule would shift upwards to the right. Opposite will happen if interest rates are expected to fall (write the sequence of events). Notice that here the relationship between the rate of interest and liquidity preference or demand for money becomes positive while it was negative with supply. (See Figure 11.7.) Recall the distinction between movement *on* a demand curve and the movement off a demand curve. Failure to make this distinction may land you in confusion on the topic.

3. The theory regards interest as the 'reward for parting with liquidity'; an incentive for 'not hoarding'. But how can people surrender liquidity unless they already have liquidity? Also, how can liquidity exist without prior savings? The positive connection between interest as an incentive and savings as the result is lost in the Keynesian analysis. It has also blurred the distinction between savings and hoarding of money. This distinction is vital because Islam also does not approve, rather condemns, the hoarding of money.

The distinction between savings and hoarding seems to be a matter of *intent*. Hoarding of money may be the consequence of the lust for amassing wealth. Savings may be the result of precautionary motives plus a desire to earn an income by converting it into investment. Where the process of holding money for savings stops and hoarding begins, an economist—mainstream or Islamic—can hardly say; God alone knows what people have in their hearts; what they really intend. But *zakat* is payable on savings only if money stays unspent until a year, implying probably a 12 month time demarcation between the two.

11.6   WHY ISLAM PROHIBITS INTEREST?

There are few topics in economics that have attracted as much attention of Islamic scholars as the question of interest. Over the years, a consensus has evolved, though dissentions are not entirely absent, that Islam prohibits both the giving and taking of interest, irrespective of whether the loan is in the form of money or commodities; it is taken for meeting consumption needs or for production; it comes from a person or an institution like the modern bank, and whether the interest is charged at a simple or compounding rate.

> Over time, a consensus has emerged among the scholars that Islam prohibits the giving and taking interest on all sorts of borrowings. Disagreements from this verdict are rare.

Islam requires that exchange of anything with one of its own kind should not take place except on the basis of equality of measure; 1 carat of gold for 1 carat of gold, 1 kilogram of barley for 1 kilogram of barley, 1 litre of milk for 1 litre of milk, 100 dollars for 100 dollars on the spot or over time. Any excess paid or charged over what is given is interest that Islamic law prohibits. If excess is involved in hand-to-hand or spot transactions, such as one measure of white sugar for one and a quarter measure of brown sugar, it is called *riba-al-fadl*. If time for repayment of the debt is allowed, the excess charge it is called *riba-al-nasiah*. In either case, it is the similarity of the goods involved despite the difference in their quality that attracts the prohibition. Different qualities of a good should pass through the market sale and purchase process for valid exchange.

> Interest *(riba)* is of two types. One involves time dimension and is called *riba-al-nasiah,* while the other called *riba-al-fadl,* may arise in spot transactions. The prohibition of the first comes from the scripture but of the second follows from the Sunnah.

For the faithful it is reason enough to avoid transactions involving interest as submission to their belief system. However, as an academic discipline, Islamic economics must provide justification for the prohibition. The reasoning on the point has two aspects, negative and positive.

11.6.1   Interest Payments are Illogical and Unjust

Islamic economics borrows a plea against interest from Keynes' *General Theory*. It is argued that the schedule of expected profit rates is rarely in tune with the schedule of interest rates, the latter being much sticky. When profit expectations run high and wide of interest rates, the economy is on its way to inflation. On the other hand, when profit expectations are falling faster than the slow-responding interest rates, the economy faces deepening deflation and unemployment. Alternating booms and depressions hinder the long-run growth and stability of the economy.

Again, the marginal productivity theory, whatever its other weaknesses, cannot explain the payment of interest. Islamic economics need not deny that capital, even if liquid may have productive attributes in a factor combination. But more fundamental is the question whether interest matches its productivity? We know that the level of interest rates in a country is essentially determined by the state of opinion in the bond market, and the manipulation of its monetary policy by the central bank. What has the productivity of capital to do with either of them?

Furthermore, all funds, whether owned or borrowed, are inseparably intermixed in the business of a firm and are exposed to the *same* degree of risk in its business. How does the productivity or exposure to risk of the owned and borrowed funds differ from the viewpoint of the firm or society? Why the two sorts of capital should then be differently rewarded: one with variable uncertain profit and the other with prefixed interest? Social conventions or legal fictions need not always be just as well; interest is no exception.

Finally, interest payments cannot be shown patterned to meet the norms of social justice at the macro level. Borrowings in the past resulted in the flow of money from the rich to the poor in society. Interest rates were high, often exorbitant and loans often financed the fulfilment of bare survival needs; the poor suffered. Today, the situation has reversed in the sense that savings largely come from the middle classes of society who contribute to pension funds, take insurance policies, buy units in mutual trusts and put money in fixed deposits. This pool of small men's savings goes to finance the business tycoons via the financial institutions. Interest rates are kept low. Real interest rates (nominal interest rate minus inflation rate) may even become negative. Cheap money policy is the order of the day. Small savers part with their money just for a song if we compare what they get as interest with the profits their savings help generate. Many times when the interest rates rise in an economy due to a change in monetary policy, the banks are quick to pass the increase to the borrowers but drag their feet to raise the rates on customer deposits. Thus viewed, interest was an institution of perpetual injustice in the past, it remains so even today. The weaker sections of the society have always been its victim.

11.6.2   Islamic Alternative

On the positive side, let us begin with a clarification. Note that the Islamic prohibition of interest has nothing to do with either the *productivity* of capital or the *fixity* of interest rates as some Islamic economists argue. The objective is the removal of an instrument of injustice and exploitation from the economic scene.

Islam seeks to treat *all* capital in trade, industry and commerce on an equal footing in a scenario where the business is growing risky and its outcome so uncertain. It proposes the sharing of the profits and losses of business among providers of capital on an equitable basis without any prior claims on the firms' net revenue. While all losses are to be borne in the ratio of contributions to business capital, sharing of profit ratios could be negotiable. In addition to profit-sharing finance, internal or external, the Islamic scheme admits a time value for money in deferred payment contracts, where markup or cost plus profit pricing of products is allowed.

It is evidence of the vitality of the interest-free finance system that Islamic banking is making rapid progress in competition with interest-based conventional banks. Even the latter embracing the Islamic modes and instruments with elation.

C. PROFIT

11.7 INDIFFERENT ATTITUDE

Profit plays a central role in the free enterprise economies, including Islamic economy. Price theory, the core of economic science, cannot stand erect if its basic assumption of profit maximization is withdrawn. Also, few growth models would look as neat as they do without some profit concept. Yet, to questions such as what is profit, what causes or determines it, and to whom it really belongs, economists have hardly provided convincing or conclusive answers. Modern textbooks on economics either do not discuss this vital subject or relegate it to some dusty corners. Books and journal articles on the subject are rare and far between.

Empirical studies on business profits are also rare. An interesting feature in print media reports on corporate profits is the non-availability of rates of return on equity, net worth, sales or on total capital employed in a firm. What is usually reported is by what percentage the amount of profit of a corporation changed over the previous year. Can you say why there is much reluctance in talking or reporting about profits? Discuss among yourselves.

11.7.1 Issues in Profit Theory

Profit theory is one of the most confusing, controversial, neglected and shifty areas in economics. Going against the tradition, we shall not discuss here each profit theory as a separate unit. Instead, we shall examine some of the main *issues* in the area. This would help avoid overlaps, economize space and clear some cobwebs in the arguments on the subject.

Concepts of profit

The division of the factors of production into *hired* and *unhired* is helpful in the discussion on profit. The unhired factors guarantee, under contract, the agreed payments—wages, interest and rent—to the hired

Most issues concerning profit—its definition, locale, cause and source, division, measurement and role remain in dispute.

factors for their cooperation in the process of production. The division is a social necessity for producing goods and services to satisfy human needs under *uncertainty* of business outcome. Uncertainty divides people into those who prefer to work for assured, even if fixed, incomes and those who provide such assurance in the expectation of larger incomes even if uncertain. They are unhired factors and bear the risk and uncertainty of business; they are the *entrepreneurs*. From the sale proceeds of output they first meet their obligations to the hired factors, what remains is theirs. If contractual payments exceed sales revenue they suffer a loss; if revenue is more than payments they earn profit. We discussed this view as accounting profit in Section 6.4 of Chapter 6. To repeat, we also explained there the concept of normal profit and identified its elements. Normal profit is now treated as part of production costs; surplus additional to normal profit is pure or economic profit or now simply profit. Profit that theory seeks to explain does not include monopoly revenue and scarcity rents. Islamic economists do not make such conceptual distinctions; they make the notion too abstract and atomistic. They rather take an integrated holistic view of profit. But the distinctions mainstream economists make have analytical significance.

Source of profit

To explain the emergence of profit and identify its source, economists usually start with no-profit model constructed on the basis of some assumptions. Then they seek to uncover what makes those assumptions inoperative in the real world and regard them as the source of profit. Interestingly, the no-profit models economists make virtually end up in a perfect competition picture that you already know. Perfect competition is a static model. The source of profit is, therefore, *dynamic change*.

In a dynamic change, profit sources may be varied—innovation, imitation, windfalls, monopoly gains, etc.

Dynamic change makes predictions difficult and information incomplete. Expectations may not come true. Capital invested in business may be lost. Business is risky and profit is the reward for taking that risk. However, with the appearance of insurance on the scene, we may transfer many business risks to others by paying a premium. So, businessmen bear only uninsurable risks, technically called *uncertainty*. Following Frank H. Knight, many regard profit as a reward for bearing uncertainty.

However, uncertainty theory makes profit a *windfall*, income independent of human thought or action. Uncertainty is a fact of life like sun or rain. We have to take it in our stride; why should a payment incentive be needed to bear it in business? According to Joseph A. Schumpeter, what causes dynamic change is *innovation*. Innovation means introducing new ideas or products, or better ways of doing old things. For example, introduction of power looms to replace hand looms in textile industry was an innovation. Product improvement in electronics, hand phones and computers are the result of ever-increasing innovations. The act of innovating is venturesome. It is moving away from tradition as swimming against the current. It involves risk; many try, not all succeed. Those who innovate are the entrepreneurs Joseph

Alois Schumpeter pleaded in his *Theory of Economic Development* (1932). But he soon realized that the function of innovation had already been institutionalized: university departments, research laboratories and research and development teams in large corporations are doing the work; innovation is no longer the area for individual explorations. Thus, in his *Capitalism, Socialism, and Democracy* (1946), Schumpeter threw his notion of innovation as the source of entrepreneurial income into the dust bin of 'obsolete ideas'.

In summary, we do not have a single unified theory of profit. We have a variety of them, each providing at best some partial truth about the source of profit.

Profit and entrepreneurs

Economists have invariably regarded profit as a functional return—the reward for entrepreneurial services. Knight provides the leading example that still seems to underlie the common view on the subject. He argued that since uncertainty breeds risk that cannot be eliminated or met at cost, everyone is not equally inclined or equipped to assume the role of decision maker in the realm of business. Only those who have confidence in their own judgment as well as the ability to put their opinion into operation, specialize in decision-making and are ready to bear the consequences. They are the entrepreneurs.

> Profit going to the entrepreneur cannot always be justified as reasonable or deserved.

BOX 11.2

Productivity and Factor Rewards

The problem of distribution has ever been to determine the relative shares of the factors of production, say labour and capital, in the net revenue (NR) a firm earns, in a just manner. Economic science has met with one of its major failures from David Ricardo to J.B. Clark in this regard. The latter put forth his marginal productivity theory to resolve the issue. After the initial elation subsided, the critics found little difficulty in demonstrating that it is the relative scarcity of factors that determines both their rewards and marginal productivity.

The productivity of any individual factor is unrealistic. The skill of a worker, the ability of a manager, the usefulness of a machine or the location of a factory are admittedly qualities in themselves affecting their market value; but they do not operate in a vacuum. For production, they are meaningful expressions only when conceived as operating together in appropriate *combinations* for organizations engaged in the process of production. Individual contributions do matter in a factor combination but cannot be separated. For the firm, significance of the individual is on the wane; team work is gaining importance. Thus, in empirical researches, the concept of combinational (total) is gaining ground. The net revenue/profit of a firm is the measure of total factor productivity and must be shared.

Source: Zubair Hasan (1975)

The entrepreneurs translate business ideas into action for which they hire other factors of production. The services of the hired factors do not involve the exercise of judgment in the same sense as it does in the case of the entrepreneurs. The hired factors work for him in return for contractual payments. The objective requirement for entrepreneurship, according to Knight, is the possession of property since no empty-handed person can ensure contractual payments to the hired factors of production. Interestingly, Schumpeter did not consider the owning of capital necessary for the entrepreneur, though control on it could be an advantage. Sufficient for being an entrepreneur to him was to have a new bright saleable business idea. To find a financier may not then be difficult. Possibly, being an economic historian, Schumpeter took a cue from the popularity of *mudarabah,* the dominant business model in the flourishing Muslim lands until the close of the 14th century. (In *mudarabah,* one person does business with money supplied by another, both sharing profit in an agreed ratio and the loss being borne by the financier alone.)

The above view of an entrepreneur sees him as a person; with business ideas and organizational talent profit being the reward for making business succeed in the face of uncertainty. The concept is a legacy of the old days' model of tiny owner operated business units. It fits well even today to cases of small business. But since the rise to dominance of the modern corporate form of organization both the functions and the identity of the entrepreneurs have come under attack. Put briefly, the argument is as follows.

> With the rise of modern gigantic corporations as the dominant form of business organization, the link between profit and entrepreneur has only become ritualistic. If it is difficult to identify the entrepreneur in such organizations, it is even more so to specify his functions.

The promoters bring the corporation into existence and the stockholders provide the risk capital which is often supplemented by institutional finance. The decision-making function and the ownership of the organization are in quite different hands. Ordinarily, those who make decisions are the salaried people and they seldom bear the consequences of their decisions. Further, decision-making is divided among a large number of fairly independent functionaries all of whom may not have the same aims or motivation. Who then are the entrepreneurs and what functions do they perform in the era of large corporations?

Small and closely held corporations are no different from the proprietary businesses. The notion of an entrepreneur is still valid in their case. But in large corporations, the ownership rights of the small, widely dispersed and unknown stockholders are largely nominal, representing a mere claim to a 'dividend wage' for their capital determined by the management. It is the rights of the owners of large blocks of stocks that alone are real in the sense that they often manage to acquire effective control over the affairs of their corporations. The perfection of the proxy machine (influential shareholders collect authorization from small scattered ones to vote on their behalf at company meetings) and some other techniques tend to help in the emergence of 'control ownership' in large corporations. Though the control may rarely pass into the hands of a single person, the possibility of a small group of stockholders enjoying such power is widespread. The entrepreneur in this sense, survives as a 'unit of interest and control' even in large corporations.

To conclude, profit defined as a surplus of business earnings over the contractual payments is a non-functional surplus whose origins lie in progressive dynamic change. Its appropriation in a free enterprise system is essentially institutional; market is a poor arbiter in the matter. The real issue in profit theory is whether contractual payments, especially wages as determined by the market forces, can be shown to be just on the contribution to output basis. More than that, can profits in the hands of control ownership be always shown as judiciously utilized? We have explained in the previous chapter that from an Islamic viewpoint, profit-sharing schemes in big businesses may presumably be the solution to the issues such questions raise.

Summary

- The three distributive shares—rent, interest and profit—in national income largely go to the same social class, the capitalists, in free enterprise economies. The basic issue, therefore, is how the division of revenue output between labour and capital takes place in modern business.

A. Rent

- Economic rent may be defined as the price paid to the landowners for the use of land that includes all natural resources God has provided to benefit mankind and other living beings.

- Ricardo regarded the payment as compensation for using the original and indestructible qualities of soil in the process of production. He highlighted differences in the quality of various pieces of land in his illustration of using land for growing corn. Nevertheless, his theory can be shown as applicable even when all land is assumed as being of the same quality.

- More of less fertile land has to be cultivated to meet the increasing demand for corn as population grows. At any point in time, the least fertile land under cultivation is the *marginal land*; the cost of production on marginal land is the highest. The price of corn in the market must cover this cost as society needs the output of the marginal land to meet the demand.

- However, all corn has to be sold in the market at a uniform price. Such price will yield a surplus over cost for all land graded better than the marginal land. This differential is economic rent for Ricardo.

- As price just equals the cost of growing corn on the marginal land which receives no rent, rent does not enter price, according to Ricardo.

- In the final analysis, what the theory of Ricardo says is that more fertile land will get higher rent than the less fertile land. This is no more than saying that a better article will always fetch a better price. But his theory has had far-reaching socio-political fall out.

- Modern theory of rent sees rent as an element in all factor rewards if it commands a higher price in any use over and above its transfer earnings or opportunity cost. The supply of land for alternative uses not being totally inelastic; rent becomes a part of price in a particular use.

- In Islamic economics, we still do not have an agreed position regarding the ownership of land or the determination of rent for its use.

B. Interest

- Early writers in the area of economics regarded interest as a nominal rate of payment for the use of money. The real rate of interest to them was the return to capital as determined by its marginal productivity. They also sought to establish some relationship between the nominal and real rates of interest.

- Modern economists use the term interest as denoting only the payment for the use of money. They separate the return to investment from interest maintaining its link with productivity. Thus, interest and profit both are returns to the same factor—capital—in its different forms. The rationale for paying interest is that capital, even in money form, has opportunity costs or transfer earnings. Interest, when a *sunk cost*, should not be counted in comparing alternatives to achieving the same goals.

- The loanable funds theory explaining the determination of interest rate is the application of the familiar demand and supply apparatus to the capital market transactions. Demand for loanable funds usually arises for partial financing of investment in fixed assets, working capital and liquid funds requirements in trade industry and commerce. Consumers too need loans to buy durable goods. The credit card culture is fast catching up in the developing world as well.

- Supply of funds comes from individual savings, free reserves of joint stock companies, public enterprise surpluses, pension funds, insurance companies, and unit trusts.

- The position of hoarding money in the loanable funds theory of interest is not clear. The theory does not provide a determinate solution: there seems to be circular relationships between savings, borrowings and the rate of interest.

- The liquidity preference theory sees the need for paying interest to overcome common desire of people to keep a part of their money incomes with them to carry on daily expenditure until the next inflow of income, to meet unforeseen emergency expenditures and to take advantage of expected turns in prices.

- There is an inverse relationship between interest rate and liquidity demand for money. Since money is scarce in relation to the demand for it, its price or interest rate cannot fall beyond a point. Beyond that point, any additional supply of money put into circulation is retained by the people for speculative purposes; additional money moves into the liquidity trap, interest rate stays stuck at the minimum level it had reached.

- If the liquidity preference schedule remains unchanged, the rate of interest varies inversely with money supply. On the other hand, if money supply stays unchanged the interest rate varies directly with changes in the liquidity preference schedule.

- Since the groups that demand money for its liquidity attributes are not the same who supply money to the market, schedules of interest rates and profit expectations rarely match with reference to interest rates. The economy is rarely in a state of disequilibrium. Interest is a hindrance to both growth and stability, as Keynes saw it. Islamic economists endorse this viewpoint.

- Islam prohibits interest in all forms and purposes of borrowings. The reason is neither the pre-fixity of interest nor its murky relationship with productivity. It is the act of eliminating an instrument of injustice and exploitation from the social scene that interest has always been.

- In the old days, the flow of money was from the rich towards the poor of the society; interest rates were rather exorbitant. Today, the bulk of the loan money flows from the middle classes to the rich in business via the banks; interest rates are kept rather low as a matter of policy. Interest was exploitative of the weak then; it is exploitative of them today. The real interest rates even become negative when interest rates lag behind inflation rates.

- Furthermore, all capital in the business of a firm is exposed to identical risk and uncertainty. From the viewpoint of the firm or society, why should the two parts of it—owned and borrowed—be rewarded differently?

- The remedy lies in sharing of profits with workers in mass production corporations. Such schemes are becoming common and popular to ensure industrial peace. Islam is not averse to such arrangements.

C. Profit

- Profit plays a central role in free enterprise economies. Yet, economics textbooks no longer pay much attention to a discussion on the subject. Journal articles, let alone books, are rare and far between on profit. Empirical research in the area too is scanty. This is surprising.

- Much confusion surrounds the concept of profit: distinction is not clear between normal, pure, economic and monopoly versions of profit. There is no one-on-one correspondence between profit and risk or productivity for which it is claimed to be a reward.

- There is also confusion regarding the source of profit—dynamic change, risk, uncertainty, innovation or monopoly power. Nor is it logically settled whose profit one talks about in a large corporation: the shareholders, the entrepreneur or the corporation? The seat of profit is unclear because the identity as also the functions of an entrepreneur have become blurred beyond recognition in large corporations that control the bulk of the industrial output in modern economies.

- In essence, the source of profit is dynamic change. Its appropriation is institutional; market forces have little to do with it. Islam hails profit as a bounty from God and would want a share for labour in its distribution.

Glossary

Quasi-rent The concept rent originated in Ricardo but the word has since assumed several different meanings in economics. The commonly used meaning sees rent as an excess of what any factor of production earns over its transfer earnings. A quasi-rent is different; it is a reward granted to a factor over and above its opportunity cost to work as an incentive. For example, to get it an Islamic bank manager may have to come up with a new Shari'ah compliant saleable product. Quasi-rent is a temporary short-run phenomenon. In the long run, the new product imitates the old, and economic profit the latter brought in is competed away.

Rent seeking In economics, rent seeking refers to the endeavour of an individual, organization or firm to make money by manipulating the economic and/or legal environment rather than through productive contributions. Most of the scams involving politicians such as food for oil program in Iraq are the result of rent seeking. Earning extra money through match fixing in sports is another example. Rent-seeking behaviour is the mother of all corruption the world over. An *operative* Islamic economic system can significantly dampen rent-seeking behaviour of individuals and organizations.

Risk and uncertainty Risk management has assumed much importance in Islamic economics because of the proliferation of Islamic financial institutions. It is therefore essential to know what risk is. In this connection one cannot ignore the vital distinction between risk on the one hand and uncertainty on the other. Some risks can be measured and therefore can be met at a cost. Measurability of risks is the foundation of all sorts of insurance business in the world. But there are risks which cannot be measured because they do not submit to statistical probability measurement. A student, for example, cannot insure the risk of failure at an examination nor can a football team get insurance against losing a match. Insurable business risks are in fact no risks as they can be met at a cost. True risk lies in the uncertainty about the future outcome of an action that cannot be insured against. How can one manage such uncertainty is the question.

Share cropping This is a system of cultivation in which a landowner allows a tenant to use the land in return for a share of the crop. The system flourished in the pre-Islamic era and Islam allowed its continuation as a social convention in preference to other modes of owner–tenant relationship in agriculture under the term *muzara'ah*. However, Islam granted many concessions to the actual tillers of the soil exhorting landowner to be considerate and benevolent in dealing with their tenants.

Concepts for Review

- Dynamic change
- Entrepreneur
- Hoarding
- Innovation
- Institutional appropriation
- Interest
- Islamic prohibition of interest
- Liquidity preference
- Liquidity trap
- Loanable funds: demand and supply
- Marginal land

- Money supply
- Profit-sharing
- Profit-risk mismatch
- Pure profit
- Quasi-rent
- Rent
- Rent seeking
- Risk and uncertainty
- Share cropping
- Speculative motive
- Transfer earnings

Case Study   11.1

Real Interest Turns Negative

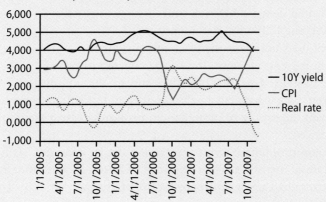

Real 10-year T-note yield since 2005 in the USA

Figure 11.9 *Subtract the 12-month change in the consumer price index from the month-end Chicago Board Options Exchange (CBOE) 10-year treasury note yield ($TNX)*

Source: Federal Reserve

In the above figure, the vertical distance between the nominal rate of interest (black line) and the rate of inflation measured by the consumer price index or CPI (grey line) measures the real interest rate (dotted line). Study the three lines carefully and answer the following questions.

Case Questions
1. Explain the rising trend of real interest rate during the year 2006. Why did this rate show a falling trend earlier?
2. Mark when the real rate of interest turned negative and state for what reasons.
3. Can you picture how the figure would look like if the economy were operating without interest? Could the dotted line show the level of profit in the economy?

Case Study   11.2

Islam and Residence Renting

A in India takes a residential apartment on lease for a period of three years. He pays INR 1 million for the lease. *A* will hand over the apartment to the owner on the expiry of the lease period and get back the lease money INR 1 million he had paid. The agreed maintenance charges have to be paid for the apartment each month. Some Islamic scholars feel that this sort of arrangement, though popular in many places, is not permitted in Islam. The waiver of rent is, they argue, the *interest* paid in this case.

Source: <bigpicture.typepad.com/comments/2007/12/real-interest-r.html>, accessed 1 April 2014.

Case Questions
1. Do you agree that the renting contract in the above case is not Shari'ah compliant? Give reasons for your answer.
2. Will it make the contract Islamic if *A* pays a nominal rent to the owner of the house in addition to the present lease arrangement? Explain.

Test Questions

11.1   What is marginal land? How does rent rise and increase as the margin of cultivation extends? Use the information given in the upper part of Table 11.2 to fill its blank cells. Fill the last row of the table if supply is to match the indicated demand for each year.

11.2   Reconcile the following statements:
   (a) Rent does not enter the price of a product.
   (b) Rent is a cost element. It must be covered in price.

11.3   Why is an interest paid? Critically examine the liquidity preference theory of interest. What happens to the rate of interest if liquidity preference rises faster than the supply of money in an economy? Use a diagram to illustrate your answer.

11.4   Why Islam prohibits interest transactions in an economy? Is it the fixation of the rate of interest before the results of business operations are known, or because money capital is not productive? Discuss.

11.5   Write notes on:
   (a) Quasi-rent,
   (b) Rent seeking,
   (c) Transaction motive, and
   (d) Entrepreneurs land profit.

Table 11.2 *Price, marginal land and economic rent (imaginary data)*

Year	1998	2000	2002	2004	2006
Grades of land	A	B	C	D	E
Cost of production per ton	50	60	70	80	90
Output in tons	100	100	100	100	100
Price per ton	50	60	70	80	90
Demand in tons	100	200	300	400	500
Total rent					
1998					
2000					
2002					
2004					
2006					

Web Exercise

Search the Internet for material on the notion of an entrepreneur in economics, his role in modern economies, and write an essay on his functions in modern economies.

Forward Link

The final chapter of the book is devoted to a broad discussion of environmental issues that confront the world with an impending catastrophe. We shall discuss the source of these issues, their nature, possible solutions and difficulties in resolving them.

Markets, Environment and Sustainability

LEARNING OUTCOMES

This chapter should enable the student to understand:

- The welfare theorem and the environment
- Some basic questions in environmental economics and the extension of scarcity and efficiency notions
- Market failures: Externalities or spillover
- Pollution: The two versions
- The tools for analysis: Marginal benefits and marginal external costs
- Environment and Pareto optimality
- Remedial measures: Market versus government intervention
- The Coase theorem, standards, taxes, subsidies and tradable permits
- Sustainability, environment and Islam

12.1 MARKETS VERSUS WELFARE

Markets do not include environmental costs in commodity pricing.

In the previous six chapters, we have explained how free markets allocate the scarce resources of the community to the production of various goods and services and distribute the resultant output among the participating factor owners. Markets are great social institutions and undisputedly the cheapest way to administer an economy. However, the cheapness of a system alone may not always justify the consequences it leads to from the viewpoint of overall social well-being. The performance of markets needs a fresh look, especially because freedom of markets is assuming compulsive overtones under the rising wave of globalization crossing national borders unrestrictedly.

12.1.1 The Fundamental Theorem

It is invariably claimed that markets allocate resources efficiently and distribute the fruits of productive effort equitably among the participants. The achievement of this two-fold objective is expressed in the *fundamental theorem of welfare economics* as derived from the Pareto optimality conditions as:

$$MRT_{YX} = MRS_{XY}$$

The price mechanism operating in the product markets on the one hand and in the factor markets on the other equate the two marginal rates, i.e. the marginal rate of transformation (MRT) of Y into X and the marginal rate of substitution (MRS) of X for Y. (Recall production possibilities curve of Chapter 1.)

Figure 12.1 explains the theorem. Here, Y measures the quantity of herbal cold drinks such as Rooh Afza of Hamdard and X the quantity of aerated waters such as Coca Cola. The initial equilibrium of the Pakistan economy with reference to these drinks is at point D on the production frontier AF. But D is a static point. Tastes, technologies, resource availability, income distribution and assortment of goods are all in a process of dynamic change in modern economies. For example, improvement in the acidity consciousness among people may shift consumer demand away from Coca Cola to Rooh Afza, the herbal drink. As demand for Rooh Afza increases because of a change in tastes, it would make the entire production chain from farm to factory better off. On the other hand, as the demand for Coca Cola shrinks, its price must fall affecting the welfare of those connected with its production and distribution all along the line. This must affect the relative incomes of people as well.

> The fundamental theorem based on Pareto optimality says that social welfare is maximized when MRT equals to MRS in the case of all commodities that pass through the market.

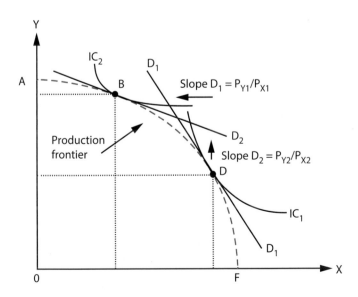

Figure 12.1 *Fundamental welfare theorem requires MRT$_{YX}$ = MRS$_{XY}$ at both points B and D*

The essential point of this example is that even as people are influencing each other's welfare, *all* of the effects are transmitted via changes in the market prices. A new optimality is bound to emerge, say at point B on the frontier, technology remaining unchanged. The economy would be producing more of the herbal drink and less of the aerated waters than before. Thus, free markets eventually provide an efficient solution to the central problems of an economy. Simultaneously, markets are also supposed to ensure equity in distribution. These claims of efficiency and equity are being increasingly put to scrutiny in more recent times.

12.1.2   Three Basic Questions

Broadly, three questions are being raised.

1. What is it that the welfare theorem includes in resources on which markets put the price tags? The question has necessitated a relook on the notion of scarcity in a general broader context.
2. What do we mean by efficiency? What assumptions underlie the notion and how realistic are they?
3. Finally, how do we define equity for the purpose of the welfare theorem, and how valid is that definition?

Environmental costs extend the concepts of scarcity and efficiency.

These questions remain relevant even if we ignore the fact that economies are for most of the time, in a state of disequilibrium which the fundamental theorem simply does not deal with.

Scarcity: a broader view

We use the word 'resources' here as referring to natural resources that God has provided in the air, water and the crest of the Earth for all his creatures. His provisions are inexhaustible. Their availability to mankind is restricted by the state of our knowledge, exploration and discovery that involve costs; so resources remain scarce in relation to our wants. Those who bear costs to own and acquire resources can make or allow others their use to produce goods and services for sale. The market puts a valuation on them for compensating the owners.

But firms use in the process of production not only resources that involve ownership rights. People use for production (and consumption) resources such as fresh air and water, grass, plants, trees, animals and marine wealth which no one owns. Their use does not pass through the market. Nobody pays for their use although they are extremely valuable for promoting the common good and social welfare. They are the common property of the community, in some cases, of the mankind in general.

The unpaid use of this 'common wealth' adds to the resource scarcity in three ways. First, non–payment for them keeps prices of goods lower than they would otherwise be. This leads to a relatively faster use of the resources that pass through the market, aggravating in particular the scarcity of exhaustible resources, minerals of various types, fossil fuels and crop lands, for example. Second, being available free of charge, these natural resources are themselves being rapaciously exploited. Animals, birds and reptiles are all killed for their flesh, skin, teeth, poisons and bones. Many species are becoming extinct or rarer. Biodiversity is losing its balance leading to a number of problems, especially the spread of new and deadly diseases. What were once shimmering rivers and scenic lakes have vanished due to the diversion of their waters to irrigate the crops. The Dead Sea in Jordan and the Lake of Earl in Central Asia converted into salt deserts are leading example of man's greedy exploitation of nature.

Non-inclusion of environmental costs in product pricing has led to over use of natural resources and caused their rapid exhaustion.

Finally, the natural agents of land, air and water—in a word, the environment—have been bestowed by divine wisdom with immense self-cleansing properties. Man naively thought that this ability of the environment has no limit. He could, therefore, throw any amount of human and industrial waste increasing with every growth in population and production in the dustbin of the environment and forget about it. This was not true. The Qur'an had long warned man that God has created things in due proportions and that man should not spread corruption on the Earth to disturb the balance of creation. Far-sighted individuals did draw our attention to the impending environmental calamity. A. C. Pigou and K. E Boulding were perhaps among the first to fire the warning shots in *Limits to Growth,* which appeared on the scene much later. Meanwhile, the degradation of the environment continued unabated. Deteriorating air quality, acid rain, muddying waters, deforestation, melting ice caps, rising sea levels and the heating globe all stare us in the face. Environment is deteriorating fast and no satisfactory solution seems in sight, for every ones responsibility is rarely any ones responsibility. Extension of the concept of scarce resources to environmental goods and creation of property rights in them can presumably ease the situation.

Externalities or spillovers

Environmental issues owe their origin and aggravation to the failure of the markets to account for externalities. We may define an externality as:

A cost 'A' has to incur, or the benefit he enjoys because of 'B'—an outsider to 'A's market transactions with others—without 'B' compensating 'A' for the cost imposed, or 'A' compensating 'B' for the benefit received.

If the person has to incur a cost, no one compensates him; likewise if he receives a benefit, he does not pay for it. Such costs and benefits are called *externalities* because they accrue to a third party external to the market transaction. Let us give us an illustration to clarify the point.

Beekeeping and honey selling is a lucrative trade in many countries. The bees visit orchards and flower beds of others to collect nectar. But in the process, they help gardeners to have richer crops through cross-pollination of plants. This is the balance in beneficial externalities that nature maintains for mutual advantage. The gardeners do not grudge the bees taking nectar; nay, they invite beekeeper to plant their hives in their orchards and gardens for better results.

The cost we incur due to the economic activities of others or the benefits we reap on that account are called externalities. They do not pass through the market—they are external to it.

The above was the example of a two-way beneficial externality. It need not always be so. Your neighbour across the street keeps his house always well painted and maintains a well laid out flowery lawn. Every morning you enjoy the refreshing sight from the window of your bedroom. Do you (or would you) pay for the enjoyment? In Malaysia, the highways are well maintained and decorated. The landscaping around them is tasteful. They are dotted with gleaming vehicles. Often, you feel better on the roads than in your house, which lends meaning to joy rides. Does the government charge you extra for the externality you cherish? When you meet each other even if strangers give a smile is an Islamic cultural edict. Do you see its wisdom as an externality?

Alas! The examples of beneficial externalities that we come across are rare and far between. What surround us, and at an increasing pace, are *harmful* externalities. They impose costs on us for no fault of ours. They are the consequence of pollution.

Pollution is the discharge of waste material into land, air or water that makes them physically harmful for consumption and may create psychological disquiet in human beings. The net result is the loss of welfare in its widest sense.

The physical effect of harmful externalities may show up in ill-health, respiratory problems or eye irritation, spread of cancer or species imbalance, for example. Chemical reaction through acid rain may weaken buildings, railway tracks and reduce fish production. Psychological disquiet may manifest in signs of distress, irritation and anxiety caused, say, by day in and day out advertising noise during TV programmes, even in between the news. How many of you enjoy that sudden noise in the middle of a soothing programme?

As pollution does not pass through the market, the gross domestic product (GDP) package for whose growth we always aspire wraps in together with goods and services we need to satisfy our ever-increasing wants, also the polluted air, toxic waste, poisonous water and deafening noise. The increasing amount of impurities in GDP brings us face to face with our second question: the norms for efficiency.

> Harmful externalities impose costs on us for which no one compensates us. Beneficial externalities benefit us but we do not pay anyone for the benefit received.

Efficiency norms

Economic efficiency is a criterion that can be used in several ways to input usage and to the determination of output levels. For example, in Chapter 7 (equation 7.3) we defined equilibrium output as efficient in the competitive factor market with reference to the private cost involving labour and capital if the following conditions were met:

$$\frac{\text{Marginal product of labour}}{P_0} = \frac{\text{Marginal product of capital}}{P_0}$$

But if we could add to private cost the cost inflicted by the producer on others through pollution, we shall get the social cost of production. The addition will shift the supply curve upwards, restrict output and raise price. There will be efficiency gain from a social viewpoint. We shall explain this point later when we come to Figure 12.6. However,

> The mechanism economics employs for achieving maximum social benefit from the use of resources does not take into account the intensity or urgency of individual wants. It treats the benefit of a Riyal income of equal value in a rich and poor person.

even if market could in this way, make production efficient from a social viewpoint, the welfare of the community may not be maximized. The reasons are not far to seek.

The process of maximizing net social benefits does not bother to whom these benefits accrue: efficiency does not distinguish among people. A Riyal of benefit to a rich person is considered worth a Riyal of benefit to a poor person. Likewise, a 1000 Riyal benefit to one person is thought to be the same thing as a one Riyal benefit to 1000 persons. This implies that an efficient outcome may still not meet the norms of justice. And, this brings us to our third question that is of equity.

Equity and welfare

We have seen in the preceding chapter that the notion of equity is closely linked to the personal and functional distributions of incomes in a society. If these distributions could be regarded as just, then one could also accept the distribution of output through the market as equitable. But distribution of income is and would remain unfair because competition cannot stay perfect due to asymmetric information, moral hazards, risk aversions and restricted factor motilities which the market is not able to overcome. Under the circumstances, the efficiency criterion, however defined, would remain narrow and misleading. But at the same time, let it be said that in judging economic outcomes, the trade-off between efficiency and equity would always remain a matter of controversy because the notion of justice is largely a matter of taste and on a more important side, it primarily belongs to the political arena.

Thus, the impurities in GDP packet we mentioned earlier would remain. The basic question for environmental economics is not of their elimination but of their maximal reduction. An obvious way to that end is to make polluters pay for the harmful externalities they inflict on others in a society. Let the market system internalize the damage. Theoretically, this does not pose much of a problem.

> Pollution is harmful if externality GDP is over estimated as it does not take note of external costs.

12.2   TOOLS FOR ANALYSIS

Under perfect competition, price equals marginal cost (P = MC). What surplus producers get on each of the inter-marginal units is the measure of marginal net private benefit (MNPB). Figure 12.2 explains how MNPB can be obtained. In panel A, the lined area shows the marginal profit (P − MC) for each unit as output increases up to Q_1 where marginal cost equals marginal revenue. Panel B takes profit on Y-axis and the lined area shows marginal profit as an inverted image of panel A, X-axis operating as if the price line. The MC assumes the form of marginal profit curve, the MNPB. Remember that the shape of the MNPB will depend on the shape of the MC. Here it is convex to X-axis so MNPB is concave to the origin. If MC increases at a constant rate, i.e. the curve is linear, the MNPB will also be linear. Finally, if MC increases at a diminishing rate, i.e. the curve is concave to X-axis, the MNPB shall be convex to the origin as we use this in some figure later.

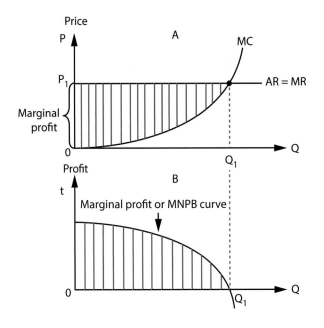

Figure 12.2 *Derivation of the MNPB curve*

The instruments for theoretical analysis in environmental economics are based mostly on the assumption of perfect competition in the markets.

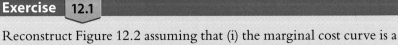

Exercise **12.1**

Reconstruct Figure 12.2 assuming that (i) the marginal cost curve is a straight line, and (ii) the marginal cost curve is concave to the X-axis.

Minimization of external cost leads to maximum social benefit.

Now, suppose the MNPB curve in Figure 12.2 is of a steel mill operating in the neighbourhood of a fishery. The fumes and gases containing droplets of sulphur oxide (SO_2 and SO_3) and nitrogen oxide (NO_2) emitting from the mill rise up in the atmosphere. They remain suspended in the air and mix up with the clouds to make acid solution that drops with rain into the fresh water of the fishery. This acid rain reduces the quantity of dissolved oxygen in the water depleting the fishermen's catch. The fishery has to incur extra cost to maintain its output level. Figure 12.3 gives the marginal external cost (MEC) the mill imposes on the fishery. The curve rises at an increasing rate as more and more of steel is produced.

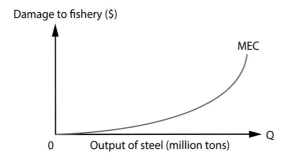

Figure 12.3 *Marginal external cost the steel mill imposes on the fishery*

We superimpose the MEC of the fishery on the MNPB of the steel mill to obtain Figure 12.4. Here, MEC crosses the MNPB at point T or Q_1 level of output. Let us analyze this position from a social standpoint. The perpendicular TQ_1 divides the figure into four sections A, B, C and D. Now, consider the following statements.

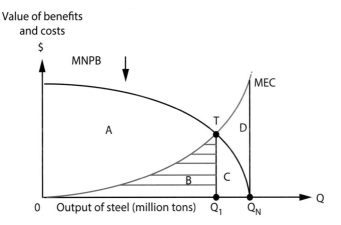

Figure 12.4 *Environment and Pareto optimality*

1. The area under the MNPB i.e. A + B + C shows net private benefit. So, left to itself, the mill would like to produce Q_N tons of steel where its marginal profit is zero and total profit maximum. Of course, private gain is part of the social gain as well.

2. However, in the process of producing steel, the society suffers the damage measured by the MEC (B + C + D) inflicted on the fishery. For the society then, we must balance the benefit and loss. Let us bring the benefit of the mill and the value of damage to fishery together to assess the gain to the society. We have:
Net social benefit = (A + B + C) − (B + C + D) = A − D

3. Area D is at once irrelevant to the situation because it is not part of even private gain. It can be eliminated if we reduce output to Q_1. But that would eliminate area C also, a part of private gain. This gain has to be sacrificed to eliminate D and maximize net social gain as A. Note that area C < area D (the implication?)

4. Note that area C + D is Pareto *relevant* externality because its elimination would improve social welfare. The optimal trade off between social benefit and externality takes place at point T where MNPB = MEC. The policy implication of the figure is that living beings on the Earth have to tolerate in some measure their slow poisoning measured as area B for economic progress.

For efficient use of resources, the price of a commodity must cover not only explicit marginal cost (MC) but also the implicit social cost (MEC).

However, even to keep externality at an optimal level, it must pass through the market, the price covering not only private cost but social cost of production as well. It is easy to see what this cost shall be. From Figure 12.2 we have:

$$MNPB = P - MC \qquad (12.1)$$

Figure 12.4 tells us that:

$$MNPB = MEC$$

Through simple substitution we have:

$$P - MC = MEC$$

The market price from the social viewpoint must therefore, be:

$$P = MC + MEC = \text{Marginal social cost or MSC} \qquad (12.2)$$

12.2.1   Pollution and Absorption

The argument that pollution should be penalized only if the absorption limit of the environment is crossed is valid in theory, but is extremely difficult to put into operation.

Some writers, however, seek to purify the definition of pollution we have used to construct the above figures. They argue that all environmental agents, for example, land, air and water, have a self-cleansing property which we talked about earlier as well. From total pollution, they suggest, we ought to take out the part which environment absorbs to arrive at the factual externality. The MEC must start from somewhere after the origin. Figure 12.5 illustrates the point. You may note that the area showing optimal externality is reduced (identify it in the figure) and Q_0 steel can be produced without causing any damage to the fishery or others for that matter.

This modification of the definition of pollution we employed until now is valid in principle. But, from a practical viewpoint it is very difficult to lay down for each case where the absorptive capacity of the environmental good in question ended and pollution started causing damage, the more so in a dynamic socio-economic scenario. On a more fundamental side, the treatment of the absorptive capacity would depend on the view you take of property rights in the environmental goods. If we take the stand that such rights are in general with the people, little objection can be raised to the proposed modification in the definition of pollution. However, if we say that environmental goods belong to the society as a whole, we may count the use of environment from zero onwards; it would be immaterial when pollution turns hurting. Of course for that reason we shall not have to pay for inhaling fresh air or swimming in shimmering common waters. Whatever position we may like to take, current discussions on the issue imply social ownership of environmental goods and external costs are invariably measured from the origin.

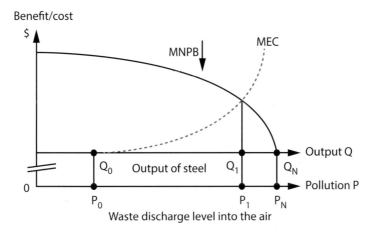

Figure 12.5 *Restrictive definition of pollution*

12.2.2   Demand and Supply Framework

The determination of optimum output that we demonstrated in Figure 12.4 can be explained in the usual demand and supply curves format also. As it has the advantage of integrating externality with the market determination of equilibrium price and output, we present in Figure 12.6 the necessary adjustments in the usual price–output equilibrium diagram.

To keep things simple, we show here the MEC imposed on the fishery of our illustration by the steel mill as a constant. The initial equilibrium price–output combination for steel is $P_0 - Q_0$ given by the intersection of demand and supply curves at point T_0. If we add MEC to private cost-based supply curve S_P, it will shift upwards to the S_S level, including the social cost of production. The equilibrium price–output combination would now be $P_S - Q_S$. The message of the figure is that internalization of the externality will tend to make output smaller and the price larger than before. At private levels, the change may be unwelcome to both the producer and consumers of the product.

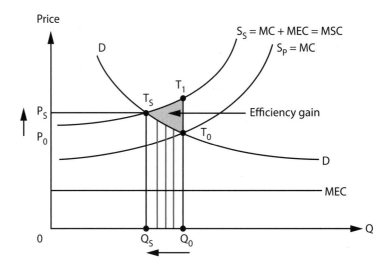

Figure 12.6 *Adjustment for externality raises price and reduces output to optimize social welfare*

Interestingly, the change is conducive to social well-being. The reduction in output from Q_0 to Q_1 reduces consumers' benefit by $T_S Q_S Q_0 T_0$, the area under the demand curve. But it also reduces the cost of production to the extent of $T_S Q_S Q_0 T_1$, the area under the supply curve. Note that:

$$T_S Q_S Q_0 T_1 - T_S Q_S Q_0 T_0 = + T_S T_0 T_1 \qquad (12.3)$$

$T_S T_0 T_1$ enclosing the shaded area shows the excess of reduction in cost over the reduction in the consumer benefit; it is efficiency gain from the social welfare viewpoint as hinted at earlier.

Exercise 12.2

The following statements are based on Figure 12.4. Do you agree with these statements? Give reasons for your answer.
(i) A + B is the area showing the optimal level of net private benefit for the steel mill.
(ii) C shows the level of private benefits unwarranted from the social viewpoint.

12.3   REMEDIAL MEASURES

The damage pollution is causing is vast and its proliferation is fast. The world is, therefore, seized with the designing of appropriate measures to deal with the problem since long. The moral norm is: *do unto others as you would have others do unto you.* The implication is that before you indulge in some economic activities assess its marginal benefits and costs with empathy for others. As this usually does not happen, remedial action becomes necessary. The traditional methods to deal with environmental damage include a system of standards enforcement, pollution charges and tradable pollution permits. These remedies involve public intervention and we shall soon discuss them. But in recent years, a few interesting suggestions were made in an effort to keep freedom of the markets and enable them to deal with externalities. Let us first have a look at such suggestions.

> Pollution cannot be eliminated altogether. We can attempt to minimize it using appropriate methods.

12.3.1   Coasian Theorem: Creation of Property Rights

We had said earlier that the problem of externalities arises because no one has property rights in environmental goods, and this is the main cause of market failure to ensure social efficiency in resource use. Ronald Coase, a British Nobel laureate in economics, revived the idea of creating property rights in environmental goods and leave the parties bargain for their use. An important demonstration of Coase was that it hardly matters to whom we give the property rights—the polluter or the sufferer—the market would lead to the same socially efficient equilibrium price and output combination. Public intervention in the market was not needed. Figure 12.7 illustrates the point. Here, AQ** is the MNPB curve of the steel mill. The area it encloses with the axes X and Y is the total net benefit of the mill. If air were the free gift of nature, the mill would produce Q** tons of steel for that would maximize its profit. But the emissions it releases into the air inflicts extra cost on the nearby fishery which is the area of the Δ 0BQ**.

> Ronald Coase believed that the market can internalize social costs if we create private property rights in environmental goods like fresh air.

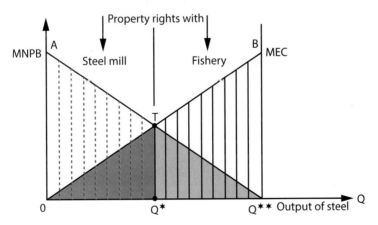

Figure 12.7 *Whether property rights in fresh air are with the steel mill or with the fishery bargain will lead to the same steel equilibrium output, Q**

Now, suppose the property rights in fresh air are granted to the mill, the polluter. Clearly, it will like to produce Q** tons of steel to maximize its profit, the area A0Q**. The resultant pollution would inflict on the fishery extra cost measured by the area B0Q**. Note that beyond Q* level of steel output, the external cost to the fishery (TBQ**Q*) is much more than the profit (TQ*Q**) the mill earns over Q* to Q** range of output. There is then scope for *bargain* between the parties who, you should note, do not know each other's benefit or cost. The fishery would offer money to the mill for reducing steel output long as the payment is smaller than the MEC: height of unbroken lines. On the other hand, the mill will accept any offer from the fishery so long as it is higher than its marginal benefit it will forego in reducing output. The bargain will continue until Q* is reached, i.e. where MNPB equals MEC. The eventual compensation paid to the mill will equal TQ* per ton of reduction in steel output. The total payment fishery would make is the light-shaded triangle while its net gain will be net savings in external cost measured by the area BTQ**. The total net gain of the mill will also not decline as the reduction due to smaller output will be made up by payments from the fishery.

But what if the property rights in fresh air were given to the fishery, not to the mill? Coase showed that the result would remain unchanged. The mill would not take the production of steel beyond Q* because for producing an additional ton of steel, the compensation rate payable to the fishery would be more than its marginal net gain. The dark-shaded area of the triangle T0Q* shows the total payment it would make to the fishery; its net gain being the AT0 area.

Criticism of the theorem

Creation of property rights in environmental goods is an elegant idea at the theoretical plane, but to put it in operation has many pitfalls. The important ones we discuss here under.

> The Coase theory is valid but it is extremely difficult to put into operation.

1. **Narrow outlook**: One latest and more dangerous discovery for living beings on Earth than even global warming is what we call *global dimming*: the increasing reduction in the volume of sunshine reaching the crest of the Earth day by day. This is caused by the clouds absorbing chemical droplets and gas particles hanging in the polluted air, open burning, air transport, indiscriminate carpet bombings in wars as in Afghanistan, Iraq and Lebanon, or frequent volcanic eruptions resulting in widespread haze. All these block substantial amounts of sunshine from reaching the globe. For example, the pollution coming from the European industry blankets the Indian Ocean south of Africa and the increasing *dimming effect* does not allow enough cloud formation for rains in Northern Sahara leading to persistent crop failures, spread of famines and diseases. The result is widespread deprivation and population movements, causing death and misery for millions over vast tracts of the continent. To put the brakes on this catastrophic phenomenon, who should bargain with whom? The Coasian theorem is too restrictive and atomistic to deal with international or regional pollution issues though possibilities are not entirely non-existent.

2. **Insufficient information**: Even at the local level, we do not come across many examples of bargains taking place except that some nuclear power stations do negotiate with local populations to accept them in their neighbourhoods. One great hindrance is the non-availability of full and correct information about the other party. In our illustration, for example, the fishery would rarely know exactly the loss of private benefit to the mill of any reduction in the steel output, nor could the mill be sure of the MEC to the fishery due to from air pollution it causes. The bargain takes place in a vacuum. The agreed rate of compensation like T_0Q_0 would usually be the result of guess work, bluffing and hoodwinking between the parties. The Islamic commitment to transparency and brotherhood—if it were there—may help improve the situation.

    > The Coase theory cannot be applied to all cases in pollution as sufficient information may not be available, transaction costs may be prohibitive and free riding may be a serious problem.

3. **Transaction costs**: Pollution is pervasive. We require numerous bargains all the time in an economy. If the polluters are not willing to negotiate or negotiations break down for one or the other reason, legal action may have to be taken. This would involve cost in terms of time and money. The court processes are slow, identification of polluters difficult and the estimation of damage for compensation not easy. For example, the source of air pollution causing harm to the fishery in our example may not be the steel mill alone. The moving sources such as automobiles could be the main culprit in some cases, but can easily avoid negotiations. Costs involved in the legal process may keep people away from the courts and suffer in silence.

4. **Free riding**: As sufferers are often many, each may wait for someone else to take legal action against the polluter, and enjoy himself the benefits of a win free of cost. The free-riding temptation is real and may greatly weaken the bargaining power of the sufferers. To illustrate, suppose it is not only the fishery but also an apple garden in the area that suffers from acid rain caused by the emissions from the mill. The joint action on the part of the fishery and the garden may give better compensation to each than if any of them singly takes the action against the mill. Consider the illustrative data in Table 12.1 that Figure 12.8 presents in a diagrammatic form.

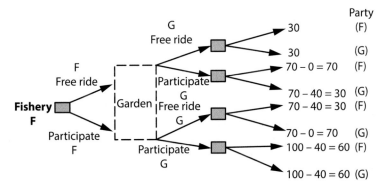

Figure 12.8 *Consequences of participation and free riding in negotiations*

Table 12.1 *Participation and free-riding effects on negotiation outcomes*

	Fishery	Garden
	F	**G**
If both participate in negotiations, each will gain	100	100
If one of them goes to court, the case is weakened, each gets	70	70
If none of them takes action, each will get from the mill	30	30
The cost of going to court for each is	40	40

Exercise 12.3

List the main difficulties in the operation of the Coasian theorem. Assume two students, Mansor and Jacob, share a rented room. Jacob is a smoker while Mansor is averse to the smell and smoke of tobacco. To avoid confrontation and save himself the trouble, he offers Jacob a payment of RM1 a day, if he does not smoke in the room more than two cigarettes per day. Jacob values his own discomfort from abstaining equal to RM12 and thinks that the discomfort Mansor would avoid through the bargain is worth more than RM10. So, he makes a counter offer for agreeing to the request if Mansor could raise the payment to RM12 a day. Mansor feels that Jacob's loss of welfare in not smoking in the room is not worth more than RM12. Can there be a successful bargain between the two? What will happen if friends of Jacob, knowing the bargain, come to see him and smoke in the room? Argue your case.

5. **Identification problem**: Even when transaction costs are not prohibitive and bargaining promises net gain, bargain may not take place for two broad reasons. *First,* many pollutants stay in the air for long periods and their damage may unveil itself in many cases after decades, even centuries. Many toxic chemicals, radioactive waste, global dimming and greenhouse gases fall, among others, in this category; the sufferer may even have died before he could think of taking action. *Second,* sufferers may be unaware what and whose pollution has hit them or what damage it is causing. Regulatory authorities may fail to identify all the polluters and estimate the value of damage they are causing to others.

It may be difficult to identify the polluters as well as the sufferers—a one-on-one correspondence is almost impossible to establish.

6. **Market imperfections**: Finally, the Coasian theorem is based on the assumption of perfect competition in the markets for goods and factors. We reproduce below what we have shown earlier. Under perfect competition we have:

$$MNPB = P - MC \qquad (12.1)$$

Therefore,

$$MNPB = MEC$$

This implies that,

$$P = MC + MEC = MSC \qquad (12.2)$$

It is this demonstration that allowed the mill to treat its MNPB as the bargain counter. But note that for a firm operating under perfect competition (MR − MC is the marginal profit curve), equation 12.1 is valid only because AR equals MR. This condition is not met if competition becomes imperfect. In imperfect markets MR = MC < AR = P. Therefore, (P − AC) not (P − MC) gives the net profit for equilibrium output; (P − C) cannot serve as the bargain counter. Thus, under imperfect competition the basis of bargain for the theorem is knocked out completely.

Due to the cumbersome nature of the legal process, lack of adequate information about the polluters or sufferers, absence of perfect markets and free rider temptations, the Coasian theorem is unlikely of being much practical value. And, this makes a case for public intervention in the market. We discuss below a few forms the intervention takes.

12.3.2   Standard Setting and Pollution

The oldest and the most popular form of state intervention in the environmental matters is the setting of standard limits for allowable pollution coming from a source, fixed or mobile. Factories and automobiles are examined periodically to see if emission standards are being observed. In many cases, standards are governed by preset levels of permissible pollution. For example, so many micrograms per cubic meter of air or per cent dissolved oxygen in water, or decibels for the noise level are not to be exceeded. These levels are usually fixed with reference to some health considerations.

Standards invariably go with a system of penalties, if not observed. The important question is: are penalties effective in keeping pollution within the limit the standard prescribes? Figure 12.9 deals with this issue. The X-axis has a dotted parallel line below it showing the pollution levels corresponding to output levels. The familiar MNPB and MEC curves intersect at T_o indicating Q_o and P_o as optimal output and pollution levels respectively. However, the government estimation of damage caused by the steel mill to the fishery is valued at P_S for standard fixing and the corresponding penalty at level B_1. It is easy to see that the standard is too high and penalty for not meeting it is too low. There is *additional* gain to the mill measured by the $\Delta T_S T_O T_P$ in violating the standard and paying the penalty. In practice, this usually is the fate of standards.

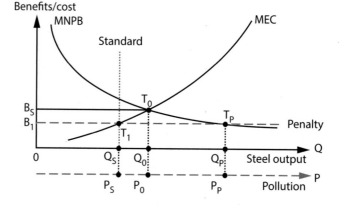

Figure 12.9 *Standard fixing may not ensure optimal externality*

Pollution abatement costs

One way for firms to escape the cumbersome standards and penalties system is to incur costs for pollution control or *abatement*. For example, factories may use filters and scrubbers in their chimneys to diminish harmful particles going up with smoke in the air. They may also use cleaner coal or replace it with gas. Abatement measures involve *additional cost* and producers compare them with, say, penalties to choose the alternative. Figure 12.10 helps us to understand this choice making on their part. Note that:

1. The marginal abatement cost (MAC) curve slopes down to the right and is convex to the origin.

2. Pollution is measured outwards along X-axis but reduction in it is measured inwards.

3. The implication of (1) and (2) is that the cost of pollution abatement rises at an increasing rate for additional reductions in pollution. The reason is that it is stickier and finer pollution that you now have to deal with in the process; it may require the use of higher technology and costlier methods to reduce it.

4. It is assumed that the standard and the accompanying penalty is fixed such that now, moving inwards along the pollution abatement scale, the firm will compare pollution reduction cost both with the alternative of paying fines and its net profit to make an economic choice. You may note that in the inward movement process MAC remains less than both the penalty and the net profit until we reach E. The firm will clearly gain by incurring abatements costs than pay for emissions the penalty which, unlike MAC, is more than the MNPB as well.

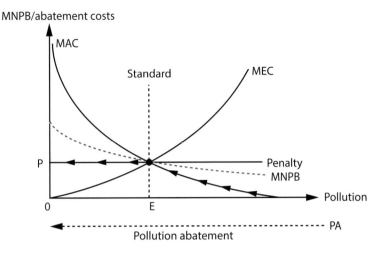

Figure 12.10 *Standard versus abatement costs*

But notice that beyond E, penalty is less than the abatement cost and even the MNPB: it is now cheaper for the firm to pay penalty rather incur abatement costs. The arrow heads mark the trade-off path as we move in along the abatement scale.

12.3.3 Pollution Charges

A. C. Pigou proposed a fiscal solution to curtail pollution, i.e. impose tax per unit of output to curtail damage. This could make the market internalize externalities through adding tax to the cost of producing commodities. It is reasonable to presume that the rise in costs would tend to reduce output and profit margins. For achieving the objective, the tax per output unit must equal the optimal externality. Figure 12.11 helps to explain the position. Without tax, the firm would like to produce Q_N output as that maximizes its net profit. But MNPB equals MEC at T level of output. Therefore, the government imposes a pollution charge equal to LT on per unit of output. This lowers the net profit curve to $(MNPB - t)$. Notice that (a) the output is reduced not to T but even more, that is to Q_0 $(Q_0 < T)$, and (b) net profit is not reduced by the full amount of tax $(t < T)$. The reason is that part of the tax effect on profit is offset by a reduction in the MC of the firm as output decreases from Q_N to Q_0.

A.C. Pigou had suggested the imposition of pollution charges to curb the evil but had difficulty in practice, especially in cases of mobile sources of pollution.

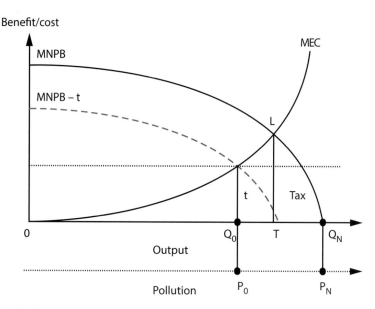

Figure 12.11 *Optimal pollution tax*

Difficulties

There are a number of difficulties in using pollution charges as an effective control measure. These are:

1. **Property rights issue**: The charges do not exempt the pollution falling within the absorption capacity of the environmental elements. This is a matter, as indicated earlier, of how a society views property rights in these elements. To repeat, if these rights are assumed to be with the society, no exemption is necessary, otherwise the demand is valid.

2. **Double loss**: A more serious difficulty is that once the firm under the threat of taxation has reduced the output to optimal pollution levels, why should such output then be subject to charges? Clearly, the firm is burdened with two sorts of losses. (Refer to the for explanation to Figure 12.11). The firm reduces output from Q_N to Q_0 and loses profit for the Q_N Q_0 range of output. But it still has to pay t-tax per unit on Q_0, the optimal output. This is one reason, among others, as to why charges are unpopular. Taxes are indeed, rare in practice.

3. **Damage estimation difficult**: It is commonly felt that it is very difficult to measure pollution caused damage in practice; different experts are likely to give different estimates. Damage figures are easy to manipulate. The idea that the amount of an optimal pollution charge can be calculated is unrealistic. Some damage, we noted earlier, takes time—years, even decades—to reveal itself. Necessary information is often not available.

4. **New idea**: Controlling pollution through taxation is a relatively new idea. It failed to catch the imagination of policy makers

and the bureaucracy stuck to the conventional standard penalty system for pollution reduction.

Subsidies

Taxation being unpopular, grant of subsidies to reduce abatements costs is sometimes used. Subsidies work as an incentive to the firms for reducing pollution. The measure does not require damage estimation and compensation norms for the sufferers. It operates as Figure 12.12 explains. The firm produces an output (Q_0) that keeps pollution at the optimal level P_0 shown in the diagram. However, from the social viewpoint it is considered desirable to reduce it further to P_S. This has to be done without reduction in output Q_0 which is optimal. The grant of subsidy $T_0 T_S$ per unit of pollution the firm reduces beyond P_0 to meet the standard at P_S can do the trick. The advantage, among others, is that unlike taxation a reduction in output is not required; Q_0 remains intact.

Some think subsidies are an effective way to deal with pollution.

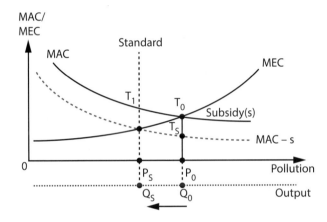

Figure 12.12 *Subsidies cut pollution0*

12.3.4 Tradable Pollution Permits

Another incentive-based method of pollution reduction is to issue tradable pollution permits. Let us see how the measure works.

Tradable permits to pollute have been tried but found little success.

Firms value the right to emit pollution because it enables them to produce goods and earn profit: they are willing to pay for obtaining pollution right. But the value various firms assign to emission rights is not the same. These facts give rise to two questions:

1. What criterion would ensure an efficient distribution of these rights among the firms?
2. How can this criterion be put into operation?

Figure 12.12 helps us fix and understand the criterion for an efficient distribution of rights. It shows when the two hypothetical firms, A and B, would be in a state of efficient distribution of these rights with reference to the value each puts on them. Emissions of firm A increases from left to right and of B from right to left. Likewise, MG_A and MG_B curves provide the marginal valuation they put on the emission rights. The lower position of MG_B indicates that B puts a smaller valuation than A on the gains from rights.

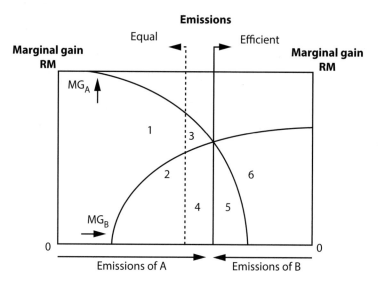

Figure 12.13 *Efficient emissions*

The dotted line shows equal distribution of rights between A and B. In that case the total gain for firm A is the area (1 + 2) and for B the area (4 + 5 + 6). Efficient allocation of rights takes place when marginal gains of the two firms become equal. Now, firm A gains equal 1 + 2 + 3 + 4 and for B, area (5 + 6). Compare the total gains arising in each case.

Total gain under efficient distribution = 1 + 2 + 3 + 4 + 5 + 6
Total gain under equal distribution   = 1 + 2 + 0 + 4 + 5 + 6

Thus, there is additional gain of area 3 under efficient solution. But it is difficult for anyone to establish in reply to our second question what the optimal volume of aggregate pollution would be? Tradable emission permits can do it without any cost to society. The pollution control authority decides, even if arbitrarily, an aggregate quantity of a particular pollution forms and divides it into small parts for making permits. You may liken it to the division of authorized capital of a joint stock company into parts for issuing share certificates. The pollution permits can then be given to the polluter, the sufferer or even to a third party, for sale, making little difference to their final distribution. Pursuit of self-interest will lead the parties to reach an optimal gain that Figure 12.12 identifies.

Tradable emission permits have several merits. They constitute a flexible way to control pollution. If new firms enter an industry, increase in competition would raise the permit price, if their supply were kept fixed. Alternatively, authorities may increase the supply of permits through new issues. Figure 12.14 illustrates the point. The initial supply of permits is fixed at E_0 for emissions into the atmosphere corresponding to aggregate output Q_0. The demand for permits D_0 determines their price at P_0 per unit of emissions. The demand for permits may rise from D_0 to D_1 as new firms enter the industry. If the authorities do not increase the supply of permits, their price would climb up to P_1 resulting in realignment of outputs individual firms produce. On the other hand, if it were deemed fit to increase the permit supply to say E_1, their price may rise, or even fall, depending on the relative pull of the altered demand and supply conditions.

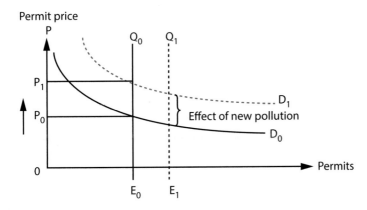

Figure 12.14 *Price, demand and supply of permits*

The equilibrium obtained will satisfy the efficiency condition:

$$\frac{\text{Marginal gain of A}}{P_A} = \frac{\text{Marginal gain of B}}{P_B}$$

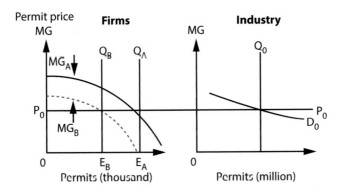

Figure 12.15 *Gain maximization from permits*

The price of permits being the same for each of the firms, the market forces will so allocate the aggregate output Q_0 among them that their gains are equalized. Figure 12.15 illustrates the point. Here, we measure, unlike Figure 12.12, the marginal gains of both the firms along Y-axis in the same direction, MG_B falling below MG_A. The price P_0 equates the marginal gains of the firms A and B when they buy E_A and E_B permits, respectively, and produce the corresponding outputs Q_A and Q_B. Note that E_0 in the industry panel of the figure is measured in millions but in thousands for the firms. Firms A and B are price takers; P_0 is determined by the demand and supply forces operating in the industry. Emission permits bought by the two firms are part of E_0 and so are their outputs as part of Q_0.

Even as tradable emission permits have, as mentioned above, several advantages over other measures of pollution control, the method is not free of governmental supervision. Given that market enables firms to buy emission permits efficiently, it has yet to be monitored if their emissions remain within permit limits. This is difficult for a variety of reasons, sufficiency of inspectors and absence of corruption being the leading ones. Like taxation, use of emission permits has not been popular on a noticeable scale. They have been used in some US cities but not with much success.

12.4 SUSTAINABILITY

After 1980s, the word sustainable is invariably attached to any concept of economic development. A long-run view of things is implicit in the notion of sustainability. Unclear, however, is what we want to sustain. A review of the literature shows that sustainable development may refer to any of the following:

1. Maintaining the long-run rate of economic growth.
2. Achieving intergenerational equity in the use of natural resources.
3. Restricting as much as possible the increase in pollution emissions from the processes of production and consumption, rather roll them back if possible.

The views on sustainability in the three versions of development are interrelated. Sustaining growth over the long run demands conservation of resources and environment will not deteriorate as fast as it is currently doing. Still, the focus on one to the neglect of the others may lead to different policy mix and preferences. In 1987, the World Commission on Environment and Development gave a definition of sustainable development with intergeneration equity occupying the centre of stage. In its opinion, such development is that which meets the needs of the present generation without compromising the ability of future generations to meet their own needs. It implies more than conservation of resources.

Sustainable Development and the Environment in Islam

While the concept of sustainable development is Western in its origin and understanding, the implications of this idea extend to Islam in which, as in the other Abrahimic faiths, an essence of this idea can be found. Dr Zubair Hasan examines the debate on the meaning of sustainable development in Islam and attempts to expound upon a concrete, Islamic definition for sustainable development. As Dr Hasan explains, the issue of sustainable development is intricately linked to the environment as any definition of sustainable development ends with environmental concerns. Such a concept represents an important development as it regards Islamic Finance for it could provide the framework for a positive-screen methodology. Currently, the mainstream of Islamic Finance is based upon negative-screen methodology, relying upon averting investments and actions contrary to Islamic law rather than positive investment in socially responsible concerns. While organizations such as the Islamic Development Bank do engage in development projects, this issue, and particularly the environment, is absent in most of the criteria of Islamic financial institutions. The development of a definition for Islamic sustainable development implies another opportunity for convergence between Islamic Finance and other ethical investments. With the growing popularity of socially responsible investment principles in the world of conventional finance, perhaps an Islamic counterpart would provide an opportunity for collaboration, particularly given the great liquidity of the Gulf region at this time.

Source: *Convergence – New Directions in Islamic Finance*, (Seminar proceedings, 2011), AFF the Arab Financial Forum, Harvard, <http://www.melafrit.com/education/Finance/FinanceIslamique/documents/Report_islamic_financeAFF.pdfhttp://www.melafrit.com/education/Finance/FinanceIslamique/documents/Report_islamic_financeAFF.pdf>, accessed 1 April 2014.

12.4.1   Islamic Viewpoint

From an Islamic angle, a healthy and balanced economy is one that is as much concerned with the fulfilment of our spiritual needs as it is concerned with the meeting of our material needs, especially the basic human requirements. It must aim at preserving the natural foundations of life. Such development calls for a fair distribution of goods and opportunities. Performance efficiency and an effective economic organization are vital for using natural resources, but social solidarity and cohesion deserve no less attention.

> The issue of pollution of the environment emerged to attract attention much after the advent of Islam. However, the Qur'an provides some valuable guidelines to care for the environment.

It is interesting to note that these Islamic ideas find recognition in the report of the Commission. It explicitly relates sustainable development to three domains: economy, society and the environment. The integrative view of the Commission on sustainable development is now treated as standard in the literature. However, debate on the subject often drifts to focus on environmental issues in the field of development. Environmental issues, local, regional and international, are assuming alarming proportions day by day, rather hour by hour. It would be naïve to claim that Islam provided solution to current environmental problems we face today. These problems simply did not exist even after centuries when Islam made its appearance on the scene; they are of recent origin. What Islam did provide were unmistakable general warnings about treating nature with care so that it does not take revenge on mankind. The sum of these warnings, as mentioned earlier also, is that Divine wisdom has created things in due proportions, maintaining a balance among them. Take note of the following verses from the Qur'an:

6: 3 – It is He Who created the heavens and the earth in true (proportions).

30:41 – Mischief has appeared on land and sea because of (the need) that hands of men have earned.

39: 5 – He created the heaven and the earth in true proportions.

54:49 – Verily, all things we have created in proportion and measure.

67:3 – He Who created the seven heavens one above another; No want of proportion will thou see in the creation of Allah the Most Gracious. So turn thy vision again. Seest thou any flaw?

67:4 – Again turn thy vision a second time (thy) vision will come back to thee dull and discomfited, in a state worn out.

Exercise 12.4

Check and understand the interpretation of the above verses from some authentic commentary on the Qur'an.

The Qur'an warns of punishment for those who do mischief and spread corruption in the land of God. Mischief and corruption include acts that work to disturb the delicate balance God has built in creation on the Earth.

BOX 12.2

The Assisi Declarations on Nature, 1986: Universal Environmental Ethics of Islam

In 1986, the WWF International invited five leaders of five of the major religions of the world—Buddhism, Christianity, Hinduism, Islam and Judaism—to meet and discuss how their faiths could help save the natural world. Afterwards, three more faiths—Baha'i, Jainism and Sikhism—produced similar declarations. The meeting took place in Assisi in Italy. From this meeting arose key statements by the five faiths outlining their own distinctive traditions and approach to the care for nature.

The Muslim Statement
Unity, trusteeship and accountability, that is *tawheed*, *khalifa* and *akhirah*, the three central concepts of Islam, are also the pillars of the environmental ethics of Islam. They constitute the basic values taught by the Qur'an. It is these values which led Muhammad, the Prophet of Islam (pbuh) to say:

'Whoever plants a tree and diligently looks after it until it matures and bears fruit is rewarded', and: 'If a Muslim plants a tree or sows a field and men and beasts and birds eat from it, all of it is charity on his part,' and again: 'The world is green and beautiful and God has appointed you his stewards over it'.

Environmental consciousness is born when such values are adopted and become an intrinsic part of our mental and physical makeup. Muslims need to return to the nexus of values, this way of understanding themselves and their environment. The notions of unity, trusteeship and accountability should not be reduced to matters of personal piety; they must guide all aspects of life and world. Shari'ah must not be relegated just to issues of crime and punishment, it must also become a vanguard for environmental legislation.

We often say that Islam is a complete way of life, by which it is meant that our ethical systems provide the bearings for all our actions. Yet our actions often undermine the very values we cherish. We must judge our actions by them. They furnish us with a world view which enables us to ask environmentally appropriate questions, draw up the right balance sheet of possibility, properly weigh the environmental costs and benefits of what we want, what we can do within the ethical boundaries established by God, without violating the rights of His other creations.

If we use the same values, the same understanding in our work as a scientist and technologist, economist or politician as we do to know ourselves as Muslims—those who subject themselves to the will of God, then, I believe, we will create a true Islamic alternative, a caring and practical way of being, doing, and knowing, to the environmentally destructive thought and action which dominate the world today.

Source: <http://www.the ecomuslim.com/2011/10/islam-environment-ethic-assisi.html>, accessed 30 April 2014.

Summary

- From the viewpoint of social welfare, the performance of the markets calls for a relook. This essentially involves an appraisal of the claim that markets allocate resources efficiently and distribute the fruits of productive effort equitably. The fundamental theorem of welfare economics summarizes the claim in the equation $MRT_{XY} = MRS_{YX}$.

- The theorem raises three questions for inquiry: What is included in resources that pass through the market? What do we mean by efficiency? And, how do we define equity?

- Market transactions include only those resources that have ownership rights attached to them. It fails to take note of harmful externalities resulting from pollution that detract from human welfare locally, regionally and globally. The definition of scarcity calls for an extension to include environmental goods and generate property rights in them so that market may put a price on them.

- An externality is cost imposed or benefit conferred on an outsider by any of the parties to a market transaction without any compensation passing to or from the outsider. Thus, externalities could be harmful if they cause damage to the outsider; they could be beneficial if they benefit him. No payment is received for damage or made for the benefit involved. The bulk of externalities has harmful effects on individual and social welfare.

- As externalities that pollution causes are not priced by the market, the GNP package includes apart from welfare promoting goods also the polluted air, toxic water and soil erosion.

- Efficiency norms based on Pareto optimality must include external cost for the estimation of social welfare. Equity norms also must take into account the impact income distribution patterns; a 1 dollar gain by the rich is not the same thing as a 1 dollar gain by the poor.

- The analytical tools of economics have to be modified to internalize externalities so that social costs are reflected in the market pricing of goods and services.

- Coase revived the idea of creating private property rights in environmental goods to make externalities pass through the market bargains. He demonstrated that whether these rights are given to the polluter or its sufferer or even to a third party, bargain among them would lead to an optimal solution. The theory looks elegant but has difficulties in implementation. Its outlook is narrow to cover regional and international environmental issues like pollution of mighty rivers flowing through several countries or global warming. Insufficiency of information, transaction costs, free riding and identification of the polluters or their victims and the damage estimate are among the other stumbling blocks in its way.

- Standards are very difficult to administer. Pollution charges suffer from internal inconsistencies and are unpopular for a variety of reasons, abatement costs free the firms from public interventions in their affairs, and provision of subsidies may encourage and widen their use. Tradable emission permits can help efficient distribution of gains among the firms. They are flexible on the demand and supply sides but there are difficulties in monitoring their honest use.

- The notion of sustainable development is vague; what do we want to sustain, long-run rate of economic growth, intergenerational equity or environmental quality? The World Commission on Environment and Development focuses on intergenerational equity and other social considerations such as spirituality, and social cohesion and solidarity. Many of its observations seem to echo Islamic norms.

- Islam does not discuss or provides solution to specific environmental problems that we face today but the Qur'an contains many verses to provide broad policy framework to deal with environmental issues.

Glossary

Abatement costs In addition to penalizing producers for causing pollution the government may encourage them to use better though costlier technology to reduce (abate) pollution. To encourage firms for using pollution-reducing technology, the government may give subsidy as an incentive.

Externality An externality is the economic loss (gain) for one who is not a party to a transaction between the buyer and the seller/producer of a commodity in the market. It is *external* to the market. The third party is not compensated for the loss cost it suffers (pays for the gain).

Free riding This refers to waiting in the hope that someone else from the sufferers would incur cost to take action against the polluter, so that you will benefit due to non-exclusion if reduction in pollution takes place as a result.

Fundamental welfare theorem The general version of the theorem says that a competitive equilibrium leads to Pareto efficient allocation of resources for which the condition is:

$$MRTS^A_{KL} = MRTS^B_{KL}$$ for any pair of outputs (A, B) and any two factors, K and L.

Pollution It is a harmful externality, a loss inflicted by the activity of an economic agent on someone entirely unrelated to the activity without paying any compensation. The measurement of the harm caused depends on who has property rights in environmental goods.

Sustainable development This is a term that gained currency in economic writings after the 1950s as awareness and concern of environmental degradation spread. Interestingly, while people do not today talk of development without adding the prefix sustainable, but not all are aware or sure of what the qualification really means. To some it refers to the sustenance of the rate of growth over the long run while some interpret it to mean sustaining the inter-generation equity in the use of resources of an economy. But whatever interpretations are presented, they all converge to the sustainability of environmental goods.

Concepts for Review

- Abatement costs
- Absorption capacity of the environment
- Coase theorem
- Efficiency norms
- Equity in distribution
- Externalities or spillovers
- Free riding
- Fundamental welfare theorem
- Global dimming
- Islamic view of balance and environment
- Marginal external cost
- Marginal net private benefit

- Net social benefit
- Optimal externality
- Pareto irrelevant externality
- Pareto optimality
- Pareto relevant externality
- Pollution
- Pollution charges or Piguo taxes
- Property rights
- Scarcity and the environment
- Standards for emissions
- Subsidies and abatement costs
- Sustainable development
- Tradable pollution permits

Case Study 12.1

Climate Change: Who is Responsible – Humans or Nature?

In the last 50 years, the proportion of CO_2 pumped into the atmosphere that remains there has risen from about 40 to 45%, thus fuelling the greenhouse effect. This effect has been causing climate change, discussed at the Copenhagen Summit, 2009. The Summit listed some alarming signals for oncoming climate change.

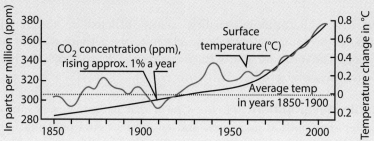

Figure 12.16 *Rise in Earth's temperature/CO_2 levels*

   The 2014 authentic report of the Intergovernmental Panel on Climate Change (IPCC) produced by 1,250 international experts and approved by 194 governments only intensifies the alarm. It warns that carbon emissions have soared in the last decade and are now growing at almost double the previous rate. But its comprehensive analysis found rapid action can still limit global warming to 2C, the internationally agreed safe limit, if low-carbon energy triples or quadruples by 2050. It finds that averting the catastrophe is eminently affordable. Diverting hundred of billions of dollars from fossil fuels into renewable energy and cutting energy waste would shave just 0.06% off expected annual economic growth rates of 1.3%–3%, the report concluded.

   There has emerged, however, a parallel opinion that does not deny that global warming is taking place, but what or who is responsible for it is vigorously denied. For example, Maurice Newman declares: 'We know that there are a whole host of scientists out there who have a different point of view, who are highly respected, reputable scientists. So the 97 per cent does not mean anything in any event because science is not a consensus issue. Science is whatever science is and the fact remains: there is no empirical evidence to show that man-made CO_2 and man-made emissions are adding to the temperature on earth. We have not had any measurable increase in temperature on earth for the last 17.5 years. If you look back over history, there is no evidence that CO_2 has driven the climate either. So I know that this is a view which is peddled consistently, but I think that the edifice which is the climate change establishment is now starting to look rather shaky because Mother Nature is not complying'.

Source: The New Straits Times, Kuala Lumpur, Sunday, 6 December 2009.

Case Questions

1   What in your opinion, are the main causes of global warming? List some of its main consequences. Can the world go in for more economic development? Argue your case.

2   Name the major areas of the world that face greater danger of vanishing first due to rising sea levels. What do you think is the position in your country?

3   Do you think Islam provided clear hints of possible environmental degradation taking place and warned mankind on this score? Elaborate your answer.

4   Comment on the behaviour of the two curves and their relationship in the above figure.

5   Would you support the view that it is not *man* but *nature* that is responsible for climate change? Give reasons for your answer.

Case Study   12.2

Ice Melt Threatens Drought for 1.3 Billion

KATHMANDU More than a billion people in Asia depend on Himalayan glaciers for water, but experts say they are melting at an alarming rate, threatening to bring drought to large swathes of the continent. Glaciers in the Himalayas, a 2,400 km range that sweeps through Pakistan, India, China, Nepal and Bhutan, provide head waters for Asia's nine largest rivers, lifeline for the 1.3 billion people who live downstream.

But temperatures in the region have increased between 0.5 to 0.6 degrees Celsius each decade for the last 30 years, dramatically accelerating the rate at which glaciers are shrinking. As world leaders gather in Copenhagen for a climate change summit, campaigners warn that some Himalayan glaciers could disappear altogether within a few decades; within 40 years the scientists predict.

Experts say the effects of glacier warming are already being felt in the region. In Nepal and Bhutan, the receding glaciers have formed vast lakes that threaten to burst, devastating villages downstream. In China, studies have shown that the rapid melting of the glaciers will result in an increase in flooding in the short run and in the long run, the continued retreat of the glaciers would lead to a gradual decrease in river flows. Even in low-lying Bangladesh prone to severe floods, rivers could run dry by the end of the century.

The deal reached in Copenhagen will have huge ramifications for the lives of hundreds of millions of people living in the Himalayan drainage systems who are highly vulnerable due to widespread poverty.

Source: New Straits Times, Monday, 7 December 2009.

Case Questions

1. Melting of glaciers must bring more water to the Himalayan rivers threatening floods. What raises the alarm for droughts? Explain.
2. What do you find in the Copenhagen Climate Change Summit's decisions for allaying the fears of 1.3 billion people living in the region? Do you have any suggestions?

Test Questions

12.1 'Pollution is an external cost. It arises only when one or more individuals suffer a loss of welfare'. Explain. Why then, do economists not talk of eliminating externality but recommend its maintenance at an optimal level?

12.2 Explain briefly the Coase theory of creating ownership rights in environmental goods and allowing bargain in the market to arrive at an optimal solution. Do you think the theory can be put into practice? Give reasons for your answer.

12.3 In explaining the Coase theorem, we used Figure 12.7 assuming that the property rights are given to the steel mill. You argue that the result would have been the same if property rights were with the fishery.

12.4 Construct a case where you may like to be a free rider. Make a policy suggestion that will remove your temptation to act as a free rider. Do you think Islam would endorse free riding? Give reasons for your answer.

12.5 Explain the concepts of MRT and the MRS. What role do these rates play in the fundamental welfare theorem?

12.6 How will you react to the following survey results?

(a) Smoking releases carbon monoxide in transport buses.

(b) The practice of not using both sides of a sheet of paper for writing answers in university examinations involves cutting down of more trees.

(c) Burying toxic industrial waste pollutes underground water reserves.

12.7 Which one will you prefer, taxation or subsidy for abatement as a measure for emission control? Explain your answer.

12.8 Explain how tradable emission permits work to satisfy the equimarginal principle. Why are such permits not in common use?

12.9 Islam does not provide readymade solutions to current economic problems, but it does indicate a broad framework for action to find solutions to these problems. Elaborate.

Web Exercise

Collect material and write a critical essay on the Copenhagen Summit 2009's decisions concerning climate change.

Forward Link

We had briefly referred to the role of money in modern economies. The following Chapter 13 takes you into the area of monetary economics. We shall discuss why and how money came into existence, what forms is assumed over time; what is the relationship of money with real economy at the macroeconomics level, etc. You may find the discussion interesting.

13

Money Banking and Prices

LEARNING OUTCOMES

This chapter should enable the student to understand:

- Specialization, division of labour and exchange
- Money and its evolution
- The definitions of money: Commodity versus functions
- The nature and significance of money
- Money, banks and finance
- Islamic view of money and banking

13.1   MONEY: DEFINITION AND FUNCTIONS

From the very dawn of civilization, humans had come to realize that an individual could not produce with ease what he wanted to have for satisfying even his few and simple wants due to natural limitations of ability and time. Specialization increased production but generated surpluses of what they individually produced. Thus, societal living started with some crude specialization in the area of production. Exchange of what one had in surplus with what others had in excess was essential for wider want satisfaction and societal progress. This was possible only through a system of exchange that came to be known as barter: a person exchanged whatever good or service he had to offer with the goods or services others possessed. The system required a *double coincidence of wants*—B should not only have what A wanted but must also be in need of what A could offer in exchange. This was restrictive of transactions that could be made, consumed more time and curtailed specialization.

Money can be defined in terms of the commodity that works as money or in terms of the work that the commodity does.

The frustrations barter imposed on human ambitions led people to discover by experience something in each society that most people needed for want satisfaction. That commodity became commonly used as medium of exchange on way to evolution of what in course of time was called money. Thus, to define money one just had to identify in the beginning the *commodity* that was commonly used for exchanging goods in a society The story of what commodity worked as money over time and space in various societies was indeed romantic: from hides and skins to cowrie shells, salt, spices, grain and precious metals to bank deposits i.e. the promise to pay was a fascinating journey of human ingenuity. In this journey, the commodity used got primacy in identifying money for its *functional* view was nonfigurative. But the uniformity of definition over time and space could only be seen in the functions money performed even as the substance performing those functions changed. Thus, a more unifying definition of money emerged *money is what money does.*

This functional definition sees the significance of money in serving as (i) a medium of exchange, (ii) as a measure of other goods' value expressed as their prices (iii) as a standard for comparing commodity values and (iv) as a store of purchasing power or value in general. In that, money imparts liquidity to other assets. Money acts as a unit of account for quoting prices and recording transactions in the currency indicated. One reason why the USA invaded Iraq and Libya in recent times was that these countries wanted to use Euro as the unit of account instead of US dollar for quoting crude oil prices for their exports. Money also facilitates the transfer of value within and across countries at a very low cost.

Money works a medium, a measure, a standard and a store but if you want you may add liquidity and transfer more.

Of the various services money renders, its medium of exchange function is more important, for it tears apart the two sides of the barter coin—sale and purchase. You can convert what you have into money, keep that money with you and use it to buy whatever and whenever you may want. In barter, the sale and purchase of commodities have to go simultaneously; no time gap is possible. Note also that the ultimate exchange is between real goods and services at both ends; money works merely as a go-between. If paper, plastic or book entry can perform the functions efficiently, why use much more valuable things like gold or silver to serve as money? Money derives its significance from its *general acceptability* and that acceptability stems from its value remaining reasonably stable, not from of what it is made. Money is the vehicle of human progress and prosperity. It is the cornerstone of modern finance, the lifeblood of trade industry and commerce.

The following are two statements about money:

(i) Money satisfies our wants. Therefore, money carries a price in the form of interest

(ii) Money is not wealth; we cannot remove poverty by printing notes and distributing it to make people rich. It should not carry any price tag.

Comment on these statements, giving reasons for the position you take in each case.

13.2   STATE AND MONEY

After centuries of experience, civil society had settled to the use of metallic coins largely made of gold and/or silver. Early coins were made by private manufacturers. But such coins lacked uniformity in shape, weight and purity. The standardization process required that gold (or silver) was pre-alloyed and coins were weighted for uniformity before they were put into circulation. As long as people knew the manufacturer and had trust in him, no touchstones were needed. At the time when Islam made its appearance on the scene, the gold and silver coins in circulation carried the stamping of pagan idols. The fact that the Prophet (pbuh) allowed their continuation in circulation testifies that faith was no limitation to their use.

> State soon acquired the monopoly of issuing money to put legal force behind its customary acceptability, and to standardize its units and control of supply. Moreover, it was a profitable project for the government.

However, governments soon started stamping the coins with an emblem to strengthen the process of standardization and widen acceptability. The emblem was a guarantee for the weight of the coin, its degree of purity and its value. The facility gave people the satisfaction of carrying value *within* their money, but it could not prevent the loss of precious metal in the circulation process through normal wear and tear and more than that, through dishonest greedy clipping of coins for recycling. Carrying money in pockets and over space involved inconvenience cost and risk. Governments soon discovered that coins derived their value essentially from the emblem; people often debased the coins to lower their precious metal content. To that end, coins became no better than notes printed on metal. This led Gresham to postulate during the Victorian era that bad (debased) money drives good (full-bodied) money out of circulation. That could possibly be the reason why the Qur'an condemned the hoarding of gold and silver so vehemently (9: 34-35).

13.2.1   From Metals to Paper

To overcome the above mentioned difficulties of commodity money—the coins—banks began to issue paper receipts to depositors stating that the receipt was redeemable for the precious metals the bearer had already deposited with them. Soon the receipts started circulating as money because everyone started taking them as good as gold. They were *representative* of the yellow metal. The suggestion for enforcing a 100% reserve requirement today in Islamic economics perhaps derives its inspiration from the policy of that era.

It soon became apparent that spending money and toil to dig the glittering metal out from the earth bowls only to lock it back into the dark vaults of banks as currency reserve was an avoidable folly. But representative money proved just a short step to usher in the practice of banking based on the fractional reserve system. Banks were soon printing receipts above and beyond the amount of yellow metal deposited with them. It benefited traders and enriched the bankers. Paper notes had appeared in China as early as the year 806 AD—less than 200 years after the advent of Islam—and dominated the scene until the middle of fifteenth century. China stopped using paper notes in 1455 because their overproduction led to high inflation. But the fractional reserve system, being an easy and effortless way for self-enrichment, the banks could not curb the temptation to over issue notes. Intermittent bouts of inflation became rampant across countries. If the linkage of money to gold (standard) at its zenith could not stop the emergence of the malady; on what basis can one advocate for its revival today to promote stability? Inflation could not, as it cannot, sustain itself for long because it carries *within* its fold the weapons for its own demise. Sooner or later, it must turn its tail upward to nose dive. The slump that the burst of the bubble generates is found to be much more sticky and damaging. We shall return to the issue in some detail in one of the chapters later. Presently, we turn to the two interesting developments in monetary history that the recurrence of inflation triggered.

The first was the emergence of the state as a monopolist for the conversion of gold into coins and of coins into gold at the official mint. Initially, this service to people was rendered free of cost but later on a small fraction of gold (or silver) brought to the official mint for coinage was used to be taken out to cover manufacturing costs. The deduction was known as the *seignorage*—the right of the king/lord over the possessions of the commoners. Thus, free coinage did not mean free of cost. It meant that people were free to bring for conversion into coins at the indicated precious metals—gold or silver. The main reason for acquiring monopoly power in coin-making was its profit churning potential. The need to put a tab on money supply for curbing inflation and keep its supply commensurate with the overall needs of the economy was of smaller significance. Thus, money creation could not be left entirely to the private discretion. And this brings us to the second major development in monetary history.

The advent of paper money in China in the year 806 AD.

The main reason the state assumed monopoly of coinage was *seignorage* cut out of the metal people brought for conversion into coins and which kings and lords appropriated for self-enrichment.

The expanding international trade and the resultant complexity of foreign exchange issues added further to the growing governmental interest in the monetary affairs. Even as the authorities were attracted to money creation for a variety of reasons, especially the profit it was sure to bring in, they did not consider it expedient to put their finger in the business directly; they chose to raise a cover—the central bank.

13.3   THE RISE OF CENTRAL BANKS

The process of the government taking over the creation of money proceeded on a slow pace. The first to come in were the regulations to curb the credit creation power of banks as we will discuss in Chapter 20. They had to cope with organizational restrictions including the continuation of the partners' liability as unlimited in banking far longer than in other businesses. But at the same time, the risks bankers took were sought to be reduced through severe penal provisions including in places even capital punishment for payment defaults. Recall the 16th century drama, *The Merchant of Venice* by William Shakespeare.

> Central banking emerged out of the need to coordinate, integrate and supervise financial institutions and banks especially in an economy to promote growth, employment and price level stability.

Centuries later, the rise of democracy and the concern for human rights brought in some relief for the borrowers in the form of increased transparency in dealings and lowering of interest rates. The industrial revolution that started in England spread fast to other countries in Europe and their control over colonies got stabilized. International trade expanded fast. The growth of wealth and prosperity of European nations became increasingly dependent on the colonies for obtaining industrial inputs and for selling finished products in their vast markets. Private banks still had the sway in facilitating these activities and their coalitions that had already started emerging in the face of rising liquidity shortages.

However, a large number of banks collapsed during the inter-war period for a variety of reasons which called for increased public intervention in the banking system. The collapse led to the expansion of central banking across countries. The process took the semblance of a natural evolution as initially some private banks were asked to operate as government bank. State ownership emerged only gradually. Gorton and Hung (2001) provide some interesting data on the rising numbers of the central banks with the passage of time. We reproduce the expansion data in the following Table 13.1. It is interesting to note that the number of central banks contracted after peaking in the year 1990. Today we have no more than 145 central banks in the world.

Table 13.1 *Growth of central banks over time*

Year	1900	1950	1990
Number of central banks	20	59	161

Among the various functions of a central bank, the crucial ones are the issuing of currency notes and maintaining stability in the value of money.

One of the leading objectives of establishing central banks was to have an institution devoted to keeping stable the value of its currency both at home and abroad. For achieving these objectives along with others the central banks were given some monopoly powers. For instance, they were to act as bankers to the government, that is, they were to perform functions for the government that ordinary banks performed for the public at large. They were given the sole right to issue currency notes and could adopt measures to control the creation of credit by commercial banks. They had to operate as the lender of the last resort for commercial banks to help them out of temporary difficulties. In view of these and other privileges granted to central banks, they were not to compete with ordinary banks for business in the financial markets. They had to supervise and guide the latter with a view to promote growth and achieve stability in the value of money. Since coins of gold were already in circulation in many countries, central banks were to streamline the system for the issuance of currency with a linkage to the yellow metal. The rules for maintaining such a linkage were embodied in what came to be known as the principles of note issue that we presently discuss.

13.3.1   Issuance of Currency Notes

The issuance of currency notes in the modern era owes its origin to the letters money lenders and traders in one town wrote in the distant past to their counterparts in other places certifying the amount the bearer of a letter had deposited with the letter-writer. The letter also contained a request that the presenter may be paid the indicated amount of money on behalf of the issuer. In the course of time, such letters developed to work like modern banking cheques. As trade within and across countries expanded, state authorities started sharing the task of issuing notes with the commercial banks but eventually assumed its monopoly via the central banks. However, this act did not slow down the growth and expansion of financial institutions, especially banks, over time and space. The note issue was governed by two alternative principles: the currency principle and the banking principle.

13.3.2   The Currency Principle: Representative Paper Money

Under the currency principle of note issue, gold worth the face value of each currency note is to be physically kept in the reserve.

The reason for public authorities assuming the sole right for the issue of currency notes was apparently the need to bring order and regularity to the supply of money in the economy. But it also carried some political prestige and was an effortless source of wealth to monarchs in the past. However, in later eras, governments could not ignore the psychological attachment that money should equate to something valuable in the public mind, just as the centuries-old use of gold (and silver) coins had embedded in their minds. As such, the first currency notes were issued as 'representative paper money'. Public authorities announced that gold worth every note issued was kept in the reserve, and anyone was free to convert the notes they possessed into gold at the public mint. This system is known as operating on the 'currency principle'.

13.3.3   The Banking Principle: Convertible Paper Money

With the growth of output, money markets and foreign trade in national economies, the demand for money expanded fast and the non-availability of gold at the required price made retaining a 100% gold reserve costly and cumbersome. This led to the argument that it was the assurance regarding the convertibility of notes into gold that the public needed, not the percentage of note issue that the metallic reserves covered. In normal circumstances, most people were not expected to present their notes for conversion; a less than 100% metallic reserve could safely lend flexibility to the money supply to meet the growing needs of the community. This came to be known as the banking principle of note issue.

> The banking principle requires a less than 100% reserve for note issue. The extent of coverage follows alternative but set rules.

Under the currency principle, the money supply was less elastic but more secure. The banking principle reversed this position; the money supply became more elastic but relatively less secure. The ideal method needs to seek a judicious balance between the two requirements.

13.4   METHODS OF NOTE ISSUE

The abandoning of the 100% reserve system brought to surface the question of striking an appropriate trade-off between the flexibility and security of a note issue scheme. How much less than a 100% reserve could ensure a safe level of flexibility and convertibility? This question leads to a discussion on the methods of note issue. The main methods used for the purpose are as follows:

> Keeping less than 100% reserve for note issue raised the problem of striking a trade-off between the covered and uncovered portions i.e. between the desired flexibility and needed security—primarily a matter of judgement.

1. **The fixed fiduciary system**: The Bank Charter Act of 1844 established the fixed fiduciary system in Great Britain. The Bank of England, the central bank of the country, was authorized to issue notes up to a fiduciary limit (up to which the government took responsibility for people's money) without the necessity of a gold reserve to cover the currency. Government securities were considered sufficient for the purpose. However, beyond that limit, the coverage in gold had to be pound for pound. The fiduciary limit could be raised for currency expansion under a 1928 Amendment to the Act. The presence of the limit acted as a check on a possible over issue of notes. Today, in the absence of convertibility, the system has little relevance but survives as a matter of tradition.

Methods of note issue under the fractional reserve system define how the covered and uncovered portions of the issue will be determined.

2. **The proportional reserve system**: Here, the central bank was not allowed to let the gold backing of notes in circulation fall below a certain percentage. Beyond that limit, any quantity of currency in circulation needs no metallic content. This system was prevalent in Europe. For instance, France kept a 35% reserve for all notes in circulation, Germany and the USSR each kept a 40% reserve. With some modification, it was also followed by the Federal Reserve System of the USA. Until 1956, India also followed the proportional reserve system with 40% coverage, the reserve being a mix of gold and pound sterling securities. The percentage could be lowered with the permission of the government for a limited period and the asset proportions in the reserve could also be varied.

The judgment was influenced by the monetary requirements of the country and the position of its reserve level and its composition, especially with reference to gold.

3. **The fixed minimum reserve system**: However, the Reserve Bank of India replaced the system in the same year with a fixed minimum reserve regimen. A minimum holding of foreign securities worth INR 40 billion and of gold reserve worth INR 11.5 billion became the basis of note issue. In 1957 it was cut to INR 2,000 million, including gold worth at least INR 1,150 million. This drastic, reduction was necessitated by the rapid depletion of foreign exchange reserves due to an adverse balance of payments. Thus, the system India adopted was a mix of the fixed fiduciary and the minimum reserve systems; it imparted a much needed element of adjustability of currency supply to the fluctuating needs of the country. The Reserve Bank of India could not use the fiduciary limit to frustrate the public finance pressure for the printing of additional notes. Of course, today, all currency in India is inconvertible fiat money.

Exercise   13.2

There is an opinion that money convertible into something of value, say gold or silver, is like the moon—it has no glow of its own, but is illuminated by the light of the sun. In contrast, fiat money is the sun itself—it has its own glow. Do you agree? Give reasons for your answer.

13.5   MONEY AND ECONOMIES

Ibn Khaldun (Introduction, 1406) had recognized the use of money as being an essential factor in the expansion of economic activity and in the rise of human civilization. This emphasis was again highlighted far down the stream through Adam Smith in his equally monumental work, *Wealth of Nations* (1776). Money as a medium of exchange, a source of liquid credit and a facilitator of remittance had already assumed importance in trade and commerce expanding fast within and across nations. Specialized institutions, banks in particular, took little time to emerge as organizers of money and financing.

One reason for the rapid expansion of financial institutions was that those who save money in a society are not generally the ones who need money for productive or other purposes. Intermediaries were needed. Banks were the first to fill the gap. Other institutions followed later. Banks in particular operate as the intermediaries between the savers and the users of money.

They collect large and small amounts from the savers in the form of deposits and advance the same as loans to those who need financing. The revenue banks earn from their lending operations minus what they pay to attract deposits constitutes the *bank margins*. From this gross income (margin) banks take out their operating expenses to arrive at the net profit for their owners. Collectively, these profits are the cost that society has to pay to the banking system for performing the mediation function so vital for wealth creation and distribution.

Banks initially came into being when trade and commerce were the dominant economic activities and the industry was yet to assume importance. As a result, they became known as *commercial banks* and began as providers of short-term finance to trade, small businesses and artisans, supplying working capital or to meet seasonal shortages of cash.

Banking has undergone a sea of change with the passage of time, within and across countries. These institutions have expanded their financing activities in terms of coverage and timeframes under what is now known as *universal* banking, but the nomenclature—commercial banks—is still their collective description. Apart from banks, many *special purpose* institutions, such as mutual funds, unit trusts, investment houses, insurance companies and cooperatives, have emerged, and these operate to meet the different types of financial needs of businesses and other consumers in modern economies. These institutions constitute the financial markets for money, stocks, bonds, foreign exchange and so on.

A major development in recent decades has been the *formal* addition of Islamic finance to the system. But Islamic finance did not stem, as some believe, from the womb of the conventional system; rather, it owes its emergence to religious movements in the Muslim lands, which worked for the restoration of Islamic values and glory, especially after these countries had won their independence from colonial rule. In practice, Islamic financial institutions operate side by side and in competition with their conventional counterparts across the world, including in Muslim countries. Despite their similarities, however, Islamic finance has, we shall see, its own distinctive features. Islamic finance now operates in over 75 countries—the size of its assets crossed the USD1.8 trillion mark in 2013. It is the fastest-growing segment of

> Those entities in an economy that save money out of their incomes are not mostly the same entities that need that money for use.

> Banks operate as the intermediaries between the two; they collect money from the savers (depositors) and channel the same to borrowers needing the funds.

> Islamic banks operate as financial intermediaries in the market but their modes are different from the conventional banks.

the global finance system, with rates of growth varying between 15% and 25% a year. However, it remains small; its share in global financial assets is still less than 1%.

The fast expansion of banking and finance has led to viewing the economies as divided into the *financial* and the *real sectors*. We may broadly describe finance in the context of this division as concerned with the provision and management of money and credit, including related assets, with a view to promoting the growth of the real sector that produces goods and services for meeting human needs both mundane and spiritual. However, over time pure financial transactions have come to far exceed those involving real goods and services increasing the frequency of devastating financial upheavals.

The setting of performance standards and the framing of regulations for financial institutions is an integral part of the system. The modifications initiated to make concepts, instruments, norms and practices Shari'ah-compliant have helped to create the structure of Islamic finance at the national and international levels. Such modifications are an ongoing process to improve a system that is still in its infancy. As Islamic finance operates in a dual and competitive financial system, its study can be more fruitful in an integrative reference frame.

> The course of economic activities like the course of weather never runs smooth. Price levels fluctuate for a variety of reasons.

13.6   MONEY AND PRICES

> Price index numbers are constructed to measure price level change. They link prices in a time unit to a base taken as equal to hundred.

We noted that money acts as a measure of value. One characteristic of all measures is that their own value, relative to what they measure, remains unchanged in the measuring process—a yard is always of three feet and a kilogram of a thousand grams. But money is a different sort of measure in that its own value is never independent of the value of what it measures. The measure of money value is its purchasing power. If a money unit buys less than before, its value is reduced; it is increased if it buys more. So, we buy less when prices rise and more when they fall, other things remaining unchanged. Thus, the purchasing power of money or its value varies inversely with changes in the prices of goods and services in an economy.

However, prices of goods and services in an economy do not all change simultaneously or in the same direction or by the same proportion over time. So, when the price of a commodity (or commodities) rise and fall, how do we measure the changes in the values of money? This problem is resolved by the construction of price indices. Index numbers measure relative changes in the *general price level* over the years relative to prices in the *base* year, which is taken as equal to 100. Different sorts of indices are constructed for different purposes, but those intended to measure the changes in the value of money are usually the wholesale or purchasers price index numbers.(See Table 13.2.) Note that in index numbers, the first suffix identifies the base period and the second the current period for which the index is constructed.

Table 13.2 *Simple average of price relatives*

Commodity	Price		Price relatives P_1/P_0
	Period 0 P_0	Period 1 P_1	
A	C	D	E
Rice	2.6	3.0	1.15
Potato	1.0	1.2	1.20
Sugar	1.8	2.5	1.39
Cooking oil	1.5	1.5	1.00
Chicken	8.0	10	1.25
Coffee	12.0	10.0	0.83
Coal	1.0	1.2	1.20
Total (N = 7)			**8.02**

However, of late, consumer price indices are increasingly being used for measuring the temporal fluctuations in the purchasing power or value of money. We cannot explain at length the process of constructing index numbers, their types, uses and limitations here, but below we provide an example based on a simple average of price relatives so that you understand how we measure the change in the general price level. We use imaginary data for constructing the price index for period 1, with period 0 as the base = 100.

Example 13.1 We may calculate the index (P_{01}) for period 1 with period 0 as the base by taking the simple arithmetic mean of price relatives:

$$P_{01} = 1/N \ \Sigma \ P_1/P_0 \times 100$$
$$= 1/7 \times (8.02) \times 100 = 114.6$$

Thus, the price level in period 1 was higher by approximately (114.6 − 100) = 14.6% compared to base period 0. The purchasing power of money thus fell to (100/114.6) × 100 = 87%. In other words, the purchasing power of money fell by (100 − 87) = 13%. (Why not by 4.6%?)

Exercise 13.3

In the above illustration, take prices in period 1 as the base and calculate the index for P_0 symbolized as P_{10}. Interpret the result as a change in the value of money. Is $P_{01} \times P_{10} = 1$? If not, why?

13.7   PRICE LEVEL CHANGES

Price level changes
are important as they
change the relative price
structure and so alter
income distribution in the
society.

Changes in price levels are not generally welcome to the common man. But no one would bother if the prices of all goods and services were to rise or fall by the *same* ratio, however large it is. The people's income will also change by the same ratio. It is not the fluctuations in the level of prices *per se* that matters. The source of worry is that these fluctuations change the   *relative price structure*. Some prices rise (or fall) faster than others, altering in the process, the pattern of income distribution and employment in the economy. The two broad descriptions for these fluctuations are *inflation* and *deflation*. Inflation takes place when prices in general rise and continue rising over time. The opposite happens during deflation; the economy is declining and prices tend to fall unceasingly. Inflation and deflation invariably alternate in national economies and tend to move across borders in a ripple effect. Their sequences constitute what we call *trade cycles*. A typical cycle passes through four phases. (See Figure 13.1.)

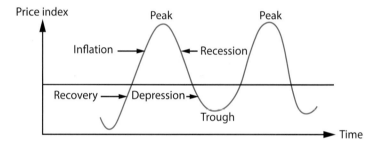

Figure 13.1 *Phases of a trade cycle*

The upward leg of trade cycles are usually longer and downturns sharper in comparison with their lows or troughs, which are shallower and broader, with the upturn being delayed and painful, causing significant economic hardship. Trade cycles are also known as business cycles and affect almost every aspect of an economy. A trade cycle shows up in the variations of national GDP and its rate of growth. During periods of inflation, money income expands at a faster rate than the production of real goods and services, aggregate demand runs ahead of aggregate supply and pushes the prices up all the more.   Costs lag behind prices; profit margins rise. Traders and manufacturers gain, as the rise in cost is slower, but farmers generally gain more because the supply of farm produce cannot readily be increased to meet rising demand. Those who are leasing items or renting property tend to suffer most in real terms because rents are contractually fixed and cannot be revised immediately with the rise in prices. Income inequalities tend to sharpen even as the economies

Inflation refers to a
situation when prices in
general rise –employment
output, and income
chasing one another in an
upward direction.

operate at full employment. Price controls tend to create black markets. Rising interest rates dampen people's willingness to invest, growth slows down, and employment may suffer. This creates *stagflation*, which has been a worrisome specter in many economies in recent decades—the economy tends to stagnate and unemployment exists even when inflation is taking place.

The hardships of inflation apart, rising prices keep the sun shining on the economy. The story of deflation is entirely different. Something pricks the prosperity bubble at the peak of inflation and the booming economy takes a downward plunge until the recession finds its lowest point in a depression. Figure 13.2 illustrates the actual ups and downs around the average, which price fluctuations bring about in the economy.

> Eventually the spiral of inflation takes a downturn pushing the economy into deflation.

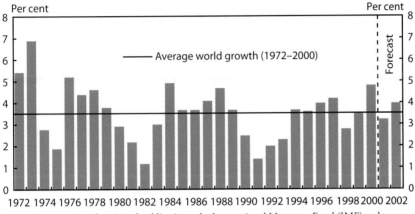

Source: Various national statistical publications, the International Monetary Fund (IMF) and treasury
Note: World GDP growth rates are calculated using GDP weights based on purchasing power parity.

Figure 13.2 *Annual growth in world GDP has not been steady*

What causes trade cycles is a difficult question to answer. A helpful and simple approach is perhaps to search for price level determinants. There are many factors that influence the prices of goods and services via their demand and supply. However, the demand and supply of most goods and services need not normally change at the same time and in the same direction, as happens during the inflationary or deflationary phases of a cycle. Some other force in addition to their demand and supply must be operating in the system to push prices up or down in general. Of the several forces that have been identified as causing fluctuations in price levels, economists find that variations in the money supply are on the whole decisive. There is ample empirical evidence that variations in money supply, price levels and national GDP move in tandem during the up and down swings of a trade cycle. Figure 13.2 depicts the actual phases of a trade cycle.

There have been several models linking price level changes to money supply as a causative factor, but Irving Fisher's classical quantity theory of money is the principal model. We briefly discuss this theory, which goes by the name of the *exchange equation* in the literature. It relates the general price level to the quantity of money in a country, as follows:

$$MV = PT \qquad (13.1)$$

Where M is the quantity of money, V the transaction velocity of money, P the average price index of the goods traded in the market per unit of time, and T the volume of such transactions. This expression is an *identity* because V here assumes an *ex post* value. Thus, the theory says that money receipts and payments in an economy will always be equal. V indicates the average number of times a unit of money, say one ringgit, is used for making payments in the economy. Consider the following example. Suppose, at a point in time, the physical quantity of goods T is 48 billion units, the price per unit P is RM100 and the stock of money M is RM400 billion. The monetary volume of goods in the economy PT would then be 100×48 billion $= 4,800$ billion. We can now define the transaction velocity of money as the number of times a ringgit is used on average in accomplishing transactions:

$$V = \frac{PT}{M} = \frac{4,800}{400} = 12 \qquad (13.2)$$

The transaction variable (T) in the above example includes the sale of both currently and previously produced goods as well as financial assets. Therefore, V is called transaction velocity of money. If we include in T only final goods, the formula would give us V as income velocity of money, but that refinement is not needed for the current use of the concept.

The exchange equation (1) above expresses the truism that income (MV) always equals expenditure (PT) in an economy; it explains nothing. However, if we take all the symbols, save (P) the price level, in the expression as *equilibrium* values for the economy determined by other forces, the exchange equation helps determine the price level. As Fisher wrote: *We find that under the conditions assumed the price level varies (i) directly as the quantity of money in circulation (M), (ii) directly as the velocity of circulation (V), inversely as the volume of trade done by it (T). The first of these relations here is worth emphasis. It constitutes the 'quantity theory of money'.*

The velocity of circulation of money does not play a role in the current explanations of the price level changes. How fast or slow people spend money in a particular situation depends on their psychological reaction to that situation. The velocity concept is dependent on this reaction and helps us to explain why the recovery phase of the cycle is sticky and slow, and why inflation may sometimes get out of control. Thus, it was not the lack of money supply (M) at the bottom of the 1930s Great Depression that hindered the way to recovery; it was the failure of the velocity of money to recover quickly. The increases in M and cheap money policy failed to allay the fears of the entrepreneurs who had suffered losses. Increases in money supply could not revive the economy; people simply hoarded it instead of investing. Likewise, what was more important in fuelling hyper-inflation in Germany in 1923 was not so much the expansion of money supply M as the public loss of faith in the German currency that sky-rocketed its velocity of circulation.

> Inflation and deflation are phases of longer duration in a cycle, velocity of circulation being more active during the turns.

Exercise 13.4

In the equation of exchange MV = PT, you are given M = 10,000; V = 5, and T = 5,000. Find the price level, P and complete the equation.

Now, the government wants to acquire 10% of goods for infrastructure development. It has no money to purchase the required goods from the market. It has two options (i) raise the money putting a sales tax on goods or (ii) print notes to buy the goods. Find the impact of each method on price level, P. Which course would you prefer to adopt and why?

BOX 13.1

War and Inflation

The German economy during the early 1920s presented a classic example how wars can completely shatter the economy of the vanquished. The reparation the allied powers imposed the on the country after the First World War was so heavy that the payments devastated the economy of Germany as never before in history. The annual national income plus the liquidation of the accumulated wealth of the Germans was not sufficient to maintain the payments schedule. On the one hand, the central bank was printing notes day and night so that the government could purchase goods from the market for export to meet the schedule dates, while on the other the Germans needed basketfuls of currency to beat the spiraling inflation—in one year, prices rose 1,013 times. Inflation ran parallel to the depreciation of the German mark that in fact had caused it. The table and figure (constructed using data) below present the depreciation drama of the epoch.

Table 13.3 *Exchange rates: 1USD value in German marks*

Date	Mark/USD	Date	Mark/USD
Jan 1918	5.21	Mar 1923	21,190.00
Jan 1919	8.20	Apr 1923	24,475.00
Jan 1920	64.80	May 1923	47,670.00
Jan 1921	64.91	Jun 1923	109,966.00
Jan 1922	191.81	Jul 1923	353,412.00
Apr 1922	291.00	Aug 1923	4,620,455.00
Jul 1922	493.22	Sep 1923	98,860,000.00
Oct 1922	3,180.96	Oct 1923	25,260,000,000.00
Jan 1923	17,972.00	Nov 1923	2,193,600,000,000.00
Feb 1923	27,918.00	Dec 1923	4,200,000,000,000.00

Source: School History (2004), The Seeds of Evil: The Rise of Hitler, <Schoolshistory.org.uk> assessed 1April 2014.

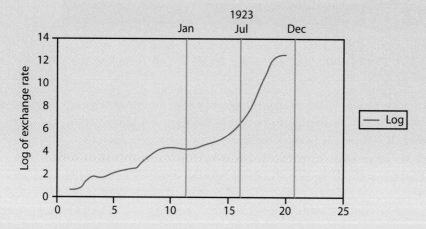

Figure 13.3 *German mark/US dollar exchange rate depreciation, 1918–1923*

Germans fought two world wars within a span of 30 years (1914–1945). They lost both. Each time their economy was completely shattered. The vanquished had to pay crippling reparations to the victorious. And yet, German economy is the strongest in Europe, why, because war cannot destroy the knowledge, skills, work culture and determination of a people.

13.9 THE RISE OF ISLAMIC BANKING

Although Islamic banking, along modern lines, emerged around the middle of the twentieth century, it gained momentum after the 1960s with the rise of Islamic revivalist movements across the world. However, the growth pattern and structure of the fast-expanding Islamic finance differs from country to country, and common and cohesive elements are yet to be established. The development of Islamic banking comprises three broad elements:

1. Since conventional banks were the common experience, the pioneers of the Islamic banking system naturally based the theory of Islamic banking on similar principles, with the exception of the ban on interest. Their roadmap was dominated by much of the colours they saw around them.

2. This led to a mismatch between the compulsions of the structural choice and the objectives that the Islamic ethos expected a financing system to address. Conventional models suited the short-term liquidity needs of trade, industry and commerce, whereas Islamic finance has to prioritize and make resources available for long-term development goals. Structural diversification now seeks to remedy the situation.

3. Islamic banking was conceived as competing with the mature and large Western banks. This led to a convergence of the Islamic system towards mainstream banking practices in terms of product development and regulatory requirements. The pros and cons of convergence for Islamic finance remains a moot point.

> Although modern Islamic finance is of recent origin, it has picked up fast and growth of Islamic banks has been spectacular.

The development and growth of Islamic banking and the challenges it faces today, or may face tomorrow, can be better understood and analyzed if these elements are taken into account. Islamic banking, like its mainstream counterpart, is no more than a means of financial intermediation: a 'neutral' means of transmitting funds from those who have them in surplus to those who need them for the parties' mutual benefit. Certainly, Islamic banks also have to play this role, but once we bring their ethical norms and their contribution to Islamic developmental goals into the equation, they have to move beyond mere intermediation.

13.10   THE DISTINCTIVE FEATURES OF THE ISLAMIC APPROACH TO FINANCE

Academics, practitioners and system regulators often begin their discourse on Islamic finance with a reference to its special features, as these are what give it a distinctive and superior quality over the traditional modes of financing. A survey of the literature reveals that there are no uniform features in the Islamic approach to finance; an individual's selection is purposive. Three interpretations of this approach are clearly identifiable, although they do tend to overlap. First, there are those who see the system's humanistic theory and rule compliance as being its distinctive features. Second, there is the group who think it is the financial instruments that the system uses that sets it apart. Third, there are still others who consider the regulations and procedures that oversee the system in operation as its distinguishing features. Presently, we shall base our discussion here on the first of these approaches, although we will mention the others too in the subsequent chapters.

13.10.1 Ban on Giving or Taking Interest

Islamic finance emerged and derived its strength essentially from the ban the Scripture imposed on the institution of interest. After some short-lived controversy over what constitutes *riba* (interest), which Islam declares as unlawful, consensus has been built around the idea that modern, interest-based financial activities fall within the concept of *riba*. It does not matter whether the purpose of taking or giving a loan is for consumption or production. Nor does it make any difference whether the loan is in the form of money or a commodity. It is this ban on interest that is the most distinctive feature of Islamic finance and all other features revolve around this. We shall discuss the ban and the reasons for it in the following section.

The ban on interest implies that the only legitimate means for survival can be the creation of value in real terms. Islamic finance ensures a close linkage between the real economy and finance, the former dictating and the latter following. The linkage is obvious as in principle, Islamic financial institutions treat their customers as partners in investment and financial services. They cannot sell what they do not own and possess. Economic activities are, by definition, value-creating activities. Because it remains asset-based, Islamic finance helps the real economy to expand. In essence, the real sector directs the allocation of resources which finance is supposed to follow. In contrast, conventional finance only requires the existence of real assets as a point of reference. This allows trading in commercial and financial papers as representing pure debt. Thus, *debt mountains* grow relative to real assets in modern economies.(See Figure 13.4.)

13.10.2 Avoidance of Gharar or indeterminacy

Islam aims at shaping all exchange relations among people on the principle of cooperation, mutual benefit and fair play. It directs them not to expose themselves to or inflict on others an injury (loss) that is possible to avoid. These principles lie at the heart of the celebrated Islamic notion of *gharar*, translated as indeterminacy or hazard. Contractual relations must, as far as possible, be free of *gharar*. Prophet Muhammad (pbuh) is reported, for instance, to have instructed that fruits on trees should not be sold until they show clear signs of ripening or standing crops should not be sold until

**BOX
13.2**

Time Value of Money

Money by itself is barren. Marking time alone does not create anything. So, Islam in general does not permit putting a time value on money. However, money has purchasing power and opportunity cost. It is the most liquid asset and imposes disadvantages on the creditor to the advantage of the debtor. But Islam insists on symmetrical treatment for the parties to a transaction. It therefore allows time value to money on certain conditions. The early Islamic jurists hold that 'time has a share in price' (*lil zamani hazzun filth aman*) in the case of deferred sale, provided there is an underlying asset, and price is nothing but the expression of value in terms of money. Indeed, this juristic position is the fulcrum of all deferred obligations on which Islamic financial institutions tend to thrive today. For example, this is the basis of cost-plus sale (*murabahah*), with the deferred receipt of the price, or leasing (*ijarah*). Figure 13.4 shows when money has or does not have a time value in business transactions.

Islam does not grant a time value for money but allows time a value in deferred price.

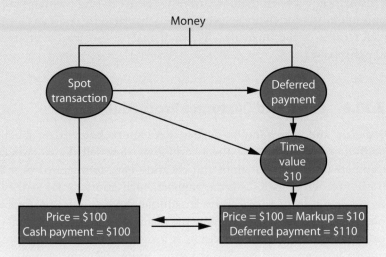

Figure 13.4 *Time value of money in Islamic sale*

the grain-ears have turned golden and the danger of damage through natural calamities has reasonably passed. The prohibition on selling what one does not possess at the time of the contract is another example of the *gharar* application, because deals such as these have the potential to cause harm to either of the parties. For example, if a crop is sold before it has ripened, it can harm the buyer if a sudden storm destroys the crop before it is harvested, and the transaction cannot be completed. The buyer is worse off. Thus speculation is not allowed. Speculative activities in the financial markets are not approved for this reason.

13.10.3 Participatory Financing

Avoidance of *gharar* or indeterminacy is a precautionary measure. It curtails the risk involved in business transactions, but it does not eliminate it altogether. The outcomes of current actions are only revealed in the future and may betray expectations. In order to ensure the symmetrical treatment of parties to the contract, Islam encourages, rather prefers, participatory financial arrangements. Financiers lose in terms of capital, entrepreneurs in terms of their reputation. Participatory financing thus rests on sharing business risks and the profits of business.

The high point of participatory finance is that it is in principle based on risk sharing, not on risk transfer as in its conventional counterpart. The consequences that follow are so vast that some scholars consider the risk treatment alone sufficient to account for the widening gap between the two systems—Islamic and conventional. Opinions on the point differ but that does not detract from risk treatment being an important point of distinction between them. Currently, profit-sharing contracts are not common in Islamic finance; rather, it is dominated by contracts yielding fixed returns to the financiers. We shall analyze this state of affairs in a later chapter.

13.10.4 Enhanced Customer Protection

Producers and merchants invariably have more knowledge about the qualities and usefulness of the commodity they sell. Laws protecting customers from manipulations and cheating have proliferated over time within and across nations. Islam supports such efforts as far as they go, but has some distinctive features in addition to the usual insistence on honesty with regard to measurements, quality, pricing and information. For instance, one Islamic provision is a significant departure from the modern business practices. Islam insists, writes Ghazali, that not only should sellers desist from undue praise of their wares, they are also under an obligation to reveal to the prospective customer defects, latent or patent, if any, in the goods offered for sale. The provision fixes some norms for marketing. Advertising should be essentially informative, transparent, educative and purposeful, and it should resist the temptation to be over-glamorous or to attempt to overpower consumers' discretion and distort their preferences.

13.10.5 Asset-based Finance

The distinctive features of the Islamic financial system that lend it superiority over the conventional system are both the effect and cause of real assets underpinning the transactions. The emphasis on this linkage is based on the Qur'anic ban on interest. The point in the literature is stretched to the extent of regarding the real and financial sectors in modern economies as entirely separate entities. This is not correct. Any transaction taking place in the financial market must have a counter-transaction somewhere in the real goods market. Past transactions can be the support for current transactions.

Of course, the transactions need not take place simultaneously. Papers traded in the financial markets cannot command value without a real asset connection somewhere in the economy. However tangled, roundabout or long the chain may be, the chain is always there. The moon only shines because the rays of the sun reach it. In conventional finance, the credit creation power of banks, as we shall see in the next chapter, has been so vast that secondary deposits have grown into shaky, inverted pyramids with their real base becoming smaller and smaller in proportion to the expanding top.

Exercise 13.5

Two interesting developments have recently taken place. First, some Muslim countries are engaged or interested in exchanging oil for gold. Second, in debt-ridden Greece, people are also reported to be reverting to the barter system of commodity exchange instead of using their currency as the medium. Can you explain why?

Summary

- Money evolved as a social convention because of the difficulties of the barter system, i.e. exchanging goods for goods. The main difficulty was the mutual matching of wants—A must not only have the good that B wants, but B must also have to offer what A wants in exchange. Thus, only something that everyone generally required worked as money in society. Thus, there was a need to find something generally acceptable in exchange for other goods and services, and that something eventually acquired the status of money in society. Money came to perform the function of the medium of exchange.

- In its role as the medium of exchange, money also measures value in exchange of commodities, expressed in their price, which can be compared. In addition, money serves as a store of value because it is the most liquid form of wealth. It also works as the standard of value in the discharge of payments and as a unit of account.

- Money is the go-between in the act of exchange; eventually the exchange takes place between the real goods and services of one and those of others. Money flows in one direction in the economy, and goods and services move in the opposite direction. Mapping the flows of money is quite complicated.

- The identification of money does not lie in what is used as money, for items that were used as money have had no uniformity over time and space. In contrast, it is the function of money that dictates its universality. Money is what money does. But money is also a measure of value. It cannot perform that function well unless its own value remains stable over time.

- The general acceptability of money (whatever form it takes) comes from the stability of its value, i.e. its purchasing power. This does not necessarily mean that what works as money must be valuable in itself, although for centuries money has been made from precious metals—gold and/or silver.

- Paper money appeared as a way to economize on the use of precious metals, especially gold. The link with gold came to an end in 1971. Since then paper currency serves as money across the globe.

- Initially private banks issued paper currency but this lacked uniformity in currency notes and led to their over issue. Countries gradually established central banks to perform those functions for the government agencies which private banks did for the ordinary citizens. They were given certain special rights and powers including the sole right to issue currency notes.

- Central banks use different methods to issue paper money. The common point of these methods was to decide the portion of note issue covered by precious metals kept in reserve for convertibility. 100% reserve soon gave way to fractional systems.

- However, note issue law cannot make people accept paper currency if something happens to make them lose faith in the stability of its value. This is what happened in Germany in the early 1920s and it is happening in Greece today.

- The concept of a general price level is different from the notion of individual commodity prices, although it depends on the prices of individual commodities. The general level of prices is measured through the construction of relevant price indices that have a reference base. The value of money, i.e. its purchasing power, varies inversely with, and proportionate to, the general price level.

- Price level changes *per se* are of little consequence and assume significance because they alter the relative structure in the economy. This brings about changes in the income distribution and employment level in an economy. A persistent rise in the general price level is called inflation and leads to a boom, and a fall is designated as deflation and plunges the economy into depression. The repetitive chain of events is called a trade cycle.

- A typical trade cycle comprises four identifiable phases: boom, deflation, depression, and recovery. Inflation favours businesses and leads to full employment. It hurts those on fixed incomes, such as retirees. It also skews the distribution of incomes towards the rich. Anti-inflationary policies, especially interest rate hikes, sometimes discourage investment and increase unemployment, and the economy experiences what is termed stagflation.

- In contrast, deflation dampens the business outlook, investment tends to shrink, unemployment spreads, and recovery is slow and painful. Thus, inflation and deflation both cause disequilibrium in the economy but of the two inflation, within limits, is perhaps less harmful.

- What determines the value of money? Given the demand for money, economists in general regard the quantity of money as doing this job. The lifespan of Fisher's theorem, $MV = PT$ seems to have lengthened indefinitely. Many insist that the theorem is an identity expressing the truism that there cannot be an income unless there is a corresponding expenditure somewhere in the society. But Fisher explained the assumptions that could link the money supply to the general price level and suggested remedial measures for containing inflation and deflation. The role of V in the equation is important as variation in it may play a significant role in aggravating booms and depressions.

- Finance is based on money and banks are the institutions that collect money in the form of deposits and channel these deposits to their users in the form of loans. This service is known as financial intermediation and the income they bring to the banks is called bank margins.

- Islamic banks emerged in formal shape in the last quarter of the 20th century and are making rapid progress. They differ from conventional banks in some important ways including the avoidance of interest, ambiguity and over speculation in business; they keep their financing firmly linked to real economy.

Glossary

Deflation This is a situation opposite to inflation. Prices in general continue falling until they hit a bottom called depression. National income, savings, investments, employment, wages, interest rates and other macro variables all move pushing one another in a downward direction. Businesses are hit hard; agriculturists the hardest and fixed income groups that remain employed, gain.

Gharar Justice and fair play are the foundation stones of all contractual relationships in Islam: parties to a transaction must avoid as far as possible causing harm to each other. Any chance of financial injury to any of the parties due to the indeterminacy of the subject matter, modes of operation or interpretation of clauses is not permitted— *gharar* must be avoided.

Inflation The prices of goods and services in the market fluctuate in response to changes in their demand and supply conditions. Normally, these conditions for all commodities need not change at the same time and push prices in the same direction, but it is common experience that most prices are at times seen to be rising (or falling) together. This phenomenon is called inflation. Yet, in economics, inflation is a technical term. Inflation is not a one-off general rise in prices; it is a trend that feeds on itself. Factors which set the ball rolling are varied and complex. Earlier economists thought it was a purely monetary phenomenon: too much money chasing too few goods described inflation. The failure to establish the relationship firmly led to a refinement in the approach: inflation was taking place when money income—not the quantity of the money supply—were expanding faster than growth in the real economy. Still, others saw a circular relationship between various macro-variables and defined inflation as a state of disequilibrium in the economy where prices, the quantity of money, or its velocity, and employment are pushing each other in an upward direction. Creeping inflation is a tonic for prosperity; galloping inflation is an agent of destruction. Inflation alters the income structure in favour of the relatively rich in society but keeps the poor in jobs.

Legal tender money This refers to money that the law of a country declares as a legally valid offer in payment of a price or a debt. The law discharges the person making the offer from responsibility if the seller or the creditor refuses to accept payment. The money serving as a unit of account in a country, such as the dollar, euro or rupee, are domestic units of account and serve as unlimited legal tender in their respective countries. All money forms which represent any part of a unit of account are legal tender up to a predefined limit only. For payments beyond that limit, the seller or debtor can refuse to accept payment in that form. Such money is called token money.

Seignorage In general it refers to the right of a king or a lord over the property of his people. Restricted to money, it was the crown's right to a percentage cut on bullion anyone brought to mint for conversion into coins. The application of the term to inconvertible fait money of today is misleading; no one asks the government to print notes for him and pays the printing cost.

Velocity (V) of circulation of money A unit of money is used again and again in the act of exchange. How many times, on average, a unit passes from hand to hand as a medium of exchange is called its velocity of circulation. It is related to M_0. The behaviour of V is largely a matter of the psychological state of mind of the people. A rise in V increases the money supply even as M_0 remains constant, and vice versa.

Concepts for Review

- Barter system
- Barter system of exchange
- Central bank
- Convertible paper money
- Currency principle of note issue
- Deflation
- Legal tender money
- Liquidity
- Representative paper money
- Time value of money
- Trade cycles

Case Study   13.1

The Rising Public Debts

Public debt is the total amount of money owed by the government to creditors. It is usually presented as a percent of gross domestic product (GDP). Because of the global financial crisis and the Euro zone sovereign debt crisis, advanced economies have followed a particularly dangerous trajectory of indebtedness in recent years. Total debt for OECD countries was at 74.2% of total OECD GDP in 2007 and is now growing to 112.5% in 2014 (estimated). Individual countries within the OECD ranged in 2012 from a low of 14.5% of debt to GDP in Estonia to 224.3% in Japan.

Source: Tina Aridas and Valentina Pasquali, <http://www.gfmag.com/global-data/economic-data/public-debt-percentage-gdp>, accessed 9 July 2014.

Case Questions

1. Why are public debts rising fast in developed economies such that a few in Europe have reached the brink of bankruptcy since 2005? Explain.
2. It is sometimes pointed out that internal borrowings and their repayment are not worrisome; it is the burden of external debt that can lead a country to trouble. Do you agree? Give reasons for your answer.

Case Study   13.2

Islamic Finance: Asset Distribution Worldwide

In 2010, the global size of Islamic finance was estimated at around USD800 billion. But its distribution over various financing schemes was narrow and uneven, as Table 13.4 succinctly shows.

Table 13.4 *Global distribution of Islamic finance assets 2010 (USD800 billion)*

Items	Share
Islamic Banking	83%
Sukuk	11.3%
Islamic Funds	4.6%
Takaful	0.8%

Source: Kuwait Finance House Report (2010)

Case Questions

1. Islamic banking dominates Islamic finance. Why? Are there any significant regional differences to consider?
2. Why does *takaful* remain a tiny element in the spread of Islamic finance? What can be done to improve the situation?
3. In your opinion, what reasons have caused the proliferation of *sukuk* issuance in recent months? Explain.

Test Questions

13.1   Explain the difficulties of exchanging goods through barter. 'Islam was the first social order that disliked the bartering of goods and encouraged their exchange via the market.' Give evidence supporting this statement. What, in your opinion, were the Islamic reasons for instructing trading through the market?

13.2   Money separated the act of purchase from the act of sale. What functions of money followed from this basic facility that money provided? Explain, providing the linkages between the different functions of money.

13.3   Is it necessary that money in itself, be valuable or should it be convertible into something that commands a value in use? Argue your case.

13.4   Inflation is a purely monetary phenomenon. Do you agree? Give reasons for your answer. If a choice has to be made between inflation and deflation, which one would you prefer to see and why?

13.5   The equation of exchange only exhibits the truism that money receipts and payments would always be equal in an economy. It has no analytical value. Discuss.

13.6   Distinguish between representative and convertible forms of paper money. What principle of note issue governs each?

13.7   It is said that inflation is unjust while deflation is inexpedient but of the two, deflation is worse. Do you agree? Explain reasons for your answer.

13.8   Write a note on the rise of Islamic banking. How is Islamic banking different from mainstream banking? Explain clearly.

13.9   Write explanatory notes on the following:
  (a)   Barter system: its limitations and current uses,
  (b)   Principles and methods of issuing currency notes, and
  (c)   Banks as financial intermediaries.

Web Exercise

Search the Internet for articles on the content and scope of macroeconomics and how is it based on microeconomic theories you have studied in the preceding chapters. Provide a cross over from microeconomic theory to macroeconomic theory. Analyze which is more policy oriented. In the next chapter we shall discuss what macroeconomics is about, i.e. what is its subject matter, scope of limitations and significance.

Forward Link

This chapter was a cross over from microeconomics to macroeconomics. In the next chapter we shall introduce you to the nature and content of broad aggregates like national product, national income and national expenditure, and their variants.

CHAPTER 14

Macroeconomics: Nature and Significance

LEARNING OUTCOMES

This chapter should enable the student to understand:

- What is macroeconomics and how it differs from microeconomics
- The objectives and problems macroeconomics addresses
- The principles for allocation of economic resources to alternative uses
- The concept and importance of opportunity costs in an economy
- Role of the state in a market economy: Freedom versus intervention
- Globalization: Content and impact
- Growth and human welfare

14.1 MACROECONOMICS: CONTENT AND SCOPE

We explained in Chapter 1 that economics is the study of human behaviour in relation to scarce resources employed to satisfy ever-increasing human wants. Wants, being unlimited, keep human beings under perpetual pressure to have more and more of goods and services for their satisfaction, while the scarcity of resources constantly tends to keep their supply restricted. Prices maintain the equilibrium between the two opposite forces of demand and supply. We may look at this scenario for the relationship between demand, supply and prices either with reference to small individual entities like firms, farms and industries, as we have done so far, or collectively as aggregates of, say, national output, savings or investments. The first is the micro aspect of economics, the second macro. Until the mid-thirties of the last century, economists treated both the micro and macro issues of economics in a single unified framework.

The propositions that are valid for microeconomics may not be valid for macroeconomics.

However, after the 1930s, Great Depression had overwhelmed the world, economists felt the need to study their subject under two distinct schemes of analysis—microeconomics dealing with the behaviour of individual economic entities and macroeconomics concerned with relationships between such entities in an aggregative framework. *Microeconomics* is concerned with topics such as the contribution of individual farms firms and industries to total output, the role of consumers and producers in the market price formation, and the allocation of individual resources to competing uses. In contrast, *macroeconomics* deals with national aggregates of micro variables such as the volume of output, rate in its growth, the overall level of prices, employment position, resource allocation, foreign trade, quantity of money and so on. Here, the centre of our interest is the *totality* of an economic phenomenon, not its small partial components. The reasons for the bifurcation of economics into micro and macro parts are not far to seek. It was realized, although late, that issues relating to the individual economic units do not always or entirely remain the same when we look at their aggregative behaviour. Concepts, definitions, relationships, implications and consequences often tend to change. Let us take a few examples to make the nature of such differences clear.

Individual drops of water from the morning dew, is cool and pleasing. The same drops together in a tornado may become agents of fear and destruction. Likewise, savings in money terms may be, as we shall see later, a virtue in the case of individuals for a variety of reasons. But a community of individuals cannot save in terms of money; it has to save in real terms. (Why? Argue.) Again, think of money as wealth. An individual may become rich in assets through savings from his money income but can a community become rich by printing more of its own currency notes? (Yes or no? Why?)

Macroeconomics helps in achieving social goals.

Even as there are important differences between microeconomics and macroeconomics, the two remain inseparable. Microeconomics provides the main concepts and data for macroeconomics studies. Likewise, changes in aggregate national income affect the size and distribution of individual earnings. More importantly, the tools and analytical framework of the two branches are not much different. Both employ the demand and supply apparatus to arrive at the equilibrium price–output combinations. To illustrate this, microeconomics deals with the determination of and changes in the prices of individual commodities. The demand and supply of individual commodities is affected by varied factors; prices of all of them are not likely to move in the same direction during a time span. But we do find that prices are, in general, often rising or falling together. At times, fluctuations could be abrupt, even violent. Macroeconomics sees such fluctuations in *price levels* as resulting from changes in the *aggregate demand* and *aggregate supply* of goods and services in the system. As price level changes are of vital significance for growth, employment, and distribution of incomes and wealth in an economy, they call for remedial action. Macroeconomics thus deals essentially with policy issues. Over time, numerous models have appeared as solutions to macroeconomic problems with much ideological content and controversy.

14.2   POLICY OBJECTIVES

The commonality in policy objectives stems from the circumstance of human existence on Earth i.e. the scarcity of resources available for use in the face of multiplicity of wants and the desire of the mortals to maximize satisfaction from their use. The problem of 'resource scarcity and want multiplicity' is part of the divine scheme of things that lends meaning to *maqasid-al-Shariah*. The macroeconomics policy objectives are thus in harmony with the *maqasid*; the initial ones include growth, employment, distributive justice and stability. Environmental care, poverty eradication and self-reliance were later additions to the list.

> Macroeconomics seeks to improve social welfare.

14.2.1   Growth

Even as other objectives of economic policy were well-recognized, growth in gross national product (GNP) has always occupied centre stage. It was believed that growth would take care of employment and promote stability as well. The conflict between growth and distribution was alone considered substantive. The issue *was* vital for developing countries where distributive inequalities were indeed acute. However, without growth, nothing save poverty could be distributed more evenly. One hoped that the imputation process would make growth income eventually *trickle down* to the lower rungs of society, and the upcoming industrial centres would *spill*, growing prosperity far and wide with the passage of time. Other goals were thus conditioned by the primary requirement of improvement in the per capita real income growth in developing economies.

The single-minded pursuit of growth did produce results. The GNP per capita of developing countries grew at an average rate of 3.4% per annum during 1950–75. This was faster than either the developed or developing nations had grown in any comparative period prior to 1950. Indeed, the total output of the world during the later half of the twentieth century far exceeded what humanity could produce during the entire period of its existence before the War (Hasan, 1995). However, the expected trickle down did not take place: the gulf between the rich and the poor widened unabated both within and across nations. (Refer to Table 1.2, Chapter 1.) Likewise, the centres of growth did not radiate prosperity around: instead they became the whirlpools of affluence sucking in men and material from all around, leaving the far flung areas in deep deprivation. In addition, fast development brought in a frightful degradation of the environment including ozone depletion, melting of ice-caps, global warming, rising sea levels, deforestation, and species extinction. In sum, rapid growth was characterized with aggravating poverty and inequalities topped with awesome environmental deterioration. Thus, it is being asked:

> Growth alone or by itself cannot ensure increase in human welfare.

1.   What sacrifices do the production of goods and services impose on a society?

2. What type of goods and services does the GNP packet contain i.e. what is the product mix?

3. How are the contents distributed among the people and institutions?

It is difficult to answer these questions but these (and the like) are questions that have to be answered if growth has to be meaningful. Some of the reasons why such questions are avoided are discussed briefly as follows:

- Growth invariably causes pollution that encroaches on the quality of environment and depletion of natural resources for future generations.
- Long hours of work may increase output but would unduly reduce workers' leisure, especially in less developed economies, and affect their health.
- Rapid unregulated growth may accentuate income inequalities within and between nations, giving rise to social unrest.
- Finally, one of the leading social objectives of modern economies is, or should be, the fulfilment of basic needs of their nationals, irrespective of caste, colour or creed. In fact, need fulfilment is so vital that the constitution of the Islamic Republic of Iran makes its achievement obligatory for the state. There is agreement in general that food, clothing, shelter, education and healthcare are to be the minimum contents of the basic needs basket. However, the range, quantity and quality of its contents would vary with the level of economic development a country may have reached at a point in time. Some concern was shown about the non-fulfilment of basic needs in developing economies during the 1980s, especially in the United Nations development Programme (UNDP) publications. But the concern has since been on the wane and growth again seems to be leading development goals. The reason is that basic needs fulfilment requires a major shake-up of the planning priorities for which the needed political will is lacking. Still, the issue remains for the developing world an inescapable challenge.

14.2.2 Full Employment

Economies need to grow, and they should grow at a pace and in a manner so as to ensure full employment to the growing population. This has been the case indeed for the globe as a whole and over the long run. But individual counties—developed and developing—have both experienced rounds of agonizing unemployment. The non-economic factors causing unemployment have of late been rising. Frequent wars as a means of satisfying human lust and lure, menacing corruption and increasing natural calamities—floods and earth-quakes—and incurable diseases, are now swelling the ranks of the unemployed. Each of us wants amelioration but nobody seems to know how. We shall discuss the more technical economic aspect of the problem in a later chapter.

But what do we mean by employment in an economic sense? It is quite logical to say that one is employed if he were not unemployed, as economists find it more convenient to explain what unemployment is to help them fix the volume of employment in a country. Note carefully the following unemployment concepts.

> What is employment or unemployment is a matter of definition.

1. **Voluntary unemployment**: 'A' had a job, but he was not satisfied with the working conditions. So, he left the job and is searching for a new one. Job hopping is common these days. For example, in Malaysia, seven out of ten persons are reported to change their job every five years. Technically, A is not considered as unemployed. Similar is the case of 'B' who has had several job offers but joined none; he decided to wait until he gets a job of his choice.

2. **Structural unemployment**: 'D' was an owner–operator taxi driver in Penang but due to the fast expansion of cheaper public transport systems, he is not able to earn enough for a comfortable living. He sold his vehicle for scrap and is waiting to find a job in the new transport set up. He, too, is not considered unemployed. The common and visible source of structural unemployment is the transformation of an economy from agriculture to industrialization.

3. **Cyclical unemployment**: 'E' was working in a coal mine. In the 1930s depression, he was laid off because coal was piling up unsold at the pithead. He got back his job only after the economy overcame the turmoil.

4. **Involuntary unemployment**: 'C' is desperate to find a job and would work at the going wage rate for any firm. Still, he remains jobless. Cyclical unemployment, too, falls in the same category. People who lose their jobs due to war, riots or natural disasters such as earthquakes, fires or floods are modern times entrants to the involuntary categories.

Apparently, people falling in any of the above categories are jobless but economists have different ideas. They consider only people who do not find jobs, though they are *willing* to work at the going wage rate, as unemployed. Voluntary and structural employment categories are excluded. People in these two categories are expected to be absorbed soon on completion of the readjustment processes working in the economy. If involuntary unemployment remains around 3%, it is not seen as a cause of much concern. It is a serious matter if involuntary unemployment crosses that limit. Germany, the largest of the European economies, is currently facing a worrying problem on this score; unemployment there stood at over 8.7% at the close of 2007.

> Presumably, the definition of employment needs a relook in economics.

14.2.3   Distributive Justice (Equity)

Of all the policy objectives, the most talked about since the dawn of civilization is the ensuring of justice in the distribution of wealth and income in a society. And yet, it is on this front that human beings have met their worst defeat. Perceptions of unjust distribution have often been shared but perceptions of a distribution being just have been rare. Islam emphasizes distributive justice more than any other social system. The Qur'an says: *Behold: God enjoins justice, and the doing of good, and generosity towards one's fellow men, and he forbids all that is shameful and all that runs counter to reason, as well as all envy, and He exhorts you repeatedly so that you might bear all this in mind (16:90).*

The concept of a fair and just distribution needs clarity and precision.

It follows that to call a distribution Islamic, it must be fair in some clear sense. That sense has remained perceptive or interpretive. In fact, much bloodshed has taken place among the believers due to interpretive differences on the notion of justice. But this does not mean that there is lack of possible measures to improve distribution which patently is much skewed in favour of the rich. Fulfilment of basic needs of the masses alone can go a long way in ameliorating the situation and sharing profit with labour can do much good.

Economic justice in an Islamic economy can be further improved through strengthening the belief in the teachings of Islam, promoting cooperation rather than competition in the markets, and improving the political system with reference to freedom of expression, transparency in applying regulations and non-partisan treatment of individuals, groups and institutions. In sum, the effort should be to create an economic order beneficial and benevolent for all devoid of discrimination.

There may, at times, be a clash between policy objectives, especially between growth and equity. There is ample empirical evidence for an inverse relationship between growth and equity: the weak are expected to be left farther behind in a speedy and long race. Thus, of the two situations—(a) faster growth with increasing inequalities, and (b) a less speedy growth with greater equity—presumably (B) would be preferable.

However, distribution of the GNP has two aspects (i) personal or size distribution i.e. what an individual gets from various sources and (ii) what share does each functional group—labour and capital—get in the national income. In other words, what proportion dowages and profit have in national income? The two types of distributions interact with one another. Table 14.1 shows their mutual relationship.

Table 14.1 *Functional and personal income distributions (INR'000)*

Household	Payment made as				Personal distribution of income (Total)
	Wages	Rent	Interest	Profit	
A	–	13	12	100	**125**
B	9	5	1	10	**25**
C	–	10	5	8	**23**
D	10	–	–	5	**15**
E	6	2	2	2	**12**
Functional distribution of income (Total)	**25**	**30**	**20**	**125**	**200**

Note: Reproduced here from Chapter 1 for ready reference

However, in macroeconomics, the issue of justice or equity is primarily concerned with the functional distribution of income in a country. The data on the division of national income between wages and profit is rarely available, particularly for Muslim countries. In the global view of macroeconomics distribution of income, disparities among nations also become important even as their influence on national income distribution may be roundabout and indirect. Refer to Table 1.2, not only is the gap (b − a) between the per capita income of the developed and developing nations large, it is increasing alarmingly with the passage of time even as the ratio (b/a) declines.

In economics, the norm of equity is taken as having been met if each factor of production—labour and capital—gets equal to what it contributes to the total output. Assuming perfect competition in both the product and factor markets, economists use the celebrated marginal productivity theory to show that capitalism is a just social system with reference to the income distribution among factors of production; both labour and capital get equal to what each contributes to GNP. If wages the workers get were a just payment, profit, which is equal to GNP minus wages, cannot be unjust. It is dubious reasoning, for, if profits could be shown as a just reward, wages paid to workers equal GNP minus profit must automatically be just. We shall not elaborate the point here because you have learned in detail about the marginal productivity theory of distribution and its weaknesses in Chapter 9.

14.2.4 Stability

An interesting fact came to light in a research work. The income inequalities in developing Muslim countries were found to be significantly smaller than in other developing nations as Table 14.2 reveals. How can this be explained?

Current income inequalities are vast and formidable.

Table 14.2 *Income inequality comparisons*

Particulars	Countries			
	Muslim (n = 20)		Non-Muslim (n = 63)	
Measures	Ratio	Gini	Ratio	Gini
Mean	6.26	36.45	10.41	40.85
σ	2.10	5.23	7.65	10.44
CV %	33.54	14.35	73.68	25.55

Notes:
1. Construction of the table is based on UN data downloaded from Wikipedia.
2. The countries have been selected on the basis of their survey year falling within the 2000–2003 period.
3. The income ratio used is of top 20% to bottom 20% income.

The course of economic activity, like that of weather, seldom runs smooth. There are frequent ups and downs, big or small. We are facing a boom here and a recession there. These fluctuations are sudden, random and may at times be quite violent. Take any macro variable and plot it against a time scale; you will seldom find a smooth curve that is free of fluctuations. Figure 14.1 is illustrative of such fluctuations showing the quarterly growth domestic product (GDP) of Malaysia for the years 2002–2006.

Keeping tabs on the fluctuations in key economic variables including price level, interest rates, balance of payments and supply of money is crucial for the health and smooth expansion of output and prosperity in an economy. Figure 14.1 for example depicts the fluctuations in the level of the Malaysian GDP and its rate of growth over the first decade of the century.

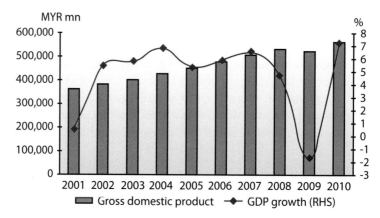

Figure 14.1 *GDP – Level and growth rate, Malaysia (2001–2010)*
(adapted from CEIC Data Blog, Malaysia)

14.2.5   Environmental Care

In view of the increasing pace of ozone depletion, global warming, climate change, species extinctions and spread of diseases; environmental degradation poses the greatest challenge for mankind in years ahead. Environment protection is listed in the World Development Indicators 2003 Report as among the major millennium development goals. Pollution of environment poses a threat to people everywhere. Damage done to environment in one location may affect the well-being of plants, animals and humans in other locations; protection of environment is the nations' common responsibility.

Tracking the damage from pollution, let alone measuring it, is difficult even as its indicators have already been quite developed. Environmental issues are attracting much attention in the micro part of economics, but macroeconomics is yet to incorporate the problem in its theoretical models. Ethics provides generic awareness of environmental issues that may be useful guides for specific action for developing economies.

14.2.6   Poverty Eradication

Poverty has emerged as a major issue in the developing economies since the mid-1970s and has invoked international concern. The World Summit on Social Development held at Copenhagen (1995) regarded eradication of poverty as an ethical, social, political and economic policy imperative.

It is difficult to define poverty and identify the poor. But efforts are made to conceptualize poverty and measure it at the national and international levels. Poverty essentially is a relative concept as it involves perceptions but its measurement could only be possible if defined in some absolute term. A reference base is required. For this, national and international poverty lines are defined. For example, the World Bank publishes data of the number of people in poverty on the basis of two expenditure lines: (i) < 1 USD a day and (ii) < 2 USD a day for individual countries in terms of both urban and rural categories for the survey years. A poverty index is also published. Many countries define their own poverty lines in local currencies as World Bank benchmarks are too unrealistic for them.

14.2.7   Self-reliance

Perhaps this objective of macro policy is a reflection of increasing external indebtedness of developing countries to the developed. It implies that these countries must attempt to stand on their own feet through better management of their economies and more efficient use of resources at their disposal. The objectives need not be stretched to mean economic self-sufficiency, i.e. a country producing everything that it may need. Self-sufficiency is neither desirable nor can be achieved in an age of globalization. Self-reliance only requires that a country be able to export enough to pay for what it would need to import: it must cut the coat according to its cloth. Self-reliance promotes self-esteem.

14.3   CONFLICTS AND TRADE-OFFS

As already hinted, the simultaneous pursuit of the above objectives is complicated and difficult; there are conflicts between them that have to be resolved. Stability and growth go along well while self-reliance seems to be a neutral objective. However, this is not so with other inter-objective relationships.

To begin with, growth and equity do not harmonize. Income inequalities allow more savings for investments that is conducive for growth. The low per capita income economies may find it inadvisable to go in for reduction of inequalities in the early stages of development, as such a policy would only redistribute poverty. Thus, until the middle of 1970s, growth remained the unchallenged darling of development economics. But growth ran into disrepute when inequalities, mass poverty, and despair increased and became visibly rampant despite economies in general registering elating rates of growth in their GNPs.

Growth and equity may clash because the rich can save relatively more than the poor.

The assumption that benefits of growing at higher income levels will, in due course, filter down to the lower levels, proved unrealistic. Also, it was not found appropriate to believe that increase in the consumption of the poor due to redistributive measures will necessarily lower growth as national savings would be reduced. It was a late realization that improvement in the living of the poor because of income transfers to them is an investment in human capital: it must ultimately increase labour productivity. In addition, increased spending on consumption was likely to increase, almost immediately, the size of the market for the sale of goods and services. Thus, in the context of growth, what the economy loses on the swings, it will gain on the rounds.

The above argument adds meaning to the earlier argument on the fulfilment of basic needs and poverty removal. In any case, if the choice were between (i) a slower rate of growth accompanied with better income distribution and (ii) a fast rate of growth with aggravating inequalities, many would presumably prefer to have (i) and not (ii).

Growth generally creates more employment opportunities.

Another clash is between growth and employment. The use of more capital provides less employment in the short run for producing the same volume of output. Modern technologies including organizational forms emanating from the West mostly fall in this category. Developing countries such as India, Pakistan, Bangladesh and Indonesia are capital short, but have large populations with high unemployment rates. Such economies face a dilemma having little option. They have to rely on foreign technology which multinationals alone can bring in. But multinationals come in areas of their choice; host countries do not have much say in the matter. The result is that the products and technologies developing economies perforce import often turns out to be inappropriate for them. They may possibly not remain so in the long-run; employment may eventually increase. But to many, this might be a poor consolation. How long the long-run would be seldom clear; the consequences may remain vague and controversial. Education and training, innovation and adaptation seem to be the answer.

Normally, stability must promote employment but sometimes what is conducive to maintain stability may create problems on the employment front. For example, the downward rigidity of wage structure tends to deepen recession.

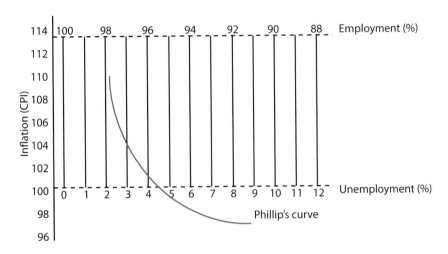

Figure 14.2 *Inflation–unemployment relationship*

Again, it is found, as per the Philips curve, that there is a trade-off between inflation and unemployment: the higher the rate of unemployment, the lower is the rate of inflation. It shows an empirical relationship between unemployment and wage-induced inflation. Figure 14.2 presents a typical downward-sloping Philips curve. The message of the curve is that the economy must put a tab on rise in wages to maintain stability andemployment. It also sharpens the conflict between growth and equity. Interestingly, in some recent studies the validity of the relationship has been questioned, especially for the developing economies.

Policy makers make decisions concerning allocation of scarce resources to various uses with reference to these and other policy objectives. The process of how this is done was discussed in Chapter 1.

for you all that is in the Earth (2.29) looks small but its ramifications are vast: it is the epitome of *maqasid–al-Shari'ah*. The macroeconomic objectives of Islam flow from this divine declaration like water from an open tap. Men have to use whatever is given to their possession—individually or collectively—according to the terms and conditions of the Creator.

The trusteeship idea attracted the attention of Mahatma Gandhi, the father of the Indian nation. He regularly wrote on social trusteeship exhorting the Indian industrialists to hold the wealth they create as trustees for the nation to ameliorate the fate of the poor.

Shari'ah law codifies these terms and conditions. The difficulty is that man has been granted freedom of action. Thus, if men follow the rules of the game, the law will reward them here and in the hereafter. And, in case of defiance, the same law will punish them. Thus some of the leading objectives of Islamic macroeconomics are as follows:

1 Social justice

Justice is the essence of Islamic faith but no precise definition of justice is available in the juristic literature, why? The reason is that justice cannot be defined independent of the nature and circumstance of a situation and carries in some measure a perceptive ingredient. Also, it has to be pronounced with contextual reference. Thus, it is the application of Shari'ah norms to specific situations—individual or collective—that would decide what is just and what is unjust. Otherwise, only broad directions alone are available in most macroeconomic matters. They are the clearest with reference to the fulfilment of the basic needs—food, clothing, shelter, education and healthcare—of all people normally living in a country. In several Muslim countries, this is a constitutional responsibility of the state.

2 Education

Presumably, Islam is the only religion that started with the instruction *iqra* i.e.(you) read. For, knowledge is power. It was the passion of Muslims and their contributions to various sciences—physical, technicaland social—that soon made them the teachers of the world; it was the key that opened to them the doors on treasures of the world. Islamic norms of education created a community of believers imbued with morality compassion, contentment and self-awareness which created a social order that won the day for them—they ruled the world for centuries. Again, it was the reversal of the scales in favour of the West. Muslims ran away from education; glory ran away from them even faster. Today, Muslims are on the lower rungs of the ladder; their contribution to knowledge is meagre. They are over 20% of global village but contribute no more than 7 to 8 percent to the GDP of the world. This is the position even as they hold a substantial portion of world resources: they are mostly sellers of resources, not their users. 22 of the 57 Muslim countries are classified among the least developed of the world.

3 Distributional equity

Islam is a pro-poor religion but unlike socialism it is not anti-rich; it behaves as trustees for the poor—it believesthe poor have a rightful share in their riches. The beauty of the Islamic system is that it does not use communism-like compulsive measures for achieving equity. It allows differences in distribution because of natural or acquired differences in talent or skills. It is also needed to promote individual initiative. But to make corrections beyond that Islam has in-built measures like *infaq, sadaqaat, zakat,qard, hasan* and *awqaaf* to mitigate inequalities and poverty. It is well to note that empirical investigations have revealed that distributional differences in Muslim developing economies are significantly lower than in comparable non-Muslim developing nations.

4 Growth

The macroeconomic goals of an Islamic economy like its conventional counterpart cannot ignore growth in per capita income. For, if the emphasis on equity ignores growth efforts at improving distributional equity it will only be redistributing poverty. Growth is imperative for most of the Muslim world steeped in grueling poverty and where in addition wars, mostly not of their own choice, have of late been taking a heavy toll on life limb and civil infrastructures. It also has to be guided more by utility than glamour. Moderation in consumption and avoidance of waste can go a long way in making less look more. Expenditure on education must rise and environmental care cannot be ignored.

14.4   ROLE OF THE STATE

In the fixing of macro objectives, designing of policies to achieve them and in putting those policies into operation, the state plays a crucial role in all modern economies. Private enterprise never had an absolutely free run in history. The legal framework for its operation and control, especially of monopoly power, in social interest, was always provided by the state authorities. Public utilities, infrastructure development and energy supply have for long been, and in most developing countries, still remain in the public sphere.

However, the important macroeconomic issue concerning the state is the division of spheres of economic activities between the public and private sectors, it designs and enforces. This is usually a generic and flexible division. To illustrate, the 1948 Industrial Policy Resolution of India declared that all key and heavy industries including atomic research, space exploration, oil and natural gas, ship building, aircraft manufacturing, heavy electrical, rail and air transportation, and any further expansion of iron and steel industry will fall in the public sector while the remaining industries, road transportation, finance, insurance and agriculture were left open for the private sector. During the 1960s, a joint sector was introduced where the state and private enterprise both could operate and even have partnerships. During the last two decades, the classification in India has been much diluted: the joint sector expanded fast and many public enterprises, especially the losing ones, have been sold to the private sector under the wave of globalization, which is now sweeping the world. Significantly, the 14 commercial banks nationalized in 1969 to meet certain social priorities remained untouched by the ongoing privatization process.

> State intervention in the running of an economy is unavoidable. The dispute is about the form, areas and extent.

BOX 14.2

Crises, Islam and Stability

A. Frequency of crises

The economic history of the world is replete with recessions and depressions. From the bursting of the British South Sea Bubble and the French Mississippi Bubble in 1720, (which at least one economic historian claims delayed the industrial revolution by 50 years) to the industrial depressions of the 1870s and 1930s, to the Latin American middle income debt crisis, African low income debt crisis, ex-Communist output collapse, and East Asian financial crisis, crises have been a constant of market capitalism. Add to that the collapses that have accompanied non-economic shocks like wars, hurricanes, earthquakes, volcanoes, fires, pests, droughts and floods, and it is a wonder that anyone in the world has economic security.

More recently, economic crises have often tended to go hand in hand with financial crises whose frequency and severity in developing countries has increased over the past quarter century. The causes and nature of these crises have differed. For example, those that characterized the debt crises of the 1980s were precipitated by profligate governments with large cash deficits and uncontrolled monetary policies. The more recent ones have occurred in countries which, for the most part, were following prudent macroeconomic policies, some of which had quite sophisticated institutional arrangements. The marked differences in the downturns in Latin America in the early 1980s and in East Asia in the late 1990s (and the Mexico crisis of 1994-95) means that we need a general framework for thinking about macroeconomic fluctuations—one that can encompass differences among countries. Furthermore, economic volatility is of importance not just because of the short run adverse effects on the poor. It has been shown to be negatively correlated with economic growth. There are thus ample reasons for trying to understand better the determinants of economic volatility.

Source: Wiliam R. Easterly, Roumeen Islam and Joseph Stiglitz, (2000*) Shaken and stirred: explaining growth volatility,* <http://econ.worldbank.org/WBSITE/EXTERNAL/EXTDEC/EXTRESEARCH/ EXTPROGRAMS/EXTMACROECO/0,,contentMDK:20340423~menuPK:4279583~pagePK:64168182~piP K:64168060~theSitePK:477872,00.html>, accessed 1 June 2014.

B. Islam and stability
With both assets and liabilities subject to amounts of risk-sharing sufficiently balanced to protect the banks from runs on funds, Islamic finance makes banking system as a whole more stable. Conventional banks carry liabilities including demand, time and savings deposits which they fully guarantee. Their assets are, however, mainly risky debt. Default on the asset side of the bank, if happens in significant proportion, would imply inability to meet the bank's obligations on the liabilities side. Such default can be expected in a crisis, be it banking or macroeconomic in nature.

An Islamic bank guarantees only demand deposits while investment deposits are kept on profit and loss sharing basis. This reduces total risk on total deposits compared to conventional banks where all deposits carry interest risks. In conventional finance, present money is traded for future money which carries more risks compared with Islamic banks where money transactions carry a real commodity attachment. These and other features of Islamic financing make it less risky and more stable.

Source: Iqbal, M. and Ahmad, A. (2005), *Islamic finance and economic development,* Palgrave: Macmillan, p.19–20.

14.5   TWO APPROACHES

One may come across in literature two broad approaches to the role of the state in contemporary economies. The distinction rests on as to which of the policies—monetary or fiscal—would be the preference in resolving national economic issues.

Monetary policy is designed and implemented by autonomous institutions—the central banks—which various countries have established for the purpose. Bank Negara Malaysia and the Reserve Bank of India are examples of such central banks. In the US, the Federal Reserve System, a consortium of privately-owned banks, plays the role of the central bank. The weapons a central bank has in its monetary arsenal to influence the course of economic events include those meant to bring about changes in the quantity of money or influence its price through manipulation of the bank rate. The latter is rate of interest at which the central bank lends money to commercial banks and discounts their bills. The central bank also has much persuasive influence on the system. The advocacy for employing the monetary policy implies a preference for keeping public intervention in the economy to the minimum.

Fiscal policy, on the other hand, is framed by the central government of a country to achieve predetermined socio-economic goals. The policy broadly includes changes in the revenue and expenditure patterns of the government. Tax structure determination, capital controls and budgetary allocations are the main instruments of fiscal policy in a country for promoting the goals discussed above.

Monetary and fiscal policies are not entirely or always independent of one another. Often they are used to supplement each other for achieving the desired objectives. They are parts of the overall financial system of an economy and cannot operate at cross purposes. The government, for example, has in many cases, the power to issue currency notes of small denomination (Government of India—not the Reserve Bank—issues one rupee notes or mint coins). More importantly, it may cover its budget deficits through borrowings from the central bank against its securities. In such cases, it may affect the supply of money in the economy beyond the central bank intentions.

> Fiscal and monetary policies have always worked together, but the influence of fiscal policy has of late been rising fast.

There is controversy over the relative efficacy of the monetary and fiscal policies to keep the economy progressive and stable. The debate seems to have ideological overtones. Those who perceive market arbitration in economic choice-making conducive to societal well-being prefer a limited role for public sector in the economy. They argue that the major problem economies face today is of stabilization and the cure lies in monetary action. On the other hand, their opponents point out that stabilization implies contra recreation policies where, following Keynes, fiscal approach has proven its worth and propriety. The division between the monetarists and the Keynesians is sharp in the US probably because operation of monetary policy is in private hands while fiscal policies involve public intervention in the economy.

One basic attribute of monetary and fiscal policies is that their consequences are difficult to predict both with reference to their timing and their impact on aggregate demand and supply of goods. Historically, central banks are found slow to move and tend to underkill for fear that they might overkill. In a crisis, the state authority tends to act faster. This of necessity lends a political edge to macroeconomics. Political dominance on macroeconomic policies is vivid even in nations that advocate for private ownership of property, open markets, non-intervention and globalization.

> Monetary and fiscal policies work together to ensure stability.

14.6   BASIC ASSUMPTIONS

Assumptions imply
ethical choices.

Irrespective of the debate and controversy about approaches, objectives, priorities and treatment of the issues in macroeconomics, the underlying assumptions of the subject remain the same as in microeconomics. These include private ownership of property, freedom of enterprise, competition, *laissez faire* and cosmopolitanism or globalization. That there is in general a harmony between individual and social interests, that the pursuit of self-interest brings out the best in human beings, that maximizing behaviour improves efficiency in the face of scarcity and that more is preferable to less are treated as axiomatic in modern economics.

Ethically, one may find these assumptions inadequate for the promotion of human well-being, rather a hindrance in ameliorating the lot of the poor and the deprived. Many would agree that these assumptions are useful analytical tools but need modification, not rejection, in the light of ethical teachings. The deciding factors are how self-interest is being promoted, what is being maximized, how and to what end. Thus viewed, the pursuit of self-interest or its maximization may look value neutral: but questions may still be raised about the efficacy of their impact on the human mind and behaviour.

14.7   GNP GROWTH AND HUMAN WELFARE

Growth and welfare do
not always go together.

We will discuss the issues of poverty and distributive justice in some detail in a later chapter of the book but a brief review of the linkage between GNP growth and human welfare may not be unsuitable here. There are many difficulties and pitfalls in the way of exploring this linkage. In general, increasing wealth brings power, pleasure and prestige to a nation. And, its relationship with employment is crucial. For these reasons, among others, growth in GNP (more so in per capita income) has long been a cherished goal to pursue for many in this world and remains so even today for no less a number. Adam Smith's *Wealth of Nations* (1776) even after centuries remains in the reckoning; its converse of recent origin—Gunnar Myrdal's *Asian Drama* (1968)—lost significance in no time.

Doubtless, wealth creation is a laudable act and a *necessary* condition for human prosperity both mundane and spiritual. However, wealth creation is by no means a *sufficient* condition. There are many reasons for that; some of them we list below.

1.   The notion of human welfare being a whole composite; a matter of feeling and perception; it is influenced by a host of factors like economic achievements, political environment, social relations, job satisfaction, family life and even weather. From economic at

the one end of the scale you may walk to the other entirely non-economic end without crossing a ditch or climbing over a fence separating the two; they mesh into one another like shades in a painting.

2. Even if we could separate the economic from the non-economic component of welfare, another concern confronts us: what is the product mix in the GNP packet? Clearly if it contains more of butter than guns, economic welfare will be larger than if guns in it were more than butter.

3. Even when GNP has more of butter, i.e. goods for civilian consumption, than guns or the military hardware, does it contain more for meeting the basic needs of the poor or devotes more of scarce resources to the production of luxuries including products like cigarettes or drugs injurious to health? It is easy to see that the impact on welfare would be different in the two cases.

4. GNP does not take into account the value of leisure as a measure of human well-being. We can, and in some cases we do, increase the GNP by lengthening the working hours of labour and putting children to work at a tender age. But will the increase in wealth so obtained promote welfare of the masses?

5. We have markets missing in environmental goods like fresh air and the societal commons like shimmering waterfalls or scenic beaches. Pollution has long been causing incalculable damage to all life forms on the planet Earth to push up GNP growth all around the globe. We must ask, is net economic welfare (NEW) increasing?

6. Market directs resources to production of various sorts of goods proportionate to the purchasing power groups of people possess, not according to their needs. Unless wealth created is distributed on an equitable basis, the rich may have festive celebrations even for their dogs in luxury hotels while across the street the poor may die of hunger.

Summary

- Economics is the study of human behaviour in relation to scarce resources having alternative uses employed to satisfy ever increasing human wants. One may look at both resources and human wants in two different ways: individually, i.e. microeconomics or collectively, i.e. macroeconomics.

- Macroeconomics looks at an economy on the whole; the important areas it studies are aggregate demand, aggregate supply, price levels, savings and investment, exports and imports, and monetary and fiscal policies in relation to pre-fixed goals. Even as microeconomics provides the basic notions and data for macroeconomic analyses, the two branches of economics have distinctive features of their own. What may look rational at the micro level need not remain so for the aggregate.

- Macroeconomics is by nature policy oriented and often tends to assume political overtones. As such, it cannot stay amoral and value free.

- Resource allocation at the macro level gives rise to alternatives based on certain norms and assumptions. Production possibility curves have certain important properties including the increasing marginal rate of transformation of Y into X or of X into Y. MRT_{YX} is defined as DY/DX.

- Macroeconomic policies are geared in developing economies to achieve some predetermined objectives, the major ones being: growth, full employment, stability, poverty eradication and self-reliance.

- These objectives are not always compatible with one another. Typically, growth and equity do not go together. Likewise, an inverse relationship is claimed to exist between inflation and unemployment. Trade-offs among conflicting goals have to be constructed.

- As macroeconomics deals with issues, there often is a clash on the efficacy or otherwise of a policy. The broad division is as to which one is better to pursue: monetary manipulations or public action. Honest difference of opinion is pervasive on the point.

Glossary

Basic needs Human wants differ in their intensity and importance. Those which have generally been recognized as basic have the first claim on resources for their satisfaction. Opinions differ on what to count as the basic needs but few deny that food, clothing, shelter, education and medical care constitute the basket. The content, quality and the range of goods included would vary with the stage of economic development and the pace of growth in each economy. The constitution of the Islamic Republic of Iran makes it obligatory on the state to meet the basic needs of its citizens if the same are not being fulfilled otherwise.

Efficiency The term efficiency has several meanings in economics. At the elementary level, it is sufficient to say that an economy would be using its resources efficiently when the rate of transformation of one bundle of goods Y into another bundle of goods X equals their price ratio. In symbols, it will be so when MRT_{YX} equals P_Y/P_X.

Employment The economy is at full employment level when all those willing to work on the current market wage find jobs.

Equity This refers to justice in the distribution of incomes in a society. Justice is essentially a matter of individual and social perception. Objectively, it is related to the concept of productivity. The general criterion is that each worker must get equal to what he/she contributes to total output while social system must take care of those who are unable to contribute at all or enough for valid reasons.

Fiscal policy Policy means action designed to achieve given objectives. Fiscal policy refers to the action plan public authorities make for raising revenues and spend it on promoting given social ends. Annual budgets of public authorities are expressions of fiscal policies.

Growth rate This refers to the rate at which the gross national product or GNP of a country expands over time, usually from one year to another. It is a dynamic process involving structural changes in an economy and is positively related to social well-being.

Income distribution It can be viewed in two ways: (i) horizontal or personal or size and (ii) vertical or functional. In personal distribution, we count the income of a person from what he gets from all sources, however varied. On the other hand, in vertical distribution, we identify sources like rent, interest, wages and profit and add what each person receives under each single head. This gives us information about the relative shares of various functional groups in the GNP. Functional distribution of income significantly affects their personal distribution. You see that wage earners usually have much smaller incomes than the landlords or businessmen.

Inflation It shows in itself an unrelenting sort of rise in the general level of prices. All prices do not rise by the same proportion. Some prices rise faster than others, changing the relative price structure. This sort of change favours certain groups and works against others. Inflation thus inflicts social injustice. What causes inflation is difficult to say; it is a very complex phenomenon.

Monetary policy It studies changes in the demand and supply of money and the factors underlying them. It deals with fluctuations in money supply and its consequences for the economy, especially the impact of credit creation on the level of prices which it works to keep stable.

Opportunity cost Resources are scarce and have alternative uses. We can have more of butter only by reducing the production, say of guns, which we consider the next best use of what we have. The number of guns we have to sacrifice for producing an additional ton of butter is the opportunity cost of that ton.

Self-reliance This term is used as a desirable objective developing countries are advised to pursue among others. Self-reliance does not mean that a country must produce everything it may need. It implies that a country should normally be able to produce enough to pay for what it would like to import.

Concepts for Review

- Aggregate variables
- Basic needs
- Employment
- Fiscal policy
- Growth
- Income distribution
- Inflation
- Policy objectives
- Resource allocation
- Self-reliance
- Stability
- Unemployment

Case Study   14.1

Malaysia: A Successful Growth Story

Malaysia is a small country but has some big achievements to its credit in the field of economic development. Starting as a low income country in 1957, it has long climbed up the ladder into the upper middle grouping in the World Development Reports. Its per capita income at constant prices rose from USD306 in 1965 to USD5,490 in 2007 and its economy with GDP worth 357.9 billion US dollars occupied the 29th position in the world with per capita income ranking at 57 the same year.

Geographical location, an abundance of natural resources, a small population with low density, a work friendly climate and a plural social order were the initial advantages the country enjoyed. However, there was a lack of capital, and a shortage of both skilled and unskilled manpower. The size of the domestic market was too small to warrant industrialization. Expediency demanded that the country evolve a policy design that could cash in on its strengths and convert its deficiencies into advantages keeping at the same time, the country's options flexible.

Central planning has been a major factor in shaping the economic destiny of Malaysia. It has been instrumental in achieving social goals like the redistribution of wealth, and the provision of major public utilities. The transformation process adopted an open economy model, choosing trade as its engine of growth. The country provided infrastructural facilities, tax concessions and remittance freedom to attract foreign capital. The country had a long-run view for development from the very start eventually culminating in what is known as Vision 2020.

Malaysia started its economic journey with dependence on rubber, tin and oil palm. These three commodities along with other raw materials had already set her economic tempo prior to independence. During the seventies, the country decided on shifting from the primary sector to manufacturing under a protection regimen. Foreign assistance from Japan and the West eased and hastened the process of transformation. Exports of manufactured goods were soon fuelling her growth. The structure of the economy underwent rapid transformation. The share of the primary sector declined progressively from 42.7% in 1970 to a mere 16.7% in 2006. The industrial and services sectors both expanded but the share of the services grew much faster.

Table 14.3 *Sector contribution to GDP (%)*

Sectors		1970	1980	1990	2000	2006
Agriculture	1	29.0	22.9	18.7	8.6	7.9
Mining	2	13.7	10.1	9.7	7.5	8.8
Primary	**1 + 2**	**42.7**	**33.0**	**28.4**	**16.1**	**16.7**
Manufacturing	3	13.9		27.0	32.3	31.1
Construction	4	3.8	4.6	3.5	3.3	3.1
Secondary	**3 + 4**	**17.7**	**24.2**	**30.5**	**35.6**	**34.2**
Services	5	36.2	40.0	42.3	53.6	51.8
Others	6	3.4	2.8	−1.2	−5.3	−2.7
Tertiary	**5 + 6**	**39.6**	**42.8**	**41.1**	**48.3**	**49.1**

Source: The table has been constructed using information in the Statistical Annexure in the Bank Negara Annual Reports for the relevant years.

Case Questions

1. How can you say that Malaysia presents a successful growth example?
2. What factors do you think have been mainly responsible for the rapid economic growth in Malaysia?

Case Study   14.2

World Population and Its Growth Rates: 1950–2050

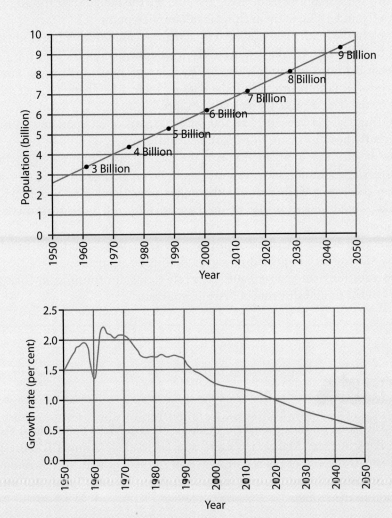

Figure 14.3 *The world population and its growth rates: 1950–2050*

Case Questions
1. World population was nearly 3 billion in 1960, which year was it almost double of that?
2. The rate of population growth has been falling since 1990, why is the population increasing?
3. Can you determine in how many years the world population tends to roughly double on an average?

Test Questions

14.1 Distinguish between microeconomics and macroeconomics. Do you think that the assumptions underlying the two are the same? State the assumptions briefly and evaluate them from a welfare viewpoint.

14.2 Explain the main policy objectives of macroeconomics. What modifications in them, if any, would you make from an ethical angle?

14.3 What is a transformation curve? Why is it concave to the origin? Construct a transformation curve using the data in Table 1.1 (Chapter 1) but taking X as Y and Y as X. Compare it with Figure 1.1.

14.4 Distinguish between private and public sectors of an economy. Which has recently been growing in importance and why?

14.5 Define full employment. Explain the factors that cause unemployment in modern economies. How can more jobs be created?

14.6 Can there be a clash between the policy objectives of an economy? If yes, how would you reconcile them? Discuss with reference to growth versus equity.

14.7 Can you define distributive justice precisely? What are the difficulties, if any, do you face in providing such a definition. Explain.

14.7 Do you think the government has a role to play in running an economy? If yes, what should this role be? Argue your case.

Web Exercise

Table 14.3 is based on data published in Bank Negara Malaysia's Annual Reports. Visit the Bank Negara Malaysia website and go to their Annual Report for the current year. At the end of the report, you will find tables with Key Economic and Financial Statistics for the country for several years. Update Table 14.3 using the information in the report.

Forward Link

You have learnt in this introductory chapter what macroeconomics is, what is studied under it and the types of problems it deals with. In the next chapter, we shall get you familiar with the subject matter of macroeconomics: national income, its variants and significance and also the methods we use to measure it.

CHAPTER 15

National Income: Variants and Measurement

LEARNING OUTCOMES

This chapter should enable the student to understand:

- The concept and role of national income accounting in an economy
- The nominal and real income flow and their mutual relationship in a closed economy
- The distinction between:
  - Productive and unproductive activities
  - Intermediate products and final products
- The nature, importance and uses of simple input–output tables
- The different methods of measuring national income and their relationships
- The adjustments needed in gross national product to arrive at net national income
- How to get from national income at factor cost to personal income
- The treatment of some typical transaction classes in national income estimation
- The elements of national output from the income and expenditure sides
- The special problems of accounting for national income in developing economies

15.1 NATIONAL INCOME AND ACCOUNTS

Countless exchange transactions take place day and night in an economy. People buy their daily needs. Firms pay wages and buy raw materials. Governments collect taxes. Second hand cars are sold. Retirees receive pensions. Imports arrive at the ports; exports leave them and so on. To understand the way in which an economy operates, such transactions

The multitude of transactions taking place in modern economies calls for summarizing them in manageable classes on some common bases.

The factors that help in answering the questions one may want to investigate become the bases for classifying the transactions.

National income: Data can be presented in any of the three forms:
- On the pattern of commercial accounts
- As a set of interrelated equations
- In the input–output tables

have to be classified in a systematic summary form. We cannot begin to examine such questions as to whether national product or income is rising or falling or what is its current level unless we know which transactions should be included in its measurement and which should not. We shall, for example, see that some of the transactions mentioned above are not included in accounting for national income.

Economic transactions can be classified in numerous ways but the classes have to be exhaustive and mutually exclusive. Also, no system of classification is likely to help provide the data to answer all the questions one may seek to investigate. For example, to study the extent of inequalities in the distribution of income, it would be necessary to classify cases with reference to the size of personal income. On the other hand, if the objective were to investigate the contribution of individual factor services to national productive effort, one must classify income according to economic functions such as rent of land, wages of labour and profit of capital.

However, the basic classification currently in use for taking account of national income has largely been influenced by the need to see what factors determine its level in the short run and in the long run. To design a classification for this purpose implies taking into consideration what variables cause national income to change over time in volume and content. More specifically, the classification must respond to the questions economists usually ask about an economy, for instance, what makes an economy grow or how fast, if at all, is it growing? In fact, there has been a rapid growth in national income accounting during the recent decades because of a major breakthrough in economic theory which J.M. Keynes ushered in to explain the causes that make national income fluctuate in the short run. Indeed, what causes economic instability was the question economists had unceasingly been asking in the wake of the 1930s Great Depression. Notions of aggregate demand, aggregate supply, saving and investment, price levels, their interrelations and so on have since become the stock-in-trade of macroeconomics. Systematic presentation of the classified data pertaining to these variables constitutes what we call the National Income Accounts of a country. Table 15.1 provides a simple specimen. These accounts are constructed on the same double entry principles as business accounts. For having uniformity in definitions and consolidation processes across nations, the UN has evolved a System of National Accounts and each country is expected to supply economic data to the UN in that form.

Economists are interested not only in the short term fluctuations in the economic activity; they are also interested in the long run growth of the economy, efficiency in resource use, structural changes, employment expansion and so on. For analyzing long run issues, it may be necessary to classify data according to the outputs of different sectors, industries and regions. Functional classification of income may be needed. Classification of transaction for national accounting is always in a process of modification and change. Despite their importance, national income

Table 15.1 *Specimen of a production account*

Debits (income)   Credits (expenditure)

Particulars	Symbol	Particulars	Symbol
Wages, interest, rent and other distributed income	Y_H	Private consumption	C_P
Direct taxes paid by firms	T_F	Government consumption	C_G
Depreciation and undistributed profit: Savings of firms	S_F	Gross domestic capital Formation	GDCF
Net indirect taxes (Indirect taxes − Subsidies)	T_I	Exports less Imports	X − M
Total = Gross national product at market price	GNP (MP)	Total = Gross national product at market prices	GNP (MP)

Equation: $Y_H + T_F + T_I + S_F = C_P + C_G + GDCF + (X - M)$

accounts merely provide data for an argument; they do not generate an argument on their own.

15.2   A SIMPLE TWO-SECTOR MODEL

Private and public records of economic transactions are consolidated and published as national income statistics. This statistics is the initial source of information on key variables needed to explain and analyze macroeconomic issues for policy making. We shall discuss these variables in detail in the following chapter but let us briefly identify them here. For this purpose, the economists invariably start with a simple closed model of an economy. They assume away the existence of government and external economic relations. What remains are two sectors: business firms or producers and consumers or households. The classification is functional; the same individuals may appear in both categories simultaneously. Two sorts of flow are visualized as circulating between them, real flow and money flow. The two are linked together by price mechanism in a market economy. Figure 15.1 shows the circulations between firms and households.

Real flow and money flow generally match each other but not always. Some flows of goods and services are not matched by any money flow. For example, in rural India, Pakistan and Bangladesh many people construct their own houses, grind their own corn, wash their own cloths and work on their own farms. These self-services though real and valuable are not paid for: no corresponding money flow is generated. Thus, there is substantial economic activity that does not pass through the market for money and escapes accounting for the national product. Likewise, no real flow takes place in the reverse direction corresponding

Money flow in an economy corresponds to real flow; though the two move in opposite directions.

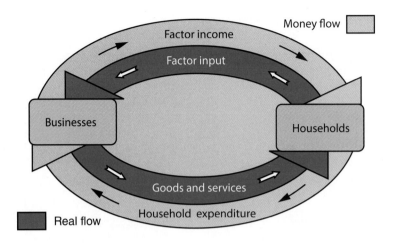

Figure 15.1 *Real flow and money flow run counter to one another in an economy as shown in this two-sector closed model*

to some money flow in an economy. Donations and charities are an obvious example. Speculative transactions in currency and stock markets, especially involving derivatives, constitute another category.

In the following chapters we discuss money flow and their classification and shall pay little attention to the corresponding real (reverse) flow. The reasons are: (i) it is usually obvious what these real flows are, and (ii) it is possible to add or subtract different real items only in money terms. Consider this: can you add an apple to three oranges or deduct two cars from a house in any other way?

15.3   PRODUCTIVE AND UNPRODUCTIVE ACTIVITIES

The history of economic thought tells us about much confusion and debate on what is productive or unproductive. For example, some thought trade alone was productive; others rejected the idea and argued that only agriculture was productive. Today we regard trade, agriculture, manufacturing and services as productive.

To understand what determines the growth and stability of the national product or income you must have a clear idea of the transactions that contribute to these variables. For this purpose, a distinction has to be made between (i) transactions that are related to the productive activities, and (ii) others which are simply meant to redistribute the goods and services produced among different societal groups. Transactions falling in the latter category are called *transfer payments*. The pocket money your father gives you falls in this category. Unlike productive activities, such payments are merely transfers of purchasing power from one economic entity to another; they do not have a counterpart adding to the output of an economy. Old age pensions, gifts and donations are some examples.

Another point is that the demarcation between transfer payments and productive activities is at times arbitrary. Soviet economists, for example,

Russia, regarded payments for many services like entertainment, as income transfers on the plea that they are not productive of anything tangible. Ideology and conventions also contribute to the arbitrariness of the distinction. For example, to supplement his pocket money, a boy may (a) wash his father's car, or (b) deliver milk packets to households each morning. In both cases, a matching service is provided. But convention in many countries treats activity (b) as productive, but (a) as unproductive. Zakat payments in Islam are for the most part, income transfers. But, if the money is used as allowed to win freedom for a slave, we may probably treat it as a productive activity. For what could be more productive than restoring the right of freedom to a human being?

> Similar confusion exists on a distinction between transfer payments and productive activities.

15.4   INTERMEDIATE PRODUCTS AND FINAL PRODUCTS

Even as *all* transactions must be classified into productive and unproductive for reckoning the aggregate national product, we cannot simply add the values of those called productive to estimate it. A further distinction *within* the productive category has to be made between:

- Intermediate products, and
- Final products.

Intermediate products are the ones used in producing other goods and services. In contrast, final products are demanded for their own sake. For example, the production of cement is a productive activity and so is the production of houses. Suppose cement, valued at RM50,000 is sold to real estate developers who use it to construct houses worth RM400,000. Now, if you count the whole value of houses in the estimate of national product, you must not include the value of cement RM50,000 in arriving at the gross national product estimate; it has already been counted in the value of houses. The output of cement here is an *intermediate* product; the houses constitute the final product. Alternatively, if you want to count cement in the national product you must count in the houses after deducting the value of cement from their value. *Double counting must be avoided in estimating the national product.* You cannot have your cake and eat it too; here cement has been used up in constructing the houses.

> Both transfer payments and intermediate goods stand outside the production boundary but for different reasons.

Notice that the reason for keeping out transfer payments from the national product estimation is not the same as for the exclusion of intermediate products. Transfer payments are excluded because they are not part of the productive activities from the very beginning. In contrast, intermediate products are, but they stand out of the estimate to avoid *double counting.*

15.5 INPUT–OUTPUT TABLES

Input–output tables throw light on the structure of an economy and the cause of changes in that structure.

Intermediate transactions all take place among the producers within the left-hand side 'business firms' box of Figure 15.1; they do not cross its frame also known as the *production boundary*. Final transactions alone move out. In agriculture, a part of the crop of a year may be used as seed for the next year. It supplies, say, cotton to textile mills. Steel may be used to make tractors or cars. Thus, transactions in the box may take place within or between various sectors. However, flour, cloth, passenger cars, computers and a host of other things are sold for final consumption across the boundary. The two product types—intermediate and final— are closely linked in terms of quantity and quality. The linkage helps us to plan for the future output targets. Table 15.2 provides a simple two-sector input–output matrix where (A) represents agriculture, (I) industry and (F) final consumption of the households. Reading down the columns, we find that out of the total output valued at 14,000 in agriculture, the sector itself uses, say as seed, 2,000 or 1/7 of the total; 4,000 or 2/7 it sells to industry as raw materials; and the remaining 8,000 it distributes to the households as income. Likewise, the industry sells 1,500 or 3/40 of its total output of 20,000 to agriculture; 5,000 or 1/4 to self; and the remaining 13,500 it provides as income to the households. Row-wise we get the breakup of total output of each sector into intermediate products and final products. Thus, for agriculture, the division is 3,500 and 10,500, respectively; for industry, it is 9,000 and 11,000. The households sell factor services to the sectors valued at 8,000 + 13,500 = 21,500.

Table 15.2 *An imaginary input–output matrix (Rs. million)*

Category	Intermediate product		Final product (Households)	Total output
	Agriculture (A)	Industry (I)	(F)	(T)
Agriculture (A)	2,000	1,500	10,500	14,000
Industry (I)	4,000	5,000	11,000	20,000
Households (H)	8000	13,500	–	21,500
Total input (T)	14,000	20,000	21,500	55,500

The proportions of their respective outputs that the sectors sell to self or to each other are called *technical coefficients*. They have technological orientation and remain stable over the short run. The coefficients help generate sets of simultaneous equations to estimate input requirements, for a given change in final demand. To illustrate, the above example would give us the following set of equations.

$$A = \frac{1}{7}A + \frac{3}{40}I + F_A \qquad (15.1)$$

$$I = \frac{2}{7}A + \frac{1}{4}I + F_I \qquad (15.2)$$

Now, suppose we want to increase the output in agriculture by 2,175. The above equations allow us to find out how much more must be produced in agriculture and industry to achieve that target. The final demand for agricultural output will now be 10,500 + 2,175 = 12,675. Putting the values in the equations, we have:

$$A = \frac{1}{7}A + \frac{3}{40}I + 12,675 \qquad (15.3)$$

$$I = \frac{2}{7}A + \frac{1}{4}I + 11,000 \qquad (15.4)$$

These can be written as:

$$\frac{6}{7}A - \frac{3}{40}I - 12,675 = 0 \qquad (15.5)$$

$$-\frac{2}{7}A + \frac{3}{4}I - 11,000 = 0 \qquad (15.6)$$

Multiply (15.6) by 3:

$$-\frac{6}{7}A + \frac{9}{4}I - 33,000 = 0 \qquad (15.7)$$

Add (15.5) and (15.7):

$$\frac{87}{40}I - 45,675 = 0$$

$$I = 21,000$$
$$A = 16,620$$

Table 15.3 shows the final changes in the input–output matrix.

Table 15.3 *Input–output matrix after change in final demand for agricultural output (INR million)*

Category	Intermediate product		Final product (Households) (F)	Total output (T)
	Agriculture (A)	Industry (I)		
Agriculture (A)	2,375	1,575	12,675	16,625
Industry (I)	4,750	5,250	11,000	21,000
Households (H)	9,500	14,175	–	23,675
Total input (T)	16,625	21,000	23,675	61,300

The following exercises will help you check your understanding of input–output tables.

Exercise 15.1

Compare Tables 15.2 and 15.3 carefully. Note down their differences and state how a change in final demand for agricultural output has affected industry and income generation because of inter-sector linkages. Does the income of the households equal their expenditure?

Exercise 15.2

Use the data given in Table 15.1 and assume that due to recession in the economy the final demand for industry products falls by 1,000. Work out the impact of this change on the input–output matrix and construct a new table to record the changes.

BOX 15.1

Islam and Social Accounting

Until the beginning of the second half of the 20th century, what we know today as National Income Accounting was called Social Accounting in mainstream economics. The change was to make the name revealing of the content and coverage of the subject. In the mid-1960s, the UN introduced a standard set of National Income Accounts making it obligatory to use the format in reporting national economic data to its data reporting organs. Standardization facilitated comparisons of economic position and performance over time and across countries.

It is reported that from the early years of Islamic Caliphate in seventh century A.D, the collection classification and maintenance of records of data pertaining to the state revenue and expenditure under various heads were systematically maintained under the supervision of a *mahasib* (accountant/auditor). The process was expanded and refined over time and space until the close of the 15th century, when Muslims lost the year Columbus discovered America.

Since the early years of communal living, economies were small and simple private sector was of little significance. State enterprise dominated national economies. Thus, Social Accounting has presumably had its origin in earlier State craft.

Source: The pioneering mega work of Maulana Hifz-ur-Rehman Seoharvi in Urdu – *Economic system of Islam: An outline* (1936), p.107–9.

15.6 METHODS OF MEASURING NATIONAL PRODUCT

The most comprehensive description of the national economic performance is the gross national product or the GNP; it is the value of all *final* goods and services the labour and capital of a country working on its natural resources produce per unit of time, usually a year. The meaning of final goods and services we have already explained while indicating the distinction between intermediate and final products. In Table 15.2, for example, the final products of the two sectors add up to RM21,500 and constitute the value of GNP.

On the other hand, intermediate products having a higher value of RM34,000 are not part of the GNP. Broadly, three alternative methods are available for measuring the value of final product based on accounting for national expenditure, national output and national income.

> Value of output is distributed among factors of production as their income. This becomes their expenditure when they spend it on purchasing goods and services to satisfy their wants. Thus, in our closed model, the three—national expenditure, value of national output and national income—are equal.

15.6.1   Expenditure Method

The expenditure on final product measures the value of national output from the side of demand for it. The value of final output equals final expenditure. The relationship between national income and national expenditure is even more intimate as no income is generated in an economy unless there exists somewhere a corresponding expenditure. The two are but the sides of the same coin. The GNP is also the income that the household can spend for buying the final product. In a simple closed model of an economy that Figure 15.2 presents, you see that the three methods of measurement yield identical results.

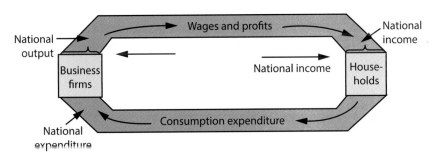

Figure 15.2 *Money flow: national output, national income and national expenditure*

The components of national expenditure or final demand are consumption and investment both private and public including net exports. We shall discuss them in detail in Section 15.9.

Apart from highlighting the nature and components of final demand, the expenditure method is important for another reason. There are certain components of GNP that are difficult to value otherwise. There is, for instance, no good way to put value on the services of the police force and the public administration. It is also difficult to measure, for example, the output value of domestic servants and shop assistants or teachers. Often the market puts no value on them. Their value is indirectly measured by the employers' expenditure on them.

15.6.2   Output Method

Writers often discuss output measure of national product together with its income measure as the value of national output equals national income: the receipts from the sale of output must accrue to someone as income. The buyers of bread are indirectly paying for services of the farmer, the miller, the baker and the retailer. In the income form, the payments can also be classified as wages and profits. We may begin with a discussion of national output method of GNP estimation.

A common way to estimate the final product is the value added or output method. This is also called the *origin of industry* method. The concept of value added implies the value each sector or industry adds to the raw materials or goods and services that it buys from other industries before passing on its products forward to other industries in the production chain. Consider an economy that has no other transactions at all except the following:

Agriculture sells wheat to a flour mill for	RM5,000
The mill sells flour to a bakery for	RM12,000
The bakery sells bread to households for	RM25,000

The sum of all these transactions is RM42,000. But it would be wrong to consider that amount as the value of total product the economy gets from the three sources. The grain worth RM5,000 the mill took from agriculture is an input and so is the flour the bakery got from the mill for RM12,000. The correct procedure must exclude these intermediate products from the GNP estimation as shown in Table 15.4. Here, we see that the value added by the three activities to the GNP is worth only RM30,000.

Table 15.4 *Value added by economic activities*

Source	Value added (RM)
Agriculture	5,000
Flour mill (12,000 – 5,000)	7,000
Bakery (25,000 – 7,000)	18,000
Final product	30,000

The upper part of Figure 15.2 shows GNP as annual flow of the *final* products from firms to the households. Households receive them as income for factor services they provide. In the lower segment, the income flows back as expenditure to the firms on the final goods and services they sell. The income method counts them at the point where they enter the household box, while the expenditure method counts them at the point where the same income enters the firms' box.

Exercise 15.3

The following are the only transactions that take place in an economy.

Aamir sells goods to Rana for	INR 5,000
Rana sells goods to Sana for	INR 8,000
Sana sells goods to final demand for	INR 3,000 and to Noor for INR 4,000
Noor sells goods to final demand for	INR 8,000

(i) What is the total national product at market price?
(ii) What is the value of intermediate goods?

15.6.3   Income Method

The income method looks at the value of the national product from another angle, i.e. in terms of the income accruing to the basic factors of production used in producing the national product. We need not discuss here on what constitutes the factors of production. We shall follow their broad conventional classification into labour and capital receiving wages and profits, respectively. Islam does not allow interest: it is merged into profits. This makes division of income into wages and profits fall in line with Islamic norms.

Labour can be thought of as consisting of all the human contribution to output whether by an employer or an employee. So defined, labour includes entrepreneurship. All the rest is capital; it covers land along with sub-soil resources like mines, and man-made instruments of production such as machines and railroads. All payments of income originating in the process of production can be attributed to these two categories of factors: labour receiving wages, salaries and commissions; and capital getting the remainder of the catch-all category, profit. Profit is what does not go to labour. Part of profit is usually transferred to individuals in the form of interest which Islam prohibits, or as dividends or rent, which Islam allows.

The broad classification of factors into labour and capital is meaningful because eventually, these basic categories of factors receive all income that production generates in an economy. Other payments the firms make in the course of production, such as buying raw materials, transportation, insurance, energy and other inputs do not generate any income, though they help generate income. The firms supplying the inputs in turn, pass on their net value added to the factors of production; labour and capital, that help produce them.

Not all profits of a firm need always be distributed. Still, profit that remains undistributed belong to the individuals to whom they initially accrue in the firms. Thus, the sum total of all factor payments must equal the sum total of value added by industry, which we have seen above equals the value of sale to final demand. The value added shown in Table 15.4 could, for example, be distributed as in Table 15.5.

For the equality of value of national output with national income the two tables demonstrate, we have to make two adjustments to arrive at net national income, the NNI.

Table 15.5 *Distribution of value added between production factors*

Value added		Shares of labour and capital	
Activity	Value added	Wages	Profit
1. Agriculture	5,000	4,000	1,000
2. Flour mill	7,000	4,000	3,000
3. Bakery	18,000	5,000	13,000
Total	30,000	13,000	17,000

Exercise 15.4

Compare from Table 15.5 the wage-profit ratio in agriculture with that of bakery. Can you explain the reasons for the difference in the two cases?

Capital consumption

If we eat all the wheat we grow in a year, we will not have seeds to grow wheat next year. The wheat we use as seeds are in the nature of capital. We must save that much wheat from the current output to continue production in future.

The physical capital, like buildings and plant and machinery, continually lose in value through wear and tear in the process of production; they are, so to say, unseeingly being absorbed by the goods and services they help to produce. This loss is recovered from the value of products as *depreciation*. Depreciation is the part of GNP set aside to maintain the productive capacity of the economy. It is usually shown as *capital consumption* in the national income accounts. It is difficult to keep record of national capital assets and estimate depreciation for each year for aggregative purposes. Therefore, depreciation is often estimated as a percentage of the GNP, say 10%. GNP minus capital consumption is the net national product, the NNP.

Market price versus factor cost

Unless mentioned otherwise, GNP is the value of goods and services expressed in *market* prices. Market prices of many commodities, however, include taxes the government imposes on their production, sale or export. These are *indirect taxes* as they are realized from the people not as a direct obligation, like income tax, but through addition by sellers to product prices. Such taxes cause difference between the market price of goods the buyers pay and the sellers of goods receive. Their receipts net of indirect taxes is the amount they can pay to the factors of production.

Governments do not affect the market prices of products by imposing indirect taxes alone; they often grant subsidies also that make it possible to sell goods at prices lower than their factor cost. Subsidies may be treated as negative indirect taxes; they flow in the reverse direction. In most economies, there is a mix of indirect taxes and subsidies. Hence, national product at market prices will be greater than at factor costs if indirect taxes are more than subsidies and vice versa.

Indirect taxes minus subsidies can be viewed as a special kind of transfer payments. They do not directly affect like any transfer payment the total national income or the physical product of the basic factors. They are unlike other transfer payments in that they cross the production boundary. But the value of national product remains the same because they cross the boundary *twice*. First, they go in and raise the price of the product they are added to. They cross the boundary again on their way out to the treasury. Thus, they leave the output value unaffected. Figure 15.3 illustrates the point. Here, the position before tax is that the firms produce 500 units of the commodity. The demand and supply forces clear the market at a price of 10 ringgit a piece. The sales give firms net revenue of RM5,000. This amount is received by the households as income which they, we assume, spent all to buy the commodity. Thus, the value of output = National income = National expenditure = RM5,000.

Now, suppose the government had already imposed a 10% tax on the sale of the commodity. Other things remaining the same, the tax enters the production boundary and raises the price of the commodity by 10%, i.e. to RM11 a unit. At this higher price, the households with their RM5,000 will be able to purchase 5,000/11 = 454 units of the commodity. From the receipts (RM5,000) the firms will pay 10% or RM500 to the government. Taxes cross the boundary a second time. With the tax money the government would buy 500/11 or 46 units of the commodity. The market is cleared again despite a rise in price: 454 + 46 = 500 units. The price rise through taxation has made the people poorer in real terms to let the government have resources for welfare works (or war).

> The value of output is distributed as income to factors of production but its market value is higher than factor cost because government imposes taxes for income to perform its duties. The sellers add the taxes to the cost of the commodity. Thus, the value of output at market becomes higher.

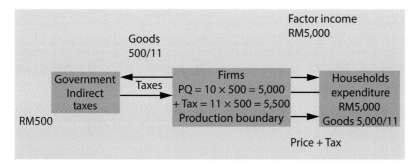

Figure 15.3 *Indirect taxes cross the boundary twice, raise prices and divide physical output*

GNP at market price is in most cases greater than GNP at factor cost. From the GNP at market prices, we have to take out capital consumption and indirect taxes minus subsidies to arrive at the net national product at factor cost or the net national income (NNI). Table 15.6 illustrates the adjustments using the data from Malaysia.

Table 15.6 *GNP and National Income of Malaysia in 2000 (RM million)*

Gross national product (at market price)	**118,780**
Less:	
Capital consumption (10% of GNP)	11,878
Equals: Net national product	**106,902**
Less:	
Indirect taxes minus subsidies	18,017
Net national product (income) at factor cost	**88,885**

Source: Bank Negara Malaysia, Annual Report 2000

Exercise 15.5

If in Table 15.6 capital consumption is measured at 20% of the output and indirect taxes constitute another 5% of the GNP, find (a) net national product and (b) national product at factor cost.

15.7   PERSONAL AND DISPOSABLE INCOMES

The money one gets annually from contribution to production is not all available to spend. For example, taxes reduce incomes for spending.

National income is a measure of what a country gets from the current production of goods and services. However, it may be useful to know for some purposes the income *persons* receive in an economy during the accounting period. Personal income is the measure of income person receives irrespective of the source. When we take out personal tax payments from personal income we obtain disposable or after tax personal income.

To get from national income at factor cost to personal income variants, we subtract elements of national income that are not received by persons and add the income they receive from sources other than current production of goods and services.

Table 15.7 shows the necessary adjustments in the case of Malaysia for year 2001, based on data provided by Bank Negara Malaysia's Annual Report, 2002.

Table 15.7 *Personal income and personal disposable income for Malaysia, 2001 (RM billion)*

Gross national product at current price	**193.4**
Less: Depreciation 10% (assumed)	19.3
Net national product	**174.1**
Less: Indirect taxes	
Export duties	0.9
Import duties	3.2
Excise duties	4.1
Sales tax	7.4
Service tax	1.9
Others	1.9
	19.4
National income at factor cost	**154.7**
Less: Direct taxes	
Companies	20.8
Petroleum	9.9
Cooperatives	0.1
Taxes on income	30.8
Real property gain tax	0.2
Stamp duty	1.7
Others	0.8
Taxes on property	2.7
	33.5
	121.2
Add:	
Debt service charges	9.6
Pensions and gratuities	4.7
Other grants and transfers	13.6
Subsidies	4.5
	32.4
Personal income	**153.6**
Less: Personal income tax	9.4
Personal disposable income	**144.2**

The advantage of the output–income equality is that even if the estimators cannot obtain data on the net output (value added) of each industry, they may be able to obtain data at the national level of the total wages and other incomes people received. For example, income tax returns and land revenue records may help in this matter. The expenditure method can also provide information on some items not covered by output or income methods. Spending on defence is one example.

15.8   SOME SPECIAL TRANSACTIONS

We have noted earlier that transactions in an economy may sometimes be difficult to identify as transfer payments, intermediate products or final expenditures though broad criteria are quite clear. A few cases are discussed below.

15.8.1   Sale of Second-hand Goods

National product is the value of the flow of goods and services produced in an economy over a span of time. The definition implies that we are dealing with economic activities of a country that took place during the *current* year, not in earlier periods. As such, a whole class of transactions must stay outside the estimation process irrespective of the consideration whether they belong to the productive or unproductive category. These are the transactions that relate solely to the transfer of capital assets from one owner to another.

For example, if you sell your car of year 2000 make to a friend for RM40,000 in 2007, the amount should not be added to the national product of the year for it does not match any addition to the current flow of goods and services. The car had already been counted once when it was produced; its inclusion in the GNP of any subsequent year would involve double counting. No country can become richer by selling its existing assets back and forth among its nationals. Transactions in second-hand goods only bring about changes in the assets and liabilities sides of the individual balance sheets. This last point brings us to another category of transactions which is discussed in the following section.

15.8.2   Interest on Public Debt

Interests people pay on internal debt are the income of the creditor. National income is not reduced. What if interests were paid to foreigners on money borrowed from them?

Factor payments made by the government do not include as a standard practice the interest it pays on public debt the nationals hold. The payment is not counted in measuring the national income. The reason for exclusion is that it constitutes a *transfer* of income from one set of people, the tax payers, to another set of people, the bond holders, in the economy. There is no corresponding real flow of goods and services, say from government buildings or other capital assets matching the payments.

Such a problem does not arise in the case of business interest as the payments are offset by a corresponding reduction in business profits; interest plus profit may be regarded as measuring the contribution of capital. The contradiction in the conventional treatment of public and private capital assets is obvious. (How?)

15.8.3 Stock Market Transactions

Financial activities such as sale of bonds and shares on stock markets are another class of transactions which obviously cannot form part of national product; it would be easy to raise national product manifold by simply passing bonds and shares back and forth at an ever increasing pace. For that reason, a rise or fall in the capitalization of the stock market is of little consequence to the volume of physical assets or to their productive potential in an economy. Islam does not regard money by itself as productive and calls for the abolition of interest on borrowings. Even if interest exists in the society, Islam would insist on its merger with profit for the GNP estimates.

However, it must be mentioned that the profit dealers make in the trade of second-hand goods such as cars or houses during the accounting year would form part of the national product for providing retailer services. The case of stock market transactions can be a questionable matter, for profits and losses here constitute a zero sum game.

15.9 DOMESTIC VERSUS NATIONAL PRODUCT

Our discussion so far remained confined to the drawing of the production boundary with reference to, which of the economic activities would lie within it. However, there is another question that calls for attention in settling the boundary issue: *whose* activities it would contain? In particular, we may talk either of (i) the production taking place on a geo-political area, i.e. within the *domestic territory* of a country irrespective of the nationality of the people involved; or we may talk of (ii) the production activities attributable to the *nationals* of a country irrespective of whether such activities are taking place within or outside the territory. In other words, a distinction has to be made between the *domestic* product and the *national* product.

> Domestic product refers to what is produced within the national boundaries of a country irrespective of who produces it—nationals or foreigners.

Domestic product (gross or net) refers to what is produced within a country: who produces it is immaterial. On the other hand, national product (gross or net) is what the nationals of a country produce; where they produce it—within or outside the country (including the return on assets they own)—does not matter. In countries where a large part of the capital is owned by the foreigners such as in oil-rich West-Asia, foreigners may be making substantial contribution to the domestic product. But, as much of this contribution does not enter the national product of these countries, the difference between their national product and domestic product could be large and negative. This difference (GNP – GDP) is called the *net property income from abroad* and could of course be positive or negative. The economies of Pakistan and Malaysia since the year 2002 presented in Table 15.8 is an interesting contrast on the point.

Notice that the GNP of Pakistan has been greater than her GDP during the period, the excess averaging around 2% a year. In contrast, Malaysia's GNP has all along been lower, the deficit on an average being about 5% a year.

Table 15.8 *Difference between GNP and GDP of Pakistan and Malaysia compared (data at current prices)*

Year	Pakistan (PKR billion)			Malaysia (RM billion)		
	GNP	GDP	GNP – GDP	GNP	GDP	GNP – GDP
2002	4,170	4146	+ 24	337	362	– 25
2003	4,686	4534	+ 152	373	395	– 22
2004	5,375	5251	+ 124	426	450	– 24
2005 F	6,257	6123	+ 134	471	495	– 24
2006 R	7,279	7129	+ 150	527	546	– 19
2007 P	8,387	8227	+ 160	568	590	– 22
Mean	6,026	5902	+ 124	450	473	– 23
% of GNP			+ 2.1			– 5.1

Source: National Economic Accounts of Pakistan and Bank Negara Malaysia's Annual Report, 2006.

Note: F stands for final, R for revised and P for provisional estimates.

15.10 COMPOSITION OF FINAL OUTPUT

15.10.1 The Expenditure Side

Final output is what an economy obtains in the end of all economic activity. The remaining output, i.e. the 'intermediate product' is a means for achieving that end. We have seen that the value of final output is received as income by the households in payments for the services they provide. As indicated earlier, they spend this income for buying the same output that they helped produce and their expenditure becomes a measure of its value. Thus, the circular flow of economic activity, as shown in Figure 15.2, assumes different names—value of output, national income or national expenditure depending on the point where we wish to look at it. The three (value of output, national income or national expenditure) are obviously equal representing the same thing, the outcome of a nation's economic activity. Because of their basic equality, the three are often represented by a common symbol, Y.

It follows that we can describe the composition of the final output either from the income side or from the expenditure side. If we look at it from the *expenditure* side, Y has two main components: (i) consumption (C) and (ii) investment (I). Consumption is that part of the national output which is used up for its own sake, e.g. food, clothing, shelter, medicines and education that people buy day and night. Investment, on the other hand, is what is not consumed out of the final product but is used to help production in future. Thus, we have a basic identity from the expenditure side constituting the value of output.

$$Y = C + I \tag{15.8}$$

A classification of the final product along these lines is often referred to in the world or country statistical tables as the *use of resources*. The resources under reference are not the labour time, raw materials, or machines and so on used up completely or partially in the process of production but the *final output* of the economy.

> What we produce (Y) is partly consumed (C) and partly invested (I) to continue and increase production.

Consumption

Bulk of the national expenditure is on consumption even as its proportion in the aggregate expenditure, called *propensity to consume*, tends to decline as output in an economy grows over the years. Consumption is divided into two parts: (i) private and (ii) public. Table 15.9 gives us the consumption in Malaysia for selected years.

Table 15.9 *Aggregate consumption (RM billion)*

Year	1995	2005
Private consumption	106.6	215.9
Public consumption	27.5	64.1
Aggregate consumption (A)	134.1	280.0
GNP (B)	212.1	471.3
(A) as % of (B)	63.2	59.4

Source: Bank Negara Malaysia's Annual Reports, 1999 and 2006.

The reason for dividing aggregate consumption into two broad categories (public and private) is that their size and components are determined by very different forces, and transactions in national accounts have to be arranged in classifications such that they would enable the economists to understand the forces shaping the course of an economy. Private consumption is the expenditure of the households on items such as food, clothing, shelter and lighting; the taste of individuals, their incomes and the relative prices of the products they purchase are its main determinants. On the other hand, public consumption refers to the government expenditure for providing education, health care, defence, law and order, justice and so on to the people. The level and pattern of public expenditure on such heads is determined by socio-political considerations, need and extent of directing the course of economic events in times of crisis, and resource constraint.

1. **Private consumption**: Private consumption covers the expenditure of people in their personal capacity on products for *current* use. These products may include: (i) durable goods, (ii) non-durable goods and (iii) services. Of these *durables* like television sets, automobiles, fridges and washing machines raise some problems. It might be argued that such goods should be included in investment because they do not meet the criterion of current use in the hands of the consumers. But if the durables mentioned here were treated as part of investment, not of consumption, they would have to be counted as additions to national wealth. However, the difficulty is that they do not, as they cannot, help create wealth in future like investment goods. One way of including them in consumption is that we spread the cost of a durable over its useful years and include the average value so obtained each time in current consumption. But in practice, this would raise many difficulties. To avoid complications, it is accepted to include as an accounting convention the entire value of a durable in the consumption of the year of its acquisition.

One important exception to the convention is the purchase of new residential houses. These are excluded altogether from private consumption and are counted as part of investment of the economy like all other new buildings such as those purchased by real estate companies or public authorities. The purchase of buildings not constructed in the current year only changes their ownership; they had already been counted in national output the year they were constructed. They are not an addition to the current production. The three components of private consumption expenditure behave very differently during the economic downturns. Table 15.10 provides the per cent change in consumption expenditure of the US economy during the Great Depression 1929–1932 and also the value of output, national income or national expenditure for a longer period (1929–1965) that includes the depression. Calculations are based on constant prices (1958 = 100). Notice that during the Depression, aggregate consumption declined by 18% but expenditure on durables went down by 48% and on services slightly less, i.e. by 46%; non-durables remained relatively sticky, falling by 19% only. During 1929–1965 also the relative positions of the components did not change, the rise in expenditure on durables being the highest. The reason is that people can more readily postpone the purchase of durables in bad times when incomes fall and unemployment spreads: an old car can do for another year, purchase of furniture and appliances can be delayed. But expenditure on food, medicine and rent payments cannot be much curtailed even if one may have to liquidate assets or resort to borrowings.

Durables have special treatment in estimating consumption.

Table 15.10 *Behaviour of consumption expenditure in the US*

Item	Percentage change	
	1929–1932	1929–1965
Aggregate consumption	−18	+ 182
Durable goods	−48	+ 302
Non-durable goods	−19	+ 156
Services	−46	+ 181

Source: Schultze C.L. (1970), *National Income Analysis*, 2nd edn., Prentice Hall (Indian Reprint), p. 29.

2. **Government or public consumption**: Public consumption, as noted earlier, is a category of final expenditure on national product. Like private consumption, it too includes only *current* spending on goods and services. As such, it does not include (i) investment and (ii) transfer payments made by public authorities. Capital formation undertaken by the government agencies such as the construction of roads, school buildings or dams is included in public investment. Transfer payments like interest on public debt, current grants to persons or local authorities plus subsidies and capital grants that make part of public expenditure are excluded from public consumption since such payment flows do not have a corresponding output flow in the economy. Thus, statements like the one that government expenditure constitutes 35% of the national income to emphasize the burden of administration on the economy would be grossly misleading if transfer payments are brought into reckoning; transfer payments do not divert goods and services to public authorities. Nevertheless, high levels of defence expenditure are invariably at the expense of civilian consumption and well-being.

Investment

Unlike consumption, investment is that part of final output which consists of goods and services that are used up not in one accounting period, a year, but over a number of years. Investment is a means of adding to the stock of national wealth, i.e. to its capacity to produce more incomes and satisfactions in the years ahead. It is important to distinguish between *income* and *wealth*. Income is the current *flow* of goods and services while wealth of a nation is the *stock* of capital that enables the creation of this flow. The distinction between flows and stocks is, in fact, among the most important ones in economic analysis and assumes significance in resolving many problems. Thus, investment is the portion of current output that adds to the stock of existing capital for raising the potential income flow of the economy in future. Potential income is what an economy is capable of producing; actual income that it generates annually may fall short of the potential for a variety of reasons. (For a comparison of actual and potential GNP versions, see Glossary.)

> What an economy can produce may be different from what it is producing.

It is possible for a nation, like an individual, to have an increase in its wealth without a sacrifice of current consumption in the form of a windfall such as the discovery of an oil or gas field. Such windfall additions to wealth are ignored in defining the part of current output which is employed as investment; it is by definition the part of output that is not consumed. It is the part of output used to produce plant, equipment, houses and other instruments of production. In summary, it provides *capital goods in real terms* which when combined with skilled labour force and technological progress may enable us to have abundance of production to reduce poverty and raise living standards.

Total gross investment serves two purposes: Each year part of the national capital is lost in the act of producing current output and new methods of production make some existing equipment obsolete. As such, each year new plant and machinery must be produced and installed merely to *maintain* the existing stock of capital, i.e. to make up its depletion; the remaining investment represents a net addition to capital stock of the economy. As it is very difficult to measure depreciation, it is a convention to show investment in gross figures. Investment has three main components:

- Gross domestic capital formation,
- Changes in inventories, and
- Export minus imports.

Gross domestic capital formation (GDCF) is investment made at home, i.e. within the political boundaries of a country. It consists of only long-lasting capital goods such as newly made plant and machinery; buildings constructed or under construction; hence the name fixed capital. Obviously, fixed capital does not cover items such as stock of raw material, semi-manufactured goods and finished products. These three elements put together are called inventories. From the end year inventories, we deduct the beginning year inventories. The balance, positive or negative, measures the change in inventories which forms part of current year investment.

Change in inventories is kept distinct from changes in fixed inventories for the reason that what motives of investing in each case are not the same. The two have different sorts of uses and their impact on the economy is also different. Generally, business firms engage in fixed capital formation if the future demand for the goods produced looks attractive, i.e. profitable. It is based on intention. Changes in the inventory may be random; forced and entirely unintentional.

Exports minus imports (X – M) is the third and final component of investment. It can be a positive or negative value. Exports measure the expenditure foreigners make on the purchase of our goods and services; imports on the other hand are the expenditure we incur on purchasing what others produce. However, goods constitute only the *visible* portion of this item in the sense that we can see them being loaded into and unloaded from cargo ships and planes at our ports. But there is an *invisible* part as well which service constitute. Invisible exports include expenditure of foreigners in our country on tourism, embassies, education, medical treatment, investment, aid and so on. Invisible imports add up to what we have to pay for such items to foreigners. All sorts of exports and imports (visible or invisible) are recorded in a country's balance of payments. The balance could be in its favour or against it. If favourable it increases current domestic capital formation; the effect is opposite if negative. Exports minus imports are taken as ($\pm$) net investment abroad. Table 15.11 gives the summary description of the GNP components from the expenditure side using Malaysian data for the year 2005. The expenditure equations that follow from the table are:

$$C = C_P + C_G \tag{15.9}$$
$$I = GDCF + (X - M) \tag{15.10}$$
$$Y = C_P + C_G + GDCF + (X - M) \tag{15.11}$$

Equation 15.11 can also be written as:

$$Y = C + GDCF + G + (X - M) \tag{15.12}$$

Where, $C = C_P$ and $G = C_G$.

Table 15.11 *Components of Malaysia's GNP, 2005 (RM billion)*

Consumption			
Private	215.9	C_P	
Public	64.1	C_G	
		280.0 = C	
Fixed investment	44.4	I_P	
Private	54.6	I_G	
Public	99.0	DFCF	
Change in inventories	−0.2	I_N	
		98.8 GDCF	+
Export	611.1	X	
Import	−494.5	M	+
Others	−23.9	M	
		92.7 (X − M)	
Investment		91.5 = I	
GNP by demand aggregate		471.5 = Y	

Source: Bank Negara Malaysia's Annual Report, 2006, Table A.4.

15.10.2 The Income Side

Let us now have a brief look at the estimation of the GNP (Y) from the income side. Income that people receive has two basic uses: It may be consumed (C) or saved (S) or may be divided between the two. Thus, in symbols we have another identity:

$$Y = C + S \tag{15.13}$$

Part of income may be consumed and part of it may be saved. Thus, consumption plus savings must exhaust income.

Looking at the GNP as income received and identifying its components is important not only from the viewpoint for completing the other side of the production accounts, but it also has much wider significance for macroeconomic analysis. For instance, the topic of income inequalities within and among nations is, among others, the most worrisome issue that confronts the world today as never before. The supply or income side of macroanalysis has countless economic, political and social dimensions.

One statistical concept most commonly used with reference to economic inequalities, as well as in connection with other economic issues, is the share of wages in national income as distinct from the share of profits. The concept is of much significance for the traditional microeconomic analysis of the production process in the context of rewarding the basic factors of production—land, labour and capital. According to one version of conventional theory, these factors earn respectively rents, wages (and salaries) and profits (plus interest). In Figure 15.2, what we have shown as payment for factor services is the sum of these three incomes.

Income tax may reduce both savings and consumption.

The income side valuation of the national product includes the following items: wages and salaries (compensation of employees); distributed profits (Y_H), direct taxes paid by firms (T_F), direct taxes paid by households (T_H), depreciation plus undistributed profits (or savings) of firms (S_F) and net indirect taxes (indirect taxes minus subsidies) (T_I). Thus, from the income side we have the gross national product valued at market prices:

$$GNP = Y_H + T_F + T_H + T_I + S_F \tag{15.14}$$

Household disposable income may have two components: consumption and savings. Thus,

$$Y_H = C_H + S_H \tag{15.15}$$

Taxes constitute the income of the government; it may be consumed but part of it may also be saved. We have:

$$Y_G = T_F + T_H + T_I$$
$$= C_G + S_G \tag{15.16}$$

Combining (2.14), (2.15) and (2.16) we get:

$$GNP = C_H + C_G + S_H + S_F + S_G \tag{15.17}$$

Adding up we have:

$$GNP = C + S; \tag{15.13}$$

The same as given in Table 15.11

The proportion of savings (S) in national income is called *propensity to save*, and increases over the years as an economy grows.

It may be noted that the two sides of the national production account (at market prices) as shown in Table 15.12 are equal. We shall later see that it is an important result.

Table 15.12 *National production account summary*

National income		National expenditure
C + S	=	C + I
Therefore,	S = I	is an important result

Exercise 15.6

Savings and investments are shown to be equal in Table 15.12. But savers and investors are largely different groups of people and their motives are also not the same. How can savings and investment always be equal then?

Savings versus hoarding

Here, we must make a distinction between hoarding of wealth and savings. To be sure, hoardings and savings are both leakages from the income stream in an economy. The difference is that savings are backed with intention to invest for earning a return to augment future income. The leakage is expected to return to the stream thus maintaining, if not enhancing, its level. Hoarding, on the other hand, is meant to merely have the pleasure of amassing wealth and thus remains a leakage from the income stream. We know that all savings do not instantly come back to the income stream: there is invariably a time interval between savings and their eventual investment. Savings cannot be distinguished from hoardings objectively with reference to intention. Arbitrarily, we may say that if an amount of money stays with the saver for over a year, it may be regarded as hoarding. This seems to be the position in Islam.

> Savings and hoarding are both leakages from the income stream. Intention makes the difference. Savings are intended to put back an investment into the income stream, while hoardings are not. Thus, Islam encourages savings but condemns hoarding.

15.11   MEASUREMENT OF GNP IN DEVELOPING COUNTRIES

Measuring national income in any circumstance is not easy but it presents additional problems in most developing economies including the Organization of the Islamic Conference (OIC) members. We list below some of the major difficulties in measurement of GNP in their case.

In many developing countries in Asia and Africa, there still exists a large sector where money is not used in economic transactions; the barter system or the use of commodity money, usually grain, still prevails. It is very difficult to put for accounting a money valuation on such transactions.

Many economic activities like cooking of food, washing and stitching of clothes, constructing one's own house, sowing and reaping crops, nursing of the babies and the sick, and so on absorb millions of labour hours year after year but escape the accounting net because they carry no price tags. Commercialization of many activities has not yet taken place in the developing countries.

Even in manufacturing, both in towns and villages, many goods and services are produced in the unorganized sectors where no systematic records of transactions are kept, sometimes deliberately to bypass the taxation laws.

Many countries are poor in data collection and its publication. They seldom care to supply the required information to international organizations like the World Bank, the IMF or the UNDP. In the publications of these institutions, one often comes across blank rows for such countries.

Adam Smith, the writer of *The Theory of Moral Sentiment* in 1758, did not take long to leave his ivory tower and imbibe the realities of life to give the final shape to his ideas in his *Wealth of Nations*. Some lament that the philosopher killed morality to invent economics.

BOX 15.2

Why Are We Rich and They So Poor?

The above is the title of an article published in the West—a pertinent question. There is no dearth of writings in the literature answering this question and the reasons listed are mostly valid. Some writers lament that Muslims remain behind because they failed to develop the institutions, especially corporate form of business organization, because of their faith. Let it be what it is, but the question: why are we rich and they so poor misses one crucial reason to mention: the centuries long exploitation of the now developing economies by their imperialist rulers—has continued unabated even after they became independent during the decades after the WW2. Table 15.13 provides a glimpse of this exploitation. Comparison of Europe with the third-world and of UK with undivided India is of special interest.

Table 15.13 *Exploitation of nations for wealth of nations: Colonial plunder—1750–1900; per cent share of world manufacturing output*

Region	Country	Year				
		1750	1800	1830	1860	1900
Europe		23.2	28.1	34.2	53.2	62.0
	Russia	(5.0)	(5.6)	(5.6)	(7.0)	(8.8)
	UK	(1.9)	(4.3)	(9.5)	(19.9)	(18.5)
USA		0.1	0.8	2.4	7.2	23.6
Third World		73.0	67.7	60.5	36.6	11.0
	Undivided India	(24.5)	(19.7)	(17.6)	(8.6)	(1.7)

Source: Paul Kennedy, (1987) The rise and fall of great powers, New York: Random House.
(Produced from Prof. Khursid Ahmad's IDB/IRTI lecture, PowerPoint 2007 slides)

Smith could visualize great inventions and innovations on the way and found capital accumulation growing fast. The *nature and causes* of this accumulation escaped his attention. He just saw industrial revolution knocking at the door of England. He is known for his optimism flowing not from his *moral sentiment* but from his acumen as a system builder: he is the architect of capitalism.

Summary

- Countless transactions take place in an economy daily. To understand and analyze the way an economy operates we have to sort out transactions relevant to our objectives and classify them in some summary form. The classification helps us provide the system for National Income Accounting.

- The UN has standardized the format for presentation of National Income Accounts with a view to achieve uniformity across nations in data reporting.

- National income accounts aim at providing data on economic aggregates like consumption, savings and investment to make us understand and analyze the workings of an economy; to know about its performance concerning the pace of growth, distribution of income, sector contributions, employment patterns, price level changes, etc.to help formulate policies.

- Gross national product or the GNP is the key variable to measure. But all transactions taking place in an economy are not productive in the sense that they all do not contribute to national product. Donations, charities, gifts and the like are merely *transfer payments*. They are simply unproductive and stand out of the GNP estimation.

- To understand the basic macroeconomic variables and their mutual linkages, we usually start with a simple two-sector closed model with business firms on one hand and households on the other. In physical terms, households supply inputs—materials, tools and labour hours—to the firms which the firms then use to produce goods—bread, butter, haircuts, guns, etc. The goods become available to households in payment for the inputs supplied.

- But transactions in physical terms are cumbersome to calculate aggregate output (Q). It is difficult to add apples and oranges. A common denominator is needed. Money is that denominator and puts value on goods and services in terms of price (P). All PQs can be easily added to have the value of national product in terms of money.

- Thus, there are two types of flow circulating between firms and households: the flow of real goods and services and the other of their money values moving in opposite directions as shown in Figure 15.1. The value of national product is received by the households as payment for the inputs supplied.

- All transactions, even when related to production, do not enter the measurement of national product. Many of these transactions take place among the producers within the box of business firms; they do not cross its frame known as the *production boundary*. For example, agriculture retains a part of say the wheat crop to be used as seed for the next harvest; it sells some wheat to the flour mills who sell a part of the output to bakeries. Bakeries sell their products to the households. Of course, agriculture and flour mills too can sell parts of their output to the households directly. The point is that in general, the products that stay within the boundary are intermediate products and those that cross it constitute final products. Only the latter are counted for estimating the GNP.

- The distinction between intermediate and final products gives rise to input–output tables. The proportions of a sector's output needed internally or by other sectors for production are called *technical coefficients*. The coefficients signify sector linkages and remain fairly stable in the short-run. Input–output tables have many important uses, especially in the area of economic planning.

- The fact of money flow being circular between firms and households is of much help in measuring the value of national product and the verification of the estimate. The method of measurement would depend on the point where we decide to look at this flow. When it is entering the household box it is being received as income, when it is entering the firms' box it is *expenditure* on their products and when it is leaving the same box it is the value of final output (Figure 15.2). As such, there are three methods for measuring the GNP: expenditure method, output method and income method with necessary adjustments; the three yield identical results.

- People and the government may both incur expenditure either on buying consumption goods or investment goods. The latter include also the net foreign investment. From the expenditure side, we have a basic identity: $Y = C + I$. The output method leaves out intermediate products and adds up the value added to the intermediate goods bought from other sectors of the economy. For some of the services it takes what employers spend on hiring them as the value of their contribution to output. Finally, the income method adds up all incomes people receive from business or employment net of transfer payments and receipts obtained within the production boundary to avoid double counting. Income got may either be consumed or saved. Thus, on the income side too we have an identity, that is, $Y = C + S$.

- We have numerous total product concepts. It is difficult to list them all. However, a few guiding principles may be stated. If we take out depreciation from gross national concepts, we get their net versions. If net indirect taxes are added to the aggregates at factor cost we get the corresponding values at market price. Finally, if we add net income from abroad to national versions we get the corresponding domestic figures.

Glossary

Factor cost The money value of output produced each year is distributed among the participating factors of production as their remuneration. The sum of what the factors so receive is called the value of GNP at factor cost. It is the sum of what people receive from current production as wages, interest, rent and profit in an economy.

Final demand The value of that part of output which is meant to satisfy directly the needs of ultimate consumers is called the final demand of the economy for production.

Gross domestic capital formation For maintaining and enhancing the growth rate in an economy, addition to its stock of capital goods is essential. In addition, the economy must replace whatever capital it has currently used up in the process of production. Since it is difficult to measure the second component, we take as gross (not net) capital formation the additions to the beginning year capital stock.

Intermediate products   The goods and services that are all used up in producing the final output constitute intermediate products. They do not cross the production boundary.

National income accounts   National income and expenditure are opposite of one another but basically the two are equal in an economy. This allows us to present the data in the form of commercial accounts maintained under the double entry system. Each transaction is recorded on opposite side in the giver and the receiver accounts. National income accounting has developed as a separate subject. A standard set of national income accounts has been developed by the UN. Each country is required to present its national income statistics in the given format each year. This has helped the consolidation and standardization of national income statistics for global use.

Potential GNP   It is the 'full employment' level of gross national product. Actual GNP tends to fall short of an economy's potential. However, we know that full employment does not mean zero per cent unemployment. Workers in the process of changing jobs may remain unemployed for a while or declining industries may be laying off workers even in the best of times. Thus, a margin of 3 to 4% unemployment of workers is usually ignored and economy is taken as operating at full employment. In addition, potential GNP is also related to the physical production capacity of an economy. If around 97% of labour force in an economy is at work and over 90% of its productive machinery is being used, the economy is considered as producing to its full potential. The gap between the actal and potential GNPs of an economy is a measure of a nation's economic prosperity and performance. The gap assumes importance as a measure of prosperity during periods of recession an economy experiences; the wider is the gap greater is the loss of prosperity and vice versa.

Price level   It is the average of all prices in an economy at a point of time usually a year with reference to a base assumed as equal to 100. Price index numbers is the technique used to measure price level and changes therein.

Production boundary   It is an analytical imaginary tool that separates the production and use of intermediate goods from the final demand (output). Intermediate goods do not cross the boundary. What moves out of the boundary is called final output. The distinction has importance in input–output analysis and economic planning.

Transfer payments   Payments which people make to others without receiving any compensation in money or real terms are called transfer payments. They are not counted in the national income as there is no real flow matching them in the economy.

Value added   If we take out from the output of a firm the value of what it took from others to produce the product, the remainder will be the value added by the firm in the process of production.

Concepts for Review

- Capital consumption
- Change in stocks
- Disposable income
- Domestic fixed capital formation
- Domestic product
- Factor cost
- Final demand
- Input–output tables
- Intermediate products
- Macroeconomic identities
- Money flow
- National income accounts
- National product

- National savings
- Net income from abroad
- Net indirect taxes
- Personal income
- Production boundary
- Propensity to consume
- Propensity to save
- Public consumption
- Real flow
- Technical coefficients
- Transfer payments
- Value added

Case Study   15.1

Components of Malaysian GNP

The 2007 forecast values for Malaysia as per Bank Negara Malaysia's Annual Report in billion ringgit at constant prices were approximately GDP = 590; Consumption = 335; Investments = 126; Change in stocks = 2; Exports = 726; Imports = 595 and Net factor payments abroad = 22.

Case Questions

1. Will it be correct to say that the forecast for the 2007 GNP of the country must have been RM568 billion? Make an explanatory table to support your answer.
2. Find the gross domestic capital formation (GDCF) forecast for the year.
3. Is the balance of trade negative? Justify your answer.

Test Questions

15.1 (a) Define the term gross national product (GNP). Explain what sort of transaction is not included in the estimation of the GNP.

(b) What do you understand by the term national income? Why is it not equal to GNP?

(c) Distinguish between personal income and disposable income. Explain the importance of the distinction.

15.2 What do you understand by the term transfer payments? In what ways do transfer payments differ from intermediate products? Explain.

15.3   The following Table 15.14 is an imaginary input–output table. Find the technical coefficients and work out the changes and show them in a new table if the final demand is to increase by 40 in industry A. Does factor cost rise from 205 to 252? Verify.

Table 15.14 *Input–output matrix*

Category	Intermediate product		Final product (Households) F	Total output (T)
	Industry A	Industry B		
Industry A	10	30	60	100
Industry B	10	45	145	200
Households (H)	80	125	–	205
Total input (T)	100	200	205	505

15.4   In the economies (a) and (b) below, only the given transactions take place. Indicate the value of national product and find the value added by industry of origin. Assume there is no change in stocks.
   (a)   Rafiq sells for INR 6,000 to Noor
         Noor sells for INR 10,000 to Ilyas
         Ilyas sells for INR 120,000 to household consumption
   (b)   A sells for Riyal 500 to B and for Riyal 500 to C
         B sells for Riyal 800 to C and for Riyal 200 to household consumption
         C sells for Riyal 20,000 to final consumption
15.5   Salim is a dealer in watches. He goes to Switzerland on a holiday. He spends INR 25,000 there on hotel accommodation and another INR 10,000 on food and travel. He also buys 200 new watches for INR 20,000. He pays 10% import duty on the watches at the airport when he returns to India. He sells them for INR 500 a piece.
   (a)   Indicate the direct effect of all these transactions on the GNP at market price.
   (b)   What would be the effect if he gives away 10 of the watches as gifts to his relatives and 20 remained in stocks at the end of the accounting period?
15.6   Find the GNP and private consumption, if in terms of the symbols used in this chapter we have:
         $I = 150$; $S_H = 100$; $S_F = 50$; and $Y_H = 850$.
15.7   (a)   If GNP = 1000; $Y_H = 900$ and $S_H = 100$, what is the investment (I)? Is your answer $I = 20$?
   (b)   Firms make no savings and pay no taxes but CG = 25,000. After spending on private consumption and paying taxes ($T_H = 35,000$), households have $S_H = 5,000$. What is investment (I)? Is it 17,000?
15.8   Given below is information for an economy in million units of money. Find: (a) personal income, (b) disposable income, and (c) personal savings. What is the rate of personal savings in the economy?

National income	2,450
Corporate profit	253
Social security contributions	165
Zakat transfers	375
Interest adjustments	106
Dividends	68
Personal taxes	432
Private consumption	1,992
Service charges paid	58
Transfers to foreigners	6

15.9 The following data is available from Bank Negara Malaysia's Annual Report, 2002 of the Malaysian economy for the year 2000.

	RM billion
Private consumption	145
Public consumption	36
Public investment	44
Change in stocks	5
Export of goods and services	427
Import of goods and services	328
Net factor payments abroad	− 29
GDP	342

Find: (a) GNP and (b) private investment in the economy.

15.10 Fill in the blanks in the following table:

	Billion Dollars
Gross national product	6,264
Depreciation	510
National product	xxx
Net indirect taxes	xxx
National income	5,908

15.11 From Bank Negara Malaysia's Annual Report, 2006, the following information is available for the year 2005. Figures are in RM million.

Public gross capital formation	54,570	
Public surplus	15,936	
Private savings	103,905	
Gross domestic capital formation	98,730	
Balance on current account	75,681	(16.1% of GNP)

Find: (a) GNP, (b) public savings and (c) private capital formation and aggregate consumption.

Web Exercise

From Bank Negara Malaysia's Annual Report, find how close were the forecast values given in the Case Study above to the estimates for the year 2007.

Forward Link

You now know that macroeconomics broadly deals with various sorts of aggregates centring on national output. In the next chapter, we look at these aggregates forming the demand and supply sides of an economy so that we may link them to the general price level and study the conditions pertaining to its equilibrium. In other words, you will learn about the form and nature of the tools we use in macroeconomic analyses.

Aggregate Demand and Aggregate Supply

16.1   AGGREGATIVE CONCEPTS

Macroeconomics deals with demand and supply of products including their components and prices in aggregative form for reckoning the money value of national output. We have seen in the preceding chapter that this value equals national income as well as national expenditure. However, for an analysis of national income or expenditure the demand and supply concepts assume different meanings and their determinants also do not remain the same as you studied them in Chapter 4 from the microeconomics perspective. Aggregate demand (AD) refers to the amount of money people plan to *spend* on consumption and investment. You are on the credit side of the production account (Table 16.2). Likewise, aggregate supply (AS) refers to the amount of *income* people can get from different sources—wages, salaries, interest rent and profit—to meet their aggregate demand. An economy is in an overall equilibrium when aggregate supply matches aggregate demand. This chapter deals with the meaning of price levels, aggregate demand and aggregate supply in this context. We begin with a brief explanation of what equilibrium means, because in the subsequent chapters too this concept will be frequently used.

> The concept of market equilibrium of demand and supply at the macro level is in form similar to their equilibrium at the micro level.

16.1.1 Equilibrium

Equilibrium may conveniently be thought of as a situation where opposite forces are held in balance like a momentary stalemate in a tug of war. You have come across this view of equilibrium earlier in the discussion on price theory. The price of an individual product is at rest or equilibrium if at that price the demand for the product equals its supply. In macroeconomics, the equilibrium price level is the one that holds the demand and supply aggregates for the economy in a state of balance. The demand clears the market and is termed as effective demand. This is a good working definition of equilibrium. But there are deeper meanings of the term that you must always keep in mind for a better understanding of economic forces at work. Ideally, an economy would be in a state of equilibrium when all economic agents are able to choose those quantities out of the alternatives available to them that they prefer to produce and to consume.

> The concepts of aggregate demand, aggregate supply and price level are a bit complicated though not difficult to understand.

Some Islamic economists have interpreted that equilibrium means *moderation*—an Islamic norm exhorting the believers to avoid behavioural extremes and follow the middle course. Such interpretations must be avoided as they are misleading as to how the term equilibrium is used contextually in economics.

For understanding the remaining concepts—aggregate demand and aggregate supply—it may be helpful to start with an equilibrium diagram and then explain the theoretical structure that holds it together. We can easily see that if prices in general were lower, people are expected to buy more of goods and services than if it were higher. Also, profits and output will be smaller at lower prices than at the higher ones. Consequently, supply will be reduced. Opposite will be the effect, if price levels rise. However, things are not as simple as they look. Let us start with the question: what do we mean by price level?

Exercise 16.1 will help you to experience the shapes and slopes of the aggregate demand and aggregate supply curves and their equilibrium price level.

Exercise 16.1

Given the following data for an economy, construct an aggregate demand and aggregate supply intersection graph showing the equilibrium price level and the GDP values.

Table 16.1 *Price level, demand and supply*

Price level (index number)	Real output (billion dollars)	
	Aggregate demand	Aggregate supply
110	59	69.5
105	62	68.0
100	65	65.0
95	68	60.5
90	71	53.0

Is the aggregate demand curve a straight line? Explain your answer.

16.2   PRICE LEVEL

Prices of all goods and services tend to rise or fall together due to monetary expansion or contraction. In microeconomic equilibrium, this factor is assumed to remain constant.

Trees in a grove are of different heights, but when we see the same trees from a distance, we are able to form some idea about the height of the grove itself from the sky line. Two or more of groves can be compared for their level in a sense. This level is distinct from the height of *individual* trees though it depends on how tall the trees in general are. Similar is the notion of a general level of prices. Changes in the price of an individual commodity depend on variations in its demand and supply determinants. But, it is most unlikely that these determinants will change for most commodities at the *same* time to push them all in the *same* direction, up or down. However, it is not uncommon to find prices of almost all commodities sometimes rising and sometimes falling together: the economy may be experiencing *inflation* or suffering from *recession*. At times, the change is quite sharp and abrupt. Price level changes are the result of some out-of-market pressure on the price mechanism. This pressure comes from the monetary side of the economy.

Price level changes marked on the Y-axis of Figure 16.1 have two important characteristics that are absent in the microeconomic equilibrium diagrams. First, the concept of a price level implies the existence of a reference *base*; a *change* in price level measures the departure from that base. Second, we have techniques of combining the prices of commodities and their corresponding quantities into price index numbers which link the current year average to that in the base year with a percentage. We shall discuss the details of constructing index numbers in Chapter 23. Here, it is sufficient to indicate that it is price indices that we have shown on the Y-axis in Figure 16.1.

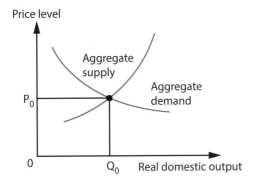

Price level

Figure 16.1 *Aggregate demand and aggregate supply equilibrium*

16.3   AGGREGATE DEMAND

Aggregate demand is the sum of various sectoral demands for current output of the economy. The sectors include households, businesses, government and the foreign buyers of domestic exports. However, the definition need not tempt us to strike a parallel with the concept of demand in microeconomics. In microeconomics, we conceive demand for a commodity as a schedule of its quantities that buyers are willing to purchase at various prices at any point in time. But this view may be misleading if applied literally to macroeconomics; it does not help us explain why an aggregate demand curve should slope downwards. Microeconomic demand curves in product markets assume that the real income of the buyers remains intact and prices of related goods and services do not change. Thus, if price of a commodity falls it is often substituted for relatively expensive alternatives such as tea for coffee; people buy more of tea whose price has fallen. Likewise, people now spend less money for buying earlier quantities of tea. Some income is released for use elsewhere. Consumers may use part of this income to have a little more of tea. It follows that demand for a commodity may increase under substitution and income effects, with a fall in its price; the normal demand curve must slope downwards. This explanation does not work in the case of an aggregate demand curve.

Markers on the Y-axis of Figure 16.1 do not show *alternative* positions as in microeconomic diagrams. Here, they indicate *successive* price levels; in the form of index numbers geared to a base. A price level rise means a fall in real income of the people and vice versa. But beware, a fall in the price level does not necessarily show a corresponding increase in real income. On the contrary, it may lead, as it often does, to a contraction of real income in the wake of widespread unemployment that it causes, as losses collapse businesses. Thus, no income effect operates here because real income does not remain constant. Substitution effect cannot even be conceived of as an operator in the case of aggregate demand; it simply does not exist. What then causes the aggregate demand curve slope downwards?

16.3.1   Why Do Aggregate Demand Curves Slope Downwards?

We have already seen that the answer to this question is not the same as to why the demand curve for an individual product slopes downwards. In Figure 16.1, when we move down the aggregate demand curve, the entire economy moves down from a higher to a lower price level. The circular flow diagram of Figure 16.2 tells us that if households would for any reason, pay lower prices than before for the goods and services they purchase, smaller income flows back to them as rent, wages and profits including interest as payments for the factor services they supply to businesses. *This would by itself be of little consequence if all prices in the product and factor markets in the economy fall by identical proportion say 10% (think why?).* The economy would only be operating at a lower price level than before.

Income distribution effect

The crucial aspect of price level changes is that whenever it rises or falls, the change is *on an average*. Individual prices on which the average is based change much differently: the structure of *relative* prices undergoes a change. This alters the income distribution in society even if the circular flow level remains the same. Lower price levels change income distribution in favour of the fixed income groups. Workers especially gain. Their purchasing power increases. As they consume larger proportions of their income, they tend to contribute to the expansion of aggregate demand as the curve shows. The crucial assumption here is that lower prices do not cause such unemployment as would shrink the income flow more than proportionately. But this assumption may not remain valid for long. The circular relations would eventually make the snake eat its own tail. Opposite will be the consequence when price level rises: aggregate demand would tend to shrink.

There are a number of factors (real and nominal) that may affect the level of aggregate demand and cause changes in it.

Real balances effect

People generally do not spend all of their income. A part of it they save. They keep these savings usually in the form of liquid assets: deposits in banks, investments in gold, units, bonds and equities that can be readily sold in the market if cash were needed. These balances have purchasing power, a value in real terms at current prices. What happens to real balances when price level departs from its current position? Evidently, if prices in general move up the real value of the balances fall: their purchasing power is reduced. A household may decide not to buy a television set, or postpone its purchase for now, so as to increase nominal savings for maintaining real balances intact. Aggregate demand will decrease. When price level falls people may liquidate some of their assets to buy things such as a car at cheaper rates even without reducing real balances. Aggregate demand would expand.

Interest rate effect

An underlying assumption of the aggregate demand curve is that the supply of money remains fixed. However, when prices in general rise both households and businesses need more money to carry on with the same volume of transactions. But money has a price, the rate of interest in mainstream economics. It may have to be raised enough to neutralize the effects of monetary expansion. Interest rate has to increase also to compensate the savers for the price level rise so that real rate of interest on deposits may remain intact. In any case, the assumption that money supply remains fixed goes. Rise in interest rates leads to a reduction in investment expenditures eroding aggregate demand in the economy. While high interest rates may curtail aggregate demand to contain rise in prices, the opposite may not be true; a cheap money policy may not revive investment spending and pull the economy out of a low level equilibrium. As the saying goes: taking the horse to the water does not ensure that he will drink it too unless he is really thirsty. Cheap money policy may fail to revive aggregate demand during recessions.

Foreign trade effect

Finally, the aggregate demand curve may slope downward due to a foreign trade effect. If the price level of a country rises relative to its trade partners, its exports may decline and imports increase. The effect of an adverse balance of trade would be a decrease in the aggregate demand for goods and services in the country. Devaluation of the domestic currency is invariably suggested as the remedy, especially by the International Monetary Fund (IMF). However, the policy may not succeed unless both exports and imports are price elastic. (Why?) This not being the case during the 1960s in India, the devaluation of the rupee in 1966 could not help dampen demand for imports and raise exports much.

> Factors affecting the level of aggregate demand can be internal as well as external.

16.4   DETERMINANTS OF AGGREGATE DEMAND

It is important to know, that the effects causing the aggregate demand curve to slope downwards as discussed above do not mechanically operate in the opposite direction. The reasons and consequences of a fall in the price level are not a mirror copy of those when the price level rises. The two situations—inflation and recession—are qualitatively different. We shall talk about this point in some detail when we discuss monetary and fiscal policies. For now, let us focus on a more general but important issue. This is not about the rise or fall in the aggregate demands along a curve; it is about what determines the level of the curve and shifts it bodily in the plane. Like most micro demand curves for individual goods, macro or aggregate demand curves too may shift up or down as shown in Figure 16.2. Here, AD_0 is the initial aggregate demand curve; AD_1 indicates a decrease in aggregate demand while its shift to AD_2 shows an increase.

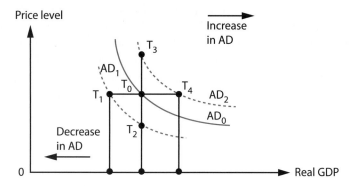

Figure 16.2 *Increase/decrease in AD*

Formally, we may define an increase in the aggregate demand at a given price level as when the buyers are purchasing more goods and services than before (movement from T_0 to T_4) or even with a rise in the price level they do not reduce their purchases (movement from T_0 to T_3).

Exercise   16.2

Define decrease in aggregate demand and illustrate it using the curves in Figure 16.2. Also, mark the given price in the figure.

What brings about a shift in the aggregate demand curve is not far to seek. We have identified and explained the broad components of aggregate demand in the foregoing discussion of methods used for measuring the GNP. Consider Table 16.2. It provides data on Malaysia's GNP by demand aggregates at constant (1987 = 100) prices for three years (2002–2004). Let the central year 2003 be the point of reference for comparison such that the lower values of the variables in 2002 show a decrease in them and their higher values in 2004, an increase. Constant prices imply that the price level between the years has remained unchanged. Change in the variable values, therefore, implies the change in their *physical* or *real* volume. Thus viewed, the GNP value for 2002 in the last row of the table records a decrease in aggregate demand from that of the benchmark volume for 2003 while that for 2004 shows an increase.

Table 16.2 *Malaysia: GNP by demand aggregates, 2002–2004 (RM billion)*

Item head	Year		
	2002	2003	2004
Consumption	**132.9**	**143.2**	**156.8**
Private	102.0	108.7	120.2
Public	31.0	34.4	36.6
Investment	**63.2**	**65.0**	**67.0**
Private	22.2	22.2	29..0
Public	41.1	42.7	38.0
Change in stocks	**3.2**	**– 1.0**	**5.8**
Exports – Imports	21.2	21.0	19.0
GDP at purchasers' value	**220.4**	**232.5**	**249.4**
Net factor payments abroad	– 17.3	–15.2	– 16.0
GNP at purchasers' value	**203.2**	**217.3**	**233.4**

Source: Bank Negara Malaysia's Annual Report, 2006, Table A.4.

Figure 16.3 is an illustrative depiction of these changes. It presents a replica of the three aggregate demand curves of Figure 16.2 showing the movement along the points T_1, T_0 and T_4. Let us now explain the determinants of aggregate demand as listed in Table 16.2.

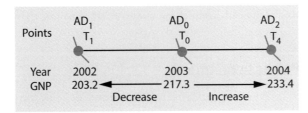

Figure 16.3 *Increase and decrease in aggregate demand*

16.4.1 Private Consumption

Private consumption comes out of the disposable income of the households. If they decide to save more of this income, consumption will be reduced and vice versa. Likewise, if taxes on commodities or personal incomes are reduced (increased), private consumption may rise (fall). Transfer payments meant to benefit the poor would tend to raise private consumption. In addition, the factors that make an aggregate demand curve slope downward may also make it shift. These especially include changes in consumers' expectations and their real assets.

16.4.2 Public Consumption

Government current expenditure on routine functions such as civil administration, health and education, law and order, and defence, except accommodation for the army personnel, falls in the public consumption domain. In Malaysia, this expenditure is on the rise in absolute amounts but has remained virtually unchanged in relative terms: from 15.26% in 2002 of the budget it crawled up to a mere 15.68% in 2004. The rise in public consumption has been slower than the growth rate of the GNP indicating an increasing privatization of the Malaysian economy. Thus, the relative significance of public consumption for aggregate demand in the country is on the decline.

16.4.3   Private Investment

Investment spending—the purchase of capital goods—is a major determinant of aggregate demand, more so in developing economies. Private investment proportion in the package has in general been on the rise under the globalization wave now sweeping the world. An increase in private investment would shift the aggregate demand curve to the right, a decrease in it to the left. Profit expectations are the main influence on private investment decisions. Government policies, taxation especially, also matter. In Malaysia, for example, private investment took a back seat after the 1998 financial crisis: its share in total investment fell in 2002 to around 35% but it is again climbing up being 45% of the total in 2007. Also, there has been an unmistakable trend in the country towards reducing corporate taxes: the 2008 budget brought them down further to less than 30%.

16.4.4   Public Investment

Public sector plays a significant role in most developing economies for a variety of reasons—including social and ideological—even as privatization is in general on the rise. Exploration for new resources, public utilities, transportation and key industries are the popular public preserves. Public investment is also an important policy variable used for directing the economy to achieving national goals. Increase in public investment adds to aggregate demand and vice versa.

16.4.5   Net Expenditures on Exports

The increase in foreign spending on domestic exports minus payments for imports would increase aggregate demand while a reduction would decrease it. Table 16.3 illustrates the impact of changes in net exports $(X - M)$ on aggregate demand using Malaysian data around the financial crisis in 1998. Foreign trade plays a crucial role in the Malaysian economy, $(X + M)$ being more than double of the GDP. Thus, the large negative balance of trade in 1998 (41% of her GDP) largely contributed to the negative rate of growth, while the positive trade balance helped it to become positive in the following year.

16.4.6   Income Variations Abroad

In modern times, national economies are interrelated through various bonds: trade, finance, transportation, tourism, sports, diplomatic contacts and so on. The prosperity in one country gets in part transported to another country almost automatically; adversity may even be faster to spread as the financial crisis that afflicted Malaysia in 1997–98. If America sneezes, Europe catches cold is an old adage.

Table 16.3 *Impact of balance of trade (X − M) and net foreign income on aggregate demand in Malaysia (RM billion)*

Description	Year		
	1997	1998	1999
Export of goods and non-factor services	186.5	187.4	212.5
Import of goods and non-factor services	199.7	162.2	179.8
Balance of trade (X − M)	−13.2	−74.8	+32.7
GDP at purchasers' value	**196.7**	**182.2**	**192.8**

BOX 16.1

Islam on Savings and Investment

The explanation that Prophet Yusuf (pbuh) provided for the then king of Egypt's dream that seven thin cows were eating seven fat cows and that there were ears of corn, seven green and seven dry, contained the divine instruction of saving from the current output for contingency and for using as seed (investment) for the next crop.

The interpreters of the king had dismissed the dream as a puzzling mix of things which they did not possess; skills to give meaning. But the prophet (pbuh), knowing things from God, explained the dream as follows: *For seven years you sow diligently and reap the harvests as usual. But you eat (consume) little of the crops leaving the rest in the ears. The years of prosperity will be followed by seven years dreadful years of drought but you would then live in comfort on what you had reaped and stored in the preceding years minus only little that you had eaten. After the seven years period of drought has passed there will be a year of plentiful water and people will press wine and oil* (Qur'an 12: 46-50).

This story from the Qur'an should not be mistaken as predictive or supportive of modern microeconomics. It only highlights the importance of aggregative analysis and its components in economic analysis. It also was perhaps the first announcement on the inevitability of cyclical fluctuations in economic activity and at the role of natural factors in trade cycles.

16.4.7   Foreign Exchange Rate

Changes in the exchange rate of a currency may affect aggregate demand via the trade routes. When the currency of a country depreciates in terms of other currencies, their one unit buys more of the domestic currency, e.g. a US dollar would purchase more of Pakistan rupees than before. Pakistani exports become cheaper in the US and other countries: her exports are likely to expand. On the other hand, Pakistani goods would become costlier for other countries. (Why?) On balance, net aggregate demand from abroad could increase.

Exercise 16.3

Explain how aggregate domestic demand is likely to be affected if the currency of a trade partner depreciates (or is devalued) relative to the domestic currency.

16.5 AGGREGATE SUPPLY

Aggregate supply, like aggregate demand, is also a schedule concept; it is the sum total of real outputs that various sectors of an economy would be willing to produce at different price levels. These sectors include business firms, government, and the foreign sellers of goods and services the country imports. The aggregate supply schedule gives a curve where price and output levels are positively related. Supply takes time to adjust to changes in demand. For this reason, supply curves have a classification with reference to time. We have short-run supply curves and long-run supply curves.

16.5.1 Short-run Supply Curve

The short run is defined in macroeconomics as a period which is not sufficient enough to allow resource prices, especially wages, to adjust to changes in the price level given the productive capacity of the economy. In contrast, long-run is a period in which the process of resource prices adjustment is expected to complete and production capacity can also be expanded. Figure 16.4 shows a short-run aggregate supply curve. The Y-axis measures the price level again in terms of index numbers and the GDP at each point on the curve is the value of corresponding output measured on X-axis.

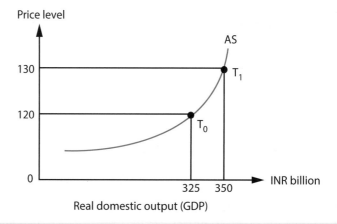

Figure 16.4 *A short-run aggregate supply curve*

When price level rises by 8.3% from 120 to 130, real output increases by 7.7% from INR 325 billion to INR 350 billion. Thus, the rise in real output is less than proportionate to the rise in prices. The reason is that in the short-run some resource prices take time for adjustments with the general rise in prices. The short-run aggregate supply curves, therefore, tend to be convex to X-axis.

But **why should the short-run supply curve slope upwards?** This requires explaining as to why a rise in price level increases real output and a fall in price level decreases it. The curve for aggregate supply is no different in shape from the supply curve for a single product to the extent that per unit cost of production lies behind them both. We can easily obtain this cost of production in either case through dividing the total cost of production by the number of units produced. In the short run, the per unit production cost of the aggregate output matches the price level for that output. As an economy expands, the short run per unit production cost tends to climb up because increasingly smaller quantities of fixed resources remain available for fuller use of each addition to the variable factors. More so, if the economy is already operating at close to full employment level. Simultaneously, the prices of variable factors may also rise and push up costs.

The movement along a short-run aggregate supply curve shown in Figure 16.4 is in response to price level changes. But output can change (increase or decrease) with price level remaining unchanged; there can also be a movement off the supply curve. Thus, in Figure 16.5, AS_0 is the initial aggregate supply curve from which AS_1 shows a decrease in aggregate supply and AS_2 an increase.

> Sellers are willing to sell more at higher prices to increase their profits and less at lower prices to avoid or reduce losses.

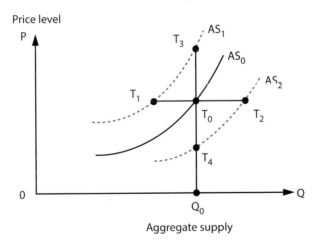

Figure 16.5 *Price level and short-run aggregate supply curves*

Notice that supply increases from T_0 to T_2, price remaining unchanged. It also increases if quantity supplied remains unchanged at Q_0 even with a fall in price level from T_0 to T_4.

To check your understanding of an increase or decrease in aggregate supply, you may find the answer to Exercise 16.4.

Exercise   16.4

Using Figure 16.5, define a decrease in aggregate supply along the same lines as we have explained an increase in supply above. You may use the T points in Figure 16.5 for illustrative purposes.

16.5.2   Long-run Supply Curve: Full Employment

The production responses of firms to changes in the price levels may not be the same as in the short run. As indicated earlier, resource prices in the long run have more flexibility to adjust with the changes in price levels. Consequently, one limiting case for an aggregate supply curve could in the long run be vertical at full employment level as shown in Figure 16.6. The argument for such a case is as follows. Suppose the price level (index number) is 100 and the GDP is valued at $400 billion composed as $320 billion wages plus $180 billion profit. Now price index moves to say 200, that is, the price level doubles. Clearly, the value of output at *current* prices would be $800 billion. The argument assumes that *real* wages in the long run would remain constant. Nominal wages would rise to $640 billion and profit, the remainder, will be $360. In real terms, profit will also not change; it will stay at $180 billion (360/2). The producers will have no additional incentive to expand output.

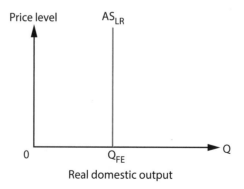

Figure 16.6 *Long-run aggregate supply curve (AS_{LR}) is vertical at full employment output* (Q_{FE})

The assumptions of the above argument are quite stringent. Firms may, for example, resist increase in nominal wages to neutralize fully the rise in prices. They may attempt to replace workers with labour saving devices to increase the profit share in the stagnating output. Output stagnation coupled with expanding unemployment was the worrying feature of the US economy during the 1980s and brought the supply side economics to the fore.

The long-run and short-run aggregate supply curves may differ only in degree, the former being steeper than the latter. As we allow more time for readjustment between the overall output and factor prices to work out, the gap between the long-run and short-run aggregate supply curves may tend to narrow down as shown in Figure 16.7.

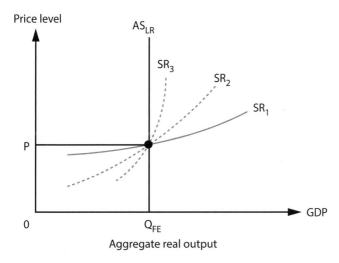

Figure 16.7 *Short-run supply curves tend to become flatter with the extension of time; so do the long-run supply curves*

The period becomes longer as we move from SR_1 towards AS_{LR} passing through curves like SR_2 and SR_3.

16.6 DETERMINANTS OF AGGREGATE SUPPLY

The search for the determinants of aggregate supply makes us look to the income based measure of the national output because the quantity and quality of goods an economy supplies is a function of the input availability for producing them. Input availability depends on the level of their prices. The linkage gives us the following as some of the main factors influencing aggregate supply of goods and services in an economy. We have shown the shifts in aggregate supply (increase or decrease) under their impact in Figure 16.5.

Supply needs time to adjust to the changes in demand at the aggregate level as well. The curve rotates to the right as time allowed increases.

16.6.1   Input Prices

The proportion of wages and salaries in business costs is quite high in modern economies; for example, it is currently around 70% of the total in the US. However, the high percentage share of wages in costs need not convey that the proportion of goods the workers use is equally high in the GDP, especially in developing countries. The higher costs of luxury goods pull up the price level and make wages and salaries lag behind the productivity of the workers. The point that reduction in wages reduces per unit cost and helps increase in production is invariably highlighted: the supply curve shifts downward to the right. A rise in wage rates will, on the other hand, curtail output and shift the curve upward to the left. The point is valid in so far as it goes but it does not go far enough. In a labour–capital factor model, the price of a commodity is finally made up of two elements: wages and profits. But whenever there is talk of reducing prices to increase output, the suggestion invariably is to cut wages, not profit, why? Discuss this point in your class.

16.6.2   Prices of Imported Resources

Both internal and external factors including productivity cause changes in aggregate supply over time.

A country is seldom self-sufficient in resources it uses in production. Most economies import men, money and materials in large or small quantities from abroad to keep production process going and expanding. For example, in more recent years Malaysia has been importing electronics, machinery, petroleum products, plastics, vehicles, iron and steel products, and chemicals in that order of importance from a number of countries. These items make 70% of ingredients in her exports. More than 1.85 million foreign workers working in the country constitute about 15% of her labour force. Again, foreign capital has played a significant role in the economic development of the country. Other things remaining the same, if prices of these imported resources used per unit of output rise, the aggregate output would decrease; the supply curve would shift upward to the left. The opposite will happen if prices fall.

16.6.3   Market Corrections

Developing countries producing basic raw materials like cotton, cocoa and petroleum mostly do not get fair prices for their exports relative to what they have to pay for things they import. The import prices climb up because of the market power the producers supplying them have. In comparison, the prices of what developing countries export increase at a much slower pace. The gap between the two sets of prices tends to widen moving the terms of trade to the disadvantage of the developing nations. To remedy the situation, the producers of oil could alone join hands successfully in a loose association called the organization of petroleum exporting countries or the OPEC.

Helped by unprecedented expansion of demand, OPEC could see oil prices rise to remunerative levels: they rose ten-fold since early 1970s; becoming four times during the past six years alone, thanks to the uncertainties the American led invasion of Iraq created in the market. The sharp rise jolted the world, especially the oil hungry American economy itself. The US per unit cost of production rose sharply shifting its aggregate supply curve to the left abruptly. The American economic policy at home and abroad centred so much around oil that Alan Greenspan, the former governor of the Federal Reserve, in his recent book *The Age of Tolerance: Adventures in a New World* (2007) confirms the widespread belief that the 'Iraq war was all about oil.' He concludes that the Republicans 'swapped principles for power. They ended up with neither. They deserved to lose' the congressional elections.

> Dependence on external demand or supply may even tempt nations to launch wars.

16.6.4   Productivity

Productivity per unit of inputs in an economy is a simple concept. Divide the units of output by the units of input they help produce. Thus, we have:

$$\text{Productivity} = \frac{\text{Units of output produced}}{\text{Units of input used}}$$

Productivity is a measure of efficiency in resource use. An economy must attempt to obtain as much real output per unit of its limited resources as possible, given the technology. Over time, it must work to improve technology itself through research and development. Improvement in productivity reduces the cost of production and shifts the aggregate supply curve downward to the right. Replacing old machines and plant with the new ones, improved management, educating the masses, training the workers on job to improve skills and maintaining industrial peace are some of the ways to improve productivity. Islamic behavioural norms of responsibility, mutual trust and cooperation prescribed for the producers and workers can help enhance productivity unabated.

Exercises 16.5 and 16.6 will help you to understand the concept of productivity.

> Productivity is a measure of efficiency in resource use and equity in factor rewards.

Exercise 16.5

Suppose the output of a product is 1,000 units and the firm uses 25 units of a single resource to manufacture it. Find the productivity per unit of input. If the product is sold at $10 a piece, and the input price is $8 a unit, find the average cost of production.

> ### Exercise 16.6
>
> Suppose in the above exercise the output and input prices change to $15 and $11, respectively. Will productivity change or cost of production or both? Give reasons for your answer. What if prices do not change but output increases to 1,100 units due to improved supervision?

16.6.5   Taxes and Subsidies

Increase in taxes on the sale, production or import of commodities increases per unit cost of production to the extent that they are not transferred to the buyers. Aggregate supply will decrease. A rise in wages not without a corresponding increase in productivity will have similar effects. So will be the effect of raising the mark-ups in Islamic finance to enhance profits.

Taxes and subsidies both distort free-market prices: taxes tend to raise it, subsidies lower it.

In contrast, a payment by the government to producers to meet part of costs and keep prices down i.e. a subsidy, increases short-run aggregate supply. A leading example is the subsidy Malaysia is providing to the oil industry to keep transportation and energy cheap for business. But for meeting the objectives of a subsidy scheme, some control on the demand for the subsidized commodity is essential to curb black marketing; Malaysia is losing millions of dollars to neighbouring countries as it is deficient in controls over illegal taking out of oil from the country.

16.6.6   Regulation Policy

Public policy and social environment have their impact on employment and also affect aggregate supply in an economy.

Liberalization is one of the main elements in the globalization wave now sweeping the world. Its supporters argue that to comply with government regulations is, in general, costly for businesses: increase in regulations raise per unit cost of production, decreases aggregate supply and shifts the curve upwards to the left. Opponents argue that deregulation may result in accounting manipulations, cornering of products and monopolization (that Islam condemns). It may open doors for the exploitation of consumers and workers alike under the impulse of promoting self-interest and profit maximization. Much honest differences of opinion exists on the merits and demerits of regulations. However, business in developing economies probably need more of public controls as appropriate institutions are lacking in number and maturity to make development process self-regulatory. Islamic systems will out of necessity have higher levels of regulation to see that Shari'ah requirements are met. Islamic finance, for example, is already having Shari'ah compliance regulations additional to mainstream rules.

16.6.7   Socio-political Environment

Finally, social institutions, such as *zakat* and *awqaf* in Islam and legal frameworks such as the anti-trust laws in USA, play an important role in affecting the volume of aggregate supply. Attitudes of countries toward war and peace not only influence output volume and composition at home but in other countries as well. More recent examples are the periodic communal killings in India; recent American adventures in West Asia and the civil war like conditions in Pakistan. War increases production costs, peace lowers them.

Before closing our discussion on demand and supply aggregates, it is well to point out that factors we discussed influencing each of them above are not always mutually exclusive. For example, investment spending, changes in exchange rates, taxes and subsidies operate on both the demand and supply sides of the market. So is the case with public regulation of the economy, social attitudes and political institutions. Also, the nature, quality, range and impact of these factors will not be the same in all economies, especially the developed and the developing ones.

> Factors that influence demand and supply aggregates need not altogether be different.

Exercise 16.7

Argue which variable aggregate demand or supply or both will be affected by the following:
- The Malaysian currency appreciates against the US dollar.
- The government increases per unit tax on the production and sale of tobacco products.
- Malaysian Airline System raises air fares and freights to avoid recurring losses.

16.7   CHANGES IN EQUILIBRIUM

We had started this chapter with the explanation of the three macro variables—price level, aggregate demand and aggregate supply in a state of equilibrium as shown in Figure 16.1. We explained separately what factors give shape and cause shifts in the demand and supply curves. The next logical step obviously is to see how shifts in one or both of the curves would affect the equilibrium price level and the GDP of a country.

Table 16.4 *Distinction between price level and the change in price level*

Year	1999	2000	2001	2002	2003	2004	2005
Price level (index numbers)	96	100	104	**108**	105	100	94
Change in price level (%)	4.3	4.2	4.0	**3.8**	− 2.8	− 4.8	− 6.0

Inflation and deflation are states of disequilibrium in an economy. Both can change relative price structure; inflation increases income inequalities in society, deflation increases unemployment.

Such a change could result in **inflation** or **deflation**, the terms which must be distinguished from the changes in price level itself. Look at Table 16.4 to better understand the distinction between the two. The year 2000 is the base for the index number series indicating the price level in the table. The price level rises up to 2002 after which it starts declining. On the other hand, the *per cent change* in the price level declines continuously but remains positive till 2002; inflation is taking place in the economy at a falling rate. There is a turn of events after 2002. The price level decreases, as well as the amount of change in it, that too at a faster rate. The economy moves into deflation, usually termed as **recession**. *Price level is a point on the index number curve; a change in it is the slope of that curve (positive or negative) at that point.* Fluctuations (rise and fall) in output and employment resulting from the price level *changes*, calculated on a point-to-point basis are termed as **cyclical fluctuations**.

Exercise 16.8

Show calculations to arrive at changes in price level in Table 16.4 for the years 2000 to 2005. Find out whether the entries in the third row of the table are correct.

16.7.1   Changes in Aggregate Demand and Equilibrium

To facilitate analysis and understanding, we shall take shifts in one of the curves— demand or supply—at a time assuming that the other remains constant. We begin with changes in aggregate demand and their impact on equilibrium.

Increase in aggregate demand

Increase in aggregate demand, supply remaining constant, is likely to increase both price level and the real national output. The change may reveal either of the two things: demand-pull inflation or expansion of output absorbing the existing unemployment in the economy.

Figure 16.8 depicts the impact of an increase in aggregate demand on price level and the volume of national output, the supply curve remaining unchanged. Here, the demand curve AD_0 intersects the supply curve AS_0 at T_0; P_0 and Q_0 being the *initial* price level and the corresponding GNP.

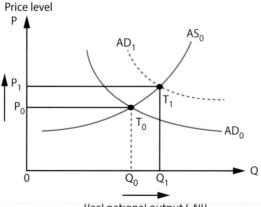

Figure 16.8 *Impact of increase in aggregate demand*

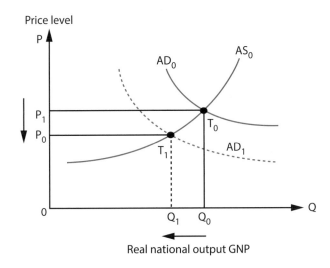

Figure 16.9 *Impact of decrease in aggregate demand*

Suppose that aggregate demand shifts to AD_1 moving the equilibrium point to T_1. The price level and GNP both increase to P_1 and Q_1, respectively.

Figure 16.8 helps to explain the two possible effects of an increase in aggregate demand.

If the initial equilibrium at T_0 were at the *full employment level,* the increase in demand has caused what we term as **demand-pull inflation**; the real GNP remains unchanged at Q_0. You may wonder, what then does the movement from Q_0 to Q_1 in the figure show? Well, it measures the gap between the *actual* (Q_0) and the *potential* GNP (Q_1) of the economy as the point is on the aggregate supply curve. Potential GNP is the value of the final output the economy could produce at the full employment level. Actual GNP is not always equal to potential GNP.

If the economy were operating at less than full employment at T_0, the point of initial equilibrium, the price rise in response to increase in demand would enhance profits as incentive for growth leading to an expansion in both employment and real output at T_1, the new full employment point.

Decrease in aggregate demand

Let us now examine what happens when decrease in aggregate demand takes place. Consider Figure 16.9: T_0 is as before the initial equilibrium point where P_0 is the price level and Q_0 is the real domestic output at the *full employment* level. Let aggregate demand decrease for any reason and the curve shifts downwards to the left from AD_0 to AD_1. We again have two possibilities.

The supply curve is concave from below implying that production as a whole is taking place under diminishing returns or increasing costs. This means that some reduction in costs is automatic if production level has to be reduced in response to a decrease in aggregate demand. Producers are able to readjust costs through improved efficiency and reduction in some resource prices to remain on the supply curve AS at point T_1. But some unemployment will still take place due to reduction in output to Q_1.

However, if the cost structure were so rigid that no reduction whatsoever in per unit cost was possible, recession will be stickier and unemployment prolonged like the one the world witnessed during the Great Depression of 1930s. Such unemployment is *cyclical* in nature. We explain it in some detail below.

Aggregate demand—depression and unemployment: Many things looked paradoxical during the Great Depression. The shops were full of merchandise. The buyers wanted to buy them and sellers wanted to sell them but exchange would not take place. The plant and machinery was there with full capacity and ability to produce; there was also no dearth of workers, skilled and unskilled. The system was as efficient as ever before but stood still. There was no coal in the house because there was too much coal in the market; the miner was laid off losing income as coal piled up at the pithead. Aggregate demand was grossly deficient to clear the market. It was loss of jobs and incomes that deepened the misery. The causative factors were as follows:

1. **Fall in consumption expenditure**: Economists blamed the rigidity of wages denying cost reduction needed to arrest closure of businesses and spread of unemployment. The resulting loss of incomes led to a sharp fall in consumption demand. But it is interesting to note that not workers alone; the employers too did not want to cut wages. Lower wages might have impaired workers' morale and work effort. The loss of productivity might not have helped reduce the production costs. Finally, even if the wages could be readjusted, the demand need not have revived to clear the market; increase in incomes was the cure.

2. **Fall in investment expenditure**: Piling up of inventories on shop shelves was a frightening sight. Even as funds were available at low interest rates, the business psychology was dominated by a fear complex and risk aversion. It is interesting to note that in the US businesses beyond a minimum size were still making reasonable profits at the bottom of Depression as WL Crum showed in his book *Corporate Size and Earning Power'* published in 1932. Scale economies have probably been since considered as an effective hedge against recessions. Recall that banks in Malaysia were virtually made to merge into six bigger units after the 1998 downturn for that reason.

3. **Fall in export demand**: Before the close of the thirties, the world was on gold standard, a monetary system that transmits

both prosperity and adversity originating in a major economy to rest of the world. Hence, after the onset of Depression in the US, gold standard was its first casualty leading to an era of freely fluctuating exchange rates. There was competitive depreciation of currencies in an effort to sell abroad. Uncertainties only reduced the volume of international trade. Fall in external demand for goods and services deepened the crisis all the more. The colonial countries, such as India, were lured to take advantage of the goods like plant and machinery available from the developed nations at throw away prices: Depression, indeed, helped the industrial development of that country.

> Recession in countries importing domestic goods causes a contraction in aggregate demand.

16.7.2   Changes in Aggregate Supply

Changes in aggregate supply (AS) take more time to work out than changes in aggregate demand for the reasons we have already explained. Their impact on equilibrium price level and employment is also of wider ramifications. In explaining their impact, we take the aggregate demand curve as fixed. Changes in aggregate supply like those in aggregate demand are of two types: increase and decrease. Let us begin with a decrease in supply.

Decrease in aggregate supply

Suppose, a US inspired Israeli attack on the uranium enrichment facilities of Iran severely disrupts world oil supplies and drives up the already escalating oil prices by 200%. Imagine the consequences! The higher energy prices would have a ripple effect the world over. Developing economies will be hit all the more severely.

The production and distribution costs of a wide variety of products will sharply rise. Even the aggregate supply curve of an oil producing country like Malaysia would jump up to the left as Figure 16.10 illustrates. P_0 and Q_0 show the full employment equilibrium position at T_0. Now, the cost of production per unit of output rises due to the jump in oil prices and the aggregate supply curve shifts upwards to the right. It intersects the aggregate demand at point T_1. However, there would be no change in real output. (Why?) The inward output movement from Q_0 to Q_1 only shows how much less would have been produced compared to Q_0, if Q_1 were the initial full employment equilibrium output. The rise in price level to P_1 is termed as cost-push inflation.

> Increase in production costs may cause a decrease in aggregate supply pushing up prices. For example, the recent rise in oil prices is the major cause of inflation these days in the Indian sub-continent and else where.

Exercise 16.9

Compare Figures 16.8 and 16.9 and explain the similarities and differences you note between them.

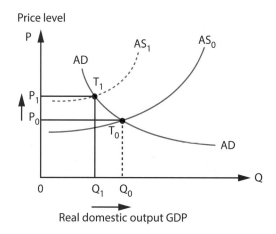

Figure 16.10 *Impact of decrease in aggregate supply*

Increase in aggregate supply

For a decade (1988–1997), Malaysia experienced strong economic growth with full employment and low inflation. Aggregate output rose at an annual rate of 8.72%, and unemployment hovered around 3.5%. Aggregate demand also expanded during the period but expanding supply neutralized considerably its impact on prices and the rise in their level averaged below 4%. Figure 16.11 is a schematic depiction of these interesting cross currents. The intersection of AD_0 and AS_0 at T_0 gives us the *initial* equilibrium at P_0, (price) and Q_0 (output levels) with full employment. Now, if there is an increase in aggregate supply, aggregate demand AD_0 remaining unchanged, the equilibrium will move to point T_1 corresponding to a lower price level P_1, the full employment output remaining at Q_1. The increase in supply could have been due to discovery of new resources, or technological improvements, their benefit being passed on to the consumers.

Mixed cases

What would be the likely effect of simultaneous change in aggregate demand and supply on the price level and output is difficult to say unless we know the magnitude and direction of the changes in the two variables. Even safe predictions may not be possible.

In contrast, if there were an increase in aggregate demand *alone* to AD_1 in Figure 16.11, the equilibrium will have moved to point T_2 with price level at P_2 and output again remaining unchanged at Q_1, the change resulting in what we have already explained as *demand-pull* inflation. However, the *simultaneous* increase in the aggregate variables, demand and supply, which the broken curves AD_1 and AS_1 depict, illustrate a *mixed case* like that of Malaysia we mentioned above. The new curves intersect at T_3. The effect of increase in aggregate demand on prices has been partially neutralized by increase in aggregate supply reducing the inflation measure to P_0P_1. There can be innumerable combinations of shifts in demand and supply aggregates; it is impossible to list them all or discuss their possible impact on the equilibrium price–output combination.

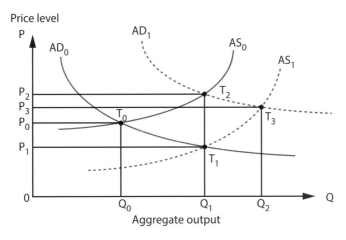

Figure 16.11 *Changes in aggregate supply and aggregate demand: the impact on equilibrium price-output combination*

We shall examine the consequences of price level changes—inflation and deflation—together with remedial measures for achieving stability in Chapter 20.

BOX 16.2

Islam, Capitalism and Marxism – The Common Point

Islam, capitalism and Marxism are vastly different economic systems but they have a common point—the growth of production utilizing nature to its maximum limit. This much is beyond economics; it is part of the divine scheme of creation. The Qur'an exhorts mankind: *Say (O Muhammad): Who has forbidden the beautiful (gifts) of Allah which He has produced for His servants and the pure and clean things (tayyabat) He has provided for sustenance?' Say:' they are (available) in the life of this world for those who believe (and) purely for them (not for the non-believers) on the Day of Judgement. Thus, We explain the signs in detail for those for those who understand* (7:32).

The decisions on what is produced and how, is governed by the doctrinal framework of each system. To illustrate, capitalism does not approve any method of increasing the product which conflicts with its notion of economic freedom. Islam rejects all those methods of increasing wealth which includes non-halal goods in the product-mix or allows discriminatory treatment of production factors. Marxism pleads for the supremacy of the labour force in decision-making processes related to production.

However, more important differences arise on the social distribution of the product. Capitalism believes in the supremacy of free markets: they ensure not only efficiency in the allocation of resources to various uses but also justice in the distribution of incomes. Islam upholds market freedom but does not trust it in achieving Islam's distributional goals. It assigns a crucial supervisory role to the state in that regard. Marxism believes that the workers cannot but be exploited under capitalism. Thus, it believes in virtual abolition of private ownership of property and puts it in the hands of social agencies, especially the government.

The literature on these issues is vast and characterized with sharp exchanges but an agreed solution continues to remain a far cry.

Summary

- This chapter explains three basic concepts and their mutual linkages in macroeconomics: equilibrium, aggregate demand and aggregate supply.

- Equilibrium takes place where two contending forces such as demand and supply, tend to balance each other. Ideally, an economy would be in equilibrium when all economic agents operating in it are able to choose those quantities from the available alternatives that they prefer to produce and to consume.

- Price level is the comparative average of prices of the goods and services at a point of time expressed as a percentage of their average at some reference point called the base. Price indices express this level. A change in price level is the per cent change in the index numbers over two points of time, for example, year on year basis. It measures inflation or deflation over time.

- Aggregate demand is the sum of demands by various sectors—households, businesses, government and foreigners—for the goods and services an economy produces. The aggregate demand curve, like the demand curve for an individual commodity, also slopes downwards but for different reasons.

- The factors that make an aggregate demand curve slope downwards are: the state of income distribution, real income effect, interest rate level and foreign trade pattern. The determinants of aggregate demand that bring about shifts in the curve are consumption and investments both public and private, income variations abroad and foreign exchange rate. Increase (decrease) in aggregate demand curve takes place when people in general demand more (less) of goods and services than before at the same price level or they do not curtail (increase) purchases even with a rise (fall) in prices.

- Aggregate supply, like aggregate demand, is also a schedule concept. Cost of production lies behind this curve that slopes upwards showing that price level and aggregate supply are positively related. We can think of aggregate supply curves in the short run or in the long run. The distinction is needed because factors affecting the upward slope of the curves and the shifts in them are not the same in each case.

- Short-run supply curves usually have an upward increasing slope. As an economy expands, the aggregate output increases, other things remaining the same, the short run per unit costs tend to climb up as reducing production capacity is available for a fuller use of the increasing variable factors units, more so if one moves closer to the full employment level.

- Long-run full employment supply curve may become a limiting vertical case implying total non-response of output to a change in the price level. A rise in price level for any reason will be purely inflationary and a fall reflective of technological improvement or discovery of new resources.

- The difference between the short and long-run supply curve shapes is essentially of degree not of a kind. Supply takes time to change; the slope of short-run supply curves decreases with the length of time considered.

- The major determinants of aggregate supply are: input prices, total productivity, business regulation policies of the government and the socio-political environment of the country.

- Changes in the equilibrium price and output levels can take place due to a change in either (i) aggregate demand, or (ii) aggregate supply, or (iii) both. If the economy is already operating at full employment level, an increase in aggregate demand only may cause demand-pull inflation and a decrease may set in a recession causing cyclical unemployment. Decrease in supply only may trigger cost-push inflation; an increase may cause depression. In mixed cases where both aggregate demand and aggregate supply change simultaneously, it may be difficult to visualize all possibilities.

Glossary

Capital consumption The money value of physical capital that is used up in producing goods and services in a year by way of wear and tear or needs replacement for improving efficiency is called capital consumption. It has to be recovered from the sales revenue like other expenses before arriving at contribution of profits to the national income.

Equilibrium It is the position of rest resulting from the equal pull of two opposite forces operating on the object. For example, price level is in equilibrium when sellers are willing to sell what buyers are willing to buy. The economy is in a stable state.

Income distribution effect It refers to the impact on aggregate demand of a change in the distribution of incomes via consumption. Reduction in income inequalities raises consumption component of aggregate demand and vice versa.

Indirect taxes Taxes that can be transferred wholly or in part to others by those who are legally responsible to pay them are called indirect taxes. Sales tax and custom duties are obvious examples; the sellers pass them forward to the buyers through addition to prices.

Productivity The concept of productivity is used to measure the performance efficiency of a factor of production, for example, labour or of the entire production process. In the case of a single factor, productivity is usually conceived as a marginal concept; other things remaining unchanged, the addition to total output if we employ one more unit of labour will be its marginal productivity. If we add together the marginal productivities of all factors we shall have a measure of total or overall input productivity.

Subsidies To keep the price of a commodity under control the government may give financial support to the producers to lower their cost of production so that they may keep the price at an indicated level. Farm subsidies to make food prices lower is one leading example. Governments these days encourage industries to use costlier but cleaner technologies to combat pollution.

Concepts for Review

- Aggregate demand
- Changes in equilibrium
- Determinants of aggregate demand
- Determinants of aggregate supply
- Equilibrium price level
- Income distribution effects
- Index numbers
- Private consumption and investments
- Productivity
- Real balances effect
- Regulation policies of government

Case Study 16.1

GDP and GNP of Malaysia

The GDP and GNP statistics of Malaysia are given below for selected years at market prices in billion ringgit.

Item	Year				
	2002	2003	2004	2005	2006
GDP	362	395	450	495	546
GNP	337	373	426	471	527

Case Questions

1. Why is GDP and GNP different? Find the difference.
2. Why is GDP > GNP?

Test Questions

16.1 Explain what you understand by the term equilibrium. Construct a diagram to show the equilibrium of an economy that has the following aggregate demand and aggregate supply schedules.

Table 16.5 *Price level aggregate demand and aggregate supply (amount in billion units of money)*

Time point	1	2	3	4	5	6	7
Price level	40	60	80	100	120	140	160
Aggregate demand	200	180	162	145	130	117	106
Aggregate supply	75	94	117	145	183	229	286

16.2 What is price level? Distinguish price level from the change in price level. Use the first row of the table given in question 16.1 to illustrate your answer. (*Hint*: Add a row at the bottom of the table for recording year-on-year inflation).

16.3 Explain briefly the factors that bring about a shift in the aggregate demand curve and reconcile the following statements in the light of your answer.
(a)   Aggregate demand decreases with a rise in price level.
(b)   Price level rises with an increase in aggregate demand.

16.4 Why does an aggregate demand curve slope downwards? Do you agree that the reason is the same as the demand curve of a single commodity for sloping downwards? Give reasons for your answer.

16.5 Construct a diagram using data (imaginary) from the table below; show the price level on Y-axis and aggregate demand on X-axis. If AS_t is the initial aggregate demand curve, show AS_{t-1} and AS_{t+1}.

Table 16.6 *Price levels and aggregate demand cases*

Year	2001	2002	2003	2004	2005	2006	2007
Price level	80	84	90	100	110	125	140
AS_{t-1}	150	165	180	195	200	240	300
AS_t	165	180	195	200	240	300	370
AS_{t+1}	180	195	200	240	300	370	400

16.6   Why should we make a distinction between the short-run and long-run aggregate supply curves? Explain the notions of (a) an increase in aggregate supply and (b) a decrease in aggregate supply. Use illustrative diagrams. What factors cause changes in aggregate supply? Discuss.

16.7   The determinants of aggregate supply make us look to the income components of GDP. Explain and indicate the main determinants of aggregate supply. What is likely to happen in the long run to the aggregate supply curve if the full employment level of output has already been reached? Explain assuming that aggregate demand rises.

16.8   Explain the impact of the following on aggregate supply:
   (a)   Total productivity per unit of output increases due to technical advancement.
   (b)   Most of the export duties are abolished.
   (c)   Petrol is made available at subsidized prices.

16.9   If aggregate supply of goods and services in an economy increases and other things remaining equal, how will price level and employment be affected? Explain using an appropriate diagram.

16.10 Suppose aggregate demand also increases with an increase in aggregate supply. What impacts may you see on price level and output of such a change? Explain using suitable diagrams.

Web Exercise

Search the Internet for the United Nations prescribed standard set of national economic accounting and carefully study the nature of entirly in each account. Focus on how entries in one account find their counter-parts in other accounts.

Forward Link

You have become familiar with the tools of macroeconomic analysis in this chapter. Now, you shall learn to use them step by step to understand macroeconomics in action. The two basic questions macroeconomics seeks to answer are: how the level of national output is determined and what causes fluctuations in that level over time. You have seen that both national income and national expenditure are equal to the value of national output. Taking advantage of this circular relationship, economists prefer to answer the questions raised from the expenditure side of national accounts constituting aggregate demand. You already know the components of aggregate demand and the factors that influence them. But you should also know how these components cause changes in the national output. The following chapter begins explains how the changes in aggregate demand that is in consumption, savings and investment would affect the level of GNP.

CHAPTER 17

Aggregate Demand: Consumption and Investment

LEARNING OUTCOMES

This chapter should enable the student to understand:

- The process of GNP determination from the aggregate demand (expenditure) side
- A new technique of studying macroeconomic equilibrium
- The form and nature of a consumption function
- Various forms of consumption function and their relationships
- Propensity to consume and propensity to save: Their meaning and significance
- GNP determination from the expenditure side: Its components and processes

17.1   INTRODUCTION

In the preceding chapter, we demonstrated how equilibrium GNP is determined by the forces of aggregate demand and aggregate supply but employing the micro style diagrams. However, in macroeconomics we generally use diagrams based on departures from equality positions. The basis of such diagrams is the equality between national income and national expenditure, both in turn being equal to the value of national output as explained in Chapter 15. The bifurcation of the plane at 45° gives us a line such that points on it are at equal distance from the two axes, X and Y. Figure 17.1 is an illustration of this sort of line.

Here, each of the three points T_1, T_2 and T_3 is equi-distant from the X and Y axes, illustrating that each point on the line, income equals expenditure. We shall use this line to explain equilibrium positions in this and the following chapters. However, we can derive the aggregate demand and aggregate supply curves from the equality based figures.

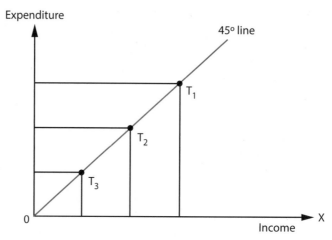

Figure 17.1 *Income received is all spent at any point of the line*

To simplify matters, we begin our discussion below with the assumption of a closed economy without a public sector and without any external transactions. All income (Y) generated in the economy is either consumed or saved, i.e. Y = C + S. All expenditure (E) is either on consumption (C) or investment (I) goods, i.e. E = C + I. As Y = E, we may also write Y = C + I.

17.2   CONSUMPTION AND SAVINGS FUNCTIONS

The notion of a function is mathematical. You will avoid confusion in understanding its meaning if you remember that the word function here simply means 'depends on'. For example, a consumption function specifies the factors on which aggregate consumption depends. We know that consumption (C) depends on the disposable income of households and the relationship between consumption and disposable income defines the consumption function. Of course, you may find wide variations in the consumption behaviour of individuals; rich households tend to spend more on consumption goods than the poor. High income generally goes with high consumption spending.

But expenditure on consumption must be seen in relation to overall income level. What fraction of their disposable income households spend on consumption is called their **propensity to consume**. If we multiply this proportion by the ratio of all household disposable income to the GNP, we get households' propensity to consume for the economy as a whole.

Let us illustrate the point. Assume that in a year, out of their aggregate RM75 billion disposable income, households consume 50 billion worth of goods and services. Their propensity to consume with reference to their disposable income will be 50/75 or 2/3. If the GNP for the year were RM150 billion, the ratio of disposable income to GNP would be 75/150 or 1/2. We can get the households' propensity to consume in terms of GNP by multiplying the two ratios, i.e. $[2/3 \times 1/2] = 1/3$ for the economy. Note that we can arrive at the same result by dividing household consumption expenditure directly by the GNP, thus: $50/150 = 1/3$.

As the data on household consumption and disposable income are not regularly collected and published in most economies, propensity to consume is generally calculated for the economy as a whole by relating aggregate consumption (private + public) to the GNP. Propensity to consume can be thought of in two ways:

1. Average propensity to consume or APC: It is obtained for the households by dividing the annual consumption expenditure by the GNP for the year.

    $$\text{Average propensity to consume} = \frac{\text{Consumption expenditure}}{\text{Gross national product}} \qquad (17.1)$$

2. Marginal propensity to consume: Here, we take the difference of consumption expenditures and the GNPs of the two consecutive years to calculate the ratio. Thus,

    Marginal propensity to consume or MPC $= (\Delta C/\Delta Y)$ \qquad (17.2)

    As income not consumed is by definition income saved, average propensity to save or APS is:

    $$\text{APS} = (1 - \text{APC}) \qquad (17.3)$$

    And marginal propensity to save or MPS, would likewise be:

    $$\text{MPS} = (1 - \text{MPC}) \qquad (17.4)$$

> Remember that in our closed model, GNP will equal the disposable income of the households.

How the values of APC, APS, MPC and MPS behave with reference to income level changes and how they are mutually related is shown in Table 17.1, using imaginary data.

Table 17.1 *Household income, consumption and savings (amount in RM million)*

Income (Y)	Consumption expenditure (C)	Savings (S)	Average propensity to consume (APC)	Average propensity to save (APS)	Marginal propensity to consume (MPC)	Marginal propensity to save (MPS)
2,000	2,150	−150	1.08	−0.08		
3,000	3,100	−100	1.03	−0.03	0.95	0.05
4,000	4,000	0	1.00	0	0.90	0.10
5,000	4,850	150	0.97	0.03	0.85	0.15
6,000	5,650	350	0.94	0.06	0.80	0.20
7,000	6,380	620	0.91	0.09	0.73	0.27
8,000	7,050	950	0.88	0.12	0.67	0.33
9,000	7,670	1,330	0.85	0.15	0.62	0.38
10,000	8,180	1,870	0.82	0.18	0.51	0.49

Exercise 17.1

Explain how the following values have been obtained for Table 17.1: APC = 1.03, MPC = 0.80, APS = 0.06 and MPS = 0.27. Why are the first two values for the APS in the table negative?

At low levels of income, people may not be able to meet even their minimal basic needs of food, clothing and shelter without external assistance—donations or borrowing. Consumption expenditure is more than personal disposable income.

The above discussion concerning consumption expenditures, savings and their respective propensities need not convey that household income alone affects these variables. There are many other influences that affect the decisions of a family on consumption and savings. Some of these, for example, are the number and age composition of the family members, especially the children. The sources of income, past accumulations, future income expectations and the like also matter. Thus, it is not necessary for any two households with identical income to have the same consumption patterns and identical propensities to consume and save. However, in economics we do not deal with each individual case; we are interested in knowing the broad average pattern of behaviour of the households. Even on average, wealthy families spend much more on consumption than the poorer ones. The consumption functions we shall be dealing with will show the general sort of relationship between consumption expenditure and income. This relationship has a central position and role in the analysis of what determines the level of the GNP and cause it to change over time.

Propensity to consume or save is a *ratio* to GNP not an absolute amount. For, in absolute terms consumption values are invariably much larger than the savings figures.

Notice that with an increase in income, the average propensity to consume falls while the average propensity to save rises. The opposite is true when income decreases; average propensity to consume rises and to save falls. This confirms in actual life the common observation that the rich are able to save a larger proportion of their incomes than the poor. At very low levels of income, savings are in fact negative as we find in Table 17.1; savings are negative until income touches the RM4,000 million mark.

17.2.1 Why Do Average and Marginal Propensities Differ?

The reason is that an average propensity relates the relevant variable (consumption or savings) to the level of income *at one point of time*. On the other hand, marginal propensity is the ratio of *change* in the variable (consumption or savings) to the change in income *over two points of time*. For example, look at Table 17.2 that gives private consumption and savings data as also the GNP figures for three years. Note that APC and APS moved in the opposite direction with an increase in GNP and the relationship between MPC and MPS is no different.

Table 17.2 *Marginal propensities to consume and save for Malaysia, 2003–2005 (amount in RM billion)*

Year	Private consumption (C)	Private savings (S)	GNP =C + S	APC	APS	MPC	MPS
2003	172.4	76.0	248.4	0.694	0.306		
2004	192.8	85.9	278.7	0.692	0.308	0.67	0.33
2005	215.9	103.9	319.8	0.675	0.325	0.59	0.41

Source: Bank Negara Malaysia, Annual Report 2007, Tables A.4 and A.5.

As income can either be consumed or saved, the two propensities are counterparts of one another. If we know any one of them, we may easily find the other as follows:

$$Y = C + S$$

Divide by Y; we get:

$$\frac{Y}{Y} = \frac{C}{Y} + \frac{S}{Y}$$

Thus, we get:

$$1 = APC + APS$$
$$APC = 1 - APS,$$

and,

$$APS = 1 - APC \qquad (17.5)$$

In Figure 17.2, the consumption curve is concave from below. It is so because marginal propensity to consume, i.e. the slope of the curve decreases as disposable income increases. At point T, the economy is in a state of equilibrium in the sense that here, national income, national expenditure and the value of national output, Q, are all equal with zero savings. But if output increases to Q_1, then income, BQ_1, will be greater than consumption, C_1Q_1; and their difference, B_1C_1, becomes savings. The economy at Q_1 is in a state of disequilibrium. Savings B_1C_1 is a leakage from the circular income flow; its level will shrink, recession will set in and unemployment will spread unless the leakage is injected back into the flow.

> Savings are a leakage from the income stream and unless injected back into the flow at some point, recession is likely to set in.

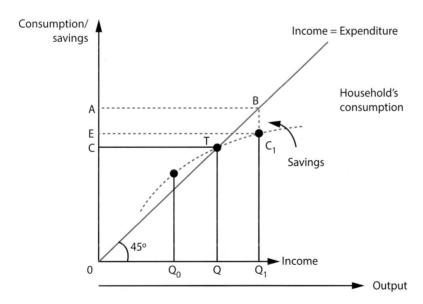

Figure 17.2 *Consumption, income and output equilibrium in a closed model*

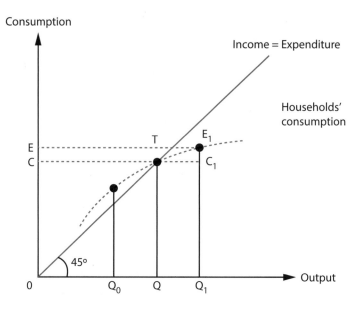

Figure 17.3 *Consumption, income and marginal propensity to consume*

We may modify the diagram as in Figure 17.3 to explain the concept of marginal propensity to consume (Equation 17.6) and obtain marginal propensity to save as well by deducting MPC from 1.

$$MPC = \frac{\text{Change in consumption}}{\text{Change in income}}$$

$$= \frac{E_1Q_1 - C_1Q_1}{0Q_1 - 0Q}$$

$$= \frac{E_1C_1}{TC_1 = QQ_1}$$

(17.6)

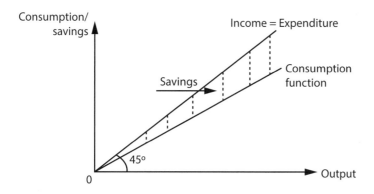

Figure 17.4 *Savings need not always be negative at low levels of income*

Many economies, especially the developed ones, are in a position to meet the minimal needs of their population even at very low levels of income through say withdrawals from past accumulations of wealth. In their case, the consumption function does not cross the equality of income and expenditure line. Figure 17.4 above explains such a situation.

> All consumption curves need not always cross the 45° line.

BOX 17.1

Marginal Propensity to Consume and Islamic Macroeconomics

It is not worth devoting time to determine what will happen to the marginal propensity to consume in a Keynesian macroeconomic framework. What is required is to recognize that the consumer behaviour in Islamic framework is a distinct behaviour compared to what a Keynesian or any other framework would imply. These distinctions are required to be incorporated into the consumption function of an Islamic economy. What Islamic economists should now be in search of is the identification of the building blocks of the Islamic economic system so that an ideal Islamic economy is presented in comparison with the Arrow-Debreu type economy and so that the outcome of the Islamic economy may be compared and evaluated with that of the Arrow-Debreu type economy. For example, we are still not clear about what the Islamic approach to the time value of resources is and whether general equilibrium with such an approach to time-value of resources will exist and be unique and stable as the Arrow-Debreu type economy is being proved to be. Confining ourselves to the MPC in Keynesian framework takes us nowhere in describing the system and the decision-making process in an ideal Islamic economy.

The consumer decision-making in an Islamic economy is not merely what Keynesian type consumption function implies. There, it is simply a consumption-income relationship. In Islamic economic framework, consumption function is much more than merely a consumption–income relationship.

Unlike the Keynesian function, the consumer behaviour in Islamic framework is not important simply because it determines savings in the economy which in turn determines investment and hence growth of the economy. It is important in Islamic framework because it first determines distribution of income and wealth in the economy before it implies savings and hence growth.

17.3   SOME COMPLICATIONS

The expenditure on consumption does rise (fall) with an increase (decrease) in disposable income but the behaviour of consumers is not as simple as Figures 17.2 and 17.3 make them out to be.

To begin with, the proportion of its income that a household may want to spend on consumption is likely to depend not on the income it gets but also on the amount *relative* to the average income of others around. People want to be well off but they want more to be ahead of others. Keeping up with the Joneses' is an old adage but ever fresh. Relative income hypothesis is part of advanced explanations of consumer behaviour.

> People do not want to become rich, they want to become richer.

Another complexity of consumer behaviour that has important implications for stability; one of the major goals of macroeconomic policies; is that consumers' purchases in the short run do not fluctuate so sharply as their disposable income. There is empirical evidence that consumers have a tendency to adjust their consumption pattern to their long term income possibilities. The presumption gave rise to the life cycle theories of consumers' behaviour. Both relative income and life cycle theories are part of higher studies in macroeconomics; we do not discuss them at the present introductory stage.

> Long-run income prospects have greater influence on consumer behaviour than short-run considerations.

Finally, the nature of income (temporary or permanent) affects propensity to consume in a considerable measure. Retirement benefits including pensions, health care facilities and insurance schemes tend to make people care free for the future: propensity to consume tends to rise at all income levels in general. The thriving credit card business and culture provides evidence on the point.

> Why is MPC less than 1?

In spite of these and other complications in understanding consumer behaviour, the fact that consumption expenditure tends to rise and fall with income can hardly be denied. Even more significant is the fact that the change in consumption is less in absolute terms than the change in income.

17.3.1   How is GNP Determined?

> Consumption is part of national expenditure while saving is unspent income.

Figure 15.1 demonstrated money flow circulating between businesses and households in a closed economy and why they assumed different names—value of output, factor incomes and consumption expenditure—depending where one chooses to look at the circular flow. In Chapter 3, we discussed the components of aggregate demand and aggregate supply, the factors that determine each of them and how the two are equal at the equilibrium price level. All these are relevant matters for understanding the basics of macroeconomics. However, these are no more than building blocks for answering the vital questions: how national income is determined and what causes it to fluctuate, at times violently? Here, we start this discussion focusing on the consumption and saving components of national output. Remember that in this discussion we can drag items such as savings from the income side into analyzing expenditure using negative sign because they are two sides of the same coin: National income = Y = National expenditure. (In Chapter 2 under national income account, we have C = Y − S.)

17.3.2   Consumption, Savings and Investment

Recall that in our closed model, no government or external transactions exist. Let us make this model still simpler: assume further that savings in the economy are all done by the households. Businesses save nothing; they surrender all gross profits to the owners. In this scenario, all national income becomes disposable income. However, businesses spend money on investments. From where do they get the money to invest shall be discussed later. It is easy to see in this model the aggregate demand that determines the level of GNP will have only two elements: consumption expenditure of the households (C) and investment expenditure of businesses (I).

There will also be no difference between GNP and NNI. Why?

Example 17.1 Assume the consumption function for an economy is:

$$C = 250 + 0.6Y \qquad (17.7)$$

The savings function will then be: $S = Y − C = −250 + 0.4Y$ (17.8)

Assume further that businesses keep investments constant at $\bar{I} = \$150$ million irrespective of what output the economy produces. The aggregate demand (AD) function will then be:

$$AD = C + \bar{I} = (250 + 0.6Y) + 150$$
$$= 400 + 0.6Y \qquad (17.9)$$

These assumptions help us produce Table 17.3 which shows that the economy is in a state of equilibrium when the value of output is $1,000 million because here the GNP or Y equals the aggregate demand expenditure, i.e. C + I. Figure 17.5 depicts these facts.

Table 17.3 *Consumption, savings, investment and equilibrium output[†] (million Dollars)*

GNP (Y)	Consumption (C = 250 + 0.6Y)	Savings (S = Y − C = − 250 + .4Y	Investment (Ī)	Consumption + Investment (C + I = 400 + 0.6Y)
0	250	−250	150	400
250	400	−150	150	550
500	550	−50	150	700
750	700	50	150	850
1,000	**850**	**150**	**150**	**1,000**
1,250	1,000	250	150	1,150
1,500	1,150	350	150	1,300

[†]Data illustrative and imaginary

In Figure 17.5, C + I is the consumption function plus the amount of investment spending. It tells us that for every level of output there is a matching amount of income generated. The consumption function informs us how much of that income will be spent on consumption (C) and if we add to it the amount spent on investment (I) we get total spending or aggregate demand. The curve C + I is, therefore, total spending of the economy or the aggregate demand schedule as given in the last column of Table 17.3.

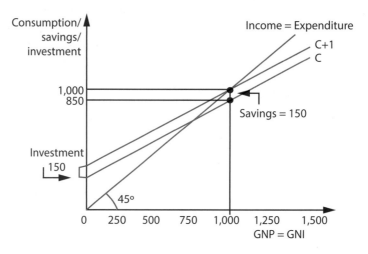

Figure 17.5 *Determination of GNP: expenditure or aggregate demand model*

Exercise 17.4

Add a column to the right of Table 17.3 and enter into each cell the excess or deficiency of aggregate demand compared to aggregate supply. Explain why the economy is in a state of equilibrium when the GNP is $1,000 million.

Exercise 17.5

Use Equation (17.7) to derive the corresponding savings function and use it to verify if the values entered into the savings column of Table 17.3 are correct. Show your calculations. Add a row at the bottom of the table and see if you can fill in the cell details.

Actual savings always equal actual investment but this need not be true for what savers plan to save and investors plan to invest in the year ahead.

But Figure 17.5 shows that only one of the outputs, where C + I = 1,000 as given in Table 17.3, will be produced. It is the equilibrium output. Recall that we had asked the question: from where do the funds for investments come? This can now be answered. These funds come from the savings of the households out of their income. The people who make the decisions to invest are not the same ones who have saved part of their income; how then does savings equal investment as the example shows? It is a matter of definition: income is equal to expenditure. Income not consumed is savings. This means expenditure on consumption must leave some of the goods unsold. Value of goods remaining unsold is counted as investment. Thus, savings must equal investment if the income = expenditure identity is to remain intact. But remember that savings = investment is an accounting imperative. Accounts present *ex post* data; they record what *has* happened. The savers and investors being different groups of people are guided by different motives, so savings and investment in their *ex ante* version need not be equal.

Ex ante versions mean planned savings and planned investments. If the two were per chance equal, as at Q_1, the economy will presumably be in a state of equilibrium at full employment level. However, if aggregate demand (C + I) falls short of aggregate supply, i.e. households decide to save more than businesses plan to invest as at Q_2, recessionary trends may set in the economy pushing output back to Q_1 to restore equilibrium. In contrast, if the output were Q_0, planned investments will exceed planned savings (equal to zero) making aggregate demand larger than aggregate supply. Prices will tend to rise enlarging profits. Expansionary pressures will push output up towards Q_1, the equilibrium level.

> Aggregate demand and aggregate supply are in equilibrium when planned savings equal planned investments.

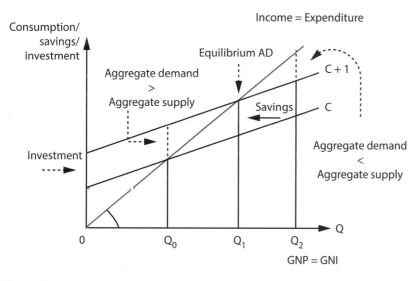

Figure 17.6 *Aggregate demand model: equilibrium and disequilibrium*

It follows from the above discussion that for stability of an economy, the equality of planned investments and planned savings is necessary; for that alone can keep aggregate demand equal to aggregate supply. Figure 17.7 illustrates this point. Investments remain constant at all levels of GNP. You can see that savings stay negative until output expands to $625 million. After that, growth in GNP takes place until savings completely matches investment at point T = $1,000 million.

To repeat, remember that the process leading to the equality of savings and investments does the full productive potential of an economy.

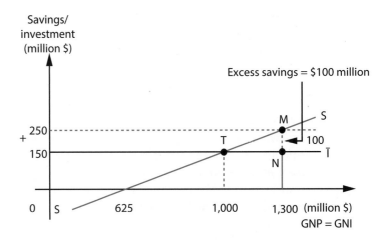

Figure 17.7 *Demand and supply are in a state of equilibrium only where S = I*

For example, if in Figure 17.7, excess savings of $100 million at M were used to raise investments by that amount, the potential of the economy could be utilized to push up GNP to $1,300 million. This last point leads us to an important concept in macroeconomics.

17.3.3 The Multiplier

You see that in Figure 17.7 if savings = investments, investments rise by MN = 100, income increases from T to N, that is, by $1,300 - 1,000 = 300$. If we divide 300 by 100 we get 3. Thus, income increases three times of the increase in investments. The number of times an increase in investment causes increase in income (GNP) is called the **investment multiplier**. To formalize the concepts, let C, $\bar{I}$ and Y be the initial values of the three entities. Also, let the change in C, $\bar{I}$ and Y be denoted as ΔC, $\Delta \bar{I}$ and ΔY, respectively. Now, if $M_{\bar{I}}$ were the investment multiplier, we have:

$$M_I = \frac{\Delta Y}{\Delta I} \tag{17.10}$$

We can express the multiplier with reference to consumption function as follows:

$$C = a + cY, \text{ where } a \text{ and } c \text{ are some constants.}$$
$$S = Y - C$$
$$= Y - a - cY$$

$$= -a + (1-c)\,Y \tag{17.11}$$
$$S + \Delta S = -a + (1-c)\,(Y + \Delta Y) \tag{17.12}$$

Equation (17.12) − (17.11),

$$\Delta S = (1-c)\,\Delta Y \tag{17.13}$$

If I = S then,

$$\Delta S = \Delta I$$

We may write equation 17.13 as:

$$\Delta I = (1-c)\,\Delta Y$$

Dividing by ΔI we get:

$$1 = (1-c)\frac{\Delta Y}{\Delta I} \tag{17.14}$$

But c is the marginal propensity to consume or MPC.

So, we may write equation 17.14 as follows:

$$(1-\text{MPC})\frac{\Delta Y}{\Delta I} = 1, \text{ or}$$

$$\frac{\Delta Y}{\Delta I} = \frac{1}{1-\text{MPC}}$$

But $1 - \text{MPC} = \text{MPS}$ and $\dfrac{\Delta Y}{\Delta I}$ is the investment multiplier (M).

Thus, finally we get $M = \dfrac{1}{1-\text{MPC}}$ or

$$= \frac{1}{\text{MPS}} \tag{17.15}$$

Here, we have introduced the concept of multiplier to make you familiar with it but its significance comes to light in the analysis of economic dynamics which we shall discuss later.

Exercise 17.7

Suppose the consumption function for an economy is as follows (expressed in billion dollars):

C = A + cY, where A and c are constants. You are required to:
  (i) Derive the savings function for the economy.
  (ii) Find the multiplier (M) for investment (Ī) which is independent of the level of output, i.e. the GNP.
Given A = 300 and c = 0.7, find the current GNP if Ī = 30 and initial GNP = 2,000.

17.3.4   Business and the GNP

We have so far discussed the simple case of circular flow in a closed economy with only one form of leakage: personal savings. The case had the advantage of keeping GNI equal to disposable income. Businesses or

Equality of *ex ante* savings and investment alone ensure stable macroeconomic equilibrium.

governments did not absorb income. We now remove these restrictions as we have already seen in Chapter 3, that disposable personal income constitutes only part of the gross national income. Businesses today are among the main carriers of economic change and progress. One part of the remaining GNI goes to business firms as retained earnings and depreciation reserves which have increasingly become a surer and safer source of self-financing; though external sources remain important. These we call gross business savings. The other part goes to the government in the form of tax revenue. But for the time being, let us continue assuming away the existence of the government and consider gross national income consisting of only two broad components: personal disposable income and gross business savings.

With growth in GNP (= GNI) business profits also tend to rise in volume. Unfortunately in most economies, especially the developing ones, published data on profits is scanty and unreliable. Business reports in the media do at times provide information on the rate of growth in absolute amounts of major firms' profits in a country but information on profit rates on capital or sales is rarely available. Income retention data may be obtained only if one chooses to glean through the periodic accounts of firms for information and add up the relevant figures for overall aggregates. Government statistical organizations can fill an important gap in national data needed for a variety of uses if only they realize their significance.

Profits are intimately related to the level of business activity. Part of profit is paid out to the shareholders in the form of dividends; the remaining is retained in business. Thus, for each level of GNI we have a corresponding level of gross business savings, but note that it does not form part of disposable income as discussed earlier; it is retained in business. To sum up, out of each additional dollar worth of income generated in an economy, one part flows into disposable personal income and the other part goes to gross business savings. An illustration may help. Suppose GNP (= GNI) increases by $1,000. The possible consequences are presented in Table 17.4.

Table 17.4 *Impact of increase in income on savings: personal + business*

Treatment of additional income = $1,000	Personal disposable income	Business profit
A. 40% flows to business profits; 60% to personal disposable income	600	400
B. 20% is paid to shareholders as dividend from business profits	+ 80	− 80
C. Total	680	320
D. Savings from personal disposable income if MPC = 0.75	170	
E. Total savings of the economy 170 + 320	490	

Exercise 17.8

Calculate the marginal propensity to save for (i) the households, (ii) business and (iii) the economy. Comment on the difference between the first two.

Table 17.4 brings out a few important facts as follows:

1. There is a distinct level of personal disposable income associated with each level of GNP because a part of the additional income generated invariably flows to households.
2. For every level of personal disposable income, we have an associated level of household consumption.
3. It follows that a change in GNP will also change consumption via the relationships stated in 1 and 2 above. However, the change in consumption will be smaller than the change in GNP.
4. Business savings notably raise the marginal propensity to save for the economy as a whole because no part of retained earnings is consumed.

Thus far, we discussed consumption with reference to personal disposable income in the economy. However, the first three points above establish a direct link between aggregate consumption and the GNP. This enables us to detach the concept of marginal propensity to consume from disposable income and link it directly to GNP. We distinguish this linkage from the one with disposable income by attaching k as subscript to the symbol, that is, we write marginal propensity as MPC_k.

> We now relax our assumptions of having no business income or no government.

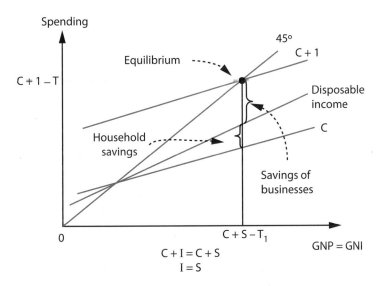

Figure 17.8 *In equilibrium, household + business savings equal investment*

Figure 17.8 helps us understand the implications of the change in the linkage of MPC with disposable income to GNP. The generation of a gross national product equal to OT_1 or ET_1 would generate an income that is equal to (C + I) spending.

Exercise 17.9

(a) The increase in GNP = GNI of an economy over the previous year is estimated to be equal to $800 billion of which 40% is disposable income. If private consumption increases by $200 billion, show that the MPC_{GNP} will be 0.25. Will it be greater or smaller than if consumption were related to disposable income? Calculate and compare.

(b) Suppose MPC_{GNP} = 0.5 and disposable income is 60% of the GNP; what will the MPC be in relation to the disposable income?

We may now link consumption directly to GNP.

17.3.5 Government and the GNP

Governments have to spend money on numerous social services they are called upon to provide to the community and invariably undertake substantial production activities in various fields, especially defence. You have already learnt the details in Chapter 2. Government obtains money for performing its functions through taxation of business and personal incomes as its main sources of revenue. It also participates in the savings and investment processes of the economy. Here we bring in government or the public sector into the process of GNP determination focusing on its spending and tax revenue.

The introduction of the government requires two modifications in our earlier model.

1. The consumption–GNP relationship needs readjustment to incorporate in it the leakage from the circular income flow because of taxation.

2. We have to include in consumption, the government spending on economic activities it undertakes. (See if you can identify the relevant items in Table 17.1.)

Imposition of taxes tends to lower household spending on consumption and, therefore, aggregate demand. But at the same time, government purchase of goods and services from the market tends to compensate for the leakage. In any case, we have to think of aggregate demand now as including consumption, investment and government purchases of goods and services. To be precise, GNP will tend to settle at a level where output would equal the sum of these three elements. Aggregate demand will, in equilibrium, equal total output when the part of income *not* spent on consumption will match personal savings + business savings and + government tax revenue or when total savings plus taxes match investment plus government spending. Figure 17.9 depicts the impact of these adjustments on equilibrium of the economy.

Exercise 17.10

Let us go back to Table 17.4 and introduce government into the picture assuming:

(i)   That the households have to pay income tax at 10% on personal disposable income.

(ii) That business has to pay a corporate tax at 30% on profits before dividends.

(iii) That the current spending of the government on goods and services matches its tax revenue.

Redraw Table 17.4 incorporating these facts. Check if your results are the same as in Table 17.5.

Table 17.5 *Impact of increase in income on savings: personal + business*

Treatment of additional income = $1,000	Personal disposable income	Business profit	Government
A. 40% flows to business profit; 60% to personal disposable income	600	400	
B. 20% is paid to shareholders as dividend from business profits	+ 80	− 80	
C. Total	680	320	
D. Taxes	− 60	− 120	+ 180
E. Consumption	465	0	− 180
F. Savings from personal disposable income if MPC = 0.75	155	200	
G. Total savings of the economy 155 + 200 + 0		355	0

Show and explain your calculations clearly.

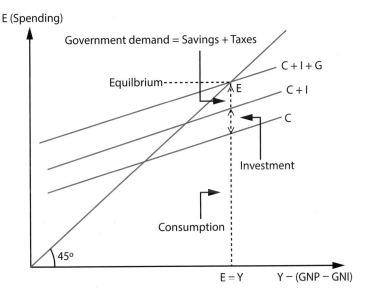

Figure 17.9 *Determination of equilibrium GNP with inclusion of government*

17.3.6 Multiplier versus Stabilizing Operators

Automatic stabilizers moderate mild fluctuations in investments or other spending; they are powerless to impact major turmoils.

The discussion on multiplier in Section 17.3.3 focused on its technical aspect and illustrated its application with reference to its linkage with an *increase* in investment. Now we add that the concept of multiplier applies equally to any type of reduction in investment. It works the same way in response to changes in other forms of spending, especially governmental. Multiplier effect on national income is of relatively greater concern when it operates in the reverse direction. The larger the multiplier, the greater the chances that a reduction in initial investment or other spending will lead to a serious downturn of the economy; recession would be deeper and longer. Fortunately, multipliers have not been large in modern economies after the 1930s. In addition, there are some automatic operators in market economies that attempt to counter the adverse impact of a declining multiplier and keep them relatively stable. Operators that tend to stabilize an economy include, among others, the following variables mentioned below.

Business savings

We shall illustrate later that business savings absorb a large proportion of change in national income in most economies and help stabilize disposable personal income. Profits react much to the slightest change in the level of economic activity; they drop off fast with falls in GNP. In addition, corporations in general tend to follow a stable dividend policy even when profits become leaner. Thus, gross business savings fall much more rapidly than other forms of income; they work as shock absorbers.

1. **Government tax collection**: As national income increases (decreases) the tax collections of the government automatically rises (falls), the rates remaining unchanged. Most business taxes use income, profit or sales as the levy base. Thus, a portion of the fall in national income is soaked by the government revenues. The extent of the fall in disposable personal income is thus reduced by what the government soaks in. To illustrate, assume that the national income last year was 10,000 and the tax rate was 10%. Other things being equal, disposable personal income would be 9,000 and tax revenue 1,000. Now, suppose this year the national income falls to 9,000. Of this, disposable personal income would be 8,100, the remaining 900 going to the government as tax. Between the two years, the fall in disposable personal incomes is of 900 and government tax collection 100. What the government soaks in (100) people have to pay less; total reduction 900 + 100 = 1,000.

2. **Transfer payments**: Transfer payments originating from the government automatically increase during the periods of

falling income and employment. In most developed economies, unemployment allowances and other social security benefits reduce the impact of the falling GNP on wage income.

3. **Living standards rigidity**: Finally, despite the fall in disposable income, households attempt to maintain their earlier living standards as far as possible. They think that the fall in their income is only temporary and good days will soon return. Reduced earnings during recessions do not make most of them cut back on their consumption outlay at the same pace as the fall in income. The above discussed automatic stabilizers operating in modern economies keep MPC_G relatively small during moderate variations in GNP. Obviously, MPS_G stays relatively large and multiplier ($M = 1/MPS$) therefore is smaller. It follows that changes in the initial investment or government spending are less likely to lead to major depressions or violent inflations. However, stabilizers have their limitations. They are expected to be effective to neutralize moderate variations in investment or government spending. They are like boot straps and powerless to lift the weight of major upheavals.

BOX 17.2

Impact of *Israf* and *Zakat* on Aggregate Consumption

Writers in the area of Islamic macroeconomic theory seem obsessed with a desire to introduce moderation—avoidance of *israf*—in their models as a compensatory factor for the consumption increasing potential of *zakat*. They are usually haunted by the fear that increased consumption would reduce savings and investment in the economy slowing down its rate of growth compared to a secular model. Such obsession is meaningless, and its fear misplaced. What is important for believers is not primarily the superiority or otherwise of the Islamic models over the secular ones, but the molding of their thinking, behaviour and social institutions according to the dictates of the Shari'ah. What then follows must be welcomed as the best.

On a rational plane, one must recognize that the concept of moderation in consumption is vague as *israf* is not a verifiable quantity. The consumer himself may not usually be able to separate *israf* from legitimate requirements. An external observer like an economist is all the more a poor judge in the matter. In contrast, *zakat* including voluntary expenditure in the way of Allah, is at once objective and a quantifiable variable. It is better to desist from obscuring its impact on aggregate consumption by introducing negative *israf* i.e. moderation as a balancing factor in an Islamic model.

Such models can rarely have descriptive utility or predictive value. Presumably one should prefer analyzing the impact of *zakat* on consumption in an Islamic model with the assumption that the level of *israf* is zero. Then one can describe how the results are likely to change if *israf* does take place. We may explain this approach by using a familiar type of diagram.

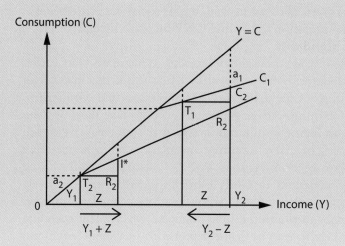

Figure 17.10 *Impact of zakat and israf on aggregate consumption*

Here C_1 is the consumption function of the *zakat* payers with Y_1 income and a_1 the minimum consumption constraint. The corresponding values for *zakat* recipients are $C_2 Y_2$ and a_2. Z is the amount of *zakat* transfers—calculated on appropriate basis—from the payers to the recipients. The amount could be gross or net depending on whether Z includes or excludes collection charges and intra-payer transfers. The slopes of C_1 and C_2 indicate that the MPC of the payers is smaller than the MPC of the recipients. Before *zakat* transfers, the entire Y_2 is consumed by assumption ($y_2 = a_2$). After transfers, Y_2 increases to $Y_2 + Z$ and Y_1 is reduced to $Y_1 - Z$. As a consequence, the consumption of the payers is reduced by $T_1 R_1$ and of the recipients increased by $T_2 R_2$. The slope of C_2 being greater than of C_1, so $T_2 R_2 > T_1 R_1$. Thus, for any given Y, aggregate consumption must increase as a net result of *zakat* transfers, savings are obviously reduced.

Now, if *israf* is introduced into the picture, the slope of C_1 will tend to rise as extravagance of the rich increases. The positive effect of *zakat* on aggregate consumption will not, however, be reversed—though progressively reduced—so long as the increasing slope of C_1 under the impact of *israf* remains less than that of C_2. It will be zero when the two slopes become equal. The net *zakat* effect would be negative because of it, aggregate consumption would be less and savings more—only when *israf* makes C_1 become steeper than C_2. Such possibilities are expected to be rare in an Islamic economy. Therefore, the conclusion drawn in the above paragraph is likely to remain intact. To my mind it is not *israf*, but some other factors which require more serious thought and investigation in formulating a consumption function in an Islamic economy. Some of these are briefly indicated below. An individual's consumption expenditure depends *inter alia* on his total resources. There is an *a priori* expectation that his consumption will rise with the level of resources but in such a way that it takes a smaller proportion. However, in the long run, increased consumption of the poor due to *zakat* receipts may increase their productivity contributing to a net rise in Y.

Summary

- In this chapter we have looked at the process of GNP determination from the side of aggregate demand (AD) including its broad components: consumption, savings and investment.

- We use a new technique for dealing with macroeconomic issues—the 45° line—based on a few identities such as $C + S = Y$, or $Y = C + I$, or $S = I$. Points on this line are at equal distances from the Y and X axes.

- Function means 'depends on'. Consumption function specifies the factors on which consumption of individuals depends. For example, its linear form is $C = a + cY$, where a and c are some constants and Y can be disposable income or GNP.

- What is not consumed is saved, i.e. savings or $S = Y - C$, i.e. $S = Y - a - cY$ or $S = -a + (1 - c)Y$.

- In the consumption function, $C = a + cY$, a is the minimum consumption level needed for survival of the people independent of the level of income Y; c is the proportion of current income (disposable or GNP) that flows into consumption.

- The money value of goods and services consumed in a year divided by the income of that year is called the *average propensity to consume*. On the other hand, the division of *change* in consumption by the *change* in income causing it is called the *marginal propensity to consume*.

- The average or marginal propensity to consume do not depend only on the size of income other influences are also there; the important ones are the relative position of a person on the income ladder and his long-run income level and security expectations. However, the consumption linkage with current income remains valid and vital.

- The circular flow of money in the economy ensure the value of national output. National income and national expenditure are essentially different names of the same flow; what we call it depends at what point we look and account for it.

- In a simplified two sector closed model, we deal with the determinants of GNP from the side of aggregate demand (AD) with reference to consumption, savings and investment. The income is determined at the level where $S = I$. Departures from this equality create excess of savings over investment or vice versa causing disequilibrium (instability) in the economy which sets into motion adjustments to equate savings and investment to restore equilibrium.

- Equality of actual savings and actual investment is an accounting imperative; an accomplished fact. Savers and investors in an economy are different sets of people and the motives that regulate their acts are also different. So, the amounts of intended savings and intended investments seldom coincide. Thus, economies are usually in a state of disequilibrium with forces at work to restore equilibrium.

- Unlike consumption, investment has the characteristic of multiplying output (income) several folds. The part of wheat crop that we eat away i.e. consume, does not replace itself. But each grain of wheat that we use as seed (investment) reproduces in due course into hundreds of wheat grains to replace itself. The number of times investment (a seed grain) multiplies itself in generating income is called investment multiplier. Thus, $M = \Delta Y/\Delta I$.

- But, $\Delta I = \Delta S$. This is linked to consumption function as $\Delta S = (1 - c)\Delta Y$. Investment multiplier (M) is then equal to $\Delta Y/(1 - c)\Delta Y$, which gives us $M = 1/(1 - c)$. As $(1 - c)$ is MPS, we finally have $M = 1/MPS$.

- In our simple closed model, we restricted our discussion to disposable income of the households as equivalent to GNP (= GNI). We can relax that restriction to bring business activities into the model.

- One part of business earnings is distributed to the owners in the form of dividends and adds to personal consumption and savings. The remaining part is retained in business as (i) addition to depreciation (capital consumption) fund to replace fixed assets in future and (ii) to increase free reserves. Both constitute business savings.

- As business propensity to save (MPS) is equal to 1, their retained earnings boost national savings. Aggregate savings (household + business) provide matching investments to boost national economic growth.

- Finally, we bring government into the picture with reference to its spending and taxation activities in the economy. Government spends money on providing services to the people, for example, in terms of education, health care, civil administration and defence. It runs sometimes selected key industries and invests in infrastructures.

- Government raises money for undertaking these activities through taxation among other sources. Even in developed economies of the world 20 to 30% of the GNP is absorbed by public sector activities. The percentage is much higher in the case of developing economies.

- The spending and taxation activities of the state must be seen as complementary to one another not in isolation to have a balanced view of the public sector role in developing countries.

Glossary

Automatic stabilizers Operation of multiplier tends to make market economies prone to undesirable fluctuations in incomes and employment. However, there are some automatic stabilizers in such economies that reduce the multiplier impact in case of both inflation and depression and thus tend to moderate the fluctuations. Business savings and public taxation/ expenditure operate as the main shock absorbers.

Function Here, function means 'depends upon'. For example, if we say that economic growth is a function of investment, we imply that growth of GNP depends on investment. The relationship a function expresses has a dependent variable such as the growth rate in our example and independent variable(s) as investment that determine it. A function can be monotonic where only one value of dependent variable is caused by the independent variable or non-monotonic where a value of independent variable is associated with more than one value of the dependent variable. A variable can be a decreasing function of another variable as quantity supplied is an increasing function of price; it can also be a decreasing function as quantity demanded of price.

Investment multiplier (M) It is the number of times an increase in investment multiplies GNP, i.e. $M = \Delta Y/\Delta I$. The concept of multiplier is valid for other forms of spending as well, especially public expenditure.

Propensity to consume It is the ratio of consumption expenditure (C) for a period to a defined income concept (Y) such as disposable or national. We may think of it in terms of average or marginal. Average propensity to consume (APC) equals C/Y while marginal propensity to consume (MPC) is incremental, i.e. $\Delta C/\Delta Y$.

Propensity to save It is the counterpart of propensity to consume; for savings is income not consumed. Thus, S/Y is the average propensity to save; it equals $(1 - APC)$. Similarly, marginal propensity to save is $\Delta S/\Delta Y$, which is the same thing as $(1 - MPC)$.

Concepts for Review

- Average propensity to consume
- Components of aggregate demand
- Equilibrium and disequilibrium
- Function
- Government and the GNP equilibrium
- Investment multiplier
- Life cycle hypothesis
- Marginal propensity to save

- Profits-growth interaction
- Propensity to consume
- Propensity to save
- Relative income theory
- Savings and investment equality
- Taxes and subsidies
- Temporary versus permanent income hypothesis
- 45° line

Case Study   17.1

New Fuel Subsidy System in Malaysia

The following Table 17.6 provides summary statistics for three years about Malaysian economy at current prices after the 1998 financial crisis. The figures have been approximated to RM billion.

Table 17.6 *Summary data of GNP and its components for Malaysia (RM billion)*

Item	Year			Difference (Δ)	
	1999	2000	2001	99–00	00–01
Consumption	158	181	193	23	12
Private consumption	125	144	150		
Public consumption	33	37	43		
Investment	66	88	83		
Private investment	32	44	35		
Public investment	34	44	48		
Change in inventories	1.5	5.0	− 3.7		
Goods and services					
Exports	365	427	389		
Imports	290	357	328		
GDP at purchasers' value	301	342	335		
Net factor payments abroad	− 21	− 29	− 26		
GNP at purchasers' value	280	313	309	33	− 4

Case Questions
1. Fill in the blank cells in the last two columns of the table.
2. Calculate the marginal propensity to consume for each of the years 2000 and 2001 and compare them.
3. Find the rates of fixed investment to GDP for each of the years and comment on your results.
4. Find the trade balance of the country for each year and compare.
5. Compare GDP with GNP year wise and comment on the difference between the two.

Case Study   17.2

Malaysian Economy after the 1998 Financial Crisis

The government will scrap fuel price controls by August and raise pump prices to market levels under a revamped subsidy system to be unveiled today. The fuel subsidy provides Malaysians with Asia's second cheapest pump prices but is eating up a third of the national budget. The new subsidies would be part of a need based system, rather than the current arrangement which lowers the cost of petrol for all users no matter what their income. The government is considering mechanisms including offering cash payments or setting quotas. Based on the latest floating market prices in Singapore, a litre of petrol costs about RM5.07. But in Malaysia where a litre of petrol now costs RM1.92, prices are not expected to rise so steeply.

Case Questions

1. State what changes the government introduced in the subsidy system for petrol the following day. (You may refer to any Malaysian newspaper of 5 June 2008.)
2. Do you think that the new subsidy scheme meets the objectives stated in the above declaration? Give reasons for your answer.
3. Compare the per litre petrol price in the free market with what users have to pay on an average today in Malaysia.
4. Did the rise in petrol prices due to reduced subsidy affect the GNP growth in the following years? Provide evidence if possible to support your answer.

Test Questions

17.1 Explain the advantages of using a 45° line for studying equilibrium positions in macroeconomics.

17.2 Explain briefly what you understand by the term 'consumption function'. If $C = a + cY$ is a consumption function, identify the variables and constants. Assuming $a = 100$ and $c = 0.7$, construct a table to show the values of consumption (C) for the income levels (Y) 1,000, 2,000, 3,000, 4,000 and 5,000.

17.3 Derive from the consumption function, $C = a + cY$ above, the corresponding savings function. Add a column to the right in the table you have already constructed to show savings for each of the given income levels calculated using the savings function you have derived. Check for verification that consumption and savings add up to equal income in each case.

17.4 Attempt the following questions based on Table 17.7.
  (a) Fill in the blank cells in the table.
  (b) The consumption function for Malaysia on the basis of the data below is estimated as $C = 20 + 0.55Y$. Find the estimated consumption for each year in the table. Compare your results with the original figures and comment on the validity of the function.

Table 17.7 *Consumption and savings propensities in Malaysia*

Year	GNP (RM billion)	Consumption (RM billion)	Savings (RM billion)	Average propensity to consume	Average propensity to save	Marginal propensity to consume	Marginal propensity to save
1999	280	158					
2000	323	181					
2001	309	193					
2002	337	209					
2003	373	227					
2004	426	252					
2005	471	280					

17.5 (a) Using the consumption function stated in question 17.4(b), derive the corresponding savings function for the Malaysian economy.

(b) Using the savings function obtained in (a) above, calculate savings for each year for income figures provided in the table given in question 17.4 and compare with the actual savings. Put your results in an appropriate table.

(c) Include a column in the table you constructed in (b) to show the investment multiplier for each year using the estimated savings.

17.6 In Figure 17.11 below, replace the question mark in the text box with an appropriate caption for each of the unlabelled arrows.

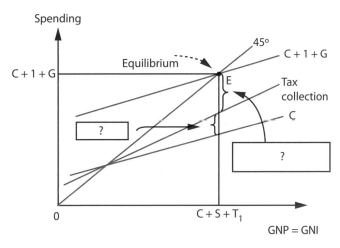

Figure 17.11 *Introduction of government taxes and expenditure*

17.7 In an economy which is in a state of equilibrium the rate of growth is 6% and the savings function, S = 0.04Y. Will you agree that the investment multiplier here must be 1.5? Give reasons for your answer.

17.8 What do you mean by the term 'automatic stabilizers'? How do they operate? Give examples. Are such stabilizers always effective? Explain their limitations.

17.9 Bank Negara Malaysia in its Annual Report for 2007 available online states in page 2 as follows:

'In budget 2007, the government introduced the reduction of corporate tax by two percentage points in two stages; to 27% in 2007 and 26% in 2008. This helped reduce further the cost of doing business and accorded companies with greater capacity to expand capital spending. Public investment grew at a supportive pace of 8% while public consumption also increased steadily by 6.4%'.

(a) What do you understand by a reduction of 'two percentage points'? Would it make a difference to call the budget provision as 'tax reduction of 2%'?

(b) Private investment increased by 5.3% over the year 2006; government spending (tax + consumption) by 0.4%. The growth rate in 2007 was higher by 0.4%. Would you say that higher growth was due to the tax incentive the budget provided to the corporate sector or the result of increase in government spending?

Web Exercise

Search the Internet for Bank Negara Malaysia's Annual Report 2007, p. 2 and review your answer.

Forward Link

In this chapter, you have learnt the role of main components of aggregate demand (AD) on the determination of national income and output, and the supply side of the system as given. The aggregate supply schedule was assumed to be represented by points on the 45°line. In the following chapter, you will learn about the factors operating on the supply side of the economy; you will know what determines the volume and content of aggregate demand in greater detail than what was discussed in Chapter 2.

CHAPTER 18

Aggregate Supply: Factor Incomes and Savings

LEARNING OUTCOMES

This chapter should enable the student to understand:

- Developments on the supply side of goods and services in an economy
- The role investment plays in determining the level and composition of the GNP
- What determines investment and capital formation in an economy
- Accelerator and the checks
- The role of wages in determining the equilibrium level of output
- How price, wages and employment are linked together
- The adjustment process of supply to disturbances originating from the demand side
- The supply side shocks and their treatment
- The significance and limitations of supply side economics

18.1   SUPPLY SIDE ECONOMICS: ORIGIN AND CHARACTERISTICS

In the preceding chapter we looked at the decomposition of national output Y into demand for consumption and investment goods in terms of their money value. Now we shall see the division of the same output value as the supplier (generator) of income which is distributed among the factors of production as interest, rent, wages and profit. The recipient can either save or consume their income and we get the equation Y = C + S. If we equate income and expenditure, we are left with the equation S = I. Recall Figure 15.1 to see how financial intermediation tends to help convert savings into investment. However, production of goods to generate income is a vast subject. Here we introduce you to some of its broad features.

Recall the built-in stabilizers operating in an economy discussed in the preceding chapter.

Supply side economics made its appearance earlier than its demand side counterpart, as discussed in the preceding chapter. It originated essentially in the writings of classical economists (1776–1873). They put emphasis on *real* as opposed to monetary factors in determining the *Wealth of Nations*. An increase in the stock of production factors—capital and skills—and technological advancement were the real determinants of economic growth for a nation. To them, there was no disharmony between individual and social interests. Thus, they stressed the reliance on optimizing forces of free markets and were sceptical of state actions beyond what was essential for maintaining competition. The classical writers agreed that money facilitates transactions by serving as a medium of exchange but in their view most questions in economics could be better answered without any reference to the role of money.

The resurgence of supply side economics was in response to stagflation afflicting the US economy during the 1880s.

The two main positions of classical writers: (i) the emphasis on the real factors in economic growth and (ii) the faith in the efficacy of market forces to ensure social good with minimal state intervention were generally discussed with a long run developmental perspective and remained the focus of controversies in the literature. The modern supply side economics addresses issues for accumulation of capital and provision

BOX 18.1

Production and Factor Rewards – Capitalism versus Islam

In capitalism, production generally centres on the main factors—capital, labour, land and enterprise—engaged in the process. The theoretical idea of distributing the output value among them as interest, wages, rent and profit treats the factors on an *equal footing*, the (just) share of each determined by its demand and supply in the market.

Islam rejects this view of production; for, it neither puts factors of production on an equal footing nor considers the fixation of their respective shares fixed by the market forces of demand and supply as satisfactory. On the contrary, the general economic theory of Islam regards production from the natural raw materials as the property of the producing man—the workman—alone. As for the material means of production and the tools the workman uses in the process for breaking in and harnessing nature, these have no *share* whatsoever in production. Their owners excluding the workman have a claim on the latter; he has to pay them for their contribution but the payment would not represent the share for example of the owners of land or tools and implements themselves in the output.

Thus, in Islamic theory the producing man is the real owner of the materials produced and other contributors have property claims therein. But they have a right to demand from the producing man compensation as his servants and not as his partners.

A most important phenomenon that reflects this material difference between the two theories—Islamic and capitalist—is the standpoint of the two systems of economics regarding the capitalist of natural raw materials. The capitalist doctrine permits capital to practice this in production. Capital has the power to hire labourers for cutting the wood from the forest or extracting petrol from the well and pay them their wages which represents all their share in the output and the capitalist becomes the owner of whatever be the quantity of wood cut or petrol extracted, selling it at the price that suits his fancy as his right. In Islamic theory there is no room for such production.

Source: Baqir-as-Sadr, (1884), *Our Economics*, p.12–15.

of incentives to spur growth in a rather narrower perspective. Still, it is inspired by the classical positions. Its resurgence took place during the 1870s. Economists subscribing to the notion maintain that changes in aggregate supply play an important role in the determination of inflation, employment, investment and growth levels in an economy. To control these variables, aggregate supply rather than aggregate demand has to be the focal point of attention. Let us begin with the role investment plays on the supply side of the economy.

18.2 INVESTMENT, CAPITAL FORMATION AND PRODUCTION

We have already discussed in the preceding chapter the relationship between savings and investment. Taking investment as a given (autonomous), we showed how equilibrium income will be determined if the economy adjusts consumption to release matching savings. In this context, we also explained what investment multiplier is and how it works. Here, we shall discuss the role investment plays in an economy on the output or supply side. We begin with a discussion on production function.

Production function informs us what factors the real (physical) output (Y) of goods and services in an economy depends on and the sort of linkages it may have with them. To keep matters simple, we condense factors of production into two categories: labour (L) and capital (K). We may then write the production function as:

$$Y = F (L, K)$$

The above formula states that the volume of real output (Y) would depend on the quantity and quality of labour (L) and capital (K) combining together in the process of production, given the state of technology in an economy. The procedure that usually follows is to take one of the factors (labour or capital) as fixed, and see what causes changes in the other and how it affects output. Let us begin with investment that may cause fluctuation in the capital stock of a country.

> A production function tells the way in which output of a commodity depends on the input used.

18.3 INVESTMENT: TYPES AND CHARACTERISTICS

Throughout the history of modern economic development, major changes in GNP growth rates have taken place with changes in investment spending. Fluctuations in investment have often been sharp and the multiplier effect caused even larger absolute changes in total spending and output. To understand why some economies grow faster than others and what brings in inflationary booms and depressions accompanied with widespread unemployment of men and machines, you must know the factors that influence investment decisions.

The production and installation of machines, construction of buildings and the extension of infrastructural networks increase the formation of productive capital in a nation. But the changes in capital stocks are not in general, smooth and steady. The spurts and declines in them are often sharp and abrupt. To understand the reasons for sudden changes, it may be helpful to examine certain aspects of investment.

18.3.1   Plant and Machinery Purchases are Irregular

Business investments are by far the major carriers of economic change, more so in the current era of privatization and liberalization. Inventions, innovations and new techniques of production are typically incorporated in new machines, new plants and improved equipment. Innovations in railroads, energy provisions, expressway constructions, automobiles, aeronautics, ship-building and others have prompted waves of new investment activity, at first swelling then receding. Business investments at any given time are directly related to new developments and fluctuations in new lines of production. The investment in such lines of production tends to fluctuate, often quite violently.

18.3.2   Fixity of Capital in the Short Run

Investment in plant, machinery and equipment is mostly long-lived. These assets take years before being fully used up in the process of producing goods and services. The size of capital stock firms may want to have will depend on the capital-output ratio and the desired level of production. But new innovations may make the still useable equipment inefficient and non-completive in the wake of improved machinery becoming available in the market. In the textile industry, for example, power looms drove out hand looms but were themselves replaced later by automatic looms.

The amount of capital per unit of output or the capital-output ratio would depend on the character and the waiting period for assets' availability, their prices and the cost of borrowing funds to acquire them. The wages of labour that capital would replace will also count. The faster we need the replacement, the more acute the problems tend to become.

18.3.3   Investment in Inventories

A modern economy not only requires machines and workers in order to produce an assortment of goods and services, it must also have ready-at-hand adequate quantities of raw materials, stores, semi-finished (work-in-progress) and finished goods in stock for carrying on production uninterrupted. Firms cannot afford stoppages of production while waiting for input to come from suppliers after each round of production. Collectively, we call the indicated elements as stock-in-trade or *inventories*. Inventories absorb funds, making them unavailable for other uses and they have carrying costs.

Firms normally have what they perceive to be the optimal level of inventories determined by trade practices and experience. For example, many industries in India *normally* carry average inventories sufficient to keep production uninterrupted for three months. Meanwhile, they continue to replenish stocks of various kinds as and when considered advisable. If inventories tend to pile up on the shelves, the excess over the norm represents *involuntary investment* signalling bad times ahead. Inventories falling short of the norm show increase in demand, upward pressure on prices and tend to fuel profit expectations; inflation seems knocking at the doors.

> Inventory component of investment is relatively more prone to fluctuations than others.

When we include both voluntary (planned) and involuntary inventories in investment, savings and investment (ex post) are always equal. Savings and investment are rarely equal if their involuntary components are not counted.

18.4   ROLE OF EXPECTATIONS AND PROFITS

Investment in plant and machinery invariably entails expectations about the *future and* risk as well. The assets are valuable to the investing firms because they are a source of future production, sale revenue and profit. Future outcomes being uncertain, the expectations of businessmen play a crucial role in determining the volume of investment during a given period. Expectations are influenced by a host of factors and not by rationality alone. Animal spirit, gut feeling, perception, exuberance and the like have been the words that economists have often found to describe what overcomes reason in business assessment of future course of events, causing, more than that, aggravating, economic turmoil.

> Perceptions about the course of future events play a major role in the formation of expectations, especially concerning profits.

18.4.1   Role of Profit

The primary objective of businesses remains the earning of profits for their owners even as their social responsibility aspect is now being increasingly emphasized for a variety of reasons. (What are they?) In the case of GNP accelerator prompting increase in investment due to sales expansion, capacity is added not for its own sake but in the expectation of earning higher profit rates. Again, firms introduce cost reducing equipment and technology in the hope that the savings in the labour or material costs will exceed the corresponding investment costs making net additions to existing profit rates.

Furthermore, remember that even though expected profits are the major incentive for investments, current profits are an important source of funds to finance additional investments. Thus, profits play the twin role in the area of investment, as an incentive and as a source of financing. The report cards of the past serve in part as useful guides for future investment actions.

Having discussed the components and role of investment on the supply side of an economy, let us examine the role of labour as a cost element in the production of goods and services at the macro level. We shall do so assuming that the capital stock remains fixed; that is, the production capacity does not change.

> Expected profits guide investment into various channels; realized profits are a major source of internal financing.

18.5   THE ACCELERATOR AND THE CHECKS

Given the efficient (optimal) amount of capital needed per unit of output, the required amount of capital would depend on the size of the market for the goods, i.e. on the expected volume of output and sales. Multiplying the capital needed per unit of output by its volume will give the amount of money required. If production were expected to remain stable over an extended period, additions to fixed capital will not be desirable except for replacement purposes. No net additions will be called for.

> The accelerator indicates the positive relationship between GNP growth rates and investment. Investment tends to magnify rates via the multiplier.

However, rising output and sales expansion may give rise to net increases in investment; firms will purchase new equipment and machinery over and above the normal replacement needs. The faster the rate of increase in output and sales, the larger the net capital required to maintain the optimal level of capital stock. Fluctuations in sales and therefore in production is one of the major sources of instability in investment spending. The level of investment is very sensitive to change in output growth. The direct relationship between the level of investment and the GNP growth rate is called the accelerator. To illustrate, suppose an expansion of RM1 million calls for an additional investment of RM2 million. Thus, if sales increase by RM3.5 million, net investment would have to be worth RM7 million.

The accelerator theory helps us identify some destabilizing effects of investment spending. However, there are factors in an economy that tend to reduce their rigour, for example, it takes time to order, produce and install new equipment. Businessmen are usually hesitant to install additional capacity, as they are prone to believe that the increase in their sales is only temporary. There is a limit to how fast firms can effectively absorb new technology. Finally, purchases of new plant and machinery may hit financial barriers.

18.6 DEMAND FOR LABOUR

Let us begin with the question of how much labour a firm would want to employ? The decision is made at the margin that the firm will not stop employing additional workers so long as there is addition to total revenue because increasing output remains less than the additions to total labour costs. The point where additional revenue equals additional cost will determine how much labour the firm will employ. The contribution of additional labour to output, with constant capital, is called the marginal product of labour or MP_L. The MP_L declines as output and employment increase. For this reason, the curve is concave to X-axis in Figure 18.1A. The wage rate is tangent to the curve at M with slope a/b and equilibrium employment L_0.

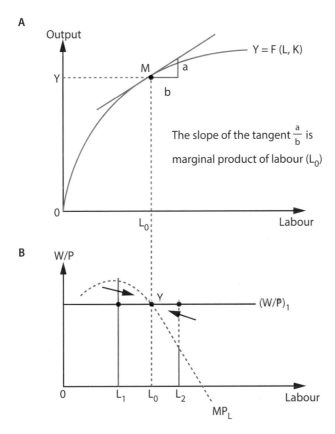

Figure 18.1 *Labour market equilibrium under perfect competition*

Our next task is to find what it will cost if we employ L_0 units of labour. This would depend on the market money (nominal) wage rate. Wage rate is the price paid per unit of labour service for a specified time—an hour, a day, a week, a month or a year. Under perfect competition, the market wage is determined by the interaction of demand and supply of labour. For individual firms, supply of labour at that wage rate is perfectly elastic. But our model deals with *real* values. A real wage is the amount of goods and services a worker can buy with the nominal wage he receives. To convert money wage (W) into *real* wage, we divide it by the price level (P). Thus, real wage equals W/P. Firms will employ workers until the MP_L of labour equals the real wage rate. This means that the curve operates as the demand for labour curve. Figure 18.1 shows the equilibrium of the labour market at Y output where real wage equals $(W/P)_1$ for L_0 labour. If at the given wage rate, employment were L_1, i.e. $< L_0$; the real wage will be higher than the MP_L of workers that will increase their supply until the real wage equals the given rate $(W/P)_1$ at Y. In contrast, if at the given wage rate $(W/P)_1$ employment were L_2, i.e. $> L_0$, the wage rate will be higher than the MP_L of labour; firms will incur losses and curtail employment so that it equals L_0. Thus, competition would tend to maintain optimal employment (L_0) in the economy, given $(W/P)_1$ as the real wage rate.

The distinction between real and money (nominal) wage is crucial. Consider for example the case where a report says that country A is becoming wealthier each year than country B because wage levels are rising there by an average of $200 compared to $120 in country B. However, an examination of data reveals that country A has been having an inflation rate of 50% while in country B, the rate is virtually zero. Taking inflation into account, the conclusion is quite different: Despite nominal wages in country A rising much faster than in country B, real wages are falling significantly because the currency loses half its value each year.

> The extent of the use of a factor in production is determined by what it would contribute in real terms to output compared with what has to be paid for it in real terms if one more unit of it were employed, other factors remaining unchanged.

Exercise 18.1

Explain what the broken portions of lines at L_1 and L_2 are in Figure 18.1A.

Exercise 18.2

Suppose an agriculture-based economy employs 50,000 workers and pays them 50 million tons of wheat per crop as wages. The arrangement helps optimize the use of its farm capacity with agriculturists making only normal profits. Assuming that these were the only facts known about the economy, answer the following questions.
  (a) What is the per worker real wage rate for the economy?
  (b) How will equilibrium be restored if:
      (i) The wage rate were 125 tons per worker?
      (ii) The wage rate were 95 tons?

In Figure 18.1, let us assume that (a) ML_0 is the labour supply curve and (b) Y is the full employment equilibrium point (output) with $(W/P)_1$

being the wage rate for L_0 labour. These assumptions imply that we are now moving from the short- to long-run equilibrium of the economy. For in the long run alone, the labour supply curve is perfectly inelastic as the L_0 is at full employment output. We also assume for the moment that the curve is independent of the real wage rate i.e. labour supply is *fixed*. This implies that demand for labour alone would play an active part in the determination of the real wage rate (W/P) as Figure 18.2 illustrates. However, the immediate adjustment of real wage to a change in demand to maintain full employment is not possible unless we assume that:
- Money wages would rise or fall readily to keep labour market in equilibrium.
- Prices of goods would rise or fall instantaneously to clear the market.

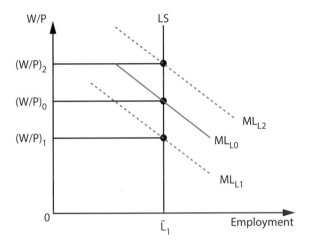

Figure 18.2 *At full employment labour supply (L_0) becomes inelastic and real wage rate varies with changes in demand for labour*

To find out how realistic these assumptions are, we must investigate the process of determination of the *money wage rate* (W) and the *level of prices* (P) in the system.

18.6.1   Money Wage and Price Level Flexibility

Under the classical model, the flexibility of money wage ensures that they will rise or fall with any change in the level of prices such that real wage appropriately adjusts to the requirement to keep the labour market in equilibrium at whatever price level. Thus, firms would always maintain full employment and the corresponding level of output (Y). Figure 18.3 illustrates the point. The figure combines an aggregate demand curve with the classical long-run aggregate supply curve showing full employment equilibrium at P_0 price level that corresponds to P in the real wage $(W/P)_0$ of Figure 18.2. We take it as a given position without investigating the price level response to shifts in aggregate demand or supply to bring about the result. The important point to note is that in the classical scheme of things, the system *automatically* tends to have this kind of equilibrium in the long-run. However, the argument rests on certain assumptions:

1. Given the equilibrium price level P_0, the money wage will change as we have already stated such that the real wage would be (W/P_0).

2. Not only do wages and prices change in harmony, firms revise their production decisions quickly enough in the light of such changes.

3. Workers are able to move rapidly between jobs as some firms' contract and others expand, ensuring continual full employment equilibrium in the labour market.

4. Disturbances like increase in money supply or technological improvements are immediately reflected in wage-price variations needed to restore full employment.

The classical full employment model is unrealistic as it is based on unfulfilling assumptions but it has a benchmark value.

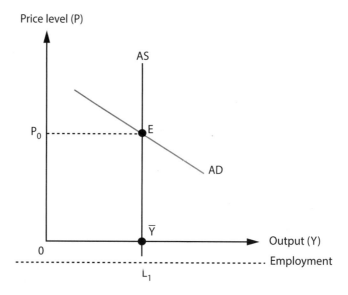

Figure 18.3 *Output, price level and employment*

These assumptions are very stringent, yet the classical model may serve as a useful reference point for studying many real world macroeconomic situations. For, it underlines the plausibility of an economy converging in the *long run* to full employment with commodity and factor markets both in the state of equilibrium. It informs us that in the short run, transaction costs and information problems may complicate the finding and taking of jobs. Also, contractual provisions make both wages and prices sticky and may affect the adjustment process. Thus, in the short run we do expect transitory disequilibrium and temporary unemployment in the economy. The weakness of the classical model is that it ignores the importance of time in the equilibrium analysis.

18.6.2   Money Wage Floor Model

We saw that the classical model assumes complete wage-price flexibility that ensures perpetual full employment; it cannot explain the possible existence of unemployment in modern economies. The explanation of unemployment is therefore provided today in some measure by assuming a *wage floor.*

The assumption implies that the short-run *money* wages cannot be reduced at all but are freely movable upward. The assumption presumably draws its inspiration from the classical view that wages in the long run cannot depart from *subsistence* levels.

Figure 18.4 shows labour supply as the function of *money* wage. Here, L_1 is the full employment labour such that the labour supply curve (LS) is completely inelastic at that point. But at employment levels less than L_1, the same curve is perfectly elastic at W_1 wage. This follows from the assumption that perfect competition prevails in the labour market with W_2 as the floor below which wages cannot be reduced. Figure 18.4A contains two additional demand curves for labour, DL_1 and DL_2,

Downward inflexibility of wage rates results in short-run unemployment of workers.

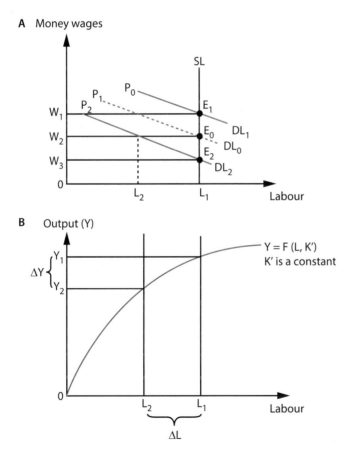

Figure 18.4 *Money wage floor and full employment model*

corresponding respectively to price levels P_1 and P_2. At full employment price level P_1, the demand for labour DL_1 makes the wage exceed floor by E_0E_1. Notice that point E_0 at the broken line labour demand curve is also at a position of equilibrium but at the floor wage rate W_2. At any point to the left of E_0 on the horizontal part of the labour supply curve (LS), the system would still be in a state of equilibrium as at point E_2 but with unemployment existing from L_2 to L_1. This unemployment may be eliminated if wage rate could be forced down to W_3. This is not possible as wages are inflexible downward for adjustment because the floor equals just the minimal survival wage in the model.

Figure 18.4B shows that if employment falls from L_1 to L_2 it would cause output to fall from Y_1 to Y_2. Thus, during the downturn of the cycle, unemployment spreads as aggregate demand for goods falls short of aggregate supply.

Exercise 18.3

(a) In Figure 18.4A, can you say what area the rectangle W_1, E_1, E_0 and W_2 shows? Justify your answer.

(b) In Figure 18.4B, why is ΔY smaller than ΔL? Explain your answer.

18.6.3   Evaluation of the Model

We have argued that the wage floor model serves as a benchmark to measure departures from the full employment ideal. It tells us that shortfalls in aggregate demand can lead to the spread of unemployment in the economy. The classical analysis saw long-run wages stuck to subsistence *both* ways, not allowing any movement upwards. In contrast, the wage floor model sees money wage free to move up but resistant to any reduction even when it is above the subsistence level. Thus, the model is a significant improvement over the classical analysis and a step closer to ground realities. Nevertheless, it has some serious limitations as stated below.

> The wage floor model is a useful benchmark but it has some serious limitations.

1. There is a sharp contrast in the labour wage on the two sides of point E_0. It is not that the wage is fully flexible once labour demand crosses the full employment level. Output can, for instance, be above the full employment level Y_1 if labour hours are extended or paid holidays are reduced. It is true that there are hindrances to the downward adjustment of the wage especially because of terms of contract or the minimum wage law but it is not valid that no downward adjustment is possible or actually made. Under the wage floor model, we are in a vacuum once the

economy is somehow caught in an unemployment trap such as at E_2. Figure 18.4 does not provide any clue to the linkage between unemployment and possible change in wage rates. It is much more realistic to presume that wages rise gradually when output is rising beyond the full employment level and fall gradually when demand for goods is falling faster than their supply.

2. The wage floor model relies on the distinction between money wage and real wage. However, the behaviour for the real wage (W/P) as seen in the model is questionable. It assumes that in moving from E_0 to E_2, prices fall from P_0 to P_2 with a decrease in aggregate demand and output (from Y_1 to Y_2) but money wage remains unchanged at W_2 implying that in recession, real wage rises. Conversely, in a forward movement from E_2 to E_0, prices rise but money wage again stays constant at W_2. Thus, real wage falls during expansion. This conclusion that real wage moves inversely with the cycle held for quite some time. However, numerous empirical studies conducted to test the hypothesis, in the US especially, remained inconclusive on the point. The facts do not testify for a key implication of the wage floor model.

18.7   EMPLOYMENT AND WAGES IN THE SHORT RUN

In view of the limitations of the wage floor model, the wage-employment relationship is now explored under a more realistic assumption. It is that over time money wages change in response to the changing conditions in the labour market and wages are neither too sticky nor too flexible. Figure 18.5 helps explain this sort of wage behaviour. The three curves W_1, W_0 and W_2 show the wage-employment relationship in the short run at three different time points. The higher the level of employment in the current period, the higher is the wage rate. In addition, there is a dynamic relationship between employment in the current period; let us say W_0, and the future wage rate. Suppose output (Y) in the current period (W_0) is such that it can only offer less than L_1 employment. In other words, if the current period is experiencing unemployment, the wage curve in the subsequent period will shift down to W_2. Thus, prevalence of unemployment in the economy lowers short-run wage rates. Conversely, if the output in the current period is expanding such that it can absorb more than L_1 labour, the wage curve in the next period will shift to W_1. The implication is that employment expands with growth of an economy.

> Wages (and employment) rise and fall with output.

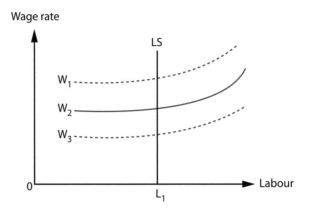

Figure 18.5 *Money wage rate and employment*

18.7.1 Why are Wage Rates Sticky Downward?

We have already indicated above that passing factors like contractual compulsions and minimum wage legislation make wages sticky. Additional and perhaps more fundamental is the long term nature of relationship between business firms and their workers. Both gain by smooth production operations. Better capacity utilization lowers costs and thus increases profit. Workers save time and income involved in job hopping. Firms are saved from incurring expenditure on finding and training new workers. Both may gain if they stay together. Firms are therefore, hesitant to cut wages when there is unemployment. Reputation is also involved. Workers too prefer patience in the hope that wages will get a raise without delay when times change for the better.

Gains of industrial peace make wages sticky.

In consequence, the response of wages to dynamic change remains sluggish; the adjustment is not immediate. Unemployment leads to lower wages slowly. Likewise, on the upswing of cycle, wages lag behind prices, employment though expands. Adjustment of course takes place over time but much time lag characterizes the process. Both features of wage response are central to modern macroeconomics.

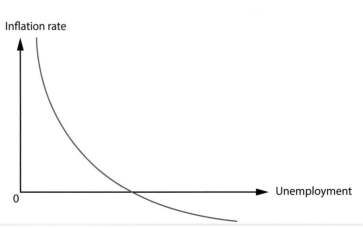

Figure 18.6 *The Phillips curve*

18.7.2   Phillips Curve

Figure 18.6 shows the Phillips curve. The curve is an application of the law of demand to the labour market where the wage rate treated as price is shown in an inverse relationship with unemployment. It is an obvious corollary of the positive wage–employment relationship but the form of presentation lends it different meanings. The curve fitted to real life data over a long period was found *convex* to the origin. The implication was that, the higher the rate of unemployment, the lower is the rise in price level (in W/P). The implication rapidly made the curve a tool for policy analysis in macroeconomics. Expansion in employment caused the rise in wages but it was erroneously termed as *wage inflation*. The misnomer suggested that if inflation were to be controlled, demands for increase in money wage rates had to be curbed. While there is an empirically proven relationship between wages and productivity, the Phillips curve puts that relationship under wraps. In that, it loses contact with the process of modern dynamic change.

Today, in many developing countries experiencing inflationary pressures, public policy tolerates money wage lagging behind productivity to stay competitive in world markets. Real wage rates tend to be eroded on the *relative* income scale. Under the circumstances, using the term *wage inflation* as the cause of malady looks intriguing. Broadly, price is composed of two elements: wage and profit. During inflation, profits rise at a much faster pace than wages. Will it then not be more appropriate to speak of *profit inflation* than focusing on wage rates?

> The Phillips curve has a misplaced focus.

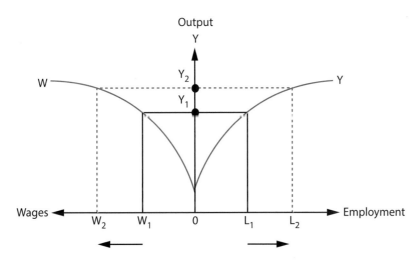

Figure 18.7 *Relationships between output, wages and employment*

18.7.3   Wages, Output and Productivity

Employment is an increasing function of output; jobs expand with growth. Likewise, wages increase with a rise in employment and vice versa. Putting the two together, we find wages and output tied in a positive relationship. Figure 18.7 depicts the relationships between the three variables. Points Y_1, L_1 and W_1 show their initial equilibrium position. With an increase in output to Y_2, employment expands to L_2 and the rise in demand for labour raises wages to W_2. But economies are characterized with dynamic changes. We have described in Chapter 17 the types of changes that take place on the demand and supply sides of an economy. Here, we shall explain how such changes affect the *relationships* between wages, output and employment. Even though demand for goods matters, more vital for growth of output in the long run are factors that operate on the supply side. Some of the important factors are discussed below.

Increase in resource use

An economy can increase its real output and income through increase in resource or input use. Consider the following equation:

$$\frac{\Delta Y}{Y} = \beta_1 \frac{\Delta L}{L} + \beta_2 \frac{\Delta K}{K} + \frac{\Delta A}{A} \tag{18.1}$$

In Equation 18.1, $\Delta Y/Y$ is the rate of growth in output, $\Delta L/L$ in labour and $\Delta K/K$ in capital while b_1 and b_2 are some constants. The last term $\Delta A/A$ is the rate of technological change. Here, it is zero by implication; growth in output is determined by increases in labour and capital inputs alone. If we treat one of the factors, say capital, as fixed, expansion in output shall be a function of employing more labour as Figure 18.4B shows.

Increase in productivity

The increase in factor productivity is another, rather more important, source for output expansion because it works even when input availability is quite restricted. Productivity may be thought of with reference to individual factors of production, say labour or capital. However, we have in addition the notion of total productivity. We begin with productivity of labour. Labour productivity is defined as the ratio of a volume of output to a time measure of labour input. Gross domestic product (GDP) or gross value added (GVA) are normally used as the volume measure of output at constant prices, i.e. adjusted for inflation. For labour input, the three most commonly used measures are: hours worked, workforce jobs and number of people in employment. Thus, labour productivity will differ on our choice of output and labour input definition.

Two types of labour productivity may well be distinguished: average and marginal. For any given amount of labour, the average productivity measure is total output divided by labour units used. To begin with, for obtaining the average productivity of labour, we divide a measure of output with the corresponding measure of labour used in its production. We may choose, for example, in Figure 18.8, any amount of labour units along the labour axis, such as L_1, and read off the corresponding value of total output on any of the three curves Y_1, Y_2 or Y_3, respectively,

Productivity of an individual factor is difficult to measure compared to total productivity.

to calculate average labour productivity. In each case, labour units used remain unchanged at L_1. The average productivity of labour rises as more and more capital becomes available per unit of the *same* amount of labour to work with. This we call capital deepening as the increasing use of capital $\bar{K}_1$, $\bar{K}_2$ and $\bar{K}_3$ for L_1 shows in the figure. However, as we move along any of the curves, additional capital is needed with increase in labour to keep its availability per worker the same as before. This is called capital widening which is not likely to raise labour productivity.

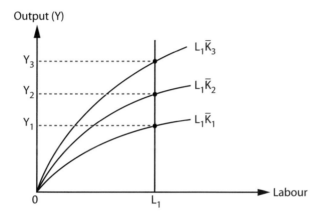

Figure 18.8 *Increase in the use of capital may improve productivity of labour*

It follows that labour productivity varies as a function of the accompanying input factor such as capital. However, it also varies with the *efficiency* with which a factor combination is used (total productivity). This implies that two firms or countries may have equal total factor productivity but labour productivity could be higher for the one that uses more of capital or better technology.

In contrast, marginal productivity of labour is obtained as indicated earlier (Figure 18.4) by dividing the *increase* in output by the corresponding *increase* in labour units used, i.e. $\Delta Y/\Delta L$; it is provided by the slope of the tangent at any point on the curve. Marginal productivity is not a thing by itself. It essentially is a mathematical concept, the ratio of two differences. The difference ratio is affected by technological change which is a long run phenomenon and is denoted by factor A in Equation 18.1. Factor A is taken as fixed in the above discussion; thus factor A does not influence labour productivity in the short-run. However, A may vary in the long-run due to a variety of reasons.

Also, labour productivity in the long run is additionally a function of improvement in the quality of labour force due to education, training and healthcare. Socio-political environment, regulatory frameworks, technological changes and cyclical fluctuations in economic activity also matter. Together, these factors make the measurement of long run changes in labour productivity a complicated uphill task.

However, Equation 18.1 links together the growth rate of output and *total* productivity elements to help understand the concept. The equation

Increased use of capital may raise labour productivity in the short run but technological improvement is a long run factor.

conveys that the rate of growth in total productivity of an economy may be defined as the amount by which output would increase as a result of improvement in the quality of factors it depends on ΔL, ΔK and ΔA for *given* measures of L, K and A. Note now that constant β_1 in the equation is the income share of labour and β_2 is the income share of capital such that $\beta_1 + \beta_2 = 1$. Thus, the message of the equation is that getting more output with the *same* amount of factors would be the evidence of growth in total factor productivity.

Example 18.1 Suppose the income shares of labour and capital were 0.20 and 0.8, respectively. Labour force grows by 2.5% and capital stock by 4%. Finally, suppose that technical progress is estimated at 1.5%. Feeding the information in Equation 18.1 we get:

$$\Delta Y/Y = 0.20 \times 0.025 + 0.8 \times 0.04 + 0.015$$
$$= 0.005 + 0.032 + 0.015$$
$$= 0.052 \text{ or } 5.2\%$$

Thus, growth in total productivity is worth 5.2%.

Exercise 18.4

Given the following information, use Equation 18.1 to verify if the income shares of labour (L) and capital (K) were 25% and 75% respectively.
$\Delta Y/Y = 6.5\%$; $\Delta L/L = 2.5\%$; $\Delta K/K = 3.5\%$ and $\Delta A/A = 3.25\%$

18.8   AGGREGATE SUPPLY AND TAXATION

The impact of taxation on incentives to save and invest is quite uncertain.

The impact of taxation on output growth is a key issue in supply side economics. It is said that the tax system may impair incentive to work, save and invest; high tax rates work against productivity, hamper growth and as a consequence slow the expansion of long-run aggregate output. They reduce the disposable income of people and in the process lessen the financial attractiveness of work, savings and investment. The question of how valid are these claims is vital, especially in democratic social systems where taxes can affect output by reducing (i) the productivity of labour and capital, and/or (ii) their overall supply.

18.8.1   Labour Supply

The main determinant of household labour supply is the after-tax real wage. Increase in taxation of income from work reduces wage income; a reduction in tax raises it. Incentive to work and, therefore, labour supply varies inversely with the movement in tax rates. But things are not that simple. A tax cut, for example, would increase disposable income from work. But it may generate two reactions simultaneously. First, the worker can now maintain or even increase his current income a little by working fewer hours than before. Leisure will be traded for work. We call this the income effect of a rise in real wages that reduces the labour hours supplied. But at the same time, every hour spent in leisure is costlier in terms of income foregone luring the worker trade leisure for work. This substitution effect of higher real wage due to tax cut would tempt him to increase labour. The net effect of these opposing forces, internal to a worker, is in general uncertain and difficult to predict.

Leisure versus work affects wages.

18.8.2   Supply of Capital

Capital is at any point in time, an accumulated stock of earlier investments. The stock grows if current investment is more than the depreciation of capital due to wear and tear in the process of producing goods or obsolescence because of technological progress. Such growth requires savings and their investment. Supply side economists, therefore, focus on incentive aspects of the matter. They argue that taxation of economic gains reduces the profitability attraction of investment and dampens the ability and willingness to save. What policies can help overcome such disincentives? It is pointed out that tax laws provide for a number of tax exemptions from returns from savings and reduced rate of taxes; even tax holidays are allowed, to returns from new investments to take care of incentives to save and invest. However, the empirical studies do not seem to support such claims.

We must, however, remember that the impact of taxation on output growth cannot be studied in isolation of structure of taxation apart from its level and the patterns of government spending. This makes matters all the more complicated.

Exercise 18.5

A worker in India is working for 40 hours a week at an after-tax wage rate of INR 100 per hour earning INR 4,000 a week. Now the wage rate rises to INR 125 and he can earn INR 4,750 per week by working 38 hours a week. Notice that earnings and leisure have both increased. Do you think that labour supply would necessarily decrease with a tax cut as the example seems to suggest? Argue your case.

BOX 18.2

Prohibition of Interest as the Time Value of Money

Islam prohibits the giving and taking of interest as a share in production for a variety of reasons. However, Islamic economics has not been fully able to discard in practice the use of interest in its present-future value calculus in finance. $(1 + r)^n$ formulations are still being used in the discounting regimes even as the formulations have been shown as based on compounding. One reason could be the unfamiliarity with the Islamic reason of prohibition in this case.

The Islamic notion of justice does not grant to one a share in the product unless he has worked to produce it. Islam does not permit earning without labour. One justification proponents advance for charging interest is their belief that value money carries a time value. For example, if you lent a Dinar to someone for a year, it is your right to demand more than a Dinar at the end of the year such that the amount now equals the exchange value of Dinar you had lent. The excess would be the compensation for deprivation and waiting you underwent until repaid. Thus, interest is in accordance with the difference between the present value and the future value of the Dinar lent.

The argument rests on a wrong basis. Capitalism ignores the linkage of ownership in production with the theory of product value. The theory of ownership is not the same as the theory of value. There are numerous factors that affect the exchange value of a product. The capitalist theory assumes interest to be identical with what determines ownership share in production. Interest is identified with time value of money. Islam bans it because it does not commensurate with the Islamic view that one who produces a commodity owns it and no one else.

Summary

- Early economists put emphasis on the real factors that determine the production of wealth in an economy. They saw no conflict between the individual and social interest. They put reliance on the free play of market forces to obtain optimal economic results. They opposed government intervention in economic matters except when needed to maintain competition in the market.

- Modern supply side economics focuses on the level and/or the growth rate of output which it argues could be significantly increased through policies aimed at promotion of efficiency, reduction of public intervention, and encouragement of willingness to work, save and invest. It argues for tax reduction as a major tool to achieve these ends.

- It is obvious that supply side economics centres on production and how public policy would affect the variables involved in shaping it. To make matters simple, economists usually condense these variables into labour (L) and capital (K) as determinants of real output (Y). Thus, we have: $Y = F(L, K)$.

- Investment plays a key role in the growth of an economy. It has two broad categories from the short-run viewpoint: fixed and variable. Investment in the inventories is the major component of variable; it is very sensitive to change in growth rates.

- Changes in growth rate are directly responsible for acceleration or deceleration of investment activity in an economy.

- Investment for the major part is lumpy, irregular and uncertain. Fluctuations in investments are one of the major sources causing instability in modern economies.

- Investment decisions are primarily guided by profit expectations. Profit works not only as an incentive or disincentive to invest, but also as an important source of financing investment.
- Starting with labour, we ask how much workforce a firm would employ. The straight forward answer is that it would go on employing more and more of labour so long as the addition to wage bills remains smaller than the addition to total revenue the resultant increase in output would bring. The labour measure will be determined at the level where MR = MC.
- Output (Y) is expressed in real terms by using an appropriate price index as the deflator. Likewise, money wage rates (W) are divided by the corresponding price index (P) to obtain real wage measured as W/P.
- In the long run, labour supply will become completely inelastic at full employment level. An increase in demand for labour will push up the real wage rate (W/P) and a decrease is likely to lower it.
- The classical model assumed that money wage would be flexible enough to rise or fall with changes in the price level such that real wage could appropriately adjust to keep the labour market automatically in a state of equilibrium.
- Automatic adjustment of variables in question to ensure perpetual equilibrium implies a number of assumptions which seldom hold well. But the classical model still serves as a useful benchmark to study real life departures from equilibrium.
- In the absence of complete wage-price flexibility, the classical model fails to explain the possible existence of unemployment in modern economies. A wage floor assumption is used to explain such a phenomenon.
- The wage floor model implies that money wage cannot at all be reduced in the short run but can freely move upwards. At the downswing of the cycle, all workers cannot be employed at the floor wage; stickiness of wages leads to unemployment.
- The model is a significant improvement over the classical analysis and a step closer to ground realities. Nevertheless, it has some serious limitations.
- There may be hindrances to the downward adjustment of wages due to terms of contract or the minimum wage law but it is untrue that no downward adjustment is possible or is not actually made. Also, the model can be shown to imply that real wage moves inversely with the cycle but empirical evidence does not support the proposition.
- In view of the above limitations of the wage floor model, wage-employment relationship is now studied with a short run perspective under the realistic assumption that over time money wage changes in response to the changing conditions in the labour market and wages are neither too sticky nor too flexible.
- The Phillips curve understandably shows wage rate in an inverse relationship with unemployment levels but its convexity to the origin implied that the higher the rate of employment the lower is the rise in price level: money wage (W) being constant in real wage (W/P). This led to the rise in wages due to expansion in employment (reduction in unemployment) naively called as wage inflation: something unwelcome and calls for remedial action. Thus, the Phillips curve has a misplaced focus.
- Employment normally is an increasing function of growth in output. Increase in demand for labour relative to its supply tends to push up wages. Wages and output are tied together in a positive relationship. In addition, wages also rise with an increase in resources and productivity of labour. Increase in factor productivity is an important source of output expansion, especially when resource availability tends to diminish.
- Labour productivity in average or marginal terms—average productivity of labour is obtained by dividing total output by a measure of labour defined as hours worked or number of persons employed. On the other hand, marginal productivity is defined as the addition to total output that an additional worker brings in.
- The incentive effects of cuts in taxes on savings and investment are favourable but this is a controversial claim and lacks empirical support.

Glossary

Accelerator This refers to the positive relationship between the growth rate of GNP and the investment activity. When GNP is expanding sales rise fast. Investment in both addition to capacity and inventories has to increase. Opposite will happen when the economy is slowing down.

Inventory investment For smooth unhampered process of production business firms invariably has various types of commodities—raw materials, stores, semi-finished goods and finished goods—in production pipelines. Taken together such goods are called inventories. Businesses like to keep inventories at an optimal level as they absorb a sizeable part of investment. Inventories tending to depart from the optimal level plus or minus are signals for bad or good times ahead concerning the GNP growth. The extent of departure from the optimal are measures of what is termed as involuntary investment in inventories.

Marginal product of labour We can think of the marginal product of labour in physical or money terms. In physical terms, it denotes the increase in the output of a firm or economy that results from hiring one additional unit of labour measure, all other factors of production remaining unchanged. We can convert the physical productivity (MP_L) into money equivalent by multiplying the output by the price of the commodity. In money terms, it is called the marginal revenue product of labour (MRP_L).

Production function In economics production function is an expression linking output to inputs that combine to generate that output in a firm, farm, industry or even in an entire economy. The expression can take the form of an equation, a graph or a table. Some notion of efficiency invariably underlies a production function. Thus, a production function can be defined as the specification of the minimum input requirements needed to produce specified volume of output, given the state of technology. Functions can assume linear or non-linear forms. The general expression is: $Q = f(X_1, X_2, X_3, ..., X_n)$, where Q is the quantity of output and X_1, X_2, X_3, ..., X_n are the factor inputs such as capital, land or labour.

Real wages The term real wages refers to wages that have been corrected for inflation. This term is used in contrast to money or nominal wages that have not been so corrected. The use of real wages is needed in some forms of economic analyses. For example, we must compare real wages within a nation over time, or between two nations at the same time to asses relative performances; conclusions may be misleading if nominal figures were used.

Supply side economics The term supply side economics has two different but interrelated versions. Earlier, it referred to the fact that in the long-run, supply of goods underlies consumption and living standards. Rise in income levels and living standards cannot be thought of without expansion in output. All economists subscribe to this view. However, today, supply side economics is used to describe how growth rate of output could be significantly increased through policies designed to promote efficiency, reduce regulation and cut marginal tax rates to provide incentives to work, save and invest. The latter version has of late gained much popularity.

Wage floor model This model is used to explain why inflation can exist with unemployment in modern free enterprise economies. It rests on the assumption that money wages cannot be reduced beyond a level even as they can freely move upward. The model is criticized for the non-symmetric treatment of wages on the two sides of the floor.

Concepts for Review

- Average labour productivity
- Fixed investment
- Inventories
- Labour market equilibrium
- Labour measure
- Marginal productivity of labour
- Money wage floor

- Money wage rate
- Phillips curve
- Profit and expectations
- Real wages
- Supply side economics
- Total factor productivity
- Wage inflation

Case Study 18.1

Are Deposit and Investment Accounts in Islamic Banks in Malaysia Interest Free?

Islamic Banking and Finance (IBF) provides products and services guided by the Shari'ah. Therefore, they are supposed to be different from their conventional counterparts. Islamic deposit rates should be different from conventional deposit rates. Islamic banking profit rates are supposedly less risky due to the risk-sharing attribute embedded in their structure as compared to the conventional banking interest rates on similar risk investment products. This paper addresses this concern by examining the differences in the monthly fixed deposit rates of conventional and investment deposit rates of Islamic banks and finance companies in Malaysia for the period of January 1894 to December 2012 and determines the causality relationship between profit rates and interest rates on these investments. The findings suggest that profit rates of Islamic banks are significantly linked with interest rates of conventional banks. The findings also indicate that profit rates of Islamic banks and finance companies are affected by the movements of interest rates of conventional banks and finance companies respectively and not vice versa. The findings imply that there is a gap between Islamic banking theory and practice. Lack of infrastructure for full compliance and lack of stringent for cement of regulatory requirements are possible reasons for such behavior of Islamic financial institutions in Malaysia.

Source: Anuar, K. et al. (2014)

Case Questions

1. What do you understand by risk and risk-sharing? Do you think that risk-sharing alone can be a sound basis for organizing Islamic finance? Give reasons for your answer.
2. Explain the findings of the authors. What are some of the not known or new facts brought to light by the paper? Explain.
3. Do you think that interest-based finance is entirely risk-free? Argue your case.

Case Study 18.2

The following table provides data on several productivity aspects of the US economy for the years 1890 to 2005.

Table 18.1 *Contribution of capital deepening and total factor productivity to labour productivity growth, 1890–2005*

Contributory element	Average annual growth rate			Change	
	1891–1895	1896–2001	2002–2005	1891–1895 to 1896–2001	1896–2001 to 2002–2005
Contribution of capital deepening (percentage points)	0.50	1.33	0.76	0.83	− 0.57
Contribution of total factor productivity (percentage points)	1.04	1.22	2.45	0.18	1.23
Labour productivity	1.54	2.55	3.21	1.01	0.66

Source: Congressional Budget Office, based on data from the Bureau of Labour Statistics and the Bureau of Economic Analysis.

Case Questions

1. Explain the difference between percentage and percentage points.
2. The last row of the table shows that labour productivity in the US has continuously been rising. How did this affect the long-run GDP growth in the economy?
3. Explain the meaning of 'capital deepening'. In Figure 18.7, K_1, K_2 and K_3 have been arranged in an increasing order. Why?
4. Explain how the values for labour productivity in the bottom row of the table have been obtained.
5. Why is the contribution of capital deepening to labour productivity smaller than the contribution of total factor productivity? Explain.

Test Questions

18.1 What do you understand by supply side economics? Why and when did it emerge on the scene? Explain briefly its main characteristics.

18.2 Carefully study Figure 18.9 and answer the following questions.

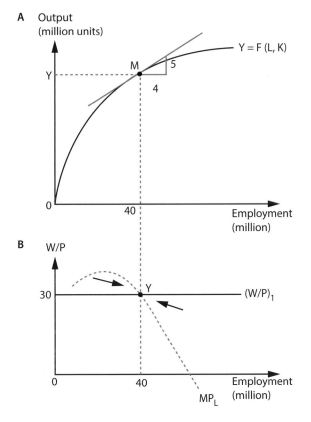

Figure 18.9 *Labour market equilibrium under perfect competition*

(a) If P = 1, what would be the amount of money wage bill? Shade the relevant areas in the figure. Can you say what would be the average real wage rate?

(b) If 8 million more workers were employed, how much will the increase be in total output? Can you indicate the marginal physical product of labour?

(c) Explain why should the market be in a state of equilibrium at point Y in part B of the figure? What do the two arrows indicate?

18.3 State and explain briefly the investment types and their characteristics. Why investment is a relatively more volatile variable than others in macroeconomics? Explain.

18.4 What role does inventory investment play in the process of production? How is it related to fluctuations in economic activity in a country?

18.5 What links money wage to real wage? If the price level at two time points remains unchanged, will money and real wage be different over time? Give reasons for your answer.

18.6   If price levels were completely inflexible, show that real wage will fluctuate directly with changes in the demand for labour. Use an appropriate diagram.

18.7   Fill in the blanks in column 4 of Table 18.2 after 1865. When you have completed the table, construct a time series graph: take years on X-axis and real wage and price index numbers on Y-axis. Note the year where the two graphs cross each other and compare their level before and after their intersection point.

Table 18.2 *Average weekly non-agricultural wages in the US*

Year	Current Dollars	1882 Dollars	Price index 1882 = 100
1	2	3	4
1860			
1865	101.5	310.5	32.7
1870	125.8	312.9	
1875	170.3	305.2	
1880	240.8	281.3	85.6
1885	304.7	276.2	110.3
1890	349.3	262.4	
1895	399.5	258.4	
2000	480.4	275.6	
2004	543.6	275.8	187.1

Source: First three columns use part of data provided in Table 30.3, p. 634 of Hughes, J. and Cain, L.P. (2007), *American Economic History*, 7th edn., Pearson Education Inc.

18.8   Why are money wages sticky downward? Explain. Discuss and evaluate carefully in this context the wage floor model.

18.9   Explain the concepts of productivity. How is labour productivity measured? What are the factors that determine productivity of labour? Discuss.

18.10   On Wednesday, 29 October 2008, the Dow Jones industrial average fell by 0.82% to close at 8,990.96. Verify if it fell by 73.73 percentage points.

18.11   The term investment represents the annual flow of newly produced capital goods which replaces or adds to the existing capital stock. Table 18.3 provides the investment requirements for an economy. What percentage of total requirement is for (a) capital widening and (b) for capital deepening?

Table 18.3 *Investment requirement estimates*

1	Replacement requirement	$60 billion
2	Capital required to provide the new workers with tools and implements	$30 billion
3	Requirement to increase capital availability per worker	$25 billion
	Total investment requirement	$115 billion

Web Exercise

Go to http://georgewbush-whitehouse.archives.gov/cea/progrowth.html and search for the article 'Pro-growth Tax Policy'. Make a summary of the article in not more than 500 words.

Forward Link

Macroeconomics deals with economy on the whole. So far, we have discussed the component variables and their mutual relationships piece by piece. In the next chapter, we shall put these pieces together. We shall discuss the nature of various types of markets—goods, assets (capital) and money—and how they together bring about the overall equilibrium of the economy.

CHAPTER 19

Markets in Equilibrium: The IS–LM Model

LEARNING OUTCOMES

This chapter should enable the student to understand:

- The equality of savings and investment that clears the goods market
- The dependence of investment on interest and income levels
- The mechanism that brings about equilibrium in the money market
- How the goods market and money market combine to set up the overall equilibrium of the economy
- The process of adjustments that integrates the markets for overall equilibrium
- The limitations of the IS–LM model
- The tools of monetary and fiscal policies for use in the following chapters

19.1 INTRODUCTION

Equilibrium is a key concept in economics. In microeconomics, we learn about the demand for and supply of individual commodities and how the two forces come together in the market to determine their equilibrium price. We learnt in the preceding chapters what determines aggregate demand and aggregate supply of goods and services in an economy and how large its total output will be. But what determines their equilibrium and how is a bit complicated. While *price* brings demand and supply together for a specific commodity, *income* is the key to an aggregative equilibrium. Furthermore, in macroeconomics we deal with the general level of prices and what brings changes therein. The assets market, especially that for money gets involved, that is, the issues relating to demand and supply of money and its price—the rates of interest—enter the field. We have to study how these factors combine to bring about money market equilibrium.

Since the determinants of overall demand and supply in the goods and services market on the one hand and the assets and money market on the other are not the same, there is no automatic correspondence in their equilibriums. This necessitates the study of the mechanism which tends to bring about adjustments between the two for setting up an integrated equilibrium of the markets for the economy. This chapter provides an elementary exposition of that mechanism based on the tacit assumption that the economy does not indulge in any external transactions.

> Components of overall equilibrium: goods and services market, money market, price level and interest rates.

19.2 EQUILIBRIUM OF GOODS AND SERVICES MARKET

The goods market equilibrium is determined by the equality of ex ante or planned income and spending on them. People and institutions save a part of their income for a variety of reasons. We have also shown that saving is a leakage from the income stream, causing it to shrink, unless it is being put back into the stream through some kind of spending. Part of this spending could be autonomous ($\bar{A}$) and the other depending on propensity to consume (c) out of income. The autonomous part will obviously be the autonomous investment (I). Let us extend aggregate demand (AD) model (with given income Y) as follows:

$$Y = AD \tag{19.1}$$
$$\text{But } Y = \bar{A} + cY \tag{19.2}$$
$$Y - cY = \bar{A} \tag{19.3}$$
$$Y(1 - c) = \bar{A}/$$
$$Y = \frac{\bar{A}}{1-c} \tag{19.4}$$

But propensity to consume relates to disposable income, that is, Y net of taxes (tY) where t is the tax rate. However, (tY) represents government expenditure G. Thus, we may expand Equation 19.2 as follows:

$$AD = \bar{A} + c(1 - t)Y + G \tag{19.5}$$

Notice that c here will be smaller than c in Equation 19.4. (Why?)
From Equation 19.1, we have $\quad Y = AD$
$$Y - C = D - C$$
$$S = I \tag{19.6}$$

What is additional here is that investment is not considered coming entirely free of cost from outside the system, e.g. from the government and the rate of interest will also be among the determinants of investment.

> Rate of interest and investment are negatively related.

19.3   INVESTMENT, INTEREST AND INCOME

When we introduce interest into the picture as a determinant of investment, the latter becomes internal or endogenous to the model. The rate of desired or planned investment is inversely related to the rate of interest, i.e. the higher the rate of interest, the lower will be the rate of investment and vice versa. The reason simply is that expenditure on investment is for additions to the capital stock—plant, machinery, tools, implements and factory buildings. Such expenditure is incurred with a view of making profit in future. Firms often borrow money to finance investment. The higher the rate of interest, the higher will be the annual costs of borrowing, cutting into profit margins generated by investment. Thus, it is the negative relationship between costs and profits that accounts for higher interest rates going with lower rates of planned investment. The relationship can be expressed in a functional form as follows:

$$I = \bar{I} - bi; \qquad b > 0 \tag{19.7}$$

Planned investment is determined by its autonomous component and interest elasticity.

Where I is planned investment, $\bar{I}$ denotes the volume of autonomous investment spending, i.e. the part of investment which is independent of income as well as of interest rate and b is a constant that specifies the interest elasticity of investment. In words, Equation 19.7 simply states that the higher the interest rate is smaller the investment spending will be.

Figure 19.1 shows the relationship between I and i of equation 19.7 as you have verified in Exercise 19.2. The figure contains two investment curves to show that (i) investment varies inversely with the rate of interest along a particular curve and (ii) it varies inversely also with the slope (elasticity) of the curve, the rate of interest remaining unchanged.

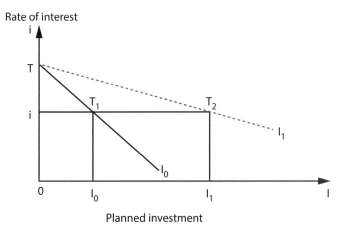

Figure 19.1 *Rate of interest and interest elasticity of investment are inversely related to the level of investment*

Exercise 19.3

Mark the slopes of the investment curves I_0 and I_1 of Figure 19.1 and compare them. Explain what relationship you find between the slope of the curves and volume of investment with the rate of interest remaining the same.

The above demonstration that investment increases when rate of interest goes down looks consistent with equation 19.7. But for the equation to hold good in a growing economy, we must additionally assume that savings will also increase with falling rates of interest to match the rising investment. Prima facie, this sounds dubious; common sense would suggest that the higher rates of interest, not the lower ones, will encourage savings. This is true if we are considering savings out of a given income. However, things are different in a dynamic situation when an economy grows through one level of equilibrium to another; the impact of rising income overpowers the influence of interest on savings. We shall explain this point further later.

19.4   SAVINGS, INTEREST AND INCOME

> Lower interest rates encourage investment which raises income and, therefore, savings. The income effect outstrips the interest impact on savings.

An important proposition underpinning the IS-LM equilibrium model is that savings are more income elastic rather than interest elastic. As increasing investment pushes up income levels, marginal propensity to consume goes down and releases larger savings out of current income: Investment, income and savings move upward in a circular relationship. You may ask from where do the initial increases in investment come to push up income in the absence of matching savings? It is an intelligent question. But recall that investment (I) in equation 19.7 includes what we described as an autonomous component ($\bar{I}$) independent of both the level of income and interest rates. This component of investment could and often does come, among others, from the government or from the financial reserves of businesses built in the past out of profits.

Figure 19.2 provides a schematic depiction of the relationships between rates of interest, investment, income and savings in the goods market in a scenario where an economy moves on from one state of equilibrium to another. The figure shows inverse relationship of interest with investment and therefore with income and savings. Since investment and savings are equal in a state of equilibrium, we mark the matching values of the two variables at equal distances from the origin on either side of the horizontal axis. The curves in the figure are drawn commensurate with this equality. The figure only puts in focus the various relationships; not their derivations or proofs.

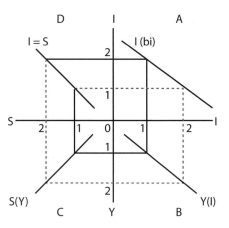

Figure 19.2 *Interest, investment, income and savings relationship*

Notice that the numbers 1 and 2 in section A match with 2 and 1 in sections B and C. Their paths make the matching clear. Section D unfolds our assumption of savings being a negative function of interest with *growing* income as also their equality with investment. This I and S equality can be shown as a function of interest rate. A rise in interest rate reduces equilibrium savings and investment (IS) and, therefore, income. Thus, we can depict the relationships as shown in Figure 19.3. The curve shows GDP (Y) as an inverse function of interest rates via their impact on investment.

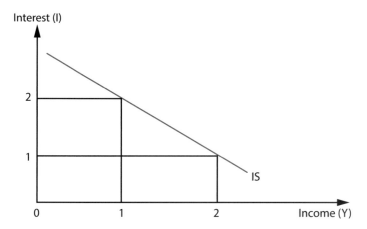

Figure 19.3 *The IS curve as derived from Figure 19.2*

The generalized version of IS curve is used to represent the locus of all possible equilibrium points where aggregate demand equals total real income Y or GDP. It shows all the combinations of Y and i that cause the market for goods and services to clear, that is, when all goods and services produced are purchased by households, firms or the government. The level of income is determined along the curve for each rate of interest. The equality of saving and investment implies that all withdrawals (leakages) from the circular flows depicted in Figure 19.2 are injected back into the flow.

> The IS curve shows equality of investment and savings for different levels of income as an inverse function of the rate of interest.

Two questions remain unanswered about the IS curve: (i) what determines the slope of this curve and (ii) how is its position fixed in the plane.

The negative slope of the IS curve begs a question. The negative relationship between rate of interest and investment is understandable but how would one explain a negative relationship between interest rate and savings? Clearly, higher interest rates should attract more savings and lower rates, less. The interest–savings curve must slope upwards. How can one show it sloping downwards in conjunction with the interest-investment curve? The reason for such an occurrence is that savings is not a function of interest rate alone; it is also a function of the income level. This latter relationship is positive—savings tend to rise with income—and stronger than the negative interest–savings relationship. Under dynamic long-run conditions, savings are more income elastic compared with their interest elasticity and can more than neutralize the negative impact of interest rates on savings to make the IS curve slope downwards.

Interest elasticity of investment

> The slope of an IS curve depends on the magnitude of interest elasticity of investment and the investment multiplier.

If investments were very much sensitive to changes in interest rates so that b in equation 19.7 were large, a rise in interest rate would much depress income compared to a situation where b were smaller and the IS curve less steep.

Impact of the multiplier

Let us now consider the impact of the multiplier size on the slope of the IS curve. Figure 19.4 uses aggregate demand curves corresponding to different multipliers derived as stated below.

Equation 19.2 above showed that in equilibrium:

$$AD = Y = \bar{A} + cY \tag{19.8}$$

$\bar{A}$ includes the autonomous part of investment ($\bar{I}$). Bringing in the non-autonomous or planned part of investment into the picture using equation 19.7, we may write the aggregate demand function as:

$$Y = \bar{A} - bi + cY \tag{19.9}$$

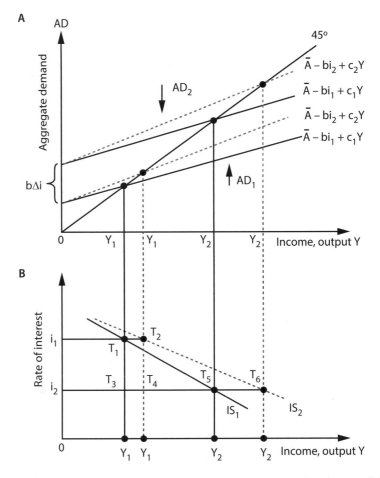

Figure 19.4 *Determinants of the slope of IS curve—interest elasticity of investment and the magnitude of the investment multiplier*

Notice that in Figure 19.4A, the slope of the parallel AD curves the unbroken lines show is different from those shown with broken lines, even as each has the same investment gap ($b\Delta i$). We can find the slopes for corresponding IS curves with reference to the interest axis from Figure 19.4B as follows:

The IS curve shows equality of investment and savings for different levels of income as an inverse function of the rate of interest.

$$\text{Slope of IS}_1 \text{ (derived for set 1)} = \frac{T_3 T_5}{T_1 T_3} \text{ and IS}_2 \text{ (derived for set 2)} = \frac{T_4 T_6}{T_2 T_4}$$

Thus, for the same change in the rate of interest $i_1 i_2 = T_1 T_3 = T_2 T_4$, $T_4 T_6 > T_3 T_5$ because $T_1 T_2 = T_3 T_4 < T_5 T_6$, while $T_4 T_5$ is common to both the numerators in the calculations. Thus, the slope of IS$_1$ is smaller than IS$_2$. The smaller slope of the IS$_1$ results in smaller rise in income ($Y_1 Y'_1$) compared with the larger slope of IS$_2$, i.e. ($Y_2 Y'_2$) for a given change in the interest rate. (Why is this so?) Note that the slope of the two IS curves in Figure 19.4 corresponds to the marginal propensity to consume and $_1$ is smaller than $_2$. And the larger the c, the greater the investment multiplier ($1/[1 - c]$) and expansion of income. Thus, multiplier is another factor in determining the slope of the IS curve.

19.4.1   Position of the IS Curve

Figure 19.4B shows two IS curves, IS$_2$ lying over IS$_1$. What causes the gap between the two and how much is the gap? In other words, what determines the relative positions of IS curves in the plane? The straight forward answer is the magnitude of autonomous expenditure $\bar{A}$. Other things remaining unchanged, if increase in $\bar{A}$ is $\Delta\bar{A}$ and λ is the multiplier, we will have expansion in income, $\Delta Y = \lambda\Delta\bar{A}$. Figure 19.5 illustrates the shift in the position of an IS curve.

Notice that an increase in the aggregate demand by $\Delta\bar{A}$ in Figure 19.5A shifts the curve upwards from T_1 to T_2. The two curves remain parallel because all other factors are assumed to remain unchanged. The points of intersection of the curves at T_1 and T_2 mark the equilibrium of the economy before and after the change in $\bar{A}$. The rise in $\bar{A}$ causes expansion in income from Y_1 to Y_2, that is, more than one time of its own magnitude. This helps generalize that any increase (decrease) in autonomous spending may have a multiplier effect on income. The concept of multiplier is prominently associated with investment because the purpose and character of investment have no other target except income and the act is much more repetitive here than in the case of other kinds of spending.

All autonomous spending not only on investment goods has a multiplier effect on income.

Figure 19.5B clarifies the association of a different IS curve with each level of equilibrium income resulting from a change in $\bar{A}$. The two IS curves are far apart by the same distance as the change in income. The two are parallel to one another for the same reasons that keep aggregate demand curves in that position in Figure 19.5A.

Exercise 19.4

Compare carefully Figures 19.4 and 19.5 and list the similarities and differences you find between them. Do you think b∆i and ∆A give you identical aggregate demand curves in the two figures? Also, could the two cases be identical? Give reasons for your answer.

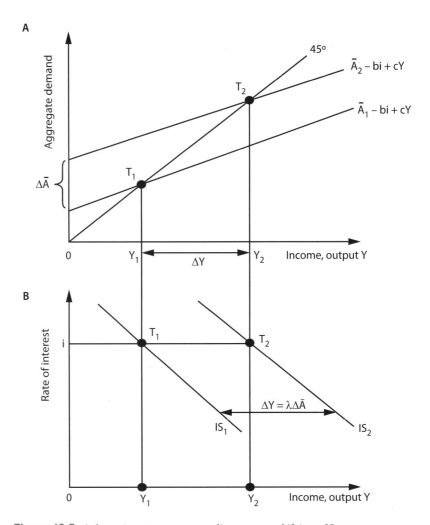

Figure 19.5 *A change in autonomous expenditure causes a shift in an IS curve*

19.5 MONEY MARKET EQUILIBRIUM: THE LM CURVE

We have explained above the nature of significance and mathematical expressions of the demand for real output needed for final consumption or for use as investment in goods and services for future production. In this explanation, we assumed the supply of resources (in money terms) as given. Now, we relax this assumption and we see how the money market adjusts to given demands and how the LM curve is fixed.

19.5.1   Demand for Money

Money market equilibrium, like any other market is determined by the forces of demand and supply. The supply or quantity of money in an economy remains almost completely under the control of the central bank of the country such as Bank Negara in Malaysia. The demand for money can be viewed from two angles. Money goes on rounds to serve as medium of exchange but it also works as the store of value: it sits on the hands of people as the most liquid asset. For this dual role of money, the notion of money demand is a bit intricate. Given the supply of money M, if more of it is demanded for transacting real goods and services, that is, to work as medium of exchange, less will be available to hold as cash. You can easily visualize that if an economy moves from one level of national income (Y_1) to a higher level (Y_2), the volume of transactions would increase and more money will be required to serve as medium of exchange. Thus, there is a positive relationship between money demand and the level of national income. The rise in the transaction demand will push up the price of money, that is, the rate of interest. However, this will increase the cost of holding money in the form of earnings foregone from other assets. People will tend to move out of money and into (say) bonds. The demand for real balances—liquidity (L)—will fall. Thus, to conclude, demand for money is directly related to income levels but is inversely related to rates of interest. Figure 19.6 is a schematic demonstration of the relationships.

> Money demand and income levels are positively correlated but the relationship between money demand and rates of interest is negative.

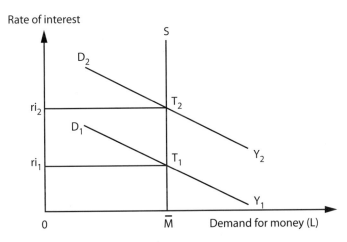

Figure 19.6 *Rate of interest, demand for money and income level: mutual relationships*

19.5.2   Nominal Money and Real Money

Demand for money is not only influenced by income levels and the rate of interest, but it is also influenced markedly by the changes in the general level of prices (P). For example, if prices of real goods and services double, we may reasonably expect the transaction demand (P × Q) for money to be twice as much. PQ is the nominal demand for money. But if prices remain constant then $\bar{P}Q$ will constitute the demand for real money. To avoid complications, the discussion in the present chapter is based on the assumption of prices remaining unchanged; we are dealing with real income and real demand for money. We shall present this general notion in a formal equation below.

19.5.3   Supply of Money

The supply or quantity of money (M) mostly remains, as discussed earlier, under the control of the central bank of a country. An earlier theory of money supply or quantity linked it to the value of final goods and services or national income (Y) in a simple expression as:

$$MV = Y \tag{19.10}$$

It was assumed that the velocity of circulation of money (V) remained unchanged during the short period. Velocity refers to the number of times a unit of money changes hands 'on an average' as medium of exchange during a given period, say a year. Income (Y) was the sum of values obtained as product of goods and services (T = Q) and their corresponding prices (P). Thus, Y = PT, where T excluded the transactions in intermediate products. On the assumption that V and P remained unchanged in the short run, supply or quantity of money M was a positive function of income Y. In other words, an expanding economy would require an appropriate expansion in money supply to run the show smoothly.

Later refinements in the quantity theory of money coming from Cambridge shifted the focus from the medium of exchange function of money to its store of value function. In that, the discussion in a sense incorporated demand for money into the supply side of the market. It was easy to do so because income and expenditure at the macro level were the two sides of the same coin. It was argued that the quantity of money could be expressed as a fraction of Y that people wanted (demanded) to keep with them in the form of cash (i) for meeting day to day transactions need, (ii) to serve as a precaution for meeting exigencies or (iii) to take advantage of change in prices. The transaction or precautionary motives of holding cash were considered stable. So, what could make money supply volatile was the switching of wealth between money (liquidity) and speculative assets. However, for the moment, the important point is that motives apart, people wanted to keep a portion of their income in money form. Equation 19.10 could then be written as:

$$M = (1/V)Y = kY \text{ where } 0 < k < 1 \qquad (19.11)$$

Notice that k and V are inversely related; the implication being that if more money is used as medium of exchange less is available to hold as cash.

These developments led to the forging of more sophisticated weapons to formulate and analyse macroeconomic issues for policy making: the IS–LM model was developed to improve understanding of how the economies operate. Income (Y) remains at constant prices, i.e. Equation 19.11 assumes that there are no changes in the price level; it just says that the amount of money people may want to keep with them—rather spend—is a fraction of their real incomes. However, the equation is an identity; for, by definition k must change to whatever value that could keep the equation intact.

Economists further altered the quantity of money equation. The fraction k now identified the fraction of money income that people desired on an average to keep with them, and that desire depended on the amount of income they expected to receive in the future. Thus, k was converted to a behavioural variable and Equation 19.10 can be read as follows.

Demand for money (liquidity):
$$L = kY, \text{ where Y is expected income.} \qquad (19.12)$$

Fraction k in equation 19.12 was assumed to remain stable so as to express demand for money as a function of expected income. This equation is qualitatively different from equation 19.12 in that it tells how people may want to act, whereas equation 19.11 informs us how they have actually acted. Let us examine briefly the implications of income expectations. We saw that people can keep their assets (i) in liquid form, i.e. money, where they earn no interest or (ii) non-money forms, where they can earn interest. How they switch between these alternatives will depend on changes in the rate of interest, given the quantity of money. It is easy to see that when higher rates of interest are expected, more people will spend on acquiring non-money assets, say bonds, in other words, lower will be the demand for holding money as cash and vice versa. The rising interest rates will make keeping funds idle more expensive in terms of their opportunity cost. Investment spending will rise. To bring in the influence of interest rates on the demand for money, we may modify equation 19.12 as:

$$L = kY - mi \qquad (19.13)$$

Where i is the rate of interest and m measures the interest elasticity of money demand L.

19.5.4   The LM Curve

We may now put the demand and supply of money together to obtain the equilibrium of the money market. Let us go back to Figure 19.6. Here we have no axis for income Y. In Figure 19.7, we take Y on the X-axis

The new interpretation of the demand for money helped economists to incorporate demand and therefore interest into the supply side of an economy.

The Cambridge refinements in the theory focused on the portion of real income people wanted to keep with them in the form of cash.

LM curve is the path of points equating the demand for money (L) with its supply (M).

and mark off on it the two income levels associated with the money demand curves. Corresponding to each Y level, we have an interest rate. We can use the coordinates (Y_1, ri_1) and (Y_2, ri_2) to fix points T_1 and T_2 in the plane. The line passing through these two points will chart the equilibrium path of the money market as Figure 19.7 shows.

The LM curve shows how much spending any fixed quantity of money could support. High rates of interest like ri_2 induce rapid spending of money that could maintain Y_2 level of income. In contrast, when interest rates are at a lower level such as ri_1 the money stock supports less spending and, therefore lower, i.e. Y_1 income level. The other points representing similar combinations help generate the LM curve. The **money** market will be in equilibrium at each point on the curve as the division of money stock (supply) between its sitting and circulating portion will be such as would adequately meet the liquidity needs on both counts. In other words, k will be appropriate at each income level.

It is now easy to construct the equation for the LM curve. Let there be a fixed supply of nominal money $\overline{M}$ which we can readily convert into real money by dividing it by an appropriate price index $\overline{P}$ to get the constant money supply in real terms, i.e. $\overline{M}/\overline{P}$. We may equate this with the real money demand to obtain the LM equation as:

$$\overline{M}/\overline{P} = kY - mi \qquad\qquad (19.14)$$

Slope and position of the LM curve

The greater the size of k; which measures the income elasticity of demand for money, the steeper will be the LM curve. However, the influence of interest rate operating in the opposite direction cannot be ignored. The lower the interest elasticity of demand (m) for money, the greater will be the slope of the LM curve. Thus, the slope will depend on the relative strength of these two forces. For instance, if high value of k combines with low value of m, LM must be rising steeply.

Another implication of k and i being opposite influence on the demand for money may be noted. The LM curve is sloping upwards. A rise in interest rate (i) reduces the demand for real balances. Under the circumstance the demand for real balances can be kept at required level only if the level of income could appropriately rise as Figure 19.7 shows.

Furthermore, recall that the real money supply is held constant along the LM curve. Clearly, a change in the volume of real money supply will change the position of the LM curve. The shift will be to the right from its initial position if there were an increase in real money supply and to the left if there were a decrease; other things remaining unchanged. Figure 19.8 illustrates the point. Here, M_2 and LM_2 show the initial position. LM shifts to the left if M_2 decreases to M_1 and to the right if M_2 increases to M_3.

> The slope of the LM curve depends on the relative strength of the income and interest elasticity of demand for money and its position on changes in real money supply.

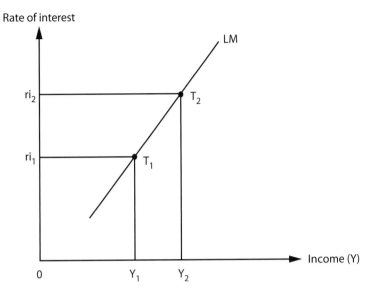

Figure 19.7 *Money market equilibrium: the LM curve*

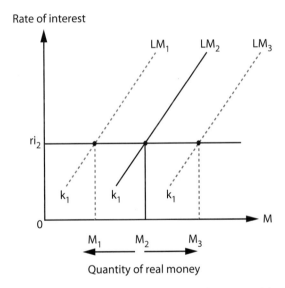

Figure 19.8 *Change in the quantity of real money changes the position of the LM curve, other things remaining unchanged*

19.6 THE IS–LM MODEL

We have now the tools ready to show and explain the overall equilibrium of the economy. To recapitulate, we have the IS curve which traces the inverse relationship between interest rates and the investment-savings equality needed for goods market equilibrium. Likewise, we have the LM curve that links liquidity requirements via the interest rates to the given supply of money in the market. We may put these curves together as shown in Figure 19.9 to fix the equilibrium of the economy compatible with those in the goods and money markets. Both markets clear at point T. In other words, equilibrium occurs when the amount of money invested equals the amount of money available for investing. In other words, the decisions by investors to invest correspond to the amount of money available with them and the interest rate they expect to receive. Demand and supply in both the markets balance each other, resulting in stable prices.

Exercise 19.5

Redraw Figure 19.9, with the following changes and comment on the consequences.
  (i) Keep the LM curve as it is and shift the IS curve upwards to the right.
  (ii) Keep the IS curve unchanged but shift the LM curve downwards to the left.

19.7   DYNAMIC CHANGE AND EQUILIBRIUM ADJUSTMENT

The IS–LM model described above shows the equilibrium of the economy at a point of time. However, economies do not stay static. Economic conditions and variables undergo changes quite frequently; these changes tend to destroy existing equilibriums and replace them with the new ones. It is, therefore, important to understand how the transition takes place over time. One element that signals the impending change is the behaviour of stocks or inventories businesses have to carry in raw materials, stores and finished and semi-finished products for running the production processes unhampered. The normal level of inventories is expressed as a fraction of yearly production. To illustrate, inventories must be sufficient enough to maintain production (say) for three months. If inventories grow beyond the normal level, resources are fruitlessly tied down in them. On the other hand, if inventory level falls below the normal, production may face stoppages along the line. Inventory behaviour is indicative of changes in factors determining the slope and position of the IS–LM curves.

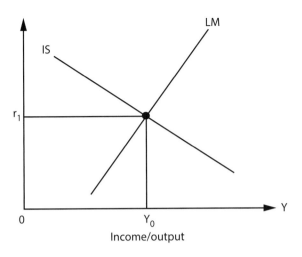

Figure 19.9 *Goods and money market equilibrium*

Is Savings Good for an Economy?

There is an old joke that if you ask twelve economists a question, you get thirteen answers: one from each, plus one from Keynes. Savings is a good example of this. In the classical theory, savings was regarded good for the economy: a high savings rate translated into higher investments, growth in the stock of capital, and increases in output and wages. This prediction was backed up by data: countries that save the most also tend to invest the most and grow the fastest.

The Keynesian story is just the opposite. A higher savings rate (the ratio of S to Y) is also a lower consumption rate, since savings and consumption sum to after-tax income. In terms of the IS–LM diagram, we can think of an increase in the savings rate as a leftward shift in the IS curve, which (in the theory) reduces output. The story is that if individuals decide to consume less, this hurts firms, who are trying to sell, and leads them to lay people off. This is a demand side story in the sense that we are talking about who demands or buys goods, rather than how they are produced. I think the story has some merit.

So who is right? Presumably, it is a little of both: the Keynesian theory fits the short term, but over periods longer than a couple years, savings clearly raises output (i.e. the classical theory is the best guide). For example, the short-run effect of a reduction in budget deficits (via a cut in spending, G, or an increase in taxes, T) may be recessionary according to the Keynesian model; however, over time, the cut in the budget deficit leads to a fall in real interest rates, less crowding-out and an increase in private investment. Over time, this increase in investment leads to a larger capital stock and an increase in potential and actual output. So, while the short-run effects of a fiscal contraction may be recessionary, the long-run effects are likely to be expansionary. This tradeoff between short- and long-term objectives is one of the tough issues facing policymakers. On the whole, I tend to worry that short-term thinking has led to policy with poor long-term consequences. Businessmen face some of the same problems: when bonuses are tied to annual performance, there may be little gain to adopting policies with long-term benefits.

Source: Nouriel Roubini and David Backus, *Lectures in Macroeconomics*, <http://people.stern.nyu.edu/nroubini/NOTES/CHAP9.HTM>, accessed 1 August 2014.

However, the possible effects of shifts in the position of these curves are so numerous and complicated that it is difficult to comprehend them without making some heroic assumptions. The two assumptions commonly made are as under.

1. Any demand for goods and services in excess of their supply will lead to an increase in output while a short fall in demand will cause output to decrease. The assumption implies that firms will readily be able to adjust the production process to any uncalled for accumulation of inventory or short fall therein.

2. An excess of demand for money would cause a rise in the rate of interest while an excess of supply would initiate a fall in it.

19.8 LIMITATIONS OF THE IS–LM MODEL

> The merit of the IS–LM model is that it allows the use of standard economics tools of demand and supply at macro level analysis, but it has limitations as well.

The model has since long been a standard design to study macroeconomic policy issues. It gained popularity primarily because it could transfer to macroeconomics the familiar tools of demand and supply which make the understanding of issues so easy in the realm of microeconomics. However, macroeconomics of necessity needed more compressed aggregation of data; the reduction of the entire economy to two markets and five variables seems too high a degree of condensation for worthwhile understanding and analysis of the macro issues. In addition, the following weaknesses are also worth noting.

1. The model hinges on the rate of interest even in the goods market where profit expectations lead the decision-making process, interest being just one cost element.

2. Even though IS–LM is a key model of macroeconomics, economists have seldom put it to empirical testing or for making predictions about the expected levels of national income.

3. One is not sure whether the model explains the equilibrium income/output in the short run or in the long run. The behaviour of the variables involved, especially of k and m, may be quite different over the two periods. k may fluctuate considerably in the short run while m may not remain constant in the long run.

> The model relies on too much condensation of information about an economy and has little explanatory or predictive value.

4. The assumption of stable price level for real value of income or rate of interest is quite confusing from a practical angle; all problems in the construction of index numbers creep in. Interestingly, the model claims to give stable results by a prior assumption of stability.

19.9   MODIFICATIONS IN THE IS–LM MODEL

To overcome the above mentioned limitations of the initial IS–LM model, some modifications in recent years have been suggested in its initial structure. A discussion of the changes incorporated falls outside the scope of this introductory work but a few points may be briefly mentioned. The new model goes under the names of optimizing IS–LM model or expectations based IS–LM model. The reason is that it uses micro foundations and rational expectation for constructing its building blocks. It departs from the initial version in that it does away with distinction between real and nominal values of monetary measurements, interest rates or national income. This not only removes the element of arbitrariness from their estimation but imparts realism to the model. It provides the central banks with a factual policy target for controlling inflation. Furthermore, in macroeconomics we deal with the general level of prices and what brings changes therein. Interest rate behaviour in that context, helps us understand the limitations of the model in the realm of monetary policy.

**BOX
19.2**

Islamic Macroeconomics Model in the IS–LM Framework

This model focuses on the monetary side of the economy and seeks to establish the following:
    If Muslim countries move to profit-and-loss-sharing- (PLS-) based financing that should not be a cause for concern for policy makers at the international level. PLS-based banking is not an entirely new idea. A PLS-based financial system is likely to be more stable than the interest-based system. There would be no difference in the working of monetary policy as at present.

Assumptions:
- The economy consists of three markets: a market for goods, a money market and a capital market.
- All real income goes to capital rather than being divided between capital and labour.
- Banks are the only intermediaries. The savers deposit all their savings with the banks and all investments in the economy are undertaken by borrowing from banks.
- When the savers deposit their saving with the banks, they essentially buy 'shares' of banks whose nominal value is not guaranteed and the rate of return on them are not predetermined and can vary.

Symbols:
    y = real income (GDP)
    r = real yield or real rate of return on shares
    S = nominal value of shares
    P = price level
    s = real value of shares

Capital market:

Demand for bank shares: $s = S/P$
Supply of bank shares: y/r
Equilibrium condition: $s = S/P = y/r$
Balance sheet of the banking system and adjustment in the capital market:

Assets	Liabilities
y/r	S/P

When losses occur, nominal value of shares (S) is wiped off and the capital market instantaneously returns to equilibrium.

Money market:

Economic agents hold their total real wealth (W) in the form of either real money balances ($m = M/P$) or shares of the banks ($s = S/P$), where $P = 1$ (constant). That is: $w = m + s$.
All money in the system (M) is outside money or currency supplied by the government.

Working hypothesis:

People always maintain a constant ratio of real balances (m) to shares ($s = S/P$) that in turn, is an inverse function of real rate of return (r):

$$m/s = g(r), \qquad g' < 0$$

Money market equilibrium condition:

$$m = g(r).s = g(r).(y/r)$$

Aggregate demand (y^d) equals consumption demand (C) plus investment demand (I).

$$C = C(W, r), \ C_W < 0, \ C_r > 0; \ W = m + s = m + (y/r)$$
$$I = I(r); \quad I_r < 0$$
$$y^d = C(W, r) + I(r)$$

If producers are offered in real terms y, they would supply output worth y. Thus, $y^s = y$.
Goods market equilibrium condition: $y = C(Y, r) + I(r)$
Adjustment mechanism: as usual.

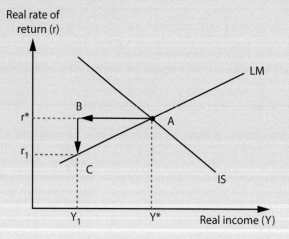

Figure 19.10 *Equilibrium in IS–LM framework; capital market assumed as being in equilibrium*

Source: Mohsin S. Khan (1986), Islamic Interest-Free Banking, IMF Staff Papers, 33(1), based on Syed Tahir's IRIT, DL–10 (17 Nov 2009) lecture in PowerPoint.

Summary

- This chapter introduces the concepts of aggregate demand and aggregate supply as they operate in the product and money/assets markets and how they set up equilibriums in each of these markets. The discussion is based on the assumption of a closed economy.

- In macroeconomics we deal with the general level of prices and what brings changes therein. Thus, the issues relating to changes in the demand and supply of money and its price—the rates of interest—enter the field.

- The goods market equilibrium is determined by the equality of planned spending and planned income. Income apart, people and institutions save for a variety of reasons.

- Savings is a leakage from the income stream causing it to shrink unless the amount is put back into the income stream through some kind of spending. Part of this spending could be autonomous ($\bar{A}$) and the other depends on (c) the propensity to consume.

- The autonomous part would invariably include autonomous investment ($\bar{A}$). From the aggregate demand model of Chapter 17, we take and extend:
$$Y - cY = \bar{A}$$
Thus, the equilibrium level of income (Y) at which aggregate demand (AD) would equal output is:
$$Y = \bar{A}(1 - c)$$

- If aggregate income (Y) = AD (aggregate demand), we have:
$$Y - C = AD - C$$
$$S = I$$

- The rate of desired or planned investment is inversely related to the rate of interest, i.e. the higher is the rate of interest the lower will be the rate of investment and vice versa. The relationship can be expressed in a functional form as follows: $I = \bar{I} - bi$, where I is planned investment, $\bar{I}$ is the volume of autonomous investment spending, i.e. the part of investment which is independent of income as well as of interest rate, and b is a constant that specifies the interest elasticity of investment.

- Higher interest rates must normally increase savings. However, expanding income overpowers the negative influence of lower interest rates on savings and we find that in a dynamic situation, lower interest rates go with higher incomes, and higher rates of interest with low incomes.

- Planned savings and planned investment must be equal in a state of equilibrium given the rate of interest. The magnitude of this equality is negatively correlated to the rate of interest but has a positive relationship with the levels of income. Thus, the equality of savings and investment or the IS curve slopes downwards as a function of falling interest rate and expanding incomes.

- The higher the interest elasticity of investment, the steeper will be the IS curve. Given the rate of interest, the larger the marginal propensity to consume and therefore the investment multiplier; will result in flatter IS curve. The slope will be greater. On the other hand, the magnitude of autonomous expenditure ($\bar{A}$) determines the position of the IS curve in the plane.

- The IS curve explains how the equilibrium of demand and supply takes place in the product market. The money (assets) market is explained by the equality of demand (L) and supply of money (M) too via the interest rate. Here, we have the LM curve that depicts the equilibrium of demand and supply path of the market.

- Given the supply of money ($\bar{M}$) and demand for money (liquidity) varies inversely with the rate of interest along the curve and directly with the level of income indicated by the shift of the curve.

- Supply of money required can be seen with reference to the medium of exchange function of money or in its role as a store of value. The first approach gives us the classical quantity theory of money MV = PT, where T represents the quantity Q of all transactions exchanged in the market through money. It is an identity because income (MV) would always equal expenditure (PT) for the economy as a whole.

- Later, intermediate transactions were dropped from PT, T included the quantity of only the final goods and services and the equation became MV = Y, but it still remained an identity with V taking any appropriate value to keep the two sides equal.

- The Cambridge version looked at the equation from the demand side. It thought that the quantity of money must be enough, not only enabling money to do the exchange work efficiently but to also meet the demand for money to hold as a store of value.

- The Cambridge version saw the store of value function as reciprocal of its velocity to make the equation read as M = 1/V(Y). 1/V was put equal to k. The equation now was written as M = kY, where k represents the fraction of real income (Y) people wanted on an average to keep with them in the form of money both for carrying exchange transactions as well as to meet their other liquidity needs.

- The merit of the Cambridge modification was that it incorporated the demand for money into its supply side so as to link it to the rate of interest. The rate of interest brought in on both the sides of the equation enabled the construction of the demand and supply curves providing a stable combination.

- The equilibrium of demand and supply gave a unique and stable combination of interest rate (i) and national income (Y).

- The IS–LM model explains the equilibrium of the markets at a point of time but economies are dynamic. In the real world, the changes are so numerous and their consequences to complex that the model loses much of its explanatory and predictive value. Modern texts on macroeconomics at times tend to skip over it.

- The model lacks clarity; it is not policy oriented and hence has little practical value.

Glossary

Assets market We may think of asset in physical terms such as tools, machines, buildings and so on or in terms of financial papers like bonds, units, stocks, bills or money. For the purpose of this chapter the asset market refers to financial instruments.

Autonomous investment Autonomous investment is that part of investment which is not explained by changes in the level of output. For example, the investment in public services—utilities, civil administration or defence—which is determined by government policy falls in this category. It is also called exogenous investment.

Interest elasticity of investment The interest elasticity of demand for investment is the responsiveness or sensitivity of investment to changes in the rate of interest.

IS curve When we construct a graph showing what the equilibrium income is for each level of interest rate, we get a curve called the IS curve, and its name comes from the condition for equilibrium, i.e. investment (I) must equal savings (S).

LM curve It is an upward sloping curve that traces the path of equilibrium points of demand for money with its fixed supply as associated with different interest rate and income levels.

Nominal money Nominal money is the quantity of money expressed in units of currency of a country and is intimately correlated with the price level in that country.

Planned investment Planned investment refers to what capital firms intend to invest in business in times ahead usually a year. It is an ex ante concept and is affected by such factors as rate of interest, profit expectations and the risk involved. This sort of investment need not equal planned savings though such equality is an equilibrium condition for the economy.

Real money Real money is the quantity of money measured in terms of constant prices using index numbers; it is connected to nominal money as follows:

Real money = Nominal money/Price level, i.e. M/P

Concepts for Review

- Assets market
- Autonomous investment
- Demand for money
- Dynamic change
- Income elasticity of the demand for money
- Inflation
- Interest elasticity of investment
- Interest elasticity of money demand
- IS curve
- LM curve
- Nominal money
- Planned investment
- Real money

Case Study 19.1

Bolivian Stabilization

Bolivia in the mid-1980s suffered from rates of inflation in excess of 1,000 per cent per year. On the advice of Jeffrey Sachs of Harvard, they adopted one of the cleanest examples of an orthodox stabilization: fiscal budget balance, slower money growth and market-oriented policies. What we saw was a dramatic fall in the inflation rate, as you might predict from the classical theory. We also saw a substantial decline in output, as the Keynesian theory predicts for the short-run. This suggests that the kinds of price inertia we are talking about are also present at very high rates of inflation (which should tell you why it is so hard to get rid of inflation once you get it). Sachs remarked on the latter: 'When I came, Bolivia was a poor country with very high inflation. Now, Bolivia is simply a poor country'.

Source: Nouriel Roubini and David Backus, Lectures in Macroeconomics, < http://people.stern.nyu.edu/nroubini/NOTES/CHAP9.HTM>, accessed 1 August 2014.

Case Questions

1. Following the advice of the advisor, what were the steps Bolivia initiated to control inflation? State and explain why the country could succeed in their anti–inflation policy.
2. Why did the success in curbing inflation leave the country poorer? Explain.

Case Study 19.2

Causes of the Current Meltdown

09 February 2009

The classic explanation of financial crises is that they are caused by excesses—frequent monetary excesses—which leads to a boom and an inevitable bust. This crisis was no different: A housing boom followed by a bust led to defaults, the implosion of mortgages and mortgage-related securities at financial institutions, all resulting in turmoil.

The Fed (Federal Reserve System) held its target interest rate, especially in 2003–2005, well below known monetary guidelines. Keeping interest rates on the track that worked well in the past two decades, rather than keeping rates so low, would have prevented the boom and the bust. The effects of the boom and bust were amplified by several complicating factors including the use of subprime and adjustable-rate mortgages, which led to excessive risk-taking which was encouraged by the excessively low interest rates. Government action also helped prolong the crisis considering that the financial crisis became acute on 9 and 10 August 2007, when money-market interest rates rose dramatically. Interest rate spreads, such as the difference between three-month and overnight interbank loans, jumped to unprecedented levels.

Source: Paraphrased from the writings of Prof. Taylor in the WSJ (edited from the Web).

Case Questions

1. In the above case, interest rates were lower than the equilibrium rate. Which side of the LM curve should the disequilibrium point be—left or right?
2. What can restore the equilibrium of the economy: increase in quantity of money resulting in the expansion of income or raising of interest rates curtailing credit? Argue your case within the LM framework.
3. How is the policy choice you make in (2) likely to effect the IS curve? Explain.

Test Questions

19.1 (a) Suppose in an economy, autonomous expenditure is $3,000 billion and the propensity to save is 40%. Do you agree that the level of national income would be $5,000 billion? Show your calculations.

   (b) Suppose the national income of a country was estimated at $6,000 billion and her autonomous expenditures were $3,000 billion. What must have been the propensity to consume for the country?

19.2 If the consumption function for an economy were C= 300 + 0.8Y with national income equal to $6,000 billion, what must have been the equilibrium rate of savings and investment in the economy? Show your calculations.

19.3 It is obvious that the higher the rate of interest, the higher will be the cost of borrowing funds and smaller will be the level of planned investment. Can you provide at least two reasons why this may not always be the case, i.e. investment could rise despite increase in the rate of interest?

19.4 In Figures 19.4 and 19.5, the slopes of the aggregate demand curves remain constant. Does it mean that the propensity to consume will also have to remain the same as equilibrium income changes? Argue your case.

19.5 Suppose the national income of a country at constant prices is $16,000 billion and people normally hold 25% of it in the form of cash under liquidity motives. It is also known that the interest elasticity of demand for money is stable at 200. Estimate the demand for money if the interest rate were (a) 18% and (b) 15%. Compare the two results and account for the difference in their levels.

19.6 Given $\bar{M}/\bar{P} = 700$ and L = 0.5Y − 40i. Specify the equation for the LM curve. If the rate of interest were 20, at what level of income would the money market be in a state of equilibrium? What would the income level be if the rate of interest falls to 15%, other things remaining unchanged? Using the two points, plot the LM curve on a graph paper. Explain what makes the curve slope upwards.

19.7 In Figure 19.11 point 'a' is above the IS curve. Will there be excess supply or excess demand in the goods market at point 'a'? What would your answer be if the economy were below the IS curve at point 'b'? Give reasons for your answer in each case.

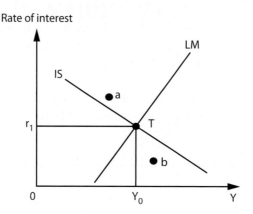

Figure 19.11 *Goods and money market equilibrium*

19.8 (a) Explain why the IS curve slopes downwards and the LM curve slopes upwards in Figure 19.11.

(b) Notice that point 'a' in the figure is above the IS curve while point 'b' is below it. Likewise, point 'a' is to the left of the LM curve but point 'b' is to its right. Explain in the case of each curve, whether there will be an excess of money supply or of money demand in the market at a particular point? Justify your answer.

19.9 What shall be the effect on equilibrium income if taxes were (a) increased or (b) decreased? Explain your answer.

19.10 What would be the effect on equilibrium income if (a) money supply (M) is decreased or (b) increased? Explain your answer.

Web Exercise

Search the Internet and add up the amounts of money countries spend on programmes to pull their economies out of the first global economic meltdown of the current century.

Forward Link

The next section of the book takes you to macro-policy frameworks commonly used to deal with issues in range and depth that modern economies face today. The next chapter deals with topics that monetary policy deals with for maintaining inter market equilibriums in modern economies; especially in the face of recurrent financial problems like the meltdown the world is facing today. Various types of markets—goods, assets (capital) and money—and how they together bring about the overall equilibrium of the economy.

20 Monetary Policy: Bases, Goals and Instruments

LEARNING OUTCOMES

This chapter should enable the student to understand:

- The meaning and significance of economic stability
- Price level measurement and value of money
- Demand for and supply of money: Their role as bases for economic stability
- Quantity theory of money: Fisher and Cambridge versions
- Inflation and deflation: Meaning, causes and consequences
- Goals and instruments of monetary policy
- Leverage gains: Lure and stability – a new control policy tool

20.1 MONEY AND ECONOMIC STABILITY

Monetary policy aims at keeping an economy stable.

Economic policy is action designed to achieve specified goals. The primary goals of macroeconomics are to promote growth, full employment, distributive justice and stability. Of these, the monetary policy of a country is directly concerned with maintaining economic stability. If economic variables especially savings and investment fluctuate violently, the other goals—growth, justice and employment— become hard to achieve. Price level changes make other economic variables like national income, production, consumption and profits lurch with them. The lurching variables soon get into a circular causation spiralling up and down. Such up-down movements form patterns known as trade cycles.

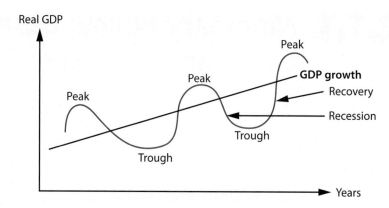

Figure 20.1 *Trade cycles and phases*

General level of prices is a sort of average of all prices at a point of time with reference to some base. It measurement requires construction of price indices.

We have already explained in Chapter 16 the concept of a general price level being distinct from the prices of individual commodities and shall revert to the topic in more detail later in Chapter 23. We shall explain the phases of the cycle as marked in the figure later; the matter of immediate interest is different. We know that the prices of individual products are determined by the demand and supply of each separately. Normally, we do not expect the demand and supply conditions of all or most products to change such that their price would move together in the same direction. But we often see this happen. (Why?) Clearly, in addition to the factors internally affecting the demand and supply of individual products, there is some external force that operates on their prices, pushing them together in the same direction, up or down. That force is the volume of money in a society. When the volume of money, that is its supply, is more than the demand for it, prices in general tend to rise, and when it is less, it tends to fall.

People demand money (i) to purchase goods and services where it is passed hand to hand, say V times, and (ii) to hold a fraction, k, as a store of purchasing power for future use.

Money is demanded in a society mainly to work as a medium of exchange or as a store of value. These two functions are competitive; out of a given stock of money, if more is in circulation as the medium of exchange less is available to store value and vice versa. However, if the speed of money in circulation rises, the same volume of money can meet increase in demand for exchange functions. The measure of this speed is the number of times the money unit performs on an average, the act of exchange during a time span say a year, and is called money's velocity of circulation. However, the measurement of money demand is much more cumbersome. The demand as medium of exchange depends on the volume of transactions, which is difficult to estimate for a variety of reasons. (What are they?) The demand for holding money back from circulation is all the more difficult to estimate due to its dependence on psychological factors. Monetary policy has therefore preferred to focus on the process of money supply, adjusting to given demand for money, and that preference takes us to the quantity theory of money we briefly referred to in an earlier chapter.

Exercise **20.1**

Compare Figures 20.1 and 20.3 and comment on their similarities and differences.

20.2 QUANTITY THEORY OF MONEY

Money is a measure of the exchange value of goods and services expressed in their prices. But money is different from other measurements like metres or gallons. In measuring the value of other goods and services, it contains a measure of its own value. If price level rises, the value of money goes down; its purchasing power reduces. For this reason, a relationship between the quantity (supply) of money and the level of prices has long been expressed in what is known as the quantity theory of money. In simple words, the theory says that there is a direct and proportional relationship between the supply of money and the general price level—double the quantity of money and the prices in general are doubled, and vice versa. This concept is usually put in the form of an equation relating money supply and prices to other economic variables.

Jean Bodin (1530–1596), a sixteenth century French jurist and political philosopher, is credited as the first to put the relationship between money supply, M and price level, P in the form of an equation: $M = kP$, with k being some constant. He observed that in 16th century Europe, prices were rising fast in most countries due to expansion of (silver) money as new mines for the metal were found. Later, we find a chain of economists from Irving Fisher to Milton Friedman who have made valuable contributions to the subject. For most of these, Fisher's equation of exchange and its Cambridge version have served as the base. We have already discussed them both in Chapter 19 Section 19.3.

You must have noticed there that the Cambridge modification transforms the equation to focus on the demand for holding money to help construct the IS–LM framework. However, its relationship with Fisher is simple and straightforward, as the part of money supply which the public holds (demands) is not in circulation. Thus, $k = 1/V$, i.e. k and V are inversely related. This provides some clue to the impact of change in k relative to V and its impact on price level leading to inflation or deflation as Figure 20.2 depicts. We see that if out of a given income, Y_0, people hold back a larger proportion, k, deflationary pressures tend to develop in an economy. On the other hand, if they indulge in overspending; V rises relative to k, inflation may take place. Thus, moderation in spending as Islam advocates seems to be an appropriate policy.

Quantity theory of money states that there is a direct proportional relationship between money supply, M, and price level, P. The Fisher equation is $MV = PT$.

The Cambridge equation sees the money quantity from the demand side of money. The equation is $M (1/k) = PT$; (T = Income Y). V and k are inversely related.

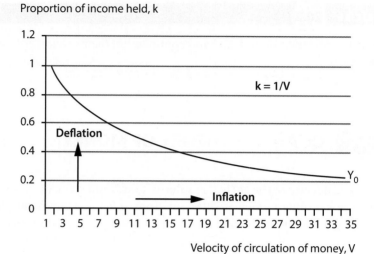

Figure 20.2 *The impact of relative changes in k and V*

One factor that has made world economies more volatile and crisis prone in recent decades is the much faster expansion of the monetary sector of the economy relative to the growth of the real sector. The reason is that much of the monetary sector expansion is the result of the rising and reckless speculation and the growing mountains of black money that fuels consumerism. One indicator of this trend is the rising GDP share of the financial industry in modern economies such as the US economy, as exemplified by Figure 20.3.

Figure 20.3 *Rising GDP share of the financial industry in the US (adapted from Philippon, 2008)*

Looking at matters from the side of demand for money, the Cambridge equation brought the standard equilibrium analysis to the money market. Let us see why people demand money to serve as the store of value rather than let it remain in active circulation.

Exercise 20.2

Why has the financial sector fast outgrown the real sector in most countries in recent times? In what way has this growth affected the stability of global economies? Elaborate your reasons.

20.3 DEMAND FOR MONEY

We have already examined and evaluated in Chapter 11 the demand side of money. In that context we explained the liquidity preference theory in some detail. Money sitting idle in the safe does not provide any income; its investment can. Why should people *demand* money to hold as a liquid asset? People want to keep a part of their money income with them for a variety of reasons. These include the need to bridge the gap between receipt of income and daily expenditure. Some money must be at hand to meet exigencies. Also, people may want to take advantage of a favourable turn in prices. Money is the purchasing power, the most *liquid* form of wealth *readily* convertible into any asset. They want incentives to part with liquidity. Keynes defined interest as that incentive: *it is the reward for not hoarding.*

The relationship between the demands for money and interest like all prices is direct; both rise and fall together, given the supply of money. However, this relationship is qualified: The nominal rate of interest cannot fall beyond a limit. There is a liquidity trap concept which was explained earlier. (See Figure 11.7 for clarification.) This helps explain why increases in money supply and cheap money policies do not put economies on the road to recovery once they get stuck in the mire of depression. Additions to money supply simply walk into the liquidity trap instead of raising the effective demand and clearing the market. Note that contrary to the general rule, speculative demand for liquidity may be inversely related to the rate of interest. To keep matters simple, we assume that the only alternative people have to the holding of money is to invest it in bonds carrying fixed rates of interest. When rates of interest are expected to rise, bonds fall in value in the market. People are spurred to sell existing bonds to have money to avoid possible capital losses. On the contrary, if interest rates are expected to fall, bond prices climb up. People move out of money; they purchase bonds. It follows that there is an inverse relationship between the expected rate of interest and the speculative demand for money. In other words, if the rates of interest rise, demand for money would fall, and if the interest rates fall, the demand for money would increase.

> Liquidity preference theory states that people want to keep a portion, k, of their income, Y, with them to bridge income–expenditure time gap, to meet contingencies and to wait for favourable price changes.

> The distinction between savings and hoarding of money depends on intention and the period of holding. In Islam, wealth held more than a year is hoarding.

20.4 MONEY SUPPLY COMPONENTS

We have discussed the demand for money and its relationship with the rate of interest, supply remaining unchanged. But supply of money does not remain constant; it changes over time for a variety of reasons. (What are they?) Thus, to understand the monetary policy of a country, we should know what constitutes money supply that is, we have to identify its components; the things that serve as money in an economy.

At the very onset of the discussion that follows, you need to understand two things about the supply of money. First, the supply of money refers to the *stock* of money at a point of time. By specifying this stock repeatedly at different points, we can generate a time series of money supply. The change in this stock over time is a flow. Thus, money supply is a *stock* variable. Here, the rate of change in the stock over time is a flow variable. Contrast it with say real income, which itself is a flow measured each year.

> Supply of money is a stock concept; only change in this stock over time is a flow concept,

Second, the stock of money always refers to stock of money held by the public. It is always smaller than the total stock of money in existence. The word public here includes all economic units—individuals, firms and institutions except those producing money, such as the government (central and state) and the banking system (the central bank plus banks that accept demand deposits). Thus, by implication, the term 'public' includes all local authorities, non-bank financial institutions and non-departmental public sector undertakings. Even the foreign central banks, governments and the International Monetary Fund (IMF), who hold a part of the domestic money locally in the form of deposits with the central bank of the country, are included in the term. In the standard measure of money, money held by the government and the banking system is excluded.

> Money has several components, symbolized as M_1, M_2, M_3, etc. But their definitions or their choice for defining money supply is not standardized.

The primary object in measuring the stock of money by indicating who is included and who is not is to keep separate the producers or suppliers of money from those who demand it for holding under the above stated motives. Such a separation is essential for both monetary analysis and the designing of monetary policy. As the objectives of monetary analysis or policy may vary over time and space the user of the concept decides on the measure to suit his purpose. We cannot therefore answer for sure what measure of money supply to use and why? It should suffice to indicate here is that by M or M_1, M_2 and M_3 specifications. We define:

$$M \text{ or } M_1 = \text{Currency held by the public} + \text{Net demand deposits of banks} + \text{Other deposits of the central bank}$$

$$M_2 = M_1 + \text{Total deposits with small savings institutions like post offices or unit trusts}$$

$$M_3 = M_1 + \text{Net time deposits of banks}$$

M_2 is also used to indicate the aggregate monetary resources (AMR) of the country. The M series can be and at times is extended to M_4 and beyond. Money produced by the government plus that produced by the central bank of a country is at times called the high-powered, base or reserve money; it is part of M_1. Managing the quantity of base money is no problem in implementing monetary policy. Demand deposits with commercial banks pose real issues for monetary policy managers—the central banks. The reason is that the fractional reserve system allows banks to create deposits many times the base money they have. This power of the banking system taken as a whole is indeed vast and has been the major source of instability in modern economies. Let us have a look at the process of credit (money) creation.

20.5   CREDIT (MONEY) CREATION BY BANKS

The volume of currency in an economy provides commercial banks the base for generating credit money. Part of currency always remains inside the central bank while the remaining is held *outside* by the public. People deposit a part of the money they hold in commercial banks as demand or time deposits which together constitute the *cash* deposits of the bank. The banks have to keep a portion of deposits, say 10%, as a statutory reserve to meet the daily withdrawal needs of the depositors. The remaining $90 out of, say, $100 cash deposit, they can lend on interest or invest in the Islamic profit-earning instruments. In conventional banks, the sum loaned ($90) is credited to the account of the borrower—what we call credit deposits. The banks make no distinction between the two sorts of deposits—cash and credit—for their lending operations. For instance, the bank will treat $90 the same way as a cash deposit and, keeping $9, will lend forward $81. The process will continue until total deposits approach the limit of $1,000, the cash $100 with the bank serving as a 10% reserve. Thus, loans create deposits in the banking system. (Recall the banking principle of note issue discussed above.) These loans and deposits appear one for the other as contra entry in the bank balance sheet.

> The fact that all depositors do not withdraw all their money at the same time lies at the heart of the credit creation process and the power of commercial banks.

> Banks do not pass across the counter the entire loan granted to clients; they ask them to deposit it in their accounts with the bank. Thus, loans create deposits.

For the economy as a whole, let us assume that the amount of currency or base money circulating in a country at a point in time is $100 million. People keep half of this amount, i.e. $50 million, with them for daily transactions, to meet exigencies or for speculative purposes. They deposit the remaining $50 million with the commercial banks. Suppose banks on an average, retain F fraction of their cash deposits as a reserve to meet the daily withdrawals, while the central bank wants them to maintain with it a minimum fraction R of their deposit—cash plus credit, how much credit can a bank create with these constraints? The credit multiplier M provides the answer. It can be calculated as follows:

$$M = 1/F\,(1 - R) \tag{20.1}$$

Example 20.1 Suppose a bank has $50 million in cash deposits and has to keep F = 0.1 fraction of the sum in its safe at all times to meet the daily withdrawal demands. Furthermore, suppose that each commercial bank is required to maintain 5% of its deposits—cash plus credit—in cash with the central bank, implying R = 0.05. The credit multiplier M will then be 9.5. The $50 million cash deposit with the bank will enable it to have total deposits worth 50 × 9.5 = $475 million. From that amount, if we take out cash deposits, the remaining $425 million will be the *credit* (loan) deposits the bank has generated. The multiplier will hold good for all commercial banks. Figure 20.4 presents a schematic depiction of how the process creates an inverted credit pyramid in the economy.

Total deposit $475 m = Cash $50 m + Credit $425 m

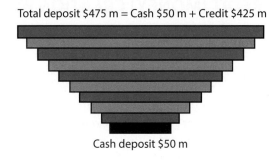

Cash deposit $50 m

Figure 20.4 *Inverted credit pyramid with F = 1/10 and R = 1/20 (multiplier, M = 9.5)*

Note that an individual bank cannot create credit disproportionate to others because, on balance, it will soon find its net cash inflow reducing via inter-bank clearances. The cash string forces it to remain with the group. However, the credit creation power of the banking system is, on the whole, tremendous. The interest received on this amount minus the part of it payable to cash deposit holders and other operating expenses will all belong to the bank owners. Banking is thus, an exceedingly lucrative business. Collectively, banks may generate a huge inverted credit pyramid, as Figure 20.4 shows, for our illustrative bank. Easy renewals can convert them into long-term funding. Leverage gains tend to make businesses over-adventurous. But continued pumping in of funds ultimately makes the credit balloon burst, economies roll downhill and unemployment tends to become rampant. This has largely been the cause of the global financial turmoil since 2008 and there still seems to be no way out.

20.5.1   State Intervention

The credit creation power of banks brings huge profits to commercial banks in the shape of leverage gains. That lure has led the industry players to stretch that power beyond safety limits. Eventually, even the mightiest of banks can crash under the weight of their own creation. Massive bailouts from state revenue are akin to allowing 'private folly at public cost'. The credit (money) creation ability of banks also provides state authorities in many countries with a way to cover up yawning fiscal deficits through borrowings from the banking system for financing massive unproductive expenditures, including spending on wars and political manipulations. Many sovereign and corporate debts have already been downgraded by leading rating agencies, sending quivers through the stock markets. The debt crisis in Euro-zone countries—Greece, Portugal, Spain, Ireland and Italy, for instance—has revealed the urgency to engage in an unprecedented fiscal consolidation process without delay. The situation has deteriorated to a level that the number of banks facing liquidation is increasing because of the sovereign debt defaults. Disputes have erupted over the magnitude of the potential bailouts and the fixing of responsibility for raising the money that is needed. Indeed, there is room to presume that the European Union could eventually disintegrate because of the unmanageable debt crisis. The deepening crisis in Europe has created the dilemma of choosing between markets and the people. No one knows for sure where the trade-off between austerity and growth lies.

> The leverage gain lure has brought down mighty banks, and even states, leading to economic downturn and political chaos across the globe. ▸

> Seasonal variations in the demand for money provide the rationale for credit creation. ▸

BOX 20.1

Credit Creation and Islamic Banks

Before we discuss the issue whether Islamic banks should or should not create credit, we need to find out if credit creation is essential for the smooth running of modern economies. For even in mainstream economics, there are advocates of a 100% reserve system wherein banks are required to retain at all times, the money people deposit in their accounts. They are opposed to the prevalent fractional reserve system—the key to credit creation.

In the absence of credit creation, the only source for meeting the money demand in the economy would be the supply of legal tender or base money. However, the demand for money is of necessity, even volatile in modern times, if we ignore its speculative component. Fluctuations become inevitable because of seasonal factors. Festivals, climate change, social ceremonies and availability of industrial inputs, such as cotton, sugarcane, oil seeds, and juicy fruits, all impart seasonality to a variety of economic variables. The supply of base money has to be kept at a level so that seasonal rise in demand is fully covered and can be reduced in the off-season (as shown in Figure 20.5). However, this may cause some serious difficulties in monetary management.

- Keeping the base money supply all the time at a level that is sufficient to cover a seasonal rise in demand requires a prior measure for such a rise, but this can only be arbitrary. Furthermore, the issuance of base money involves cost in terms of maintaining larger monetary reserves at all times.
- In the off-season, part of the money will remain in idle stock, locking resources.
- Base money creation (or withdrawal) takes time. Legal procedures have to be completed.

- The supply of money cannot readily match changes in demand.

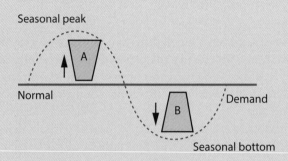

Figure 20.5 *Base money, normal demand and seasonal variations*

Commercial banks and their functions evolved over time in response to the changing and expanding needs of trade, industry and commerce. A substantial part of these needs has been of a seasonal or short-term character, the base money supply being unsuitable to meet the demands for the reasons explained above. By dealing with temporary seasonal variations, the credit money that banks create helps the growth of base money to remain smooth over time. This aspect of money supply adjustments has not been explored in writings on Islamic banking and financing modes save only in occasional and cursory discussions.

Islamic banking emerged on the scene late and, interestingly, chose to follow in the footsteps of the same system that it rose to replace. Islamic banks have imitated the instrument designs and trade practices of conventional banks but have so far hesitated to follow them in the matter of credit creation. To be sure, credit is not always a loan of the usual sort. All deferred payment contracts in Islamic finance involve credit creation. The time is not far off when Islamic banking will stand on an equal footing to challenge the conventional system in Muslim countries, if not globally. For the reasons stated above, the creation of credit is a social and economic imperative that Islamic banks cannot afford to shun in a dual system. Depositors know or should know the process. If the safety of their money is not threatened, they need not be alarmed. The safety of deposits is a function of efficient bank management and the alertness of the regulators, supplemented by adequate deposit guarantee schemes.

In time, credit creation may become an imperative for Islamic banks as the system acquires status and maturity. Arguably, by that time, the credit channel of monetary policy may have weakened because of the Islamic banks' insistence on keeping financial transactions firmly linked to real economy. The pressure on central banks for an inclusive control policy must become irresistible. The matter poses perplexing problems when the two banking systems—Islamic and conventional—operate side by side in an economy in an interactive mode. However, the problem will have to be addressed sooner rather than later.

Source: Hasan, Z. (2014), *Islamic Banking and Finance – An Integrative Approach*, Oxford, p. 42–43.

20.6   DEMAND AND SUPPLY MISMATCH

Mismatch between the demand for and supply of money causes instability and trade cycles.

The determinants of demand for money and economic entities involved in it are inevitably different in an economy from the sources of money supply and its determinants. Money markets are most of the time in a state of disequilibrium. Sometimes, there is excess of demand at others supply of money is more than needed. In either case, the general level of prices tends to fluctuate. Mild fluctuations are not worrisome. The self-correcting market mechanism is able to restore balance. The economy can sail through the phases of the cycle shown in Figure 20.1 smoothly. The difficulty however, is that more often the departures from normalcy are large, sticky and persistent. The price level is rising—inflation taking place culminating in a boom. But once the inflationary spiral has touched its peak, the bubble bursts and the economy is going downhill; prices continue falling until deflation touches a bottom. Recovery is slow and agonizing. We discuss below the various aspects of inflation and deflation, their causes and the damage they inflict on the society.

20.6.1 Inflation

For the layman, inflation refers to a general rise in the prices of goods and services; every dollar buys a smaller quantity of goods than before. This view is true in so far as it goes, but it does not go far enough. Technically, a one-off rise in prices does not constitute inflation. Inflation is the persistent tendency of the price level to rise over an extended period of time; it is a more enduring rise in prices. There have been numerous descriptions and explanations of the phenomenon of inflation throughout history. They are based on factors such as its speed, public reactions to it, and its causes (both real and perceived), not to mention its propensity to generate cycles. Fascinating though it is, such an examination lies outside the scope of this introductory book.

Inflation at a low level is considered to be beneficial for the economy. It keeps investors in good humor and illuminates growth prospects. This sort of slow-paced increase in prices is called the *creeping inflation. Malaysian economy has experienced long periods of such inflation*. Over a span of 41 years, the consumer price index (CPI) increased by about 90 percentage points; thus the mean rise was no more than 2.2% a year. But most countries have not been able to manage their economic affairs so expediently and have fallen victim to double-digit inflation in recent times, including some of the most developed economies.

Today in most countries, inflation is the major economic problem. Two alarming features of the current worldwide phase of inflation are (i) acceleration in the rate of inflation with the passage of time, and (ii) high and rising rate of unemployment. This has already earned the much maligned names of stagflation and slumpflation. Acceleration may cause *running* inflation. Economists have not fixed any upper limit for such an inflation, but if the rise crosses 20%, we enter the era of 'galloping inflation'. Such inflation is said to occur when prices are rising at double- or triple-digit rates of 20%, 100% or 200% a year. The Indian economy experienced a sort of running inflation (below 25%) after the devaluation of its currency in 1965. Argentina, Brazil and Israel witnessed inflation rates above 100% in the 1980s. Galloping inflation may degenerate into

> Inflation has earned a few nicknames—creeping, running, galloping and hyper—depending on its speed and magnitude.

what we call hyper-inflation, like that which overtook Germany in the early 1920s.

Much work has been done on various aspects of inflation, but here we shall restrict the discussion to two major ones—demand–pull inflation and cost–push inflation.

Demand–pull inflation

This sort of inflation is caused by excess of demand over supply. Here we have two competing theories—the Keynesian and the monetarist. The latter we explained in our discussion on the quantity theory of money. (See also Example 20.2.) The former is discussed as follows.

Inflationary gap analysis

The inflationary gap is opened by an excess of aggregate demand (expenditure) over the supply of money. It is a purely monetary phenomenon. Inflation per se adds nothing to national wealth.

Keynes gave his excess demand explanation of inflation in his petite book, *How To Pay For War* (1940) which was in fact an application of the static aggregate demand model of his *General Theory* (1936). The concept of the inflationary gap is quite simple and straightforward. It arises when the level of aggregate demand is above the full employment aggregate supply. However, this explanation has given rise to a welter of models that do not always present the same situation. Opinion is divided on whether the gap is a cause of inflation or is a consequence of it. Figure 20.6 helps explain this point. Note that the inflationary gap occurs *at* full employment output (Y_F), as measured by the distance AB. Y_E would be the equilibrium output if aggregate demand was E_2. However, if E_1 were the aggregate demand, E_2 would exceed aggregate supply, Y_F. Thus, the gap defined as the excess of demand over supply at full employment would be the *cause* of inflation. Note that the distances between AB and $Y_F Y_E$ are purely monetary and have no real content: inflation per se does not add to social wealth.

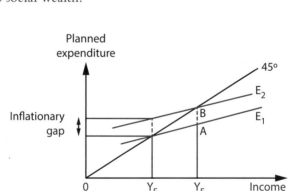

Figure 20.6 *Two ways of looking at the inflationary gap*

The relationship between inflation and employment has also become dubious. The Phillips curve attempted to establish a seemingly obvious fact: the rise in price levels reduces the level of unemployment. In other words, inflation increases employment. In fact, the result follows from our discussion of the relationship between growth and inflation, in some respects. Go back to Figure 14.2 that clarifies the relationship. There we measure price level changes in terms of the consumer price index, setting the index base at 100 from the onset. The Phillips curve is convex to the origin, implying that with a rise in the inflation rate employment rises but, at a decreasing rate. Notice also that if the index falls below 100, deflation may be taking place as unemployment rises faster along the downward-sloping curve. (Why?)

Exercise 20.3

The following information is available from an index number series

Time point	1	2	3	4	5	6	7	8	9	10
CPI	96	98	100	102	104	106	108	110	112	114

Find out the rates of inflation in the economy over the period and interpret your results.

However, from the late 1970s onward the world witnessed a phenomenon that seriously discredited the explanatory value of the Phillips curve: many countries found themselves with slowing growth and with unemployment and price levels both rising together. There was a sort of sticky stagnation period overlaid with rising inflation. Economies were intrigued by what was termed 'stagflation', and the painful experience continues unabated across the globe even to this day. Rising oil prices and food scarcity, costly wars and mounting corruption are apparently among the leading causes of stagflation. Economists struggle to find remedial measures: classical supply-side economics was turned upside down to find a cure, but it failed to provide any answers. Even labour participation in profit and management could not prevent the recurrence of such economic crises.

> Inflation tends to assume the form of an upward moving spiral; the key variables chasing each other in a circular relationship. The causal link is lost.

Cost–push inflation

Cost–push inflation came to notice after the mid-1950s and is also called sellers' or markup inflation. As Islamic banks are largely relying on markup use in their financing activities, they might unwittingly get involved in pushing up price levels even as the markup has to be revealed to the customer.

The cost–push theories emerged as a refutation of the demand–pull explanation of inflation theories. It pleaded that it was the autonomous increase in some cost components that was the primary source of rising inflation. Three of the sources are invariably mentioned:

- Rising costs of raw materials, energy and transportation,
- Labour unionism and collective bargaining pushing up compensatory remunerations, and
- Rising prices of production related imports.

In all these, the contributory role of public policies on price regulations, taxes, subsidies and tariffs is usually brought in.

20.6.2   What Causes Inflation?

Inflation can best be viewed as a state of economic disequilibrium in which all major macro variables, such as prices, output, incomes, profits and investment, are chasing one another in an upward spiral. It is a circular ascent and one cannot say which of the variables is pushing up the others in the spin. At the heart of this definition is what is sometimes called *cost–push inflation*. Economists have attempted to identify what causes this malady. In most cases, the stated cause is taken to be the defining characteristic of the phenomenon. The common definition of inflation—'too much money chasing too few goods'—began to be questioned when no sizeable difference was found in the quantity of legal tender money circulating at the peak of inflation than was seen at the bottom of depression: thus, the abrupt change in the velocity of money circulation was blamed as the main culprit. In addition, it was pointed out that much of the money in circulation was being absorbed by the *intermediate* production processes, and to that extent money did not impinge upon the purchase and sale of the *final* consumables. The Cambridge economists therefore refined the definition: inflation, they thought, takes place when money incomes are expanding at a faster rate than the availability of the final consumable goods and services. This approach to inflation won wider acceptance than the 'too much money' approach, and still lingers in the literature.

History bears testimony that natural calamities, such as droughts, floods and earthquakes, may at times cause shortages of essential commodities and trigger a general rise in prices. Economists call this *scarcity inflation*. Wars also generate scarcities of a sort. Supply takes time to respond and match the rising demand. The consumerism of the modern era has aggravated such scarcities all the more. The credit card culture has led our generation to live on future incomes—for example, each person in the USA carried an external debt of more than $50,000 on 26 June 2012. In most developing countries, the debt burden is much lower; the United Arab Emirates tops the list with over $24,000 per head at the end of 2010.

The impact of inflation

Generally, producers and traders gain during inflation as supply lags behind demand. (Why?) But among the producers, farmers benefit more than others. The reason is that crops, once sown, take time to grow and mature. Supply cannot be increased to fully meet the rising demand until the next cultivation cycle starts. Fixed-income earners, such as salaried people, wage labour, landlords and money lenders, all suffer during inflation because their real income falls. Employers, businesses, tenants and debtors gain. How these gains are distributed among the individuals in the society depends upon the nature of their contracts, including their terms, termination conditions and the duration of those contracts.

In general, there is an environment of prosperity and elation during a period of inflation, so long as prices can be contained, because growth is brisk, employment expands and per capita incomes tend to rise in real terms.

An important aspect of inflation is its connection with the government's fiscal policies because inflation can be used to divert real resources from private consumption to public use. The diverted resources can be employed for promoting productive or non-productive activities. Inflationary financing has the advantage of being invisible and costless. The following illustration, though crude, will help you to understand the *modus operandi* of deficit financing.

> Inflation has increasingly become a fiscal policy tool. Printing notes annoys no one; taxation scares away voters.

Example 20.2 Suppose an economy depending solely on the cultivation of land produces annually 100 million tons of wheat, the public has $500 million in cash and the velocity of money circulation is 5. We know the Fisher exchange equation is MV = PT. So, putting the information in this equation, we get:

$$500 \times 5 = P \times 100$$

This gives us the price of wheat as: P = $25 per ton

Now, assume that the government wants to have 25 million tons of wheat for, say, the public distribution system to benefit the weaker sections of the society. It has two ways to do it, the velocity of money remaining unchanged. First, it may impose a 25% flat tax on income to gain $625 million as revenue, leaving $1,875 million with the public. Note that total purchasing power in the society remains the same ($500 × 5 = $2,500 million). Only the distribution of purchasing power undergoes a change. It is easy to see that in the market, the government would gain from tax revenue the required 25 million tons of wheat (625/25) and the public, the remaining 75 million tons (1,875/25). Tax on income did not cause inflation.

However, taxes are seen as being taken from people's pockets. The government may want to avoid tax increases for a variety of reasons. There is a second way to achieve the same objective: to cover the budgetary gap by printing currency notes worth $25 million. Consumers and the government will compete in the market, raising the demand for wheat more than its supply (100 million tons) at the earlier price. With supply remaining unchanged, the price must rise to restore the equilibrium. The exchange equation will now be as follows:

$$(500 + 25)\, 5 = P \times 100$$

Giving: P = $26.25 per ton of wheat

At this higher price, the distribution of wheat between the public and the government will produce the same result as the solution under taxation. How can you verify this?

The classic example of choice between the two methods is provided by the Indian economy during the Second World War. Britain was at war, but at home they raised revenue for war mainly through taxation. India was not at war, but the British made the colony contribute to the war effort in men and materials, printing money to make payments. The result was that India had higher rates of inflation than Britain during and after the war. C.N. Vakil, a noted Indian economist, observed that inflation was worse than robbery. The robber is visible; inflation is invisible. The robber can be caught and brought to a court of law; inflation is legal. The victims of the robber are a few people; the victim of inflation is the whole nation. Interestingly, India successfully used deficit financing (inflation) to mobilize resources for her first Five Year Plan, but inflation is a double-edged sword: it cuts both ways. India ended up in serious trouble when it attempted the trick on a larger scale in its Second Five Year Plan.

20.6.3   Deflation

After inflation has reached its peak, something happens that makes the spiral take a downturn, putting the economy on the road to deflation. Deflation is a state of economic disequilibrium in which important macro variables—savings, investment, profit, interest, wages, employment and national income—are all found to be chasing one another in a downward direction. As in inflation, the variable that triggers deflation can be fixed, usually on a case-by-case basis. Here, psychological factors take control of human conduct. Depression presents a seemingly odd scenario. Shops are full of useful goods which sellers are eager to sell and people desperately need, but exchange does not take place. Workers are willing to work, but machines stand idle. 'There is no coal in the house because there is too much coal in the market'. (Can you guess why?) It is difficult to reverse the process before the economy is fully in the grip of depression.

The causes of deflation are complex and difficult to specify because human psychology—not the objective facts—dominate in shaping the phenomenon. Explanations usually start with the concept of a deflationary gap, which is usually based on the Keynesian framework, like the one we used to explain inflation. Figure 20.7 depicts the concept.

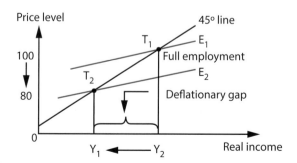

Figure 20.7 *The deflationary gap*

Here, T_1 is the full employment equilibrium point, corresponding to Y_1 income with the price index set at 100. Deflation is a departure of the economy from T_1 to a less than full employment level, such as T_2, due to a fall in effective demand from E_1 to E_2, shrinking the economy to a lower income, Y_1. The shrinkage sets into motion another round of lower prices, a wider output gap and increased unemployment, and thus the snake goes on eating its own tail.

Deflationary gap is caused by the lack of effective demand needed to clear the market. Goods pile up unsold.

Exercise 20.4

Compare Figures 20.6 and 20.7. Note all the similarities and differences, and comment on these.

Consequences of deflation

The socio-economic consequences of deflation are the reverse of what we noted for inflation. Fixed income recipients gain: the purchasing power of their earnings rise. They include people like landlords, bondholders, salaried people and wage earners. Producers suffer. Profits dwindle. Among them, farmers suffer more because the supply of agricultural produce cannot be adjusted to falling demand without a time lag. Unemployment spreads; workers in general suffer. Employees who are able to escape retrenchment, such as in government services, gain. Creditors gain in terms of purchasing power if defaults do not occur, whereas debtors lose. Society as a whole is worse off, as growth slackens and output falls.

Deflation changes the relative prices structure against producers; agriculturists suffer more. Renters gain, so do workers but only those who manage to retain employment.

Deflation is more harmful than inflation. It spreads gloom and feeds disincentives. So, recovery is slow and painful. One can slow or stop a galloping horse, but it is very difficult to make a frightened horse move forward. A car going up a hill can be stopped by turning off the engine, but one going down the slope requires the application of brakes. Monetary policies may succeed in curbing inflation through the raising of interest rates or a reduction of the money supply, but lowering interest rates may not induce businesses to borrow and invest. An increase in money supply also does not help; it just moves into the liquidity trap. In Figure 20.7, the area shaded with unbroken lines under the L curve shows what part of the total money supply Q^* people would like to hold back (they prefer to retain liquidity) rather than lend or invest at different rates of interest. During deflation, the central bank of a country often continues to increase the money supply, reducing the rate of interest, in an attempt to revive investment. But the interest rate cannot fall beyond a limit, r_i, if expected rates of profit remain below the interest rate. Any increase in the quantity of money will be hoarded i.e. it will move into the liquidity trap. This accounted for the ineffectiveness of monetary policy to lift economies out of depression during the 1930s. Rather, Keynes suggested that spending money on large public projects would act

Inflation and deflation are both harmful but deflation is more injurious and difficult to cure.

as an alternative method for economic revival. It is interesting to see that even Keynes' detractors eventually saw the wisdom in his prescription during the global turmoil 2007–2008.

BOX 20.2

Current Financial Turmoil and Islamic Banks

The current financial turmoil that started with the 2007 property market crash in the US caused devastation across countries such that the world had not experienced since the Great Depression of the 1930s. In view of the global search for remedial measures, some scholars have suggested the replacement of the interest-based conventional system with the Islamic interest-free model.

One evidence in support of their proposal is that Islamic banks have shown greater vitality and resilience in facing current crisis as compared to their conventional counterparts for the reasons that they have had comfortable liquidity buffers, low leverage ratios, better managerial skills and more customized products.

The point that Islamic banks have faced the crisis better than conventional banks has substance. The reasons given have some truth. It is pointed out that Islamic finance is yet too small in terms of the market share; it has not yet developed sufficient connectivity with the global system to catch the cold. Overall, Islamic banks do have better liquidity cushion but probably more as a problem rather than strength—many are not able to use effectively the investible surplus they are able to generate in terms of deposits. The overall argument is as follows:

- Trade is the transmission channel for the spread of a contagion across countries; its volume measures the strength of their mutual connectivity.
- The economies of 57 OIC countries are a highly heterogeneous group; 22 of them are among the least developed nations of the world; 19 are the fuel exporting rich.
- The share of OIC countries in the global trade was just 10% in 2010. Furthermore, this share remains very unevenly distributed; the major portion going to the oil-rich exporters. And, it was the magnitude of these countries trade that some gulf banks did come to grief during the turmoil.

Interestingly, the 2013 Stability Report of Islamic Financial Services Board (IFSB) also negates the common perception that Islamic finance was not affected by the current crisis. The following figure depicts the behaviour of three variables—assets, financing and savings—for Islamic financial institutions over the years 2006–2011.

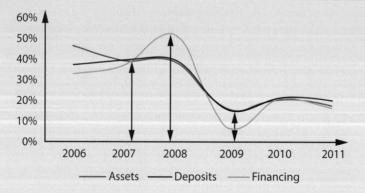

Figure 20.8 *Islamic banking global growth trends*

Source: Based on IFSB's Survey Report 2013.

Note that in 2007 the three variables mentioned were almost equal. In 2008 the industry was booming–financing was much higher than deposits. However, by the end of 2009, the crisis had reversed that relationship—financing and assets were both at their lowest ebb leaving much of deposits unutilized. Notice that, the overall trend for the variables has been sharply falling.

The shrinkage in GDP and trade was *the* conduit for the transference of the crisis across borders, not the much talked about financial markets.

20.7 GOALS AND TARGETS

In recent writings on monetary economics a distinction is often made between the goals and targets of policy. To fix ideas, we list down the variables usually included in each category.

Goals
- Maximization of output from given inputs or minimization of inputs to produce a given output,
- Growth rate acceleration to achieve high levels of performance,
- Price level stability (working for optimal inflation),
- Improvement in the distribution of incomes and wealth in society, and
- Sound management of balance of payments.

Targets
- Money supply,
- Bank credit, and
- Interest rates.

Goals and targets of monetary policy are inter-related. Changes in the target variables and the direction of change become indicators of policy impact.

Change in the magnitude and direction of the targeted goal is the measure of policy success or failure. Of the listed targets, monetary policy mostly focusses on the credit creation power of the commercial banks. The instruments it uses for the purpose are discussed below.

20.8 CENTRAL BANKS AND CREDIT CONTROL

The principles of economics help us to design policies, i.e. actions to achieve predetermined objectives. Policy objectives in any area of economic activity can never be unchanging, even if the long term direction is clear. Short term changes in policy objectives require no less attention than the long term goals, for the latter may, of necessity, need to be re-examined because of temporal demands. It is expedient to define short term goals.

20.8.1 Bank Rate Policy

Central banks design and operate the credit control policies in modern economies with a view to maintaining, *inter alia*, the stability in the internal and external value of the national currency which is needed for promoting growth. They mainly focus on two points for this purpose. The first is the *price* the borrowers have to pay for obtaining funds from the banks, i.e. the rate of interest. This rate follows the 'bank rate', which is the rate at which a central bank advances loans to commercial banks or rediscounts their bills. To put it briefly, a raise in the bank rate normally increases production costs and cuts into profit expectations. The alarm it causes among the banks and the borrowers leads to the curtailment of credit creation and helps curb inflation. Likewise, when the economy is sluggish, lowering the bank rate normally leads to lower market interest charges, making borrowing cheaper and increasing profit margins, although the measure may or may not meet business expectations. If it does not, the policy fails to meet the objective. We shall come back to the measures later in the discussion.

20.8.2 Statutory Reserve Variations

The focal point of the policy is the volume of credit banks can generate. The central bank attempts to change this volume broadly in two ways: (i) by buying or selling securities, i.e. indulging in what is termed as the 'open market operations', and (ii) by manipulating statutory cash-deposit ratios that the banks are obliged to observe. One of these is the ratio of deposits that commercial banks are required to keep with the central bank in the form of cash. This ratio for long term deposits is higher than for the short term deposits. The other is a minimum 'cash to deposit' ratio that banks must maintain internally. We shall discuss the instrument of 'open market operations' later. Here, we continue with the manipulation of ratios.

The central bank has the discretion to raise or lower these ratios separately or simultaneously. The raising of these ratios reduces the cash base for credit creation and the multiplier magnifies the reduction in credit to curb inflation. During recession, the lowering of ratios leaves more cash with the banks for multiple credit expansion. However, low profit expectations may still not create the needed demand for funds and economic expansion may not start.

20.8.3 Profit–interest Linkage

Using the cash-deposit ratios as a weapon for credit control looks permissible from the Islamic viewpoint. The difficulty lies on the first count—the rate of interest—as Islam makes the instrument unavailable to the central bank. What can replace it? The early Islamic economists thought that the profit-sharing ratio (PSR) that the bank and the firm agree upon would replace the interest rate. It is now realized that the idea was ill-conceived. The profit-sharing ratio is not a 'price' like the rate of interest; it cannot directly equate the demand and supply of funds in the market. Where can we go from here? Below, we have outlined a generic argument on this point. It is based on the reality that in Islamic finance product pricing is closely linked to the interest rate in the present dual system, although Islamic banking will eventually have to move away from the dominance of the fixed return transaction to profit-sharing instruments.

Thus, let us explore how the profit-sharing ratio is likely to be determined in a dual banking system where Islamic banks operate in competition with conventional banks. In a conventional profit-sharing model, the bank provides a portion (λ) of the total capital employed (K) in a project. In other words, it contributes λK, the other part of investment, i.e. $(1 - \lambda)$ K the firm provides. If there is a loss, it is shared by them in the λ: $(1 - \lambda)$ ratio. In *musharakah* or the Islamic partnership structure, the profit- and loss-sharing ratio of the parties can be the same, but in *mudarabah* or participatory finance, the story is different. Here, the resultant profit (P) has first to be divided in the same ratio as the capital contributions of the parties, i.e. λP going to the bank and $(1- \lambda)$P to the firm. Of λP, the proportion σ^* would go to the bank and $1 - \sigma^*$ would be retained by the firm for providing entrepreneurial services to the bank as a matter for negotiation between the parties before entering into the contract. Profit-sharing arrangements of the sort, i.e. *mudarabah*, dominated the business scene in the Muslim world until the close of the 13th century. In current practice, this ratio is 30–40% for the bank.

> The profit-sharing ratio for the bank is mainly a function of the *ex ante* profit rate loan on capital leverage, the rate of interest and the risk premium estimate. The profit-sharing ratio is directly related to the interest rate, other things remaining unchanged.

Example 20.3 The illustration in Figure 20.9 makes the process clearer. Here, we take λ = 0.4 and σ^* = 0.5 and rate of profit, r = 20%.

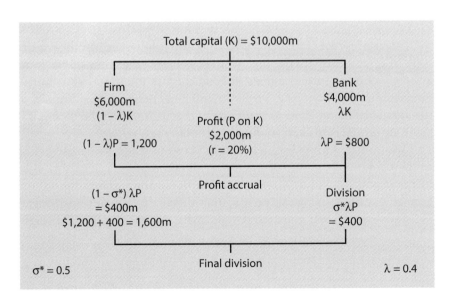

Figure 20.9 *Profit-sharing in mudarabah*

It follows from Figure 20.9 that firms enjoy leverage gain in Islamic finance as well. Here, if K were all owned by the firm, the rate of return would have been 20%. Sharing has raised it to 26.67% on reduced equity. It may be noted that we can express the sharing ratio (say, σ) for the bank in terms of total profit (P) as well, because σ P must equal $\sigma^*\lambda P$. Here σ = 400/2000 or 0.2. In our illustration also, $\lambda\sigma^* = 0.4 \times 0.5 = 0.2$. This is an important result. It enables us to discuss the relevance of the sharing ratio as a credit control measure.

It is easy to see that in a dual financial system, a firm will opt for profit-sharing finance if it expects the volume of profit left for it to be more or at least equal to what would remain if it borrows on interest. Since sharing will give the advantage of transferring part of the possible loss to the bank, it must be willing to give the latter profit more than interest as a risk premium (say, σ), for uncertainty of profit.

Thus, we can show this as: $(1 - \sigma) P \geq P - r_i\lambda K - \alpha\lambda K$

Dividing by K, we get: $(1 - \sigma) r \geq r - r_i\lambda - \alpha\lambda$ $(P/K = r)$

Solving, we get: $\sigma \leq \lambda/r \, (r_i + \alpha)$ (20.2)

If we look at the matter from the side of the bank, it will not go for profit-sharing unless it expects to receive profit more or at least equal to the interest it can earn plus compensation for sharing the risk.

From the bank side, we can then show this as:

$$\sigma P \geq r_i\lambda K + \alpha\lambda K$$

Dividing through by K we get: $\sigma r \geq r_i\lambda + \alpha\lambda$

This gives: $\sigma \geq \lambda/r \, (r_i + \alpha)$ (20.3)

A comparison of equations 20.2 and 20.3 shows that the only possibility of negotiations on sharing coming through is that both parties would agree to:

$$\sigma = \lambda/r \, (r_i + \alpha) \quad (20.4)$$

> It follows that the profit-sharing ratio σ is a function of the expected rate of return on capital, leverage ratio, interest rate and risk premium.

It transpires that main determinants of the profit-sharing ratio for the bank in agreement with the firm would be the expected rate of profit (r), leverage ratio (λ), rate of interest (r_i) and the risk premium estimate (α). For bringing the sharing ratio α in the ambit of credit control measures of the central bank, we have to think of the sharing ratios at the theoretical plane as some sort of averages for the economy as a whole.

Equation 20.4 provides a useful link between the profit-sharing ratio of the banks and the rate of interest in a dual monetary system. Let us merge α with r_i and put $\lambda/r = \mu$ to make the analysis easier. Take μ as a constant, while r and λ can vary, so that their ratio remains unchanged. We now have a linear equation $\sigma = \mu r_i$, which passes through the origin μ being its slope. It sets up a positive relationship between the profit-sharing ratio, σ and r_i, the rate of interest as shown in Figure 20.10. It follows that for the same r_i, the profit-sharing ratio, σ may fluctuate with changes in leverage, λ or profit expectation, r or both. But it can also remain constant, if changes in λ and r take place in the same direction, so that μ remains unchanged.

Assuming that all other determinants of the profit-sharing ratio remain unchanged, we can establish a relationship between σ and r which operates in the opposite direction. Combining the two relationships, we can explain the financial factors that may influence GDP growth in an economy in a dual banking system.

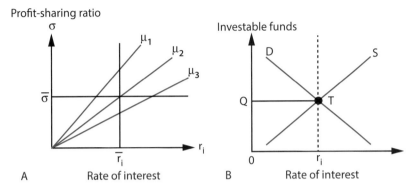

Figure 20.10 *Profit-sharing procedure in Islamic finance*

Figure 20.11 carries the story further. Its upper part (X) shows the inverse relationship between the profit-sharing ratio and the expected return on total capital employed in business. σr = A where A is a constant. The curve it provides gives the locus of a point that moves in the plain in such a way that the product of its distance from two right-angled straight lines is always the same. The data in Example 20.4 helps us to understand the point.

The curve has been flipped over to the left on the σ axis to harmonize it with the lower section Z of the figure. The depiction here is a bit complicated. Essentially, it shows the impact of (for example) lowering the profit-sharing ratio σ for any reason in addition to a reduction in the interest rate as being conducive to savings investment and growth. One can understand the diagram easily if one is familiar with the working of the IS–LM model of macroeconomics. Here, IS is the equal savings and investment curve, whereas LM is the equality of demand i.e. liquidity and money supply curve. Even if not, following the matching of variable changes shown by the numbers 1 and 2 used as super/subscripts marking, the variables may prove helpful. The message of the demonstration is that changes in interest rate will most likely change the profit-sharing ratio to play a support role in a dual financial system. Of course the ratio will have the same limitations too.

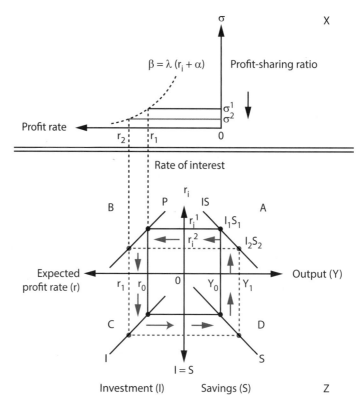

Figure 20.11 *Relationship of profit-sharing ratio with national income*

The demonstrated positive and close relationship that may persist between the profit-sharing ratio and the rate of interest will make the credit control point the same for the Islamic banks as for the conventional banks. In other words, interest rate policy can take care of both. But the problem of delayed or inadequate response of σ to interest rate change may at times create problems. Again, the interest rate is a blanket measure as changes in it affect all economic activities irrespective of their economic significance or social priorities. Qualitative credit control demands and allows discriminatory treatment of such activities. The bank rate for financing such activities can be different. For example, funds made available to agriculture, small enterprises, cooperatives, housing projects and for promoting the amelioration of the environment may be charged at lower rates or granted refunds after the agreed-upon conditions are fulfilled. Socially desired activities in Islamic countries may need such favoured treatment in finance allocation.

Example 20.4

$$\sigma r = A, \text{ where A is a constant}$$

σ	1	2	3	4	6	9	12	18	36
r	36	18	12	9	6	4	3	2	1
$\sigma \times r = A$	36	36	36	36	36	36	36	36	36

The curve generated is called a rectangular hyperbole.

Exercise 20.5

The following are the demand and supply functions for loanable funds in a dual money market:

$D = 220 - 20R_1$ and $S = 10 + 15Ri$ where R_1 is the per cent rate of interest for three months. Find the equilibrium rate of interest. Suppose the leverage ratio λ for a bank is 0.528 and the expected rate of profit is 6.6%. Estimate the value of profit-sharing ratio σ for an Islamic bank.

(*Hint:* Use $\sigma = \mu R_i$)

To reduce or increase the quantum of base money in the economy, central banks indulge in what we call 'open market operations'. We did not discuss it in sequence with the manipulation of cash deposit ratios because the bank rate policy and open market operations go hand in hand.

20.8.4   Open Market Operations

Normally, the central bank of a country does not enter the money market but occasionally uses the right to encourage credit expansion or contraction through impacting the credit creation base of the commercial banks. It can do so because it always carries a stock of first-class treasury and commercial securities. Open market operations affect the cash base of commercial banks and thus, their credit creation ability.

> Open market operations refer to the selling or buying of securities by the central bank in the market to reduce or increase the base money supply in the economy in order to stabilize the price level.

When the economy is climbing up, money income tends to expand at a faster rate than real output. (Why?) Prices rise and the economy soon finds itself in the grip of inflation. To reduce the cash base with commercial banks, the central bank starts selling securities in the open market, competing with other sellers. The people purchasing these securities issue cheques on their banks. Cash moves out from the banking system into the coffers of the central bank. The credit multiplier is expected to work in the reverse direction, exercising a dampening effect on credit expansion and the price level. The policy is reversed if the economy turns its direction and starts going downhill—deflation is taking place. The central bank starts buying securities in the open market. Papers pile up with the bank, money is being pumped into the system and the credit-creating ability of commercial banks is enhanced. The policy may not succeed if people retain the proceeds of the sale or demand for funds or stay unresponsive. (One can guide a horse to the water but cannot make it drink against its will.)

Open market operations have some serious limitations as a measure of credit control. During inflation, the prices of fixed return securities—Islamic or non-Islamic—tend to fall because better income avenues are now available for free funds. Thus, in all probability, the central bank must sell securities at lower prices than it may have paid to purchase them. In the same way, it must purchase securities at higher prices during a recession compared to new investments. Again, it is likely to incur losses on purchases. How much of a loss of money the bank can take—and justify it—in a democratic set up is an important question.

Exercise 20.6

What do you understand by open market operations? Explain. Can the measure be applied to Islamic banks? What limits the central bank's ability to use this weapon for credit control? Discuss.

20.8.5 Moral Suasion

As the central bank has special privileges and power, especially as the lender of the last resort, it acts as a philosopher, friend and guide to all commercial banks in the system. Banks listen to its advice. Sometimes a circular issued to the banks concerning credit management may have the desired impact. Thus, 'moral suasion' is counted among the methods of credit control.

There have been claims that Islamic banks withstood the current crisis better than their mainstream counterparts. But such claims have been disputed as well. The debate remains inconclusive. The fact is that Islamic banking is at present a very tiny element in global finance. Islamic banking is too small and has not yet developed the connectivity with the global system for attracting infection. Many Islamic banks did come to grief, especially in the Middle East. Kuwait has recently refused to bailout its defaulting banks.

> There is no conclusive evidence that Islamic banks have been affected by the current financial crisis.

20.9 THE AILMENT AND THE CURE

Behind most financial crises we face, locally or internationally, can be found the human desire for wealth and the power it brings to whoever can acquire it (wealth). Credit multiplication, as explained above, enables banks to bring in huge leverage gains that continue to magnify the banks' profits and commissions. To explain the process, let us use the data from Example 20.1 in a tabular form. (See Figure 20.12.)

Example 20.5 The facts of the case: Amount in billions of dollars, Bank's contribution, $(1-\lambda) = 0.575$; Depositors' contribution, $\lambda = 0.425$; Investment multiplier, $M = 9.5$; Total deposits = 475; Cash deposits 50 +

Credit deposits 425; PSR, i.e. $\sigma^* = 0.5$, Return on capital, $r = 20\%$; and Rate of interest, $r_i = 10\%$.

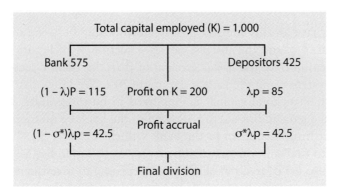

Figure 20.12 *Banks and leverage gains*

Here, we have kept the value of σ^* such that under conventional finance, the return to depositors remains the same at a 10% rate of interest, as in profit-sharing under the Islamic system. Note that $425 \times 10\% = 0.5 \times 0.425 \times 200 = \$42.5$ billion—the leverage gains in both cases. This gives the bank 7.391% profit on its \$575 billion investment in addition to a 20% return on total capital, K employed in the business. Again, note that we can express the leverage gain as part of the overall profit-sharing ratio (PSR) in Islamic finance because σP equals $\sigma^*(1 - \lambda)P$. In other words, $\sigma = \sigma^* (1 - \lambda)$. For our illustration, it verifies as $\sigma = 0.5 \times 0.425 = 0.2125$, and $0.2125 \times 200 = 42.5$ validates the relationship.

In Example 20.5, the leverage gain is 7.4% in both cases. Actually, under interest finance, it must be much greater if we take into consideration the fact that \$425 billion constitutes a credit deposit on which the bank pays no interest. Their expansion base is a mere \$50 billion cash deposit for which at 10%, the bank pays just \$5 billion. This is why banks—big or small—are insolvent all the time, in the sense that they cannot meet public withdrawal demand if there is a 'run on the bank' for any reason. In the current crisis-prone banking environment, no regulatory reform can be more urgent and effective than curbing the leverage gain lure in modern banking.

The lure can be tamed if central banks can use an instrument we designate as the β level. The β can be defined as the maximum leverage rate any bank can be allowed over what total capital employed earns in the firm or project it finances. The remaining surplus, if any, should be deposited in a common Banks Support Fund in each district, which is maintained by the bankers under the supervision and patronage of the central bank. An Apex National Banks Support Fund may receive contributions from the local funds for research and development.

Leverage gains lure banks into overstepping risk limits in credit expansion and eventually lead to defaults, dragging them into bankruptcies. These gains are also available in Islamic banking although to a smaller extent.

However, the major task of the funds would be to rescue banks if any falls into trouble. The industry can thus do its own firefighting instead of inviting public displeasure because of massive bailouts financed at their cost.

As we have already found a positive relationship between the profit-sharing ratio, σ and the interest rate (see section A of Figure 20.11A), we can demonstrate the *modus operandi* of β in the Islamic sector of the banking system using the facts in Example 20.4. We know that the rate, r of profit, P on total capital, K employed in business equals P/K. Let the leverage gain additional to r allowed to the bank be no more than β. The upper limit for return to the bank will then be $(r + \beta)$. The profit allocable to the bank on its investment $(1 - \lambda)$ K would be $(1 - \lambda)$P. But it would also get σ^* fraction of the profit accruing to investment deposits i.e. λP. Thus, we may set up:

$$\frac{(1-\lambda)P + \sigma^*\lambda P}{(1-\lambda)K} \leq (r + \beta) \tag{20.5}$$

$$\frac{P(1-\lambda + \sigma^*\lambda)}{(1-\lambda)K} \leq (r + \beta) \tag{20.6}$$

$$\frac{r(1-\lambda + \sigma)}{(1-\lambda)} \leq (r + \beta); \quad \sigma^*\lambda = \sigma \text{ as shown earlier} \tag{20.7}$$

$$r - r\lambda + r\sigma \leq r - r\lambda + \beta + \beta\lambda \tag{20.8}$$

This reduces to:

$$\sigma \leq \frac{\beta}{r}(1 - \lambda) \tag{20.9}$$

We can find out in a given situation the leverage gain level β by inserting the relevant values in equation 20.9. If the central bank finds the margin too high, it may fix a lower β as a control measure to dampen the leverage lure. We may put an upper limit on β such as

$$\beta \leq r$$

It is obvious that for any given value of r and λ, the profit-sharing ratio, i.e. σ, would vary directly with β. The relationship allows the central bank to use β as a cost-free instrument for credit control. In our example, $(\lambda P + \sigma P)/\lambda K = 0.2738$. Of 0.2738, r = 0.2 and 0.0738 is the full value of β accounting for the leverage gains. Now, if the central bank wants to curb the leverage lure, it can discourage credit creation by lowering β to, say, 0.7. To see the impact of restriction on the rate of return via a reduction in σ, let us put the values into equation 20.9. Thus, we have:

$$\sigma = \frac{0.575}{0.2} \cdot 0.07$$
$$= 2.875 \times 0.07$$
$$= 0.20125$$

The reduced σ does verify the restricted leverage profit rate as = (200 × 0.20125)/575 = 0.07. The leveraged rate of profit, r will rise only to 0.2 + 0.07 = 0.27. The bank would get: 200 × 0.20125 = \$40.25 billion as leverage gain. Of the total profit, \$42.5 billion has already gone to the depositors. From the remaining \$157.5 billion, the bank will get: 575 × 0.27 = \$155.25 billion, including the leverage gain, while the balance of \$2.25 billion will go to the local banks' support fund.

> Leverage gains can be controlled by varying the allowable margin between the rate of return on total capital employed and the rate on the owners' equity. ▶

Exercise 20.7

The facts of a case with amounts in millions of dollars are as follows:

Total capital employed 800; Bank's contribution, $(1 - \lambda) = 0.25$; Depositors' contribution, $\lambda = 0.75$; $\sigma^* = 0.2$, Profit = 256 and Rate of interest, $r_i = 6\%$.

Find:

(a) The per cent leverage gain in each case, i.e. in interest finance and Islamic finance.

(b) The value of β if the leverage gain does not exceed 15%.

(c) The amount going to the local banks' support fund.

We have established a positive relationship between the rate of interest, r_i, commercial banks charge and the profit-sharing ratio, σ of Islamic banks. In our example, Figure 20.12 perfectly matches the 10% interest rate in results with a profit-sharing ratio $\sigma = 20.125\%$. Figure 20.11 links the rate of interest, r_i to the profit-sharing ratio, σ and Figure 20.12 links their relationship to other macro variables of the economy operating on its growth. The linkages allow for regulating leverage gains via β in the conventional system and automatically in the Islamic system as well, to the same end.

The measure can be used in both the Islamic and the conventional system for qualitative financing. The value of β can be varied between uses and spaces to encourage or discourage economic activities across the board for promoting the overall economic well-being of the community. The establishment of the proposed Banks Support Funds managed by the industry under guidance from the central bank may make the financial system more resilient, sustainable and progressively free of political intervention and the public gaze. Even a marginal value of β can pile up liquidity for the system beyond expectations. The money can be invested outside the financial sector to promote priority growth sectors. Figure 20.11 links σ and other macro variables of the economy operating on its growth. The linkages allow for regulating leverage gains via β in the conventional system and automatically in the Islamic system as well, to the same end.

Summary

- Monetary policy is concerned with the promotions of the welfare goals of an economy like growth, full employment, distributive justice and stability. Since maintaining stability is basic to the realization of other monetary policy focuses on this variable.

- What has to be kept stable is the general level of prices which is a sort of average of all prices at a point of time with reference to some base. We use price indices to measure changes in the price level. Price level and the value of money i.e. its purchasing power are inversely related. If prices in general rise, the value of money falls; it can purchase a smaller basket of goods and services. Opposite happens when prices in general fall.

- Interest is the conventional price for using money. Like all other price. Interest too is determined by its demand and supply forces. But the demand for money and its supply have some distinctive features. Money is not demanded as are other goods for its own sake, nor is money manufactured like them in factories. We need to understand the notions of money demand and supply.

- People demand money (i) to purchase goods and services where it passed from hand to hand, say V times, during a period and (ii) to hold a fraction, k, of their income, Y as a store of purchasing power for future use. The more of a given income people keep with them—k increases—the less goes to circulation—V falls.

- The quantity theory of money provides the first explanation about changes in the general price level, given the demand for money. It states that there is a direct proportional relationship between money supply, M, and price level, P. The Fisher equation is $MV = PT$. Quantity theory of money is supported by modern monetarists as a valid explanation.

- In contrast, the Cambridge equation sees the volume of money from the demand side of the market. Known as the liquidity preference approach, it states that people want to keep a portion, k, of their income, Y, with them to bridge income–expenditure time gap, to meet contingencies and to wait for favourable price changes. The equation can be written as: $M1/k = PT$; (T = income Y), where V and k are inversely related and k < V.

- The liquidity preference theory says that given the supply of money, the rate of interest is completely dominated by the demand for money and normally varies directly with it. The theory helps what are known as inflationary and deflationary gaps.

- Money supply has several components symbolized as M_1, M_2, M_3, etc. But the definitions of components and their inclusion in defining money supply depends on the discretion of the user.

- Mismatch between the demand for and supply of money causes instability and trade cycles. Inflation and deflation are the results of such mismatch. Inflation has been the global worry for a long time now and has earned a few nicknames—creeping, running, galloping and hyper—depending on its speed and magnitude. Inflation tends to assume the form of an upward spiral; the key variables chasing each other in a circular relationship. The causal link is lost.

- Inflation changes relative prices. Individuals gain or lose depending on their income source. For example, producers and debtors gain, wage earners and renters lose in real terms. Inflation has increasingly become a fiscal policy tool Printing notes annoys no one; taxation scares away voters. The causes of deflation are complex, often intractable as psychological factors tend to overpower reasoning.

- Deflationary gap is caused by the insufficiency of effective demand to clear the market. Goods pile up unsold.

- Deflation changes the relative prices structure against producers; agriculturists suffer more. Renters gain, so do workers but only those who manage to retain employment.

- Inflation and deflation are both harmful but deflation is more injurious and difficult to cure.

- Goals and targets of monetary policy are interrelated. Changes in the target variables and the direction of change become indicators of policy impact.

- The main objectives of the credit control policy that the central bank operates are to maintain the internal and external value of domestic currency in order to achieve sustainable economic growth.

- Direct manipulation of interest rate, open market operations, variations in statutory ratios and moral direction are the instruments central banks use to control and allocate credit to various uses. They affect the price as well as the volume of credit in an economy.

- The problem in a dual financial system where interest based and interest-free banks operate in competition with one another is of having a common instrument. This need not be a problem because profit-sharing ratios are found firmly linked to interest rates and most other instruments are interest neutral. Interest rate changes initiated by the central bank would make the profit-sharing ratio move in tandem in a supportive way.

- The profit-sharing ratio σ is a function of the expected rate of return on capital, leverage ratio, interest rate and risk premium. Assuming that all other determinants of the profit-sharing ratio remain unchanged, we can establish a relationship between the sharing ratio σ and r, the two moving in the opposite direction. Combining the two relationships, we can explain the financial factors that may influence GDP growth in an economy in a dual banking system.

- Leverage gains lure banks into overstepping risk limits in credit expansion and eventually lead to defaults, dragging them into bankruptcies. These gains are also available in Islamic banking although to a smaller extent. It is demonstrated that leverage gains can be controlled by varying the allowable margin between the rate of return on total capital employed and the rate on the owners' equity.

Glossary

Inflationary gap The inflationary gap is a situation when aggregate demand exceeds full employment aggregate supply of goods and services in an economy. The shortfall tends to push up price level. Inflation results due to the demand–supply gap but at times inflation may itself become the cause of this gap.

Monetization In a literal sense, monetization refers to establishing something, such as gold or silver in the past, or today, paper notes as the legal tender of a country. With reference to an economy, it means sectors or areas where the barter system has given way to the use of money. In many developing economies, such as Pakistan or India, the barter system of exchange still prevails in rural areas. The real income generated in the non-monetized sector tends to escape the national income–accounting net. Monetization acts as a stimulus to economic growth and employment in an economy. The degree of monetization is one of the indicators of its level of development.

M_0 This measure combines any liquid or cash assets held within a central bank and the amount of physical currency circulating in the economy. It is the most liquid measure of the money supply. It only includes cash or assets that can quickly be converted into currency.

M$_1$ This is M$_0$ + demand deposits, which are checking accounts. The M$_1$ is a very liquid measure of the money supply as it contains cash and assets that can quickly be converted to currency. It quantifies for us the amount of money in circulation.

M$_2$ This is M$_1$ + small time deposits as defined in a country, savings deposits, and non-institutional money-market funds. M$_2$ is a broader classification of money than M$_1$. It is a key economic indicator used to forecast inflation.

M$_3$ This is M$_2$ + all large time deposits, institutional money-market funds, short-term repurchase agreements, along with other larger liquid assets. As the broadest measure of money, it is used to estimate the entire supply of money within an economy.

Phillips curve In 1958 a New Zealand economist called Phillips, using a long time series from the UK, established an inverse correlation between inflation (in the context of wage levels) and unemployment—a relationship which, *prima facie*, was very obvious: inflation boosts economic growth, reducing unemployment. In 1960, Samuelson and Solow carried the work further, confirming Phillips' findings. However, in the mid-1970s the US economy saw the surprising phenomenon of unemployment co-existing with inflation. The Phillips curve was discredited. However, it has historical resonance in the economics literature.

Stagflation It is a situation that defies the Phillips curve theory, which provides the common sense explanation that inflation must reduce unemployment. Here, unemployment and inflation go hand in hand. It dominated the US economy during the 1970s. The supply-side economy was thought to remove stagnation and control inflation.

Supply of money It is the amount of money in circulation. It is classified into two categories: narrow money and broad money. They are usually defined in terms of M$_0$, M$_1$, M$_2$, and M$_3$.

Velocity of circulation of money Units of goods once consumed cannot be consumed again. You cannot eat the same piece of cake twice. It is a different story with money. A unit of money can be used several times in exchange for goods and services. How many times a unit of money, say a ringgit, is used in a year to perform the act of exchange in an economy is called its velocity of circulation. The concept plays an important role in reckoning the quantity of money incomes (MV) in an economy. It also helps us to understand the limitations of monetary policy in controlling inflation or deflation.

Concepts for Review

- Deflationary gap
- Inflationary gap
- Leverage gains
- Liquidity preference
- Liquidity trap
- Leverage control measure

- Recession
- Recovery
- Stagflation
- Supply of money
- Trade cycles
- Value of money

Case Study   20.1

Islamic Finance Instruments and Opportunity for Financing Infrastructure in India

Infrastructure growth is *sine qua non* of the growth and development of an economy. India has been suffering from demand–supply mismatch in terms of funding requirements to finance infrastructure projects. Funding deficit of INR 1,460,784 crores has been estimated for the twelfth five year plan (2012–2017). Introduction of Islamic finance can play a crucial role in order to bridge the gap and support India in achieving anticipated growth projections. There is great possibility of funding infrastructure in India through Islamic financial instruments. The methodology consists of estimating infrastructure funding requirements in India. What is needed is the understanding of the development and status of Islamic finance in the global context, exploring basics of Islamic banking system along with its various financial instruments especially *sukuk*, as well as identifying challenges and the way forward.

Source: Majeethia, Y. and Bose, T. (2014), Islamic Finance Instruments and Opportunity for Financing Infrastructure in India, *Journal of Business Management & Social Sciences Research*.

Case Questions

1 Explain the meaning and components of infrastructure. Why is the development of infrastructure an imperative for economic development, especially for a country such as India?

2 How can the opening of Islamic financial institutions contribute to the huge monetary requirements of the infrastructural development? Explain.

Case Study 20.2

The US Subprime Crisis

The term 'subprime' refers to the credit status of the borrower, which is always less than ideal. 'Subprime lending' is a general term that refers to the practice of making loans to borrowers who do not qualify for the best market interest rates because of their weakened and deficient credit history. They may display reduced repayment capacity, as measured by credit scores, debt-to-income ratios, or other criteria.

Subprime lending is also called B-paper, near-prime, or second-chance lending. Subprime lending encompasses a variety of credit instruments, including subprime mortgages, subprime car loans, and subprime credit cards, among others. A subprime loan is offered at a rate higher than A-paper loans due to the increased risk. The subprime lending crisis, which began in the United States, has become a financial contagion and has led to a restriction on the availability of credit in world financial markets. Hundreds of thousands of borrowers have been forced to default and several major subprime lenders have filed for bankruptcy.

Subprime lending carries greater than normal risks. Although most home loans do not fall into this category, subprime mortgages proliferated in the early part of the twenty-first century. About 21% of all mortgage loans during 2004–06 periods were subprime, totalling $600 billion by the end period and accounting for about one-fifth of the US home loan market.

Source: <www.banknetindia.com/banking/subprime.html>, accessed 28 June 2012.

Case Questions

1 What do you understand by the term 'subprime lending'? Explain. In what ways do subprime loans differ from paper loans?
2 The US economy is one of the strongest in the world and their financial system is mature and efficient. How is it that a financial crisis such as one that now engulfs the world, could originate from that country?
3 It is often claimed that Islamic banks remained unaffected from the crisis originating from the US-subprime fiasco. Do you agree? Give reasons for your answer.

Test Questions

20.1 What are the major goals economies strive to achieve? Show how stability is related to other goals.

20.2 Explain and illustrate the quantity theory of money. Do you think it adequately explains booms and depressions in trade cycles?

20.3 Suppose an economy depends solely on the production of cloth and produces annually 2,000 million metres of standard linen. The public has $1,000 million in cash and the velocity of money circulation is 2 a year. What will the price of cloth per metre be, if we use Fisher's exchange equation to determine it?

20.4 What is a liquidity trap? When does an economy experience it and why? Explain using an appropriate diagram. Do you think such a trap is likely to emerge in an Islamic economy? Give reasons for your answer.

20.5 What causes an 'inflationary gap'? Explain. What measures would you suggest to close such a gap?

20.6 'Inflation is unjust; deflation is inexpedient. Of the two, deflation is perhaps the worst'. Comment.

20.7 Central banks have goals and targets. How do the two match and differ? Explain.

20.8 In Example 20.5, the bank gets an enhancement of 7.35% over the rate of return, r as leverage gain. Suppose the central bank wants to grant an increase to 8%. Find the value of the profit-sharing ratio for the bank that would give it an additional 0.65% leverage gain and verify your result.

Web Exercise

Search the Internet for material on the Phillips curve and assess its validity for modern economies.

Forward Link

The fiscal policy of the government affects not only the monetary policy of the central bank, it has impact on both the supply of money and prices. In the next chapter we examine the workings of fiscal policy of the state.

21

Fiscal Policy: Public Revenue and Expenditure

LEARNING OUTCOMES

This chapter should enable the student to understand:

- The significance of government role in an economy
- The sources of public revenue and the economic effect of using them
- Principles of taxation, tax types and their incidence
- Allocation of public expenditure: Objectives and consequences
- Fiscal policy in Islam: Sources of revenue and expenditure rules

21.1 GOVERNMENT AND ECONOMY

There has been a continual debate in literature on whether or not the government should play a role in market-run economies and if yes, what that role and its limits ought to be? This debate still lingers but the Keynesian advocacy for an active public involvement in promoting some basic economic objectives seems to have won the day as opposed to the liberals' view that market freedoms can achieve better results. The increase in the frequency of financial crises and their intensity in recent decades have made governmental action almost obligatory. Islam had assigned from its very inception, an important role to the state in guiding the economy on to the 'right path'.

In the preceding chapter, we discussed monetary policy for addressing certain goals. But monetary policy alone cannot work to that end because governments also contribute to and affect money supply in several ways. Furthermore, monetary policy helps promote economic goals only indirectly. To be effective, it has to work in tandem with the fiscal policy of the government. Fiscal policy includes measures governments employ for smooth running of the economy through manipulating the level and structure of taxation and government spending to achieve certain goals.

> In the present era of liberalization, the state is assuming an increased role in the running of economies because of the increase in the frequency of financial crises.

These goals are to achieve or maintain full employment, and a high rate of economic growth. Both policies also seek to stabilize prices and wages. The establishment of these goals for governmental policy and the development of tools with which to achieve them are of recent origin; the product of the preceding century.

A policy—monetary or fiscal—is action designed to achieve specified goals. Broadly, these goals are well-known and we have already explained the same at some length in Chapter 14. The fiscal policy of a country is more intimately related to achieving these goals than its monetary policy. In fact, taxation has become a tool of both monetary and fiscal management for 'fine-tuning' the economy so that employment and productivity may expand. Fiscal policy of a country manifests itself in the annual budget series of the central government. Changes in sources of revenue, especially in taxes and subsidies, and allocations for various heads under economic development, are important to achieve short-run targets on a long-run trajectory.

> Monetary and fiscal policies are instruments of intervention the government uses to direct economic forces to achieve desired goals.

Exercise 21.1

'It is the worldview of a community that determines the role of a government in its economic life'. Elaborate and illustrate.

21.2   SOURCES OF REVENUE

The government provides a number of services to its nationals and foreign visitors, charging **fees or prices** for the same. Examples are public utilities such as postal services, immigration work, supply of water and electricity, and issuing of various sorts of licences and certifications. In many countries, the government provides commercial services and runs public enterprises for **profit**. However, the major source of revenue collection is **taxation**. Borrowings at home or abroad and printing notes to cover the deficits have assumed importance in recent times. Taxes are not only the most important source of public (government) revenue, they are also the instruments of policy for directing resources to desired uses, for narrowing income and wealth disparities, and for reducing poverty.

> Fiscal matters relate to the raising of revenue and spending the money in addition to administrative work but on economic development in an effective manner.

A tax is a compulsory payment of money made to the government by people without any direct compensatory benefit accruing to them. This is in contrast to fees or prices that are paid as stated for direct and proportionate benefits received. Taxes are in the nature of general contributions to the revenue of the government to meet the expenditure incurred on the provision and maintenance of services the government provides to the public; maintenance of law and order and defence readiness being the leading examples. The payable amount is determined either as a specific sum or as a percentage of some variables such as income, wealth or windfalls.

21.3 THEORIES OF TAXATION

Adam Smith in his *Wealth of Nations* (1776) had laid down some basic principles (canons) of taxation. A leading one was that every person should give tax to the government according to his ability to pay. With the passage of time, however, two more theories appeared on the scene. Some argued that the government incurs expenditure to provide services to the people. To recover this amount, cost of service should be the basis of taxation. Others argued that not everyone may need the services provided or benefit to the same extent as others; therefore, benefits received should be the basis of charge. But such cost/benefit theories of taxation could not survive ultimately. Today, if they are mentioned, they are mentioned for their faults, not merits.

Ability-to-pay has won the day for its simple, straightforward logic. Scholars and laymen alike agree that taxes ought to be paid by those who can pay them, not by those who cannot. The approach appeals as it delinks the issues of public revenue from those of public expenditure.

21.3.1 Ability-to-pay Theorem

Under this approach, taxes are based on taxpayers' ability to pay without any quid pro quo. Taxes paid are seen as a sacrifice by taxpayers; this raises the issue of tax making the sacrifice of taxpayers equitable. Here, we need to distinguish two types of equity or justice: (a) *horizontal equity*; which means that people in similar situations are to be treated equally—that is people with the same amount of income must pay the same amount in tax, there should be no discrimination between them. However, there is the question of how can equality of sacrifice in taxation be achieved among people with different levels of income? This brings us to what we call the issue of ensuring (b) *vertical equity*. It may be mentioned at this stage that concepts of horizontal and vertical equity are commensurate with the Islamic norms of justice. There are two bases to say what could be just—psychological or subjective—or factual or objective.

Subjective approach

Here, the concept of *sacrifice* which the taxpayer undergoes (in parting with the amount as tax) becomes central: the payer feels a pinch—he perceives disutility. The sacrifice is measured in terms of utility lost. Three measures are considered.

1. **Equal absolute sacrifice**: The principle requires that the tax burden in terms of utility loss should be the same for all the payers. Let U be equal to total utility and Y income, T being total utility. We can now say that $U(Y) - U(Y - T)$ must be the same

for all taxpayers to meet the norm of equal absolute sacrifice. In Figure 21.1, for the taxpayer in the low income group 0 – P, the utility of money is expected to be more than the taxpayer in the higher income group, 0 – R. If tax makes the sacrifice of utility (area in green) equal to sacrifice (area in grey), then tax would make the absolute sacrifice of the two equal. It must however be added that achieving equality in practice accurately is almost impossible. A taxpayer himself has little idea of what sacrifice he is making let alone an outsider—the tax manager.

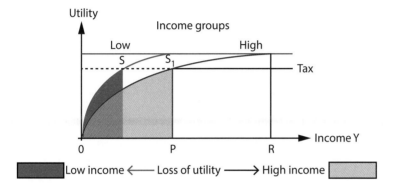

Figure 21.1 *Taxation – equal absolute sacrifice*

2. **Equal proportional sacrifice**: This means that the same proportion of each payer's income should be taken as tax. It is simple; impose a percentage tax on all income, low or high. Adam Smith advocated the imposition of such a tax. However, a proportional tax would impose a greater sacrifice on lower income recipients because for them the utility of the money is higher as indicated above.
3. **Equal marginal sacrifice**: The instantaneous loss of utility (as measured by the derivative of the utility function) as a result of taxation should be equal for all taxpayers. In terms of our figure, the tangents at two points, S and S_1 of the utility curves should become parallel. This will minimize the total sacrifice.

The principle needs the adoption of progressive taxation. In simple terms, the conditions are as follows:

1. Equal absolute sacrifice = $U(Y) - U(Y - T)$,
    where U stands for utility, Y for income and T for tax.

2. Equal proportional sacrifice = $\dfrac{U(Y) - U(Y - T)}{U(Y)}$

3. Equal marginal sacrifice = $\dfrac{dU(Y - T)}{U(Y - T)}$

Utility is a perceptive matter. It is useful to have relative comparison but to put utility based notions in tax schemes is very difficult.

21.4   CHARACTERISTICS OF A GOOD TAX SYSTEM

There are many ways to structure a tax system. The question as to what in general are the *basic qualities* that a good tax system must have becomes important. The following are often indicated for guidance. Relative emphasis may vary and additions can be made to meet local needs.

1. **Fair and equitable**: The individual contributions to tax revenue should be non-discriminatory and fair. This means that (i) taxpayers in similar financial conditions should pay similar amounts, and (ii) taxpayers who are better off should pay at least the same proportion of income in taxes as those who are less well off. Fairness in the latter sense leads to classifying taxes as *regressive*, *proportional*, or *progressive*.

   - **Regressive tax**: A tax is regressive if those with low income pay a larger share in taxes than those with higher income. Almost any tax imposed on necessities of life is regressive because lower income people have spent a larger proportion of their income on necessities and thus, in taxes. Islam prohibits gambling not only for moral and social reasons, but presumably also because a state lottery operates as a regressive tax, taking heavily from the poor, even though voluntarily. History tells us that resorting to lotteries have led governments toward corruption and decadence. State lottery is akin to a last-ditch effort by a wasteful government to fill its coffers in desperation.

   - **Proportional tax**: A tax is proportional if people of all levels of income are to pay tax at a flat rate, say 10% of their income to the government. In practice, no taxes are indeed proportional. Property taxes often come closest because there is a close relationship between a households' income and the value of the property in which they live. Corporate income taxes often approach proportionality as a single rate which applies to most corporate income.

   - **Progressive tax**: This requires higher income individuals to pay a higher share of their income in taxes. The philosophy behind progressive taxes is that higher income people can afford and should be expected to provide a bigger share of public services than those who are less able to pay. While no system of taxes is perfect, it is important to seek horizontal equity because taxpayers must believe they are treated equally. It is just as important to seek vertical equity so the government does not become a burden to low income residents.

2. **Adequacy**: This means that taxes must provide enough revenue to meet the basic needs of society. A tax system meets the test of adequacy if it provides enough revenue to meet the demand for public services; if revenue growth each year is enough to fund

> Fairness, ease in collection, productivity, variety and progression are some of the characteristics that a good tax system must possess.

the growth in cost of services, and if there is enough economic activity of the type being taxed so rates can be kept relatively low.

3. **Transparency**: This means that taxpayers can easily find information about the tax system—rates, exemptions, rebates and credits—and how tax money is used. With a transparent tax system, we know who are being taxed and how much they pay, and what is being done with the money. In other words, we can find out who in general pays the tax and who benefits from public expenditures.

4. **Administrative ease**: It means that the tax system is not too complicated or costly for either taxpayers or tax collectors. Rules are well known and fairly simple, forms are not too complicated, it is easy to comply voluntarily, the state can tell if taxes are paid on time and correctly, and the state can conduct audits in a fair and efficient manner. The cost of collecting a tax should be small in relation to the amount collected.

5. **Productivity**: A good tax system should have automation, which means tax revenue tends to grow even without imposing new taxes. In this regard, taxes on commodities are more productive than taxes on wealth or windfalls. Also, taxes charged as rates are more flexible and productive than the in the lump sum category.

21.5   TAX TYPES – DIRECT AND INDIRECT

Terms used in economics usually carry different meanings from the common language. In taxation theory, three words, impact, shifting and incidence are also of the same sort. The impact of a tax is on the entity who is legally obliged to pay it to the government; it carries the *immediate* money burden of the tax. People in general attempt to evade or avoid tax woes and legal payments. To the extent that when they cannot do so, they attempt to pass it on to someone else in the circular flow of money. For example, sellers tend to add the tax amount to the commodity prices, to pass it on to the buyers to pay. This is called *tax shifting* that uses some mechanism. The *incidence* of a tax is said to be on the entity that ultimately bears the money burden of a tax. (We speak here of the *money* burden of tax. Are there other burdens too?)

The terms we explained above help us understand the nature of various taxes better, especially of their classification into *direct* and *indirect* taxes. Taxes levied on income, wealth and gains are called *direct taxes*, those targeted on goods—their sale or purchase within or outside the country is called *indirect taxes*. The legal obligation for paying a tax is of the person on whom it is imposed. This decides the impact point of a tax. Tax reduces the consumable income of a person. So, few people like to pay tax cheerfully. Generally, they first attempt to evade or avoid

A public finance system based on a single tax is history. Modern states have a variety of taxes in the system. Broadly, these taxes are of two sorts: direct and indirect. Direct taxes are on ex post variables such as income, wealth or inheritance. Indirect taxes are mostly on current flows such as sales, production, exports and imports.

payment. If they cannot, they attempt to pass the tax on to someone else. Transfer of tax involves a mechanism of shifting the tax obligation backward to factors of production or forward to the consumers.

Direct taxes include tax on income of individuals and corporate businesses, taxes on capital gains (what are these?), national insurance contributions, statutory payments, inheritance, petroleum revenue, student loans, stamps, construction industry schemes and the likes. These direct tax sources need not be taped in every country; they are illustrations from various countries.

Leading examples of **indirect taxes** are taxes on sale (purchase) of goods and services, excise duties on production and taxes levied on the export and import of commodities (custom duties). Indirect taxes can be shifted to others fully or in part, depending on the circumstances of a case. We study these circumstances under incidence of a tax. The consequences of the shifting also become an important part of the study.

> People whose legal obligations to pay a tax are often able to transfer the money burden via the price mechanism to others in part or in full. Indirect taxes are generally easy to shift.

21.6   PRICE ELASTICITY AND INCIDENCE

> The impact of a tax is on the person who pays it to the government, but if he is able to shift it to others, the incidence of tax is ultimately on those who pay it.

We have discussed taxation and its effects under monopoly conditions in Chapter 7. Thus, we discuss the issue here under competitive markets. Essentially, two factors are relevant to determine the incidence of taxation and the consequent distribution of the tax (money) burden among the parties involved: (i) the elasticity of demand and supply for the product, and (ii) the law of production applied in its production i.e. the cost conditions.

1. **Elasticity of demand and tax**: To focus on the effect of elasticity of demand, we take two extreme cases of perfectly inelastic and perfectly elastic demand with identical supply conditions; the supply curves of the firms having identical slopes. Figure 21.2 illustrates the case. Here in A, demand is perfectly inelastic. Price rises by the full amount of tax i.e. the seller is able to shift the entire shaded area of tax to the customer. In contrast, in case B, the demand for the product is perfectly elastic. Price of the commodity does not change at all and the money burden of the tax remains on the seller. Notice that when the demand is perfectly inelastic, the quantity bought and sold does not change; only the price rises. But in B, the price and quantity bought and sold both remain unchanged.

    Thus, we may generalize that other things being equal, the more elastic the demand for a commodity, the greater will be the proportion of tax the seller will have to pay and vice versa. If the demand for the commodity is unity, the tax amount will be equally shared by the parties. (Why?)

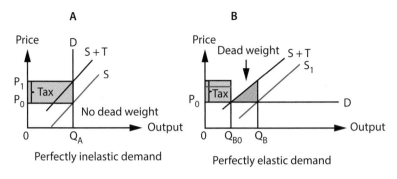

Figure 21.2 *Elasticity of demand and incidence of taxation*

2. **Elasticity of supply and tax**: As in the case of elasticity of demand, we use Figure 21.3 to illustrate the consequences of elasticity of supply for the incidence of taxation, other things remaining unchanged. Here the case is reverse; if the supply is perfectly inelastic, the seller has to pay the entire tax but if the supply is perfectly elastic the customer has to bear the full tax. Thus, as a general rule, the less elastic the supply, the larger will be the tax burden on the seller than on the customer and vice versa. Output bought and sold here also remains unchanged.

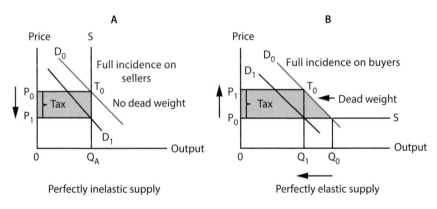

Figure 21.3 *Elasticity of supply and incidence of taxation*

It follows from the above discussion that the money burden of a tax is shared by the buyers and sellers of a commodity in ratios determined by the relative elasticity of its demand and supply. We take a typical case of a commodity produced under perfect competition as Figure 21.4 illustrates.

3. **Mathematical generalization**: Here, D and S are the initial demand and supply curves for the commodity in equilibrium at T_1, with P_0 as the price. Q_1 is the quantity bought and sold. Now, a tax LT_0 is imposed on the sale of the commodity. The supply curve shifts upwards to the left to position S + T; the

We can show the division of an indirect tax payment between the sellers and the buyers specifically in mathematical terms.

equilibrium point moves to T_0 and price rises to P_1. The total payable tax is the area $L_0LT_0P_1$. The question is how would the parties share this total tax?

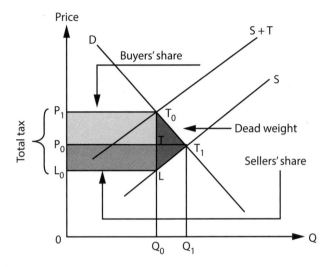

Figure 21.4 *Tax incidence – a generalized case*

Notice that the price of the commodity rises from P_0 to P_1 that is not by the full rate of tax LT_0. It falls for the seller from P_0 to L_0. The buyers share is $P_0TT_1T_0P_1$. Thus, the incidence of tax on buyers equals T_0Q_0 (because $0Q_0 = P_0T$). Likewise, the share of the sellers is TQ_0 (because $0Q_0 = L_0L$). Thus, the incidence of tax on buyers is TT_0 and on sellers is TL, Q_0 being the common multiplier. We may therefore write:

$$\frac{TL}{TT_0} = \frac{\text{Incidence of tax on sellers}}{\text{Incidence of tax on buyers}} \tag{21.1}$$

$$\text{Price elasticity of demand} = \frac{\Delta q}{\Delta p} \cdot \frac{p}{q}$$

From Figure 21.4, we get price elasticity of demand:

> The more elastic the demand for a commodity relative to the elasticity of its supply, the greater will be the payment share for the sellers, and vice versa. Thus, if the demand is perfectly inelastic, buyers will pay the whole amount to the sellers. On the contrary, if the demand is perfectly elastic, the sellers will pay the entire tax.

$$E_{DP} = \frac{\Delta q}{\Delta p} \cdot \frac{p}{q} = \frac{Q_0Q_1}{TT_0} \cdot \frac{P_0}{Q_1} \tag{21.2}$$

Likewise, we may express the elasticity of supply in terms of our figure as follows:

$$E_{SP} = \frac{\Delta q}{\Delta p} \cdot \frac{p}{q} = \frac{Q_0Q_1}{TL} \cdot \frac{P_0}{Q_1} \tag{21.3}$$

We may now write the ratio of the two elasticities as:

$$\frac{E_{DP}}{E_{SP}} = \frac{\dfrac{Q_0Q_1}{TT_0} \cdot \dfrac{P_0}{Q_1}}{\dfrac{Q_0Q_1}{TL} \cdot \dfrac{P_0}{Q_1}} = \frac{TL}{TT_0} \text{ as in (21.1)} \tag{21.4}$$

Suppose a tax t per unit is imposed on a commodity, by definition we have $t = TL + TT_0$ (21.5)

From (21.4) we get $TL = \dfrac{E_{DP}}{E_{SP}} TT_0$

Inserting this value of TL in (21.5) we obtain:

$$t = \frac{E_{DP}}{E_{SP}} TT_0 + TT_0 = TT_0 \left(\frac{E_{DP}}{E_{SP}} + 1 \right)$$ (21.6)

This gives tax $t = E_{SP} \left(\dfrac{E_{DP} + E_{SP}}{E_{SP}} \right)$ (21.7)

We may get the ratio of the sellers' share in the tax as follows:

$$\frac{E_{SP}}{t} = \frac{E_{SP}}{E_{DP} + E_{SP}}$$ (21.8)

We may find the share of the buyers by replacing the numerator in equation 21.8 by E_{DP}.

Thus, equation 21.7 gives us the measure of a unit commodity tax incidence on the sellers, the remaining tax falling on the buyers of the commodity.

Example 21.1   Assume the following information is available.

Demand for the commodity, $Q_D = 150 - 30P_b$

Supply of the commodity, $Q_S = 60 + 40P_s$

Tax per unit t sold = 0.5

In equilibrium, $Q_D = Q_S$.
Thus, we have:

$\qquad 150 - 30P = 60 + 40P$

Solving it we get:

$\qquad P = 3; \quad Q = 60$

Also, $\quad t + P = 3 + 0.5$
$\qquad\qquad\quad = 3.5$

After the tax is imposed, the quantity of the commodity will shrink due to the rise in price and the consequent fall in its demand. We have as new values:

$\qquad$ Demand $= 150 - (30 \times 3.5) = 45$
$\qquad$ Supply $= 60 + (40 \times 3.5) = 200$

Using the old and new P and Q values, we may calculate the demand and supply elasticity values as:

$$E_{DP} = \frac{\Delta Q}{\Delta P} \cdot \frac{P}{Q} = \frac{60 - 45}{3.5 - 3} \cdot \frac{3}{60} = 1.5$$

$$E_{SP} = \frac{\Delta Q}{\Delta P} \cdot \frac{P}{Q} = \frac{200 - 60}{3.5 - 3} \cdot \frac{3}{60} = 14$$

The tax amount the government would receive will be $Q.t = 45 \times 0.5 = 22.5$. The amount will be shared as follows:

$$\text{Sellers will pay} = \frac{E_{SP}}{E_{DP} + E_{SP}} \times \text{Tax amount} = \frac{14}{14 + 1.5} \times 22.5 = 20.32$$

$$\text{Buyers will pay} = \frac{E_{DP}}{E_{DP} + E_{SP}} \times \text{Tax amount} = \frac{1.5}{14 + 1.5} \times 22.5 = 2.18$$

$$\text{The price sellers would not receive would be} = \frac{\text{Total sale value} + \text{Tax share of buyers}}{\text{Quantity bought and sold}}$$

$$= \frac{(3 \times 45) + 2.18}{45} = 3.048$$

Exercise 21.2

Suppose the elasticity of demand for a commodity is 0.10 and elasticity of supply is 0.5. Using this information, find how total tax = $20 million will be shared between the sellers and the buyers of the commodity, other things remaining unchanged. Who will pay more and why?

BOX 21.1

Is *Zakat* a Tax?

Some early western writers on Islam characterized *zakat* as a tax presumably because of the obligatory nature of payment in both cases; they called *zakat* a poll or charity tax levied to help the poor with the revenue raised. Many Islamic economists innocuously followed the western description in their writings on the subject.

Admittedly, *zakat* is a compulsory extraction for the specified purposes, essentially for helping the poor and the oppressed. Still, to equate it with a *tax* does not commensurate with the Shari'ah spirit and intention. As stated above, the very notion and mention of a tax is associated with adversity in human psyche giving rise to thoughts of evasion and avoidance. On the contrary, *zakat* is the third pillar of Islam, after only *iman* and prayers. The verse of the scripture that made its payment obligatory uses the word *sadaqa*, not *zakat*. After that, the instruction for prayer and *zakat* appear tied together 34 times in the Qur'an. To call *zakat* a tax is to betray ignorance of its dignity and place in the Islamic scheme of things.

Furthermore, a tax can be imposed and abolished by public authorities at will; its rates structure, objectives and application coverage can be amended. So is not the case with *zakat*. No Act by the parliament or juridical pronouncement can abolish it, nor can the heads of expenditure; it is meant for basic exemptions and rates can be subjected to substantive alterations. For all these reasons: *Zakat* is not a tax.

21.7   COST AND INCIDENCE

We have so far looked at the incidence issue purely from the side of trading in the market. But goods bought and sold in the market have costs of production and their relationship with supply of goods and prices is even more consequential for tax incidence. Firms operate under increasing returns, constant returns or diminishing returns; phases which correspond to decreasing, constant or increasing costs respectively. Let us examine the impact of each phase on the incidence of taxation.

Of the three, constant return (cost) is not effective, the issue being decided by demand and supply conditions. The supply curve becomes perfectly elastic as in Figure 21.3B. Otherwise, the analysis and the discussion remain unchanged. Thus, what is important appears to be the decreasing and increasing cost cases, the latter especially for being more common. The case of increasing costs is the same as Figure 21.4 helped us explain. Suffice to say that the rising supply curve specifies the case of diminishing returns or increasing costs. So, let us see what happens in the third case—increasing returns i.e. decreasing costs for commodity X. Here, not only the demand curve, but the supply curve also slopes downwards as in Figure 21.5.

Here, we see that the supply curve slopes downwards but the fact seems to make no difference to the sharing of the nominal amount of tax between the sellers and the buyers. Notice that the demand curve is much steeper (less elastic) than the supply curve. Thus, it is the greater elasticity of supply relative to demand that allows the sellers shift a larger share of tax to the buyers.

> In contrast, returns applied in production costs do not affect incidence. The matter is decided by the relative demand and supply elasticities.

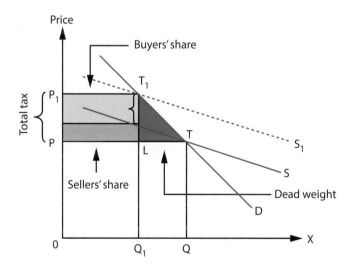

Figure 21.5 *Increasing returns and tax incidence*

Exercise 21.3

In Figure 21.5, let T be the initial equilibrium point with P = $20 and quantity of the commodity bought and sold at that price, Q = 50,000. The sellers raise the price by the tax amount to P_1 = $22 a unit. However, with a rise in price, the demand for the commodity contracts to Q_1 = 40,000, T_1 becoming the new point of equilibrium. The sellers find at this point, the net price T they get is no more than $1.30 a unit. Given this information, find the following:

(i)   The total tax the government would receive from the sellers.
(ii) The incidence of tax on the sellers and the buyers respectively.
(iii) Dead weight loss.
    (**Hint**: Find the area of the triangle TLT_1.)

21.8   OBJECTIVES OF FISCAL POLICY

Largely, the main objectives of fiscal policy are the same in the Islamic economy as in the conventional. More objectives are added, and the content and focus in others change to incorporate ethical norms.

The basic objectives of fiscal policy look alike in names for various economies but they may differ widely in their content and scope from economy to economy. Important differences for example, may exist between developed (rich) and the developing or emerging (poor) economies, the latter involving most of the global population. We may, therefore, look at the objectives of fiscal policy from the developing countries viewpoint. In these countries, wherein most Muslims live; the government plays a very active role both in the mobilization of resources and their allocation to various uses. Put briefly, the main objectives of fiscal policy in these countries are as follows:

1. To mobilize resources for public sector projects to play a strategic role in the overall growth of the economy, especially infrastructural development. If the government squeezes more or less, societal savings would be available to the private sector, crowding out must be avoided.

2. To provide incentives for the private sector to participate effectively in the growth process. As public and private sectors both draw on the same pool of resources.

3. To promote equitable distribution of income and wealth and alleviate poverty, especially through the expansion of voluntary sectors including promotion of cooperatives and *awqaf*.

4. To help allocate resources including finance to social priority areas, especially to meet the basic needs of the populace for food, clothing, shelter, healthcare and education.

5. To promote human resource development, targeting the young and the unemployed.

6. To draw up sustainable development demands measures to sustain the environment.

The list is of course not exhaustive; temporal and spatial adjustments have to be made. Taxation is a universal phenomenon. Even the verse that made *zakat* obligatory for the believers provides scope for imposing other taxes if need be. Thus, in the Middle-East income is tax-free and an important attraction for foreign workers. In most countries however, other sources of revenue rising have to be tapped for capital formation. Fiscal policy can encourage voluntary savings via tax exemptions; it can also force savings through deficit financing as explained in an earlier chapter. Tax and control concessions can be used to attract foreign capital. Money can be borrowed at home and from abroad. In fact, many countries, especially in the developed world, are dangerously living on borrowings.

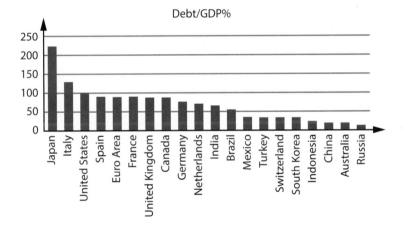

Rising public debt from abroad causes instability and crises in modern economies.

Figure 21.6 *Public debt to GDP ratios for selected countries as of 31 December 2013 (adapted from the United States Debt to GDP data)*

It is interesting to note that the debt to GDP ratios have been rising in the developed countries presumably because borrowing is an easier way to raise money as raising taxation carries political risks; it may shy away voters, and may result in losing elections. Also, borrowed money may help cover both inefficiency and corruption. But over-indulgence in borrowing implies using tomorrow's earnings today; it tends to leave future generations impoverished. It also operates against the concept of sustainability, however defined. Figure 21.6 provides the debt-GDP ratios of selected countries as of 31 December 2013.

BOX
21.2

Hidden Taxes

The tendency of taxpayers to revolt against high taxes causes tax collectors to try and hide the tax burden so that the taxpayer will hardly be aware of what is happening to him. If this process takes place at a time of rapid growth in the economy, levels of living may rise at the same time that taxes are increasing. Without an understanding of what might have been, people can truthfully proclaim: 'We never had it so good!'

An effective method of hiding taxes is the withholding of the federal, state, and local income taxes by employers from the wages of employees. Most workers are inclined to think only of their take-home pay, and give little thought to the tax they are paying.

The social security tax is not only hidden through withholding, as is the income tax, but is otherwise disguised as well. If he thinks of it at all, the employee is likely to consider only his share of the tax, not realizing that the employer pays an equal amount on his behalf. Further, many who pay in the name of social security view it not as a tax but as savings for their old age.

Perhaps the most cleverly hidden tax is inflation. When the national government fails to cover its expenditures through taxes, it must borrow the difference, either from individuals or the central bank. If the latter, a multiple of that debt is likely to be added to the money supply, which is inflation. Inflation is usually accompanied by rising prices and erosion of the purchasing power of the dollar. Since 1939, the dollar has lost about half of its purchasing power. This is a tax upon savings, as truly a tax as any of the many other ways of raising revenue. From a political standpoint, it has the advantage of being hidden. Also, it is possible to make people believe that the cause of inflation is the raising of prices by greedy businessmen or of wages by labour unions.

Taxes are hidden in other ways too. Many are incorporated in the prices of things we buy and we rarely realize that a tax has been added. Taxes on liquor, cigarettes, automobiles and gasoline are examples.

Source: W. M. Curtiss, (1967), *Taxation Theory*, <http://www.fee.org/the_freeman/detail/taxation-theory>, accessed 30 September 2014.

21.9   *SUKUK* AND PUBLIC REVENUE

Sovereign sukuk has made a big appearance in the budget financing of states in both Muslim and non-Muslim countries.

After the turn of the century, Islamic finance emerged as the fastest growing segment of the global system. Most of this growth has so far been around debt-based transactions where *sukuk* replaces conventional bonds. Their characteristics include a firm linkage with the real assets and share in project profits (losses). Figure 21.7 illustrates how rapid the growth of *sukuk* has been over the years in Malaysia, the leading country in Islamic finance.

A distinctive feature of *sukuk* is that the instrument is now being used by governments to finance productive projects, especially infrastructural development. Even the Islamic Development Bank has entered the field with that end in view. Thus, there has recently been a notable rise in the issuance of sovereign *sukuk*, 2014 becoming a landmark year with even non–Islamic countries such as the UK, Hong Kong and South Africa entering the market in a big way. The surge is indicative of a significant change in the future size, depth and liquidity of Islamic financial markets.

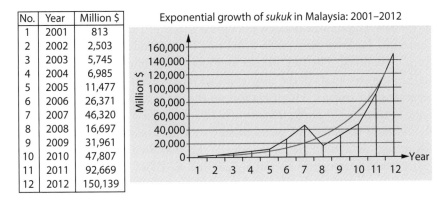

No.	Year	Million $
1	2001	813
2	2002	2,503
3	2003	5,745
4	2004	6,985
5	2005	11,477
6	2006	26,371
7	2007	46,320
8	2008	16,697
9	2009	31,961
10	2010	47,807
11	2011	92,669
12	2012	150,139

Figure 21.7 *Growth of sukuk in Malaysia*

The total sovereign *sukuk* is today estimated as accounting for more than 36% of the $296 billion of outstanding *sukuk* and is likely to reach around $30 billion by the end of 2014, crossing the 2013 levels. Malaysia and more recently Indonesia, have been driving the growth in sovereign *sukuk* with sales in domestic markets; together the two account for around two thirds of total sovereign issuance. Factors contributing to their popularity include investors growing familiarity with their relatively complex structures, the increasing financing needs and the leverage lure of some Muslim countries. Other contributory factors include a desire to have a share in stronger investment trends, faster growth in Asian economies and increasing efforts by the governments of Muslim countries to support Islamic banking and finance.

21.10   PUBLIC EXPENDITURE

Historically, public expenditure for social benefit received relatively less attention in governmental finance than sources of revenue. The latter provided for the needs, comforts and luxuries of the royalty and the armies they maintained for security, conquests and plunder. Little was the concern to ameliorate the living conditions of the masses, save occasionally. Islam was born in the full view of history and for that reason we find pointed attention of the state to improve individual and collective living. General well-being and prosperity of the Muslim lands remained exemplary until the close of the 15th century when the slide began. Ibn Khaldun recorded the causes of the rise and fall of nations around the close of the 14th century in his famous *Introduction* (1406).

The dawn of civilization that industrial revolution ushered in its train on the wheels of scientific inventions and innovations in England spread to other countries of Europe in the course of time. It was the exploitative treatment of workers that soon unveiled the true face of capitalism and attracted much criticism of its ways and consequences from men of letters

The primary objective of all public spending is to achieve maximum social advantage. The goal is complicated but provides a direction.

and faith. Economists followed suit. Notions of welfare urging reforms spread fast. Capitalism underwent a great metamorphosis and the process continues. Role of the state in economic life expanded despite resistance from orthodoxy. The importance and reach of public finance expanded. In fact, the two parts of the subject are so interwoven that it is difficult to separate their impact. Hugh Dalton, in the second chapter of his famous book *Principles of Public Finance* (1922), explained how governments should raise revenue and spend money so as to obtain 'maximum social advantage' as a total impact. Indeed, the maximization rules look so many and relationships so entangled that to those who may find the task daunting, the author advises to remain content with the old Greek saying: it is difficult things that are beautiful.

However, for analytical ease, we study the parts separately for better understanding of the whole. Public expenditure is divided into two broad categories operational or non-developmental and developmental. Table 21.1 lists their main elements in the government budget framework. The main expenditure heads are discussed below.

Table 21.1 *Basic elements in the government budget framework*

Government expenditure	Tax	Transfer payment
Operating expenditure	**Direct tax**	
Salaries and emoluments	Corporate tax	Pensions
Pensions and gratuities	Personal tax	Unemployment benefits
Debt servicing	Petroleum tax	
Grants to statutory bodies and state governments		Welfare (transfer) payments
Subsidies		
Scholarships		
Loans		
Retraining programmes		
Development expenditure	**Indirect tax**	
Economic sector	Export duties	
Social sector	Import duties	
Security sector	Excise duties	
General administration	Sales and service taxes	

Rising defense expenditures in developing countries, especially Muslim, are wasteful. Import of arms only encourages to fight with and not without.

Expenditure on defence: Expenditure on armed forces and weaponry has always been a prior claim on government revenue; 'defence is more important than opulence' is an old saying in public finance. In recent times, expenditure spending has been on the rise across countries as wars—hot or cold—continue unabated. Trade in arms has become a lucrative business. The expenditure has especially been on the rise in Muslim countries as Table 21.2 vividly brings out. Compare values in columns c and f horizontally to see how steep has been the rise in the purchase of arms over the period. These purchases mostly come from the Western countries. What the Arabs have been receiving as petro-dollars on one hand, they have been returning part to the givers for purchasing arms on the other. Who are these weapons for and why are they being used are the questions to ask.

Table 21.2 *Muslim countries and the purchase of arms (amount in billion USD)*

Purchaser country	1992			2001			2001/1992	
	Country import	Value of arms	% (b/a) 100	Country import	Value of arms	% (e/d) 100	Import d/a	Value of arms e/b
	a	b	C	d	e	f	g	H
Arabs	69.29	6.63	9.6	113.22	148.45	13.1	1.63	13.10
Others	129.10	3.95	3.0	230.96	7.36	3.3	1.79	1.92
All	169.39	10.58	5.5	344.14	155.81	6.5	1.73	2.13

Seller country	1992			2001			2001/1992	
	Country export	Value of arms	% (k/j) 100	Country export	Value of arms	% (n/m) 100	Export m/j	Value of arms n/k
	j	k	L	m	n	p	r	S
USA	420.82	25.57	5.6	1,356.30	63.75	4.7	3.22	2.71
UK	190.48	6.29	3.3	418.99	7.96	1.9	2.20	2.27

Source: Constructed using the data extracted from WDR 2002 and World Development indicators 2003.

Next to defence is the expenditure on development. Let us see what fiscal policy can do to achieve the goals.

1. **Capital formation**: It is an important requirement for economic development. Capital formation is a function of investment which needs curtailment of consumption to save more. Thus, in poorer economies, development is not possible without tears. Compulsory contributions employees have to make to pension funds or for health insurance constitute assortment of forced savings on the community. Savings also come from the commercial departments of the government. In some countries, public enterprises make substantial contributions to public revenue. For example, Indian Railways has to pay a 4% annual dividend to the Centre on capital sunk in running the services, from before independence in 1947. The government can use fiscal policy to promote **voluntary savings**. Tax concessions in the form of lower rates, exemptions, allowances and rebates on savings are often used. Unit trusts are run and small savings programmes are launched. Borrowings—internal and external—encouraging foreign capital inflow and obtaining remittances from nationals working abroad have become major sources of capital formation in many countries. Fiscal policy plays a vital role in all these areas.

   > Some of the important non-defense objectives of public expenditure are capital formation, workers training and infrastructural development.

2. **Equitable distribution**: It is essentially the perceptions of justice or equity in the distribution of income and wealth and

how to achieve the same that have divided the world into various economic systems and their shades. In democratic market-run societies, including the Islamic variations, distributive justice is also the core economic issue. Taxing the rich and spending the money more to benefit the poor is a thumb rule of fiscal administration. It wears different garbs, but the objective is the same—transferring welfare from the rich to the poor. Public transport, means of communications, fixation of minimum wages, fair price shops, low cost housing, mid–day school meals, public health networks, poor houses, social security arrangements and the like are all meant to ameliorate the condition of the poor to narrow the gap between them and the rich. But the gap within and among nations is still vulgar and in many ways, tends to widen.

3. **Economic stability**: A leading objective of fiscal policy; where it intimately interfaces with monetary policy managed by the central bank of the country on behalf of the government, is the maintaining of the internal and external value of the domestic currency. We owe the place of importance public expenditure has gained in economic matters globally to the writings of J.M. Keynes culminating in his *General Theory of Employment, Interest and Money* (1936). He explained how public expenditure by raising aggregate demand can play the crucial role in the determination of national income and employment in developed countries; how it could be used as a lever to lift the economy out of recession. He argued that the increase in public expenditure under recessionary conditions on public works or on any other head—even defence—will lead to a multiple increase in income and employment. Figure 21.8 helps explain the multiplier effect of public expenditure. Notice that increase in income Y is more than the increase in public expenditure, $\Delta_2 > \Delta_1$ such that $\Delta_2/\Delta_1 > 1$.

> J.M. Keynes accorded the rightful place to public expenditure in fighting economic stability.

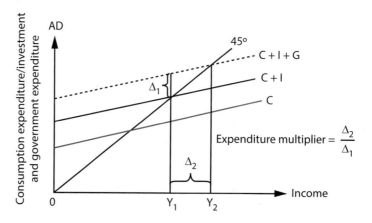

Figure 21.8 *Government expenditure multiplier of income*

21.11   ISLAM AND FISCAL POLICY

Is there any similarity between conventional and Islamic fiscal policies? We have already shown in the earlier chapter that there can be much in common of the anti-cyclical monetary measures in a dual financial system. Likewise, manipulating effective demands for augmenting that policy too can be pursued with appropriate adjustments to meet Islamic requirements. The primary difference between the two is revenue sources and expenditure priorities as *maqasid* of Shari'ah are not entirely commensurate with secular objectives of economic policies; adjustments have to be made.

> Islam never had a fiscal policy as we understand it today. In fact, given the socio-economic conditions of the early Islam, there was little deliberation on having a policy.

Four main sources of Islamic government revenue are taxation, *zakat, jizyah* and government service fees. Other sources are equity financing, public enterprises, *kharaj, al-ushr, waqf* and *sadaqah*. We will discuss them below.

Government expenditure from the Islamic perspective covers many areas, permanent as well as modern, that need to be financed from government revenue. The areas are also explained.

Exercise 21.4

Which statement regarding Islamic finance is incorrect?
  (i) Equity financing is encouraged in Islam but the Islamic state must be selective on the kind of equity allowed by Islamic principle.
  (ii) Tax is a major source of government revenue in a modern Islamic welfare state.
  (iii) *Zakat* revenue can serve all the fiscal needs of an Islamic state.

Exercise 21.5

The following are related to Islamic fiscal policy. Choose the incorrect statement.
  (i) Public expenditure of an Islamic state must be welfare oriented.
  (ii) Decision on public expenditure should be left only to the state.
  (iii) Public expenditure should aim for full realization of the goals of an Islamic state.

21.11.1   Sources of Revenue

1. **Taxation**

   Taxation is a major source of government revenue in a modern Islamic state. The government has the right to impose taxes

Sources of revenue were land or trade based. Zakat collections were enough to meet all the needs of a welfare state of the Islamic concept. At one stage, the prosperity due to conquests was so widespread that there were no people to receive zakat distributions in the land.

because it is responsible for the fulfilment of the needs of its citizen such as education, health, infrastructure, housing, research and development, and to raise capital in accordance with the level of socio-economic status of the country concerned. The classical Islamic scholars also give justifications for taxation as a source of revenue. Imam Malik, among others, is said to be the advocate of taxation. He says: *If there were no funds in the treasury or the needs of the army increased above the capacity of the treasury, the state has the right to levy taxes on the rich up to the level that satisfies the need immediately and until the revenue of the treasury appears.* (See Mohammad Abu Zahra, Imam Malik, Cairo; 1963, p. 400–01)

There should not be any injustice involved with taxation policy in an Islamic state, for example, even if they have the right to impose taxes on the poor, it should minimize their burden. The bulk of tax revenue should come from the rich because they are more capable to contribute, i.e. direct taxes should be more stressed than indirect taxes normally borne by the poor. Similarly, the imposition of taxes must not kill incentives to work.

2. **Zakat**

Zakat is an obligatory financial levy on all surplus wealth and agricultural income of the Muslims. Its objective is to provide financial support to specified categories of people such as the poor and the needy. It is charged at varying rates and collected by the state. It is levied at the rate of 2.5% on all financial assets and stock-in-trade of business, at the rate of 10% on all agricultural produce of rain and at 5% on the produce of artificially irrigated cultivation. The rates differ for livestock reared for sale. *Zakat* is like tax and is simple to administer. *Zakat* rate is fixed for each type, i.e. it is just like proportional tax, the actual money paid to *zakat* centres vary to the amount of wealth/income one owns. Again the impact is direct to the recipient and of course to the national income of a country.

Zakat is a major instrument for providing social security, eradicating poverty, curbing excessive income disparities and stimulating economic activity by transferring a certain amount of purchasing power to the have-nots. There are two types of *zakat*: *zakat fitr* and *zakat al-maal*. *Zakat fitr* is *zakat* on self and is paid during the month of Ramadan by the lead of a family for himself and his dependents. This *zakat* is solely for consumption by the poor and needy so that they could celebrate *Id-ul-Fitr* feast.

Zakat al-maal is *zakat* on wealth of Muslim payable after the ownership is above the specified length of time (haul) and the wealth has reached the specified limit (*nisab*). Types of *zakat* are shown in Figure 21.9.

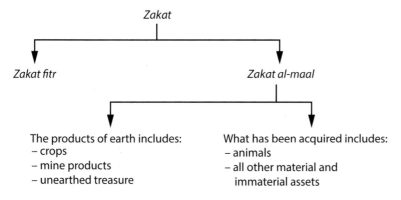

Figure 21.9 *Types of zakat*

In Malaysia, the most common wealth heads subject to *zakat* payment are as follows:

- Personal income (e.g. salary),
- Goods in trade and business,
- Animals and livestock,
- Crops,
- Savings,
- Gold and silver,
- Investments (i.e. shares/stock), and
- EPF.

Uses of *zakat* collection

Zakat fund can only be given to eight categories of recipients (asnaf). This is clearly stated in *Al-Quran*:

> *Zakat is for the poor (faqir) and the needy (miskin), and those employed (amil) to administer and collect it, and the new converts (muallaf), and those in the bondage (riqab) and those in debt (gharim) and in the cause of Allah (fisabilillah), and the way farer (ibn al-sabil), a duty ordained by Allah, and Allah is the all-knowing, the wise* (Sura Al-tauba: 60).

During recession or inflation those affected may approach zakat centre for help as they may now be categorized as the poor or the needy. Similarly those with debt may approach zakat centre.

3. ***Jizyah***

Jizyah was the tax the non-Muslim adults living in an Islamic state had to pay in the early days of Islam as they were exempted from military duties. This was then customary in the tribal culture. The Islamic government provided the security to their lives and properties and ensured all other social rights.

However, *jizyah* was gradually abolished as Muslim rule spread to vast areas of the globe. It was abolished in India under the reign of Akbar the Great who obtained a *fatwa* (religious edict) from the *Al-Azhar* school for its abolition. Akbar had non-Muslims in his army and administration, and had taken a Hindu princess as one of his wives.

4. **Service fees**

   In the modern world, many social and economic services are provided by the government and these are partly covered by fees charged by the government. However, the fees charged should not exceed the cost of services given to the public and only permissible services are allowed.

5. *Kharaj* **(tax on land)**

   Kharaj is a tax on agricultural land. It was a sort of rental fee on the land that becomes a property of an Islamic government as a result of its liberation by Muslim troops. Muslim jurists agreed that such land be kept as public property and be taxed so that future Muslims may benefit from these lands. The rate for tax depended on the qualities of land such as the level of fertility, irrigation requirement, etc. Today, no such need exists and *kharaj* has become a defunct source of state income.

6. *Al-ushr*

   Al-ushr is a commercial or business tax—which is similar to export and import tax. It is collected from three different traders. For traders from foreign countries the rate is 10% a year, for non-Muslim local traders the rate is 5% a year and for local Muslim traders the rate is 2.5% a year.

21.12   PUBLIC EXPENDITURE AND ISLAM

An Islamic government, like others, is responsible for a number of economic functions. The revenue collected from taxation, *zakat*, etc. will be spent on the needs of the country and the people in accordance with Islamic principles. The basic imperative in public expenditure is that an Islamic state must be welfare oriented and aimed at a fuller realization of the goal of an Islamic state which is to establish a good society with justice, tranquillity and security.

It is therefore important that any decision on public expenditure be made in a democratic way which would necessitate the need for consultation with relevant people on common interest as it is the people's money, trusted with the government.

An Islamic government cannot embark on any project prohibited by Shari'ah or that may jeopardize the Islamic environment and public interest.

Listed below are eight permanent heads of government expenditure of an Islamic state:

1. Defence,
2. Law and order,
3. Justice,
4. Public administration,

5. Basic needs fulfilment,
6. *Da'wah* activities,
7. Enjoining right conduct and forbidding wrong, and
8. Fulfilment of socially obligatory duties when the private sector fails to perform.

There are another five heads of essential expenditure of an Islamic state in the modern era. These are:

1. Protection of the environment,
2. Economic development,
3. Scientific research,
4. Subsidies for priority sectors, and
5. Expenditure and stabilization policies.

It must be noted here that public expenditure in an Islamic state must follow priorities, i.e. the necessary (*dharuriah*), the needs (*hajiah*), the commendable (*tahsiniah*) and the luxury (*kamaliah*). The necessary is to be given priority followed by the needs. The needs take precedence over the commendable. Expenditure functions of an Islamic state are classified into three groups. These are:

1. Expenditure functions assigned by the Shari'ah on a permanent basis,
2. Expenditure functions derived from the Shari'ah on the basis of the institution of *ijtihad* for the present situations, and
3. Expenditure functions assigned to the government by the people through the process of consultation.

Summary

- Government plays an important role in an economy in identifying its goals and in achieving them. For performing this role effectively, the government raises revenue using various means and spends the money to meet the given goals. Government actions concerning revenue raising and expenditure allocation to various uses constitute its fiscal policy.

- Government obtains its revenue from a variety of sources. They include taxes, loans, fees and fines, profit from public enterprises, foreign capital inflow and grants.

- Government spends money on defence, healthcare, education and civil administration, internal security arrangements and dispensation of justice.

- The ultimate objective of fiscal policy operations taken as a unit is to maximize net social advantage.

- Several theories of charging taxes have been in advocacy over time and space. Ultimately, the ability to pay won general acceptance. Progressive taxation that divides taxable income ordered slabs and charges tax on increasing rates as we move from the lower to the higher slabs. Flat rate on all incomes or proportional taxation is regressive. Its real burden is more on lower income groups.

- Taxes are broadly classified as direct and indirect. Taxes on income, wealth, property, inheritance and windfalls are examples of direct taxes. Taxes on commodities—their production, sale, purchase or transfer, import or export, and the like are indirect taxes.

- One distinction between direct and indirect taxes is on the basis of their shift-ability. People like to shift the money burden of the tax they are obliged to pay to others, if possible. If others can be made to pay the tax fully or partly, *incidence of taxation* to that extent is on them. It is not possible to shift direct taxes to others; indirect taxes can be shifted via the price mechanism.

- How much of an indirect tax, say an excise duty, can be shifted to the buyer of a product depends on the relative elasticity of its demand and supply. The more elastic the demand relative to supply, the greater will be the share of the sellers in the payment and vice versa.

- Another factor affecting tax shifting is the law of returns (costs) applying to the production of the commodity. In the case of constant returns, the supply is perfectly elastic; the buyer will pay the tax. Under increasing returns, the incidence will be more on the buyer. Under diminishing returns, relative elasticity of demand and supply will be decisive.

- If we know the values of the demand and supply elasticity, it can be established that the sellers share of tax T will be $\dfrac{E_{DP} - E_{SP}}{E_{SP}}$, and the remaining will be the share of the buyers.

- *Sukuk* has attracted much attention of governments across countries—Islamic and non-Islamic—as a source of revenue and is seen as Islamic bonds. This money contribution source carries both economic and political advantages.

- The main sources for raising revenue in Islamic public finance, in additional to *zakat*, are disposable income, goods in trade, livestock, crops, savings, gold and silver, investments and EPF.

- Heads for expenditure are many and varied but special concern is about the fulfilment of basic needs plus environmental care, reduction in income and wealth inequalities and helping the weak and deprived.

- In Islamic public finance, both sources of revenue and expenditure get their direction from the intention of promoting the objectives of the Shari'ah.

Glossary

Ability to pay One principle of taxation is that it should be so structured that it is least felt by the payers and is non-discriminatory in fact and perception. Three bases were initially discussed in the literature as commensurate with the principle: Tax according to benefit received by the payer, charge to cover the cost of service and take from each according to his/her ability to pay. The first two soon ran into disrepute for a variety of reasons, especially because of their link with benefit received. Tax being a general contribution had to be independent of a *quid pro quo*. Thus, to scholars and ordinary people alike, the common sense principle appealed: let those who can, pay the taxes. This is the essence for providing finance for the common good.

Dead weight This is not a joyous expression. What does it mean? It is coined by the proponents of public non-interference in the operations of the markets, say through taxation. Tax imposition tends to reduce output which could contribute to increasing social welfare. Taxation eliminates such gain and therefore kills the fruition of productive effort. However, such formulations do not see the live impact of public expenditure made possible by dead weight theorem on public welfare.

Government budget Budget presentation of the central government of a country is an annual exercise in most countries. It contains the income expenditure briefs of the preceding year, proposals for raising money and allocations for the current year plus a review of the performance and future programs and policies of the government.

Incidence of taxation Theoretically, one can visualize two sorts of burdens the payment of a tax may impose on the payer. The money burden is obvious. The pocket is lightened by the payment—one can purchase less goods and services including entertainment than before. *Value in exchange* is reduced. But the loss of the same value in exchange may inflict on the payers different loss of value-in-use. Such losses constitute the *real burden* of a tax. Admittedly, real burden is the measure of the merits of a tax. However, despite this recognition, equalization of real tax burden of taxpayers cannot be measured and the concept has little practical value. Discussions are thus restricted to who bears the money burden of a tax. This burden can be transferred to others via incorporation into contracts for sale and purchase of goods. Whether the shifting will be complete or partial, and to what extent will depend on the relative elasticity of demand and supply of the product as also the law of returns applying in the production of the commodity.

Public debt Public borrowing has become an increasing source of public finance. Government can borrow money in the domestic market from native financiers but it can also borrow from external sources. Internal borrowing poses few problems: loans and their repayment are essentially like inter-pocket money transfers in an economy. Foreign debts have been on the rise and present in developing countries.

Tax A tax is a compulsory payment under the law to any public authority in a specified jurisdiction of a country without any direct benefit to the payer as compensation. A tax can be levied as payable by an economic entity—individual, business, or institution—the basis of charge being income, wealth, and commodities produced or sold. A tax is computed on ex post measurable values only. Taxes can be progressive, proportional or regressive. Tax evasion and tax avoidance is a general tendency among the people.

Concepts for Review

- *Awqaf*
- Basic need
- Equal absolute sacrifice
- Impact of a tax
- Land revenue
- Nature of *zakat*

- Progressive taxation
- Proportional taxes
- Tax burden
- Tax shifting
- *Ushr*
- *Zakat*

Case Study   21.1

Voluntary Taxes

With compulsory taxes absorbing so high a proportion of income, it may appear paradoxical to speak of voluntary taxes. But what is a government lottery, if not a voluntary tax? Certainly, a person may avoid the tax by not participating in the lottery.

The state of New York spends millions of dollars each year to try to prevent illegal gambling. One might conclude that the lawmakers believe gambling is an evil which should be suppressed. But no; we find the state permitting and even encouraging certain types of gambling. Bingo is permitted under certain conditions and betting at race tracks where the state gets a heavy 'cut' is encouraged. And now, the state-wide lottery to raise money for 'education'! The state felt it needed more general revenue than it could raise through its many tax sources. So, why not try a 'voluntary' tax like a lottery, and call it 'education'? This might remove the onus for some who think gambling is a little bit evil, and who do not realize that this is just another way of swelling the general revenue of the state.

Source: W. M. Curtiss, (1967), *Taxation Theory*, <http://www.fee.org/the_freeman/detail/taxation-theory>, accessed 30 September 2014.

Case Questions

1. We have defined taxes as compulsory payments to the state from those entities on which taxes are levied. In what sense then is a state lottery called a voluntary tax? Explain.
2. Lotteries are regarded as unethical. Why do governments then resort to raising revenue through lotteries, especially for such a noble cause as education? Explain.
3. Give some examples of legal and illegal gambling. Does Islam allow any?

Case Study   21.2

An Alternative Theory of Government

There doubtless are those who look upon taxation as a means of redistributing wealth, in the belief that some have too much income and some too little. The progressive income tax is an expression of this belief, as are current discussions of a guaranteed annual income for all.

The use of tax policy for social control—for levelling wealth—is not a new development. The US official who said recently he would take property from those who had more than they need and give it to those who do not have enough, was merely expressing the major tenet of socialism.

The alternative theory of government, increasingly popular among Americans, would plunder the property of individuals for the supposed benefit of others. This is socialism. And the tax policy of socialism is to confiscate all private property.

Source: W. M. Curtiss, (1967), *Taxation Theory*, <http://www.fee.org/the_freeman/detail/taxation-theory>, accessed 30 September 2014.

Case Questions

1. What the second paragraph in the passage labels as the 'major tenet of socialism' is in fact Islamic. Do you agree? Give reasons for your answer.

2. If you do not agree with the statement in the above question, what in your opinion are the Islamic ways of reducing present income and wealth inequalities in modern societies?

Test Questions

21.1   Globalization, privatization and liberalization have been the dominant undercurrent increasingly shaping economic policies across countries until a decade ago. But there seems to be a reversal of this trend, especially in the developing and emerging economies, why? Discuss in the light of Islamic position on the issue.

21.2   What in your opinion should be the characteristics of a good tax system? Do you think that the tax system of your country meets the requirements of such a system? Explain and illustrate.

21.3   What is incidence of taxation? Explain how the incidence of a commodity tax is affected by the relative elasticity for its demand and supply using a diagram.

21.4   What do you understand by dead weight of tax? Explain using a diagram. What in your opinion is the economic consequence of dead weights?

21.5   What are or should be the objectives of fiscal policy? In what ways do these objectives differ from mainstream objectives of fiscal policy? Compare and contrast.

21.6   Distinguish *zakat* from a tax. Is it appropriate to call *zakat* a tax? Elaborate the reasons for your answer.

21.7 You are provided with the following information about the business of a fig importer.

Demand function, $Q_D = 380 - 20P$

Supply function, $Q_S = 80 + 30P$

Government imposes a per unit import duty, $t = 0.6$

Following the procedure of the examples in this chapter, show the division of tax between the sellers and the buyers in the domestic market.

21.8 Write explanatory notes on the following:

(a) Equal sacrifice principle in taxation,

(b) Direct and indirect taxes,

(c) Deficit financing, and

(d) Crowding out.

Web Exercise

Search the Internet for the US Economic Stimulation Programme and write a note on its current position.

Forward Link

The monetary and fiscal policies discussed in the preceding chapters have a profound influence on the shape and behaviour of macroeconomic variables and the character of the overall equilibrium of the economy. This equilibrium is deeply affected by the way fiscal policy of a country affects income distribution. And, it is this issue that constitutes the subject matter of the next chapter.

CHAPTER 22

National Income Distribution

LEARNING OUTCOMES

This chapter should enable the student to understand:

- Income distribution in a macroeconomic framework
- Measurement of income inequalities
- Limitations of measurement
- Inequalities in income distribution within a nation
- How growth is related to distributional equity
- Impact of income generation process on the state of distribution.
- Influence of structure of distribution on income generation
- Why income inequality differs among countries

22.1 INTRODUCTION

> More important economic issues are claimed to arise in the field of distribution of income rather than in the area of its production.

In the area of production, *cooperation* between nature and human beings determines the outcome: the flow of goods and services which people need to satisfy their wants. On the contrary, in the area of distribution it is the *conflict* of interests that dominates the scene; for, at issue is the sharing of what factors in combination produce. It is the distribution of income over time and space that raises perceptions of justice and injustice and generates socio-political heat, sometimes leading even to revolution. Formal interest among economists in the dynamics of personal (size) and functional distribution of income goes back to the times of David Ricardo (1772–1823), if not earlier. He thought that the more interesting and important issues for economists to attend arise in the field of distribution, not production.

However, the interest in income distribution issues has been up and down over the years around the question: whether or not price theory leaves any scope for a separate theory of distribution? Once the apparatus of demand and supply simultaneously determines the prices of output and input needed to produce it, the distribution issue is automatically resolved. That price mechanism automatically brings into existence a pattern of income distribution in market economies no one disputes. What is in dispute is the efficacy of such patterns of distribution from the viewpoint of social well-being: is it fair, equitable and just? It is this issue that has led to the revival of interest in distributional studies, recently more at the macro level.

The question of achieving equity (fairness) in income distribution was included among the major macroeconomic policy goals in Chapter 14. We showed the linkage of personal or size distribution of income with their functional distribution. Studies on functional income distribution mostly focus on *theorizing*, personal income in particular. Here, disparities within and between nations are matters of *concern*.

Income distribution is one of the subjects that constitute among others an important overlap between micro and macro branches of economics. Many introductory books on macroeconomics do not discuss national income distribution, but we have included the topic in the present work because of its growing importance in the present era of globalization. The following verses of the Qur'an unmistakably draw attention to achieving distributional equity at the macro level.

Wealth is to serve useful purposes and not to be accumulated in a few hands that it may not concentrate and circulate only among those of you who are rich (Quran 59:7).

In their wealth there is due share acknowledged by them for such as who ask (for help) and such as are deprived [of what is good in the life] (Quran 70:24).

So give his due share (haq) to kinsman, and to the needy and to the homeless. That is best for those who seek the pleasure of Allah (Quran 30:38).

In this chapter, we raise and seek answers to the following questions: How can we measure income inequalities? Does growth in a market economy necessarily increase inequalities? Do inequalities in their turn affect growth? How do market imperfections affect both growth and distribution? While these and the like are the basic questions for macroeconomics, they have only recently become the focal points of attention in literature.

> Income distribution for macroeconomics is functional but it affects personal income significantly and therefore, savings, investments and growth patterns.

22.2 MEASUREMENT OF INEQUALITIES

There are a number of techniques for measuring the inequalities in the distribution of income. However, most of them are based in some way on what is known in economics as the Lorenz curve. It is a graph where the cumulative proportion of income (y%) is plotted from below, upwards, against corresponding cumulative proportions (x%) of people having that income (y%) in the group. Figure 22.1 explains its construction using data from Pakistan presented at a conference in the year 2000. The figure uses the data presented in Table 22.1. The end points are the same in all such curves; the additional points are kept small in number—only three—as the purpose is to illustrate the construction procedure. A perfectly equal income distribution would be one where every person has the same income as another; any y% of society would always have a y% share of income. This is depicted by the straight line (y = x) labelled as the 'line of equal distribution' in the figure. On the other hand, income distribution would be perfectly unequal if one person has all the income and others have none. In that case, the curve would be at y = 0 for all x < 100%, and y = 100% at the corner where x also equals 100%. Thus, in the case of 'perfect inequality' the curve will be the two sides of the triangle which has the line of equal distribution as its hypotenuse.

Table 22.1 *Population and income shares in Pakistan, 1989–1990*

Population share		Income share	
Individual %	Cumulative %	Individual %	Cumulative %
00.00	00.00	00.00	00.00
41.39	41.39	16.99	16.99
37.56	78.95	33.62	50.61
15.33	94.28	25.01	75.62
5.72	100.00	24.38	100.00
100.00	–	100.00	–

Source: Zubair Hasan (2000), Comments on *Poverty elimination in an Islamic perspective: An applied general equilibrium approach*, Fourth International Conference on Islamic Economics and Finance, Loughborough University, UK.

The farther away the Lorenz curve from the line of equal distribution, the greater the inequalities in the distribution of income and vice versa. The Lorenz curve is a general technique that is handy for measuring and comparing inequalities in other areas of enquiry too; examples could be the distribution of land among cultivators, distribution of national wealth or the spread of examination grades among students.

The Lorenz curve essentially is a comparison graph. It does not provide a simple, single, numerical measure of inequality. However, an important quantitative measure—the *Gini coefficient*—is based on the Lorenz curve. We divide the area between the line of perfect equality and the Lorenz curve by the total area of the triangle (0, 100, 100) under that line to obtain the coefficient. Its value can vary from zero to one. If we multiply the coefficient by 100, we get what is called the *Gini index*. The larger the value of the Gini index, the greater the inequality of income and vice versa.

The Lorenz curve is a cumulative percentage diagram that uses a line of equal distribution to measure income inequalities in a society as a departure from that base.

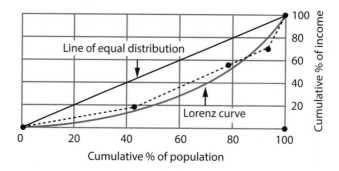

Figure 22.1 *An illustrative Lorenz curve: Pakistan 1989–1990*

It may however, be noted, that the method for calculating the Gini coefficient uses the (doted) cords joining the observed points in Figure 22.1. Thus, the area between the cords and the Lorenz curve is lost for the calculation. There is an inherent element of downward bias in the coefficient; it tends to show the inequalities smaller than the actual. However, this bias decreases as we increase through subdivisions the number of income groups, adding to the number of cords subdivisions would generate. Without showing the process of derivation, we state the formula for the Gini coefficient (G) as follows:

$$G = 1 - \sum_{i=1}^{n} p_i\,(z_i + z_{i-1}),\ z_0 = 0$$

Here p_i is any i proportion of population that gets the corresponding i proportion of income, i.e. z_i. We illustrate the application of this formula using the data given in Table 22.1.

Putting the values from Table 22.2 in the formula, we get: G = 1 − 0.6829 = 0.3117.

Table 22.2 *Calculation of Gini coefficient*

Population share		Income share		
Proportion (p_i)	Proportion (individual)	Cumulation 1 (z_i)	Cumulation 2 ($z_i + z_{i-1}$)	$p_i\,(z_i + z_{i-1})$
0.4139	0.1699	0.1699	0.1699	0.0703
0.3756	0.3362	0.5061	0.6760	0.2539
0.1533	0.2501	0.7562	1.4322	0.2196
0.0572	0.2238	10000	2.4322	0.1391
1.0000	1.0000	= 0.6829		

Exercise 22.1

The following data gives the percentage of cultivators and the corresponding percentage of land they possess in a Bangladeshi village. Construct a Lorenz curve and estimate the Gini index using the data.
- Per cent of population 36.8, 17.9, 17.2, 14.6, 12.3, 2.2
- Per cent of land held 1.6, 6.0, 9.5, 20.5, 22.4, 38.0

However, there are some serious limitations of inequality measurement in addition to those already indicated above. Some of these are discussed in Section 22.2.1.

22.2.1 Limitations

1. The data for Gini index construction emanates from sample of households living in *listed* dwellings; those covered are then surveyed with reference to their income and related information. Those who have no dwelling or live in unlisted ones are obviously excluded from the sample frame; they escape the survey net for income estimation.

2. Even if people reside in listed dwellings and are included in the sample, but are engaged in informal production or illegal activities—bribery, smuggling or stealing—their income from such sources would not be counted. Transfer payments may, on the other hand, be inadvertently included.

3. Independent household surveys such as conducted by researchers and data by the government often exhibit much divergence for the same group of income; considerable evidence is available on the point.

4. The non-response and wrong reporting, especially understatement of income is frequently noted in survey estimations. This is more likely to be the case on the upper end of the income scale. The rich may tend to conceal income especially where marginal tax rates are high.

5. The reporting time dimension for income from different sources is usually not the same in surveys, varying from a week to a year. It is obvious that the longer the reference period, the greater the chances of memory lapse and erroneous reporting.

6. If the survey is staggered over a long period, households will interpret, say a month, differently depending at what point they were surveyed during the period. Aggregation will not be uniform.

7. In many developing countries, households are not literate and most do not keep records of their income. Indirect methods for estimation are then used which may or may not give reliable results.

8. A perfectly equal distribution, as expressed by the diagonal line in the Lorenz curve is as unjust if not more, as a wide departure from it may show. For equal distribution, it rewards efficiency and inefficiency at the same rate, and treats all occupations equal, irrespective of skills required, hazards involved and training costs.

Thus, for the above and other reasons, the income estimates based on surveys are open to errors which may affect, at times seriously, the estimates of inequality and poverty. However, possibilities of errors have not deterred the use of the estimates or rendered them insignificant. Useful linkages between data of income distribution and macroeconomics

The Gini index is based on the ratio of area between the curve and the base line to the area of rectangle that contains the curve. It has a number of limitations.

theories and policies have long been established. Let us look at some points of interaction between them.

BOX 22.1

Macroeconomic Determinants of Inequality of Opportunity and Effort

Conventional wisdom predicts that changes in macroeconomic conditions significantly affect income inequality. However, the way in which macroeconomic conditions affect inequality depends on how these conditions influence the constituents of total inequality: inequality of opportunity (IO) and inequality of effort (IE). Real GDP and inflation rates are the most widely used factors in literature. To these, one may add for consideration outstanding consumer credits and public welfare and healthcare expenditures. Empirical studies show that real GDP and outstanding credits have a negative and significant effect upon IO and IE, while inflation has a positive and significant effect only on IE, and welfare expenditures have a negative and significant effect only on IO.

Source: Based on Marrero A. G. and Rodríguez, J. G. (2012), *Macroeconomic determinants of inequality of opportunity and effort in the US: 1970-2009*, working paper series, Society for the Study of Economic Inequality. <http://www.ecineq.org/milano/WP/ECINEQ2012-249.pdf>, accessed 5 June 2014.

22.3   GROWTH AND EQUITY RELATIONSHIP

Growth-equity relationship is still an unsettled matter in macroeconomics as the Kuznets curve has limitations.

The relationship between growth and income inequalities has especially been a subject of interest and investigation. More recently Simon Kuznets (1955) put forth the thesis that during the early stages of economic growth, the inequalities in the size of distribution of income would tend to grow, reaching a maximum, but in the later stages of growth they would tend to decline. Figure 22.2 depicts this inverted–U hypothesis of Kuznets. In part A, economy is in the early stages of development, as growth picks up pace, inequalities in the income distribution increase. This continues until they reach the peak, T. But as growth picks up pace, the gains begin the trickle down to the lower rungs of society. Beyond T, the economy tends to become self-propelling due to the increasing sufficiency of savings and investments. The Kuznets proposition has been put to empirical testing largely using cross country data at particular points of time. Time series analyses have been rather scant. In either case, results have largely been mixed. The difficulty is that one may never be sure at what level of income or growth rate a country would cross point T. In many countries, the much awaited trickle down does not take place though the rates of growth have been high. In both Malaysia and India, for example, inequalities tended to increase over short spans of spurting growth. But it can also be taken as evidence supportive of the position in part A of Figure 22.2.

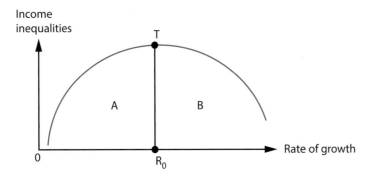

Figure 22.2 *Income inequalities and growth relationship*

However, on what happens in the long run, the evidence is inconclusive. Interestingly, the Indian economy seems to support the B part depiction of the Kuznets proposition. Figure 22.3, which is assembled using internet sources, bears ample testimony to the observation.

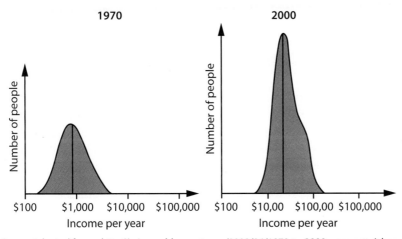

Source: Adapted from <http://mjperry.blogspot.com/2008/06/1970-to-2000-poor-got-richer-and rich.html>

Figure 22.3 *Income distribution change in India, 1970–2000*

The figure shows that under the reservation of economic opportunities for the lower caste and backward classes, their condition has visibly improved over the three decades of democratic planning—there is a marked shift of people to the right of the model income line with the income pyramid base not only shifting to higher income but becoming narrower too.

22.3.1   The Case of Malaysia

Malaysia presents another interesting and rather unique case of seeking distributive equity through social contract. It is of its own kind because here the 'haves' have voluntarily agreed to grant economic concessions to the 'have-nots,' i.e. a greater share in the national cake for reducing poverty and improving distribution. The underlying objective was the promotion of societal cohesion and harmony. The agreed policy of positive discrimination as it is sometimes called has of late been hailed as expedient on the international circuit as well. Positive discrimination took concrete shape in what came to be known as the New Economic Policy (NEP) launched in 1971 with a 20-year time span. It was basically designed to improve the economic status of Malays and other indigenous groups collectively known as *bumiputras* or the sons of soil.

> Growth and policies may cause reduction in income inequalities in the long-run: India is an illustrative case.

The concessions reserved for the group included the quotas in low cost housing, educational placements, corporate equity ownership, and preference in public sector services and contracts. During the 20 years run, the economic condition of the *bumiputras* did improve considerably but fell short of the target. So, in 1991 the policy was extended for another 10 years. A new government has taken over in March 2009 and in one of their recent announcements the racial classification of the population has been reverted to the one based on occupation: agriculturists, traders and businessmen.

Exercise 22.2

Focus on the peaks of the income distributions of 1970 and 2000 in Figure 22.3. Can you explain why the peak of 2000 is much taller than that of 1970? Notice that the difference in the height of the two distributions is much more than the difference in the width of their bases. What does this show in your opinion? Give reasons for your answer.

22.4   INCOME: GENERATION AND DISTRIBUTION

> Income distribution has a circular relationship with income generation.

In free-market economies incomes get distributed as fast as they are generated; the two processes tend to synchronize. This type of linkage between the two does not allow us to consider income distribution issues in isolation and creates a scenario of circular causation between them and related macro variables. The linkage between changes in macroeconomic variables such as factor shares, asset holdings, unemployment rates and rate of inflation on the one hand and the personal income distribution on the other is becoming increasingly complex. We discuss below some complexities arising from the linkage.

22.4.1 Asset Distribution

The distribution of productive assets—real and financial—or command over them gained through entrepreneurial activities before each production-distribution cycle starts becomes a crucial factor in determining the current income distribution patterns. Thus, unless the existing distribution of productive resources/assets remains iniquitous, measures to redistribute current incomes must remain an ever going struggle; a continuous fire fighting action that would never attack the source of fire. The distribution patterns of income generating assets, or more correctly of the ownership claims to them, are the result of evolution over the centuries. It needs both time and political will to transform it for promoting mass welfare.

22.4.2 Redistributive Measures and Intergeneration Equity

Redistributive measures that taxation and expenditure policies of the government entail not only tend to improve current income distribution, but have an impact on the future course of distributions also. This intergenerational impact of fiscal policies has recently emerged as an important concern in the formulation of what is termed as sustainable development. The idea broadly is that modern economies must grow at such a rate that resource exhaustion leaves the future generations to enjoy at least the same levels of living, if not higher as the present ones are enjoying. Notice that this view of development sees income equalization between generations via temporal distribution of resources; the renewal, where possible, plus preservation of resources have become the watch words in macroeconomic policy formulations.

> There is a two-way relationship between the generation of income and its distribution. Both affect each other.

22.4.3 Impact of Macroeconomic Variables on Income Distribution

It is easy to see that macroeconomic factors including price level fluctuations, state of employment, extent of capacity utilization, exchange rate changes, interest rate levels, public expenditure priorities and the like must and do affect in a significant manner the income distribution. The influence carriers of course are the discriminatory effects of the market system on various socio-economic groups and areas of production. Policies—monetary and fiscal—that are used for correcting macroeconomic disequilibria are also not distribution neutral. Whether the changes indicated would improve or mar income distribution depends on the direction and magnitude of the change.

> Monetary and fiscal policies for restoring equilibrium of the economy are not distribution neutral in most cases.

However, there is empirical evidence that high investment rates and improvement in terms of trade tend to improve income distribution. Policies designed to promote investment and growth in socially desirable segments of the economy—for example expenditure focused at the fulfilment of the basic needs of the masses like food, clothing, shelter, education and health care—may improve income distribution.

Presumably, noneconomic factors like religion and cultural heritage also influence income distribution in a noticeable way. For example, we found in a recent investigation that income disparities in Muslim countries are notably smaller than in other developing countries as Table 22.3 shows. The countries included in the study are those for which relevant data was available on a homogenous basis for the survey years. The lower income disparities in Muslim countries can presumably be attributed in part to the Islamic cultural heritage of benevolence, mutual help and care for the poor. Interestingly, the poverty incidence in Muslim countries for the same year was also lower in general on the criterion of income per head being less than one US dollar a day.

> Factors like religion and culture seem to influence income distribution.

BOX 22.2

Distribution of Income and Wealth – Capitalism, Socialism and Islam

There are numerous studies, related to distribution of income and wealth under capitalism and socialism/communism. While capitalism failed to ensure a fair distribution of income, a socialist economic system, despite succeeding in creating an egalitarian society, is essentially associated with a non-democratic state controlled economic system. As a whole, there is clear evidence that the reversal to capitalism and dominance of market economies, after failure of a socialist system in the USSR and Eastern Europe, is creating gross inequalities in distribution of income and wealth; though some, as a result of strong state intervention, are having a better distribution of income and wealth. Islamic economic system, not totally practiced anywhere in the world, is a non-state controlled economic system for a just and equitable distribution of income and wealth. The present study is an effort to show that how an Islamic economic system, if fully implemented, could deter excessive accumulation of wealth and also ensure an equitable distribution of income. The key variables of the system are *ushr/zakat*, elimination of interest and Islamic laws of inherence. There is visible dampening effect of zakat on accumulation of wealth besides reducing income inequalities. Elimination of interest is crucial to further reduce the inequality in distribution of income. Finally the elaborate inheritance laws of Islam distribute the accumulated wealth of a person and ensure that wealth is not concentrated in few hands. Unless all these three elements are put together and implemented in totality the expected impact on distribution of income and wealth would not be realized.

Source: S. Ghiasul Haq (2013), Distribution of income and wealth in Islam (abstract), *South East Asia Journal of Contemporary Business, Economics and Law,* Vol. 2, Issue 2 (June). *Asia Journal of Contemporary*

Table 22.3 *Income inequalities in Muslim and non-Muslim developing economies in 1994*

Country groupings	No. of countries	Mean population	Weighted mean of Gini indexes
1. Muslim	9	76.8 million	33.2%
2. Non-Muslim including India	20	79.6 million	44.1%
3. Non-Muslim excluding India	19	35.7 million	50.6%

Source: Calculations based on data in the World Development Report 1996, Tables 4 and 5.

22.4.4 Effects of Distribution on Macroeconomic Variables

Even as the two processes of income production and income distribution are involved in circular causation, the channels through which income distribution affects production of incomes have not attracted as much attention in the literature as those that operate in the opposite direction, i.e. from the side of production to distribution. The latter have been discussed above.

On the transmission line of influences from distribution to the income production process, we find the volume and composition of aggregate demand including the demand for financial assets. Current inequalities, economic and social, and also the changes therein, interact with macroeconomic variables. This interaction is considered central to alternating booms and depressions in modern economies. The current global meltdown may not be an exception: Batra (1987) rose to fame for his prediction that increasing concentration of wealth was going to push the world onto the path of depression sometime in 1990s. Is it that his prediction is now coming true, only delayed a little by the force of intervening events?

The causation circle we mentioned above closes with some aspects of the size distribution of incomes shaping some of the crucial macroeconomic variables, especially growth rates, price levels and employment. It is here that the functional distribution of incomes enters the picture because it influences the size distribution of incomes and also the macroeconomic variables like savings, investment and resource allocation. Market imperfections, unequal bargaining power of factors, asymmetric information and cyclical fluctuations all tend to make functional income distribution unfair. The inequity is summarized thus: 'Workers spend what they get; Capitalists get what they spend'. The quote implies that the earnings of the workers are hardly sufficient to make both ends meet with little scope for savings. On the other hand, returns to capital owners rise to cover not only their luxuries but leave

Economic and social inequalities interact with macro variables. This interaction is central to alternating booms and depressions in free enterprise economies.

Equity in functional distribution of incomes is essential for their fair personal distribution.

handsome saving margins as well. Fair functional income distribution is a pre-requisite for a fair size distribution of incomes.

Here public policies matter much. We have already noted the impact of reservations and positive discrimination policies in the Indian and Malaysian cases, respectively. In Malaysia, surveys of poverty dimension and location for remedial measures, attempt at wealth redistribution and encouragement of Islamic financing have also been other important factors with great potential and promise for the future.

22.5 LIMITATIONS AND PRECAUTIONS

We find in the literature many models analysing the linkages between income (and wealth) distribution and macroeconomics. They provide useful insights into the relationship. However, they have limitations and precautions which need to be considered to overcome or minimize them. They mostly relate to quality of data and variations. Some of these are as follows.

> Limitations of studies on functional income distribution are mostly related to the quality of macro data of variables and definitional issues.

1. Household surveys and national accounts statistics mostly are the primary sources of data for studying the linkage between income distribution and macroeconomic variables. These sources usually come up with different estimates for the same variable, say, in the category of income or expenditure. There may be a number of reasons for that, for instance, definitions of variables or the methods of their measurement may differ. The time point or range used for collection of information may not be identical. A reconciliation of the different data sets to the extent possible is needed before the data can be used in any inquiry. A careful comparison of definitions, coverage, time spans, imputation procedures, benchmarking and ratios employed in various sources is essential.

2. Household income data usually suffers from errors of measurement. Unbiased errors are self-cancelling but biased errors are cumulative as the size of the survey increases. Bias apart, household income estimates are also affected by cyclical fluctuations, even climatic conditions. Models of inequality using data unedited for errors of measurement, especially biased, and cycle effects may lack in reliability of results. Interpretive difficulties may innocuously create scope for misinterpretation.

3. The non-homogeneity of data makes cross country comparisons of inequalities all the more dubious. A method has been evolved to minimize the country survey differences arising from divergent definitions, sample designs and coverage. The method re-estimates the Gini coefficients making adjustments for the known gaps. The result of the exercise is what we call the 'adjusted Gini'.

The technique is complicated and its explanation is not provided in this introductory work. But it must be mentioned that the method of adjustment is not standardized and may differ from case to case.

4. Finally, in a long run view of the matter, income distribution and its links with the production process do not remain purely economic; social, political, demographic, technological and environmental concerns all enter the train to the welfare station.

22.6 CROSS COUNTRY INCOME INEQUALITIES

Cross country inequalities in income distribution refers to why in some countries the spread of incomes is less than it is in others, in other words, why is their Gini coefficient smaller? Inequalities are in general known to be lower in developed countries compared to the developing ones. But income disparities differ between countries within the *same* category, developed or developing. Recall, for instance, Table 1.3 of Chapter 1 which shows that the per capita income inequalities between the developed and developing countries were on the rise even as the widening speed is slowing down. We discuss below some reasons for this type of differences in income inequalities.

> Cross country differences in the inequalities of income are vast and inexplicable.

1. We begin with the assumption that in the short-run income inequalities arise due to factors independent of economic policies. The Kuznets curve we presented above is based on such an assumption; it takes into account the level of per capita income and related factors as *given* at a point in time. In other words, the curve relies on a *given* state of inequalities across nations. The long run dynamics that brings about changes in a *given* state contains such factors as income expansion, financial development, cyclical fluctuations, government consumption, state of education and population growth. The evolving situations are highly intricate and complex to analyse. The dynamic changes taking place in various countries differ and that makes income inequality divergences between them also change.

2. There is empirical evidence that (i) per capita income expansion tends to increase income disparities in all countries except those classified in the high income group of World Development Reports; (ii) financial development tends to mitigate income inequalities in all countries irrespective of the stage of economic development; there is no evidence supportive of the inverted-U hypothesis between the two; and (iii) finally, government consumption, openness of an economy, and illiteracy reduction tend to reduce income inequalities among nations.

3. Empirical evidence for Kuznets inverted-U hypothesis linking inequalities to growth is at best dubious. As a country develops, the actual inequalities curve tends to fall below the standard Kuznets curve: inequalities reduce faster than predicted. This happens not because of some characteristics inherent in the processes but because of deliberate social choice: societies prefer smaller inequalities as they become more and more affluent.

22.7 ISLAMIC ECONOMICS AND INCOME DISTRIBUTION

Islam does not separate material needs of human beings from their spiritual aspirations. While their worldly requirements—say for food, clothing and shelter—spur them to produce goods and services that would make living comfortable; their spiritual self asks them to be creative, benevolent and ethical. The two aspects of human life supplement each other. Real progress means their harmonious, supportive, balanced and incremental growth. Thus, the development of *human personality* is the essence of growth in Islam. It is not material needs of mankind that alone are unlimited—a point mainstream economics focuses on—there is also, in principle, no limit to spiritual urges like creativity, benevolence, commitment and sacrifice for a noble cause. Neglect of one at the cost of or preference over the other results from how one sees the world and understands the purpose of life. In any case, there is a generic correlation between the two types of human needs and Islam seeks to keep them united. The combination gives rise to provisions that focus on and help enforce distributive justice in an Islamic system such that the wealth may not remain circulating among the rich of the community. The impact of such Islamic norms presumably has reflections in Table 22.3.

Some of these provisions we have already discussed in the preceding chapters. Some others affecting distribution at the macro level are briefly discussed below.

First, modern development models convey an implicit message that present consumption is at the cost of future output. It is argued that restraints on consumption are needed to release resources for savings and investment to push up income expansion. However, the distributional levelling which is central to Islam transfers income from the rich to the poor and reduces the savings potential of the economy; development suffers.

This argument is ill-informed. Along with the benevolent expenditure on helping the poor, Islam preaches moderation in consumption that must mitigate the impact of transfers on savings. It also condemns hoarding of wealth and encourages investment spending. Moreover, when the level of earnings is as low as it is in many developing economies, the distinction between consumption and investment is blurred. Private consumption may improve health of the workers and add to their muscle power raising their productivity the same way as investment would do. Second, and this links us with the above point, the fulfilment of the basic needs of every national that include food, clothing, shelter, education and medical care is an Islamic imperative. In fact, Iranian constitution makes this eventually obligatory on the government. The provision has far reaching policy implications. It demands a preferential treatment for basic needs in resource allocation imposing radical changes in the production structure of an economy. Technological priorities might change. Fulfilment of basic needs provides the basis for fixation of minimum wages. Distributional disparities would decline. Labour capabilities must rise pushing up growth.

Finally, Islam in principle stands for sharing of profit with labour to bring wages closer to be reasonable on the contribution criterion. Zubair Hasan argued in his *Theory of Profit* (1975) for sharing to improve functional distribution of income but the idea got currency in 1983 with the publication of Martin Lawrence Weitzman's *Share Economy: Conquering Stagflation.* The book was hailed by some as the best economic idea of the 20th century. Sharing of business profits with labour under variant schemes has become common to win workers' loyalty, increase productivity and industrial peace. Firms now see profit in sharing profit.

> Islam also provides a scheme to reduce income inequalities in society at the macro level.

Summary

- Factors of production cooperate in the act of producing goods and services; there is a harmony of interests in production. In contrast, the distribution of income that production generates is marked with conflict. The area is characterized with controversy and confusion.

- Complexities are all the more Increased because the acts of production and distribution in an economy take place simultaneously; distribution thus depends on systemic arrangements.

- In free-market economies, price mechanism brings about the distribution of income at a minimum social cost but the efficacy of distribution is often questioned on the basis of equity norms and social perceptions.

- Personal distribution of income raises real issues but concerns for functional distribution are no less important because of its close linkage with the former. Personal income distribution cannot be equitable unless functional distribution of income too meets the norms of equity.

- To consider how fair the actual distribution of income is we take perfect equality as the benchmark to measure the departures. The benchmark is questionable unless we can show the differences of attitudes, skills, hazards involved, and costs of training in money and time do not matter in deciding compensation.

- The relationship between growth and income disparities is of a dubious kind. The relationship between the two that the Kuznets curve depicts is not conclusive; departures from the prediction it makes have not been uncommon on the ground over time and space.

- The Lorenz curve provides departures from perfect equality. It is a comparison graph; it does not give a precise numerical measure of deviation from the norm. But it helps in deriving such a measure: the Gini coefficient. The measure is obtained by dividing the area between the line of equal distribution and the actual curve by half the area of the rectangle that the line divides into two equal parts. The value of the coefficient varies from zero to one. If we multiply the coefficient by 100, we get the Gini index.

- The Gini index as well as the Lorenz curve both suffer from some serious limitations relating to the comparability and reliability of the data used to construct them. Different surveys that are used to collect the data often come up with divergent results. Household income data usually has errors of measurement.

- There is a two-way relationship between acts of income generation and its distribution at the macro level. Non-economic factors like religious beliefs and cultural heritage are found affecting income distribution, both personal and functional.

- Changes in macroeconomic variables including price level fluctuations, state of employment, interest rate levels, public expenditure priorities and exchange rate variations significantly affect the patterns of income distribution.

- From the side of distribution, it is the volume and composition of aggregate demand, including the demand for financial assets that constitute the crucial elements in the drama: current inequalities—economic and social—and the subsequent changes in them interact with various economic variables. Understanding this interaction is fundamental for explaining the kind of economic turmoil the world is facing today.

- Cross country income inequalities issue seeks to answer such questions as to why income spread in one country is less than in others. For instance, they are known to be smaller in developed countries than in the developing ones. Here a distinction is made between short and long run reasons.

- It is often suggested that short-run factors affecting income inequalities shape the Kuznets curve. At each point it refers to a given state of inequalities. In contrast, the long-run view of wealth is to serve useful purposes and not to be accumulated in a few hands, *that it may not concentrate and circulate only among those of you who are rich* (Quran 59:7). *In their wealth there is due share acknowledged by them for such as who ask [for help] and such as are deprived [of what is good in the life]* (Quran 70:24). *So give his due share [haq] to kinsman, and to the needy and to the homeless. That is best for those who seek the pleasure of Allah* (Quran 30:38). This deals with the socio-economic dynamics moving the economy from one state of inequality to another.

- The long run impact on distribution comes from sources such as income expansion, financial development, cyclical fluctuations, government expenditure patterns, spread of education and population growth.

- Islam does not isolate material needs of human beings from their spiritual aspirations; it treats life as a composite whole. It rather makes the fulfilment of material needs essential for achieving spiritual solace. The Qur'an says that *buy with the wealth that God has provided you the home of the hereafter and forget not your portion of this world*. The two aspects of human life supplement each other.

- The development of human personality—a balanced combination of material and spiritual attainments—is the essence of the concept of growth in Islamic economics. This could be possible through the fulfilment of the basic needs of all humans for food, clothing, shelter, education and health care.

- Social and economic justice demands minimization of inequalities of all kinds, especially in the distribution of wealth and incomes; Islamic economic system has ample provisions to achieve that objective. It asks, for example, implementation of fair wages, profit sharing with labour and income redistribution through spending in the way of God.

- Differences in the approach to income distribution among various social orders essentially arise from systemic differences between them.

Glossary

Equity in income distribution In the context of income distribution, equity refers to each factor getting a fair share in the total national income. Various criteria to judge fairness have been proposed from time to time but share according to contribution is more widely accepted as valid. Since it is very difficult if not impossible to isolate the contribution of a particular factor from the aggregate, equity has largely become a matter of perceptions, both individual and societal.

Functional income distribution Functional income distribution is the division of national income among the factors of production such as between wages and profits. Functional income distribution is a significant factor in the determination of size or personal income distribution.

Gini index It is obtained by multiplying the Gini coefficient by 100. The coefficient is obtained through division of the area between the line of equal distribution and the Lorenz curve by the total area of the triangle to which the equality line is the hypotenuse.

Kuznets hypothesis This hypothesis says that in the initial stages of economic development inequalities in the distribution of incomes increase as growth in per capita picks up pace but the relationship is reversed—inequalities tend to narrow down—after a threshold is crossed. The hypothesis is found weak on empirical testing. There is also much confusion on the short-term and long-term aspects of the proposition.

Lorenz curve It is a graphic method of measuring inequalities from a benchmark that assumes perfect equalities to be the ideal state of income distribution in an economy. It is a cumulative frequency curve based on factual cumulative percentages of people associated with the corresponding cumulative income they receive.

Concepts for Review

- Cross country comparisons
- Equity in income distribution
- Functional income
- Gini index
- Globalization
- Income spread
- Kuznets hypothesis
- Lorenz curve
- Positive discrimination
- Redistribution
- Terms of trade

Case Study 22.1

Economic Growth and Income Inequalities in Malaysia

The poverty alleviation and inequality reduction efforts in Malaysia have met with mixed success. For instance, in peninsular Malaysia the income inequality measured by Gini coefficient was 0.493 in 1970. It progressively reduced to 0.446 due to government efforts. The narrowing of disparities was accounted for by the fall in the share of the top 20% in the GNP combined with an improvement in the share of 40% in the middle and lower middle income groups. The per capita income growth rate over the long period of two decades was 4.7%.

In contrast, after 1990 the inequality reduction process took a u-turn. The Gini coefficient for Malaysia started climbing up. It rose to 0.459 in 1993 and touched 0.522 in 1997. The average per capita income growth was the highest at 5.9% for the closing decade of the century. After the 1998 financial crisis the growth of the economy slowed down and the Gini coefficient fell to 0.492 in 1999 and further to 0.480 in 2000.

Source: Hasan, Z. (2007), Fifty Years of Malaysian Economic Development: Policies and Achievements, *Review of Islamic Economics*, 11; 2: p.101–18.

Case Questions

1 Do you notice any difference between the long term and short term relationship of growths in per capita income and reduction in inequalities? Explain your answer.

2 What relationship do you find between the two variables: pace of economic growth and income inequalities? Give reasons to support your answer.

3 Can you relate in any manner, the data results with the inverted–U hypothesis of Kuznets that Figure 22.2 depicts? Explain.

Case Study 22.2

Spatial Disparities and Development Policy

Economic activity is increasingly concentrated within countries. Across the world, an estimated three quarters of economic production takes place in cities; the more dynamic coastal regions of China produce more than half of the country's GDP with less than one-fifth of its land area, and Greater Tokyo accounts for more than 40% of Japan's total output on just 4% of its land area. In the developing world, this concentration has been accompanied by sizeable—and by some accounts increasing—spatial disparities in living standards and welfare. Per capita income differentials within countries in the developing world tend to be much larger than equivalent differentials within rich countries. Paradoxically, in a world which is rapidly globalizing, one of the most important determinants of well-being is still where a person is born: in which country, in what province within the country, and whether it is a city or the country side within that province.

But the location of economic activity in the world is rapidly changing. During the last 50 years, the share of global GDP of today's rich countries has been about 80%. Over the next few decades, projections indicate that this could fall to 40%. In other words, a substantial portion of the world's GDP will, spatially be 'in play,' shifting from developed towards developing countries. Which countries, regions and cities will get this will depend on their natural endowments and their history, and perhaps even on luck. But it will depend much more on the policies that are put in place, because policy reform at the international, national and sub-national level can initiate large and lasting changes in economic geography. What can developing countries do to attract a larger share of global economic enterprise, and how can regions and cities within these countries get more of the benefit of this growth?

Source: World Development Report 2009, p.1.

Case Questions

1   What in your opinion are the reasons for economic activity concentrating in cities, not in rural areas? Do you think such concentration helps in making distribution of income better in a country? Give reasons for your answer.

2   Why do different regions of the same country show marked inequalities in development and per capita income? What can be done to narrow these differences?

3   Are the East and West Coasts of Peninsular Malaysia equally developed? If not, why? Explain.

Test Questions

22.1   Is it valid to say that production is an area of cooperation among the factors of production while distribution is an area of clash between them? Do you agree? Give reasons for your answer.

22.2   It is argued that the beauty of free-market economies is that price mechanism solves the problems of income generation and income distribution at one go and in an efficient way. There is little point in discussing distribution at the macro level. Is this statement correct? Argue your case.

22.3   What is a Lorenz curve? Explain and illustrate the method of its construction. Do you think that the line of equal distribution is an ideal benchmark for measuring the extent of inequalities in a specific case? If not, why? Explain.

22.4   From the data given in Table 22.4 below, draw the Lorenz curves for the two colleges including their cords and calculate the Gini index for each of them. Which college in your opinion has shown better homogeneity in performance at the examination? Give reasons for your answer.

22.5   Explain the Malaysian doctrine of positive discrimination to improve income and wealth distribution in the country as well as its consequences. Will you advocate for such discrimination in favour of the poor in other developing economies? Argue your case.

22.6   Why are growth and equity in income distribution treated as rivals in development economics? Does Kuznets' hypothesis hold well in the short run as well as in the long run? Explain your answer adequately.

22.7   'Generation of income and its distribution is locked in a two-way relationship'. Show how. Explain in this context, how changes in macroeconomic variables affect income distribution and how changes in distribution, say through fiscal policies, tend to change the patterns of distribution.

22.8   What do you understand by cross country income inequalities? What gives rise to such inequalities? Explain.

22.9   'Comparison of income inequalities within or between countries is beset with a number of difficulties'. Comment on this statement explaining the kind of difficulties that are peculiar to inter-country comparisons.

Table 22.4 *Examination results of two colleges: A and B*

Marks obtained			0	10	20	30	40	50	60	70	80	90	100
Number of students A		0	4	25	36	50	40	35	20	15	8	0	
Number of students B		1	5	30	35	42	45	43	22	12	10	12	

Web Exercise

Search the Internet to compile information on the fiscal policies of USA and Japan to overcome the current (2009) global meltdown.

Forward Link

The next chapter of the book deals with the comparison of national income over time within the same country and at a point of time between countries. It deals with measurement problems one faces in each kind of comparison, how the same can be overcome and to what extent. The discussion is largely technical.

CHAPTER 23

Inter-temporal and International Income Comparisons

LEARNING OUTCOMES

This chapter should enable the student to understand:

- What is meant by time-to-time (inter-temporal) comparisons of income and why such comparisons are needed
- The kind of problems faced in comparing national income over time and how we seek to overcome them
- Problems in making temporal income comparisons special to developing countries
- Why international comparisons of income are required and what is the basic principle underlying such comparisons
- The methods used to convert data to a common currency: The problem of exchange rate adjustment
- The usefulness, reliability and limitations of international comparisons

23.1   INTRODUCTION

> Economists are more interested in the comparison of real income aggregates over time than in their money values.

In the preceding chapters of the book, we remained occupied with the national income aggregates including their product and expenditure versions as measured in monetary terms at current prices and expressed in domestic currencies. However, for a number of purposes, economists and policy makers are not so much interested in the *monetary* figures as in the *real* values of these aggregates. They are more interested in *comparing* real aggregates over time than in the movements of their money values. One reason, among others, is that it is more appropriate to relate an increase (decrease) in real income to a rise (fall) in economic welfare of the people. As prices change, current dollar aggregates move differently from physical outputs. But our interest being human welfare, we may need to know, for example, if the *real* national output of Indonesia in 2008 was higher or lower than it was a year back in 2007 and how much was the difference? Or, in view of the global meltdown the world is currently facing, we may be interested to know whether Malaysian national product in *real* terms is likely to be lower this year by say 2 or 4% compared to the preceding year.

But if real values of income or output are of importance for purposes of comparing changes in welfare over time or space, what is the difficulty in obtaining them? The problem is that various goods and services are measured in different units: tons of steel, barrels of oil, metres of cloth and hours of work cannot be added together to estimate real or physical output of a country. Whereas, their money values—quantity, time, price—can be. Thus, aggregates of national income, output or expenditure can, in the first place, only be obtained in money terms. Index numbers help overcome the comparison difficulties.

Comparisons of income do not only pose problems over time *within* a country; such comparisons are even more difficult to make over space, especially *across* countries. One obvious source of trouble in spatial comparisons is that the national income of different countries is expressed in their domestic currencies which are mostly different from one another. The exchange rates between currencies do not remain constant for a variety of reasons. Fluctuations therein may make national income look much different even though the physical output in the two countries may have remained unchanged. International income comparisons demand that domestic currencies be equated to an acceptable common base. The UN International Comparison Programme (ICP) has been generating inter-spatial indices of prices and outputs to facilitate international comparisons of income albeit there are still problems that need to be resolved.

This chapter provides an elementary discussion of the issues in the two types of comparisons. We will see that comparing national output in real terms within a country at different time points is in principle no different from comparing them across countries. In both cases, one must allow for differences in prices either by expressing quantities directly in a fixed set of prices or by adjusting values for differences in the purchasing power of the monetary units. In inter-temporal comparisons, we use ordinary price indices to reveal the changing purchasing power of money with reference to a *given collection of goods*. In international comparisons, on the other hand, the purchasing power of the currency of one country in terms of the currency of another has to be determined by comparing prices in the two countries, again for *a given collection of goods*. However, some additional complications arise in the latter case.

The common source of information for both of them essentially remains the national income accounts. Therefore, there is a need to harmonize the concepts and methods used in national accounts and the ICP for improving insights. We begin with comparison of national income within a country over time. Such comparisons are called inter-temporal.

Economists and policy makers are more interested in knowing the level real GNP values rather than its nominal estimates. Also, they are more interested in knowing the changes over time and space compared to GNP levels.

Equalization of the purchasing power of money is needed in both types of income comparison: inter-temporal and international.

Later, we shall discuss the problems and their resolutions in making international comparisons. It is important to note that due to complexity of dynamic changes perpetually taking place in modern economies, we have to make many assumptions and compromises in comparative studies of income. Thus, despite all care, income comparisons, temporal or spatial, must invariably be taken with a grain of salt.

23.2 INTER-TEMPORAL INCOME COMPARISONS

We have observed that the welfare of the people is directly related to the level and change in the physical volume of goods and services an economy produces and that changes in their money value could be deceptive. For that reason, estimates of real GNP are one of the most familiar and widely used statistics the world over. But the exercise is interestingly of recent origin: in the US the publication of the official real income series dates back only to 1951. In most developing economies, their publication started much later. These series are obtained by *deflating* money income by appropriate price indices.

The reasons for the growing interest in real income or constant price figures are many and varied. To have real income data is almost an imperative for insights into the nature, magnitude and consequences of long-run cyclical fluctuations in economic activity or study of production trends. The analysis and treatment of various kinds of short-term economic crises or shocks also needs real income information. Without these statistics, our ability to peep into the future and project formation will be much crippled. In more recent years, the overall rate of growth in real GDP seems to have again been singled out for attention, presumably because of its wide variation from country to country with wide political implications and for formulating policies to improve economic performance.

> We need to compare national income/output over time to assess the improvement in the living standards of people.

Furthermore, it is real income data that helps us allocate resources to various uses efficiently. Refer to the illustrative Figure 1.1 of Chapter 1. The efficient allocation of resources for the economy takes place where the slope of the indifference curve expressed by the price ratio coincides with the slope of the transformation curve. Recall as well that the ratio equals the indifference curve slope—the marginal rate of substitution between the goods—in a state of equilibrium. Now, the indifference curve is not the main element in the diagram for satisfaction cannot be measured. What we set out to measure in that figure is in fact the 'real income' even as the invisible indifference curve provided the basic concept underlying that measurement. For a clearer understanding of the point, consider Figure 23.1. Here, we have put together two indifference curves and a transformation frontier, given the resources and technology. The

> Resources are scarce and have alternative uses. Their efficient use is essential to maximize peoples' welfare.

focal point for discussion however, is not the equilibrium level of output; but rather we want to highlight some characteristics of an underlying pattern of change. It would imply that TT is the transformation curve and the economy will move around until it reaches point 1, where its slope equals the slope of the societal indifference curve, IC_1. The production capacity is now fully utilized with Y_1, X_1 being the output produced. The economy would not prefer to produce any other combination as it has reached the highest possible indifference curve. The output is optimal, given the possibilities open to the economy. It would have been grossly inefficient if the economy had stuck to produce a pattern of output such as at point 2 on the frontier, as it would be having a smaller output than it has the potential of getting from the given resources.

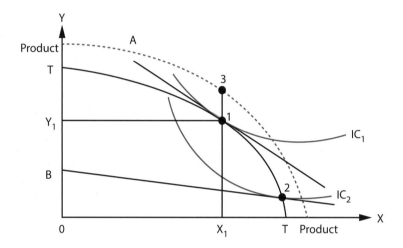

Figure 23.1 *Output pattern, given the resources*

Despite various assumptions (including perfect competition) and qualifications, price mechanism is believed to be such as would generate forces to ensure the economy reaches point 1 in the figure. For example, suppose the economy was producing at point 2, not 1. This implies that the consumers were in equilibrium at this point: the ratio of prices expressing their marginal rate of substitution. But the ratio is the slope of the B line, which is tangent to a lower societal indifference curve, IC_2. Notice that it is not, as it cannot be, tangent at the same time to the transformation curve (TT) at point 2. At this point, the line B cuts the TT curve; resources are not being used to produce optimal output.

Exercise 23.1

'At point 2, the price of Y relative to X is higher than the opportunity cost of producing Y relative to X'. Do you agree with the statement? Give reasons for your answer. Shall the economy attempt to move around until it reaches point 1? If yes, explain why.

The figure brings out the linkage between economic welfare—the real income—and output levels. Welfare is optimal when the price line is tangent to both transformation and indifference curves at a common point. On the other hand, optimal output from given resources is a matter of being, if possible, on a higher transformation curve such as point 3 on the dash-line curve. It may or may not be the point of consumers' equilibrium in the same sense as on point 2; no price line needs to be tangent to the transformation curve here.

The important point that emerges *inter alia* from the foregoing discussion is that an aggregation of output is possible in terms of money. But as the level of prices, as well as their relative structure continues changing, we face the problem of taking out from the money aggregates the component of pure price change. This brings us to price indices.

Money measures the value of goods and services. But it is a measure different from other measures like metres and grams in the sense that in the process of measuring the value of products, it gets its own value measured. If the money value (price) of goods and services doubles the value of money, its purchasing power is halved. To illustrate, if bananas have a price of $2 a dozen, the value of $1 is 6 bananas. Should the price of bananas rise to $4 a dozen, the value of $1 will become 3 bananas, that is, half of what it was before. Price indices measure the changes in the value of money and are used to arrive at real income figures. Real income change is reciprocal of the price change. If prices are in general halved, the purchasing power of money and therefore real income, are both doubled. Let us briefly look at the construction, nature and limitations of price index numbers.

> Prices, value of money and real income are involved in a causal relationship: If prices rise, value of money and real income falls.

23.3 REAL INCOME MEASUREMENT: QUANTITY AND PRICE INDICES

If prices of goods and services remain constant over the years of comparison, the difference in their money value will measure the change in real income or output. The time point (year) we compare the change with is called the base point, indicated by (0). Consider Table 23.1 which provides change in output with 2007 as the base.

Table 23.1 *Change in output with constant prices*

Commodity	2007			2008		
	Quantity	Price	Value	Quantity	Price	Value
	q_0	p_0	$q_0 p_0$	q_1	p_0	$q_1 p_0$
Wheat	10,000 tons	$50 per ton	$500,000	12,300 tons	$50 per ton	$550,000
Scooters	100 units	$1,500	$150,000	120 units	$1,500	$180,000
Total		$\Sigma q_0 p_0 = \$650,000$			$\Sigma q_1 p_0 = \$730,000$	

In Table 23.1, we have kept the prices unchanged but physical output of both commodities increased; so did the value of output from $650,000 to $730,000. The increase in the value of output by $80,000 is *real* in the sense that it represents the value of 2,300 additional tons of wheat plus the value of 20 more scooters produced in 2008 [2,300 × 50 + 20 × 1,500 = 80,000].

Table 23.1 provides us with what we call quantity index, Q_{01}, as we are taking the ratio q_1/q_0, evaluating both q_1 and q_0 at p_0 (constant) prices. We have the quantity index as:

$$Q_0 = \frac{\Sigma q_1 p_0}{\Sigma q_0 p_0} \qquad (23.1)$$

Putting in the values we get:

$$Q_{01} = \frac{730,000}{650,000}$$
$$= 1.1231$$

Thus, real income increased in 2008 by $(1.1231 - 1.000) \times 230$ or 12.31% compared to 2007. Is the result correct? (Verify.)

But prices of products do not remain constant; they change over time, and we have to eliminate the effect of price change from the money value of output to see if any real (physical) change in output has taken place. Table 23.2 repeats the above illustration, keeping this time for simplicity, the output of the two goods unchanged combined with changes in their prices. Year 2007 is again the reference or base year. Here, the focus is on the relative change in price or p_1/p_0.

Table 23.2 *Constant output with change in prices*

Commodity	2007			2008		
	Quantity	Price	Value	Quantity	Price	Value
	q_0	p_0	$p_0 q_0$	q_0	p_1	$p_1 q_0$
Wheat	10,000 tons	$50 per ton	$500,000	10,000 tons	$60 per ton	$600,000
Scooters	100 units	$1,500	$150,000	100 units	$1,800	$180,000
Total		$\Sigma p_0 q_0 = \$650,000$			$\Sigma p_1 q_0 = \$780,000$	

With a change in prices, the money value of output increases by $130,000. But note that the prices of both commodities have gone up by 20%. If we reduce the year 2008 value of output by 20%, we have the same value of output as in year 2007. Thus, there has been no increase in real output in 2008; the addition of $130,000 is a mere price change component in the money value of output at $780,000 for 2008.

The data given in Table 23.2 can be used to construct a price index, P_{01}, as follows:

$$P_0 = \frac{\Sigma p_1 q_0}{\Sigma P_0 p_0} \qquad (23.2)$$

Putting in the values from Table 23.2 we get:

$$P_{01} = \frac{780,000}{650,000}$$
$$= 1.2$$

Thus, there has been a 20% rise in 2008 relative to base year 2007. We may arrive at real income if we deflate, that is, divide the money income of 2008 by the price index as follows:

$$\text{Real income (2008)} = \frac{780,000}{1.2}$$
$$= 650,000$$

This verifies that income in 2008 has not changed in real terms; the entire increase in money income is inflationary.

Exercise 23.2

The cloth produced in an economy was valued at $230 billion in 2007 and at $1,200 billion in 2008. Other things remaining unchanged, explain how the welfare of people would change in each of the following cases. Assume that the price of cloth in 2007 was $23 a metre.

  (a) Price of cloth had risen by 20% in 2008.
  (b) Price of cloth did not change over the years.
  (c) Price of cloth fell by 20% in 2008.

Can you say what must have been the physical output of cloth in 2008 in each case?

23.3.1   Chain Base Indices

In the above illustration the indices presented are of aggregative type, as we used value aggregates in their derivation. We compared real income over two years only. Such exercises yield what we call 'point-to-point' or 'binary' comparisons of real income. Fixed base indices—where the reference point remains unchanged for comparison—are not always appropriate for the purpose. Their underlying assumption is that the value shares (weights) of commodities remain the same in the current period as they are in the base period. However, as the time distance between the two points increases, this assumption tends to break down; consumption patterns between period points changes. To overcome the difficulty, we make use of the *chain base* index numbers, not of those with a fixed base.

> If we use fixed base indices, the current year always measures change from the base period; while the use of chain base index numbers allows the estimation of change with the preceding year as the base, i.e. they facilitate point-to-point comparisons.

In the chain base technique, we first compute the *primary* indices for adjacent time points such as $P_{01}, P_{12}, P_{23}, P_{34}, P_{45}$ and so on. The chain base indices are then obtained as follows:

$$\bar{P}_{00} = 230$$
$$\bar{P}_{01} = 230 \times P_{01}$$
$$\bar{P}_{12} = 230 \times P_{01} \times P_{12} = \bar{P}_{01} \times P_{12}$$
$$\bar{P}_{23} = 230 \times P_{01} \times P_{12} \times P_{23} = \bar{P}_{12} \times P_{23}, \text{ and so on.}$$

In general, chain base indices will give a different result from those with a fixed base.

Exercise 23.3

Check the calculation of chain base indices in the following table and point out the discrepancies, if any.

Table 23.3 *Calculation of fixed base and chain base indices given the primary price ratios*

Particulars	Year					
	2000	2001	2002	2003	2004	2005
Index symbols	P_{00}	P_{01}	P_{12}	P_{23}	P_{34}	P_{45}
Primary price ratio	P_0/P_0	P_1/P_0	P_2/P_1	P_3/P_2	P_4/P_3	P_5/P_4
Value	1	0.9752	1.0164	1.0119	1.0847	1.0904
Chain base index number	100	97.52	99.12	230.30	238.80	118.63

We do not explain here all the types of index numbers, the techniques of constructing them or their uses, because such a discussion falls outside the scope of this book. But, we briefly explain the main steps taken in the construction of price indices.

23.4   STEPS IN THE CONSTRUCTION OF PRICE INDICES

The construction of index numbers was referred to in Chapter 7. Here we discuss in some detail the steps involved and the problems statisticians have to face in taking decisions. The main steps are discussed here.

23.4.1   Specifying the Purpose of Construction

To define clearly the purpose for which we are constructing the index number is essential because it determines the steps that follow and also their character. To illustrate, if we have to know the changes in the cost of constructing houses for the lower classes we need not collect prices of heavy structural steel products for the purpose. Likewise, for measuring the changes in the cost of living of the workers, we need to know the retail—not wholesale—prices of goods they consume. An index number of industrial production, in general, will equally be unsuitable.

23.4.2 Choice of the Base Year

Since index numbers are meant to facilitate comparisons, it is customary though not necessary, to select a period as the reference or base to put the values (prices) at the point equal to 230% with which we shall compare indices for other periods. The period selected is neither too short nor too long; usually we take a year as the base. All heights in geography are measured from the placid sea level. (Why not from the top of the Everest?) Likewise, a base year should be a normal year; one in which no extraordinary factors operated to disturb the index variables. It is quite difficult to define normality but it should not clearly be a war year or one affected by the influx of refugees as what is currently happening in Pakistan.

Also, for comparisons to remain realistic and meaningful, the base year should not be too far back in the past. How would it be useful to compare the price level of Malaysia in 2008 with that of 1970? Indeed, there is a practice to bring the base year forward and start a new series of indices to keep the base closer to the current periods. This is especially desirable in economies where growth and structural changes are fast. For example in Malaysia, a new series of consumer price index is started almost every five years. But we shall see that frequent change of base is not always without problems.

> Construction of price indices involves selection of a base, commodity basket, price quotations, weighting system, sources of data and a suitable average.

23.4.3 Data Collection

The data collection for a price index must be suitable to serve the objective of constructing the index number. The commodities have to be identified; markets from where data will be collected have to be chosen. How frequently, on what day and time; and from whom the price quotations will be obtained and what weights for price relatives will be used are the matters to be decided. It is difficult to answer such questions, especially in a dynamic setting. However, a few general observations may be helpful.

The commodities selected for inclusion must match the purpose of constructing the index and what it seeks to measure. For example, to measure the changes in the prices that consumers pay, we must collect information on food items commonly used, clothing, footwear, housing health care, education and so on. The price quotation choice for an index must be relevant to the purpose of its construction. For example, retail prices are needed from reliable market sources for constructing a consumer price index. On the other hand, for a general purpose index the whole sale prices would be more appropriate. Weekly collection of data is considered appropriate in most cases. The accuracy of data, their reliability, adequacy completeness and comparability must be ensured. The data must be reflective of the magnitude of change and its direction.

23.4.4   Sources of Data

Regularly published quotations or periodic special reports from selected merchants, producers, exporters or others who may supply the relevant information, can be used as sources for the collection of data for index numbers. In all cases, we must ensure that the data pertains strictly to what is being measured. Thus, if changes in the retail food prices are to be measured quotations are to be obtained from super markets, chain stores, single proprietary outlets and any other source considered important. These different sources are to be kept separate and combined using a system of weighting.

23.4.5   Deciding on a Weighting System

Changes in the prices of all commodities selected for constructing an index number series are not of equal importance. For example, a 23% rise in the price of salt is of little significance for a household compared to a 23% rise in the price of meat. (Why?) Likewise, a 20% rise in the price of chocolates will not mean the same for parents as a 20% rise in school fees. Thus, in the construction of price index numbers, the relative importance of changes in commodity prices has to be taken into account. *Weight* in statistics is the assignment of relative importance to items included in an index number construction.

What should be used as weights or to which period they should belong—base or current—depends on what is being measured and to what end. For example, if we are measuring changes in the national output over the years at constant prices we use base year prices as the weights as in Equation 23.1 above. Or, in construction price indices we may use base (or current) year quantities as the weights. See, for example, Equation 23.2. The procedure for incorporating the weights is as discussed below.

23.4.6   Combining the Data

Index numbers can be viewed as averages linked with percentages. An important step in the construction of indices is the selection of an average to be used for combining the data. The choice usually is between arithmetic mean and geometric mean. The selection depends on what *tests of adequacy* we want the index numbers to satisfy. We cannot discuss these tests here; suffice to say that there are some logical propositions that a good index must satisfy. On that criteria, the use of geometric mean scores over arithmetic mean. However, the latter is mostly used for reasons of simplicity and ease.

Equations 23.1 and 23.2 are of aggregative type, as we had indicated. But, you must remember that the same results can be obtained through an averaging process. Note that we can always express a weighted mean type as follows:

$$P_{01} = \frac{\Sigma \frac{p_1}{p_0} v_0}{\Sigma v_0} = \frac{\Sigma \left(p_1 \frac{v_0}{p_0} \right)}{\Sigma \left(p_0 \frac{v_0}{p_0} \right)} \tag{23.3}$$

Putting $v = p_0 q_0$, we get the same result as in Equation 23.2, i.e.

$$P_{01} = \frac{\Sigma p_1 q_0}{\Sigma P_0 p_0}$$

Exercise 23.4

Insert the values in Equation 23.3 from Table 23.2 and solve it to verify that there would be no difference in the results whether we use the aggregative or the weighted mean type approach for combining the data to construct price indices.

By now it may be obvious that construction of index numbers is not an easy task; a number of compromises and assumptions have to be made. The results we obtain are not without limitations. The main ones are discussed here.

23.5   DEFLATING THE NOMINAL AGGREGATES

Once we have an appropriate series of index numbers, it is easy to convert a nominal series of national income into a real income series. For each year we simply divide the nominal income (value) figure by the corresponding index number to obtain the relevant real income (value) figure. The real income series so obtained will have the same reference year as the base of the index number series (Table 23.4).

Table 23.4 *Gross national product of Malaysia in RM million at current and constant prices (2000–2005)*

Gross national product	Year					
	2000	2001	2002	2003	2004	2005
GNP at current prices	327.492	326.956	358.152	396.232	449.646	498.485
Consumer price index	100.0	101.4	103.2	104.4	105.9	108.8
GNP at constant prices (a)	327.492	322.442	347.046	379.532	424.595	458.166
GNP at constant prices (b)	327.492	331.740	351.671	376.809	402.838	424.295

Source: Department of Statistics Malaysia: (a) at consumers' prices and (b) at purchasers' prices

The process of converting nominal values into real values requires the division of nominal income of a year by the corresponding index number.

It may be noted that in Table 23.4, we have the real income (a) using the consumer price index (CPI) as the deflator but the Statistical Department uses the purchasers' value for the purpose. Thus, (b) represents the official real GNP series for Malaysia. It is notably different from (a). The reasons are not far to seek. We only need to know the differences between the implicit GDP deflator and the CPI which we discuss below.

Exercise 23.5

In Table 23.4, divide the values in the bottom row (b) with the values in the row above (a) for each of the years and comment on the behaviour of the ratios.

23.5.1   Implicit GDP Deflators and CPI Compared

GDP deflators are different from commonly-used price indices.

Both implicit GDP deflators (IGDs) and the CPI measure price changes. But while the deflators serve as a measure of overall price changes in the economy, the CPI just measures changes in the prices of goods and services that enter the consumption basket of the common households. Second, IGDs reflect the quantity weights of the *current* period, not of the base period. The implicit weights of the IGDs are updated each period with the change in the composition of consumption. They do not, thus, provide a measure of pure price component in the value change of output because they get it intractably mixed up with changes in the composition of goods and services in the basket.

The CPI on the other hand is a direct price index reflecting the quantities of the *base* period as weights. It is designed to measure the change in the money value of a fixed basket of goods and services commonly bought by the majority of households. It reflects the quantity weights of the base period. The following illustrative formulations give some idea of the differences between the IGDs and CPI. Notice that IGDs are quantity indices while CPI is a price index.

IGDs $\qquad\qquad$ CPI

$$P_{01} = \frac{\Sigma p_1 q_1}{\Sigma p_0 p_1} \qquad\qquad P_{01} = \frac{\Sigma p_1 q_0}{\Sigma p_0 p_0} \qquad\qquad (23.4)$$

23.6   LIMITATIONS OF INDEX NUMBERS

Index numbers are based on some assumptions about the working of the markets which may not always come true and tend to become obsolete quite fast due to the dynamic changes that are always taking place in an economy. Unless promptly revised, they have a number of limitations in measuring price level changes. The main ones are as discussed in the following section.

BOX 23.1

Contrast: Debt Burden is on the Rise in the West but Falling in the Muslim World

Debt to GDP ratio is on the rise in developing countries, while it shows a sharp falling trend in Muslim countries. Why is it so? Is it that the West is consuming more at the cost of future generations? Why is debt falling in Muslim countries?

	2004	2005	2006	2007	2008	2009	2010	2011	2012	2013
EGYPT	102.3	101.5	103.3	90.3	80.2	70.2	73	73.2	79.7	76.4
PAKISTAN	75.9	68.3	63.5	57.5	54.9	59.6	60.7	61.5	60.1	50.4
TURKEY	67.7	59.6	52.7	46.5	39.9	40	46.1	42.2	39.4	36
INDONESIA	60.5	55.8	46.5	40.4	36.9	33.2	28.6	27.4	25	22.1
IRAN	25.8	25.2	21.5	18.1	16.6	13.3	14.7	16.7	12.6	10.3
UAE	4.4	5.6	6.6	6.8	7.8	12.5	23.4	22.3	17.8	14.6
IRAQ	493.7	322.7	213.9	172.9	110.4	119.5	144.1	119.5	86.9	31.3

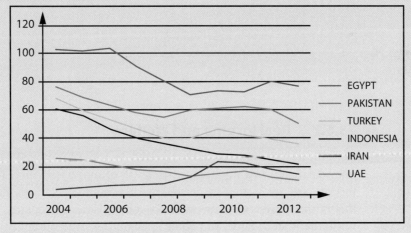

Source: Countries' Central Bank Reports

Figure 23.2A *Public debt to GDP ratios of selected Muslim countries, 2004–2013*

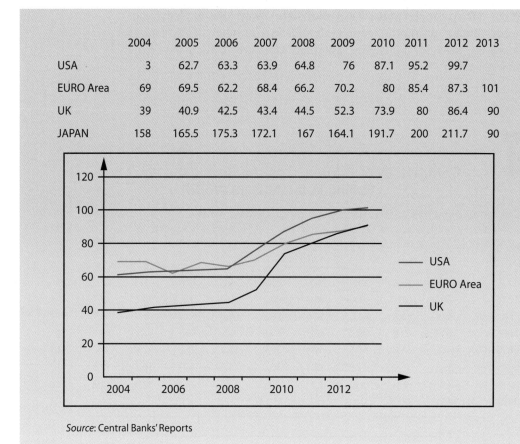

	2004	2005	2006	2007	2008	2009	2010	2011	2012	2013
USA	3	62.7	63.3	63.9	64.8	76	87.1	95.2	99.7	
EURO Area	69	69.5	62.2	68.4	66.2	70.2	80	85.4	87.3	101
UK	39	40.9	42.5	43.4	44.5	52.3	73.9	80	86.4	90
JAPAN	158	165.5	175.3	172.1	167	164.1	191.7	200	211.7	90

Source: Central Banks' Reports

Figure 23.2B *Public debt to GDP ratios of some developed countries, 2004–2013*

23.6.1   Real Income and Welfare

> We face some ticklish problems in constructing index numbers. These relate to the selection of the base year and the commodities for inclusion, the collection of data and the choice of the average to be used.

As indicated earlier, we are interested in index numbers for deflating nominal income mainly because the levels of and changes in real per capita income are very often associated with economic welfare. Presumably, this is the closest we can come to comparisons of welfare. But let us not forget that as needs of people change, the same output of goods and services will be representing different levels of consumer satisfaction. Energy supplies adequate in a warmer winter may prove deficient in a cold weather. Also, with the passage of time income distribution, work intensity and other circumstances also change; a given per capita income figure may represent different welfare levels, especially in the long run. Index numbers help obtain only rough estimates of relative changes in welfare.

23.6.2 Representative Commodities and the Weighting System

The choice of representative commodities, sources of information and frequency of obtaining quotations are based on sampling and may involve a degree of arbitrariness. In any case, the representative character of the choice tends to fade out with the passage of time due to factors such as changes in tastes and fashion, inventions and innovations, changing quality of goods, and the entry of new products into the picture even if the basket may remain the same. Likewise, the weighting system indicating the relative importance of various goods and services may become obsolete, requiring changes which do not come as fast as needed. All this may lead to arriving at fallacious estimations and conclusions.

23.6.3 Averaging the Data

Index numbers are specialized type of averages; they are subject to all those limitations that an average suffers from. Most averages do not satisfy the mathematical tests demanding logical consistency. A discussion of these tests is avoided here, but those interested in knowing them can consult any text on statistics containing a discussion on index numbers.

23.7 GNP DEFLATORS

The last two rows in Table 23.4 give us different figures of GNP at constant prices beyond the base year. The reason obviously is that we have used different types of indices to deflate the GNP at current prices. The official series of constant prices (real income) use indices especially constructed for the purpose. Here the regimen or list of commodities and weights take the overall general view of the economy. Moreover, different kind of items are deflated using different deflators say for exports, imports, and other external transactions, government expenditures, household consumption and so on. The figures so obtained are then combined to have the GNP at constant prices or its real value.

> The price index the government uses to convert nominal income into real is called a GNP deflator. GNP deflators are specially constructed price indices.

Since users of the published series of real GNP data do not know how such figures are obtained from current money values, an indirect way to know the deflator is used as follows:

$$\text{Real GNP} = \frac{\text{GNP at current prices}}{\text{GNP deflator}} \qquad (23.5)$$

It follows that:

$$\text{GNP deflator} = \frac{\text{GNP at current prices}}{\text{GNP at constant prices}} \qquad (23.6)$$

Consider the following Table 23.5.

Table 23.5 *Calculation of implicit GNP deflator for Malaysia (2000 = 230)*

Gross national product	Year					
	2000	2001	2002	2003	2004	2005
GNP at current prices (c)	327.492	326.956.	358.152	396,232	449,646	498.485
GNP at constant prices (b)	327.492	331.740	351.671	376.809	402.838	424.295
GNP deflator [(c)/(b)] 230	100.0	98.6	231.8	235.2	111.6	117.5
Consumer price index (CPI)	100.0	101.4	103.2	104.4	105.9	108.8

We often do not know the explicit deflators, but they are invariably implicit in the GNP data, giving its values at (a) current, and (b) at constant prices. We can get the implicit deflator if we divide (a) by (b).

The GNP deflator for Malaysia, as shown in Table 23.5 is an *implicit* deflator; it does not appear in the statistical tables of the country. Nevertheless, implicit deflators are regarded as the better measures of inflation in a country. Compare the deflator and the CPI given in Table 23.5 and comment on the state of inflation in the country.

23.8 INTERNATIONAL COMPARISONS

Ideally, international GNP comparisons reflect welfare differences across countries.

National income accounts of various countries provide figures in their own currencies: Indian rupees, Saudi riyals, US dollars, Japanese yen and so on. But this fact does not bar us from making comparisons of national aggregates by conversion to a common currency; say US dollars. This helps compare the size of various economies and assign them ranks. We can use *rates and ratios* for comparative purposes even without conversion to a common currency. What proportion of national income is consumed or invested? How much foreign trade contributes to national income? Which economy is growing at a faster rate? How is the structure of production currently constituted with respect to contribution of various sectors—agriculture, manufacturing and services, and so on to GNP? However, we shall see that price level differences still matter in comparisons of macroeconomic variables across countries.

International institutions—World Bank, International Monetary Fund and United Nations Development Programme—have long been publishing national income accounts data of various countries in the statistical part of their reports in tabular form. These reports are a major source of comparative information for economic studies and research. It is, therefore, important for you to know the methods of generating the data presented in the tables on national income and their limitations.

Efforts are continually made to improve GNP deflators for closer estimations of welfare differences.

Until early 1992, the official estimates of the income size of various economies were based only on their gross national income converted to current US dollars using what is known as the *Atlas method*. However, it was felt that conversion to US dollars does not make national income of various countries comparable as economic welfare indicators: the real purpose of the estimation. Clearly, the *same* dollar amount has much different purchasing power in various countries: it does not give the *same* satisfaction everywhere. To overcome this, Gustav Cassel (1918) was remembered and his purchasing power parity theory or the PPP theory was pulled out from the archives.

The theory is based on the *law of one price* which says: identical goods must have only one price, if markets were efficient. It seeks to adjust the long-term exchange rate of different currencies to equalize their purchasing power across countries for a *given* basket of goods. The use of the PPP basis is considered more logical and useful for comparing living standards in various countries as it takes into account their relative cost of living and the inflation rates, not merely the nominal income converted to current US dollars. The conversion based on the PPP yields the equivalent of national income in 'international dollars.' The World Bank now includes these equivalents in its tables. Let us briefly explain the Atlas method and the ICP conversion procedures.

23.8.1   World Bank Atlas Method

Conversion of GNP figures reported in domestic currencies into US dollars is done using the official exchange rate. For example, the GNP of Malaysia estimated in local currency for the year 2006 was RM555.2 billion. The exchange rate at the close of the year was RM3.534 to a US dollar. The 2006 Malaysian GNP expressed in US dollars would clearly be 453.8/3.534 = $157.1 billion. But the Bank systematically assesses the appropriateness of official exchange rates as a conversion factor. The Bank uses an alternative conversion factor if the official rate of any currency is judged to depart by too wide a margin from the rate effectively applied to its foreign transactions. However, this is not required in most cases and the Bank uses in all other countries the Atlas method for calculating their GNP.

The Atlas conversion factor for any given year includes: (i) the average exchange rate of a country for that year and (ii) its exchange rates for the two preceding years after adjusting them for differences in relative inflation between that country and the USA. The average of the three yearly rates is then taken to iron out fluctuations in prices and exchange rates to have the GNPs comparable across countries. The entire process is integrated in a neat formula, the method used for conversion; it is explained in the Technical Notes of the World Development Reports. The formula eventually leads to the conversion of GNPs expressed in different national currencies to the current US dollars and are divided by the corresponding populations of the countries for estimating their per capita income (dollar) values as published in annual reports of the bank. Consider the following as an illustrative case.

> The Atlas method is used for conversion to improve comparability. This method is discussed in the technical notes of the World Development Reports.

Table 23.6 *Constant output with change in prices (imaginary data)*

Commodity	Malaysia (1)				Pakistan (2)			
	Quantity	Price (RM)	Value (RM)	Value (PKR)	Quantity	Price (PKR)	Value (PKR)	Value (RM)
	q_1	p_1 (RM)	$p_1 q_1$	$p_2 q_1$	q_2	p_2 (PKR)	$p_2 q_2$	$p_1 q_2$
Rice	1,000 tons	100	100,000	100,000	10,000 tons	100	1,000,000	500,000
Scooters	100 units	1,500	150,000	1,800,000	80 units	18,000	1,440,000	120,000
Total	$\Sigma p_1 q_1$ = RM250,000				$\Sigma p_2 q_2$ = PKR 2,440,000			
	$\Sigma p_2 q_1$ = PKR 1,900,000				$\Sigma p_1 q_2$ = RM620,000			

Table 23.6 shows the production of rice and scooters in Malaysia and Pakistan along with their prices in the two countries. Note that we have also given the value of each country's product calculated in the prices of the other country in the last row of the table. How can we compare the contribution of these goods to their respective GNPs? One way that apparently comes to mind is that we may find the ratio of the value of a foreign country's output to that of its own both measured in local prices. For example, in the case of Malaysia, Table 23.6 gives us:

$$\frac{\Sigma p_1 q_2}{\Sigma p_1 q_1} = \frac{RM620,000}{RM250,000} = 2.48$$

Thus, the contribution of the two goods to the Pakistani GNP is 2.48 times to that of Malaysia. But how far is the comparison consistent if we look at things from the Pakistan side. For that country we have:

$$\frac{\Sigma p_2 q_2}{\Sigma p_2 q_1} = \frac{PKR\ 2,440,000}{PKR\ 1,900,000} = 1.28$$

The two results are not the same. Why? The reason is the difference in the relative price structure of the two countries. The demand for goods that have relatively low prices in a country is large relative to those with high prices and vice versa. Which commodity—rice or scooters—is cheaper in Pakistan relative to Malaysia in Table 23.6?

The above way of income comparison is obviously deficient. This is overcome in the Atlas method by converting domestic values to current US dollars via the average rates of exchange. Suppose these rates are PKR 70 = 1 USD and RM3.5 = 1 USD. We then have $\Sigma p_1 q_1$ = RM250,000/3.5 = \$71,430 and $\Sigma p_2 q_2$ = PKR 2,440,000/70 = \$34,857. If we compare the two contributions, we will find that it is nearly two and a half times more in the case of Malaysia compared to Pakistan (71,430/34,857 = 2.5).

We have already discussed the limitations of GNP per capita as a reflector of the human welfare in a country. Its international comparisons in current US dollars as per the Atlas method have some additional difficulties. The major one is that GNP conversions based on the official exchange rates do not reflect the relative *purchasing power* of the GNPs at the domestic level. To overcome this deficiency, the International Monetary Fund (IMF) presented the GDP data for 1992 based on the PPP of currencies in 'International dollars' under the International Comparison Programme (ICP) of the UN. The World Development Reports have since been publishing the PPP estimates of the countries' GNPs along with those in current US dollars under the old method.

23.8.2 The ICP Conversion Procedures

ICP has moved from the traditional binary comparisons into the realm of multilateral comparisons. It concentrates, for the sake of convenience, on the expenditure side of the GDP and not on its production side. It collects national annual average prices paid by the purchaser and takes GDP expenditure data from national income accounts. As expenditure equals price times quantity is an accounting identity, estimates of quantity (expenditure divided by price) are obtained in detail. Of the various formulae available for estimation, the one known as the Geary-Khamis (GK) construct is used for converting GDP values of countries estimated in national currencies into a common currency, presently the US dollar, using the purchasing power parity (PPP) ratios rather than the rates of exchange. The PPP here refers to the units of a currency required to purchase the *same* basket of goods and services in the home market as one dollar would buy in the USA.

> Equalizing the purchasing power of currencies means the equalization of prices across countries. If what RM3.56 buys in Malaysia one can get for a dollar in the US, prices in Malaysia are taken to be in that ratio in domestic currencies.

Under the programme, the prices of 400 to 1,000 items are collected and classified into over 150 basic categories covering the entire gross national product or the GDP of various countries. The price relatives of these categories are then aggregated into *average* price relatives or PPPs for the GDP components using expenditure ratios as the weights. Ensuring in this manner the equalization of purchasing power of currencies implies in fact the equalization of prices across countries.

23.8.3 Need for Improvement

If the ICP aims at price equalization across countries that objective would demand improvement in several counts.

1. **Harmonize prices**: As noted earlier, the PPPs are weighted average price relatives. The goods and services selected for a country from the overall list and also their prices in a survey must truly be representative of the expenditure pattern of that country. The specifications of goods included the selection of markets as also of the outlets must meet the same norm. Also, the items selected ought to be comparable across countries and prices

appropriate for the computation of correct national averages. The latter must also be consistent with physical quantities as embodied in the national accounts estimates. Since ideals are difficult to achieve, appropriate trade-offs have to be decided and uniformly followed.

> The ICP needs improvement in matters of items selection, obtaining price quotations, assignment of weights to various price ratios and improving the regional linkages.

2. **Source selection**: One guiding principle in ICP is to price items that are sold in large volumes with specified quality and packaging and to select markets and outlets therefrom that account for most of the expenditure on them. National price indices, notably the CPI, follow the same principle. Thus, the first source the ICP should look for a list of representative items is the list of specifications included in these indices. However, the CPI list may require additions and deletions to make it suitable for the programme. Similarly, the local indices of wholesale prices, construction and labour cost may be scrutinized for suitable information.

3. **Assignment of weight**: As CPI and ICP both use expenditure weights, countries may be advised to use a uniform expenditure classification of the type proposed in the ICP and rectify their CPI price samples accordingly so as to make the components directly comparable across countries. The sample of prices is likely to be different in various countries and expenditure weights are not usually available. For this reason, mismatching of weights to items cannot be ruled out. Thus, there presumably is a strong case for analyzing the situation to suggest corrective action.

4. **Forging global linkage**: Regional comparisons among nations are based on separate price structures of each region; this requires forging linkages between regional structures to allow and improve country comparisons across regions. To this end, several countries in each region are identified as 'core countries'. From there, additional prices are collected to improve inter-region linkage factors for better global comparison among nations.

Much has been done along the lines indicated above and data after 1994 have become more homogeneous and comparable. The developed economies have been quick to make appropriate changes and adjustments in collecting and presenting national income, output and expenditure statistics. The pace of change in developing countries has been slow for a variety of reasons, especially the cost involved in switching over to new format and designs.

Summary

- As a measure of economic welfare within a country over time and across countries at a point in time, we are interested in a measurement of the level and changes in real output rather than in its nominal or money values.

- But the real output of various goods and services are measured in different scales—inches, litres, bales, gallons,etc.—which cannot be added to form an aggregate. Their aggregation is possible only in terms of their money values, i.e. price, time and quantity. The aggregates of these values will show the change in real output over time or space only if prices in the economy remain unchanged.

- Prices invariably do not remain constant; not only do prices change, they change differently causing the relative price structure to alter. This gives rise to the issue of neutralizing the impact of price changes on the GDP over time so that we get the value of output minus the effect of price changes or GDP at constant prices.

- This objective is sought to be achieved through the construction of index numbers. An index number measures the level of a variable—single or aggregative—at a particular time point with reference to its level taken as the base point equal to 230. We can construct quantity indices with given prices as weights or price indices with given quantities as weights. Usually, quantity and price indices are or can be linked.

- Index numbers of various kinds are based on a number of assumptions including perfect competition in the market and have limitations in measuring the level of a phenomenon or changes therein. Their use demands caution and estimations need not always be taken at their face value, especially in equating change in GNP to changes in human welfare on a one-to-one basis.

- We can find the real income series by dividing each year's nominal income by an appropriate price index for the same year. However, it is not always easy to decide on an appropriate index series. Such series are especially prepared by government agencies and may not commonly be available. However, the GNP series both at (a) current and (b) constant prices are available for corresponding years. If we divide (a) by (b) we can find the deflator that has been used for conversion. This we call implicit deflator, and it can be used as a measure of inflation (deflation) in the economy.

- Implicit deflators differ from consumer price index numbers commonly used to measure inflation in a number of ways, more importantly in the former we use current year quantities as the weights, while in the latter we use the base year quantities for the purpose.

- Earlier, the IMF had been using the average rate of exchange between the USD and domestic currencies to convert GDPs of various countries to a common denominator for international comparisons. In 1992, it switched over to what is called the purchasing power parity procedure. The distinct impact of this method has been a marked reduction in the share of the developed countries in the global GDP raising the corresponding share of the developing economies. The change has been taken with some reservations in the latter set of countries. (See Case Study 23.1.)

Glossary

Implicit deflators Various countries publish a series of GNP at (i) current prices and (ii) at constant prices. If we divide (i) by (ii) we get what is termed as implicit deflator. The deflator so obtained is the measure of overall inflation in a country. It is different from the CPI with reference to the range of items included and the weights used.

International GNP comparisons Comparisons of GNP and its components are important not only over time within a country, they are important also across countries. International comparisons are in principle no different from inter-temporal comparisons: both use purchasing power of currency for the purpose. This is easy to see if the two countries have the same currency with a 1:1 rate of exchange. The additional problems arise in international comparisons as the GNP composition and currencies of countries are not the same and the exchange rates between them keep on changing. The IMF converts GNPs of countries to USD equivalents by using foreign exchange rate adjustment as the basis. The IMF has recently changed the method for such adjustment under the UN sponsored International Comparison Programme (ICP).

Inter-temporal comparisons of GNP Macroeconomic variables are invariably in a process of change. These changes have to be measured and compared. The GNP of a country is taken as a measure, however deficient, of economic welfare. Thus, a comparison of its macro variable at different time points, especially of the GNP, is a continuous and important exercise in various countries.

Nominal and real GNP Welfare is related to physical output. But physical output coming out of various economic activities cannot be added up together because measurement units are not the same for all goods and services. Aggregation is possible only in terms of their money values. As prices keep changing over time, nominal (money) values of GNP do not reveal true physical change in output. We have to use index numbers—even as they have limitations—to neutralize the price change component from the money values. We divide the nominal values of GNPs by the corresponding index number to obtain the value at constant prices or the real GNP.

Concepts for Review

- Atlas method
- GNP deflator
- Implicit deflators
- Income: real versus nominal
- International Comparison Programme
- Measurement units
- Price indices
- Quantity indices
- Weighting system

Case Study   23.1

Flaws in the New GDP Valuation Method

Gustav Cassel may be smiling in his grave. The International Monetary Fund (IMF) has rescued his purchasing power parity (3Ps) theory from fading into oblivion; albeit for a purpose he never had in mind. The Fund uses the 3Ps notion in a recent revision of its technique to revaluate the member countries gross domestic product (GDP) for 1992 and the change is intended to continue. The consequences have been startling.

The hitherto poor nation, that is, in terms of the old valuation for the same year (1992) has been made rich in one stroke. Comparisons reveal that the developing nations' share of the world's output rose sharply from 18 to 34%. Conversely, the share of the industrialized nations slumped from 73 to 54%. This is a sea change and fraught with dangerous implications. It is necessary to have a close look at the magic wand which has created wealth almost overnight, even if merely on paper. We shall discover that the new method is largely notional, even discriminatory, and must be reviewed before it roots in.

To make the argument clearer, let us preface it with a small digression making an appraisal of the 3Ps notion. Cassel's theory states that the exchange rate between inconvertible paper currencies tends to be the same as the ratio of their domestic purchasing powers. The purchasing power of a currency varies inversely with the price level changes measured by index numbers.

The limitations of index numbers are well known but their main flaw in the present context is that they specify a price level that is influenced in a way by the prices of all the goods bought and sold in an economy during the year, whereas relevant to the exchange rate determination are only the prices of those goods from the total output which enter its foreign trade. Transactions in the invisible exchange market, speculation and monetary policy manipulations affect the exchange rate but do not enter the index number construction. More importantly, the 3Ps theory insists by implication that the exchange rate must be left free to lurch with fluctuations in the relative purchasing power of the currency. This puts foreign trade in a quandary. For these and other reasons, the link between different currencies' purchasing power is invariably vague and murky. Understandably, the 3Ps theory has long ceased to be considered relevant for exchange rate determination.

It is interesting to note that in the IMF revision of the technique for GDP valuation, the issue is precisely the same as before: exchange rate versus purchasing power parity. But the direction of attack has changed. Now the target is exchange rate, not the 3Ps notion. Earlier, the IMF converted into US dollars the relevant details of a country's GDP by using the market exchange rate. To illustrate, if the GDP of a country were reported at 23,000 billion units of its currency and if the average exchange rate used were 2.5 units to a US dollars, the value of the country's GDP would appear in the international publications at USD 4,000 billion for the year in question.

However, inter-nation comparisons at a point of time remain of suspect validity. To explain, let us assume that the GDP of the country in the above illustration has a small, say 23% component of external trade. In that event, the market exchange rate for its currency at 2.5 units to a US dollar may well be out of tune with purchasing power parity (ratio) of the local currency and the US dollar. In other words, the dollar GDP values of various countries do not show under the old valuation, the well-being they confer on their respective populations.

The new method of calculation, therefore, no longer converts output into US dollar equivalent using the market exchange rates. Instead, it looks at the comparative purchasing power of currencies in an effort to get at more realistic view of GDP values for comparisons. In our illustration, if 23,000 billion units of the country's currency could purchase locally the same number of identical bundles of goods (and services) as US$6,000 billion would purchase in the US, the value of its GDP will be recorded at US$6,000 billion, not at USD 4,000 billion as calculated using the market exchange rate.

The new way of calculating the GDP values made China the third largest economy after the United States and Japan in the new IMF ranking of world economies. India rose to sixth position after Germany and France. The immediate reaction among the developing countries has been of dismay, not elation. China feels that the IMF report has over estimated her economic output, she remained a developing country and has a long way to go to catch up even with what she thinks are 'medium developed countries'. Her over one billion people are still more a liability than strength. On per capita income basis, even the revised estimates keep her well down on the list.

Comments from India express the apprehension that the new system would serve as a pretext for industrially advanced countries to slash aid to the less advanced ones, raise protectionist barriers against them and make it more difficult for them to gain access to soft loans.

The IMF argues that the traditional calculation underestimates the size of the developing economies. The new method is more accurate as it takes into account international differences in prices. The claim is infirm. Political economy of the change apart, it is unacceptable for theoretical reasons and operational difficulties. In fact, it attempts to monetize and includes in the GDP a part of the consumer surplus, people enjoy in developing economies, through the opportunity cost measures. The advanced economies do operate one high price – high income circuit. Still, the consumer surplus they enjoy is much greater as evidenced by the vast differences in the quality of life in the two types of economies.

Source: Adapted from the *New Straits Times*, 5 June 1993, p.11.

Case Questions

1. Suppose you are informed that your pocket money of RM500 a month enables you to buy in Kuala Lumpur today, one and a half times more than what you could buy with the same amount in New York. How would you react to this information? Would the information increase your satisfaction or would you feel uninterested? Give reasons for your answer.

2. The new method of converting GDPs into USD equivalents introduced in 1992 has substantially raised the share of the developing countries in the global GDP compared to the developed countries. Do you think the change has also reduced the economic welfare gap between the two sets of countries? Argue your case.

3. What, in your opinion, have been the gains to the global population by the change in the method of making GDPs comparable across countries? Explain.

Case Study   23.2

Income Disparities among OIC Countries

Income disparities among Muslim countries are quite sharp. Of the fifty seven members of the OIC, twenty two are among the least developed economies of the world with very low per capita income. Nineteen countries are oil exporters and are relatively rich. The remaining countries fall in between these two major classifications. Figure 23.3 depicts their relative positions.

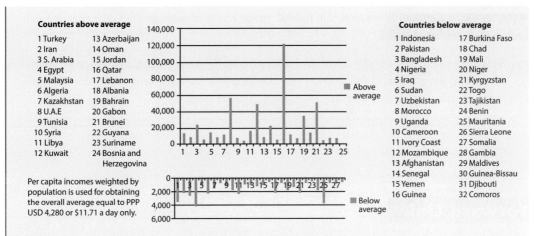

Countries above average

1 Turkey	13 Azerbaijan
2 Iran	14 Oman
3 S. Arabia	15 Jordan
4 Egypt	16 Qatar
5 Malaysia	17 Lebanon
6 Algeria	18 Albania
7 Kazakhstan	19 Bahrain
8 U.A.E	20 Gabon
9 Tunisia	21 Brunei
10 Syria	22 Guyana
11 Libya	23 Suriname
12 Kuwait	24 Bosnia and Herzegovina

Countries below average

1 Indonesia	17 Burkina Faso
2 Pakistan	18 Chad
3 Bangladesh	19 Mali
4 Nigeria	20 Niger
5 Iraq	21 Kyrgyzstan
6 Sudan	22 Togo
7 Uzbekistan	23 Tajikistan
8 Morocco	24 Benin
9 Uganda	25 Mauritania
10 Cameroon	26 Sierra Leone
11 Ivory Coast	27 Somalia
12 Mozambique	28 Gambia
13 Afghanistan	29 Maldives
14 Senegal	30 Guinea-Bissau
15 Yemen	31 Djibouti
16 Guinea	32 Comoros

Per capita incomes weighted by population is used for obtaining the overall average equal to PPP USD 4,280 or $11.71 a day only.

Figure 23.3 *Per capita GNP of OIC countries in 2013 (PPP)*

Case Questions

1. What do you understand by the purchasing power parity (PPP) version of the GNP estimation? Explain. What is an alternative measurement that you know of?

2. How is the aggregate average income obtained? Illustrate the method using imaginary values.

Test Questions

23.1 What do you understand by inter-temporal comparisons of income? Why are such comparisons needed? Do you see any difficulty in making such comparisons? Explain.

23.2 What are index numbers? Distinguish between quantity and price indices Explain the steps and problems involved in the construction of index numbers.

23.3 What are chain base price index numbers and what purpose do they serve? Explain the process of chaining using an imaginary example.

23.4 (a) It is said that the principle underlying the inter-temporal and international comparisons of income is the same. Do you agree? Explain your answer.

(b) If the underlying principle in comparing income over time and space is the same, why do their methods differ? Explain how the conversion factor is determined in the case of international comparisons.

23.5 What are implicit deflators? Why are they called implicit? How do implicit deflators differ from the consumer price index? Explain.

Web Exercise

Search the Internet for the GDP of Turkey (a) at constant prices, and (b) at current prices for the period 2000–2007. Find the implicit deflator and comment on the state of inflation in that country over the years covered.

Forward Link

So far, most of our discussion in this book has been in the framework of a closed economy model. However, in this era of globalization, the economies are open to the outside world. Movement of goods and services, men, materials and capital across national borders is an ever-expanding phenomenon. In the following chapter, which is the final chapter of the book, we will discuss the workings of an open economy with reference to trade, balance of payments and foreign exchange issues.

24 Open Economies: International Trade, Balance of Payments and Exchange Rates

LEARNING OUTCOMES

This chapter should enable the student to understand:

- Why international trade is attractive and what gains flow from it to the people in participating countries
- What makes international trade possible, i.e. what is the theoretical basis for trade
- Free trade: Is it universally desirable and does it benefit all trading countries equally
- If free trade is beneficial, why do countries erect barriers in its way and can protection be justified
- The role that governments play or should play in the area of trade and capital flows across countries
- How we define balance of payments and the role it plays in macroeconomic analyses
- What is foreign exchange rate and how do the changes in it affect trade between countries
- Which is preferable, fixed or flexible exchange rate and why or when is it preferable
- Globalization, foreign trade and developing countries: Challenges and prospects

24.1 INTRODUCTION

Most of the discussion on macro issues in this book has so far been on the assumption of a closed economy that is, ignoring economic relations countries invariably have among themselves even as exports and imports as well as balance of payments were at times mentioned. In this chapter, we remove this assumption and explain the ramifications of opening an economy to bring in the economic transactions it involves in with other nations with reference to goods, services and financial assets. The more open an economy, the more it is sensitive to economic changes taking place outside its borders. We measure the degree of openness by examining the ratio of its imports to its gross national income (GNI). On this criterion, Malaysian economy is among the most widely open ones in the world—imports exceed its GNI by a big margin as Table 24.1 shows. In contrast, India is still not a much open economy; imports constitute around 10% of her GNI. Among the foreign trade transactions between countries, goods and services constitute by far the most dominant component. The gains from trade and the related problems are enormous.

Table 24.1 *Ratio of import to GNI in Malaysia in recent years (amount in RM million)*

Years	2010	2011	2012	2013	2014*	Mean
Import (a)	608,728	664,928	708,548	728,706	769,571	696,096
GNI (b)	770,994	862,650	905,213	949,264	1038.835	905,391
A / b	0.79	0.77	0.78	0.77	0.74	0.77

Source: Bank Negara's Annual Report 2013, Table 4A, p.3 (Import and GNI figures are at 2005 prices). *Estimated

24.1.1 Gains from Trade

Islam encourages trade and holds it as the largest single source of creating wealth and prosperity. The roots of modern industrial age can easily be traced back to mercantilism which had a run of nearly three hundred years until the middle of 18th century. Thus, implicit was in the literature—both Islamic and secular—the recognition of the virtues of division of labour and specialization centuries before Adam Smith (1976). Indeed, one finds candid explanation of the phenomenon in the works of Raghibul Asfahani and Ibn Khaldun, the Muslim scholars. Trade across nations once again shot into prominence after the Second World War because of the vast and fast expansion of national incomes due to spurting growth rates and the spread of cosmopolitanism.

The volume of goods and services the world produced during the second half of the preceding century far exceeded what human beings could produce from the dawn of civilization until 1950. Today, one can buy in the domestic markets American fast food, Italian shoes, Japanese hand phones, Brazilian coffee, Indian mangoes and a host of other goods not locally produced. This is geo-distribution of prosperity and satisfaction, which is both the effect and cause of unabated expansion of foreign trade in the modern era.

As noted above, trade puts within the reach of people in a country imported goods which they may or may not like to produce at home for reasons we shall see later. For example, Bangladesh is good at producing jute specialties like sacks and carpets; it can get tractors in exchange for them from Pakistan. It follows that trade enables a country to specialize in producing goods where it has some kind of natural advantage, say in terms of raw material, as Bangladesh in our example cultivates jute at low costs and which is the best in the world. Note also that specialization would help the country to have a further reduction in manufacturing costs of jute goods.

By allowing greater divisions of labour, promoting specializations and boosting technological progress, international trade contributes to enhance the overall world production and benefit the global population in general. Of late, efforts are being made to develop frameworks for quantifying the gains of international trade in financial assets. Trade gains eventually reach every country, employment expands and scarcities caused by natural factors can be beaten off. Some gain more, some less, but none is left altogether deprived.

Exercise 24.1

What are the major gains of international trade? Identify at least three. Would you agree with the statement that developed and developing countries gain from trade in equal measure? Give reasons for your answer.

24.2   BASIS OF TRADE: THE THEORY

We have shown in Chapter 1 that efficient allocation of resources between alternative uses takes place when marginal rates of transformation or the opportunity costs of producing some commodities rather than others equal their market price ratios. This is so because the input–output prices in the market provide incentive to factor owners including workers to engage into activities where the *opportunity cost* of each is the lowest. This enables the factors use their gains from such specialization to buy goods that would give them higher satisfaction but which they cannot produce due to higher costs. Specialization and exchange of goods via trade thus tends to maximize social gain—the sum of consumers' surplus and business profits in each case. The classic pin-making parable of Adam Smith (1776) well illustrates the point: An individual on his own can make no more than 3–4 pins for himself in a day; specialization and division of labour in a factory produces millions.

> Costs in international trade theory refer to *opportunity cost* involving identical factor use in producing different kinds of goods.

24.2.1   Absolute Differences in Costs

David Ricardo later could easily extend the principle to trading between nations. Starting with the fact that countries usually differ from one another in terms of variety, quantity and quality of their factor endowments,

Absolute differences in costs occur when one country can produce a commodity at a lower cost which some other can produce only at a higher cost.

he argued that it will benefit them to specialize in the production of goods where each has an absolute advantage in producing something over others; trading would then benefit the participants. He illustrated his theory by equating cost between countries in terms of labour hours for producing a pair of goods in two countries along following lines. Table 24.2 presents a scenario where 2× units of labour—one produces wheat and the other cloth—are used in countries A and B. In the closed model M where each country produces both commodities itself, the total output is 1,500 million units in each case. But it is obvious that the resources of country A are more efficient in producing wheat and of B in producing cloth. If each uses its 2× units of labour in producing the commodity where it has absolute advantage over the other, specialization will raise as in N the total output of each commodity to 2,000 units, the gain of specialization being 500 million units in each case. Trade will distribute this gain between them. How much each country will gain would depend upon the barter terms of trade that is the rate of exchange of two goods in physical terms. The data in Table 24.2 allows for identification of the limits of the bargain.

Table 24.2 *Production under absolute differences in costs*

Situation	Wheat (million kg)	Cloth (million metres)
M. Situation before specialization		
2× units of labour produce wheat and cloth in country A	1,000	500
2× units of labour produce wheat and cloth in country B	500	1,000
4× units of labour produce total wheat and cloth	**1,500**	**1,500**
N. Situation after specialization		
2× units of labour produce wheat in country A	2,000	–
2× units of labour produce cloth in country B	–	2,000
4× units of labour produce total wheat and cloth	**2,000**	**2,000**

It is easy to see that A will not be willing to give more than 2 kilograms of wheat for a metre of cloth which it does not produce. If B demands more than that, A will find it cheaper to produce cloth at home at an opportunity cost of 2 kilograms of wheat for it. On the other hand, B will be happy if it can obtain from A anything more than ½ a kilogram of wheat for a metre of cloth, because if A offers less than that, it will pay B to grow wheat at home at a lower opportunity cost. Thus, the exchange rate will settle for 1 metre of cloth anywhere between ½ and 2 kilograms of wheat. The actual rate between these limits will be settled by the relative bargaining power of the two countries that would determine the terms of trade between them. We shall explain the concept below later in the chapter.

Assume that the exchange ratio settled at one and a quarter kilograms of wheat for a metre of cloth and country A has a surplus of 1,000 million tons of wheat; the remaining needed to meet local demand. The situation after trade is shown in Table 24.3. Notice that country A has gained 300 million metres of cloth, while country B benefited by having 500 million tons of wheat.

Table 24.3 *Availability after specialization and trade*

Country	Wheat (million kg)	Cloth (million metres)
A	1,000	800
B	1,000	1,200
Total	2,000	2,000

Exercise 24.2

In Table 24.2, if the barter rate of exchange were 1.5 kilograms of wheat for a metre of cloth, construct a table showing the division of gains between the two countries as in Table 24.3, assumptions remaining unchanged.

Under absolute advantage, the unique positions with respect to natural resources, labour skills and machines in various countries determine the assortment of goods and services that each can produce most efficiently and trade allows them to exchange items they produce with what others produce to mutual gain. For example, Indonesia, with its large population but relative scarcity of capital, specializes in growing oil palm, while Germany, with labour shortages but abundance of capital, specializes in producing machines for use in various fields including agriculture. Specialization and trade may benefit both. Indeed, trade enhances the world output of useful goods and services and expands employment and welfare all around.

24.2.2   Comparative Differences in Costs

Even when country A could produce both commodities cheaper than country B, specialization may still be advisable and trade would benefit them both, if they have comparative differences in costs of producing some goods, other things remaining the same. This implies a situation, for example, where country A may be superior to country B in producing both wheat and cloth but its superiority is greater in producing wheat than cloth; or conversely, country B is inferior in producing both the goods but its inferiority is greater in producing wheat rather than cloth. Ricardo was aware of the possibility of division of labour and specialization working to their mutual gain via trade in such a situation too. For, he asked that if he were the best lawyer in the town as well as the best typist, will it not be to his advantage to devote more time in

Even when one country is superior to the other in the production of both goods, there is a comparative difference between costs of producing them, specialization and trade will benefit both.

preparing cases and employ the second best typist available to handle his manuscripts.

However, the comparative cost theory of international trade—its bases, implications and ramifications—were more fully explained by Eli Heckscher and Bertil Ohlin, the teacher-student team that highlighted the opportunity cost differences playing the role in cross-border trade. We present the comparative cost differences case in Table 24.4 to show that specialization and trade is still beneficial to the trading countries. Note that the opportunity cost ratio of wheat in terms of cloth is 2.5 in A and 1.3 in B. (How?)

Table 24.4 *Production under comparative differences in costs*

Situation	Wheat (million kg)	Cloth (million metres)
M. Situation before specialization		
2× units of labour produce wheat and cloth in country A	1,000	400
2× units of labour produce wheat and cloth in country B	910	700
4× units of labour produce total wheat and cloth	**1,910**	**110**
N. Situation after specialization		
2× units of labour produce wheat in country A	2,000	–
2×units of labour produce cloth in country B	–	1,400
4× units of labour produce total wheat and cloth	**2,000**	**1,400**

A country can be superior to another in producing any two goods but if its superiority is larger in producing one thing rather than the other, it will benefit the country to specialize in producing only that commodity where it has greater superiority. The other country though inferior in both areas of production but would gain by trade by producing only that commodity where its disadvantage is smaller.

Now, after specialization, A will not part with more than 2.5 kilograms of wheat for a metre of cloth that being the opportunity cost of producing cloth at home. Likewise, B will not accept less than 1.3 kilograms of wheat per metre of cloth. (Why?) Suppose bargain sets the rate at 2 kilograms of wheat for a metre of cloth, the distribution will appear as in Table 24.5. Notice that the countries together are having 350 million metres of cloth more than before due to specialization and trade without any reduction in the availability of wheat in either case.

Table 24.5 *Availability after specialization and trade*

Country	Wheat (million kg)	Cloth (million metres)
A	1,000	455
B	910	945
Total	1,910	1,400

The absolute cost difference is but a special case of the generic comparative cost differences. We have explained the foreign trade theory with a two countries–two commodities set. The theory can be extended to multilateral trade but the basics remain unchanged; we do not attempt extension here to keep things simple.

Exercise 24.3

Fill in the blanks marked as xxx in Table 24.6 and show if trade will take place between the countries, giving reasons for your answer.

Table 24.6 *Production under xxx differences in costs*

Situation	Wheat (million kg)	Cloth (million metres)
M. Situation before specialization		
2× units of labour produce wheat and cloth in country A	1,000	400
2× units of labour produce wheat and cloth in country B	750	300
4× units of labour produce total wheat and cloth	**1,750**	**700**
N. Situation after specialization		
2× units of labour produce wheat in country A	xxx	–
2× units of labour produce cloth in country B	–	xxx
4× units of labour produce total wheat and cloth	**xxx**	**xxx**

24.2.3 Terms of Trade

We have referred to the terms of trade or TOT. What does this term mean? Briefly, it is the ratio of the index of a country's exports prices to that of its import prices, usually expressed as a percentage. The ratio measures the relative price position of a country in external trade. The terms of trade are said to improve if that ratio rises and vice versa. If a country's export prices rise relative to its import prices we say that its terms of trade have moved in its favour as it now receives more imports for each unit of goods exported. Abrupt and adverse changes in its terms of trade may have serious consequences for a country. For this reason, terms of trade are sometimes taken as an indicator of the relative social welfare of a nation, though such a usage is not always appropriate.

Exercise 24.4

Suppose country A exports to country B, 10 units of X commodity at a price of $20 a unit, and imports from them 10 units of Y commodity at $10 per piece. The export and import price ratio for A therefore is 2:1 and for B its reciprocal 1:0.5. Now suppose the international price of X rises to $25, with that of B remaining unchanged. Verify if the export–import price ratios are now 2.5:1 for A and 1:0.4 for B. Who has gained in terms of trade—A or B—and by how much (50% or 60%)?

A favourable change in terms of trade means that a country can import more of goods and services per unit of export than before and vice versa.

It is well to note that there indeed is a whole family of the terms of trade. For some variations you may see the glossary at the end of the chapter.

Over the past 50 years, terms of trade have in general moved against the primary producers—the developing economies.

In general, the trend after the Second World War has been the movement of the terms of trade against the primary producers to the manufacturers' advantage; most raw material prices fell very sharply from the mid-1980s barring oil. This has happened because large multinationals from the rich, industrialized nations could tilt the domestic market structure in their favour to the disadvantage of small, unorganized commodity producers in the developing economies. For instance, African terms of trade deteriorated by over 30% between 1980 and 1989 which prompted industrialization aimed at import substitution. Alternatively, there have been concerted efforts to reduce production in order to increase prices.

BOX 24.1

Financial Crisis 2007–2008 and Global Economy

What shall be the impact off this financial crisis on the global economy? The effects are complex and work across multiple channels. First, and most important, access to bank credit is likely to be highly restrained for a considerable period, as banks seek to reduce leverage and rebuilt capital bases. Bank lending standards have already been ramped up sharply, and they are likely to tighten further as weakening economies further magnify bank losses, even when governments are providing public funds to help boost capital bases. Second, access to debt securities markets has tightened dramatically, not just for riskier low-grade borrowers but even for top rated issuers and short-term securities, such as commercial paper, that are normally immune from such risks. Third, the drop in equity prices and residential property values has eroded household net wealth. For example, household net worth in the United States has fallen by an estimated 15 per cent over the last one year. Fourth, emerging economies are also facing much tighter limits on external financing, as global deleveraging and increasing risk aversion have curtailed investor interest in these markets.

How big the aggregate impact be? Some insights can be gained by looking at the historical record of what has happened to economic activity following financial crises in the past. At first glance, the evidence is mixed. The recent *World Economic Outlook* found that only about half of the 113 episodes of financial stress over the past 30 years were followed by economic slowdowns or recessions. However, the characteristics of a stress episode are a key determinant of the scale of its macroeconomic impact. Episodes associated with banking crisis tend to have a much more severe macroeconomic impact. In fact, recessions associated with banking crises tend to last twice as long and to be twice as intense, and thus to imply four times the cumulative output losses. Also, episodes in which the financial stress lasts for a longer period are likely to be more damaging.

Source: World Bank's World Economic Outlook, 2008.

24.3   BARRIERS TO TRADE

Islam stood for freedom of trade, it could be of little consequence for at the time of its advent the size of world population could hardly be conceived of being over thousands in head count—the earliest authentic estimate available for 1850, more than a thousand years after Islam, puts the population of the planet at just 50 million. Economics as a formal discipline, developed in the West during the dominance of the colonization era. As such, principles of economics have always had policy underpinnings. Free trade soon became an article of faith with the Western countries in general, because being far ahead in industrialization, free trade allowed them access to sources of raw materials as well as to markets for finished goods in the colonies under their rule. The demonstrable benefits of free trade counted above and others were so convincing that opposition to it was taken almost as a rebellion by the rulers. However, the first effective shot against the doctrine was fired from Europe.

24.3.1   Free Trade versus Protection

From 1800 to 1840, Germany experienced one of the worst patches of its economic history; it was lagging far behind England in industrialization. While movement of goods between states within the country was much restricted, their flow from abroad, England in particular, was absolutely unhindered. Frederic List (1789–1840) saw the undoing of his country in competitive trade among the unequal. The merit of his opposition to the doctrine for improving economic position of Germany lay in presenting the case for protection as a counter *theory* to the *principle* of free trade.

List introduced two ideas that were new to the economic thinking of that time. One was the idea of nationality as opposed to cosmopolitanism. The other was the idea of productive power as pitched against the idea of consumable wealth. List's *National System of Political Economy* rests primarily on these two ideas.

List argued that the plea for free trade rests on the hypothesis that men were henceforth to be united in one great community from which war would be banished. Note that the similarity with the current vision of a *borderless global village* is quite striking. On such a hypothesis, continued List, humanity was merely the sum of individuals. Individual interests alone counted and any interference with economic liberty could never be justified. But between man and humanity stands the history of nations to which the conventional wisdom was altogether oblivious. Every individual forms part of some nation and his prosperity largely depends upon the political power of his nation. Universal good is a noble end to pursue, but nations today as ever are of unequal strength and have quite different interests. A *global* union could benefit them all if they met on an *equal* footing. At present the union could benefit only the stronger.

Second, List argued that the equality of nations rests on the equality of their *productive power*, trade increases consumable wealth alone not the power to produce it. He wrote the *power to create wealth is infinitely more important than the wealth itself.* To him, this power lay in *manufacturing*, not in trade or agriculture. Manufactures permit better utilization of a country's resources: its waterpower, its winds, its minerals and its fuel supplies are better harnessed. Industry for List was a social force, the

The merit of List lies in that he forged the case for protection as counter theory to the free trade theory.

creator of labour and capital, not the *natural* result of labour and saving. Its development requires growth of dynamic culture skills and powers of a unified process of production. A nation must sacrifice and give up a measure of immediate prosperity for the sake of this qualitative growth. It must sacrifice some present advantages—gains from free trade—in order to ensure to itself the future ones; it cannot and should not wait for *natural* process to usher in industrialization. In a beautiful passage, List makes the comparison: *It is true that experience teaches that the wind bears the seed from one region to another, and that thus, waste moorlands have been transformed into dense forests, but would it on that account, be wise policy for the forester to wait until the wind in the course of ages effects this transformation?*

The tariff, apparently, was the only method of raising the wind. However, permanent protection for domestic industry was no part of List's scheme. The industries had to meet certain criteria and show potential for surviving when protection was withdrawn in course of time. It was never meant to be a shelter for inefficiency.

Current literature recognizes List's contributions in allowing temporary protection to an industry in its early stage; the axiom is: *nurse the baby, protect the child and free the adult.* However, UNCTAD XI recommendations seem to reinforce List's view beyond the infant industry argument to help developing economies.

> Protection granted to new industries until they mature benefits the country. The rule of thumb is: nurse the baby, protect the child and free the adult. Protection must be granted to industries that have potential to continue growing even when protection is withdrawn.

24.3.2   UNCTAD XI Recommendations

The Eleventh United Nations Conference on Trade and Development or UNCTAD XI emphasized that trade was only a means, not an end in itself; it was important not only to increase developing countries' share in the world trade but also to ensure that their participation helps create employment, reduce poverty and adds to masses' welfare so as to contribute towards achieving the Millennium Development Goals and World Summit Outcomes. This requires action at the international level and national level in developing countries.

At the international level

- Developing policy and encouraging participation to address the problems of communities.
- Enabling the development dimension in multilateral trade regulations.
- Strengthening and expanding the services sector in developing economies.
- Helping developing economies and those in transition in their access to the World Trade Organization.
- Addressing the problems of small and vulnerable as well as landlocked developing economies.
- Improving the understanding of using preferences and ways to stem their erosion.
- Ensuring duty-free and quota-free market access to the least developed countries.

- Developing policies that promote both trade and environmental care.
- Protecting, preserving and promoting, traditional knowledge, innovation and biological resources.
- Preventing and abolishing the use of anti-competition practices.
- Promoting the responsibility and accountability of corporate actors in the society.
- Helping increased participation of developing countries in new and dynamic sectors and promoting their creative industries.
- Promoting South-South trade and economic cooperation.

> UNCTAD XI increases the responsibilities of developed economies for providing help and support to developing and in-transition economies to promote their economic and social achievements.

At the national level in developing countries

- Initiating trade policies that suit the needs and circumstances of internal development requirements.
- Integrating trade with national development policies to ensure poverty alleviation and support growth and sustainable development.

Exercise 24.5

Do you find any ambiguities and contradictions in the actions that UNCTAD XI has recommended to be undertaken by developed countries at the international level? Explain your position clearly.

BOX 24.2

Silver Lining for Emerging and Developing Economies

In better shape

Higher foreign reserves and lower debt are providing a cushion for many, but not all emerging and developing economies during the current downturn.

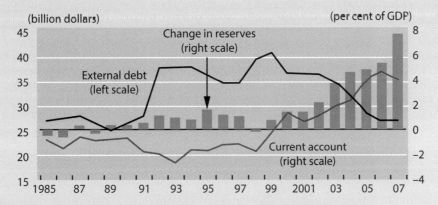

Figure 24.1 *Aggregate data for emerging and developing economies as classified in the IMF's World Economic Outlook database*

Source: IMF staff calculations.

24.4 BALANCE OF PAYMENTS

Balance of payments presents an accounting record of the external economic transactions of a country for a specified period usually a year. It has three broad sections: current account, capital and financial accounts, and official reserves.

When we talked of national income accounting in Chapter 2, we implied a system of double entry accounts underpinning the discussion. In the identity sort of expression: $C + S = Y = C + I$, we in fact were providing the two sides of the production account of an economy: $C + S$ being its debit or receipt side and $C + I$ being its credit or expenditure side. The sum of debits is the gross national product equalling the sum of all credits or national expenditure; both income and expenditure measure the value of national output. All items on the debit or credit side of the production account find a counter entry in some other account of the economy. But the $(X - M)$ on the credit (expenditure) side reaches here via the account we call as the balance of payments or BOP. But $(X - M)$ as we have so far used the expression is not the complete story.

The balance of payments is a statistical statement of external economic transactions—receipts and payments—of a country for a specific time period, usually a quarter and/or year. In BOP we record the transactions on the *accrual accounting* principle. In other words, transactions are recorded when economic value is created, transformed, exchanged, transferred or extinguished. The purpose of preparing the statement is to monitor the impact of changes in the pattern and volume of the transactions on the national economy. It shows if a country has on balance given out or received money.

Table 24.7 *Balance of payments of Malaysia: estimates for 2011 in RM billion*

Item	Value sign		
	+	−	Net
Goods	696.6	549.0	151.6
Services	110.6	116.9	−6.3
Balance on goods and services	816.2	664.9	145.3
Income	52.1	100.0	42.9
Current transfers	1.2	17.3	−16.1
Balance on current account	862.4	365.0	102.4
Percentage of national income			11.9
Capital account			−133.0
Financial account			23.3
Direct investment			−9.3
Portfolio investment			26.1
Other investment			6.5
Balance of capital and financial account			23.1
Errors and omissions			−30.9
of which foreign revaluation gains			7.6
Overall balance			94.7
BNM international reserves (net)			423.3
USD billion equivalent			133.6

Source: Department of Statistics Bank Negara Malaysia

Note: Numbers may not necessarily add up due to rounding up of figures.

The GNP–GDP differences give the state of BOP; the balancing entry being the *net* amount the country has to receive from or pay to the others under the head 'net property income from abroad'. A negative balance shows an addition to our external liabilities and results in an erosion of our foreign exchange reserves and weakens our currency. A positive balance does just the opposite. Table 24.7 presents the Malaysian BOP estimates for the year 2011. It has, like any BOP, three main components: (i) current account, (ii) capital and financial account, (iii) financial reserves.

24.4.1   Current Account

We record in current account transactions excluding those of financial character. They involve economic values and take place between the resident and non-resident entities. Major items covered include goods, services, income and current transfers. Goods mostly consist of moveable items that Malaysia exports to and imports from rest of the world.

Services include transportation, tourism, education, healthcare, construction, communications, insurance, etc., which Malaysians provide to outsiders and vice versa. They also cover royalties, license fees, income from investments, current transfers such as capital gains or losses, and expenditure on maintaining embassies. Remember, all the items mentioned constitute what we earlier referred to as invisible exports and imports.

> Current account records items including exports and imports of goods and services, incomes and payments, and income transfers.

Note that Malaysia recorded a large surplus of RM102.4 billion making 11.9% of her national income (GNI) in 2011. The US remains the largest trading partner of the country followed by Singapore, even as her trade with the Organization of Islamic Conference (OIC) countries has been showing up in recent years.

24.4.2   Capital and Financial Account

Capital account mainly covers capital transfers arising from the acquisition or disposal of non-financial assets. Direct investments of long-term interest are also included. Finally, we have here portfolio investments of short duration. It covers transactions in equities and debt securities including bonds, notes and other money market instruments. Other investments—short and long term—covered are short-term trade credits, loans, currency and deposits and other receivables and payables.

> Capital and financial transactions appear together in this section of both short- and long-term duration.

The financial section of the account records transactions pertaining to the changes in ownership of foreign financial assets and liabilities of a country. The parties involved are monetary authorities, general government, banks and others.

Table 24.7 shows substantial deficit on the capital and financial account of Malaysia (RM109.7 billion). The entire deficit falls in the capital account while the financial sector shows a small surplus. (Can you say why?)

24.4.3   Official Reserves

Items in the reserve section result from transactions in assets that Bank Negara Malaysia regarded as available for international settlements. The items include monetary gold, special drawing rights (SDRs), reserve position in the IMF, foreign exchange (currency), deposits, securities and residual claims. The reserve position of Malaysia has usually been sound. Currently their value is well over USD 100 billion or about 16% of her GNP.

24.5   EXCHANGE RATES: FIXITY VERSUS FLEXIBILITY

Once you move to an open economy model, the perplexing issues concerning foreign exchange rate enter into the picture. Exchange rate changes become a significant factor in adverse balance of payments corrections. Stable rates of exchange between currencies reduce risks of foreign trade, fluctuations increase them. The choice becomes difficult: on historical evidence, efforts for stability tend to result in rigidity while attempts to impart flexibility tend to end in chaotic movements. Managed flexibility can be a theoretical ideal but is difficult to put into operation. Thus, discussions on exchange rate norms have usually been inconclusive.

Whether a country should pursue a fixed or flexible exchange rate policy is determined a priori. The choice is determined by the circumstances of a country developing countries choice of a flexible exchange rate policy seems more beneficial.

Pursuit of stability in practical terms has two requirements. First, keep the economy *internally* stable, i.e. free of inflation or deflation. Second, keep exchange rate stable to ensure smooth and growing economic transactions with the rest of the world. The difficulty, we shall see, is that the two requirements mostly call for conflicting action. The policy choice, therefore, depends essentially on the circumstances of a country, especially the size and openness of its economy.

24.5.1   Fixed Rates

We may begin with the statement that fixed exchange rates ensure internal stability no more than do the flexible exchange rates. One can recount from the history of gold standard, no less periods of financial turmoil and sharp variations in output and prices than one can from the recent era of more freely fluctuating exchange rates. For keeping exchange rate fixed, we have to tie the domestic currency to an anchor—gold or a strong currency such as the dollar, euro or yen. The principle is the same. Because gold has served as the anchor in one form or the another over long stretches of time until 1973, we may use the yellow metal for explaining the modus operandi of fixed rates. Let us assume that currency A contains (or is regarded as equivalent to) 3.2727273 grains of gold 24/12 fine while currency B has (or equals) 10 grains of gold 9/10 fine. The pure gold equivalence exchange rates (ER) expressed as the domestic price of foreign currency in the two countries A and B will then be as follows:

$$\text{For A,} \quad \frac{10 \times \dfrac{10}{9}}{3.2727273 \dfrac{11}{12}} = 3 \text{ per unit of B} \qquad (24.1)$$

For B, reciprocal of 3, i.e. = 0.333333 per unit of A   (24.2)

In both countries, monetary authorities will be under obligation to buy and sell gold at officially fixed prices. The importers in both countries will be free to make payments either through buying foreign currency in the market or through export of equivalent gold. Remember that what are exports of one country are imports of the other whether goods or gold. But payment through gold export involves transportation costs which must affect the choice of the mode of payment.

Assume that the cost of exporting gold worth 3 units of currency A between the two countries is 0.0005 units of currency A. Thus, in the foreign exchange market of country A, the exchange rate (3 + 0.0005) = 3.0005 will be what we may call the upper gold point (UGP), and let (3 − 0.0005) = 2.9995 be known as the lower gold point (LGP). We now have the apparatus ready to explain how the gold standard would keep the exchange rate fixed between the two countries. Figure 24.2 helps explain the argument.

> Fixed exchange rates ensure stability, reduce risks in external trade and help planning, but they subject the economy to the vagaries of external forces and tend to reduce economic independence of a country.

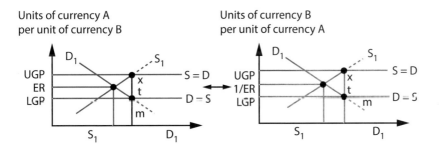

Figure 24.2 *The gold standard mechanism ensuring exchange rate fixity*

If the demand for currency B starts rising relative to its supply in country A—the balance of payments moves against it—imports are more in value than exports. The exchange rate in the market will start rising (why?) but it cannot cross the UGP as it will become cheaper for importers to buy gold in the market and export it to country B. D_1 will cease shifting up; excess demand will move out from the currency market to that of gold, allowing only a tiny (tx) departure from ER. In contrast, if the balance of payments becomes increasingly favourable to country A raising the supply of currency B relative to its demand in the exchange market, the ER will start falling. But currency A will become dearer in country B. Nevertheless, the rise in 1/ER cannot go on unabated. As soon as the rate crosses the upper gold point in B—again a small divergence (tx) from 1/ER, the importers in country B will find it cheaper to ship gold to country A rather than buy her currency in the exchange market. The upper gold point of one country is the lower gold point of the other. But in Figure 24.1, they are shown at the same level because the exchange rates in the two countries are marked as mutually reciprocals.

Under the gold standard, no country can stop either export of gold or its import. Gold standard works on the assumption that at gold points the supply of the metal is kept perfectly elastic. The impact of this requirement is indeed far reaching. The mechanism keeps the exchange rates between currencies *fixed* in relation to one another as they are tied to a common beam: the price of gold. But it does not necessarily keep the rates *stable*; it only makes them fluctuate in response to the changing demand and supply conditions of gold affecting its price. It forces a country to import inflation or deflation taking place outside via the gold tie; a stable economy thus may become unstable. Finally, what is true of fixity of rates in case of gold is true of attempting fixity of exchange rate through pegging with a strong currency. Malaysia gained by doing away with the dollar peg recently; ringgit appreciated vis-à-vis other currencies.

24.5.2 Flexible Rates

Flexibility in exchange rates implies movement confined within certain limits. Flexible rates allow more independent monetary policies, are better shock absorbers and accommodate rapid dynamic changes more easily.

The fixed versus flexible exchange rate debate is not of much relevance for developed economies. It is the developing and economies in transition which face the dilemma. We saw that in a fixed exchange rate regime domestic economic activity adjusts to the exchange rate. On the other hand, freely floating exchange rate is taken as a reflection of fast paced dynamic economic activity. In either case, the circumstances of an economy are, as alluded to earlier, the deciding factors.

Fixed exchange rates hamper adjustments; they require much flexibility in wages and prices in the domestic economy, especially because of volatile capital flows. They may put monetary and fiscal policies under much stress during cyclical fluctuations even as they have the merit of reducing transaction costs and exchange rate risks. Flexible exchange rates have the advantage of allowing a country to pursue an independent monetary policy rather than be tied down to the wishes of the anchor currency country. Again, experience shows that flexible exchange rates provide more elbow room for absorbing shocks and enhance ability to better distribute the adjustment burden between internal and external actors. Flexible rates are found more helpful in the case of small and more open economies like Malaysia.

Flexibility in exchange rates is vital to permit balance of payments adjustments. The requirement motivated the IMF recently to put in place procedures for surveillance of exchange rate policies in member countries. The implementation of these procedures calls for improvement.

Corporate governance, more so in the case of multinational, can do a lot towards economic progress with stability by more responsible and transparent behaviour.

Flexibility in exchange rates is a matter of measure and management. Freely fluctuating rates may prove no less harmful than the rigid ones. IMF from its very inception has provided for disciplined flexibility, for example, within reasonable bands dotted with occasional grant of exceptions. But its treatment of the developing economies lacks discretion; one size does not fit all.

> The difficulty with flexible rates is the non-determinate nature of the limits for change. The IMF for that reason is strengthening the surveillance system.

Summary

- How open is an economy is determined by the ratio of its imports to its gross national income; the GNI. On this touch stone, Malaysia has long been among the most open economies of the world.

- The theory of international trade is an extension of the same principles of division of labour that prompts specialization and exchange in the domestic fields of trade. Resource diversity and skills variety is much more marked among countries than within different regions of the same country.

- If each country produces goods and services where its advantage is the largest or disadvantage the least, efficiency in factor use is maximum i.e. the costs are the least and output is maximum, making welfare gains the biggest. Costs here mean opportunity costs.

- Cost differences in a two commodity–two country model may be absolute, comparative (why?) or equal. Specialization and trade are possible in the first two cases, not the third. (Why?)

- The gains from trade between any two countries are shared between them in the same ratio as their terms of trade. The terms of trade consist of the ratio of a country's exports price index to its imports price index, expressed as a percentage. Terms move in favour of a country if this ratio rises and vice versa.

- Even as free trade benefits all countries, it often erects barriers in its way as national interests differ often for non-economic reasons. These barriers assume various forms: duties, tariffs quotas, licensing, etc.

- Infant industry argument is the principled tool against free trade. Of no less importance for developing countries, is also the unfair distribution of trade gains between the developed and developing nations. The UNCTAD XI recommendations are intended to correct the tilt.

- Balance of payments records the economic transactions of a country with rest of the world for a given period, usually a year under three broad heads: current account, capital and financial account, and official reserves.

- Balance of payments is always balanced, the balancing entry being the positive or negative debt to outsiders. An adverse balance of payments may put pressure on the rate of exchange leading to inflation and depreciation of the domestic currency. Even a persistently favourable BOP could be a cause of concern. (Can you say why?)

- Fixed rate of exchange has the merits of achieving external stability and reducing foreign exchange risks in trade but it is unwelcome for reducing the possibilities for a country to pursue an independent monetary policy. Flexible exchange rate allows greater independence especially to developing countries to adjust BOP imbalances more easily.

- A flexible exchange rate policy demands restraint, sagacity and managerial skills to keep things on the right track. Thus, IMF is putting stronger surveillance procedures in place to guide monetary policies of the member countries.

Glossary

Balance of payments The balance of payments is a statistical record of the external transactions of a country for a stated period of time, usually a year. It is generally divided into three sections: (i) current account contains entries for import and export of goods and services, income and transfers excluding financial transactions; (ii) capital and financial section records the long-run and short-run flow of capital and other purely financial payments and receipts of money, and (iii) the third section holds the national assets and reserves. The BOP is always in balance. (Recall why?)

Comparative costs In principle international trade is not different from domestic trade. Both are based on division of labour and specialization as source of increased production, trade distributing the gains between the parties. The main difference is that international trade relatively involves higher costs than domestic trade. Specialization in either case gives comparative advantage to one in what he produces over others. Comparative advantage means smaller opportunity cost compared to others in producing something. Specialization benefits both countries even if one has lower costs in producing both the goods. For example, if country A can produce both cloth and shoes at lower cost than country B but the difference is greater in the case of cloth, trade will still benefit both if A produces only cloth and B shoes.

Exchange peg An exchange rate is said as pegged in modern era if its value is matched to the value of another single currency or to a basket of other currencies. It is also called a fixed rate regime as the world had for long under the gold standard. In principle, the rate can be tied to any measure of value believed to remain stable. The peg is usually used to stabilize the value of a currency in relation to the currency it is attached. This facilitates trade and investments between the two countries, and is especially useful for small open economies like Singapore, Malaysia, Kuwait or Taiwan where external trade forms a large part of their GDP.

Floating exchange rates They are also called the flexible exchange rate results when it is set for a currency by its supply and demand relative to other currencies in the foreign exchange market. Thus, floating exchange rates change freely and are determined by the foreign exchange market. This is in contrast to a 'fixed exchange rate' regime. In some instances, if a currency value moves in any one direction at a rapid and sustained rate, central banks intervene by buying and selling their own currency using reserves. For example, Bank Negara Malaysia buys and sells ringgit in the market to maintain its exchange rate flexible within a band. However, central banks are reluctant to intervene, unless absolutely necessary, in a floating regime.

Terms of trade (TOT) A country's terms of trade expresses the relationship between its import and export prices; more precisely TOT = Export prices index/Import prices index. A rise in the export prices of the country relative to its import prices, the terms of trade are said to have moved in its favour as it would now get more imports per unit of what it exports. Terms of trade are determined by the supply and demand forces of commodities at the international level. They are given data for individual countries. From around 1985, most raw material prices, with the exception of oil, have fallen very sharply as industrial nations can dominate and structure markets in developing economies to their advantage. The result is that the terms of trade have all along tended to move against the primary producers. For example, African terms of trade deteriorated by 30% between 1980 and 1989. You should know that we in fact have a family of terms of trade. The more important ones are here. The ratio of relative export and import prices is called the *net barter terms of trade* if and when the volume of trade is held constant. The *gross barter terms of trade* equal the ratio of the quantity index of exports to the quantity index of inputs (recall Chapter 10 for quantity indices). The value of exports as a ratio of import prices gives us the *income terms of trade*.

Trade barriers If there is gain for all in international trade why do most of nations resort to restrictions on the free flow of goods and services across their borders? The reason precisely is that even as nations gain from trade but gains between them are not equitably distributed. There is also clash of interest in who produces what, as Ricardo free trade has meant a policy appropriate to an advanced manufacturing nation, in its relation with agrarian nations supplying it with food, raw materials and markets. This division is still sought by vested interests. Finally, trade benefits nations as a whole but not all individual within a nation. Powerful losers make authorities raise barriers in the form of quotas, tariffs, etc. to shut out foreign goods.

Concepts for Review

- Absolute differences in costs
- Balance of payments
- Closed and open economies
- Comparative costs theory
- Exchange pegging
- Fixed rates of exchange
- Floating exchange rates
- Foreign direct investment
- Free trade
- Gains from trade
- Trade barriers
- UNCTAD XI

Case Study 24.1

Exchange Rate Pegging: Merits and Demerits

A former president of the Federal Reserve Bank of New York described fixed currencies as follows:

'Fixing value of the domestic currency relative to that of a low-inflation country is one approach central banks have used to pursue price stability. The advantage of an exchange rate target is its clarity, which makes it easily understood by the public. In practice, it obliges the central bank to limit money creation to levels comparable to those of the country to whose currency it is pegged. When credibly maintained, an exchange rate target can lower inflation expectations to the level prevailing in the anchor country. Experiences with fixed exchange rates, however, point to a number of drawbacks. A country that fixes its exchange rate surrenders control of its domestic monetary policy'.

William J. McDonough

Case Questions

1. Do you think that Malaysia gained the advantages expressed above when it pegged the ringgit to US dollar during the 1998 Asian financial crisis? Elaborate your answer.

2. Following the devastation of World War II, the IMF allowed all forty four allies in the war to fix exchange rates against the US dollar. The system collapsed in 1970. Why? Explain.

3. What drawbacks of fixed exchange rates did experiences bring to light as referred to in the second last line of the case above? Explain.

Case Study 24.2

Remittances and Their Significance for Developing Economies

Remittances sent home by migrants represent the largest source of external capital in many developing countries. This source is now being affected by the current financial crisis. Remittances were estimated at $251 billion worldwide in 2007 (World Bank, 2008), which represents more than twice the level of international aid. Adding remittances through informal channels, the number is higher by 50% (World Bank, 2008). The level of remittances has been increasing for many years but if the predictions are confirmed, 2008 risks being the first year of decreasing levels of remittances in several decades. This would set back developing countries, as remittances have a poverty reducing impact on both the sending households and the country of origin. Remittances are much less concentrated in certain countries than foreign direct investment, which tends to flow to certain countries.

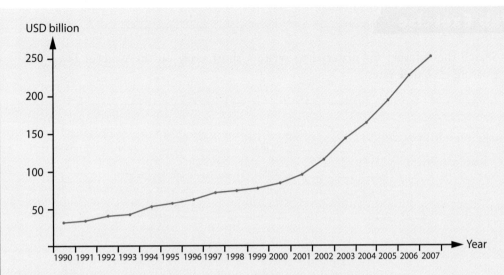

Figure 24.3 *Remittances for developing countries, 1990-2007 (USD billion)*

Source: World Bank (2008)

Case Questions

1. Nationals working outside the country bring in more money home that helps promote economic development. Why it is then that there is often clamour about the brain drain? Which in your opinion better: remittances or brain drain? Give reasons for your answer.

2. Foreign aid and foreign direct investment (FDI) are important sources of helping growth in developing economies. Which one is preferable and why?

Test Questions

24.1 Explain clearly the theoretical basis of international trade. Show that specialization and trade increases the volume of output. Is it different from the reason for domestic trade? Elaborate.

24.2 Why do countries attempt to restrict foreign trade? Under what circumstances would you justify such restrictions? Is there a general case for protecting domestic industries from foreign competition? Argue.

24.3 What is meant by terms of trade in economics? Explain. When can terms of trade be regarded favourable to a country? Explain the consequences of an adverse balance of trade.

24.4 How will you define balance of payments? Explain what its main sections contain. How would you know if the BOP is adverse or favourable to a country?

24.5 Discuss carefully the merits and demerits of a fixed exchange rate regime. Do you think that floating rates are better especially for small open economies such as Malaysia? Give reasons for your answer.

Web Exercise

Search the Internet for material to write a short essay on the issue of fixed and floating exchange rates.

Bibliography

Abraham, W. I. (1994). *National Income and Economic Accounting*, New Delhi: Khosla Publishing House.

Addas, W. A. J. (2008). *Methodology of Economics: Secular versus Islamic—A Comparative Study*, Research Management Centre, International Islamic University, Malaysia (IIUM)

Ahmad, S. (1993). '*Inter temporal and Inter-spatial Comparisons of Income—The Meaning of Relative Prices*', International Economics Department of World Bank, WPS 1157, Washington DC: World Bank.

Arndt, S. W. (1971). 'The Comparative Merits of Fixed vs. Flexible Exchange Rates', *Journal of Money, Credit and Banking*, 3/2. pp. 356-36, <http://www.jstor.org/pss/1991148> accessed 25 Aug 2013.

Bade, R and Parkin, M. (2002). *Foundations of Microeconomics*, USA: Pearson Education Inc.

Bank Negara Malaysia Annual Reports.

Beckerman, W. (1987). *An Introduction to National Income Analysis*, 3rd edn.,New Delhi: Universal Book Stall.

Bertola, G., Foellmi, R. and Zweimuller, J. (2006). *Income Distribution in Macroeconomic Models*, UK: Princeton University Press.

Boulding, K. E. (1963). *Principles of Economic Policy*, London: Staples Press.

Branco, M. (1994). '*Determinants of Cross Country Income Inequality: An Augmented Kuznets Hypothesis*', World Bank: Policy Research Working Paper, pp.1246.

Case, K. E. and Fair, R. C. (2004). *Principles of Economics*, 7th edn., New Jersey: Pearson Prentice Hall.

Coase, R. H. (1960). The Problem of Social Cost, *Journal of Law and Economics*, Vol. 3, pp. 1–44.

Coxton, F. E., Cowden, D.J. and Klien, S. (1982). *Applied General Statistics*, 3rd edn., New Delhi: Prentice Hall.

Davidson, P. and Kregel, J. A. (1989). *Macroeconomics Problems and Policies of Income Distribution: Functional, Personal and International*, Cheltenham Glos, UK: Edward Elger Publishing Ltd.

Dornbusch, R. and Fischer, S. (1984). *Macroeconomics*, Singapore: McGraw Hill.

Field, B. C. and Field, M. K. (2002). Environmental Economics—An Introduction, New York: Irwin-McGraw Hill.

Frank, R. H. (1991). Microeconomics and Behaviour, International Edition, Singapore: McGraw Hill.

Froyen, R. T. (1990). *Macroeconomics: Theories and Policies*, 3rd edn., New York: Macmillan.

Galor, O. and Ziera J. (1993). 'Income Distribution and Macroeconomics', *Review of Economic Studies*, 60: pp. 35–52.

Hasan, Z. (1975). *Theory of Profit*, New Delhi: Vikas Publishing House.

Hasan, Z. (1983). Theory of Profit: The Islamic Viewpoint, *Journal of Research in Islamic Economics*, (1,1) ICRIE King Abdulaziz University, Jeddah.

Hasan, Z. (1996). Review of Akram Khan 'An Introduction to Islamic Economics', *American Journal of Islamic Social Sciences*, (13,4) IIIT, Herndon.

Hasan, Z. (1998). Review of M. N. Siddiqui '*Teaching Economics in Islamic Perspective*', (6,1) Islamic Economic Studies.

Hasan, Z. (2006). *Sustainable Development: Meaning and Implications*, (19,2) JKAU: Islamic Economics.

Hasan, Z. (2010). '*Factors of Production and Factor Markets from the Islamic Angle*', IRTI's online teaching programme.

Hasan, Z. (2011). '*Islamic Economics: Scarcity, Self-interest and Maximization*', IRTI Laureate Lecture, IDB Headquaters, Jeddah.

Hekal, R. (2006). '*What is the Balance of Payments?*' <http//www.investopedia.com/articles/03/060403.asp> accessed 23 July 2013.

HM Treasury. (2009). '*Overview of User's Guide GDP Deflator Series*', <http//www.hm-treasury.gov.uk/data_gdp_guide.html> accessed 25 August 2013.

Hoffmann, M. (2007). 'Fixed versus Flexible Exchange Rates: Evidence from Developing Countries', *Economica*, 74: pp. 425–49

Human Development Annual Reports.

Keynes, J. M. (1957). *General Theory of Employment, Interest and Money*, London: Macmillan.

Knight, F. H. (1921). *Risk, Uncertainty and Profit*. Boston: Houghton Mifflin.

Koutsoyiannis, A. (1987). *Modern Microeconomics*, Hong Kong: Macmillan.

Landreth, H. and Colander, D. C. (1994). *History of Economic Thought*, Boston: Houghton Mifflin.

Lieberman, M. and Hall, R. E. (2005), 'Comparative Advantage and the Gains from International Trade' slides by John, F and Zambelli, *Introduction to Economics*: Chapter 18, <http//www.swlearning.com/economics/lieberman/lieberman.html> accessed 25 August 2013.

Lipsey, R. G. (1982). *Positive Economics*, London: Weidenfeld & Nicholson.

Marshall, A. (1920). *Principles of Economics*, 8th edn., London: Macmillan.

McConnell, C. R. and Brue, S. L. (2005). *Economics: Principles, Problems and Policies*, 6th edn., New York: McGraw Hill.

Munawar, I. (Ed.) (1988). *Distributive Justice and Need Fulfilment in an Islamic Economy*, Islamic Foundation, Leicester, UK.

Pearce, D. W. and Turner, R. K. (1990). *Economics of Natural Resources and the Environment*, Singapore: Harvester Wheatshead.

Rahman, H. (1946). *The Economic System of Islam—An Outline*, 6th edn., New Delhi: Daril Mussanifin.

Rehman, H., Khan, S. and Ahmad, I. (2008). 'Income Distribution, Growth and Financial Development—A Cross Country Analysis', *Pakistan Economic and Social Review*, 46/1: pp. 1–16.

Robbins, L. (1932). *Nature and Significance of Economic Science*, London: Macmillan.

Robinson, J. and Eatwell, J. (1973). *An Introduction to Modern Economics*, London: McGraw Hill.

Sadr, B. (1976). *Iqtisaduna: Our Economics*, Tehran, Iran.

Samuelson, P. A. (1967). *Economics: An Introductory Analysis*, New York: McGraw Hill.

Sarel, M. (1997). '*How Macroeconomic Factors Affect Income Distribution: The Cross Country Evidence*', The IMF Working Paper, WP/97/152.

Sayyid, T. et al. (Ed.) (1992). *Readings in Microeconomics: An Islamic Perspective*, Malaysia: Longman.

Schultze, C. C. (1970). *National Income Analysis*, 2nd edn., New Delhi: Prentice Hall.

Schumpeter, J. A. (1912). *The Theory of Economic Development*, Cambridge: Harvard University Press.

Sen, A. K. (1982). *Social Choice and Welfare*, Oxford: Basil Blackwell.

Smith, A. (1937). An Inquiry into the Nature and Causes of the Wealth of Nations, Cannon, E. (Ed.), New York: Modern Library.

Srinivasan, T. N. (1992). 'Income Distribution and the Macroeconomy; Some Conceptual and Measurement Issues', *Journal of Philippine Development*, XIX/35: pp. 1–27.

Suranovic, S. (2003), '*International Trade Theory*' (excerpts from the paper), <http//www. lotsofessays.com/viewpaper/1686687.html> accessed 26 August 2013.

Tornell, A. and Velasco, A. (2000). Fixed versus Flexible Exchange Rates: Which Provides More Fiscal Discipline? Journal of Monetary Economics, Vol. 45, Issue 2, pp. 399–436.

Weitzman, M. L. (1984). Share Economy: Conquering Stagflation, Cambridge: Harvard University Press.

Wikipedia, the free encyclopaedia, '*Fixed Exchange Rates*', <http//en.wikipedia.org/wiki/Fixed_exchange_rates> accessed 3 August 2013.

Wikipedia, the free encyclopaedia, '*Terms of Trade*', <http//en.wikipedia.org/wiki/Terms_of_trade> accessed 23 July 2013.

Word Bank, World Development Report (1992). *Environment and Development*, Oxford: Oxford University Press.

World Development Annual Reports.

Index